MCDM: Past Decade
and Future Trends
A Source Book of Multiple
Criteria Decision Making

DECISION RESEARCH, VOLUME 1

Editor: Howard Thomas, *Department of Business Administration,*
University of Illinois at Urbana-Champaign

DECISION RESEARCH

Series Editor: **Howard Thomas**
Department of Business Administration
University of Illinois

To Sharon Kinsman,
Research assistant and colleague
of excellent skill and dedication

MCDM: Past Decade and Future Trends

A Source Book of Multiple Criteria Decision Making

Edited by: **MILAN ZELENY**
The Joseph A. Martino Graduate School
of Business Administration
Fordham University at Lincoln Center

 **JAI PRESS INC.**

Greenwich, Connecticut   *London, England*

Library of Congress Cataloging in Publication Data

Main entry under title:
MCDM: past decades and future trends.

Bibliography: p.
Includes index.
1. Decision-making—Mathematical models—Addresses,
essays, lectures. I. Zeleny, Milan. II. Title: M.C.D.M.
HD30.23.M393 1984   658.4'03   84-15405
ISBN 0-89232-439-2

Copyright © 1984 JAI PRESS INC.
36 Sherwood Place
Greenwich, Connecticut 06830

JAI PRESS INC.
3 Henrietta Street
London WC2E 8LU
England

ISBN: 089232-439-2
Library of Congress Card Number: 84-15405
Manufactured in the United States of America

CONTENTS

INTRODUCTION:
TEN YEARS OF MCDM

More than ten years ago, on October 26 and 27, 1972, there was an international conference held at the University of South Carolina. It addressed a new, previously unorganized topic of inquiry: *Multiple Criteria Decision Making* (MCDM). In 1973, a volume of conference proceedings, bearing the same title and edited by Cochrane and Zeleny, was published by the University of South Carolina Press to become the seminal sourcebook for MCDM research in the decade to follow.

When commemorating the ten years of MCDM we do not wish to imply that no work, no research, or no studies explored the multiplicity of decision criteria prior to 1972. Basic groundwork for MCDM was laid down in the articles and books of Pareto, von Neumann, Morgenstern, Georgescu-Roegen, Koopmans, Kuhn, Tucker, Raiffa, MacCrimmon, Shapley, Blackwell, Bod, Johnsen, and many, many others. The South

Carolina conference would never have taken place without their impressive and competent groundwork being in place.

But it was only *after* 1972 that MCDM became an organized field of inquiry: a distinct philosophy and methodology of decision making, capable of standing on its own feet, producing its own, independent body of knowledge. Why in 1982 the most extensive bibliographies of MCDM came close to 3,000 references! MCDM is now a field covered by specific university courses, serviced by a number of excellent and exciting textbooks, becoming increasingly popular with students of business and management, engineering, social and urban studies, as well as not-for-profit organizations. MCDM researchers hold meetings and conferences on a yearly basis, either on their own or in connection with such societies as IFORS, ORSA, SGSR, TIMS, AIDS, EURO, AAAS, and many others.

Ten years ago, in South Carolina, the field of MCDM was born. Over 250 people were participating, trying to ease the birthpains. It is impossible to list them all, but gathered there, among others, were J.-P. Aubin, J. L. Balintfy, J.-M. Blin, C. W. Churchman, R. M. Dawes, W. Dinkelbach, J. S. Dyer, P. C. Fishburn, P. E. Green, J. P. Ignizio, Y. Ijiri, E. Jacquet-Lagrèze, R. Keeney, K. R. MacCrimmon, R. J. Niehaus, U. Passy, B. Roy, R. Sarin, R. E. Steuer, H. M. Wagner, P. L. Yu, L. A. Zadeh, and M. Zeleny. The ideas they brought to life, as embedded in the book of proceedings mentioned earlier, still represent the freshest, the most original, and essentially inexhaustible source of MCDM ideas today.

Ten years after South Carolina, on January 4–6, 1982, another MCDM conference has taken place, this time in Washington, D.C. The decennial MCDM meeting was held under the auspices and sponsorship of the American Association for the Advancement of Science (AAAS), the most prestigious association of scientists in the United States. Presenting MCDM to AAAS's demanding audiences was a challenging task for the leading researchers and practitioners of MCDM. The representatives of different areas of MCDM included K. E. Boulding, Ch. Carlsson, J. Cohon, N. Georgescu-Roegen, A. Goicoechea, Y. Y. Haimes, I. Kavrakoğlu, L. B. Lave, W. Stadler, T. L. Vincent, P. L. Yu, M. Zeleny, and others, with L. Duckstein, C. L. Hwang, and G. Leitmann participating in absentia. Additional colleagues—W. B. Gearhart, E. L. Hannan, J. S. H. Kornbluth, and M. Yilmaz—have joined the participants in their contributing to the MCDM decennial volume.

It is interesting to note the difference in participants between South Carolina and Washington: only P. L. Yu and M. Zeleny participated in both conferences. Otherwise, a new group of MCDM researchers has established itself in Washington, ready to carry the field into the new decade. Spanning of the two decades of MCDM, the one past and the one to come, is the purpose of the MCDM sourcebook you now hold in your hands.

It is time to recapitulate the achievements, assess the state of the arts, and trace the future directions in MCDM. It is also necessary to provide a guide through the bewildering maze of some 3,000 items of MCDM-related literature. Tutorial assessments and reliable summaries were prepared for more typical MCDM areas—goal programming, decision dynamics, compromise programming, multiobjective programming—but also for MCDM applications in economics, governmental studies, business, and management. All of these contributions are fully up-to-date and reliably exhaustive, yet they are written in a clear and engaging style, stressing concepts rather than mathematical technicalities, and emphasizing usefulness and relevancy rather than ivory-tower purity.

This volume can be characterized as an edited, multiauthored sourcebook for students, researchers, and practitioners alike. It can be used to complement any textbook on MCDM, providing the essentials of most of the published MCDM literature, evaluated and carefully screened for quality by the best in the field.

This is *not* a book of readings (all papers are originals; there are no reprints of old articles), a conference transcript (no haphazard conglomerate of uneven, narrow, unedited papers), or a festschrift (all theories and approaches are covered equally; none is given preferential treatment). Rather, we have striven to give this volume an encyclopedic quality of lasting value. Hence, we call it a sourcebook.

It is important to realize that decision making with multiple criteria is fundamentally and *qualitatively* different from "decision making" with a single criterion. In fact, there is no decision making involved in situations characterized by a single criterion of choice: mere acts of measurement and subsequent search suffice for making a choice.

For example, if you are asked to select the largest apple from a basket (criterion of size), the tallest man from a team (criterion of height), or the heaviest book from a shelf (criterion of weight), it is entirely sufficient to measure objects with respect to the criterion in question and then search for the "maximal" alternative. In real life, however, we often worry whether the largest apple is the juiciest, the sweetest, the most aromatic, and the freshest. We compare teamplayers not ony with respect to height but also according to their skills, age, reliability, and many other criteria. Under these multicriterion conditions measurement and search are no longer sufficient for making the choice. No matter how precisely we measure and no matter how efficiently we search, the decision has not been reached; there is still a need for deciding. Finding the largest apple and finding the (different) sweetest apple has not absolved us from deciding between the two.

If there is only one stated criterion, the decision has already been implicitly made; it is sufficient to make it explicit by the related acts of measurement and search. With multiple criteria the choice is never implicit in the measurement and cannot be explicated by unidimensional search. In essence, then, no unidimensional (single-criterion) decision problem can exist.

Operational sciences (operations research, management science, decision science, systems analysis) have devoted most of their history to problems characterized by a single, aggregate criterion of choice. They dealt with problems of measurement and search in connection with simple problems of limited practical interest. *All* decisions, public and private, individual and collective, are characterized by multiple, apparently conflicting, criteria. Actually, at least two incompatible or conflicting criteria are necessary in order to be able to even speak of decision making as such.

In very few problems of interest we find a single, preemptively important criterion of choice. Individuals and their organizations face multiple objectives, attributes, goals, and criteria, and their reduction to an all-encompassing single aggregate (utility function, welfare function, cost–benefit index, and so on) is no longer scientifically acceptable and practically permissible. Decision makers, in public and private institutions as well as in the government, have to learn to work with multiple and parallel criteria of choice; they have to learn some decision making in addition to simply measuring and searching.

In this volume we have identified major streams and trends within MCDM over the past decade and ventured to extrapolate them into the future. Thus, the reader finds sections devoted to goal programming and its most promising new extension, fractional programming; compromise programming; decision dynamics and the displaced ideal theories; risk and uncertainty aspects of MCDM; optimal design problems; and so on. Among applications one finds especially the areas of economics, governmental regulation, energy planning, engineering, and some others.

Any field of the scope and vastness of MCDM will necessarily suffer from inadequate coverage, even through comprehensive volumes like this. Some MCDM areas have proven to be of limited usefulness and low survivability: cost–benefit ratios, outranking procedures à la ELECTRE, preemptive goal programming, earlier utility decompositions, regression-based "capturing" models, and many others. Some approaches, although promising and potentially very useful, are not yet sufficiently developed and theoretically grounded to warrant a serious review (for example, interactive programming approaches). Other methodologies are so far only superficially treated and are often characterized by convoluted and repetitious writing—as, for example, the treatment of fuzzy sets and fuzzification of some MCDM models. We have accorded only limited space to such areas.

It is a pleasure to acknowledge the excellent cooperation of the experts contributing to this decennial volume. It was a true pleasure to work with these creative thinkers, original authors, and exciting writers: William B. Gearhart, N. Georgescu-Roegen, Edward L. Hannan, Ibrahim Kavrakoğlu, Jonathan S. H. Kornbluth, Lester B. Lave, Wolfram Stadler, Mustafa Yilmaz, and Po-Lung Yu.

My thanks go also to Professor Howard Thomas of University of Illinois for recognizing the importance and purpose of this volume and for supporting its publication. I am also thankful to Professor Burton V. Dean of Case Western Reserve University, who read the entire manuscript and was very helpful in further refining the sourcebook concept.

Finally, my appreciation goes to Sharon Kinsman, research assistant and colleague of excellent skill and dedication, who performed most of the editorial work and to whom this volume is dedicated.

Milan Zeleny
Editor

ANALYTICAL REPRESENTATION OF ECONOMIC DECISIONS UNDER MULTIPLE CRITERIA

Nicholas Georgescu-Roegen

1

NICHOLAS GEORGESCU-ROEGEN provides a spirited and long-needed discussion of decision making from the vantage point of an economist. He acknowledges that in making decisions there is never a single reason to guide us: all decisions, no matter how rarely explored by economists, are characterized by multiple criteria. Of course, no self-respecting theory of decision making should carry the label "multiple criteria," as this should be its natural, undisputable, all-pervasive aspect. The only reason for such a label is, according to Georgescu-Roegen, to emphasize the correction of the old myopic theory. Let us hope that soon and equally naturally, "decision theory" will simply do, in spite of the misuse of this label in statistics.

Georgescu-Roegen launches a devastating critique of utility theory within the context of economics. He establishes nontransitivity and noncomparability of alternatives as perfectly normal conditions of human decision making. He calls for further exploration of the seminal work of May (published in 1954) concerning the noncomparability issue. Similarly, the concept of indifference is presented as being a purely formal construct rather than a more desirable falsifiable postulate. In fact, the absence of indifference is a dominant feature of the ordinary preference structure. That is, there are no trade-offs among certain types of multiple criteria: "give to a hungry woman dresses in any number; they will not satisfy her hunger a bit."

An interesting discussion of multiple criteria related to the choice among risky propositions involves Irving Fisher's observation (made in 1906) that human choice is influenced not only by the expected value but also by the variance of the appropriate probability distribution. That is, an observation preceding those of Markowitz and Tobin by some fifty years. More significant were the ideas of John Hicks, arguing in 1934 for something that is today referred to as stochastic dominance. Actually, Karl Pearson's idea that comparing two distributions can be satisfactorily approximated by comparing two sequences in their first four moments is a strange point of attraction to which all the mean-variance Markowitz-Tobin theories and the stochastic dominance theories seem to be ultimately converging in their search for that exquisite and elusive balance between theoretical correctness and practical relevance. (A young statistician interested in pursuing these ideas should not confuse Irving Fisher with the later personage of R. A. Fisher.)

Similarly, Marschak's imperative, "everyone should maximize expected utility," is subjected to legitimate criticism. This dictate has, however, already been refuted by Allais in 1953.

As usual, Georgescu-Roegen's writing is full of stimulating ideas and topics for research and doctoral dissertations in economics. His are ideas and topics leading not to a simple cranking of the mathematical machine but to intelligent efforts for coming to grips with the complexity of facts. Not many students are independent enough or guided with enough imagination and ambition to undertake such tasks without taking substantial short-term risks. Yet, in the long run, it is Georgescu-Roegen, one of our greatest living economists, who is showing the path toward the true economics of *human* beings. At the least, for the time being, Georgescu-Roegen provides a useful bridge between economics and MCDM.

1. Those who have concentrated their scholarly activity on the problem of the decision process are legion and belong to many professions—economists, psychologists, econometricians, and management experts. But few, very few indeed, have ultimately come to see that to make decisions is a continuous activity of any awake human, that a human "must decide what [he or she is] going to do the next moment" [46]. Virtually all studies have considered only special, highly simplified situations, often characterized by some sort of gambling. Economists, in particular, have focused their attention on decisions whose outcomes consist of "money." The fact that the last Nobel Memorial Prize was awarded for contributions to the analysis of financial portfolio or to associated factors leaves no doubt about the fact that such endeavors belong to the most desirable ways that serve the aims of economics.[1]

Some actions are performed virtually without any deliberation on the part of the individual—such as running away from an attacking dog or dodging a sudden flying object; to chew or to swallow also are reflex actions involving no deliberation. All other actions are preceded by a decision, and the decision in turn by a deliberation about which the individual may not be always fully aware. And another truth, which has also been ignored in modern times, is that to reach a decision is an extremely complicated process: any actual choice is torn between multiple and often contradictory criteria associated with the possible outcomes. When we must decide on any action we never have a single reason to guide us. Not even when, for example, one wants to buy ten gallons of gasoline, for no one wants *just* to have some gas in the tank. Besides, to buy gasoline is only one link of an earlier decision in which some kinds of enjoyment were chosen instead of others. Now, gasoline is a rather homogeneous substance from the consumer's viewpoint. Complications come to the surface if the individual has decided to buy a car and must now decide precisely *which* one. In this case, the criteria are almost numberless: "price, mileage, projected maintenance costs, horsepower, appearance, expected resale value, overall appeal, and many others" [46]. No wonder that decisions involving multiple reasons have ultimately given rise to a special discipline, which, as if to make up for the past neglect of the problem, has been growing fast and in several directions during the past decade.

And if the label of that discipline still carries the qualifications "multiple criteria," it certainly is for the same reason—to emphasize the correction of the old myopic theory. Indeed, standard economics (the main seat of decision theory) considers only the superficial aspect of the decision when at checking out the individual pays cash for, say, some apples. Demand price and supply price constitute the fundamental coordinates used by

3

standard economics for its description of the economic process. Now that we have become aware of the necessity of going beyond (or rather "behind") the checking out to consider the drama of choice due to the multiplicity of human reasons, the term "decision theory" should simply do. I am sure that use of this term will gradually become the accepted practice.[2]

2. The fundamental elements of decision theory must be so chosen as to serve for the analysis of choice in any situation, say, even when Joe decides to marry Helen rather than any of the other marriageable women among his acquaintances. But the best domain for testing the merits of any decision theory—for there have been several set forth—is the economic field.

Every special discipline has some specific "building blocks": those of mechanics are mass and force; those of chemistry are the molecule and the chemical reaction. For a discipline that purports to study the process by which decisions are made we must consider, first, the constellation of reasons guiding the human individual and, second, the uncertainty of most outcomes. Both these aspects are surrounded by many analytical difficulties, some totally insuperable given the limitations of human nature. I shall go briefly over these issues in turn.

The actual world in which we live is perceived by all of us as a pluralistic mosaic. Some thinkers of great intellectual power have thus insisted on a pluralistic epistemology. It was not only William James [27], the best known expounder of this view, who attacked monism; Bertrand Russell [40], although writing during a period when it dominated the scientific temper, also struck at monism by saying that "the most fundamental of my beliefs is that this is rubbish. I think that the universe is all *spots* and *jumps,* without unity, without *continuity,* without coherence and orderliness or any other properties that governesses love."[3]

Unfortunately, the human mind feels quite uncomfortable when confronted with the task of analyzing a pluralistic structure. It has systematically sought a haven in a monistic interpretation of actuality. More than three thousand years ago Moses realized that monotheism is a more comfortable religious dogma than polytheism since it does away with the irreducible intellectual conflicts fostered by the latter. In philosophy and science, the monistic view was first thought up by Parmenides. His was the strictest form of monism, for it claims that the entire world is an *undifferentiated* One. I say "the strictest form," because other forms of monism have since been proposed, such as the pluralistic atomism of Democritus. There is even an atomistic pluralism, such as Bertrand Russell's logical atomism [41]: "When I say that my logic is atomistic, I mean that I share the common-sense belief that there are many *separate things*", a statement which is a natural consequence of his epistemological pluralism mentioned earlier.

Of all these epistemologies, one interests us here. It is a particular variant of Democritus's particular atomism that may be instructively illustrated by Karl Marx's argument for the labor theory of value: every concrete labor consists *only* of a definite amount of a homogeneous abstract, general labor (which is measured in units of unskilled labor). Standard economists have not minced words in denouncing this view as absurd. Yet essentially the same argument is implied in the prevailing consumer theory. Commodities answer to various *concrete* wants of the individual which are just various manifestations of the same general, abstract want—utility. This kind of monism was indirectly formulated by Aristotle (*Ethica Nicomachea*, 1133a-b), as he argued that there must be the same thing in all things that are exchanged against each other.

The idea of pleasure as a general undifferentiated feeling and of pain as the negative form of pleasure goes back to the earliest philosophers, but Jeremy Bentham was the main modern promoter of utility as a general, calculable and even interpersonally additive coordinate [20]. Like Plato (*Philebus*, 21C), the original architect of hedonism, Bentham, too, insisted that, in contrast to oysters, all humans calculate with pleasure and pain. Bentham was not alone in believing in the future discovery of a "moral thermometer"; F. Y. Edgeworth [4] also believed in a possible "hedonimeter"; and even in our own century F. P. Ramsey [39] opined that a "psychogalvanometer" would ultimately enable us to measure the utility felt by an individual. We do not today, I think, believe in the possibility of instrumental measurement of utility, but that every utility of the same individual can be identified by a number on a scale, at least ordinal if not cardinal, is now an undisputable tenet of economists and of psychologists as well. The utility scale is established not by an instrument but by a paper-and-pencil operation on the map of preferences constructed on the basis of the theory of *binary* choice proposed by Vilfredo Pareto.

Pareto's theory of choice, like any other similar theory, views the individual as a "black box" inside which a process decides which among the multiple attainable alternatives must be chosen. The process leading to the decision, the weighing of the multiple criteria against each other, is thus completely blacked out. This omission of conscious decision making is not an innocuous abstraction; it has facilitated the acceptance of some fateful axioms without any "due process of law," apparently only because they make it possible to erect the concept of measurable utility on the foundation of Paretoan choice theory.

There is, first, the assumption that the choice of any rational man is transitive.[4] If this statement is not to remain a plain tautology without any factual significance, "rational" must be defined by some other means as well. Without this condition, all cases of nontransitivity observed in laboratory or in ordinary life can be dismissed as displaying irrationality, thus "saving" the theory. Yet there can be hardly any doubt that normally people do not fail to prefer A to C if they prefer A to B and B to C. The main cause of actual, relevant nontransitivity is a greatly deficient knowledge, which is a perfectly normal condition of any human. No person accustomed to living with some modest income would be able to know in advance how he would spend to his satisfaction an annual income of one million should he suddenly get it. Nor would a millionaire be likely to envision the possibility of living with the low income of, say, a small clerk; otherwise, there would not have been so many suicides after Black Tuesday.

Lack of any substantial personal experience also accounts for occasional noncomparability. One who has to choose between two jobs—one in country K with a salary of 40,000 dollars per year, the other in country T with a yearly salary of 30,000 dollars—may very well find the decision very hard to make if one has never lived in either country. The alternatives are not comparable in one's mind. One may have then to toss a coin or trust someone else with the choice. Although one ultimately chooses between K and T only because refusal to make a choice would result in a situation that might be worse then either, this does not establish their comparability. We can compare and hence make a deliberate choice only between situations that are not too different from those with which we are already familiar [13]. It stands to reason that even in the case of neighboring situations the choice may not be repeatedly the same. There is only some probability, $\omega(A,B)$, that the individual should choose A over B, with $\omega(A,B) + \omega(B,A) = 1$. Just as there is no perfect material measuring instrument, no human is a perfect choosing agent. In this analytical framework, nontrasitivity affects several relations proper to such a structure [17,16].[5]

General comparability is nonetheless a stalwart assumption of standard theory of utility. There are analytical examples to prove that noncomparability does not do any damage to the incontrovertible fact that the quantity one buys of a commodity varies with the price and with one's income, which constitutes the general law of demand [15]. But it does destroy the construction of measurable relevant utility on the basis of Paul Samuelson's revealed preference approach.[6]

But noncomparability may also reflect the impossibility of the human mind to weigh in some cases one criterion against an entirely different one. This surmise may recall the fact, mentioned by May [35], that in some *Consumer Reports* ten electrical shavers were ranked according to six criteria, with the rankings revealing no ordering at all. However, I know of no attempt to explore these situations further, especially in relation to noncomparability.

3. The usual preference map necessarily implies still another assumption whose importance has generally been glossed over, again for the sake of saving the theory. The assumption is that between "preference" and "nonpreference" there always is "indifference." Proof that we are inclined to regard this statement as the purest pleonasm is the wholesale opposition I encountered when I insisted on the necessity of introducing it as a postulate, i.e., as a factual statement that may be falsified [12,19]. It was later incorporated into the axiomatic basis of Paretoan theory [45], for without it, although choices can be ordered, the order cannot be represented by a numerical scale and hence utility cannot be related to any kind of measure.[7]

With this postulate we deny (implicitly) an indisputable property of the structure of our wants, which are directly related to the various qualities of commodities, severally or jointly. Before the veil of utility was thrown over the structure of the human wants, this structure used to form the continous study object of philosophers, sociologists, psychologists, and, of course, economists. Plato (*Rep.*, II.369D) told us that "the first and chief of our needs is the provision of food for existence and life. The second is housing and the third is rainment and that sort of thing." That human wants are hierarchized is a truth recognized by all economists who have not been infatuated with the success of the mathematical tool in physics. No pertinent explanation of the so-called decreasing marginal utility exists that does not boil down to the famous fable of Carl Menger [36]. Any human in isolation would use the first bag of corn for food, the second for seeds, the third for fodder, the fourth for making some drink, the fifth for entertaining friends with food and drink, the sixth for keeping pet parrots, and so forth. The writings of many a great economist of the nineteenth century contain still other properties of the structure of wants, such as the Principle of Satiability of Individual Wants or the Principle of the Subordination of Wants.[8]

4. The reason why this rich and appropriate description of *homo oeconomicus* was completely abandoned by standard economists is simple. Want is not susceptible of analytical definition and hence has no place in any mathematical model. The point is that throwing out the qualitative structure of wants was not only unjustified but also damaging to our comprehension. Indeed, any attempt of ours to establish a satisfactory mental bridge with actuality—outer or inner—calls for two distinct kinds of concepts: the arithmomorphic and the dialectical [18,20].

As the term itself suggests, *arithmomorphic concepts* are of the essence of a number, standing in absolute isolation from all other concepts, including all other numbers. A regular polygon of a fantastic number of sides—say, of 100^{100} sides—still does not constitute a circle. And if you change however little two angles of a square, you no longer have a square. Take even one single point out of a circle, the circle is no longer there. It is because every arithmomorphic concept is *discretely distinct* from all others that they can serve as building blocks for logic as well as mathematics. Actually, these disciplines can operate only with arithmomorphic concepts, the source not only of their power but also of their limitations for our understanding.

Dialectical concepts, on the other hand, although distinct, are *not discretely distinct*. They slide into each other, especially into their opposites. The characteristic aspect of a dialectical concept is that it is separated from its opposite by a substantial penumbra, within which both A and non-A can be true. This kind of contradiction is not possible in an arithmomorphic matrix, for what separates an arithmomorphic concept from its opposite is a *void*. A crucial characteristic of dialectics is that the penumbra separating one concept from its opposite is not an arithmomorphic entity, for if this were so we could represent the whole structure by an arithmomorphic triad: A, A and non-A, non-A. That dialectical penumbra is separated by other dialectical penumbras, which in turn are separated by other dialectical penumbras, and so on in an endless dialectical regress which is ultimately reduced by a process similar to that by which Achilles overtakes the tortoise. It is because of this dialectical algorithm that it is not possible to ascertain exactly how many observations are "sufficient" to make a statistical statement compelling. We know, however, that one observation would not do, whereas a million of them is plenty.

The overwhelming majority of our most important concepts are dialectical. It is amusing, therefore, to see that those who claim that one talks "nonsense" if one uses dialectical concepts (as here defined) cannot defend their position without using continuously "muddled concepts."

At this juncture, I should hasten to explain that nothing is further from my own thought than to deny the incomparable value of analytical models. My view is that arithmomorphism—which unfortunately has nowadays given rise to arithmomania—is not the philosopher's stone; it must be used alongside of dialectics. Actually, arithmomorphic models are absolutely necessary for the simple reason that a good model represents a *simile* of a dialectical reasoning, so that, given its discretely distinct nature, the model constitutes the only tool for probing the correctness of that reasoning.[9]

5. I can now return to the dialectical structure of our wants. The principles mentioned in the foregoing section must certainly be understood as dialectical relations. Virtually any want slides into another by its own nature, as well as because the want-satisfying commodities generally are dialectical concepts.[10] The Roman sandal ultimately slides into the cavalry boot, satisfying various wants on the way. But for an analytical simile of the consequences of the multiplicity of our wants, we must interpret the principles just mentioned in an arithmomorphic way. In this, we can again find help from some of the famous writers of the past. Take the observation by Plato (*Rep.* IV.439A): "The soul of the thirsty then, insofar as it thirsts, wishes nothing else than to drink, and yearns for this and its impulse is toward this [only]." The same may be said for every want that happens to be pressing in a particular circumstance. The hungry, insofar as it hungers, yearn only for food. Any social climber, as has been observed long ago by Abbot Fernando Galliani, also thinks of social advancement before anything else. It goes without saying that the thirst of the hungry has already been quenched and that social climbers do not suffer from hunger pangs.

A very simple, yet telling, arithmomorphic simile of the dialectical structure just described is shown in Figure 1. On Ox axis are represented amounts of margarine in calories; on Oy, amounts of butter, also in calories. Let us assume that butter tastes better than margarine and taste is a superior want (criterion of choice) to hunger. Then, within the domain OAB, where AB represents the amount of calories that completely satiates hunger, the hungry individual will always prefer the combination with greater amount of calories, say, C to D. However, between two combinations of equal amounts of calories, the same individual will prefer that with more butter, say, E to C; taste, the superior want, now becomes active even for the hungry. If hunger is fully satisfied, as is the case with any combination above AB, then taste alone presides over the choice; M is preferred to N even though N contains more calories. However, between M and P the individual will choose P because with more margarine he can satisfy better the next superior want—perhaps, the want for socializing.[11]

It is hardly necessary to show how this result may be generalized [14,20]. But one consequence deserves unparsimonious emphasis. In the above simile there are no indifference curves. One combination out of

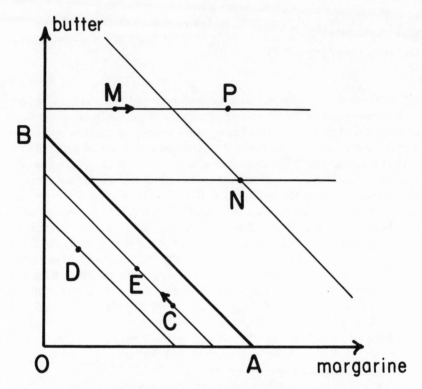

Figure 1.   An Analytical Example of Ordered but Non-numerical
Representation of Utility.

two is always preferred to the other. The indifference postulate mentioned earlier is not satisfied, and hence the preference order cannot be reduced to some measurable utility.[12]

Still more important is the point that absence of indifference is a dominant feature of the ordinary preference structure. It is a reflection of the Principle of the Irreducibility of Wants. To paraphrase a famous witticism of Joseph Schumpeter: give to a hungry woman dresses in any number; they will not satisfy her hunger a bit.

Indifference is thus related to the necessary existence of absolute substitutes, an assumption that is generally taken for granted. The most conspicuous case is none other than the standard theory of choice under uncertainty, where it is explicitly assumed that for any lottery ticket there is a ''completely indifferent'' sure alternative. The ordinalist's fallacy, as I called it [14], is precisely that of not seeing that the same axiom underpins both the ordinalist and the cardinalist doctrines. Strike that axiom out, and both edifices collapse.

6. In a world in which bananas were the only commodities, a lottery ticket would be a new commodity essentially different from a bunch of bananas here and now. Lottery tickets add an essentially new dimension to any riskless world, a truth that even those who fully endorsed the modern theory of cardinal utility of Ramsey–von Neumann–Morgenstern have recognized in one way or another.

But before proceeding further, let me point out the imbroglio created in this field by the shortcomings of our vocabulary. Late in life, Bentham complained that "utility" was a bad choice for his notion of "the greatest happiness for the greatest number." And indeed we now know the slips for which "utility" is responsible, such as when we speak of the utility of corn, meaning the usefulness of corn. In the field under consideration "uncertainty" covers two essentially different conditions, which is a source of confusion that has turned into an endless controversy.

No one can say for sure what face will come up from a future tossing of a dice. Nor can anyone predict with certainty who will be elected President of the United States at the next election. In both cases the outcome is *indeterminate* at this moment; yet there is an essential difference between the two. Frank Knight [28] is the economist who insisted on this point. In the first case, he said, the indeterminate outcome is subject to *risk*; in the second, to *uncertainty*.

One can obtain a regular insurance against risk, but not against uncertainty.

The established doctrine of standard economists and econometricians is to deny any difference between the two situations. Arrow [2] argued that Knight's concept of uncertainty seems "to have surprisingly many of the properties of ordinary probabilities, and it is not clear how much is gained by the distinction."[13] I will return to this matter in a subsequent section. For the time being, I shall discuss the case of known objective probabilities.

Even the case, say, of the probability that an atom of radium should explode during one second or that the tossing of three dice should show three "sixes" is not as free from headaches as is generally assumed. No attempt at an analytical formalization of even this most simple concept of probability has been successful. A run of hundred "tails" is no sure means for deciding whether the coin is loaded. Stochastic sequences are themselves stochastic units. This is the reason why the true base of probability is shown only by a dialectical definition (in the Hegelian sense), as follows:

Given the positive numbers d *and* e, *there is some* N *such that*

$$1 - d < \{\text{prob} \mid f_n - p \mid < e\} < 1 \qquad \text{for n} > \text{N}, \tag{1}$$

where p *is the probability of the chosen event and* f_n *its observed relative in a series of* n *observations* [21].

I have said earlier that humans cannot be perfect choosing instruments. They are not good instruments at estimating probabilities, that is, at arriving at reliable personal probabilities. Personal probabilities of exhaustible and mutually exclusive events rarely add up to one. The actuarial order of stochastic structures is often contradicted by actual preferences. There are, for example, distortions due to hard-to-explain subjective preferences for some particular frequencies [5]. All this still constitutes a matter of wonder about the choice in a field of risk.

Virtually all choices are confronted by multiple criteria. The earliest recognition of this truth seems to have come from Irving Fisher [8], who pointed out that the choice between risk propositions is influenced not only by the expected value but also by the variance of the stochastic distribution. The idea was well received by Pigou and others [1,30,38]. Psychologists began testing it: some tests confirmed it [29], others failed to do so [6]. Markowitz [31,32] erected his algebraic analysis of portfolios on the idea originated by Fisher.

In a 1934 paper, Sir John Hicks [26] went a step further than Fisher and Pigou by suggesting that a complete judgment of a stochastic prospects should be based on the frequency distribution, adding (how surprisingly!) that these curves could be arranged in the order of personal preference "in the same way as the preference-scale used by modern writers in the theory of wants." As a last thought, he also argued that instead of the curve itself, we could consider its moments, or only a sufficient number of them for a good approximation of the curve. Both ideas seem even now to be excellent novelties. The point that mean and variance provide an incomplete, albeit simple, picture of the actual distribution has been recently reflected in the protest of Zeleny [46]: "Why is simplicity often confused with correctness?" Actually, an experiment made by Coombs and Pruitt [3] seems to show that purely subjective choices are influenced by the asymmetry of the distribution as well.

7.   Hicks's ideas anticipated in a very general form the recent works on stochastic dominance (for which see Zeleny [46]). There is, however, an interesting historical background to Hicks's paper, a background that should be of great interest nowadays.

Roughly between 1925 and 1935, the theorem stating that from the knowledge of all moments of a distribution one can obtain, by a Laplace transform of the generating function, the distribution function engendered a widespread interest in the properties of moments and, understandably, with the focus on the moments of the sampling moments.[14] R. A. Fisher [9] even came out with a new concept—the cumulant, defined so that the mean of its sampling distribution should coincide with the corresponding moment about the mean, μ_i, of the parent population.

At the Galton Laboratory, we were then all animated by Karl Pearson's hope that such works could lead to a general method for arriving at the exact distribution of the sampling moments.[15] That great hope was never realized beyond the distribution of the sampling variance from a normal distribution.

However, if all could not be had, there was a partial result of great importance, namely, Karl Pearson's construction of a class of distributions determined only by the first four moments. The frequency functions, y, of these distributions are generated by the differential equation

$$(b_0 + b_1x + b_2x_2)\,dy = (x - a)y\,dx, \tag{2}$$

the four parameters being determined by the first four moments.[16]

The merit of this tool is both great and obvious. The sequence of moments

$$m_1, m_2, m_3, \ldots, m_k, \ldots, \tag{3}$$

when it exists and fulfills some relatively simple conditions (which always happens for actual distributions), constitutes an alternative way to define a distribution. The first four moments happen, not unexpectedly, to correspond to four intuitive aspects of the shape of the frequency curve: its location, its spread, its asymmetry, and its kurtosis. (This is as far as our intuition can be productive.) The sequence may thus be regarded as the decimal digits of a real number. And just as in the case of a number, the greatest information about the shape of the frequency curve is provided by the first "digit," m_1; the next greatest by the second "digit," m_2; and so forth along the rest of the "digits." Karl Pearson rightly judged that the first four "digits" provide sufficient information, in practical terms, about the frequency curve.[17]

To compare two distributions in the manner required by the stochastic dominance [46] is tantamount to comparing two, possibly infinite, sequences of moments—a possibly infinite set of individual comparisons. Karl Pearson's idea was to use only four criteria, a proposal that, to my knowledge, has never failed to provide a satisfactory approximation of an actual distribution.

The reason why this idea fell completely into oblivion belongs to the sociology of the literati. For some petty reasons, by 1930 the relations between Karl Pearson and his successor in the chair and in the position of leader of the profession, R. A. Fisher, had turned into bitterness. After Pearson's death Fisher felt no inclination to support any of Pearson's ideas, nor did the younger statisticians, who were generally interested in obtaining the literary blessings of the new pontiff.[18]

It is not too late, but rather quite proper, to make use of the four-moments tool in describing the behavior of an outcome under risk. The available data for consols are not so complete as to call for the fine instrument based on all moments. As Aristotle taught (*Ethica Nicomachea*, 1094b), an instrument is "adequate if it achieves (just) that degree of accuracy which belongs to its subject matter." At present we have no theoretical reason, I believe, to expect the yields of consols to follow a particular type of distribution—but if one exists, the application of Pearson's method to a sufficient number of consols will certainly reveal it.

8. The analysis of pecuniary prospects involving risks—namely, of prospects whose outcomes can be obtained repeatedly, possibly at will, and whose observed frequencies satisfy relation (1)—although not completely satisfactory, it leaves little to be desired, as any consummate actuary would aver. The problem is far more complicated if the yields are evaluated in utility terms (specifically, on at least a weak cardinal scale [18]). For once we introduce into the picture the subjective coordinate of utility, the imperative "everyone should maximize expected utility" [34] becomes subject to legitimate criticism. We need only recall the confession of one of the strongest supporters of cardinal utility, Paul Samuelson, that he is not sure even about his own consistency of choice among the simple alternatives such as those used by Maurice Allais [1] for refuting that imperative (quoted in Georgescu-Roegen [14]).

Add to this the indeterminacy of outcomes that cannot be repeated at all or only exceptionally and in situations so different that the significance of the successive observations hardly exists. Certainly, the state of one's mind in thinking about Scotland's becoming a separate state in 1990 or about the discovery of a cancer vaccine during the same year is definite. If *compelled,* any individual will certainly call a bet in each case. Let us say that X bets 1 against 15,000 that the vaccine will be discovered. This does not mean that Y will not call an entirely different bet, say, 1 against 100,000. On January 1, 1991, the world will know whether or not the vaccine was discovered. Who's bet made more sense? There is no answer to this question. The world situation of the 1980s cannot be repeated thousands of times for us to ascertain how many times the vaccine would have been discovered. This is, I believe, the quintessence of Frank Knight's view of the difference between risk and uncertainty.

We act even when confronted with uncertainty, for act we must always. But our actions in such cases are determined on the basis of our personal knowledge at the time of decision.

A simple fable involving only analytical data will bring to fore the dialectical issues involved in uncertainty. A satrap confronts a prisoner with three urns:

U_1, containing two-thirds white and one-third black balls;
U_2, from which a careful sample with replacements yielded 2,284 white and 1,142 black balls;
U_3, from which a careful sample with replacements yielded two white balls and one black ball.

The prisoner is asked to call a bet for ''white'' which he may be obliged to accept on one side or the other. If the individual is sufficiently knowledgeable to make adequate judgments, he will certainly bet 2 against 3 in favor of a white ball. But if the satrap then asks him to choose one urn from which the next single drawing will decide: if white, he goes free; if black, he goes back to incarceration. There can hardly be any doubt that

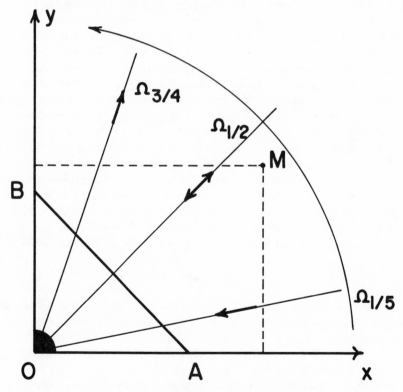

Figure 2. An Analytical Example of Non-numerical Expectation.

a knowledgeable prisoner will choose U_1, for if this fact is doubted, then, God help the theorists of choice.[19]

The analytical construction of Figure 2 will be used to prove, first, that even in the simple type of choice just described, the betting coefficient is not the only factor in choice; and, secondly, that in the same simple framework the states of mind confronted with uncertainty, even if ordered, cannot be represented on a numerical scale from 0 to 1, as numerous writers have assumed, often without any preliminary consideration [14,16].

Any possible sample with replacement from any urn containing only white and black balls can be represented by a point, such as M, in the plane xOy. Here the abscissa represents the number of black balls in the sample; the ordinate, the number of white. Samples of the same size, N, are represented by points on a straight line, such as AB, whose equation is $x + y = N$. All samples in which the relative frequencies are constant are represented on a straight line passing through the origin, say, $y = x/4$, if the frequency of white is 1/5. The point at infinity on the same line, $\Omega_{1/5}$, will represent the urn in which the true relative frequency is 1/5. Considering the case in which "white" is a favorable outcome, the preference in choosing an urn will normally be for a higher $O\Omega$. Among the urns on the same $O\Omega$, the preference is ordered by increasing N for frequencies of white greater than 1/2 and by decreasing N for frequencies smaller than 1/2. This ordering reflects what we may call the degree of credibility in the information. All urns for which the sample frequency of white is 1/2 must be normally regarded as "indifferent" in the choice for a "white" to come. The origin O represents an urn about which *nothing* is known and which would represent the highest case of Knightian uncertainty. It must therefore be left out of the picture.

The order just described is lexicographical and hence proves that even if uncertainties could be reduced to such simple situations as depicted in Figure 2 the betting coefficient would hide the important factor of credibility. In actual situations, credibility itself will hardly form a simple order. Certainly, the map of expectations is extremely anfractuous.

APPENDIX

To continuè the thought of note 17, I should like to observe that the popularity of standard deviation over the other metric measures of dispersion is due to its strict connection with the normal distribution,[20] which is the only one for which the probability of $x^2/\sigma^2 \leq z$ is completely determined for any given z.

However, the relationship between standard deviation and normal distribution has a deeper root. Let us consider the sequence of Thiele's semi-invariants [43],

$$s_1, s_2, s_3, \ldots, s_n, \ldots, \tag{4}$$

generated by the logarithm of the generating function, $G(t)$,

$$\ln G(t) = \ln \sum_0^\infty \frac{m_i t^i}{i!} = \sum_1^\infty \frac{s_i t^i}{i!}. \tag{5}$$

The case in which $s_2 = 0$ (hence $s_i = 0$ for $i \geq 2$) corresponds to the simplest possible distribution—a degenerate distribution. Next in line of simplicity is the distribution for which $s_i = 0$ for all $i > 2$. This is an alternative definition of the normal distribution, which from this viewpoint is the simplest nondegenerate distribution.

But the pragmatic reason why standard deviation is to be preferred to any other metric measure of dispersion is the Bienaymé–Chebyshev inequality valid for any distribution that has a definite second moment:

$$\text{Prob}\left[\frac{x^2}{\sigma^2} \geq k^2\right] \leq \frac{1}{k^2}, \tag{6}$$

which, obviously, is relevant only if $k > 1$. This inequality and the relation between x^2/σ^2 and the formula of normal distribution lead to an interesting generalization [21]. We may first observe that

$$\frac{x^2}{\sigma^2} \leq 1 \tag{7a}$$

represents the interior of an "ellipse" in one-dimensional space of Ox (Figure 3).

$$-\sigma \qquad +\sigma$$

$$O$$

$$x$$

Figure 3. Standard Variation for One Dimension.

The exponent in the formula for the bivariate normal distribution also is a quadratic form of two variables,

$$H(x_1, x_2) = \left(\frac{x_1^2}{\sigma_1^2} + \frac{x_2^2}{\sigma_2^2} - 2r\frac{x_1 x_2}{\sigma_1 \sigma_2}\right) \Big/ (1 - r^2). \tag{8}$$

Hence,

$$H(x_1, x_2) \leq 1 \tag{7b}$$

represents the interior of an elipse in the $x_1 O x_2$ space (Figure 4).

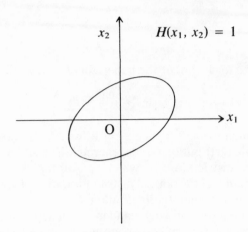

Figure 4.   Extension of Standard Variation to Two Dimensions.

In general, for n variables $x_1, x_2, \ldots, x_n$, let

$$\Delta = [\sigma_{ik}] \tag{9}$$

be the matrix of the covariances σ_{ik}, and let

$$Q(x) = (x)'\Delta^{-1}(x). \tag{10}$$

Then $Q(x)$ is the natural generalization of the quadratic form x^2/σ^2. It can also be written as follows:

$$Q(x) = \frac{\sum_i \sum_k x_1 x_k \Delta_{ik}}{|\Delta|} = \sum_i \sum_k x_i x_k S_{ik}. \tag{11}$$

where Δ_{ik} is the signed (i,k) minor of $|\Delta|$. From this last relation it is immediate that if Q^* denotes the expression obtained from $Q(x)$ by replacing $x_i x_k$ by σ_{ik}, then

$$Q^* = n. \tag{12}$$

Let now $f(x)$ be the probability density function of a distribution for which all σ_{ik} are determinate. From (12), it follows that

$$\int_{(n)} Q(x) \, f(x) \, dx = n. \tag{13}$$

We have successively

$$n = \int_{Q(x)<k^2} Q(x) \, f(x) \, dx + \int_{Q(x)\geq k^2} Q(x) \, f(x) \, dx, \tag{14}$$

and

$$n \geq \int_{Q(x) \geq k^2} Q(x) \, f(x) \, dx \geq k^2 \times \text{prob}[Q(x) \geq k^2].$$

Hence,

$$\text{prob}[Q(x) \geq k^2] \leq n/k^2, \tag{15}$$

which generalizes the Bienaymé–Chebyshev inequality. (Again, for this inequality to be relevant, k^2 must be greater than n.[21])

The ellipsoid volume of $Q(x) \leq 1$ may thus be taken as a measure of the variability of any n-variate distribution, just as the interval of the elipse (7a) is a measure of the dispersion of any univariate distribution.

Let $a_1, a_2, \ldots, a_n$ be the axes of that ellipsoid. These values correspond to the extrema of $\sum x^2$ for $Q = 1$. With a proper Lagrangean multiplier, the conditions for the extremum are

$$(\lambda/2)\frac{\partial Q}{\partial x_i} - x_i = 0, \qquad \text{for } i = 1, 2, \ldots, n. \tag{16}$$

And since Q is a homogeneous function of second degree, from (16) we obtain

$$\lambda_i = a_i^2. \tag{17}$$

The λ_i's are the roots of the equation obtained from (16) after the elimination of the x_i's:

$$\mid \lambda S_{ik} - \delta_{ik} \mid = 0, \tag{18}$$

where $\delta_{ii} = 1$, $\delta_{ik} = 0$ for $i \neq k$. From this equation, it follows that

$$\lambda_1 \lambda_2 \ldots \lambda_n = \frac{1}{\mid S_{ik} \mid}, \tag{19}$$

and since $[S_{ik}] = [\Delta]^{-1}$, we obtain

$$\lambda_1 \lambda_2 \ldots \lambda_n = \mid \Delta \mid. \tag{20}$$

By (17) $a_1 a_2 \ldots a_n = \mid \Delta \mid^{1/2}$; hence, the volume sought is

$$v_n = \pi^{n/2} \mid \Delta \mid^{1/2} \Gamma \left(\frac{n}{2} + 1\right). \tag{21}$$

For distributions of the same dimension, the comparison of the multivariate variability involves only

$$\mid \Delta \mid = \sigma_{11} \sigma_{22} \ldots \sigma_{nn} R, \tag{22}$$

where R is the determinant of the correlation coefficients r_{ij} with $r_u = 1$

Formula (22) is a pseudomeasure of the uncertainty displayed by n different criteria justified on the same analytical basis as the classical variance of a single variable.[22]

NOTES

1. In a quite rare gesture of academic elegance, James Tobin [44] wanted to make it clear that, in fact, it was Harry Markowitz [31], who first based an analysis of portfolio on an algebra that included the statistical variance along with the expected value. At the same time, Tobin seems to point out that his own contributions went beyond the analysis of portfolios of consols.

2. The only snag in this direction may be that, sometime in the 1960s, statisticians sought to increase the prestige of their discipline by labeling it "decision theory." Of course, statistical analysis does not involve multiple qualitative criteria.

3. Italics added.

4. Actual cases of nontrasitivity are easily supplied [35]. However, one must be careful to see whether the verb is *exactly* the same in each proposition; it is not in the famous paper-scissors-stone triad. If one wants a clear-cut illustration, almost any chess tournament supplies many such actual cases.

5. That this framework reflects a feature of actual behavior is seen in the fact that it explains F. W. Taussig's view of demand as a "penumbra" instead of an analytical curve [12].

6. Actually, even the comparability based on revealed preference alone cannot lead to a Paretoan utility [23, chap. 13].

7. An idea which goes back to Pareto and was later revived by W. E. Armstrong has had great currency. It is claimed that if the individual can say what alternative is equally distant from two given ones, then any order can be represented by an ordinal scale [14]. For an elementary refutation, let (x,y) be preferred to (x',y') if and only if $x \geq x'$, $y > y'$. Let us also assume that $[(x + x')/2, (y + y')/2]$ is the "midway." The order is still not representable by a numerical scale.

8. For some pertinent quotations from T. C. Banfield, H. H. Gossen, W. Stanley Jevons, Léon Walras, Alfred Marshall, F. von Wieser, Vilfredo Pareto, and Frank Knight, see Georgescu-Roegen [14].

9. This logic implies that some dialectical reasoning must already exist to justify the recourse to an arithmomorphic model. There is abuse whenever mathematical models are introduced without any previous basis—the well-known phenomenon of translating mathematics into economics. In a valuable document of the time, a young economist recognizes that nowadays it is easier to get some results by simply cranking the mathematical machine than to come to grips with the complexity of facts. (See Georgescu-Roegen [23].)

10. Nothing need to be added to recall the view that "fuzzy set theory and MCDM are joined in a lasting partnership" (Martin K. Starr, in the Preface of Zeleny [46]). A dialectical concept—want, democracy, good justice, etc.—has a "fuzzy" boundary. But we must not fail to see that between dialectics and any arithmomorphic structure—as the theory of fuzzy sets indisputably is—there can be no solid bridge [19]. Fuzzy set theory represents a valorous attempt to construct an arithmomorphic simile of dialectical concepts. To recall, R. Dedekind also aimed at representing the *intuitive* continuity by the arithmetical continuum [20, Appendix A]. But between the two programs there is an essential difference. The new element introduced by Dedekind—the irrational number that fills the "gaps" between rational numbers—is objectively operational, which accounts for the great impact it has had not only in mathematics but in the natural sciences. The other new element—the membership func-

tion—is a purely subjective coordinate, largely analogous but far less transparent than personal probability. Writing in 1964 [17], I said that dialectical reasoning awaited a new Aristotle, not a new arithmomorphic scheme; it still does.

11. One would easily recognize that this preference structure corresponds to a lexicographical order, across which I came by moving from the above economic problem into mathematics [19]. For an elementary proof that a lexicographical order cannot be represented by an arithmetical scale, see Georgescu-Roegen [18].

12. This is probably the main reason why the idea of the dialectical hierarchy of wants—nay, any consideration of wants—has failed to attract the interest of standard economists. In psychology, however, it was soon received with enthusiasm and now circulates as Maslow's Law [46].

13. Similar views have been expressed by Makower and Marschak [30], Marschak [33], and Hicks [25], among others.

14. For the history of that result, see Seal [42].

15. Myself, under the guidance of Karl Pearson at the Galton Laboratory, I also completed a long memoir on the moments of the sampling classical moments [10].

16. The class includes the normal distribution and the gamma-distribution. For details, see Elderton [7] and Georgescu-Roegen [11]. Both these works contain numerical applications.

17. In this connection I should like to take exception to the view that the use of standard deviation in the analysis of risk prospects is justified only if the distribution is normal. The standard deviation is one of the many recipes for calculating a typical value (alias an *average*) of the distribution of the deviations from the population mean. Certainly, the standard deviation is not the only way to represent the average deviation. The mean deviation as well as any $\mu_k^{1/k}$, μ_k (for k = 2m), being the kth moment about the mean, would also do. Yet in all cases of collective description we have no way other than using an "average." Therefore, rejecting the use of standard deviation in all cases is tantamount to renouncing the use of any "mean" as a statistical description of a population.

18. For the source of the animosity between the two scholarly giants as well as for the unjust silence that has surrounded Pearson's name ever since his death, see the calm, pondered judgment of E. S. Pearson [37].

19. We cannot deny that people, even knowledgeable ones, will choose U_2 explaining that "8 is my lucky number." While such phenomena should not be ignored, they concern other disciplines—anthropology, for example.

20. Nonmetric measures such as interpercentile range are far more informative than the standard deviation (except in the case where the distribution is known to be normal). The reason why economic theorists and econometricians have nevertheless preferred to use only the standard deviation seems simple: one gets more miles by using this metric coordinate.

21. It can be proved that (15) cannot be improved, that is, no function $g(k) < n/k^2$ can be found as an upper limit in (15) valid for any k [22].

22. I have referred to any "measure" of a dialectical variable as a pseudomeasure. For any such variable there are infinitely many pseudomeasures. Familiar examples are the various mathematical formulas for measuring the average of a quantitative variable in a set, or the formulas for measuring the price level [21].

REFERENCES

1. Allais, Maurice, "Le Comportement de L'Homme rationel Devant le Risque: Critique des Postulates et Axiomes de L'École Americaine." *Econometrica* 21:503–546, 1953.

2. Arrow, Kenneth J., "Alternative Approaches to the Theory of Choice in Risk-Taking," *Econometrica* 13:404–437, 1951.
3. Coombs, C. H., and D. G. Pruitt, "Components of Risk in Decision-Making: Probability and Variance Preferences." *Journal of Experimental Psychology* 60:265–277, 1960.
4. Edgeworth, F. Y., *Mathematical Psychics*. London: Kegan Paul, 1881.
5. Edwards, Ward, "The Reliability of Probability-Preferences." *The American Journal of Psychology* 67:68–95, 1954.
6. Edwards, Ward, "Variance Preferences in Gambling." *The American Journal of Psychology* 67:441–452, 1954a.
7. Elderton, W. Palin, *Frequency Curves and Correlation*. London: Layton, 1906.
8. Fisher, Irving, *The Nature of Capital and Income*. New York: Macmillan, 1906.
9. Fisher, R. A., "Moments and Product Moments of Sampling Distributions." *Proceedings of London Mathematical Society* 30(2):199–238, 1929.
10. Georgescu-Roegen, Nicholas, "Further Contributions to the Sampling Problem." *Biometrika* 12:65–107, 1932.
11. Georgescu-Roegen, Nicholas, *Metoda Statistică*. Bucharest: Imprimeria Naţională, 1933.
12. Georgescu-Roegen, Nicholas, "The Pure Theory of Consumer Behavior." *Journal of Economics* 50:545–593, 1936. (Reprinted in Georgescu-Roegen [19], pp. 133–170.)
13. Georgescu-Roegen, Nicholas, "The Theory of Choice and the Constancy of Economic Laws." *Quarterly Journal of Economics* 64:125–138, 1950. (Reprinted in Georgescu-Roegen [19], pp. 171–183.
14. Georgescu-Roegen, Nicholas, "Choice, Expectations, and Measurability." *Quarterly Journal of Economics,* 68, pp. 503–534, 1954. (Reprinted in Georgescu-Roegen [19], pp. 184–215.)
15. Georgescu-Roegen, Nicholas, "Choice and Revealed Preference." *Southern Economic Journal,* 21, pp. 119–130, 1954. (Reprinted in Georgescu-Roegen [19], pp. 216–227.)
16. Georgescu-Roegen, Nicholas, "Threshold in Choice and Theory of Demand." *Econometrica,* 26, pp. 156–168, 1958. (Reprinted in Georgescu-Roegen [19], pp. 228–240.)
17. Georgescu-Roegen, Nicholas, "The Nature of Expectation and Uncertainty." Pp. 11–29 in Mary Jean Bowman (ed.), *Expectations, Uncertainty and Business Behavior.* New York: Social Scientific Research Council, 1958. (Reprinted in Georgescu-Roegen [19], pp. 241–275.)
18. Georgescu-Roegen, Nicholas, "Measure, Quality, and Optimum Scale." Pp. 231–256 in C. R. Rao (ed.), *Essays in Economics Presented to Professor P. C. Mahalanobis.* Oxford: Pergamon Press, 1964. (Reprinted in Georgescu-Roegen [23], pp. 271–296.)
19. Georgescu-Roegen, Nicholas, *Analytical Economics: Issues and Problems*. Cambridge: Harvard University Press, 1966.
20. Georgescu-Roegen, Nicholas, "Utility." Pp. 236–267 in *International Encyclopedia of the Social Sciences,* Vol. 16.
21. Georgescu-Roegen, Nicholas, *The Entropy Law and the Economic Process*. Cambridge: Harvard University Press, 1971.
22. Georgescu-Roegen, Nicholas, "The Measure of Information: A Critique." Pp. 187–217 in J. Rose and C. Bilciu (eds.), *Modern Trends in Cybernetics and Systems,* Vol. 3 (Third International Congress of Cybernetics and Systems). New York: Springer-Verlag, 1975.
23. Georgescu-Roegen, Nicholas, *Energy and Economic Myths: Institutional and Analytical Economic Essays*. New York: Pergamon Press, 1976.

24. Georgescu-Roegen, Nicholas, "Methods in Economic Science: A Rejoinder." *Journal of Economic Issues* 15:188–193, 1981.
25. Hicks, J. R., "The Theory of Uncertainty and Profit." *Economica* 11:170–189, 1931.
26. Hicks, J. R., "The Application of Mathematical Methods to the Theory of Risk." *Econometrica* 2:194–195, 1934.
27. James, William, *A Pluralistic Universe*. London: Longmans, Green, 1909.
28. Knight, Frank H., *Risk, Uncertainty and Profit*. Boston: Houghton Mifflin, 1921. (Reissued with additions as No. 16 in "Series of Reprints of Scarce Tracts in Economic and Political Science," London School of Economics, 1978.)
29. McGlothlin, William H., "Stability of Choices Among Uncertain Alternatives." *The American Journal of Psychology* 69:604–615, 1956.
30. Makower, H. and Jacob Marschak, "Assets, Prices, and Monetary Theory." *Economica*: 261–288, 1938.
31. Markowitz, Harry M., "Portfolio Selection." *Journal of Finance* 7:77–91, 1952.
32. Markowitz, Harry M., *Portfolio Selection: Efficient Diversification of Investments*. New York: Wiley, 1959.
33. Marschak, Jacob, "Rational Behavior, Uncertain Prospects, and Measurable Utility." *Econometrica* 18:11–141, 1950.
34. Marschak, Jacob, "Why 'Should' Statisticians and Businessmen Maximize Moral Expectations?" Pp. 493–506 in *Proceedings of the Second Berkeley Symposium on Mathematical Statistics and Probability*. Berkeley: University of California Press, 1951.
35. May, Kenneth O., "Intransitivity, Utility, and the Aggregation of Preference Patterns." *Econometrica* 22:1–13, 1954.
36. Menger, Carl, *Principles of Economics*. Glencoe, Ill.: Free Press, 1950. (Original German edition, 1871.)
37. Pearson, E. S., "Some Reflections on Continuity in the Development of Mathematical Statistics: 1885–1920." *Biometrika* 54:341–355, 1967.
38. Pigou, A. C., *Economics of Welfare*. London: Macmillan, 1920.
39. Ramsey, Frank P., *The Foundations of Mathematics and Other Essays*. London: Kegan Paul, Trench and Trubner.
40. Russell, Bertrand, *The Scientific Outlook*. New York: W. W. Norton, 1931.
41. Russell, Bertrand, *Logic and Knowledge*. London: G. Allen and Unwin, 1956.
42. Seal, H. L., "The Historical Development of the Use of Generating Functions in Probability Theory." *Bulletin de l'Association des Actuaires Suisses* 49:209–228, 1949.
43. Thiele, Thorwald N., *Theory of Observations*. London: Layton, 1903.
44. Tobin, James, "Portfolio Theory." *Science* 214:974, 1981.
45. Wold, Herman, "A Synthesis of Pure Demand Analysis." *Skandinavisk Aktuarietidskrift* 26:86–118, 220–263; 27:70–120, 1943–1944.
46. Zeleny, Milan, *Multiple Criteria Decision Making*. New York: McGraw-Hill, 1982.
47. Zeleny, Milan and Martin K. Starr, *Multiple Criteria Decision Making*. Amsterdam: North-Holland, 1977.

INTRODUCTION TO DECISION DYNAMICS, SECOND-ORDER GAMES, AND HABITUAL DOMAINS

Po-Lung Yu

Po-Lung Yu has prepared an excellent overview of the concepts of decision dynamics, habitual judgmental domains, and so-called second-order games. Yu's writing is interesting because he comes to MCDM with a strong mathematical background (a student of Rufus Isaacs) and impeccable credentials in classical operations research (differential games, distribution problems, nonlinear programming). Yet he has not become an unconcerned manipulator of abstract symbols but one of the leading proponents of humanism, human concerns, and study of the human condition as related to the field of decision making. It is a deep, confident grasp of mathematics which allows some mathematicians and operations researchers to move beyond mathematics. Yu's move is an example, a reference point, for generations of young operations researchers still to come.

His first observation, his vantage point, is that applications of game theory to real-life problems are still fairly limited and far from original expectations—primarily due to the simplifying assumptions underlying the theoretical development of the topic. In reality, the minimum conditions which must be taken into account are the following: strategy sets are not fixed and foreknown—they evolve, vary, are difficult to define and predict with precision; each "player" is acting with respect to several objectives, with respect to multiple criteria, varying and evolving in numbers and kind; the perception of payoffs, single- or multidimensional, is not fixed and varies with psychological states and different contexts; human preferences are not stable and constant, for human mind is involved.

Ignoring such minimal requirements leads to mathematically elegant but pitifully empty and useless models. Relaxing these originally imposed assumptions presents a seemingly insurmountable challenge to game theorists. Normal research continues refining old models while leaving the assumptions untouched. "In order to really expand the horizon of knowledge, we must try to jump out of the existing habitual domain or break loose from the assumptions of the existing game theory," concludes Yu, an eminent game theorist. He then goes on to show how a particular breakthrough, permitting escape from one such habitual straitjacket, can proceed.

He refers to these games, which are not restricted by the assumptions imposed by the traditional game theory models, as second-order games. One should interpret this rather neutral designation as referring to nothing short of revolutionary restatement or abandonment of most limiting and unrealistic assumptions of mathematical operations research.

Expansion and/or reformulation of habitual domains appears to be one of the most powerful methods for successful problem solving and conflict resolution. Much research remains to be done, especially in connection with computer-based interactive decision aids, but the direction is unmistakeable and the foundations well laid. Professor Yu is actively coaching a whole new generation of researchers, and his contributions to MCDM, even at this early stage of his career, are long term and significant.

ABSTRACT

The concepts of decision dynamics, habitual domains, and second-order games are introduced and integrated. The description emphasizes the main conceptions and frameworks, rather than the technical details. It is hoped that the concepts and frameworks can help us cope with the difficulties of complex decision problems and second-order games, and that they provide us with a basis in the research of conflict dissolution.

1. INTRODUCTION

The theory of games [21] and differential games [11] considers decision-making problems involving more than one person (player) in which the players' payoffs are functions of their own choices as well as the other players' choices. This consideration makes the modeling of a large class of decision-making problems much closer to real life. The impact of game theory and differential games on management science, economics, psychology, social science, biology, and engineering science is immeasurable. Not only are new conceptions formed, but also new dimensions of problems are raised which are waiting for answers. Much interest has been aroused and many research results have been reported in thousands of scholarly articles. Unfortunately, the applications to real-life problems are still fairly limited and far from original expectations. Besides the mathematical difficulties, the limitations may be primarily due to the simplifying assumptions underlying the theoretical development of the topic. The following are some of the simplifying assumptions which are usually not valid in real-life decision problems:

1. In both game theory and differential games it is assumed that the strategy sets for each player (decision maker) are fixed and foreknown. In reality, strategy sets evolve and vary with time and are difficult to define precisely or predict accurately.
2. In both topics it is assumed that each player has only one criterion for maximization or minimization. In reality, each player is interested in several objectives which can vary with time, not only in the form of the objectives but also in the dimension of the objectives.
3. In both topics it is assumed that the players' perceived payoffs, measured in terms of the criteria and resulting from the decisions or strategies, are preknown and deterministic. In reality, because human perception varies with time, with psychological states, and with the constant inputs of information, the payoffs perceived by the players will not always remain constant.

27

4. In both topics it is implicitly assumed that the preferences of the players (over the payoffs) are stable and constant. In reality, because the human mind is involved, such an assumption cannot always be justified.

Due to the simplifying assumptions, many mathematically beautiful results have been derived. (For instance, see Refs. 1, 11, 15, 18, and 21.) Also due to the simplifying assumptions, the results are difficult to apply in real-life decision problems. Many people have made contributions to game theory by extending the existing results and by relaxing the assumptions. However, these contributions are so bound to the original assumptions and mathematical constructions that the new results are still hard to apply in most cases. In terms of "habitual domains" (to be described in Section 3), the research results are so much habitually bounded that their applications are difficult. In order to really expand the horizon of knowledge, we must try to jump out of the existing habitual domain, or break loose from the assumptions of the existing game theory.

This paper intends to show how one can jump out of the existing assumptions in game theory and differential games and substitute them with more realistic conceptions and models. While the technical details can be found in the references quoted, we shall concentrate on the description of the main concepts so that the reader can grasp the main ideas without getting lost in the details.

In Section 2 we focus on decision dynamics and second-order games. Section 2.1 describes decision elements and decision dynamics which form a basis for describing second-order games in Section 2.2. Section 2.3 then describes a solution concept—time stability for second-order games. In Section 3 we focus on behavior bases and habitual domains. Section 3.1 describes a model for decision/behavior processes. Section 3.2 discusses concepts and formation of habitual domains. Section 3.3 describes expansion and interaction of habitual domains. In Section 4 we integrate the concept of habitual domains with that of second-order games. The conclusion is given in Section 5.

2. DECISION DYNAMICS AND SECOND-ORDER GAMES

In Section 2.1, decision elements and decision dynamics are described. These concepts make it easy for us to compare second-order games with traditional ones in Section 2.2. Two examples are used to facilitate the comparison. Solution concepts for second-order games are discussed in Section 2.3.

2.1. Decision Elements and Decision Dynamics

In order to have a concrete feeling, let us consider a decision process of buying a house, assuming we are financially and psychologically ready for such an attempt. There are four important decision elements which are involved in the process:

i. *The set of alternatives, denoted by* X_t—The alternatives include those houses available or potentially available in the market. In a broad sense, an alternative is a package which consists of the house itself, financial arrangements, and risk sharing (guarantee or insurance) for a transaction. Clearly the set X_t under our consideration will evolve with time, information inputs, and our own thinking processes.

ii. *The set of criteria, denoted by* F_t—This set can include appearance of home, interior design, neighborhood, resale value, price, tax, number of bedrooms, number of bathrooms, etc. Indeed we used 26 criteria (attributes) identified by the American Homebuilder's Association in an experimental study of high-stake decision processes [4]. The criteria/attributes are found to change with time and then stabilize before the final decision. (See Ref. 4 for details.)

iii. *The subjective judgment of the outcomes of each alternative in terms of the criteria, denoted by* $\tilde{F}_t$—Note that the judgmental outcomes, like resale value or neighborhood, may not be precise. They involve confidence levels of judgment. These "confidence structures" are part of $\tilde{F}_t$ and are needed for consideration. Again, elements of $\tilde{F}_t$ most likely evolve with time, information inputs, and the psychological state of the decision maker.

iv. *The preference/domination structure of the decision maker over the potential outcomes of possible choice, denoted by* D_t—The preference over the number of bedrooms, the neighborhood, interior design, resale value, etc., is very important in determining the final choice of the house. As with "the number of bedrooms," it is not always the more the better. As with "interior design" and "the number of bedrooms," the preference can be changed with time, information inputs, and the psychological state of the decision maker.

Observe that for each of the above four elements, a subscript t is used to emphasize that they may vary with time. The four elements exist only as the decision maker perceives them. Their existence and variation can be strongly influenced by the decision maker's experience and psychological state.

The four decision elements can interact with one another and can be influenced by three forces:

i. *The decision maker's internal information processing*—His/her thinking processes, judgment/value processing, problem-solving patterns, self-suggested goals and illusion, defense mechanisms, attention and charge structures, physiological conditions, etc., are parts of the internal information processing—all of which may have great impact on the variation of the four elements.

ii. *Solicited information inputs, denoted by* I_t—These information inputs are actively sought by the decision maker. They may come from internal management information systems or accounting reports, or they may come from consultation with specialists, colleagues, friends, or relatives.

iii. *Unsolicited information inputs, denoted by* $\tilde{I}_t$—These inputs are collected passively. They come to us suddenly, without our actively seeking them. The sudden outbreak of a war, a sudden delivery of a threat from a rival or competitor, a sudden offer of a new job or new business venture, etc., belong to this category.

The effect that information inputs have on the four decision elements X_t, F_t, $\tilde{F}_t$, D_t, and hence on the final decision, depends to a large extent on the credibility that the decision maker assigns to the source. Source credibility depends on the channels and personal context in which the decision maker is evaluating the information.

The interaction of the four decision elements and the manner in which the three forces influence them are summarized in Figure 1. Note that the decision process starts with the decision maker's recognition of the need for making a decision to achieve his/her goals. Once the process starts, unless it is a trivial problem, the four decision elements will be, wittingly or unwittingly, produced and changed with the information inputs and the psychological states of the decision maker. As time passes, the four elements may be stabilized. But until the final solution (including abandoning the problem) is found, the process will continue and evolve. Also, the process can be shut off because other more urgent problems appear, and it can recur when no more urgent problems need to be solved. This on/off process in decision making is not unusual when one considers the decision maker as a living system who has multiple goals and equilibrium states to achieve and maintain. (See Refs. 16 and 24 for further discussion.)

Now, let $[t_1, t_2]$ be a time interval from t_1 to t_2, inclusive. We introduce the following *time-optimality* concept.

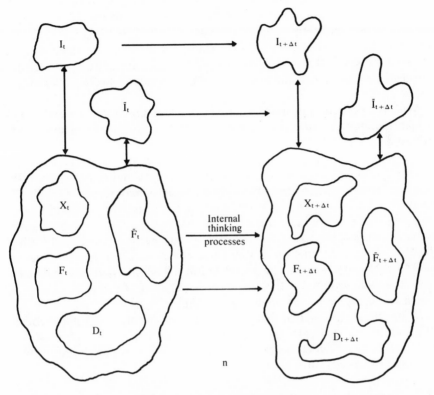

Figure 1. Decision Dynamics.

DEFINITION 2.1. An alternative x^0 is $[t_1,t_2]$-optimal iff $x^0 \in X_t$ and x^0 is the unique nondominated alternative for each $t \in [t_1,t_2]$.

Here by "x^0 is nondominated in X_t" we mean that there is no feasible alternative in X_t which is "better" than x^0 in view of the preference/domination structure of the decision maker.

Note that three conditions are implicitly imposed for x^0 to be $[t_1,t_2]$-optimal. First, x^0 must be the *unique nondominated solution*. Until this condition is satisfied, the decision maker will hesitate about which one to choose.

The second condition is that x^0 must yield a *satisfactory outcome*. One can easily construct a domination structure so that each unsatisfactory outcome is dominated. (For instance see Ref. 1.) Thus when x^0 is nondominated it must yield a satisfactory outcome.

The final condition is that the decision maker must be *convinced* that x^0 enjoys the above two conditions over $[t_1,t_2]$. This condition is built into the confidence structure of $\bar{F}_t$. Until this condition is satisfied the decision maker will continue to seek additional information, advice, or suggestions in order to increase his/her confidence in his/her own judgment.

With the definition of time-optimality one can derive a technical result which generalizes "the maximum principle." The interested reader is referred to Yu [23]. The following is worth mentioning.

Suppose that at time t_1 of the decision process the decision maker wants to reach a final decision by time $T(t_1)$. If x^0 is perceived as $[t_1,t_2]$-optimal and $[t_1,T(t_1)] \subset [t_1,t_2]$, then the decision process may terminate with x^0 as the final decision. Observe, the terminal time $T(t_1)$ may depend on t_1. Suppose that the terminal time T is fixed. As t_1 approaches T, new criteria such as *information stress* and *frustration* will, perhaps unwittingly, surface when suitable time-optimality cannot be found. These new criteria will force the decision maker to settle for a final decision which is perceived as time-optimal with respect to the new set of criteria.

On the other hand, even though a solution appears at time t_1 to be $[t_1,t_2]$-optimal, the arrival of new information during $[t_1,t_2]$ may render the solution no longer $[t_1,t_2]$-optimal. This is an important feature of decision dynamics, which we must keep in mind when second-order games are under consideration.

2.2. Second-Order Games

Any game which is not restricted in spirit to the assumptions imposed by the traditional game theory models (refer to Section 1) will be broadly called a second-order game. Using the concepts of decision dynamics from the previous section and also the appearance of the players, we can summarize the main differences between second-order games and traditional game models in Table 1.

While Table 1 is self-explanatory, the following two examples are constructed to further illustrate the concepts of second-order games.

EXAMPLE 2.1. Consider the problem of a policeman who has to guard two warehouses (denoted by 1 and 2), and a thief who tries to steal from one of the two warehouses. In traditional game models, one may define P_{ij} to the probability of catching the thief if the policeman guards the ith warehouse and the thief operates on the jth warehouse. Here, $i,j = 1$ or 2. The policeman is then to choose a strategy to maximize P_{ij}, while the thief

Table 1. Main Differences Between Second-Order Games and
Traditional Game Models

Decision Elements	Second-Order Games	Traditional Game Models
X_t	Varies with time, generated as needed	Fixed set
F_t	Multiple criteria, usually varies with time	Fixed single criterion
$\tilde{F}_t$	Outcomes specified with confidence structures which may vary with time	Decision outcome is usually deterministic and occasionally with known probability distributions
D_t	Preference, dominance, and satisficing can all vary with time	One fixed valued function
I_t, $\tilde{I}_t$ and internal information processing	Vary with time; they are important parts of "strategies" and must be considered	Rarely or never considered
Players	May be hidden or change with time	Well known to all players

chooses a strategy to minimize P_{ij}. This formulation reduces the problem into a simple zero-sum game. In real life or second-order games, the policeman's and the thief's problems are not so simple. For instance, the policeman may consider "decoy" or "adding mechanical aid" as part of the alternatives (X_t); his own life security, future promotion, and family life may be as important as catching the thief (F_t); the outcomes of each alternative choice may be very fuzzy to him ($\tilde{F}_t$); and his overall preference (D_t) among the trade-offs of his own life security, future promotion and family life may not be very clear and may change with time and experience. Similarly, the thief may consider "setting fire on another building before his operation" as an alternative (X_t); life safety, retaliation, and ego satisfaction may be part of his criteria of choice (F_t); outcomes of each choice ($\tilde{F}_t$) and the preference over the possible outcomes (D_t) may be extremely unclear, not to mention that they may change with time and experience.

EXAMPLE 2.2. (Adapted from a historical case in Ref. 26.) About 2,000
years ago there were two rival nations in Asia, designated for convenience by C (China—Han Dynasty) and
M (the invading tribes from Mongolia). M's king and
queen commanded an overwhelming army and had C's
emperor and troops surrounded in an isolated city. The
emperor, his aides and troops were desperate in the national crisis and fearful of being captured and killed. A
wise aide, Chen Ping, finally came up with an innovative
idea to dissolve the crisis. "A famous artist was asked
to paint an imaginatively charming and beautiful lady.
The painting was secretly sent to M's queen with the
message that the charming lady is going to be offered to
the king for his victory and that she is so charming and
attractive that the current queen will surely be deposed." On the same night that the painting was received, the queen, beloved by the king, kept sobbing and
weeping in front of the king at bedside before bedtime.
After many inquiries for the reason, the queen finally
told the king that she had had a very bad dream the other
night that both of them had been killed in a battle with
C. She then successfully persuaded the king to retreat
to their own country the next day, to cherish their love!

Observe that from the queen's point of view the glory of conquering C
was not as important as retaining the love of the king, and that the thought
of being deposed was not fun at all! From the king's point of view it was
much better to be alive as a king than to be killed in battle. The glory of
conquering C could of course never make up for his death.

The reader will notice that superstition was important in the thinking
processes of the king and the queen. The interested reader may also want
to reexamine how an additional person was introduced to the game in
order to effectively change the four decision elements of the players in
resolving the difficult problem of C.

2.3. Solution Concept: Time Stability

Since each player is a decision maker, he/she will, implicitly or explicitly, have the decision elements which may evolve with time, information inputs, and psychological states. The concepts of decision dynamics and time optimality become handy for a solution concept of
second-order games.

In order to make our discussion more concrete, let $\{X_t^i, F_t^i, \tilde{F}_t^i, D_t^i\}$ be the ith person's elements of decision dynamics at time t. Let $x_t^i \in X_t^i$, $x_t = (x_t^1, \ldots, x_t^n)$, and $\bar{x}_t^i = \{x_t^j \mid j \neq i; j = 1, \ldots, n\}$. The main difference between the decision dynamics of one person and that of n-person is that in the former $\tilde{F}_t^i$ is dependent only on x_t^i, and in the latter $\tilde{F}_t^i$ is dependent not only on x_t^i but also on $\bar{x}_t^i$ (that is, x_t^j; $j \neq i$; $j = 1, \ldots, n$), which is not under the control of the ith person.

Observe that tremendous uncertainty is involved in n-person decision dynamics for each player. Since $\tilde{F}_t^i$ is dependent on x_t^i and $\bar{x}_t^i$, and since the latter is not under the control of the ith person, the unpredictability of $\bar{x}_t^i$ will lead to that of $\tilde{F}_t^i$. In order to make $\bar{x}_t^i$ more predictable, the ith person may want to predict $\{X_t^j, F_t^j, \tilde{F}_t^j, D_t^j\}$ for each $j \neq i$ ($j = 1, \ldots, n$). However, such a prediction cannot always be accurate because of the gaps existing in the players' perceptions, information inputs, and judgments. The problem can be further complicated when some or all players are trying to influence the other players. Various information is given or concealed concerning decision making in such a way to influence the other players to choose alternatives that are favorable to those having the information. This complication has existed in our daily nontrivial decision problems ever since the existence of man.

Through the processes of deliberation and interpretation of information inputs (solicited or unsolicited), each player modifies and reframes his decision elements $\{X_t^i, F_t^i, \tilde{F}_t^i, D_t^i\}$. Our concern then becomes when and under what conditions the players can reach a stable settlement in their conflicting environments.

Toward this end we observe that a player will constantly look for a "better" choice until he is convinced (correctly or erroneously) that "optimality" has been obtained. Since the decision elements of the players interact with one another, a game cannot reach a stable settlement until every player in the game is convinced that "optimality" for himself is obtained. This observation yields:

DEFINITION 2.2. Let $x_0 = (x_0^1, \ldots, x_0^n)$ be such that x_0^j is an action of the jth player at t_0 (i.e., $x_0^j \in X_{t_0}^j$). We say that x_0 is a $[t_0, t_s]$-*stable solution* for the game iff, for each j, x_0^j is a $[t_0, t_j]$-optimal solution for the jth player with respect to $\{X_t^j, F_t^j, \tilde{F}_t^j, D_t^j\}$ and each $t_j \geq t_s$.

Note that the above time-stability is derived from time-optimality (Section 2.1). Although the condition is fairly strong, it can be achieved occasionally since the decision elements are subject to change from time to time. (Refer to Example 2.2.) On the other hand, the fact that x_0 is a $[t_0, t_s]$-stable solution does not guarantee that the game will be stable with each player choosing x_0^j throughout the time interval $[t_0, t_s]$. This is due to the fact that information inputs (solicited or unsolicited) will constantly reach each player and that the players' psychological states may change during the time interval $[t_0, t_s]$, which may upset the previous perception of optimality and break off the previously conceived stability.

Based on the time-stability concept, one can derive technical results which generalize the semipermeable condition of differential games. (See Refs. 11 and 23.) In Yu [23] one can find a systematic description of how one can reframe the four decision elements $\{X_t, F_t, \tilde{F}_t, D_t\}$ so as to solve the conflict problems. We shall not repeat it here.

3. BEHAVIOR BASES AND HABITUAL DOMAINS

In order to understand the working and mechanism of second-order games we need a broader comprehension of human psychology and behavior than that contained in the traditional pure mathematical description of decision making and game theory. Toward this end, we shall first briefly introduce an integrated dynamic model of human behavior and decision in Section 3.1. Then in Section 3.2 we shall focus on the concept of habitual domain, its definition, formation, implications, and main ideas. In Section 3.3 we shall discuss the expansion and interaction of different habitual domains, which form the cornerstone in second-order games.

3.1. A Model for Decision/Behavior Processes

In order to capture the main ideas as well as the dynamic and integrative features of human decision/behavior processes, Flow Chart 1 has been constructed. The following main ideas of the model are worth mentioning:

i.   Each individual is endowed with internal information-processing and problem-solving capacity, which can vary with time. *Attention (Box 6) is identified as a human's conscious time allocation of his/her internal information processing and problem-solving capacity over various activities and events.* The time could be measured in milliseconds. The allocation has direct impact on his allocation of internal body resources and external economic resources. This is a main concept which departs from traditional psychology and which allows us to use optimization of time allocation to study human decision/behavior.

ii.   A number of state variables are used to describe human physiological conditions, social situations, and self-suggested goals. A structure of the goals is listed in Table 2. Each state variable is constantly monitored and interpreted. When a variable's current value is significantly different from its goal value (ideal state), a charge (tension) will be produced. The charges produced by the various states form a hierarchical system de-

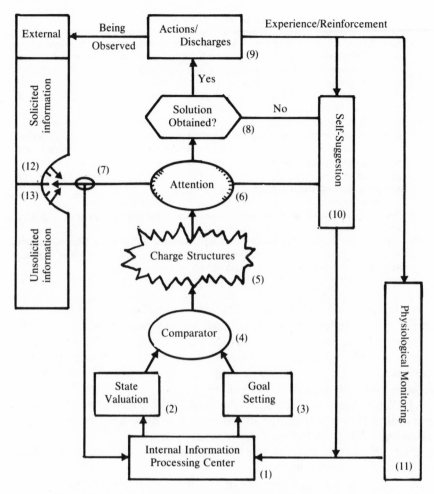

Flow Chart 1.   A Model of Decision/Behavior Processes.

pending on the relative importance of the states and on how significant the deviations of the perceived values from the ideal values are. The system can be reframed dynamically (Boxes 1–5).

iii.   *The purpose of attention* is to release the charges in the most efficient way. These ways involve (a) actions and discharges when solutions are obtained (Boxes 8 and 9); (b) acquiring external information (Boxes 7, 12, and 13); or (c) self-suggestion for internal thinking, justification, and rationalization (Box 10). All of these functions feed back to the internal information processing center.

Table 2. A Structure of Goal Functions

---

i. *Survival and security*: physiological health (proper blood pressure, body temperature, and balance of biochemical states); proper level and quality of air, water, food, heat, clothes, shelter, and mobility; safety and danger free; acquisition of money and other economic goods

ii. *Perpetuation of the species*: sexual activities; giving birth to the next generation; family love, health, and welfare

iii. *Self-importance feeling*: self-respect and self-esteem; esteem and respect from others; power and dominance; recognition and prestige; achievement; creativity; superiority; accumulation of money and wealth; giving and accepting sympathy and protectiveness

iv. *Social approval*: esteem and respect from others; friendship; affiliation with (desired) groups; conformity with group ideology; beliefs, attitudes, and behaviors; giving and accepting sympathy and protectiveness

v. *Sensuous gratification*: sexual; visual; auditory; smell; taste; tactile

vi. *Cognitive consistence and curiosity*: consistency in thinking and opinions; exploring and acquiring knowledge, truth, beauty, and religion

vii. *Self-actualization*: ability to accept and depend on the self, to cease from identifying with others, to rely on one's own standard, to aspire to the "ego-ideal," and to detach oneself from social demands and customs when desirable

---

iv.   Each event can be associated with a set of goals. Its significance can be defined in terms of the remaining charge structures when the event is removed. According to lexicographical ordering, the significance of events can be compared. The *most significant event* will command the attention. As charge structures change rapidly, the attention can switch rapidly from one event to other events.

v.   When there is a set of alternatives for discharge, the one which can reduce the current charge structures to a minimum will be chosen for discharge. This is called the *least resistance principle*.

(Note that iv and v are similar. Both of them are complex optimization problems for our "brain.")

vi.   All functions/components of the flow chart are interconnected. Through time they interact. For instance, once an action is taken (Box 9), say, publishing an article, the event and its consequence will be observed and registered in the decision maker's memory (Box 1) and will also likely be observed and interpreted by other parties (Boxes 12 and 13), which may in turn react upon the original decision maker (Boxes 7 and 11).

For more details the reader is referred to Ref. 24, in which the observations of experimental and general psychology are incorporated into eight hypotheses to describe the dynamic systems of human decision/behavior. With suitable interpretation the described system can capture most human decision/behavior. Observe that according to the model, many factors and functions can affect decision making and our understanding of decision making. These factors and functions may be the main source of fuzziness in decision making, which cannot be simply described by traditional probability theory.

3.2. Concepts and Formation of Habitual Domains

It has been recognized that each human being has habitual ways to respond to stimuli. Conditioned or programmed behaviors are some of the descriptions of these habitual ways of responses. We shall capture these behaviors in terms of habitual domains (HD).

More specifically, by the *habitual domain at time t*, denoted by HD_t, we mean the collection of ideas and actions that can potentially be activated at time t. If we return to Flow Chart 1 (in Section 3.1), we see that habitual domains involve self-suggestions, external information inputs, biophysical monitoring, goal setting, state valuation, charge structures, attention, and discharges. They also involve encoding, storing, retrieving, and interpreting mechanisms. When a particular aspect or function is emphasized, it will be designed as "habitual domain on that function." Thus habitual domain on self-suggestion, habitual domain on charge structures, habitual domain on attention, etc. all make sense. When the responses to a particular event are of interest, we can designate them as "habitual domains on the responses to that event." Thus habitual domain on job seeking, house purchasing, dealing with friends, etc. also makes sense.

In Yu [24], the existence of stable state of HD_t based on a set of hypotheses is described. For a mathematical proof, the reader is referred to Chan and Yu [28]. Roughly, as each human being learns and experiences, his/her HD_t grows with time, but at a decreasing rate because the probability for an arrival idea to be new with respect to HD_t is getting smaller as HD_t gets larger. Thus, unless unexpected extraordinary events occur, HD_t will reach its stable state. Once such a state is reached, habitual ways of thinking and responding to stimuli can be expected. If extraordinary events do not occur too often, as usual, HD_t will remain in its stable state. Thus habitual ways of thinking and acting can be manifest most of the time. This observation was the main motivation for using "habitual" as the adjective. The literature is rich with studies devoted to the formation of habits under the names of personality, human development, and the origins of intellect. Interested readers are referred to Refs. 8, 9, and 17 and references cited therein.

The following are some important implications of the existence of stable state of HD_t:

  i.   In decision analysis, the dynamics of the four elements $\{X_t, F_t, \bar{F}_t, D_t\}$ can become stable. This result makes it possible for us to apply operations research techniques to solve decision problems. In the empirical study on home purchases [4], it is reported that the cognitive structure of the decision makers (DMs) did change during the decision process, but the structures become more simplified after house touring. Acquisition of familiarity and confidence makes the DM's cognitive structure more clarified and stable.

ii.   The notion that an arriving idea is *rational* may be defined as its being contained in, or consistent with, the DM's HD_t. In conflicting situations, the rivals cannot successfully resolve or dissolve their conflict until their HDs are *expanded* or *reformed* so that there is a solution which is rational to all rivals. This observation is important for second-order games.

iii.   The existence of stable HD_t also implies the existence of personality. Therefore, the behavior of decision making, to a large extent, may depend on the DM's personality or stable HD_t. Much needs to be researched in this area!

iv.   The growth of HD_t may be regarded as a result of learning and experiencing. It has great impact on career success. If "organizations" (in a broad sense, including companies, societies, countries, international relations, etc.) are regarded as *living* entities, then they also have HD_t. The combination of an individual's HD_t and the organization's HD_t will, to a large extent, determine whether that individual will be successful, happy, and prosperous in the organization. Again, much additional research in this area is required.

In the remaining part of this section, some basic concepts of HD_t will be described in order to facilitate later discussions.

Note that through self-suggestion and/or external information inputs one idea or set of ideas can be used to stimulate or generate other ideas. This observation indicates that there exists a set of *operators* defined on a subset of HD_t which generate ideas in HD_t from the subsets of HD_t. As an example, suppose that one is interested in investing a fixed amount of cash in stocks A and B. The concept (the operator) that any portfolio (a convex combination) of A and B would also be of interest will expand the alternative set of A and B into the set of all convex combinations of A and B. Note, the operators are elements of HD_t.

Let I_t be a set of ideas with $I_t \subset HD_t$, and O_t be a set of operators which generate ideas in HD_t from subsets of HD_t. Define $R(I_t, O_t)$, called *reachable domain,* to be the set of ideas/actions that can be *reached* (or attained) from I_t and O_t. More precisely, $R(I_t, O_t)$ is the set of ideas/actions that can be cumulatively generated by any sequence of operators from the set O_t which act on I_t and the resulting ideas/actions from the operations. In the home-purchasing problem, I_t is the initial idea to purchase a suitable house and O_t is the set of existing value systems. Then $R(I_t,O_t)$ contains all the ideas generated by I_t and O_t, including some preliminary sets of $\{X_t,F_t,\tilde{F}_t,D_t\}$.

We say that $\{I_t,O_t\}$ is a *generator* of HD_t iff $HD_t = R(I_t,O_t)$, and that $\{I_t,O_t\}$ is a *basis* for HD_t iff $\{I_t,O_t\}$ is a generator of HD_t and no strict subset of $\{I_t,O_t\}$ can be a generator of HD_t.

Note that HD_t is the set of ideas and actions that can be *potentially* activated, rather than *actually* activated, at time t. In order to distinguish the difference, the latter will be denoted by AD_t, called the *actual domain at time t*. Clearly $AD_t \subset HD_t$. The relationship between AD_t and HD_t is similar to that of *the realized value* and the *sampling space* of a random variable. The set AD_t, varying with time, will be affected by the charge structures and attention at time t. The probability or confidence level for an idea/action to be activated will depend on how strongly the idea/action has been encoded and how easily the idea/action can be retrieved from its memory storage. It is also closely related to $R(I_t,O_t)$ with I_t as the set of initially activated ideas and O_t as the set of active operators around the time t. One can then formally introduce a probability or confidence structure (similar to that in Ref. 25), denoted by P_t, to indicate the probability that a set of ideas/actions in HD_t is in AD_t.

We summarize the above concepts and the related abstract symbols as follows:

1. HD_t (habitual domain)—the collection of ideas/actions that can be *potentially* activated at time t
2. AD_t (actual domain)—the set of ideas/actions that is *actually* activated at time t
3. P_t—the probability or confidence structure at time t which indicates the possibility for a set of ideas/actions in HD_t to be in AD_t
4. $R(I_t,O_t)$ (reachable domain)—the reachable (attainable) set of ideas/actions from the initial set of ideas I_t through the set of operators O_t

In studying habitual domains, we shall be interested in all of the above four concepts. Unless otherwise specified, we shall use the term "habitual domains" in a broad sense which includes the above four concepts.

3.3. Expansion of Habitual Domains

In this section we shall discuss the growth or expansion of habitual domains. Singular expansion and jumping out of habitual domain will be our focus of discussion. Some suggestions for expanding HD are also given.

Let s be the *starting* time and $R(I_s, O_s)$ be known. We are interested in the set of all reachable ideas/actions at a time t > s.

In order to facilitate our discussion, consider the problem of generating feasible investment alternatives. At time s, let $I_s = \{A, B\}$ and $O_s = \{O^1\}$, with O^1 representing the operator of "convexization," i.e., forming portfolios by convexization. Then $R(I_s, O_s)$ can be depicted as the line segment [A,B]. Note that if I_s is expanded to include C in Figure 2(a), the reachable domain will not be affected. However if D is included as in Figure 2(b), the reachable domain will be expanded. On the other hand, the operators have effect on the reachable domain. If we add an operator O^2, i.e., equal weight portfolio [thus in Figure 2(a), such operator generates E from A,B], we see that the reachable domain is unaffected by adding O^2. However, when we add operator O^3, i.e., any portfolio is acceptable as long as it does not exceed the budget, then the reachable domain expands from the line segment [A,B] to the triangle of [A,B,O], where O is the origin, in Figure 2(c). These examples illustrate that the expansion of the reachable domain is dependent on the suitable expansion of the ideas/actions set I_s and that of the operator set O_s.

In order to capture the above observation, let $\tilde{I}_t$ and $\tilde{O}_t$ respectively be the set of new ideas/actions and new operators acquired during the time interval (s,t], (excluding s but including t). Denote the resulting reachable domain of all ideas/actions at time t by $Q_{st}(I_s, O_s; \tilde{I}_t, \tilde{O}_t)$, and call it *reachable domain from s to t*.

DEFINITION 3.1. We say that during the time interval (s,t]:

(i) $\tilde{I}_t$ (or $\tilde{O}_t$) *triggers a singular expansion* [*of the reachable domain* $R(I_s, O_s)$] if $Q_{st}(I_s, O_s; \tilde{I}_t, \emptyset)$ [or $Q_{st}(I_s, O_s; \emptyset, \tilde{O}_t)$] contains $R(I_s, O_s)$ as a strict subset;

(ii) $\tilde{I}_t$ and $\tilde{O}_t$ *jointly trigger a singular expansion* [*on the reachable domain* $R(I_s, O_s)$] if $Q_{st}(I_s, O_s; \tilde{I}_t, \tilde{O}_t)$ contains $R(I_s, O_s)$ as a strict subset;

(iii) the reachable domain $R(I_s, O_s)$ *has a singular expansion* if there exist $\tilde{I}_t$ and/or $\tilde{O}_t$ which trigger a singular expansion of the reachable domain.

Figure 2(a)

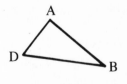

Figure 2(b)

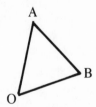

Figure 2(c)

DEFINITION 3.2. We say that during the time interval (s,t]:

(i) $\tilde{I}_t$ (or $\tilde{O}_t$) *triggers (the reachable domain to have) a jump out of the habitual domain* HD$_s$ if $Q_{st}(I_s,O_s;\tilde{I}_t,\emptyset)$ [or $Q_{st}(I_s,O_s;\emptyset,\tilde{O}_t)$] is *not* contained in HD$_s$;

(ii) $\tilde{I}_t$ and $\tilde{O}_t$ *jointly trigger (the reachable domain to have) a jump out of the habitual domain* HD$_s$ if $Q_{st}(I_s,O_s;\tilde{I}_t,\tilde{O}_t)$ is *not* contained in HD$_s$;

(iii) the reachable domain *has jumped out of the habitual domain* HD$_s$, if there exist $\tilde{I}_t$ and/or $\tilde{O}_t$ that trigger a jump out of HD$_s$.

From Definitions 3.1 and 3.2, we immediately see that triggering a jump out of HD$_s$ implies triggering a singular expansion in reachable domain. Also, a necessary condition for a reachable domain to have singular expansion without jumping out of HD$_s$ is that HD$_s$\R(I$_s$,O$_s$) $\neq \emptyset$. Note, HD$_s$ $\supset$ R(I$_s$,O$_s$).

THEOREM 3.1. (See Yu [24] for a proof.)

(i) A necessary and sufficient condition for $\tilde{I}_t$ to trigger a singular expansion of R(I$_s$,O$_s$) is that $\tilde{I}_t$\R(I$_s$,O$_s$) $\neq \emptyset$.

(ii) A necessary and sufficient condition for $\tilde{I}_t$ to trigger a jump out of HD$_s$ is that $\tilde{I}_t$\HD$_s$ $\neq \emptyset$.

(iii) The condition that R(R(I$_s$,O$_s$),$\tilde{O}_t$)\R(I$_s$,O$_s$) $\neq \emptyset$ is sufficient for $\tilde{O}_t$ to trigger a singular expansion of R(I$_s$,O$_s$). It is also a necessary condition when the multiplicativity property holds (i.e., R(I$_s$,O$_s$ $\cup$ $\tilde{O}_t$) = R(R(I$_s$,O$_s$),$\tilde{O}_t$) = R(R(I$_s$,$\tilde{O}_t$),O$_s$) holds.

(iv) The condition that R(R(I$_s$,O$_s$),$\tilde{O}_t$)\HD$_s$ $\neq \emptyset$ is sufficient for $\tilde{O}_t$ to trigger a jump out of HD$_s$. It is also a necessary condition when the multiplicativity property holds.

The following points are worth mentioning:

1. Note that (i) and (ii) of Theorem 3.1 imply that if $\tilde{I}_t$ triggers a singular expansion but not a jump out of HD$_s$, then $\tilde{I}_t$\R(I$_s$,O$_s$) $\neq \emptyset$ and $\tilde{I}_t \subset$ HD$_s$. Here the new set $\tilde{I}_t$ is generated through *retrieving* from the previously encoded ideas/actions in the memory at time s. New information inputs and/or self-suggestion could help the retrieving. However, if $\tilde{I}_t$ triggers a jump out of HD$_s$, $\tilde{I}_t$ is not in the memory at time s. The set needs to be

encoded and retrieved during the time interval (s,t]. Thus it is more difficult to get this type of $\bar{I}_t$. Again new information and/or self-suggestion may help the creation.

2. As in point 1, above, from (iii) and (iv) of Theorem 3.1 we can conclude that it is more difficult to generate a new set $\tilde{O}_t$ which triggers a jump out of HD_s than to generate $\tilde{O}_t$ which triggers a singular expansion. External information inputs and self-suggestion can help the creation of new $\tilde{O}_t$.

In the remaining part of this section, we shall suggest some methods to expand our HD and $R(I_s, O_s)$.

The largest resource for expanding our HD is other people's HDs. It is safe to say that everyone's HD is almost surely unique. That is, there is virtually zero probability that the HDs of any two persons can be identical. (See Yu [24] for further discussion.) By being aware of the difference among HDs, we may begin to be willing and able to spend effort and time encoding and absorbing those favorable ideas/operators so as to expand our HD.

Depending on the degree of cooperation, rivalry, and intimacy, humans reveal their HDs to their partners, perhaps partially, consciously and/or unconsciously. Their revealed ideas/actions or operators may be *accepted or absorbed* because they are similar to those of the partners or because the partners make a special effort to do so. The ideas/actions or operators can also be *rejected* because they are strange to the partners and/or the partners either do not care or activate their self-suggestion to distort and avoid them. The acceptance or rejection will certainly depend on the partners' charge structure and attention, etc. Usually new ideas/actions or operators can be more easily learned and absorbed if they are similar to those which are already known. Confronted with ideas which are out of our HD, we may have a tendency to reject them right away, instead of taking time and effort to absorb them. This quick rejection to totally new ideas may prevent us from expanding our HD to a higher dimension.

In real life HDs of other people are not easily observed. Recall that the actual domain AD_s is a subset (perhaps very small) of HD_s. Most of the time only a portion of AD_s is observable, and without attention even the observable part of AD_s can be ignored and/or misinterpreted. The following are some important operators/ideas for awareness and absorption of other persons' HDs: (a) *sincere appreciation and genuine interest in other persons' abilities, skills, and well-being*; (b) *open-minded frank discussion with other people*; (c) *an attitude that other persons' opinions/beliefs can be right or valid*; and (d) *the willingness to think in terms of the other persons' interests.*

The following methods can also be used to expand our HD:

i.   Expand HD by considering one higher order of the systems within which we operate. For instance, in the stock market investment problem, one can regard the stock market as a subsystem of speculation markets, which also include the bond market, option market, futures market, etc.; again, the speculation markets together constitute a subsystem of the money-making mechanism. By looking into a higher-order system, we can usually broaden our mind and see other ideas/operators which we could not otherwise see.

ii.   Expand HD by periodically being aware of our existing HD and seriously questioning the preconceived assumptions and notions in the existing HD. Different assumptions and notions will likely produce different conclusions, just like different initial points and dynamics will produce different terminal points. This awareness and questioning can make us discover new ideas and expand our HD.

iii.   Expand HD by varying relevant parameters in the thinking process. For instance, in a house purchase decision, the potential buyer can vary the parameter of how much he/she can borrow from the bank in order to see the set of feasible houses to be purchased.

iv.   Expand HD by actively using "association law." By actively trying to find the similarity and difference between two objects, we may be able to discover new ideas. For instance, in decision making, we may be able to expand the set of alternatives X_t by deliberating the other three elements F_t, $\bar{F}_t$, and D_t. Through this deliberation, some new alternatives may be derived.

v.   Expand HD on specific problems by consulting with experts and studying previous similar events and books. This consultation can usually provide us with new ideas which we could not obtain otherwise.

vi.   Retreat from the specific problem for a while when we are trapped by our HD and when the foregoing methods offer no help. Turning off the problem has the effect of turning off the sense of being trapped. Then we can start our generating process when our mind is refreshed again. New concepts and vital ideas can be obtained in an easier fashion when our mind is fresh and is not trapped by the previous pattern of thinking.

4.   SECOND-ORDER GAMES AND HABITUAL DOMAINS

In the previous sections, we have regarded human beings as living systems that try to attain a set of goals or equilibrium states. Unless extraordinary events occur, the systems will reach their steady habitual domains and have habitual ways for conception, judgment, prediction, action, and re-action to various events. In decision dynamics, unless the four decision elements reach their steady state, a formal analysis and time-optimal solution may be very difficult to obtain. A rushed solution, especially for high-stake decision problems without adequate cool study (i.e., without reaching the steady state and having a careful study), usually cannot guarantee a satisfactory time-optimal solution.

In second-order games, concepts of decision dynamics and habitual domains become extremely important both for dissolving conflict and for survival. In his classic work [27], Sun Tzu summarized the principle of war as follows:

1. Knowing yourself and knowing your enemy, you can win (or not lose) 100 times in 100 battles!
2. Knowing yourself but not your enemy or knowing your enemy but not yourself, you win 50 times in 100 battles!
3. Not knowing yourself and not knowing your enemy, you lose 100 times in 100 battles!

The above statements may at first seem to be oversimplified. But if we interpret "knowing" as knowing the details of the habitual domains, their formation and expansion, and the details of the decision dynamics of $\{X_t, F_t, \bar{F}_t, D_t, I_t, \bar{I}_t\}$ for each player involved, then we can better appreciate Sun Tsu's penetrating view of strategic matters. In war, creating and implementing a strategy which is totally outside the enemy's habitual domains is fundamentally important. The tragic 1941 Pearl Harbor event is an example of what failure to "know" the enemy can mean. Without knowing our own and our enemy's habitual domains, this kind of strategy is very difficult to create and implement. The reader may find it worthwhile to review the amusing yet relevant lesson of Example 2.2. If the wise aide Chen Ping had not had a good understanding of the habitual domains of the king and the queen of M as well as those of C itself, then the innovative strategy would not have been created and successfully implemented.

The following are some suggestive questions that may help us cope with difficulties when we are engaged in a second-order game.

i. Who are the players? What are their interests and their habitual domains? What are their four decision elements and information inputs? Can we expand our habitual domains in order to understand and absorb theirs?

ii. Do we understand precisely the respective systems *in which, under which,* and *over which* each player, including ourselves, is working? Each system may be regarded as a dynamic living entity. Do we know the charge structures and habitual domains of each related system?

iii. What are our common interests? What are the conflicting interests? What are the impacts of a decision on our and the other players' short-run and long-run careers?

iv. Can we emphasize the common goals so as to encourage cooperation and reduce competition?

v. Can we trigger a high level of "charge" on some goal functions of the other players so that for their own interest they will take an action favorable to us?

vi. Are we aware of who else can influence the other players' decisions? Do we know their interests, charge structures and habitual domain? How can we influence them to influence the other players' decisions?

vii. Can we introduce new players so that the gaming situation is favorable to us?

viii. Can we change the rules of games (the time and the habitual constraints) so that the outcomes can be in our favor?

ix. Can we reframe a one-stage decision into a multiple-stage adaptive decision, and vice versa, so that the outcomes can be in our favor?

x. Can we expand our deals into a package (including risk sharing) so that the offer can be more acceptable to each player?

xi. Can we form a coalition with other players so that a better result can be obtained?

xii. Could the consequence of the game be very significant and irreversible? If so, do we have contingency plans? How do we avoid being caught by surprise?

xiii. Do we have adequate and accurate information or intelligence to make a correct prediction and decision? Are we aware of deceptive information? How do we improve the accuracy of information and intelligence?

xiv. Do we communicate well with the other players? Do we give them enough time to digest our ideas?

Further discussion and reframing tactics for second-order games can be found in Yu [23]. We shall not repeat them here. Brown [2], Ilich [10], Karrass [13], and Shelling [19] are also worth reading.

5. CONCLUSION

We have introduced the concepts and frameworks of decision dynamics, habitual domains, and second-order games. It is hoped that the concepts and the frameworks can help us cope with the difficulties and complexity of nontrivial decision problems and pervasive second-order games. For further detailed discussion, the interested reader is referred to Yu [23] for reframing tactics, to Yu [24] for an integration of psychology, optimization theory, and common wisdom, to Shenoy and Yu [20] for inducing cooperation using reciprocative strategies, and to Kwon and Yu [14] for reframing game payoffs to achieve full cooperation or targeted goals. Many research topics need to be further explored. The interested reader is referred to those mentioned in the above works and Ref. 22, and to the references cited therein.

ACKNOWLEDGMENTS

The author wants to thank his friends Su-Jin Chan and John D. Mitchell for many constructive suggestions for improving the writing. Of course the author is responsible for any mistakes which may remain.

REFERENCES

1. Bergstresser, K. and P. L. Yu, "Domination Structures and Multicriteria Problems in N-Person Games." *Theory and Decision* 8(1):5–48, 1977.
2. Brown, J. A. C., *Techniques of Persuasion, from Propaganda to Brainwashing.* Baltimore, Md.: Penguin Books, 1963.
3. Burns, J. M. *Leadership.* New York: Harper & Row, 1978.
4. Chan, S. J., C. W. Park, and P. L. Yu, "High-Stake Decision Making—An Empirical Study Based on House Purchase Processes." *Human Systems Management* 3:91–106, 1982.
5. Carnegie, D., *How to Win Friends and Influence People.* New York: Pocket Books, 1940.
6. Conarroe, R. R., *Bravely, Bravely in Business.* American Management Association, 1972.
7. Freedman, J. L., J. M. Carlsmith, and D. O. Sears, *Social Psychology.* Englewood Cliffs, N.J.: Prentice-Hall, 1974.
8. Hall, C. S., and G. Lindzey, *Theories of Personality.* New York: Wiley, 1970.
9. Hilgard, E. R. and G. H. Bower, *Theories of Learning.* New York: Appleton-Century-Crofts, 1966.
10. Ilich, J., *The Art and Skill of Successful Negotiation.* Englewood Cliffs, N.J.: Prentice-Hall, 1973.
11. Isaacs, R., *Differential Games.* New York: Wiley, 1965.
12. Janis, I. L. and L. Mann, *Decision Making, A Psychological Analysis of Conflict, Choice, and Commitment.* New York: The Free Press, 1977.
13. Karrass, C. L., *Give & Take, The Complete Guide to Negotiating Strategies and Tactics.* New York: Thomas Y. Crowell, 1974.
14. Kwon, Y. K. and P. L. Yu, "Conflict Dissolution by Reframing Game Payoffs Using Linear Perturbations." Journal of Optimization Theory and Applications, 39(2), 1983, pp. 187–214.
15. Luce, R. D. and H. Raiffa, *Games and Decisions.* New York: Wiley, 1967.
16. Miller, J. G., *Living Systems.* New York: McGraw-Hill, 1978.
17. Phillips, J. L., Jr., *The Origins of Intellect—Piaget's Theory.* San Francisco: W. H. Freeman, 1969.

18. Rapoport, A., *N-Person Game Theory—Concepts and Applications*. Ann Arbor: The University of Michigan Press, 1970.
19. Schelling, T. C., *The Strategy of Conflict*. New York: Oxford University Press, 1960.
20. Shenoy, P. P. and P. L. Yu, "Inducing Cooperation by Reciprocative Strategy in Non-Zero-Sum Games." *Journal of Mathematical Analysis and Applications* 80(1):67–77, 1981.
21. Von Neumann, J. and O. Morgenstern, *Theory of Games and Economic Behavior*. Princeton: Princeton University Press, 1944.
22. Yu, P. L., "Decision Dynamics with an Application to Persuasion and Negotiation." *TIMS Studies in Management Sciences*, Vol. 6. New York: North-Holland, 1977.
23. Yu, P. L., "Second Order Game Problem: Decision Dynamics in Gaming Phenomena." *Journal of Optimization Theory and Applications* 27(1):147–166, 1979.
24. Yu, P. L., "Behavior Bases and Habitual Domain of Human Decision/Behavior—An Integration of Psychology, Optimization Theory and Common Wisdom." *International Journal of Systems, Measurement and Decisions* 1(1):39–62, 1981.
25. Yu, P. L. and G. Leitmann, "Confidence Structures in Decision Making." *Journal of Optimization Theory and Applications* 22(2):265–285, 1977.
26. Su, M. C., *Historical Records* (Shih-Chi), Vol. 56, No. 26, Han Dynasty (explained by Fei Yin, Sung Dynasty). (*In Chinese.*)
27. Sun Tzu. *Principle of War*. (*In Chinese*; many publishers with many diverse commentaries.)
28. Chan, S. J. and P. L. Yu, "Stable Habitual Domains: Existence and Implications." Working Paper No. 160, School of Business, University of Kansas, 1984. (To appear in *Journal of Mathematical Analysis and Applications*.)

APPLICATIONS OF MULTICRITERION OPTIMIZATION IN ENGINEERING AND THE SCIENCES

Wolfram Stadler

WOLFRAM STADLER treats the reader to an excellent survey of MCDM applications in the areas of engineering and the sciences. To the extent that engineering problems are decision problems under multiple criteria, as are many of the science problems, and to the extent that all "solutions" to engineering problems are compromises, to that extent MCDM is natural and relevant for both. That's a large extent, to say the least.

Stadler's survey is precise, comprehensive and stimulating at the same time. It provides the much needed vantage point of an engineer, mathematical economist, or mathematician. It shows that MCDM is not evolving only within a small, self-pollinating group of over-organized operations researchers but is a property of all, in all areas, under many circumstances. MCDM is interdisciplinary, intercultural, and international; it draws on knowledge offered by psychologists, economists, behaviorists, engineers, mathematicians, policy and decision makers, businessmen, and managers, computer scientists, systems scientists, and many other groups. Only a tiny and hardly significant part of MCDM can be controlled, organized, and dictated by a small group of self-appointed "experts." Stadler also shows how futile are the efforts to remove MCDM from a public domain through a misplaced entrepreneurial spirit.

Stadler, on a purely philosophical level, comes to a conclusion that optimization in the sciences and in engineering should, first of all, attempt to discover the best possible designs within the context of the physical axioms of a particular theory—"ideal designs" of sorts. The question how close one is to the physically possible optimum or ideal should then be the guide towards optimal design.

Stadler demolishes simplistic misconceptions that MCDM is about optimizing one criterion while restating others as a constraints or that it is about optimizing some sort of scalar combination or aggregate of multiple criteria. Both of these views are gross misconceptions and unscientific simplifications. They have very little to do with MCDM. Stadler's discussion of these misconceptions is very detailed and convincingly illuminating.

Inescapably, in concert with Gearhart (elsewhere in this volume), Stadler recognizes the import of approximation theory and its contributions to the Chebyshev Problem, which forms the mathematical foundation for certain classes of compromise solutions.

Stadler also notices the fact that the very first mention of the vector maximum problem in the engineering literature was a note of Lotfi Zadeh in 1963. Lotfi Zadeh then went on developing his theory of fuzzy sets and his insight became lost for MCDM, to which he never returned. Yet, Zadeh's grasp of the multiplicity of criteria at that time was sure and promising.

Stadler's paper is obviously a part of a grand design: a total and comprehensive history of MCDM (already fully completed up to 1960), a history that is being written in step with the evolution of the subject in question. One almost can't wait for the history to be completed, even though that would imply the completion of MCDM, which, let us hope, will not occur too soon.

ABSTRACT

This survey is essentially constrained to papers where the primary objective is the working of a multicriteria optimization problem rather than its use as an illustration of a numerical algorithm. In addition, the emphasis is placed on problems based on established mathematical models and an optimization with respect to physical criteria. The concept of Pareto optimality appears to be the most widely used underlying multicriteria approach in the sciences; thus, some of its characteristics and misconceptions are presented in detail along with the author's viewpoint concerning its application in mechanics. Although the subject was introduced into the sciences some 20 years ago, little concrete use has been made of its possibilities, so that there are only approximately 40 papers which fall into the above category. All of these are reviewed here in some detail. It is hoped that this survey will provide an impetus for the wider use of multicriteria optimization in the sciences and in engineering.

1. INTRODUCTION

Multicriteria optimization has been an intrinsic part of economic theory for nearly 100 years. Its historical development until 1960 was presented as a survey by Stadler [48]. With the exception of a branching into game theory, beginning with an article in 1921 by Borel [7], the subject generally found use only in connection with mathematical economics. Multicriteria optimization was established as a subject in its own right in an article by Koopmans [23] in 1951. Koopmans introduced the concept of the efficient point set together with the idea of a domination cone, a subject which has been considerably expanded and added to more recently by Yu [53]. A further article in 1951 by Kuhn and Tucker [30] treated the subject from a purely mathematical viewpoint as a vector maximum problem in connection with nonlinear programming; the subject became mathematically acceptable after an article by Hurwicz [21] in 1958 (Hurwicz gave an extensive treatment of the vector maximum problem in Banach spaces). Not until 1963 did the subject find its way into the engineering literature with a brief note by Zadeh [54]. Since then, the subject has mushroomed somewhat, so that a recent bibliography by Stadler [49] contains more than 2,300 references with articles on or related to multicriteria decision making.

In spite of this proliferation, only a small number of articles can be said to contain applications in the sciences and engineering. Of course, this statement is made within the somewhat narrow scope of the present survey. The intent here is to review papers whose primary aim is the solution of a problem rather than the use of a problem as an illustration for a numerical algorithm. It is also assumed that the mathematical model upon which the optimization process is based is a generally accepted one which may lend itself to experimental justification. In additon, it is assumed that the choice of criteria is based on physical considerations rather than economic ones. Consequently, this review is a somewhat selective one, and the author apologizes for any omissions which may have occurred.

2. SOME PHILOSOPHICAL COMMENTS

Any optimization problem usually involves the following four steps:

1. *The selection of the mathematical model for the description of the physical phenomenon*—This may vary from the standard beam equations in structural analysis to evolutionary models in mathematical biology. In any case, it is assumed that the model has been shown to be an adequate one from a physical viewpoint.

2. *The selection of the set of given parameters and the set of design parameters*—The term "parameter" should be understood in its broadest possible meaning, in that it may refer to scalars, functions, or vectors. Thus, it may refer to the cross-sectional areas of the individual members of a truss or to a time-dependent evolutionary strategy.

3. *The selection of a preference and of an optimum with respect to that preference on the set of design parameters*—Such a preference may be introduced directly on the decision set, or a preference on some other set may be used to induce a preference on the decision set. The first approach has become prevalent in economics, although even there one is immediately interested in conditions subject to which there exists a utility function over this preference; in the sciences, the latter approach is more common. That is, one usually has in mind a criterion function from the decision set into the reals, thus using the standard ordering of the reals to induce an ordering on the decision set. An optimal decision, then, is one which yields, say, a minimum of the criterion.

4. *The selection of the analytical or numerical methods to be used in the solution of the problem*—Here, the selection is extensive since a large part of the literature deals with numerical algorithms.

Clearly, step 3 is most representative of the overall design philosophy adopted by a particular author. Within the present context, the whole range of possible philosophies may best be expressed in terms of two quotes representing the extremes. Beveridge and Schechter [6] write: "The two most important criteria are the level of profit and the level of investment or their equivalent forms. Normally, technical criteria should be some reduced form of the economic criteria." Leonhard Euler [17] writes:

> For since the fabric of the universe is most perfect and is the work of a most wise Creator, nothing whatsoever takes place in the universe in which some relation of maximum and minimum does not appear. Wherefore there is absolutely no doubt that every effect in the universe can be explained as satisfactorily from final causes, by

the aid of the method of maxima and minima [Euler's terminology for the Calculus of Variations] as it can from the effective causes themselves. Now there exist on every hand such notable instances of this fact, that in order to prove its truth, we have no need at all of a number of examples; nay rather one's task should be this, namely, in any field of Natural Science whatsoever to study that quantity which takes on a maximum or a minimum value, an occupation that seems to belong to philosophy rather than to mathematics.

It would seem that optimization in the sciences is more in line with this last quotation. Indeed, there is evidence, though still scant, that what might be termed "natural laws" (expressed in terms of the axioms of a particular discipline) impose bounds on the extent to which one may optimize in the sciences. Furthermore, it seems that these bounds can be realized through appropriately formulated multicriteria problems. Such criteria, which take a designer to the limits of physical possibility, would result in the best designs one could expect within a particular discipline. Equivalently, one can also conjecture that objects and processes in nature evolve to a configuration which is optimal in this sense, with respect to natural loading and boundary conditions. Practically, one would take a discretionary look at nature and conjecture, say, that a particular shape or structure has evolved to an optimal state. One would then attempt to duplicate that state by means of an appropriately formulated multicriteria optimization problem.

In these last two situations, the usual arguments in support of a choice of one criterion or another clearly would not be needed; a close match of the physical situation would generally be extremely convincing.

In conclusion, optimization in the sciences and in engineering should first attempt to discover the best possible designs within the context of the physical axioms of a particular theory. Once these are known, one may make inquiries concerning the cost of producing these optimal designs. Cost-related approximations of the optimal design may then be made with a clear understanding of how close one is to the physically possible optimum.

3. MULTICRITERIA OPTIMAL DESIGN

In the past, optima were generally based on the use of a single criterion. The subject of this paper is the exhibition of optimal designs derived from the simultaneous minimization (or maximization) of a finite number of criteria. From the literature, it is apparent that Pareto optimality serves as a basis for subsequent refinements, and that it has become the most widely accepted concept in multicriteria optimization. The concept thus will be discussed in some detail.

Collectively, one has a decision set $\mathscr{D}$ and N criteria $g_i(\cdot)$: $\mathscr{D} \to \mathbf{R}$, resulting in a criterion mapping $g(\cdot)$: $\mathscr{D} \to \mathbf{R}^N$, defined by $g = (g_1, \ldots,$

g_N). The attainable criteria set is defined by $Y = g(\mathcal{D})$. All of the criteria are to be minimized simultaneously subject to decisions $d \in \mathcal{D}$. The usual approach in this context consists of the introduction of a preference on the criteria space $\mathbf{R}^N$, together with corresponding optimal elements $\hat{y} \in \mathbf{R}^N$. Suppose $\hat{y} \in Y$; then, an optimal decision $\hat{d} \in \mathcal{D}$ is one for which $\hat{d} = g^{-1}(\hat{y})$. For the case of Pareto optimality, the preference on $\mathbf{R}^N$ is the natural order on $\mathbf{R}^N$ given by: For $x, y \in \mathbf{R}^N$, $I = \{1, \ldots, N\}$,

$$x \leqslant y \quad \text{iff} \quad x_i \leqslant y_i, \qquad \forall i \in I;$$

$$x < y \quad \text{iff} \quad x_i \leqslant y_i, \qquad x \neq y, \qquad \forall i \in I;$$

$$x \ll y \quad \text{iff} \quad x_i < y_i, \qquad \forall i \in I.$$

The Pareto optimal elements $\hat{y} \in Y$, then, are simply the minimal elements of Y with respect to the natural (partial) order $\leqslant$ on $\mathbf{R}^N$.

DEFINITION 3.1: PARETO OPTIMALITY. A decision $\hat{d} \in \mathcal{D}$ is Pareto optimal iff $d \in \mathcal{D}$ and $g(d) \leqslant g(\hat{d})$ implies $g(d) = g(\hat{d})$, for every $\hat{d}$-comparable $d \in \mathcal{D}$.

In spite of the simplicity of the basic ideas, there are two widely held misconceptions concerning the subject. Each appears to arise from particular problems where these impressions are valid. The following is a statement of the first of these:

Multicriteria optimization is no more than minimizing one of the criteria, say $g_i(\cdot)$, with the rest of them appearing as constraints.

Or, equivalently,

The criteria in a multicriteria optimization problem may be viewed interchangeably as criteria or constraints.

Consider the attainable criteria set Y depicted in Figure 1. The set of Pareto optima consists of the heavily drawn part of the boundary of Y between c and f. Point b obviously is a minimum of $g_1(\cdot)$ subject to $g_2 \leqslant s$ and a is a minimum of $g_2(\cdot)$ subject to $g_1 \leqslant r$; neither is Pareto optimal. However, one does have the following lemma.

LEMMA 3.1. Let $\hat{d} \in \mathcal{D}$ be Pareto optimal. Then, for an arbitrary choice of $j \in I = \{1, \ldots, N\}$, one has the following: $\hat{d}$ minimizes $g_j(d)$ subject to $d \in \mathcal{D}$ and

$$g_i(d) \leqslant g_i(\hat{d}) \qquad \forall i \in I, \quad i \neq j.$$

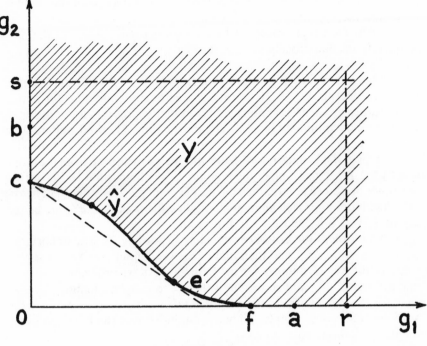

Figure 1.

Thus, the statement above serves as a necessary but not as a sufficient condition for Pareto optimality. The second statement has the form:

Multicriteria optimization is the same as minimizing a scalar combination of the criteria, $G(d) = c_1 g_1(d) + \cdots + c_N g_N(d)$, *subject to* $d \in \mathcal{D}$.

Note that all of the boundary points between c and e are Pareto optimal; however, none of them is a minimum of $G(d)$ subject to $d \in \mathcal{D}$, so that part of the solution possibilities would be omitted by this approach. Again, one has a related lemma.

LEMMA 3.2. Assume that $c \gg 0$ and $\hat{d} \in \mathcal{D}$ minimizes $G(d)$ subject to $d \in \mathcal{D}$ [that is, $G(\hat{d}) \le G(d) \ \forall d \in \mathcal{D}$]. Then $\hat{d} \in \mathcal{D}$ is a Pareto optimal decision.

The statement thus serves as a sufficient condition for Pareto optimality. It also is an example of what is known as scalarization, that is, the reduction of the vector minimization problem to a scalar optimization

problem. There are two reasons: the first is the reduction of the problem
to traditional approaches; the second is a desire for a unique solution
rather than the usual infinity of Pareto optimal ones. Some of the most
frequently used approaches are given below:

a. One introduces a "welfare" function $W(\cdot) = F \circ g(\cdot)$, which is minimized subject to $d \in \mathscr{D}$. Necessary and sufficient conditions for optima
under rather broad assumptions are given by the present author in papers
on preference optimality [44,47]. The most commonly used welfare functions are the previous linear combination $G(d)$ or some notion of a distance
function (e.g., an L_p metric), with distance being measured from the utopia
point $y^* \in \mathbf{R}^N$, consisting of the minima $y_i^* = \min\{g_i(d): d \in \mathscr{D}\}$, or from
any other preferred point. Since the utopia point generally does not belong
to Y, the latter approach amounts to finding the point $\hat{y} \in \partial Y$, the boundary of Y, which is "closest" to this point.

b. One orders the criteria completely according to their importance,
with $g_1, g_2, \ldots, g_N$, and then minimizes sequentially in the sense that,
if $\mathscr{D}_1^*$ is the set of minima for $g_1(\cdot)$, then the next problem consists of
$\min\{g_2(\cdot): d \in \mathscr{D}_1^*\}$ and so on, until there is a unique minimum for, say,
$g_i(\cdot)$; for the remaining criteria one then takes what one can get. Another
such approach is to simply minimize the most important criterion, with
the others kept as constraints.

c. One attempts to construct a scalar function $G(g)$, whose minimizing
level set coincides with the set of Pareto optima on the boundary of Y,
or a function $s(\cdot): \mathscr{D} \to \mathbf{R}^N$, whose range is the Pareto set.

At this point it is helpful to give general formulations for the multicriteria
programming and control problems. When working problems, it is useful
to convert to this general notation, since it eases the access to the mathematical literature.

i.   The Multicriteria Programming Problem.   Let Ω (open) $\subseteq \mathbf{R}^n$ and
introduce the *inequality constraints*

$$f(\cdot): \Omega \to \mathbf{R}^m,$$

the *equality constraints*

$$h(\cdot): \Omega \to \mathbf{R}^k,$$

with *functional constraint set*

$$X = \{x \in \mathbf{R}^n: x \in \Omega, \quad f(x) \leq 0, \quad h(x) = 0\}.$$

The *criterion functions* are

$$g_i(\cdot): X \to \mathbf{R}, \qquad i = 1, \ldots, N,$$

with corresponding *criteria map*

$$g(\cdot) = (g_1(\cdot), g_2(\cdot), \ldots, g_N(\cdot)).$$

The *attainable set* is

$$Y = g(X) = \{y \in \mathbf{R}^N: y = g(x), x \in X\}.$$

The basic problem statement is then: Obtain "optimal" decision(s) $\hat{x} \in X$ for $g(x)$ subject to $x \in X$.

ii. The Multicriteria Control Problem. Let the *state* $x \in A$ (open) $\subset \mathbf{R}^n$ be controlled by means of a *control* $u(\cdot)$: $[t_0, t_1] \to U \subset \mathbf{R}^r$ in the *state equations*:

$$\dot{x} = f(x, u), \tag{1}$$

with $x(t_0) \in \theta^0 \underline{\Delta}$ the *initial set* and $x(t_1) \in \theta^1 \underline{\Delta}$ the *terminal set* and with $x_n = t$, the independent variable, so that $f_n(x, u) = 1$. Furthermore,

$$f(\cdot): A \times U \to B \text{ (open)} \subset \mathbf{R}^n$$

is the *velocity function* and U is the *control constraint set*, the set of all possible values of $u(\cdot)$. It is usual to assume that $u(\cdot)$ belongs to a nonempty set $\mathscr{F}$ of *admissible controls*. A *criteria map* $g(\cdot): \mathscr{F} \to \mathbf{R}^N$ is defined in terms of the integrals

$$g_i(u(\cdot)) = \int_{t_0}^{t_1} f_{0i}(x(t), u(t)) \, dt,$$

where

$$f_{0i}(\cdot): A \times U \to C_i(\text{open}) \subset \mathbf{R}, \qquad i = 1, \ldots, N.$$

The *state space* $\mathbf{R}^n$ is augmented with

$$\dot{y} = f_0(x, u), \qquad y(t_0) = 0, \tag{2}$$

where $y \in \mathbf{R}^N$, the *criterion space,* and where $f_0 = (f_{01}, \ldots, f_{0N})$. Let $u(\cdot) \in \mathscr{F}$, and let $x(\cdot)$ be a corresponding solution of the state equations (1). Then the *attainable set* is defined by:

$$Y = \{y \in \mathbf{R}^N: y = s(t_1), \text{ where } s(\cdot) \text{ is a solution}$$
$$\text{of Eq. (2) corresponding to the pair}$$
$$(x(\cdot), u(\cdot))\}.$$

The basic problem statement is then: Obtain "optimal" control(s) $\hat{u}(\cdot) \in \mathscr{F}$ for $g(u(\cdot))$, subject to $u(\cdot) \in \mathscr{F}$.

At this point, Lemma 3.1 becomes extremely useful. As a consequence of the lemma, one can easily establish the following results:

The Kuhn–Tucker necessary conditions (including constraint qualifications) for the minimum of a single criterion function $g_0(\cdot)$ in nonlinear programming may be transformed to those for the multicriteria programming problem by replacing $g_0(\cdot)$ by

$$G(x) = c_1 g_1(x) + \cdots + c_N g_N(x) \text{ with } c > 0.$$

The maximum principle for the minimum of a single criterion functional $g_0(\cdot)$ in control theory may be transformed into that for the multicriteria control problem by replacing $g_0(\cdot)$ by

$$G(u(\cdot)) = c_1 g_1(u(\cdot)) + \cdots + c_N g_N(u(\cdot)) \qquad \text{with} \quad c > 0.$$

Precisely these results appear to be the reason for the aforementioned misconceptions about multicriteria optimization.

Some additional comments concerning Pareto optimality may be helpful in calculations. A decision $d_1 \in \mathcal{D}$ cannot be Pareto optimal if there exists another $d_2 \in \mathcal{D}$ such that $g(d_2) < g(d_1)$, that is, a decision d_2 which either decreases all of the criteria values, or at least one of them, with all others held fixed. Conversely, at a Pareto optimal decision $\hat{d} \in \mathcal{D}$, any further decrease in any criterion value requires a corresponding increase of at least one other criterion value.

The present author's experience with such problems in engineering would indicate the following general approach within the previously mentioned philosophical context:

Select N global criteria, that is, criteria which embody the behavior of the system as a whole, be it a structure, a network, a mixture, and the like, and then work an unconstrained global Pareto optimization problem. This procedure usually produces an $N - 1$–dimensional submanifold of $\mathbf{R}^N$. Subsequently, the imposition of $N - 1$ independent local equality conditions will then produce the sought-after unique solution. For example, one might use the strain energy and the mass of a structure as criteria for the structural multicriteria global optimization problem. The subsequent specification of a deflection or a stress at a point then produces a particular member of the Pareto set.

4. THE SURVEY

There is a gray area connecting cooperative game theory and MCDM, the basic difference being the number of decision makers. In the former, there generally are $N > 1$ decision makers represented by N criteria, with differing concepts of optimality (although they may ultimately agree on one); in the latter, there is one decision maker who chooses a single concept of optimality involving N criteria. There is an extensive literature in game theory, including a separate one for cooperative game theory, some of which may contain articles which would fall within the present guidelines. No specific research of such literature was made in writing this survey.

A check of the bibliography [49] and of the technical journals provides a fairly extensive list of titles which suggest applications-oriented papers. Unfortunately, in a majority of the cases, it happens that most of the paper deals with a discussion of MCDM and that the example serves as an illustration of yet another numerical algorithm. The imposition of the aforementioned guidelines results in a still greater reduction.

One of the earliest and broadest applications of MCDM methods lies at the fringes of the present guidelines. It concerns water resources planning: the earliest paper on the subject is one by Marglin [35] in 1967. Topics which fall under this general heading are river basin planning, water quality management, resources planning, and so on. For example, a river basin may be divided into several subsystems, including waste treatment plants, with each subsystem being modeled in terms of steady state mixture equations. These may involve inputs of chemical and biological wastes and outputs such as irrigation and power plants. The criterion functions usually include the cost of wastewater treatment or cost of removal of thermal pollution, and they are generally of an economic rather than a physical nature.

An additional point of interest and an explanation for the large number of articles on this topic is the extensive federal financial support of this research area. Furthermore, to the present author's knowledge, this is the only case in which actual statutory requirements based on MCDM analysis (as introduced by the U.S. Water Resources Council in 1973) are in effect within the U.S. government. A survey by Cohon [13] is of interest, along with a paper by Haimes and Hall [20], although these are not the most recent publications on this subject.

A more recent paper by Baptistella and Ollero [2] also includes the possibility of fuzzy information sets. Their basic model for the individual hydrothermal power-generating system is a linear finite difference model. The system state is the instantaneous reservoir storage determined by various inflow and discharge variables. The authors consider a system of N hydraulic and M thermal units. Their criteria essentially are the total difference in power demand and power output, total operation thermal cost, and the difference between irrigation demands and actual drawings, all of which are to be minimized simultaneously. The problem serves mainly as an illustration for a numerical algorithm, including local interactions with the decision maker. This interaction is based on fuzzy information available about the criterion values at a particular interaction. Fuzzy methodologies are used to obtain a trade-off between two criteria at a time, to generate a new set of weights. The procedure is repeated until the levels of all criteria are "acceptable." The authors indicate that their method generates noninferior solutions for the convex case, whereas the solution is not necessarily noninferior in the nonconvex case.

As indicated, this topic does not properly fall within the initially set guidelines. Since the subject has developed an extensive literature of its own, which may be traced in the *Water Resources Abstracts*, no further papers are included here. In view of the mathematical orientation of the guidelines, it is appropriate to begin with an application of MCDM in the mathematical sciences, namely, with various Chebyshev problems of approximation theory. Most of these problems only involve vector optimization in terms of scalarization, since they are generally concerned with the minimization of some norm.

The Chebyshev Approximation Problem [56].   Consider an inconsistent system of m linear equations in n unknowns of the form:

$$f_i(x) \equiv a_{i1}x_1 + \cdots + a_{in}x_n + a_i = 0, \qquad i = 1, \ldots, m. \qquad (3)$$

The Chebyshev approximation problem consists of finding a Chebyshev point for this system, that is, a point $\hat{x} = (\hat{x}_1, \ldots, \hat{x}_n)$ such that

$$\hat{f} = \max_{1 \leqslant i \leqslant m} |f_i(\hat{x})| = \inf_x \max_{1 \leqslant i \leqslant m} |f_i(x)|. \qquad (4)$$

From a geometric point of view $\hat{x}$ is the point with least deviation from the entire system of planes (3). If the n planes of (3) intersect at a point, that is, if all of the minors of the m × n matrix $[a_{ij}]$ are nonzero (Haar's condition), then this is the only case for which a Chebyshev point $\hat{x}$ is unique for any system of constants a_i.

Duris and Sreedharan [15] not only deal with this problem, but they also consider the least squares norm and the L_1 norm in addition to the maximum norm of the Chebyshev problem. For the case where Haar's condition is not satisfied, Behringer [4,5] introduces $f(x) = (f_1(x), \ldots, f_m(x))^T$ as a criterion vector and considers a corresponding vector maximum problem. He proposes a lexicographical approximation scheme which corresponds to an m-step Chebyshev approximation problem and which leads to a unique solution under somewhat weakened conditions. He also deals with conditions subject to which the solution is Pareto optimal.

The Extended Chebyshev Problem.   Consider a finite collection of real valued functions $g_i(x)$, for $i = 1, \ldots, N$, where $x \in \mathbf{R}^n$. Define

$$f(x) = \min_{1 \leqslant i \leqslant N} \{g_i(x)\}.$$

Then the extended Chebyshev problem consists of finding a point $\hat{x} \in \mathbf{R}^n$

such that

$$f(\hat{x}) = \sup_{x} f(x) = \sup_{x} \min_{1 \le i \le N} \{g_i(x)\}.$$

This problem appears frequently in game theory and in statistical analysis. Zangwill [55] presents a numerical algorithm converging monotonically to $f(\hat{x})$ for the case where all of the $g_i(x)$ are continuously differentiable and pseudoconcave. Jahn [22] introduces a constraint set X and considers the problem

$$\min_{x \in X} \| g(x) - \hat{y} \|_\infty,$$

where $\hat{y} \in \mathbf{R}^N$ is some preferred point. Since at least one solution $\hat{x} \in X$ of this problem is efficient, it follows that every unique solution is efficient. Jahn introduces a generalized Haar condition for this problem and investigates the uniqueness of the solution.

In the foregoing papers, the connection with MCDM is somewhat tenuous. The simultaneous approximation of several functions falls more obviously within the theory.

Dunham [14] considers two given continuous functions, $f_1(\cdot)$ and $f_2(\cdot)$, with $f_1(\alpha) \le f_2(\alpha)$ on [a,b]. He uses a continuous approximating function $F(x,\alpha)$ containing a parameter x, defines an error

$$e^i(x,\alpha) = f^i(\alpha) - F(x,\alpha), \qquad i = 1, 2,$$

and introduces criteria

$$g_i(x) = \sup\{| e^i(x,\alpha) |: a \le \alpha \le b\}.$$

He then calls a best simultaneous Chebyshev approximation to $f_1(\cdot)$ and $f_2(\cdot)$ on [a,b] by $F(x,\alpha)$—one for which the parameter $\hat{x}$ minimizes

$$e(x) = \max\{g_1(x), g_2(x)\}.$$

In a similar vein, Censor [11] considers a given family of real valued continuous functions $f^i(\alpha)$ on [a,b], for $i = 1, \ldots, s$, and s families $\{F_k^i(\alpha)\}_{k=1}^n$ of given real-valued continuous functions on [a,b].

For $i = 1, \ldots, s$, he defines s nondifferentiable, but convex criteria $g_i(x)$ by

$$g_i(x) = \| f^i(\alpha) - \sum_{k=1}^n x_k F_k^i(\alpha) \|_\infty = \max_{\alpha \in [a,b]} | f^i(\alpha) - \sum_{k=1}^n x_k F_k^i(\alpha) |.$$

The constrained finite simultaneous Chebyshev best approximation then consists of obtaining points $\hat{x} = (\hat{x}_1, \ldots, \hat{x}_n) \in \mathbf{R}^n$, which solve the multiobjective optimization problem:

$$\text{``min''}\{g_i(x)\}_{i=1}^s \qquad \text{such that} \quad x \in Q \subset \mathbf{R}^n,$$

where Q stands for the feasible set of the problem and $s > 1$. Censor uses Pareto optimality as the optimality concept and derives corresponding necessary conditions.

Further related treatments of these topics may be found in Bacopoulos [1], Bowman [8], Moursund [37], and in the references cited therein, some of which were not included here because they were unobtainable, others because they did not relate directly to the multicriteria aspects.

The next area of application is in mathematical biology. One example deals with optimal strategy selection in immunology, and another with optimal strategies in kin selection and evolution. Both articles are well written and should be of interest to anyone working in these areas.

Perelson et al. [41] examine the optimal strategies available to an immune system for responding to a nonreplicating thymus-independent antigen, including comparisons of these results with experimentally determined responses of natural systems. The construction of the mathematical model is described by the same authors in Ref. 40. The following dynamic multicriteria optimization problem is formulated:

Obtain Pareto optimal controls $\mathbf{u}^*(\cdot)$ for

$$g_1(\mathbf{u}(\cdot)) = \int_0^{T_1} dt \quad \text{and} \quad g_2(\mathbf{u}(\cdot)) = -M(T_1),$$

subject to the state equations

$$\dot{A} = k(L + \gamma P) \qquad\qquad\qquad A(0) = 0,$$

$$\dot{L} = buL - d_P vL - d_M wL - \mu_L L \qquad L(0) = L_0,$$

$$\dot{P} = d_P vL - \mu_P P \qquad\qquad\qquad P(0) = 0,$$

$$\dot{M} = d_M wL \qquad\qquad\qquad\qquad M(0) = 0,$$

with control constraints on $\mathbf{u} = (u,v,w)$ given by $0 \leq u \leq 1, 0 \leq v \leq 1$, $0 \leq w \leq 1$, and $u(t) + v(t) + w(t) = 1$. The state variables, controls, and parameters have the following meaning:

$A(t) =$ the number of antibodies present in the system at an instant t;

$L(t) =$ the number of large lymphocytes present in the system at the instant t (L_0 is the number present at $t = 0$);

$P(t) =$ the number of plasma cells present in the system at the instant t;

$M(t) =$ the number of memory cells present in the system at the instant t;

$k =$ antibody molecules/second secreted by the large lymphocytes;

$\gamma k(\gamma \geq 0)$ = antibody molecules/second secreted by the plasma cells;

μ_L, μ_P = death rates of the lymphocytes and plasma cells, respectively;

b,d = the large lymphocytes can either proliferate with constant birth rate b and increase the lymphocyte population or they can undergo further differentiation into mature plasma cells at a constant rate d;

d_P, d_M = the rates at which large lymphocytes differentiate into plasma cells and memory cells, respectively;

u = the fraction of daughter cells which remain large lymphocytes;

v = the fraction of large lymphocytes which differentiate into plasma cells;

w = the fraction of large lymphocytes which differentiate into non-antibody-secreting memory cells.

The criterion g_1 is the time required to secrete an amount of antibody A_1^* sufficient to neutralize the initial antigenic assault; the criterion g_2 expresses the desire to maximize the amount of memory cells at $t = T_1$, to ensure an enhanced elimination of the antigen in case of later infection.

The authors approach this problem by minimizing a single criterion:

$$g(\mathbf{u}(\cdot)) = \int_0^{T_1} dt + pT_2^*$$

with respect to u and v. Here, $T_2^*[M(T_1)]$ is the time required to complete the secondary response for a two-infection sequence, and $p \geq 0$ may be viewed as the probability of the organism encountering the same antigen again in the remainder of the reproductive lifespan. Furthermore, the authors restrict themselves to $d_M = d_P = d$.

The authors' approach thus may be classified as a penalty function approach. The corresponding necessary conditions are the same as those for Pareto optimality, and the final results are based on the extremal solutions obtained from these necessary conditions.

These results are the same as those obtained in Ref. 40 for the case without memory cells; that is, the extremal strategy is "bang-bang" and the control vector **u** takes on values only at the apexes of the unit simplex. The timing and sequence of switches depends on the system parameters $\{b, \mu_L, \mu_P, k_1, k_2, \gamma, d\}$, on the lymphocyte population L_0, on the final antibody required, and on the weighting parameter p. The authors state: "If A_1^*, the required antibody production, is larger than the same critical value, an initial proliferative stage of large lymphocytes [**u** = (1,0,0)] should be followed by (A) a switch to plasma cell differentiation [**u** = (0,1,0)], followed by a switch to memory cell production [**u** = (0,0,1)], or (B) a switch to plasma cells followed by a second switch back to lymphocyte proliferation and then a final switch to memory cell production, or (C) a switch to memory cell differentiation with no plasma cell production."

The authors carry out their calculations with realistic numerical values for the various parameters, and they state that there is some experimental evidence which indicates that memory cells may in fact be produced late in the primary response and that other evidence exists which is contradictory.

The second article is of additional interest because it presents evidence that natural phenomena may occur in a manner which optimizes several criteria simultaneously.

The paper by Mirmirani and Oster [36] contains a number of references dealing with related topics. Their mathematical model is restricted to the analysis of strategies which control the timing and allocation of resources. Let P(t) be the plant biomass which commences the season at a value $P(0) = P_0$. It is assumed that the plant can adopt but two strategies during a season: it can reinvest its resources into creating more plant biomass, and/or it can direct its metabolic resources into creating seeds whose biomass is denoted by S(t). Let $u(t) \in [0,1]$ denote the fraction of resources reinvested into creating new biomass, and let r be the resource conversion efficiency.

Consider now the situation where the plant is in the presence of a neighbor which competes for resources. To model this, the assimilation constant r for the single species is modified to include inhibition by the competition: $r_1 \rightarrow r_1 - E_2P_2$, where E_2 measures the strength of competitive interaction. For a constant supply of resources, the growth equations and seed production equations then are postulated in the form:

$$\dot{P}_1 = (r_1 - E_2P_2)u_1P_1, \qquad P_1(0) = P_{10} > 0, \qquad r_1 - E_2P_2 \geqslant 0;$$

$$\dot{P}_2 = (r_2 - E_1P_1)u_2P_2, \qquad P_2(0) = P_{20} > 0, \qquad r_2 - E_1P_1 \geqslant 0;$$

$$\dot{S}_1 = (r_1 - E_2P_2)(1 - u_1)P_1, \qquad S_1(0) = 0;$$

$$\dot{S}_2 = (r_2 - E_1P_1)(1 - u_2)P_2, \qquad S_2(0) = 0;$$

respectively. Only the symmetric case with $r_1 = r_2 = r$, $E_1 = E_2 = E$, and $P_{10} = P_{20} = P_0$ is considered with normalized time $t \in [0,1]$.

Each "player" of this competitive game for resources is assumed to manipulate its allocation control $u_i(\cdot)$ so as to maximize its reproductive output. That is, the fitness criteria are taken to be

$$J_1(\mathbf{u}(\cdot)) = S_1(1) \qquad \text{and} \qquad J_2(\mathbf{u}(\cdot)) = S_2(1),$$

where $\mathbf{u} = (u_1, u_2)$ with $u_i(t) \in [0,1]$. The authors show that the Nash equilibrium strategies for this problem are bang-bang with $u_1^*(t) = u_2^*(t)$ = 1 for $t \in [0,\tau^*]$ and $u_1^*(t) = u_2^*(t) = 0$ for $t \in [\tau^*,1]$. Thus, the plants start with vegetative growth until the switching time τ^* is reached, and then they switch to seed production.

When the symmetry assumptions are dropped, the optimal strategies are still bang-bang; however, the plants now have differing switching times τ_1^* and τ_2^*. A comparison with the single plant switching time indicates that the competition enforces earlier switching times and thus a lower overall seed production. If plant 2 has the higher conversion rate r, it can afford to wait longer to switch to seed production and end up with a larger seed biomass by season's end. Such a game, when played repetitively over several seasons, will ultimately result in plant 1 becoming extinct. The authors also point out that an important underlying assumption is that the Nash equilibrium strategy must correspond to homozygous genetic configurations. Otherwise, heterozygotes in both competing populations would have strategies deviating from the pure switching strategy. Some of these simultaneous deviations would lead to the simultaneous increase of both competitors, that is, in the direction of the Pareto set.

The authors also consider the problem of kin selection and competition between related individuals where the individual inclusive fitnesses are maximized simultaneously. Again, the strategies are bang-bang, and if both competitors cooperate, both can increase their fitness by switching earlier than provided by the Nash strategies. However, these cooperative strategies are unstable in the sense that either party can gain fitness by increasing its switching time, provided the other does not.

The all-or-none optimal strategy, with the switching time from vegetative growth to seed production as the only strategic parameter, is a fairly common type of reproductive strategy in annual plants. It is also observed in social insects and, to some approximation, in other organisms.

A paper by Burlyayeva et al. [9] deals with the extraction of insulin from frozen pancreas. The state equations are linear first-order equations with time as the independent variable. The equations contain coefficients w_j which are given by the expressions

$$w_j = b_{0j} + b_{1j}u_1 + b_{2j}u_2 + b_{3j}u_1^2 + b_{4j}u_2^2 + b_{5j}u_1u_2, \qquad j = 1, \ldots, 5.$$

The b_{ij} are given parameters and u_1, u_2, the pH and the strength, respectively, of the alcohol in the solvent, are the design parameters. The authors then scalarize the problem and optimize the choice of the parameters w_j by minimizing

$$G_1(u_1,u_2) = \sum_{j=1}^{5} (w_j - w_j^*)^2$$

and

$$G_2(u_1,u_2) = \max_j | w_j - w_j^* |, \qquad j = 1, \ldots, 5,$$

subject to $2.5 \leq u_1 \leq 3.5, 75 \leq u_2 \leq 85; w^* = (w_1^*, \ldots, w_5^*)$ is the utopia point. No discussion of the relative merits of the two approaches is given.

There is a large body of MCDM literature in electrical engineering journals; however, the application rarely is a major part of the article.

An article by Gembicki and Haimes [18] deals with an economic dispatch problem in an electric power system control for a three-bus system. The authors seek to determine an operating point for which the generation costs are as low as possible and also are insensitive to measurement errors and variations in demand. The system equations are of the form $F_i(x,u,p) = 0$, subject to operating constraints of the form $g_i(x) \leq 0$, for $i = 1, 2, 3$, where $x = (x_1,x_2,x_3)$ are the voltage phase angles (x_1,x_2) and the power (x_3) produced at the first generating bus; u is a controlled power input at the second bus; and $p = (p_1,p_2,p_3)$ are the real power demand levels at each of three system modes. The criteria are a performance index $P(x,u)$ consisting of a measure of the generating costs and a performance sensitivity index $S(v_j)$,

$$v_j = \left(\frac{\partial x_1}{\partial p_j}, \frac{\partial x_2}{\partial p_j}, \frac{\partial x_3}{\partial p_j} \right).$$

The vector optimization problem is scalarized by means of the goal programming method. Here it takes the form

$$\min_{x,u,v_j,z} z,$$

subject to $P(x,u) - zw_1 \leq P^*, S(v_j) - zw_2 \leq S^*, F_i(x,u,p^*) = 0$, $H_i(x,u,v_j,p^*) = 0, g_i(x) \leq 0, x_3 \geq 0, u \geq 0, i = 1, 2, 3$, where the H_i are the derivatives of the system equations with respect to p_i; p^* is the vector of nominal power demand values, and P^* and S^* represent given goals for the criteria; the w_i's are weighting coefficients which determine the emphasis which is placed on the attainment of a particular goal.

The authors' results indicate that an advantage can be gained by reducing the performance sensitivity and that this can be accomplished to nearly the goal value without incurring an excessive degradation in nominal performance.

Lightner and Director [34] use multicriteria optimization to optimize the operating characteristics of a MOSFET nand gate circuit. The design criteria are the transistor area, the gate switching time, and the ON voltage—the first two to be minimized, the second to be made as close as possible to zero. By using some suitable approximations for the circuit, the criterion functions are obtained from a dc analysis of the nand gate in the ON state. These criteria are to be optimized subject to certain goal constraints on the criterion values and a feasible set for the design variables. The vector optimization problem is scalarized in terms of the weighted sum, for four specified weights, and by means of a weighted L_∞ technique. The latter consists of transforming the problem

$$\min\{g: g \in \Lambda\}$$

into

$$\min_{g\in\Lambda} \| Wg \|_\infty = \min_{g\in\Lambda} \max_{1\leq i\leq N} (w_i g_i),$$

the weights w_i being generated in accordance with a prescription by the authors. In essence, the example serves as an illustration of the numerical algorithm and their particular scalarization.

It appears that most of the applications to date fall into the area of applied mechanics, in particular, optimal structural design. The remainder of the survey is concerned with papers in these areas. The first of these concern instrument design and placement.

Instrument design from an MCDM viewpoint is considered by Kryzhanovskii [29]. His example consists of the design of a gyrotachometer which is to be placed on a moving object. As criteria he chooses the accuracy, the speed of response, and the energy consumption—the first two to be maximized, and the last to be minimized. All of them are assumed to depend on the dynamic error coordinates q_i. As particular examples he introduces

$$I_1 = \int_0^T W(q)\, dt, \qquad I_2 = \int_0^T e^{2\delta t} W(q)\, dt, \qquad I_3 = \int_0^T [W(q) + kU^2]\, dt,$$

which are to be optimized subject to

$$\dot{q} = q_2$$

$$\dot{q}_2 = q_2 - Uq_1,$$

with control $| U | \leq U^*$, $U = \frac{1}{4}\xi^2$ being the relative damping factor. Here T is the terminal time, but the author defines neither the function $W(q)$ nor the parameters k and δ. The author scalarizes the problem by maximizing a weighted sum whose weights may depend on the state variables and on the time t. In the example, only a time dependence is admitted.

The optimal placement of a measuring device in an optimally controlled system is considered by Leitmann and Stadler [32,33] and by Stadler [43]. It is assumed that a dynamic system is optimally controlled by a minimum energy control. A measuring device is to be introduced into the system in such a way as to least disturb the original system. This least disturbance is characterized by the error between the state of the original system and that of the disturbed system. Two examples are considered: the placement of an accelerometer on a spinning disk, thus changing the moment of inertia of the disk; and the choice of a strain gauge or an accelerometer for a simple spring mass oscillator, that is, a choice between changing the mass or the spring stiffness, or both. Necessary conditions for Pareto optimality in the first problem indicate that the accelerometer should be placed as close to the hub of the disk as possible. For the second problem, there are three possibilities, depending on the system parameters and the initial conditions: (i) only an accelerometer should be used; (ii) only a strain gauge should be used; (iii) for a given relation between the initial conditions, a combination of the two devices should be used—one which leaves the natural frequency of the system unchanged. The nice thing about these results is that they agree with one's physical intuition.

An application to bearing design was carried out by Bartel and Marks [3]. They treat two examples. The first concerns the static optimal design of a journal bearing for fixed operating speed, load, and journal diameter. Their mathematical model is a Reynolds equation. The design variables are the bearing length L, the radial clearance C, and the oil viscosity μ. The state variables include such quantities as oil flow rate, oil film temperature rise, and minimum oil film thickness. As criteria the authors choose the oil film temperature rise and the oil flow rate, both of which are to be minimized.

The authors' second example deals with the dynamic optimal design of a big-end, full journal bearing for the connecting rod of a large diesel engine. In this problem, the design variables are the bearing diameter D, the oil viscosity μ, the radial clearance C, and the bearing length L. The state variables include the maximum eccentricity ratio, the oil film thickness, and the power loss. The analysis is based on the mobility method and on graphic relationships. As criteria, the authors choose the reciprocal of the minimum oil film thickness and the power loss, both of which are to be minimized.

For those two problems the authors generate the trade-off curves. In addition, they plot the design variables and other important parameters as functions of the position on the trade-off curve. These curves thus give the designer the ability to work from the trade-off curve into design space. For their first example, the authors indicate that a particular design on the trade-off curve is the same as one which appeared in the literature previously. For their second example, they discover a whole range of designs on the trade-off curve, with as much as 50 percent less power loss than another existing design.

The next paper is included here for two reasons: its title definitely suggests that it falls within the guidelines, though it does not; but the paper does involve the design engineer's intuitions and desires. Indeed, it would be extremely interesting to discover whether the selected trajectory as obtained by this managerial interaction is one which is also optimal from some physical point of view.

The article by Dyer and Miles [16] describes the use of decision analysis to facilitate a group decision-making problem in the selection of trajectories for the Mariner Jupiter/Saturn 1977 Project of the Jet Propulsion Laboratory in Pasadena, California. The JPL scientists participated in the process through a steering group composed of 10 team leaders of the science teams (only 10 of the actual 11 teams had been selected at the time of the analysis). As far as the authors know, this analysis provided the only example of the use of these formal decision-theoretic concepts in a significant real-world situation.

Using objectives developed by the 10 science teams as guidelines, the JPL engineers developed a total of 105 single trajectories. From these they assembled candidate trajectory pairs by picking one trajectory corresponding to the opening of the launch period and one to be launched about 11 days later. The list of trajectory pairs finally used in the evaluation by the science teams eventually contained 32 trajectory pairs.

Various utility, choice, and lottery schemes are used to assess the scientists' preferences over the set of trajectory pairs. In the process, they found that several science teams were extremely risk averse. In view of the once-in-a-lifetime chances, it was very difficult for them to consider the "no data" trajectory pair with a significant, nonzero probability. One member of a science team stated:

> the utility values indicate, in my opinion, that the team lacks gambling nature, not that the pairs are of approximately equal value to our experiment; i.e., the utilities serve more as a group Rorschach test than as a useful gauge to scientific judgments.

Dyer and Miles surmise that, in retrospect, it probably was not appropriate to request the science team to evaluate the normalization lottery—thus, in effect, handicapping themselves. Still, an ordering of the decision set was eventually arrived at and a maximal equivalence class {31,29,26} was determined; the trajectory pair 26 was ultimately selected.

The science teams believed, overall, that the ordinal rankings were a useful way to communicate their preferences to other science teams. They generally believed that the same trajectory pair would have been selected without the development of the ordinal rankings and the utility function values. The authors, however, present some convincing evidence that this would not have been the case.

From a chronological viewpoint, the next paper should have been considered first. It appears to be the first applications-oriented paper considering the vector maximum problem in engineering; it is all the more remarkable since control theory itself had only been around for a rather short time. The author was aware of Zadeh's note [54]; it appears, however, that he must have developed his approach independently. Nelson [38] considers a general dynamical problem with control constraints, terminal state constraints, and constraints on the criteria values; that is, g_k $\leq \beta_k$. His first approach consists of considering one of the criteria, say g_n, as the performance index whose value should be minimized. Since all of the remaining costs are presumed equally important, an optimal control corresponding to this approach should properly be called g_n-optimal. The author also calculates a restricted (due to the criteria constraints) Pareto set with fuel and time as the performance criteria for the satellite attitude control problem specified by the following: Obtain Pareto optimal controls $u \in \mathcal{F}$ for

$$g_3(u(\cdot)) = \int_0^T dt \leq \beta_3 \quad \text{and} \quad g_4(u(\cdot)) = \int_0^T |u(t)| \, dt \leq \beta_4,$$

subject to

$$\dot{x} = x_2, \qquad x_1(0) = x_{10},$$

$$\dot{x} = u, \qquad x_2(0) = x_{20},$$

with $|u(t)| \leq 1$, for $t \in [0,T]$. It turns out that the Pareto optimal controls are bang-bang with a switching time depending on the initial conditions. The author concludes that the efficient point set provides a suitable compromise between fuel and time optimality.

Another dynamically oriented paper is one by Tabak et al. [52]. The purpose of their study was the development of a computer-based method to aid in the design of lateral stability augmentation systems for both fighter airplanes and large manned lifting reentry vehicles. By assuming that the lateral and the longitudinal system dynamics are uncoupled, the state equations may be written in the linear form

$$\dot{x} = Ax + Bu,$$

with $x = (x_1,x_2,x_3,x_4)$ representing the sideslip angle, yaw rate, roll rate, and bank angle, respectively, and $u = (u_1,u_2)$ representing the aileron and rudder control motions, respectively. The authors then eliminate the time dependence by assuming a feedback control:

$$u = Cu_p + Kx,$$

where $u_p = (u_{p1},u_{p2})$ is the pilot's control input vector, and where

$$C = \begin{bmatrix} 1 & 0 \\ k_5 & 1 \end{bmatrix} \quad \text{and} \quad K = \begin{bmatrix} k_6 & k_1 & k_2 & 0 \\ k_7 & k_3 & k_4 & 0 \end{bmatrix}$$

are gain matrices. The k_i are the design parameters. With u_p assumed given, the state equations may be integrated. With the terminal time specified, the authors then deal with a multicriteria programming problem based on the following criteria:

$$g_1(k) = \Delta x_1, \qquad g_2(k) = \sum_{i=1}^{7} k_i^2, \qquad g_3(k) = -x_4(t_1).$$

The first of these represents the overall sideslip angle deviation from equilibrium; the last, the bank angle after the start of the rolling maneuver. The criteria are to be minimized simultaneously. The authors then present a numerical algorithm which leads to an efficient point after relatively few iterative steps. They perform sample calculations for a fighter aircraft and a heavy reentry vehicle.

A similar approach to aircraft controller design is used by Kreisselmeier and Steinhauser in several reports [25,26,28,51] and in a related article [27]. They use multicriteria design to reduce the sensitivity of aircraft closed loop controls to parameter variations due to different flight conditions.

The authors take the deviations from the trim condition for the longitudinal motion of the aircraft to be governed by a linear system of the form

$$\dot{x} = Ax + bu,$$

where $x = (\dot{\theta}, \alpha, \eta)$; $\dot{\theta}$ is the pitch rate; α is the incremental angle of attack; η is the incremental elevator deflection; A and b are the data of the particular aircraft; and $u = \eta_c$ is the incremental elevator command. The time dependence again is eliminated by using a fairly complex three-compensator feedback control structure with $\dot{\theta}$ as the feedback variable and with 10 control coefficients k_i collectively denoted by k.

A large number of criteria are introduced. As their first set of criteria, they use the sensitivity measures

$$J_i(k) = \int_0^{T_i} [\dot{\theta}_{in}(t) - \dot{\theta}_m(\alpha_i;t)]^2 \, dt, \qquad i = 1, 2, \ldots, 5,$$

corresponding to the five flight conditions under consideration, and they use the control rate measures:

$$J_{5+i}(k) = \int_0^{T_i} [\dot{\eta}_{in}(t)]^2 \, dt, \qquad i = 1, 2, \ldots, 5,$$

where $\dot{\theta}_{in}(t) \triangleq \dfrac{\dot{\theta}_i(t)}{\theta_i(\infty)}$ is the normalized pitch rate response in flight condition i;

$\dot{\theta}_m(\alpha_i;t)$ is a particular desirable reference step response; the α_i denote different time scales for individual flight conditions;

$$\dot{\eta}_{in}(t) \triangleq \frac{\dot{\eta}_i(t)}{\eta_i(\infty)} \quad \text{is the normalized rate of elevator motion; and}$$

T_i, T_i' are the response times of the flight conditions i.

The second set of criteria restricts the disturbance rejection behavior with

$$J_{10+i}(\mathbf{k}) = \int_{t_i}^{T_i} \dot{\theta}_i^2(t)\, dt, \qquad i = 1, 2, \ldots, 5;$$

$$J_{15+i}(\mathbf{k}) = \int_0^{T_i} \dot{\eta}_{in}^2(t)\, dt, \qquad i = 1, 2, \ldots, 5.$$

Here the t_i are desired settling times.

A third set of criteria is concerned with eigenvalue specifications:

$$J_{20+i}(\mathbf{k}) = [\mathrm{Im}(\lambda)/\mathrm{Re}(\lambda)]_{max}^i, \qquad i = 1, 2, \ldots, 5;$$

$$J_{25+i}(\mathbf{k}) = \exp\{[\mathrm{Re}(\lambda)]_{max}^i\}, \qquad i = 1, 2, \ldots, 5;$$

$$J_{30+i}(\mathbf{k}) = |\lambda|_{max}^i, \qquad i = 1, 2, \ldots, 5.$$

Here λ represents the eigenvalues in a particular flight condition.

The final criteria rate the controller coefficients directly with

$$J_{35+j}(\mathbf{k}) = 1/|k_j|, \qquad j = 1, 2, 3;$$

$$J_{35+j}(\mathbf{k}) = |k_j|, \qquad j = 4, \ldots, 7.$$

Thus, there is a total of 42 criteria which are to be minimized simultaneously with respect to the controller coefficients k_i.

At this point the authors scalarize the problem by considering

$$\min_{\mathbf{k}} \left\{ \frac{1}{\rho} \ln \sum_{i=1}^{L} \exp \frac{\rho J_i(\mathbf{k})}{c_i^\nu} \right\},$$

where ρ is a weighting constant used to improve convergence and where $c_i^\nu = J_i(\mathbf{k}^{\nu-1})$ is the value of the criterion for the $(\nu - 1)$st iterative step in the solution process. The authors emphasize that the minimization process is a design tool only; that is, it is used to obtain an improved controller, rather than a necessarily optimal one.

The authors provide extensive calculations for a particular aircraft, and they indicate that low-performance flight testing showed that this type of controller could be used without change. They suggest, however, that the final quality of the controller can be assured only with flight tests in high-performance aircraft.

The most extensive use of multicriteria optimization has been made in optimal structural design. The remainder of this review deals with such problems. After a discussion of various examples, the review will be concluded with the concept of natural structural shapes introduced by the present author.

In addition to the usual scalarization with respect to the Euclidean distance from the utopia point, Gerasimov and Repko [19] also introduce two additional scalarizations. Let $I = \{1, \ldots, N\}$ be an index set, and $x \in \Omega$ be a design variable. Suppose there is a criterion vector $g = (g_1, \ldots, g_N)$ consisting of n functions of x associated with the problem. Then, they propose the following:

a. *The quasiequality principle*—Normalize the criteria in some manner and denote the normalized criteria by y_k. Then an optimal member of the normalized attainable set Y_c is given by

$$y_1^* = \{y \mid \|y_i - y_j\| \leq \delta, \quad i,j \in I\} \cap Y_c,$$

where δ is to be minimized. That is, all of the local criteria are minimized with the restriction that the difference in the levels of the various criteria does not exceed δ.

b. Define the optimum by

$$y^* = \min_{y \in Y} \prod_{i=1}^{N} y_i^{\alpha_i}$$

where $\alpha = (\alpha_1, \ldots, \alpha_N)$ is an N-dimensional weighting vector which satisfies

$$\alpha \in A = \left\{ \alpha \mid \alpha_i \in [0,1], \sum_{i=1}^{N} \alpha_i = 1 \right\}.$$

That is, the levels of all the local criteria tend to equalize.

The three scalarization approaches are applied to two examples. The first concerns the pinned truss of given layout and loaded as indicated in Figure 2. Their criteria are the weight g_1, some characteristic deflection g_2, and the difficulty of manufacture, which they characterize in terms of an integer q indicating the number of different cross-sectional areas necessary for a particular design. When each of the criteria is optimized independently, the results indicate q = 10 for the minimum weight design, q = 1 for the other two minima. For the combined approach, all three yield q = 2 as the optimal solution. Their second example concerns two framed plates as indicated in Figure 3. The structure has a given layout. The cross-sectional areas and the plate thicknesses are to be chosen so as to "minimize" the criteria volume and deflection, along with the difficulty for manufacturing the structure, where q now involves the cross-

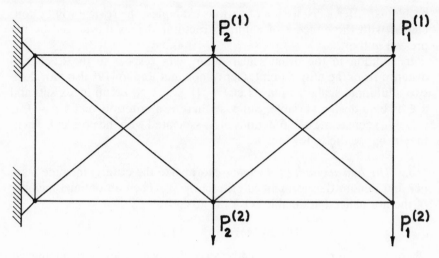

Figure 2.

sections and plate thicknesses. Two loading conditions are considered, $\{P_1\}$ and $\{P_2, P_3\}$. The compromise in terms of q here turns out to be q = 4.

In a short note, Carmichael [10] takes the so-called ϵ-constraint approach to optimize the truss in Figure 4. Suppose one first chooses g_1 as *the* criterion and calculates min g_1 subject to $g_i \leq \epsilon_i$, for $i \neq 1$. One then continues this process for each criterion in turn, all the time changing the ϵ_i, generating the entire Pareto set. The criteria are taken to be the

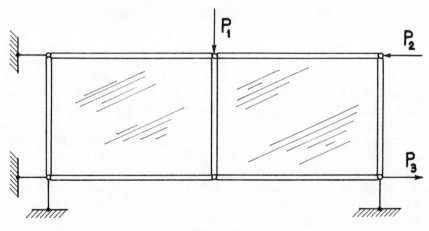

Figure 3.

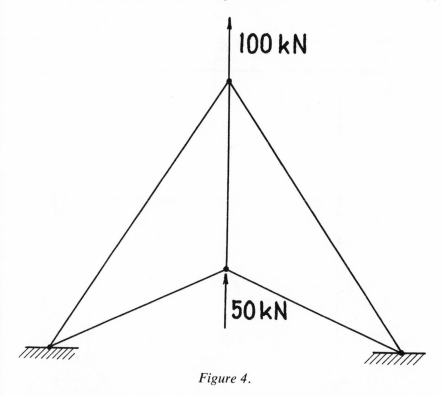

Figure 4.

weight and the sum of the vertical deflections of the central nodes. The results turned out to be $A_1 = 120.00$ mm^2 for every Pareto optimal solution, with A_2 ranging from the limiting values 87.0 mm^2 to 107.00 mm^2 as the weight increases and the sum of the deflections decreases monotonically.

Koski [24] calculates the Pareto optima for the following two examples. The first consists of the three-member plane frame shown in Figure 5. The structure is loaded by a horizontal force F at the left free node of the frame. The weight of the structure and the horizontal displacement of the left free node are the criteria to be minimized by a suitable choice of the design variables, the cross-sectional areas $A_1 = A_3$ and A_2, subject to various stress and area constraints. The Pareto optimal solutions are depicted in both the decision and the criteria space. Nearly all of the optima turned out to belong to the interior of the decision set. The author also considers the four-bar truss shown in Figure 6. The layout of the truss is prescribed and two loading conditions are considered. The criteria are the weight, the vertical deflection of the outer loaded node under load condition 1 (LC1), and the vertical deflection of the inner node under load

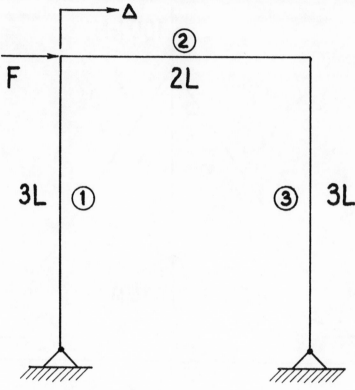

Figure 5.

condition 2 (LC2). The author again depicts the Pareto set in the criteria space, and the truss itself corresponding to the extreme points of the Pareto set.

Probabilistic aspects and the reliability of structures are discussed by Cohn and Parimi [12]. Strictly speaking, this paper does not fall within the guidelines, since a large part of it deals with the optimization of one criterion, with the others held fixed. However, the authors also consider the weighted sum, although they seem to be unaware of any of the literature in MCDM. They define failure by collapse as the formation of at least one mechanism and failure by loss of serviceability as the formation of at least one plastic hinge. They assume: (1) all loading schemes are possible and each can be described by a single random variable; (2) each possible collapse mode can be associated with at least one loading scheme. As an example, they consider a continuous three-span beam with built-in ends. The loads and plastic moment capacities are assumed to be normally distributed. The design variable is taken to be the mean value of the random variable for the plastic moment capacity. The multicriteria problem consists of maximizing P_S, the probability of survival of the structure against collapse; maximizing P_s, the probability of survival of the structure against loss of serviceability; and the minimization of the weight Z of the structure. The authors first optimize each of these with the other two subject to inequality constraints, and they then also propose a combined total cost criterion:

$$C_T = C_I + C_F(1 - P_S) + C_f(1 - P_s),$$

where C_T, C_I, C_F, and C_f are the total cost, initial cost, cost of failure by collapse and by loss of serviceability, respectively. The authors reach the conclusion that the design solution depends on the choice of failure stages and their definition. Also, the relative sensitivity of the design parameters to different failure criteria (for the beam, for example, the design is more sensitive to the serviceability criterion than to the collapse criterion) is influenced by the definition of the criteria.

Osyczka [39] introduces yet another sequential scalarization procedure. Let $x \in X$ and let $g(x) = (g_1(x), \ldots, g_N(x))$ be the criterion vector. Furthermore, let

$$g_i(x_i^*) = \min_{x \in X} g_i(x).$$

Define

$$z_i'(x) = \frac{|g_i(x) - g_i(x_i^*)|}{|g_i(x_i^*)|}$$

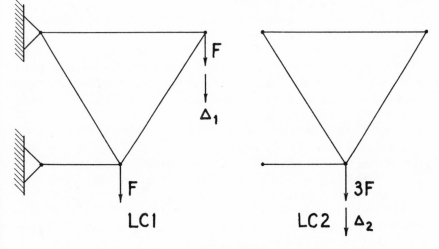

Figure 6.

and

$$z_i''(x) = \frac{|\, g_i(x) - g_i(x_i^*)\,|}{|\, g_i(x)\,|},$$

with the denominators assumed nonzero. The best compromise solution should give the smallest values of the fractional deviations for all criteria. Define

$$z_i(x) = \max\{z_i'(x), z_i''(x)\}.$$

Then the point $\hat{x} \in X$ is optimal in the min max sense if for every $x \in X$ the following recurrence formula is satisfied:

Step 1 $v_1(\hat{x}) = \min_{x \in X} \max_{i \in I}\{z_i(x)\}$, and define $I_1 = \{i_1\}$, where i_1 is the optimal index. Suppose there is a set of solutions $X_1 \subset X$ which satisfies Step 1.

Step 2 $v_2(\hat{x}) = \min_{x \in X_1} \max_{i \in I/I_1}\{z_i(x)\}$, and define $I_2 = \{i_1, i_2\}$, where i_2 is the optimal index for this step.

$\vdots$

Step N $v_N(\hat{x}) = \min_{x \in X_{N-1}}\{z_i(x)\}$ for $i \in I/I_{N-1}$.

The vector of optimal values of fractional deviations ordered nondecreasingly then is given by $v(\hat{x}) = (v_1(\hat{x}), \ldots, v_N(\hat{x}))$. When the extrema of the individual criteria are known, the desirable solution is one which gives the smallest values of the fractional deviations of all of the criteria from their extremum value. As an example, Osyczka considers a fixed-span simply supported I-beam of undetermined I-section. The beam is loaded by concentrated loads in both the transverse and the lateral direction. As criteria the author introduces the cross-sectional area and the transverse deflection under the load at the center of the beam. An optimum is calculated in the prescribed fashion subject to a strength constraint based on the ratios of the maximum moments and the section moduli. There appears to be no assurance that the author's numerical algorithm actualy converges to the desired value.

A similar approach is used by Pochtman and Skalozub [42] in the optimal design of shells. Their criteria are the mass of the shell and a quantity representing an averaging of the least shell thickness.

Some problems in viscoelasticity are considered by Leitmann [31]. As an example of a multicriteria application, he considers the usual Maxwell model for which he determines Pareto optimal stress rate histories (i) for arriving at a given stress with work and time as criteria and (ii) for a given time with work and final stress as criteria.

As a final application, the present author's concept of natural structural shapes is discussed. The concept was introduced in a somewhat lengthy paper in 1978 [46] in an attempt to present a unified approach to optimal structural design. The paper includes a fairly comprehensive discussion and review of the concept of Pareto optimality in programming and in control theory. Throughout the paper the criteria are the mass and the strain energy of a particular structure; however, the design variables range from the determination of the usual optimal cross-section distribution to the determination of an optimal hyperelastic material law. The paper contains analytic examples of axial members, beams, and a truss along with an example from nonlinear elasticity. In connection with the multicriteria problem, the extreme problems of minimum weight and minimum strain energy are also treated. As it concerns the *natural* aspect of natural structural shapes, the Pareto optimal cross-sectional distribution for the axial extension (or compression) of a bar is compared to the lower section of a *Sequoia gigantia*, with the result that it provides a better match of the outline than does the minimum weight design.

In another paper, the author [45] considers the natural shapes of uniform shallow arches. For an arbitrary distributed load, necessary conditions for the Pareto optimal initial curvatures of such arches are derived for the criteria mass and strain energy. The problem is basically a nonlinear control problem. However, as it turns out, the necessary condition for the unconstrained problem is embodied in a simple linear fourth-order differential equation which has to be satisfied by the Pareto optimal initial curvature.

The results of additional work concerning the stability implications of optimally designed shallow arches are summarized in a paper [50] presented at a conference on optimal structural design. To the author's knowledge, this was the first such conference to include a separate session on multicriteria design. The stability implications of the optimal designs of shallow arches are extremely interesting in that they indicate that there is a coalescence of stability and optimality conditions. In particular, there are examples where necessary conditions for optimality in minimum weight design are the same as sufficient conditions for instability of the corresponding optimal equilibrium, and others where the necessary conditions for a natural structural shape (for Pareto optimality with respect to the criteria mass and strain energy) turn out to be the same as sufficient conditions for stability. Consequently, this approach to optimal design may in fact open up a new avenue for the investigation of stability.

REFERENCES

1. Bacopoulos, A., "Nonlinear Chebyshev Approximation by Vector Norms." *Journal of Approximation Theory* 2:79–84, 1969.
2. Baptistella, L. F. B., and A. Ollero, "Fuzzy Methodologies for Interactive Multicriteria Optimization." *IEEE Transactions on Systems, Man, and Cybernetics,* Vol. SMC–10, No. 7:355–365, 1980.

3. Bartel, D. L., and R. W. Marks, The Optimum Design of Mechanical Systems with Competing Design Objectives. ASME Preprint Paper No. 73–DET–11, 1973.

4. Behringer, F. A., "Eine Eindeutigkeitsaussage über ein vektorielles Tschebyscheff-ausgleich problem." *Zeitschrift für Angewandte Mathematik und Mechanik* 52:T233–T236, 1972.

5. Behringer, F. A., *Tschebyscheff-Ausgleich überbestimmter Systeme linearer Gleichungen—Eindeutigkeit ohne Haarsche Bedingung durch lexikographischen Ausgleich*. Paper presented at the GAMM Conference, Graz, Switzerland, 1976. (To appear in *Zeitschrift für Angewandte Mathematik und Mechanik*.)

6. Beveridge, S. G., and R. S. Schechter, *Optimization Theory and Practice*. New York: McGraw-Hill, 1970.

7. Borel, E., "La Théorie du Jeu et les Équations Integrals à Noyau Symétrique Gauche." *Comptes Rendus Académie des Sciences de Paris* 173:1304–1308, 1921.

8. Bowman, V. J., Jr., "On the Relationship of the Chebyshev Norm and the Efficient Frontier of Multiple Criteria Objectives." Pp. 76–86 in H. Thiriez and S. Zionts (eds.), *Multiple Criteria Decision Making*. Lecture Notes in Economics and Mathematical Systems No. 130. Berlin and New York: Springer-Verlag, 1976.

9. Burlyayeva, L. F., V. V. Kafarov, R. Ye. Duzin, and A. V. Netushil, "Methods of Finding Pareto-Optimal Solutions in Problems Controlling Chemical Engineering Processes," *Engineering Cybernetics* 14(4):151–154, 1976.

10. Carmichael, D. G., "Computation of Pareto Optima in Structural Design." *International Journal for Numerical Methods in Engineering* 15:925–929, 1980.

11. Censor, Y., "Necessary Conditions for Pareto Optimality in Simultaneous Chebyshev Best Approximation." *Journal of Approximation Theory* 27(2):127–134, 1979.

12. Cohn, M. Z., and S. R. Parimi, "Multi-Criteria Probabilistic Structural Design." *Journal of Structural Mechanics* 1(4):479–496, 1973.

13. Cohon, J. L., "Applications of Multiple Objectives to Water Resources Problems." Pp. 255–270 in M. Zeleny (ed.), *Multiple Criteria Decision Making*. Lecture Notes in Economics and Mathematical Systems No. 123. Berlin and New York: Springer-Verlag, 1976.

14. Dunham, C. B., "Simultaneous Chebyshev Approximation of Functions on an Interval." *Proceedings of the American Mathematical Society* 18:472–477, 1967.

15. Duris, C. S., and V. P. Sreedharan, "Chebyshev and L_1-Solutions of Linear Equations Using Least Squares Solutions." *SIAM Journal of Numerical Analysis* 5(3):491–505, 1968.

16. Dyer, J. S., and R. F. Miles, Jr., "An Actual Application of Collective Choice Theory to the Selection of Trajectories for the Mariner Jupiter/Saturn 1977 Project." *Operations Research* 24(2):221–244, 1976.

17. Euler, L., *Methodus Inveniendi Lineas Curvas Maximi Minimive Proprietate Gaudentes*. Lausanne and Geneva, 1744. (English translation by W. A. Oldfather, C. A. Ellis, and D. M. Brown, *Isis*, Vol. 20:68–154, 1933.)

18 Gembicki, F. W., and Y. Y. Haimes, "Approach to Performance and Sensitivity Multiobjective Optimization: The Goal Attainment Method." *IEEE Transactions on Automatic Control*. Vol. AC-20, No. 6:769–771, 1975.

19. Gerasimov, E. N., and V. N. Repko, "Multicriterial Optimization." *Soviet Applied Mechanics* 14:1179–1184, 1978.

20. Haimes, Y. Y., and W. A. Hall, "Analysis of Multiple Objectives in Water Quality." *ASCE Journal of the Hydraulics Division* 101(4):387–400, 1975.

21. Hurwicz, L., "Programming in Linear Spaces." Pp. 38–102 in K. J. Arrow, L. Hurwicz, and H. Uzawa (eds.), *Studies in Linear and Nonlinear Programming*. Stanford: Stanford University Press, 1958. (Second printing, 1964. London: Oxford University Press.)

22. Jahn, J., "The Haar Condition in Vector Optimization." In G. Fandel and T. Gal (eds.), *Multiple Criteria Decision Making*. Lecture Notes in Economics and Mathematical Systems No. 177. Berlin and New York: Springer-Verlag, 1980.

23. Koopmans, T. C., "Analysis of Production as an Efficient Combination of Activities." Pp. 33–97 in T. C. Koopmans (ed.), *Activity Analysis of Production and Allocation*. Cowles Commission Monograph No. 13. New York: Wiley, 1951.

24. Koski, J., "Multicriteria Optimization in Structural Design." In *Proceedings of the International Symposium on Optimum Structural Design*. The 11th ONR Naval Structural Mechanics Symposium, Tucson, Arizona, October 19–22, 1981.

25. Kreisselmeier, G., "Controller Design with a Vectorcriterion and Its Practical Application to Adjustment Speed Reduction for Parameter-insensitive Controllers" [in German]. Research Report No. DLR–FB 77–55, 1977.

26. Kreisselmeier, G., and R. Steinhauser, "Flight results with a Parameter-insensitive Controller" [in German]. Research Report No. DFVLR–FB 78–07, 1978.

27. Kreisselmeier, G., and R. Steinhauser, "Systematic Controller Design by Optimization of a Vector Performance Index." *Regelungstechnik* 27(3):76–79, 1979.

28. Kreisselmeier, G., and R. Steinhauser, "Application of Vector Performance Optimization to a Robust Control Loop Design for a Fighter Aircraft." Research Report No. DFVLR–FB 80–14. Deutsche Forschungs—und Versuchsanstalt für Luft—und Raumfahrt, Institut für Dynamik der Flugsysteme, Oberpfaffenhofen, Germany, 1980.

29. Kryzhanovskii, G. A., "Complex Figures of Merit for Optimal Instrument Design." *Measurement Techniques* 14(3):359–363, 1971.

30. Kuhn, H. W., and A. W. Tucker, "Nonlinear Programming." Pp. 481–492 in J. Neyman (ed.), *Proceedings of the Second Berkeley Symposium on Mathematical Statistics and Probability*. Berkeley: University of California Press, 1951.

31. Leitmann, G., "Some Problems of Scalar and Vector-Valued Optimization in Linear Viscoelasticity." *Journal of Optimization Theory and Applications* 23(1):93–99, 1977.

32. Leitmann, G., and W. Stadler, "Cooperative Games for the Experimentalist (Preliminary Results)." *Proceedings of the Fifth International Conference on Systems Science*. University of Hawaii, Honolulu, 1972.

33. Leitmann, G., and W. Stadler, "Cooperative Games for the Experimentalist." *Zagadnienia Drgan Nieliniowych (Journal of Nonlinear Vibration Problems)* 18:272–286, 1974.

34. Lightner, M. R., and S. W. Director, "Multiple Criterion Optimization for the Design of Electronic Circuits." *IEEE Transactions on Circuits and Systems*. Vol. CAS-28(3):169–179, 1981.

35. Marglin, S. A., *Public Investment Criteria*. Cambridge: MIT Press, 1967.

36. Mirmirani, M., and G. Oster, "Competition, Kin Selection, and Evolutionary Stable Strategies." *Theoretical Population Biology* 13(3):304–339, 1978.

37. Moursund, D. G., "Chebyshev Approximations of a Function and Its Derivations." *Mathematics of Computation* 18:382–389, 1964.

38. Nelson, W. L., "On the Use of Optimization Theory for Practical Control System Design." *IEEE Transactions on Automatic Control*. Vol. AC-9(4):469–477, 1964.

39. Osyczka, A., "An Approach to Multicriterion Optimization for Structural Design." In *Proceedings of the International Symposium on Optimum Structural Design*. The 11th ONR Naval Structural Mechanics Symposium, Tucson, Arizona, October 19–22, 1981.

40. Perelson, A. S., M. Mirmirani, and G. Oster, "Optimal Strategies in Immunology, I: B-Cell Differentiation and Proliferation." *Journal of Mathematical Biology* 3:325–367, 1976.

41. Perelson, A. S., M. Mirmirani, and G. Oster, "Optimal Strategies in Immunology, II: B Memory Cell Production." *Journal of Mathematical Biology* 5:213–256, 1978.
42. Pochtman, Iu. M., and V. V. Skalozub, "On a Vector Model of the Problem of Optimal Design of Shells" [in Russian]. *Stroitel'naya Mekhanika i Raschet Sooruzhenii* 5:17–20, 1979.
43. Stadler, W., "Preference Optimality and Applications of Pareto Optimality." Pp. 125–225 in G. Leitmann and A. Marzollo, *Multicriteria Decision Making*. Courses and Lectures No. 211, International Center for Mechanical Sciences (CISM). Wien/New York: Springer-Verlag, 1975.
44. Stadler, W., "Sufficient Conditions for Preference Optimality." Pp. 129–148 in G. Leitmann (ed.), *Multicriteria Decision Making and Differential Games*. New York: Plenum Press, 1976.
45. Stadler, W., "Natural Shapes of Shallow Arches." *Journal of Applied Mechanics* 44(2):291–298, 1977.
46. Stadler, W., "Natural Structural Shapes (The Static Case)." *Quarterly Journal of Mechanics and Applied Mathematics* 31(2):169–217, 1978.
47. Stadler, W., "Preference Optimality in Multicriteria Control and Programming Problems." *Journal of Nonlinear Analysis: Theory, Methods, and Applications* 4(1):51–65, 1979.
48. Stadler, W., "A Survey of Multicriteria Optimization or the Vector Maximum Problem, 1776–1960." *Journal of Optimization Theory and Applications* 29(1):1–52, 1979.
49. Stadler, W., "A Comprehensive Bibliography of Multicriteria Decision Making and Related Areas." NSF Report, Department of Mechanical Engineering, University of California, Berkeley, 1981.
50. Stadler, W., "Stability Implications, and the Equivalence of Stability and Optimality Conditions in the Optimal Design of Uniform Shallow Arches." In *Proceedings of the International Symposium on Optimum Structural Design*. The 11th ONR Naval Structural Mechanics Symposium, Tucson, Arizona, October 19–22, 1981.
51. Steinhauser, R., "Systematic Arrangement of Controllers by Optimization of a Vector Criterion, Execution of the Controller Design with the Program REMVG" [in German]. Research Communication No. DFVLR-Mitt. 80-18, October 1980.
52. Tabak, D., A. A. Schy, D, P. Giesy, and K. G. Johnson, "Application of Multiobjective Optimization in Aircraft Control System Design." *Automatica* 15:595–600, 1979.
53. Yu, P. L., "Cone Convexity, Cone Extreme Points and Nondominated Solutions in Decision Problems with Multiobjectives." *Journal of Optimization Theory and Applications* 14(3):319–377, 1974.
54. Zadeh, L. A., "Optimality and Nonscalar-Valued Performance Criteria." *IEEE Transactions on Automatic Control*. Vol. AC-8(1):59–60, 1963.
55. Zangwill, W., "An Algorithm for the Chebyshev Problem with an Application to Concave Programming." *Management Science* 14(1):58–78, 1967.
56. Zukhovitskiy, S. I., and L. I. Avdeyeva, *Linear and Convex Programming*. Philadelphia: W. B. Saunders, 1966.

ANALYSIS OF COMPROMISE PROGRAMMING

William B. Gearhart

WILLIAM B. GEARHART has devoted his chapter to further mathematical and computational development of compromise programming. He observes that this particular concept is rich in mathematical content and much still remains to be explored. Building solid mathematical foundations for compromise programming is the task Gearhart has undertaken with considerable success. For example, his idea of applying a Gauss–Newton algorithm for minimax optimization is likely to lead to considerable computational experimentation and possibly to useful applications.

Again we encounter the concept of "regret" as a measure of discrepancy between the ideal criteria values and those actually achieved by selecting a particular compromise solution. A compromise solution is a best approximation to the ideal solution with respect to a distance function. It appears that approximation theory and compromise programming would benefit mutually from a two-way transfer of ideas.

Gearhart's mathematical framework for compromise programming is rich in new ideas and possibilities for research. It appears that compromise programming is general enough to encompass most MCDM methodology as special cases. For example, through systematic varying of the ideal point, one can trace out the entire set of nondominated solutions in general (not only linear) cases. Different distance functions can be associated with related families of utility functions, especially in connection with the newly emerging interest in "regret" within the utility research area. Goal programming becomes compromise programming as soon as the goal values are set intelligently, i.e., aiming for the best possible, rather than arbitrarily through ignorance. Interactive methodologies can only benefit from employing a displaceable reference solution. Compromise solutions provide a refreshingly objective optimization concept while still allowing for intimate decision maker's involvement.

As Gearhart shows, in searching for nondominated solutions, one can restrict attention to the compromise solutions only. No convexity conditions on the objective functions are needed. Furthermore, compromise solutions are properly efficient, so even that part of MCDM folklore loses its exclusivity.

It has been established that the Gauss–Newton linearization method can be successfully employed in computing compromise solutions with respect to a family of distance functions. It converges to a stationary point, and the rate of convergence is quadratic. All this behavior is true under fairly general conditions.

Studies of the mathematical properties of compromise programming have only begun. Gearhart concludes his paper with an extremely useful review of challenging and exciting research topics for both mathematicians and MCDM researchers. For example, the analysis of implicit trade-offs, a work already begun by J. G. Ecker and N. E. Shoemaker, holds a wealth of unexplored potential for providing information about trade-offs among criteria values throughout the nondominated set. Such knowledge is indispensable for the workings of any intelligent interactive procedure of decision support.

Gearhart concludes with an outline for extending compromise programming to an infinite number of criteria. This could open some interesting applications for economics and theories of general equilibrium, or, more precisely, new theories of continually displaced, dynamic equilibrium, that is, disequilibrium from a classical viewpoint.

ABSTRACT

A new abstract framework for the analysis of compromise programming is presented. After a brief review of the literature, properties of the compromise solutions in this new framework are shown. It is shown further that a Gauss–Newton method can be applied to compute compromise solutions. Finally, several important areas for future research in the theory of compromise programming are discussed.

1. INTRODUCTION

In an oft-referenced paper [21] from the 1973 seminar *Multiple Criteria Decision Making*, Milan Zeleny put forth the concept of compromise programming. The essential feature of compromise programming is the determination of solutions whose criteria values are close, according to some measure of distance, to given ideal criteria values. This subject has received considerable attention in the literature, especially by those interested in problems of practical decision making. However, compromise programming is rich in mathematical content, and much remains to be explored. In this paper we consider the mathematical foundations of compromise programming. After a brief review of the literature, we present a new abstract framework for the analysis of compromise programming problems. In this setting, the properties of compromise solutions are established. It will be shown, further, that a well-known Gauss–Newton algorithm for minimax optimization [14] can be applied to solve the general compromise programming problem. We close the paper with mention of several topics which we feel represent important areas for further research in compromise programming.

2. REVIEW OF LITERATURE

In the field of decision analysis, the concept of measuring the quality of a decision in terms of how close its criteria values are to ideal values has been used for some time. In fact, the difference between the ideal values and the criteria values attained by a decision is often called the "regret." Harris [11] and also Dinkelbach and Isermann [6] have shown how various classical decision criteria are obtained by minimization of the regret with respect to certain norms. In particular, the minimax regret and the Bayes criteria can be obtained this way.

Harris [11] uses results from approximation theory to establish properties of optimal decisions. Indeed, a compromise solution can be viewed as a best approximation to the ideal point with respect to a distance function. This idea was also considered by Dinkelbach [4] and Dinkelbach and Dürr [5], who consider the ℓ_p norms $1 \leq p < \infty$ and the ℓ_∞ norm.

Recently Jahn [13] has extended the Haar condition to compromise programming in the ℓ_∞ norm. This result is then used to identify efficient solutions. There are many concepts and techniques from approximation theory which may be applied to compromise programming, and it appears that further applications are worth investigating.

Some numerical algorithms for multiple objective optimization are based on the idea of minimizing distance to an ideal point. In particular there is the early work of Benayoun et al. [1], who use a weighted ℓ_∞ norm. Ecker and Shoemaker [7] use the ℓ_∞ norm and develop an algorithm for finding all efficient points for linear multiple objective optimization. These authors introduce the notion of the *trade-off compromise set*, which is a special subset of the efficient solutions. They show how this set provides information about the possible trade-offs among objectives. Such ideas should prove significant in the development of methodologies for searching the noninferior set.

The theory of compromise programming has been studied by several authors in addition to those mentioned above. A fairly general notion of a compromise solution appeared early with the work of Salukvadze [16], who considered the existence of solutions to dynamic optimal control problems with multiple objectives. The relationship of Salukvadze's ideas to compromise programming was pointed out by Yu and Leitmann [18]. A number of interesting properties of compromise solutions were established by Yu [17] and also Freimer and Yu [8] for the case of the ℓ_p norm. Their work also shows how compromise programming applies to group decision problems. Bowman [3] uses the ℓ_∞ norm and shows how the efficient frontier can be generated from compromise solutions by varying the ideal point. This author shows also that the same result is obtained by varying the weights of the ℓ_∞ norm with a fixed ideal point. Compromise programming has been studied extensively by Zeleny [19–25]. In particular, he has established many features important to the process of decision making.

Finally, the present author [9] has developed an abstract framework for analysis of compromise programming. In the sections below, we offer some improvements and simplifications of this framework.

3. COMPROMISE SOLUTIONS

Let $D \subset R^m$ denote the decision set, and f: $D \rightarrow R^n$ be the vector of objective or criterion functions. A point $x^* \in D$ is called efficient if there is no $x \in D$ such that

$$f(x) \geq f(x^*) \qquad \text{and} \qquad f(x) \neq f(x^*).$$

Let $Y = f(D)$ be the set of criteria values. It will be assumed that Y is closed, and for each i = 1, 2, . . . , n,

$$u_i^* = \sup\{y_i \mid y \in Y\} < \infty$$

The point $u^* \in R^n$ with ith component u_i^* is called the utopia point. If y = f(x), where $x \in D$ is efficient, then y will be called a noninferior point of Y, or, equivalently, a nondominated point of Y with respect to the nonnegative orthant R_+^n. The set of noninferior points of Y will be denoted by N(Y).

Define μ to be the max function on R^n,

$$\mu(y) = \max_{1 \le i \le n} \{y_i\}.$$

Let $A \subset [1, \infty)$ be an unbounded index set, and let a family of maps

$$\phi_\alpha: R_+^n \to R, \quad \alpha \in A$$

be given with the following properties:

PROPERTY P1. For $y \ge 0$, $\alpha \in A$, $\phi_\alpha(y) \ge \mu(y)$.
PROPERTY P2. For $y \ge 0$, $\phi_\alpha(y) \to \mu(y)$ as $\alpha \to \infty$.
PROPERTY P3. If $0 \le v \le y$, $v \ne y$, then $\phi_\alpha(v) < \phi_\alpha(y)$, for each $\alpha \in A$.
PROPERTY P4. For each $\alpha \in A$, ϕ_α is continuous and convex on R_+^n.

It is not difficult to construct families of maps with properties P1 through P4.

EXAMPLE 3.1. Let $A = [1, \infty)$ and let

$$\phi_\alpha(y) = \left(\sum_{i=1}^n y_i^\alpha \right)^{1/\alpha}.$$

This family has been considered often in the literature on compromise programming (see Gearhart [9] and Zeleny [19–25]).

EXAMPLE 3.2. Let $A = [1, \infty)$ and let

$$\phi_\alpha(y) = \mu(y) + \left(\frac{1}{\alpha} \right) \sum_{i=1}^n y_i.$$

This example appears in Refs. 6 and 9.

The maps ϕ_α, $\alpha \in A$, serve as the basis for measuring the closeness of f(x) to an ideal point $u \ge u^*$. Let

$$S_1^+ = \left\{ w \in R^n \mid \sum_{i=1}^n w_i = 1, \quad w_i > 0 \right\},$$

and for $w \in S_1^+$, denote by D_w the $n \times n$ diagonal matrix with $1/w_i$ as the ith diagonal element. For $y \in R^n$, define

$$M_{w,\alpha}(y) = \phi_\alpha(D_w y)$$

and

$$M_{w,\infty}(y) = \mu(D_w y),$$

where $w \in S_1^+$ and $\alpha \in A$. Now let $u \geq u^*$ be a fixed but arbitrary ideal point. A point $x^* \in D$ will be called a compromise solution if it solves the problem $CP_{w,\alpha}$:

$$\underset{x \in D}{\text{Minimize:}} \quad M_{w,\alpha}(u - f(x))$$

for some $w \in S_1^+$ and $\alpha \in A$. Let C denote the set of compromise solutions, and let $U = f(C)$. On occasion, the points in U will also be referred to as compromise solutions. Observe that problem $CP_{w,\alpha}$ is well defined.

THEOREM 3.1. Assume that the criteria set Y is closed and that the utopia points u^* exists. Then for any $w \in S_1^+$, $\alpha \in A$, and ideal point $u \geq u^*$, $CP_{w,\alpha}$ has a solution.

PROOF: Select $x_0 \in D$ and let

$$y_0 = f(x_0) \qquad \text{and} \qquad b = M_{w,\alpha}(u - y_0).$$

The set

$$B = \{y \in Y \mid M_{w,\alpha}(u - y) \leq b\}$$

is closed, by property P4. However,

$$B \subset B_\infty = \{y \in Y \mid M_{w,\infty}(u - y) \leq b\},$$

by property P1. But B_∞ is compact, as it is closed and contained in the rectangle $\{y \in R^n \mid u - bw \leq y \leq u\}$. Thus, the set B is compact, and so existence of a solution to $CP_{w,\alpha}$ follows.

$$\text{QED}$$

As w ranges over S_1^+ and α ranges over A, it is possible to generate essentially all noninferior points in Y via the compromise solutions. In the following theorems, it is assumed that the criteria set Y is closed, the utopia point u^* exists, and the family of maps $\{\phi_\alpha \mid \alpha \in A\}$ satisfies properties P1 through P4.

THEOREM 3.2. U is dense in $N(Y)$. In fact, let $\|\cdot\|$ be a norm on R^n, and suppose $y^* \in N(Y)$ and $\epsilon > 0$ are given. Then there is a $w \in S_1^+$ and $\alpha^* \in A$, such that if $x \in D$ solves $CP_{w,\alpha}$ for $\alpha \in A$, $\alpha \geq \alpha^*$, and $y = f(x)$, then $\| y - y^* \| \leq \epsilon$.

THEOREM 3.3. The compromise solutions are properly efficient; that is, if $x^* \in D$ is a compromise solution, then there is a constant $M > 0$ such that whenever $x \in D$ and $f_i(x) > f_i(x^*)$,

$$\frac{f_i(x) - f_i(x^*)}{f_j(x^*) - f_j(x)} \leqslant M$$

for some index j such that $f_j(x) < f_j(x^*)$.

The proofs of these theorems follow essentially those of Theorem 3.1 and Theorem 3.2 of Ref. 9, and thus will be omitted here. The point of these results, however, is that in searching for efficient points one can restrict attention to the compromise solutions. No convexity conditions on the objective functions are needed. Furthermore, in many cases the set of compromise solutions and the set of properly efficient points are the same (see Theorem 4.1 of Ref. 9). Thus, the use of compromise programming in decision making is well justified as a means to select solutions from the noninferior set.

4. A NUMERICAL ALGORITHM

For each fixed $w \in S_1^+$ and $\alpha \in A$, problem $CP_{w,\alpha}$ can be written in the form:

(P)   Minimize: $F(x) = \phi(f(x))$,
                    $x \in D$

where

$$\phi(y) = M_{w,\alpha}(u - y).$$

In studying the numerical solution of problem P, it will be assumed further that ϕ is convex and Lipschitz on all of R^n. These assumptions are not restrictive in the context of compromise programming. Indeed, each of the examples of maps ϕ_α given in the previous section can be naturally extended to convex and Lipschitz functions on R^n. In fact, if the maps ϕ_α are actually norms, as in Ref. 9, then these assumptions are satisfied immediately by the equivalence of norms on R^n.

Let us summarize the assumptions concerning problem P. Throughout this paper, the norm on either R^n or R^m is the max norm, and for $x \in R^m$, $S(x,r)$ denotes the sphere of radius r about x.

ASSUMPTION A1. $D \subset R^m$ is convex and closed.

ASSUMPTION A2. $\phi: R^n \to R$ is convex and Lipschitz, with Lipschitz constant L.

Assumption A3. The map f is defined and differentiable on an open
set W_D containing D, and for given $x^* \in D$, there are
constants $C > 0$ and $r > 0$ such that

$$\| f(y) - \ell(x,y - x) \| \leqslant C \| y - x \|^2$$

for all $x,y \in S(x^*,r) \cap D$, where

$$\ell(x,h) = f(x) + f'(x)h; \qquad x \in D, \quad h \in R^n.$$

Assumption A3 holds, for example, if f is twice continuously differentiable on W_D. By assumption A2, ϕ possesses a one-sided derivative
$\phi'_+(y,h)$ at each point $y \in R^n$ and any direction $h \in R^n$. By direct computation, it follows that F has a one-sided derivative F'_+. In fact, for any
$x \in D$ and direction $h \in R^n$,

$$F'_+(x,h) = \phi'_+(f(x), f'(x)h). \tag{4.1}$$

Definition 4.1. A point $x \in D$ is called a stationary point for problem
P if

$$F'_+(x,y - x) \geqslant 0$$

for all $y \in D$.

Equivalently, a point $x \in D$ is stationary if and only if

$$F'_+(x,h) \geqslant 0$$

for all h in T(D,x), the tangent cone of D at x. As D is convex, the tangent
cone T(D,x) is the closure of the set of feasible directions at x:

$$\{\lambda(y - x) \mid y \in D, \quad \lambda > 0\}.$$

A useful characterization of stationary points is possible in terms of a
Gauss–Newton linearization of problem P. For $x \in D$ and $h \in R^n$, set

$$F_1(x,h) = \phi(\ell(x,h))$$

and define the linearized problem at $x \in D$ by

(P_x) $\qquad\qquad\qquad$ Minimize: $F_1(x,y - x)$.
$\qquad\qquad\qquad\quad$ $y \in D$

Theorem 4.1. A point $x \in D$ is stationary if and only if $y = x$ is a
solution of P_x.

Proof: Sufficiency. Suppose x is a solution of P_x. Then for any $y \in$
D, and $t \in [0,1]$,

$$F_1(x,t(y - x)) \geqslant F_1(x,0). \tag{4.2}$$

However, observe that for any direction $h \in R^n$,

$$\lim_{t \to 0^+} \frac{F_1(x,th) - F_1(x,0)}{t} = F'_+(x,h),$$

from (4.1). Thus, taking $h = y - x$, (4.2) implies that

$$F'_+(x,y - x) \geq 0.$$

Necessity. If x is not a solution of P_x, then there is a $y \in D$ such that

$$F_1(x,y - x) < F_1(x,0) = F(x). \tag{4.3}$$

Let $p = f(x)$ and $q = f'(x)(y - x)$, so that (4.3) can be written

$$\phi(p + q) < \phi(p).$$

By convexity of ϕ,

$$\frac{\phi(p + tq) - \phi(p)}{t} \leq \phi(p + q) - \phi(p) < 0$$

for all $t \in (0,1)$. Thus,

$$\phi'_+(p,q) = F'_+(x,y - x) < 0,$$

which contradicts the stationariness of x.   QED

The basic algorithm of Madsen ([14]; see also [15]) for minimax optimization can be applied to problem P. This algorithm can be viewed as a Gauss–Newton type method in which the linearized problem P_x is used to generate a sequence of approximate solutions of P. In order that the method be a descent method, P_x is modified by introducing a bound on the distance between x and a possible solution. Thus, for $b \geq 0$, define the problem $P_{x,b}$:

$$(P_{x,b}) \qquad \text{Minimize:} \atop y \in D \qquad \{F_1(x,y - x) \mid \| y - x \| \leq b\}.$$

In general, $P_{x,b}$ is a convex programming problem. However, in some cases, it may be written as a linear programming problem. This situation occurs in compromise programming, for example, if ϕ is given by Example 3.2 and the decision set D is polyhedral. Observe that for any $b < \infty$, $P_{x,b}$ has an optimal solution, and if $b > 0$, then $x \in D$ is stationary if and only if x is a solution of $P_{x,b}$.

For a nonstationary $x \in D$, and y a solution of $P_{x,b}$, define

$$F_*(x,b) = F_1(x,y - x)$$

and

$$R(x,y,b) = \frac{F(x) - F(y)}{F(x) - F_*(x,b)} .$$

ALGORITHM. Fix $0 < \rho_1 < \rho_2 < \rho_3 < 1$ and $0 < \sigma_1 < 1 < \sigma_2$. Select $x_0 \in D$ and $b_0 > 0$, and set $k = 0$. At step k, solve $P_{x,b}$ with $x = x_k$ and $b = b_k$. Let y_k be the computed solution, and set

$$R_k = R(x_k,y_k,b_k), \quad h_k = y_k - x_k.$$

(a) If $R_k < \rho_1$, then replace b_k' by $\sigma_1 \| h_k \|$, and repeat step k.
Otherwise,
   (b) Let $x_{k+1} = y_k$, and set

$$b_{k+1} = \begin{cases} \sigma_1 \| h_k \|, & \text{if} \quad \rho_1 \leq R_k < \rho_2 \\ \| h_k \|, & \text{if} \quad \rho_2 \leq R_k < \rho_3 \\ \sigma_2 \| h_k \|, & \text{if} \quad R_k \geq \rho_3. \end{cases}$$

Go to step $k + 1$.

In Madsen [14,15], numerical experiments for the minimax case are presented. It turns out that the convergence analysis for this case, given in these papers, extends readily to problem P.

5. CONVERGENCE

The algorithm is a descent method because of the requirement at each iterate $x_k \in D$ that $R(x_k,y_k,b_k) \geq \rho_1 > 0$, which implies

$$F(y_k) \leq F(x_k) - \rho_1(F(x_k) - F_*(x_k,b_k)).$$

As problem P is bounded below, the sequence $\{F(x_k)\}$ converges monotonically. However, further results concerning $F_*(x,b)$ and $R(x,y,b)$ in a neighborhood of nonstationary points are needed to determine the convergence of the sequence of iterates $\{x_k\}$.

Using assumptions A1 through A3, it is not difficult to adapt the proofs of Madsen [14, pp. 323–325], to show the following result.

THEOREM 5.1. Let assumptions A1 through A3 hold. Then, any limit point of the sequence $\{x_k\}$ generated by the algorithm is stationary.

For the compromise programming problem $CP_{w,\alpha}$, the sequence of criteria values $y_k = f(x_k)$, for $k = 0, 1, 2, \ldots$, generated by the algorithm is contained in a compact set. Indeed, as the algorithm is a descent method, the proof of Theorem 3.1 shows that the sequence $\{y_k\}_{k \geq 0}$ is contained in the rectangle

$$\{y \in Y \mid u - b_0 w \leq y \leq u\}$$

where

$$b_0 = M_{w,\alpha}(u - y_0).$$

Thus, the existence of a limit point in the criteria set is guaranteed. If, moreover, at least one criterion function f_i is such that the "level" sets

$$\{x \in D \mid f_i(x) \geq b\}$$

are compact (when nonempty) for any $b \in R^n$, then the sequence $\{x_k\}$ generated by the algorithm is contained in a compact set. Hence, from Theorem 5.1 the distance of x_k from the set of stationary points converges to zero as $k \to \infty$.

6. QUADRATIC CONVERGENCE TO STRONGLY STATIONARY POINTS

As shown by Madsen and Schjaer-Jacobsen [15] and also by Hoffmann and Klostermair [12], the notion of a strongly (or strictly) stationary point plays a key role in establishing the quadratic rate of convergence of Gauss–Newton type algorithms.

DEFINITION 6.1. A point $x \in D$ is called strongly stationary for problem P if

$$F'_+ (x,h) > 0$$

for all $h \in T(D,x)$, $h \neq 0$.

Let $x^* \in D$ be strongly stationary. It will be assumed in this section that f' is locally Lipschitz at x; thus, for some constant L',

$$\| f'(x) - f'(x_*) \| \leq L' \| x - x_* \|,$$

for all $x \in S(x^*,r) \cap D$, where the norm of the derivative term is the matrix norm derived from the max norm. This Lipschitz assumption and also assumption A3 hold, for instance, if f is twice continuously differentiable on a neighborhood of x^* in D. Consider first the algorithm without use of the bounds $\{b_k\}$, that is, Gauss–Newton linearization.

THEOREM 6.1. Let $x^* \in D$ be strongly stationary and assume f' is locally Lipschitz at x^*. Then there is an $r > 0$ such that, for any starting point $x \in S(x^*,r) \cap D$, the algorithm without use of the bounds $\{b_k\}$ produces a sequence which converges to x^* and the rate of convergence is quadratic.

Thus, Gauss–Newton linearization applied to problem (P) is locally convergent to a strongly stationary point, and the rate is quadratic.

THEOREM 6.2. Let $x^* \in D$ be strongly stationary and assume f' is locally Lipschitz at x^*. If the algorithm produces a sequence which converges to x^*, then the rate of convergence is quadratic.

The proofs of these theorems are somewhat long; details can be found in Ref. 10. We remark, however, that the proof of Theorem 6.2 shows that if the sequence of iterates converges to x^*, then after a sufficiently large number of iterations the bounds $\{b_k\}$ will not be binding. Thus the algorithm eventually behaves simply like a Gauss–Newton linearization method.

7. FUTURE RESEARCH

Studies of the mathematical properties of compromise programming have only begun. There are, of course, many technical matters which remain open. For example, a more complete understanding is needed of the relationship between the set of efficient points and the set of compromise solutions. We suspect that under fairly general conditions these sets are identical.

Another important topic concerns the influence of the ideal point on the compromise solutions. For the ℓ_∞ norm with fixed weights, Bowman [3] has shown that by varying the ideal point any efficient point can be obtained as a compromise solution. Also, Ecker and Shoemaker [7] discovered how varying the ideal point may help provide an effective way to explore the noninferior set.

On a broader scale, however, there are two areas which we feel represent important directions for future research. The first is the analysis of trade-offs, and the second is the extension of compromise programming to cases with infinite number of criteria.

7.1. Trade-off Analysis

Knowledge of possible trade-offs among objectives is useful in arriving at a final solution. In the context of compromise programming, little has

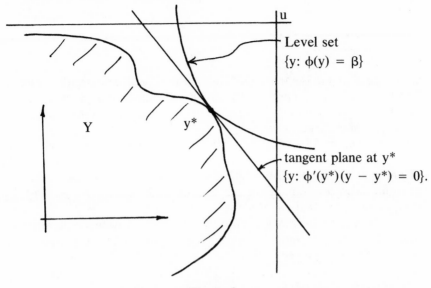

Figure 1.

been done concerning the calculation and use of trade-offs. We are aware only of the related work of Ecker and Shoemaker [7] and their idea of the *trade-off compromise set*. However, the compromise programming problem holds much unexplored potential for providing information about trade-offs among objective values along the efficient frontier. As a simple example, consider a compromise solution y* computed for a given weight vector $w \in S_1^+$ and parameter $\alpha \in A$; that is, y* solves

$$\text{Minimize:} \quad M_{w,\alpha}(u - y).$$
$$\phantom{\text{Minimize:}}_{y \in Y}$$

To simplify notation, set

$$\phi(y) = M_{w,\alpha}(u - y), \qquad \beta = \phi(y^*).$$

Then, consider the level set:

$$L = \{y \in R^n \mid \phi(y) = \beta\}.$$

If ϕ is differentiable, then the tangent plane to the set L at y* is given by the set of all $y \in R^n$ such that

$$\phi'(y^*)(y - y^*) = \sum_{i=1}^{n} \frac{\partial \phi}{\partial y_i}(y^*)(y_i - y_i^*) = 0.$$

Therefore, if the boundary of Y at y* is sufficiently smooth, the partial derivatives

$$\frac{\partial \phi}{\partial y_i} (y^*): \quad i = 1, 2, \ldots, n,$$

are proportional to the trade-offs among the objectives along the efficient frontier at y^* (see Figure 1). The trade-offs achieved at point y^* could then be compared with the desired trade-offs along the indifference curve of the decision maker at y^*.

Of course, many questions arise. Under what conditions does the boundary of the criteria set Y admit a tangent plane? Also, if the trade-offs at a given compromise solution indicate that an improved solution is possible, how does one adjust the parameters w and α, and perhaps the ideal point u, to obtain a better solution?

The discussion here has been only tentative. However, the study of trade-offs in the setting of compromise programming is very much open and worthy of further investigation.

7.2. Infinite Dimensional Compromise Programming

A theory of compromise programming for an infinite number of criteria could be important in several ways. For instance, such a theory could be applied to extend compromise programming to cases when the domination cone is not finitely generated. Also, such problems arise in decision analysis when there are an infinite number of possible states of nature.

Formally, the problem in decision analysis is easily stated. Let f: $X \times Y \to R$ (real numbers) be a payoff function where X is the decision space and Y is the space of possible states of nature. Assume that for each decision $x \in X$, $f(x, \cdot)$ belongs to a linear vector space E of real-valued functions on Y. Define the utopia point f_* by

$$f_*(y) = \sup_{x \in X} f(x,y),$$

and assume $f_* \in E$. For a decision $x \in X$, the regret is defined by

$$f_* - f(x,\cdot) \in E.$$

It is reasonable then to view an optimal decision x^* as one for which $f(x^*,\cdot)$ is close to f_* with respect to some measure of distance on E.

Can the theory for compromise programming in the finite dimensional case [9] be extended to this case of infinite criteria? In particular, is there a family of distance measures for which the compromise solutions possess the properties shown in Theorem 3.2 and Theorem 3.3? There are many challenging mathematical problems here.

Some interesting work on infinite dimensional multiobjective optimization has been done by Borwein [2], who has generalized the definition of proper efficiency. Using Borwein's results it is possible to show that, with certain separation properties in the space E and convexity assumptions on f, the properly efficient points are characterized as the solutions of the problem

$$\text{Maximize:} \quad L(f(x,\cdot))$$
$$\text{{\scriptsize }} x \in X$$

for some positive linear functional L on E. However, a solution of this problem is also a solution of

$$\text{Minimize:} \quad L(f_* - f(x,\cdot)),$$
$$x \in X$$

and conversely. Thus, considering the framework for compromise programming given in the present paper, the solutions of this latter problem could be viewed as compromise solutions.

REFERENCES

1. Benayoun, R., J. de Montgolfier, J. Tergny, and O. I. Larichev, "Linear Programming with Multiple Objective Functions: Step Method (STEM)." *Mathematical Programming* 1(3):366–375, 1971.
2. Borwein, J., "Proper Efficient Points for Maximizations with Respect to Cones." *SIAM Journal of Control and Optimization* 15(1):57–63, 1977.
3. Bowman, V. J., "On the Relationship of the Tchebycheff Norm and the Efficient Frontier of Multiple-Criteria Objectives." Pp. 76–85 in H. Thiriez and S. Zionts, eds., *Multiple Criteria Decision Making,* Jouy-en-Josas, France 1975. New York: Springer-Verlag, 1976.
4. Dinkelbach, W., "Über einen Lösungsatz zum Vektormaximumproblem." Pp. 1–13 in M. Beckman and H. P. Kunzi (eds.), *Unternehmensforschung-Heute.* Berlin: Springer-Verlag, 1971.
5. Dinkelbach, W., and W. Dürr, "Effizienzaussagen bei Ersatzprogrammen zum Vektormaximumproblem." Pp. 117–123 in R. Henn, H. P. Kunzi and H. Shubert (eds.), *Operations Research Verfahren.* Verlag Anton Hain, Meisenheim, Germany: Verlag Anton Hain, 1972.
6. Dinkelbach, W. and H. Isermann, "On Decision Making under Multiple Criteria and under Incomplete Information." Pp. 302–312 in J. L. Cochrane and M. Zeleny, (eds.), *Multiple Criteria Decision Making.* Columbia: University of South Carolina Press, 1973.
7. Ecker, J. G. and N. E. Shoemaker, "Multiple Objective Linear Programming and the Tradeoff Compromise Set." Pp. 60–73 in G. Fandel and T. Gal (eds.), *Multiple Criteria Decision Making-Theory and Application.* New York: Springer-Verlag, 1980.
8. Freimer, M. and P. L. Yu, "Some New Results on Compromise Solutions for Group Decision Problems." *Management Science* 22:688–693, 1976.
9. Gearhart, W. B., "Compromise Solutions and Estimation of the Noninferior Set." *Journal of Optimization Theory and Applications* 28(1):29–47, 1979.
10. Gearhart, W. B., *A Linearization Method for Compromise Programming.* In manuscript, 1981.
11. Harris, B., "Mathematical Models for Statistical Decision Theory." Pp. 369–389 in J.

S. Rustagi (ed.), *Symposium on Optimizing Methods in Statistics.* New York: Academic Press, 1971.

12. Hoffmann, K. H., and A. Klostermair, *Approximation mit Losungen von Differential Leichungen.* Approximations Theorie, Tagung Bonn, 1976. Springer Lecture Notes in Mathematics, 1976.

13. Jahn, J. "The Haar Condition in Vector Optimization." Pp. 128–134 in G. Fandel and T. Gal (eds.), *Multiple Criteria Decision Making—Theory and Application.* Lecture Notes in Economics and Mathematical Systems. New York: Springer-Verlag, 1980.

14. Madsen, K., "An Algorithm for Minimax Solutions of Overdetermined Systems of Nonlinear Equations." *Journal of the Institute of Mathematics and Its Applications* 16:321–328, 1975.

15. Madsen, K. and Schjaer-Jacobsen, "Linearly Constrained Minimax Optimization." *Mathematical programming* 14:208–223, 1978.

16. Salukvadze, M., "On the Existence of Solutions in Problems of Optimization Under Vector-valued Criteria." *Journal of Optimization Theory and Applications* 13(2):203–217, 1974.

17. Yu, P. L., "A Class of Solutions for Group Decision Problems." *Management Sciences* 19:936–946, 1973.

18. Yu, P. L., and G. Leitmann, "Compromise Solutions, Domination Structures, and Salukvadze's Solution." *Journal of Optimization Theory and Applications* 13:362–378, 1974.

19. Zeleny, M., "Adaptive Displacement of Preferences in Decision Making." Pp. 147–158 in M. K. Starr and M. Zeleny (eds.), *Multiple Criteria Decision Making, TIMS Studies in the Management Sciences,* Vol. 6. Amsterdam: North-Holland Publishing, 1977.

20. Zeleny, M., "The Attribute-Dynamic Attitude Model (ADAM)." *Management Science* 23(1):12–26, 1976.

21. Zeleny, M., "Compromise Programming." Pp. 262–301 in J. L. Cochrane and M. Zeleny (eds.), *Multiple Criteria Decision Making.* Columbia: University of South Carolina Press, 1973.

22. Zeleny, M., "A Concept of Compromise Solutions and the Method of the Displaced Ideal." *Computers and Operations Research* 1(4):479–496, 1974.

23. Zeleny, M., "Descriptive Decision Making and Its Applications." Pp. 327–388 in R. L. Schultz (ed.), *Applications of Management Science,* Vol. 1. Greenwich, Conn.: JAI Press, 1981.

24. Zeleny, M., "The Theory of the Displaced Ideal." Pp. 151–205 in M. Zeleny (ed.), *Multiple Criteria Decision Making: Kyoto 1975.* New York: Springer-Verlag, 1976.

25. Zeleny, M., *Multiple Criteria Decision Making.* New York: McGraw-Hill, 1982.

A THEORY OF THE DISPLACED IDEAL WITH DECISIONS UNDER UNCERTAINTY

Mustafa R. Yilmaz

MUSTAFA R. YILMAZ has started a useful new area of research related to compromise programming and to the concept of the displaced ideal: the effects of risk and uncertainty on decision making under multiple criteria. His chapter represents another encouraging departure from the prescriptive dictum of maximizing expected utility. Especially since (as it has been shown in recent years) different elicitation procedures, different analysts, even different framing of questions will, under otherwise equal conditions, provide entirely different "utility" functions. Thus, the assessed utility function can hardly represent anything in terms of correct or incorrect preferences of the decision maker, and its expected utility version even less so.

The set of feasible decision alternatives, its size, composition, and evolutionary history, is *highly relevant* to any intelligent decision making and its models. Preferences, especially human preferences, never encompass all real or imaginary prospects and alternatives: comparison of any two choices is affected by availability or nonavailability of other choices; there are no irrelevant alternatives. Decision context is an extremely important, often crucial, always changing factor of decision making under single or multiple criteria.

Yilmaz recalls that in situations characterized by risk the concept of perceived "anti-ideal" could be employed: in the context of risky decisions, decision maker's choices are realistically guided by the desire to be as far away from the anti-ideal as possible. Thus, for the individuals concerned primarily with the avoidance of risk, the alternatives that are further away from the anti-ideal are preferred to those that are closer to it. It should be added that the risk itself is a multidimensional concept (rather than a single index or ratio) and is characterized by a number of differentially perceived risk attributes. Yilmaz uses a two-attribute characterization of risk recently discussed by D. M. Holthausen.

As with most multidimensional risk measures, it can be shown that those alternatives which are nondominated with respect to their multiple attributes represent a proper subset of so-called efficiency under first-degree stochastic dominance. These results can be successfully extended to higher degrees of stochastic dominance and essentially put the so-called mean-variance analysis of efficient portfolios to its long-deserved rest.

Yilmaz has also taken first steps toward exploring the relationship between so-called utility functions and different measures of closeness (or distance) to the anti-ideal. This is potentially useful work, as it can become instrumental in bringing multiattribute utility theory (MAUT) and MCDM methodologies closer together.

There is a very interesting and instructive example where Yilmaz shows how the displaced ideal reasoning can simply and elegantly explain the well-known Allais paradox of seemingly inconsistent preferences in the sense of the expected utility model. As is true with all other such "paradoxes," they turn out not to be paradoxes at all within a broader and more general theory. That is, there can never be a "paradox"; there can only be a wrong, "paradoxical" theory. It is extremely important that research efforts be concentrated and directed toward such "paradoxes" rather than toward further refining and sharpening of paradox-spawning theories.

The issue of independent and dependent attributes is significant, and Yilmaz is aware of the need for more imaginative and relevant research of this aspect of MCDM. Yilmaz uses a nice little example at the end of his paper: observe that in terms of expected utility both prospects are equal as they are also equidistant from the anti-ideal. One can see that (10,10) is removed 14.14 points from (20,20) in terms of distance while (10,20) and (20,10) are removed only 10 points from both the ideal and the anti-ideal. So, the two propositions are very different: first, end up either 0 or 14.4 distance from the anti-ideal (or ideal); second, end up with distance 10 from the anti-ideal (or ideal) no matter what.

1. INTRODUCTION

Decision making in the presence of risk or uncertainty is an intrinsically difficult task since the available acts must be evaluated not just in terms of their possible outcomes but with respect to the element of chance as well. The most prominent prescriptive methodology for dealing with such problems is the traditional paradigm based on the Von Neumann–Morgenstern expected utility (EU) theory. In this approach, decisions are viewed in terms of pairwise preferential comparisons of acts, and certain normative conditions are imposed on the binary relation thus obtained. These conditions ensure an order-preserving numerical representation of preferences via a cardinal utility function which has the important property that the utility of a risky alternative is equal to the expected utility of its outcomes [1]. A best decision among all feasible acts is then found by the maximization of expected utility.

Since it focuses on the question of how risky decisions *ought to* be made, the EU model is not concerned with the description or prediction of actual choice behavior, and indeed it seems to perform rather poorly in this regard [7,12,13]. Although this shortcoming is often argued to be of minor importance from a prescriptive viewpoint, it has very serious consequences concerning the workability of the model in actual use. The following remarks by Tversky [15, p. 209] succintly point to the major problems in this regard:

> Decision theory demands coherence, yet it provides no clues to how it should be achieved. Given the fallibility of human judgments, what are the major sources of judgmental error? What methods, or tests, should the analyst use to detect biases and inconsistencies? How should the decision maker resolve his inconsistent preferences? Formal decision theory does not address these questions because it does not acknowledge the fallible nature of judgmental data. Consequently, the decision analyst must look elsewhere to find answers to these questions.

Perhaps the weakest link in the EU methodology is the determination of an appropriate utility function in a given decision situation. The model does not indicate a method that is certain to accomplish this task, and in fact such a procedure does not exist. Every suggested assessment procedure relies on precise indifference judgments involving artificial, arbitrarily selected pairs of choices. In addition to persistent sources of bias and ambiguity in these judgments, elicitations are almost sure to be influenced by the choices that are presented to the decision maker (DM), as well as exactly how they are worded or framed [5,16]. Thus, different procedures can produce different utility functions that are not related by linear transformations. It is therefore impossible to assert that an assessed utility function represents the true or correct preferences of the DM in any meaningfully definable sense. In their discussion of a suggested procedure, Keeney and Raiffa [8] argue that utility assessment is as much of an art as it is a science (p. 188). Apparently, the question concerning the determinacy of a DM's utility function remains unresolved.

As viewed in the EU model, the set of feasible decision alternatives is irrelevant to the analysis as long as the outcome set remains fixed. Preferences are assumed to encompass all real or imaginary prospects in such a way that the comparison of two choices is not influenced by other choices that are available. Except for the outcome space, therefore, preferences are presumed to be independent of the decision context. Under this requirement, it is irrational for a DM to concentrate only on the set of feasible alternatives. The reasonableness of this conclusion seems dubious since the preferences of real interest pertain precisely to those choices that are actually available.

Another prominent characteristic of the standard EU approach concerns its apparent neglect of the element of risk as a decision factor. The model *begins* with the assumption that the DM can precisely evaluate any pair of alternatives, and it does not distinguish between risky and riskless prospects (i.e., the latter treated as special cases of the former). Under these circumstances, it would be reasonable to demand that utility functions obtained from two different procedures—one involving gambles and the other sure outcomes—be the same. Recognizing that this is generally false, an EU theorist must painstakingly distinguish between the utility and the value of an outcome, corresponding to risky and riskless situations, respectively, although the model does not recognize such a distinction.

Over several decades, these and other criticisms of the traditional approach have stimulated many efforts in various directions. Among the proposals these efforts have produced, two ideas are of particular interest in the present discussion. The first of these concerns an explicit, multi-dimensional characterization of risk as a basis for the formation of preferences in risky choice. In the context of decisions with monetary outcomes, this idea was employed in the earlier suggestions by Markowitz [10], which were subsequently discussed by many authors, and in the recent proposals by Fishburn [2], Holthausen [6], and Zeleny [21]. The second idea concerns a process-oriented modeling of decision making that Zeleny has explicated in his well-known theory of the displaced ideal [18,19,20]. Although Zeleny's discussions were confined to multiple criteria decisions under certainty, his model is eminently suitable for risky decision situations also. Together with an explicit characterization of risk as a multiattribute decision factor, this model can serve as the basis of a flexible *decision-aid* methodology for choices under uncertainty.

The basic appeal of Zeleny's theory lies in the fact that it offers a multistage choice model which is compatible with the evolutive nature of human decision-making processes. Although direct empirical studies of the model are not widely available presently, it represents one of the few attempts to formulate a decision procedure that incorporates prescriptive as well as descriptive considerations. In this model, the selection of a decision is not viewed as an isolated activity with fixed alternatives, criteria, and preferences but as the result of a sequential process of partial decision making whereby these elements are adaptively modified. Unlike the traditional approach, the set of feasible choices at each stage *is* relevant to the analysis, both in terms of the evaluations and the criteria employed for them. Partial decisions are concerned with the elimination of inferior alternatives relative to a perceived ideal (or anti-ideal) that serves as a reference in the formation of preferences. Since the ideal is determined by the available choices, it does not remain fixed through the sequence of partial decisions, and at each stage choices are evaluated in terms of their closeness to the ideal rather than through pairwise preferential comparisons. Consequently, instead of assuming a DM's preferences to be given, the model helps *generate* them in a normatively reasonable manner. The anchoring of evaluations on an ideal alternative in this model is similar to the use of a reference value or aspiration level for the evaluation of monetary outcomes—a predominant phonomenon that has been receiving increased attention in the recent literature [2,3,6,7,12].

For a relatively self-contained presentation, we briefly discuss some aspects of Zeleny's theory in the next section. Employing a parsimonious, two-attribute characterization of risk, a displaced ideal procedure for risky decisions with monetary outcomes is presented in Section 3, and the well-known Allais paradox is briefly considered form the viewpoint of this procedure. The last section is concerned with the generalization of the procedure to the case of risky decisions with multiattribute outcomes.

2. THEORY OF THE DISPLACED IDEAL UNDER CERTAINTY

Consider a decision situation involving a finite number of feasible alternatives $x_1, \ldots, x_m$ such that each x_j is to be evaluated on the basis of r attributes (factors, objectives, criteria). Under conditions of certainty, each alternative corresponds to a sure outcome, assumed to be known, so that no distinction need be made between alternatives and consequences with respect to choices. Alternative x_j will be denoted as the r-tuple $x_j = (x_{j1}, \ldots, x_{jr})$ where x_{ji} is the status of x_j with respect to the ith attribute. Thus, the set $X_i = \{x_{1i}, \ldots, x_{mi}\}$ consists of the achievable states of the ith attribute. Letting X be the Cartesian product $X = X_1 \times \cdots \times X_r$, it is clear that the set of feasible alternatives is a subset of X.

Multiple-attribute decision problems have been approached in two conceptually distinct ways. In the usual approach represented by utility theory, it is assumed that alternatives are evaluated as complete r-tuples, formalized through an overall preference order on X, and evaluations on individual attributes are obtained as subsets of the holistic preference relation. The second approach, which is employed in Zeleny's displaced ideal procedure, reverses this process by beginning with a preference order on each attribute and then aggregating or synthesizing these into an overall ordering. A major problem with the former approach stems from the difficulty of evaluating complete r-tuples and obtaining an appropriate utility representation. To mitigate this difficulty, various decomposition models are offered which require certain independence conditions among attributes. The second approach presupposes the independence of each attribute from the others, namely, that the preference order for a given factor does not depend on the particular states of the other factors. Since this assumption is plausible in many situations, however, the latter approach is of interest in these cases, especially when a DM's holistic preference structure cannot be discovered or when it is not amenable to a utility representation.

Assuming that preferences on the ith attribute are represented by a cardinal value function f_i, or an *attribute score function* in Zeleny's terminology, each $x_j \in X$ can be described by the r-tuple of attribute scores $(f_1(x_{j1}), \ldots, f_r(x_{jr}))$. Thus, attribute state x_{ji} is preferred to x_{ki} when $f_i(x_{ji}) > f_i(x_{ki})$, and vice versa. Letting

$$f_i^* = \max_{x_{ji} \in X_i} \{f_i(x_{ji})\}, \tag{1}$$

we may refer to any x_{ji} for which $f_i(x_{ji}) = f_i^*$ as an *ideal* state of the ith attribute *given* the set X_i, and to f_i^* as its ideal value. Similarly, the r-tuple of ideal values $f^* = (f_1^*, \ldots, f_r^*)$ may be called the *perceived ideal* given the set X. If there is at least one feasible alternative that achieves the perceived ideal, then the decision problem terminates by the selection of such an alternative. It can therefore be assumed that the perceived ideal is infeasible in any nontrivial decision situation. Zeleny then proposes that holistic preferences on X are guided by the perceived ideal. Specifically, his choice axiom states that *alternatives which are closer to the ideal are preferred to those that are farther away.*

In order to operationalize Zeleny's axiom, acceptable measures of closeness to the ideal must be determined. For the ith attribute, it seems natural to employ the difference $f_i^* - f_i(x_{ji})$ as the distance of attribute state x_{ji} to the ideal value f_i^*. For measuring overall distances to the perceived ideal, it may be required, at a minimum, that the chosen measure provide a total ordering of alternatives and that the overall distance of an alternative to the perceived ideal increase when its distance on any one attribute is increased. Under the independence assumption stated above, such a measure will be a function of the distances on individual attributes, but its exact form cannot be specified without the imposition of further conditions [9, Chap. 7]. The particular class of measures proposed by Zeleny consists of the following weighted L_p metrics:

$$L_p(x_j) = \left[\sum_{i=1}^{r} \lambda_i^p (f_i^* - f_i(x_{ji}))^p \right]^{1/p}, \qquad 1 \le p. \qquad (2)$$

These functions exhibit the usual characteristics associated with a distance measure, as well as a number of other desirable properties including those mentioned above [4,17].

In (2), each λ_i is a measure of relative importance, or *attention level*, associated with the ith attribute. Zeleny argues that an attention level λ_i incorporates two distinct components: one component, called *contrast intensity*, $\tilde{\lambda}_i$ reflects the information content of the given set of feasible alternatives transmitted to the DM through the ith attribute; the second component, w_i, is a subjective assessment of importance reflecting the DM's cultural, psychological, and environmental history. For the first component, Zeleny suggests a relative entropy measure which is equal to zero when all alternatives have the same score on the ith attribute and which increase as attribute scores are spread apart. Thus, $\tilde{\lambda}_i$ is a measure of the discriminatory power provided by the ith attribute. The two components are then combined in a multiplicative fashion:

$$\lambda_i = \frac{\tilde{\lambda}_i \cdot w_i}{\sum_{i=1}^{r} \tilde{\lambda}_i \cdot w_i}, \qquad i = 1, \ldots, r. \qquad (3)$$

With a given set of attention levels and a specified value of p, minimization of $L_p(x_j)$ yields an alternative which is as close as possible to the perceived ideal regarding a particular distance function. Minimization for all values of p, for $1 \le p$, yields the locus C of all minimum-distance alternatives with respect to all reasonable geometric interpretations. Zeleny refers to C as the *compromise set* and he suggests that it can be approximated by using the three values 1, 2, ∞ for p. With $p = 1$, the distance on each attribute is unweighted except through λ_i; $p = 2$ corresponds to the usual weighting; and $p = \infty$ implies that the maximum distance is dominant. Since attention levels are also transformed differently for each value of p, imprecision in the assignment of subjective importance weights is mitigated to a certain extent by the use of several values of p. For any p, the corresponding alternatives in C are nondominated (admissible, efficient) in the r attributes, so that the compromise set is a subset of efficient alternatives.

Starting with an initial set of feasible alternatives, Zeleny's procedure consists of a sequence of partial decisions by which inferior alternatives that are far away from the perceived ideal are eliminated. Each partial decision causes a displacement of the ideal as well as a revision of attention levels. Attributes which exhibit low contrast intensity are temporarily discarded and revised weights are determined. With a new perceived ideal which is closer to the reduced set the process is repeated until a sufficient reduction of the choice set is obtained or, ultimately, a single alternative remains. Such a procedure would seem to be a realistic facsimile of human decision making, particularly as regards the context dependency of preferences and the relevance of a reference alternative in the formation of preferences.

Before turning to an adaptation of this model for risky decision situations, several observations will be made:

First, essentially the same model could be formulated in terms of a perceived *anti-ideal* consisting of the r-tuple of minimum attribute scores. In the context of risky decisions, for example, it may be more realistic to assume that choices are guided by the desire to be as far away from the anti-ideal as possible. For this reason, we shall employ the anti-ideal version of the choice axiom in the next two sections. A more intriguing possibility mentioned by Zeleny is the employment of an ideal *and* an anti-ideal so that the desire to be close to the former is accompanied by the desire to be far away from the latter. This can be pursued by switching from one criterion to the other at different stages of the decision process or by simultaneous consideration of both criteria at each stage. In the latter case, it would seem reasonable to confine the compromise set to the intersection of the two compromise sets as regards the ideal and anti-ideal, respectively. Although either of these possibilities appears to be descriptively more appealing than the use of a single criterion, they will not be further examined in the present discussion.

Second, it will be noted that Zeleny's choice axiom does not involve distance comparisons of arbitrary pairs of alternatives, and consequently all properties of a distance function are not necessary for the representation of closeness to the ideal. Although the L_p metrics in (2) are appealing for several reasons, other measures of closeness could be used as well, including ordinal measures that are monotonically increasing in individual attribute distances. Thus, for example, any positive value of p can be used in (2), and the power $1/p$ can be omitted.

Third, positive linear transformations of attribute score functions have the effect of changing the attention levels in (2). For instance, attribute distances measured in dollars would receive a different weight than if they were represented as percentage changes from a fixed dollar amount. This points to the influence of individual attribute scales on the overall measure of closeness to the ideal and, consequently, to the necessity of maintaining these scales unchanged through the analysis.

3. RISKY DECISIONS WITH MONETARY OUTCOMES

By far the most widely studied class of risky decision problems consists of those involving monetary consequences or, more generally, outcomes for which a commonly understood cardinal value scale exists. Except for temporal considerations (e.g., short-run versus long-run return), such situations are usually treated as if they involve a single criterion in terms of both the underlying value scale *and* the element of uncertainty. To the extent that both of these factors must be evaluated, however, decisions under risk or uncertainty are intrinsically multidimensional. Moreover, regardless of whether "objective" numerical probabilities are available or need to be subjectively assessed, the evaluation of risky prospects is a difficult task for most individuals. If consistency and coherence are to be required of the evaluations, it seems natural that a basis upon which risky prospects are evaluated must first be established.

There is a significant body of empirical evidence that risk is perceived by individual DM's in terms of various aspects or dimensions which we shall cryptically refer to as *risk attributes* [11,14]. In a gambling situation, for example, a DM may evaluate the lotteries on the basis of the chance of winning (or losing), and at the same time, the amount that can be won (or lost). A second prominent characteristic of observed choices under risk in the monetary context is that alternatives are usually evaluated in terms of the deviations of their outcomes from a fixed reference value (anchor, target, aspiration level) [3,7,12]. It appears that monetary outcomes are first translated into gains and losses with respect to the reference point, and it is these coded changes that are instrumental in the formation of preferences. Moreover, the direction of change from the reference point, say t, often influences an individual's risk attitude in that risk-averse behavior above t is frequently accompanied by risk-seeking behavior below t. These observations suggest that the prospects of failure and success with respect to the attainment of t are relevant areas of concern for most individuals.

Various characterizations of risk in terms of specific risk attributes have been offered by many authors including Markowitz [10], Fishburn [2], Holthausen [6], and Zeleny [21], among others. Particular risk measures employed in these characterizations include expected value, variance,

entropy, below-target semivariance, probability of loss or gain, probability-weighted losses or gains, and minimum or maximum attainable outcomes. In the present discussion, we shall consider the two-attribute characterization discussed by Holthausen mainly because it exhibits many
desirable properties, despite the basic simplicity and parsimony of the
description employed. One of its desirable features is its compatibility
with a large variety of risk attitudes as well as with the usual concepts
of stochastic dominance. Moreover, it includes many of the risk measures
in common use as special cases.

Without a significant loss of realism, let $D = \{P_1, \ldots, P_N\}$ be a finite
set of feasible decision alternatives such that each P_j is a simple probability
distribution (either prespecified or subjectively assessed) with a finite
number of possible outcomes in an interval $[x°,x^*]$. For any outcome x,
$x° \leq x \leq x^*$, let $p_j(x)$ be its probability under alternative P_j. Also let t be
a fixed reference value, $x° \leq t \leq x^*$, which we shall assume to coincide
with the status quo unless it is explicitly specified by the DM. Under these
circumstances, it seems reasonable to represent the prospect of falling
short of t by the following probability-weighted function of deviations:

$$r(P_j) = \sum_{x \leq t} (t - x)^\alpha p_j(x), \tag{4}$$

where α is a nonnegative constant. Similarly, the prospect of attaining t
can be represented by

$$R(P_j) = \sum_{x \geq t} (x - t)^\beta p_j(x), \tag{5}$$

where β is a nonnegative constant. For alternative P_j, $r(P_j)$ corresponds
to the probability of failing to meet t when $\alpha = 0$, probability-weighted
losses when $\alpha = 1$, below-target semivariance when $\alpha = 2$, and the
minimum attainable outcome when $\alpha = \infty$. For these values of β, $R(P_j)$
has similar implications in terms of the deviations above t. It seems natural
to assume that, with any fixed level of r, preferences are increasing in R,
and with any fixed level of R, they are decreasing in r. Thus, $-r$ and R
can be viewed as score functions on the two attributes corresponding to
the failure and success in achieving t, respectively.

It was shown by Holthausen that, for any $\alpha \geq 0$ and $\beta \geq 0$, the set of
alternatives that are nondominated in the two attributes is a subset of the
set of efficient alternatives under first-degree stochastic dominance. A
similar assertion holds for second-degree efficiency when $\alpha \geq 1$ and $0 \leq
\beta \leq 1$, and for third-degree efficiency when $\alpha \geq 2$ and $0 \leq \beta \leq 1$. More-
over, if the DM's preferences depend entirely on r and R, *and* if the EU
model holds, then the concomitant utility function must be of the form

$$\begin{aligned} u(x) &= u(t) - k_1(t - x)^\alpha &&\text{for all } x \leq t \\ &= u(t) + k_2(x - t)^\beta &&\text{for all } x \geq t, \end{aligned} \tag{6}$$

where $k_1 = u(t) - u(t - 1)$ and $k_2 = u(t + 1) - u(t)$. Since a large variety of utility functions can be approximated in this form, the two-attribute characterization of risk in terms of r and R would seem to be reasonably flexible in many cases.

Among the alternatives in D, there is at least one which achieves the maximum value of r, namely,

$$r^° = \max_{P_j \in D} \{r(P_j)\}, \tag{7}$$

and another alternative which achieves the minimum value of R,

$$R^° = \min_{P_j \in D} \{R(P_j)\}. \tag{8}$$

Therefore, with specified values of α and β, we may refer to $(r^°, R^°)$ as the *perceived anti-ideal*, given D. Denoting the minimum of r over D by r^* and the maximum of R by R^*, we have $r^* \leq r(P_j) \leq r^°$ and $R^° \leq R(P_j) \leq R^*$ for any $P_j \in D$.

In risky choice situations, it may be surmised that most individuals are concerned primarily with the avoidance of risk. To the extent that this is accepted, Zeleny's choice axiom would state that alternatives that are farther away from the anti-ideal are preferred to those that are closer to it. In terms of the two-attribute risk characterization considered here, it would then seem reasonable to represent closeness to the anti-ideal by the function

$$L(P_j) = \lambda_1[r^° - r(P_j)] + \lambda_2[R(P_j) - R^°], \tag{9}$$

where λ_1 and λ_2 are the attention levels associated with the two attributes. Clearly, this function is decreasing in r and increasing in R. Comparison with (2) shows that it is the particular distance measure with $p = 1$, so that the indifference curves in the (r,R) space are parallel straight lines with slope λ_1/λ_2.

To note a proximity between the utility function u in (6) and the closeness measure L in (9), suppose that D includes all degenerate distributions each of which yields a single outcome in $[x^°, x^*]$. The anti-ideal is then defined by $r^° = (t - x^°)^\alpha$ and $R = 0$. For any x such that $x^° \leq x \leq t$, its distance from the anti-ideal is

$$L(x) = \lambda_1[(t - x^°)^\alpha - (t - x)^\alpha];$$

and for any x such that $t \leq x \leq x^*$, we have

$$L(x) = \lambda_1[(t - x^°)^\alpha] + \lambda_2[(x - t)^\beta].$$

Observing that $L(t) = \lambda_1[(t - x^°)^\alpha]$, we obtain

$$L(x) = L(t) - \lambda_1(t - x)^\alpha \qquad \text{for all} \quad x \leq t$$

$$= L(t) + \lambda_2(X - t)^\beta \qquad \text{for all} \quad x \geq t,$$

which has the same form as u in (6). It is worth emphasizing, however, that the attention levels λ_1, λ_2 as defined in (3) depend on the feasible set D, whereas the constants k_1, k_2 in (6) are independent of D.

It is clear that with the risk measures in (4) and (5), the perceived anti-ideal depends on the particular values of α and β. For each of these constants, an approximate range of values can be determined through a simple preference comparison procedure. As regards α, for example, a gamble F that yields $x°$ with probability $p(x°)$ and t with probability $1 - p(x°)$ could be compared with G that yields $(x° + t)/2$ with probability 1. For these choices, we have $R(F) = R(G) = 0$, $r(F) = (t - x°)^\alpha \cdot p(x°)$, and $r(G) = [(t - x°)/2]^\alpha$. Moreover, F is preferred to G when $p(x°) = 0$ and G is preferred to F when $p(x°) = 1$. Starting with $p(x°) = 0$ and gradually increasing the value of $p(x°)$, a value p' may be reached when the DM is not willing to declare a clear preference for F over G. From $r(F) \approx r(G)$, an approximate bound $\alpha' = -\log p'/\log 2$ for α is obtained. Similarly, starting with $p(x°) = 1$ and gradually decreasing it until the preference for G over F becomes fuzzy, another bound α'' may be found. Note that coherence in preferences would dictate $\alpha'' \le \alpha'$, although this may or may not hold. In any case, it seems reasonable to employ α', α'', and $\alpha''' = (\alpha' + \alpha'')/2$ as *compromise values* of α. Obviously, compromise values for β can be determined through a similar procedure.

A compromise alternative in D is one that maximizes $L(P_j)$ with specified values of α, β and attention levels λ_1, λ_2, and the compromise set C is the locus of all such maximum-distance alternatives. This set can be approximated by employing all (α,β) pairs of compromise values along with the attention levels determined as in (3) from the contrast intensities and subjective importance weights associated with the two attributes. Although this approximation suggests a total of nine maximization problems, it is of course possible to reduce this number by employing only the compromise value $\alpha = \alpha'''$ along with the compromise values of β, or vice versa. Such a reduction would seem reasonable when the approximate range of values for α or β is relatively narrow.

We conclude this section with a brief mention of the well-known Allais paradox, which is often cited as an example of inconsistent preferences in the sense of the EU model. This example, shown in the tabulation, involves choices among the following lotteries, where M is a large monetary payoff. Faced with this situation, many individuals prefer P_1 to P_2 and P_3 to P_4, but there is no utility function which reflects these preferences and at the same time satisfies the EU model.

Outcome:	0	M	5M
P_1:	(0	1	0)
P_2:	(.01	.89	.10)
P_3:	(.90	0	.10)
P_4:	(.89	.11	0)

Since M can be obtained as a sure thing by selecting P_1, it seems likely that the reference value t may be set as t = M, in which case Eqs. (4) and (5) yield:

$$r(P_1) = 0, \qquad R(P_1) = 0,$$

$$r(P_2) = .01M^\alpha, \qquad R(P_2) = .10(4M)^\beta,$$

$$r(P_3) = .90M^\alpha, \qquad R(P_3) = .10(4M)^\beta,$$

$$r(P_4) = .89M^\alpha, \qquad R(P_4) = 0.$$

With $D = \{P_1, P_2, P_3, P_4\}$, the perceived anti-ideal is then defined by r = .90M and R = 0, and by (9), we obtain

$$L(P_1) = \lambda_1 (.90)M^\alpha,$$

$$L(P_2) = \lambda_1 (.89)M^\alpha + \lambda_2 (.10)(4M)^\beta,$$

$$L(P_3) = \lambda_2 (.10)(4M)^\beta,$$

$$L(P_4) = \lambda_1 (.01)M^\alpha.$$

It will first be noted that there are no values of the attention levels λ_1, λ_2 for which $L(P_1) > L(P_2)$ and simultaneously $L(P_3) > L(P_4)$. For any nonzero λ_1, however, it is clear that $L(P_1) > L(P_4)$ and $L(P_2) > L(P_3)$. Therefore, P_3 and P_4 may be eliminated from further consideration whenever $\lambda_1 > 0$. Upon this reduction, on the other hand, the anti-ideal is displaced ($r^\circ = .01M; R^\circ = 0$), and a new set of attention levels are formed on the basis of modified contrast intensities and subjective importance assessments [see Eq. (3)]. Consequently, P_1 may be farther than P_2 from the anti-ideal as regards the set $D_1 = \{P_1, P_2\}$, and P_3 may be farther away from the anti-ideal than P_4 given $D_2 = \{P_3, P_4\}$. At least from a descriptive viewpoint, it seems necessary to recognize such context dependency of preferences as a basic characteristic of human decision making.

4. MULTIATTRIBUTE OUTCOMES

We now consider the more general risky choice situations in which each decision alternative is a probability distribution over a multidimensional outcome set. As before, we shall let $D = \{P_1, \ldots, P_N\}$ be the set of feasible choices whose outcomes belong to the set $X = X_1 \times \cdots \times X_r$ described in Section 2. Thus, each $x \in X$ is an r-tuple $x = (x_1, \ldots, x_r)$ with $p_j(x)$ being the probability assigned to x by P_j. The earlier assumption that each attribute can be considered in isolation in the evaluation of outcomes will initially be strengthened to include risky prospects as well. Specifically, it will be assumed that if two prospects have the same marginal joint distribution on an arbitrary set of $r - 1$ attributes, then their evaluation is based only on their marginal distributions on the remaining attribute. In the usual terminology, this means that each attribute is value independent of the complementary set of attributes. Under this condition, the displaced ideal procedure of the preceding section can be adapted to multiple-factor situations in a straightforward manner.

Letting f_i be a score function for the ith attribute, the riskless evaluation of outcomes yields on r-tuple $(f_1(x_1), \ldots, f_r(x_r))$ for each $x \in X$. Following the discussion of Section 3, probability distributions on the ith attribute may be evaluated on the basis of the prospects of failure and success in attaining a reference score t_i. Accordingly, for any $P_j \in D$, the first of these risk attributes can be measured by

$$r_i(P_j) = \sum [t_i - f_i(x_i)]^{\alpha_i} p_j(x_i), \qquad (10)$$

where the summation is over all $x_i \in X_i$ for which $f_i(x_i) \le t_i$, and $p_j(x_i)$ is the marginal probability assigned to x_i by P_j. Similarly, the prospect of achieving t_i with alternative P_j can be measured by

$$R_i(P_j) = \sum [f_i(x_i) - t_i]^{\beta_i} p_j(x_i), \qquad (11)$$

where the summation is over all x_i for which $f_i(x_i) \ge t_i$. Given D, the anti-ideal (r_i°, R_i°) on the ith attribute may then be defined by

$$r_i^\circ = \max_{P_j \in D} \{r_i(P_j)\} \qquad (12)$$

$$R_i^\circ = \min_{P_j \in D} \{R_i(P_j)\}, \qquad (13)$$

and using the measure of closeness in (9) for the ith attribute, we have

$$L_i(P_j) = \lambda_{1i}[r_i^\circ - f_i(P_j)] + \lambda_{2i}[R_i(P_j) - R_i^\circ], \qquad (14)$$

where λ_{1i}, λ_{2i} are the attention levels associated with the two risk attributes as regards the ith outcome attribute.

With fixed levels of all L_j, for $j \ne i$, larger values of L_i are preferred to smaller values. Among all attainable values of L_i, we may therefore define

$$L_i^\circ = \min_{P_j \in D} \{L_i(P_j)\} \qquad (15)$$

as the least preferred score of riskiness with respect to the ith outcome attribute, and refer to $(L_1^\circ, , , , , L_r^\circ)$ as the perceived anti-ideal given D. As a measure of the closeness of P_j to the anti-ideal, we may employ

$$L(P_j) = \sum_{i=1}^{r} W_i^p [L_i - L_i(P_j)]^p, \qquad 1 \le p, \qquad (16)$$

where W_i is the DM's subjective importance weight associated with the ith outcome attribute. A compromise alternative is one that maximizes $L(P_j)$ with a given value of p. As suggested by Zeleny, the set of compromise alternatives can be approximated with $p = 1, 2, \infty$. It ill be observed, however, that each compromise requires the specification of α_i, β_i, for $i = 1, \ldots, r$. If α_i', α_i'' are bounds for α_i, and β_i', β_i'' are bounds for β_i (as in Section 3), it would seem reasonable to employ the value $(\alpha_i' + \alpha_i'')/2$ for α_i and $(\beta_i' + \beta_i'')/2$ for β_i in (14) and (15).

Clearly, the independence assumption upon which this procedure was based may be inappropriate in some situations. To cite an example mentioned by Fishburn [1, p. 149], consider a prospect P_1 that yields a two-year income stream of either ($10,000, $10,000) or ($20,000, $20,000) with probability .5 versus another prospect P_2 that yields ($10,000, $20,000) or ($20,000, $10,000) with probability .5. Then, P_1 and P_2 have the same marginal distribution on the first- as well as the second-year income, so that the two prospects are equidistant from the anti-ideal. It seems likely, however, that many people would prefer P_2 to P_1 since P_2 ensures that higher income in some period whereas P_1 does not. In such cases, the characterization of risk cannot be based on risk attributes that are defined in terms of individual outcome attributes.

It is clear that a major difficulty in the analysis of risky decisions concerns the establishment of a basis for choice, and in particular an explicit characterization of risk in the way it *enters* the decision process. On the other hand, an adequate, generally applicable risk characterization does not seem plausible in multiple factor situations. In the context of a given decision situation, however, it is often plausible to discover some of the risk factors that are deemed relevant by the DM. For example, we surmise that the probabilities of particular outcome subsets or certain combinations of attribute states are risk-relevant characteristics for most individuals. Although such attributes may not provide a complete description of a DM's viewpoint of risk, they can affect the decision task to a significant extent. For this reason, the displaced ideal procedure based on these attributes can be helpful in exploring as well as narrowing the set of choices, which can in turn simplify the selection of an ultimate decision. This, we feel, is the main purpose of any decision-aid methodology.

REFERENCES

1. Fishburn, P. C., *Utility Theory for Decision Making*. New York: Wiley, 1970.
2. Fishburn, P. C., "Mean-Risk Analysis with Risk Associated with Below-Target Returns." *American Economic Review* 67:116–126, 1977.
3. Fishburn, P. C. and G. A. Kochenberger, "Two-Piece Von Neumann-Morgenstern Utility Functions." *Decision Sciences* 10:503–518, 1979.
4. Freimer, M. and P. L. Yu, "Some New Results on Compromise Solutions for Group Decision Problems." *Management Science* 22:688–693, 1976.

5. Hershey, J. C., H. C. Kunreuther, and P. J. H. Schoemaker, "Sources of Bias in Assessment Procedures for Utility Functions." *Management Science* 28:936–954, 1982.

6. Holthausen, D. M., "A Risk-Return Model with Risk and Return Measured as Deviations from a Target Return." *American Economic Review* 71:182–188, 1981.

7. Kahneman, D. and A. Tversky, "Prospect Theory: An Analysis of Decisions under Risk." *Econometrica* 47:262–291, 1979.

8. Keeney, R. L. and H. Raiffa, *Decisions with Multiple Objectives.* New York: Wiley, 1976.

9. Krantz, D. H., R. D. Luce, P. Suppes, and A. Tversky, *Foundations of Measurement,* Vol. I. New York: Academic Press, 1971.

10. Markowitz, H. M., *Portfolio Selection.* New York: Wiley, 1959.

11. Payne, J. W., "Alternative Approaches to Decision Making under Risk: Moment versus Risk Dimensions." *Psychological Bulletin* 80:439–453, 1973.

12. Payne, J. W., D. J. Laughhunn, and R. Crum, "Translation of Gambles and Aspiration Level Effects in Risky Choice Behavior." *Management Science* 26:1039–1060, 1980.

13. Schoemaker, P. J. H., "The Expected Utility Model: Its Variants, Purposes, Evidence and Limitations." *Journal of Economic Literature* 20:529–563, 1982.

14. Slovic, P., B. Fischhoff, and S. Lichtenstein, "Behavioral Decision Theory." *Annual Review of Psychology* 28:1–39, 1977.

15. Tversky, A., "On the Elicitation of Preferences: Descriptive and Prescriptive Considerations." In D. E. Bell, R. L. Keeney and H. Raiffa (eds.), *Conflicting Objectives in Decisions.* New York: Wiley, 1977.

16. Tversky, A. and D. Kahneman, "The Framing of Decisions and the Psychology of Choice." *Science* 211:453–458, 1981.

17. Yu, P. L., "A Class of Decisions for Group Decision Problems." *Management Science* 19:936–946, 1973.

18. Zeleny, M., "Compromise Programming." In J. L. Cochrane and M. Zeleny (eds.), *Multiple Criteria Decision Making.* Columbia: University of South Carolina Press, 1973.

19. Zeleny, M., "Theory of the Displaced Ideal." In M. Zeleny (ed.), *Multiple Criteria Decision Making: Kyoto 1975.* New York: Springer-Verlag, 1976.

20. Zeleny, M., "The Attribute-Dynamic Attitude Model (ADAM)." *Management Science* 23:12–26, 1976.

21. Zeleny, M., *Multiple Criteria Decision Making.* New York: McGraw-Hill, 1982.

GOAL PROGRAMMING:
METHODOLOGICAL ADVANCES
IN 1973–1982 AND PROSPECTS
FOR THE FUTURE

Edward L. Hannan

EDWARD L. HANNAN has now critically reviewed the goal programming literature of the past decade. He dismisses the voluminous literature on so-called "applications" of goal programming which has become known under the heading, "A Goal Programming Formulation of the _____ _____ Problem," authors diligently filling in the blanks. The superficiality and intellectual damage inflicted by these papers can only be compared to a similar travesty à la "A Fuzzy Version of _____ _____ Model."

Hannan concentrates on serious goal programming research, important methodological issues, and some outlines for future research, especially at the interfaces with other disciplines and areas. Thus he only skims over the lexicographical version of goal programming (with so-called preemptive priorities) and concentrates on the question of nondominance in goal programming. Goal programming solutions must be nondominated in a vector maximum sense; otherwise its solution recommendations should not be used in situations where one searches for better rather than simply different solutions.

There is a short review of fractional goal programming problems leading naturally to the more advanced treatment by Kornbluth in the next paper in this volume. Also interval goal programming of Charnes and Cooper is shortly described. Hannan also provides a short venture into the application of fuzzy set theory to goal programming. He points out the arbitrariness of so called "maximin" concept in fuzzy sets theory, which calls, inexplicably, for maximizing the minimum membership function.

The whole area of fuzzy sets in decision making should be approached with extreme caution. First, the literature is generally of low quality, mostly mechanical "fuzzifications" of well-known, otherwise nonfuzzy models. Often, the old models are simply rewritten in a new formal notation. Second, introducing fuzzy membership functions is methodologically and technically the same as the a priori development of a utility function, the only difference being that for assessing the utility function one analyzes statements of preference while for membership functions one analyzes (or should analyze) statements of imprecision. So far, the fuzzy sets theory has avoided the issue of membership functions assessment and simply assumes them as being given.

More interesting is the possible relationship between goal programming and multiattribute utility theory (MAUT). This leads to an important conclusion that the existence of an additive separable utility function should be verified before using goal programming.

Interactive approaches to goal programming have attracted lively interest in recent years and are finally preparing ground for full incorporation of goal programming with MCDM. Interactive techniques, especially those searching for best compromise solutions, guarantee nondominated solutions, allow simple treatment of nonlinear objectives, and provide the decision maker with a variety of solutions (rather than with one, inflexible option); they also allow improvement of original goals by small increments and allow for simultaneous changes (rather than one by one) in the goal portfolio.

It seems, and Hannan confirms it, that over the past decade goal programming has become the most popular MCDM-related technique—in spite of, or precisely because of, its serious theoretical, methodological, and philosophical shortcomings. It appears that it might be its interactive version which could lead it back to respectability.

ABSTRACT

This paper summarizes methodological contributions to the goal programming literature in the last decade, synthesizes these contributions whenever possible, and ventures opinions of the role which goal programming should take in the next decade.

1. INTRODUCTION

The birth of goal programming (GP) was in 1952 when Charnes et al. [9] obtained "constrained regression estimates" for a problem involving the development of an executive compensation formula. These results were first reported in a paper presented by Ferguson et al. [19]. The term "goal programming" was first coined by Charnes and Cooper [5] in their 1961 classic text. In the subsequent decade, GP experienced only modest growth in terms of application and alternative uses. Significantly, however, researchers began to use GP for multiobjective or multigoal problems.

In the last decade, there has been a proliferation of articles pertaining to the application and theory of goal programming. A major force in this burgeoning popularity was Lee, who authored the first book devoted exclusively to GP [41]. An earlier book by Ijiri [34] applied GP to accounting problems. A subsequent text by Ignizio [30] contributed further to the popularity of GP.

The task of locating all applications of GP in the last decade would be virtually impossible. Lin [43] has provided a bibliography containing 84 applications of GP to accounting, finance, operations management, marketing, and manpower planning. This list is by no means exhaustive. Another extensive set of application papers is referenced by Ignizio [31]. As Dyer [16] notes: "It is only a slight exaggeration to suggest that an article entitled "A Goal Programming Formulation of the _____ Problem" could guarantee an author a journal publication; his only task was to fill in the blank, take a standard linear programming formulation of the problem, and shift a few constraints into the objective function following the traditional goal programming format."

Previous surveys of GP have been conducted by Kornbluth [37], Charnes and Cooper [8], and Ignizio [31]. Kornbluth's survey, written in 1973, is somewhat outdated because there have been many theoretical advances in GP in the intervening years. The Charnes and Cooper survey, conducted in 1977, contains primarily a survey of their work on such extensions as explicit methods in GP, goal interval programming, and fractional GP. Ignizio's study is primarily geared to readers not familiar with GP. It presents a historical sketch, lists applications, describes codes, and discusses areas for future research.

119

The intent of this survey is to recapitulate many of the methodological GP papers of the past decade, interrelate them whenever possible, and venture some opinions relating to the future of GP and the merits and shortcomings of GP relative to other multiple objective decision making techniques. It is assumed that the reader has already been at least superfically exposed to GP. For those who are not familiar with the subject, the works by Lee [41], Ignizio [30,31], and Hannan [23,24] will be helpful. Also, a good understanding of the impact of using preemptive priorities can be obtained by reviewing the article by Dauer and Krueger [13]. Since the present paper is part of a volume devoted to MCDM, summaries of articles which pertain to uses of GP in statistics will be omitted (see Charnes and Cooper [7] for a history of these developments, and Freed and Glover [20,21] for some additional references and for a description of the use of GP in discriminant analysis).

Before embarking, I would like to apologize to all those (I hope not many) authors whose works I have inadvertently overlooked in this methodological survey.

The linear GP problem will be defined in the following manner:

$$\min \sum_{i=1}^{k} P_i w_i + \sum_{i=1}^{k} P_i' v_i + \sum_{i=1}^{k} P_i''(w_i + v_i) \tag{1}$$

$$\text{s.t.} \quad \sum_{j=1}^{n} c_{ij} x_j + w_i - v_i = g_i \qquad i = 1, \dots . k$$

$$Fx \le f$$

$$w \ge o, \quad v \ge 0, \quad x \ge 0$$

where $x = (x_1, \dots , x_n)^T$;
          $w = (w_1, \dots , w_k)$;
          $v = (v_1, \dots , v_k)$;
          $C = (c_{ij})$ and F are matrices of dimensions $(k \times n)$ and $(m \times n)$, respectively; f and $g = (g_i)$ are vectors of dimension $(m \times 1)$ and $(k \times 1)$, respectively; and the w_i and v_i values are referred to as *negative deviational variables* and *positive deviational variables*, respectively.

For each i, exactly one of P_i, P_i', and P_i'' is nonzero, and all P_i, P_i' and P_i'' values are nonnegative. As i varies, the P_i (or P_i' or P_i'') values may be the same order of magnitude or may be of a different order. When they are of a different order of magnitude, they are called non-Archimedean weights, or *preemptive priorities*. $P_1 \gg P_2$ is used to denote that P_1 has a higher preemptive priority than P_2.

The following several sections identify some methodological areas in which advances have been made in the last decade and summarize the studies conducted in these methodological areas. The last section contrasts GP with other multiple objective methods and discusses the future of GP.

2. GOAL NORMING IN NONPREEMPTIVE GOAL PROGRAMMING

Both Widhelm [54] and de Kluyver [14] have noted that, for nonpreemptive GP problems or for intragoal weights in preemptive GP models, care should be taken in developing weights associated with the various goals. The numerical value of the deviation from each unsatisfied goal is the value of the slack or surplus variable (positive or negative deviational variable) in the goal constraint and is dependent upon the scale associated with the variable. To equalize the scales, deviations of equal geometrical distances must yield equal numerical values.

This can be achieved by associating the same Euclidean distance measure with each slack or surplus variable. Goal variables for the ith goal must be weighted by the Euclidean norm $\| c^i \| = \sqrt{(c^i)'c^i}$, where c^i denotes the ith goal constraint coefficient vector $(c_{i1}, \ldots, c_{in})$. Thus, the goal constraint

$$3x_1 + 2x_2 + 4x_3 + d_1^- - d_1^+ = 6$$

would be converted to

$$3/\sqrt{29}x_1 + 2/\sqrt{29}x_2 + 4/\sqrt{29}x_3 + e_1^- - e_1^+ = 6/\sqrt{29}$$

before determining the relative weights to assign to e_1^- and e_1^+ in the objective function. The objective function relative weights would be determined on the basis of how important it is to achieve each goal relative to the importance of achieving the other goals.

This is an important consideration in developing models which are as representative as possible of the concerns of the decision maker (DM).

3. NONDOMINATED SOLUTIONS IN GOAL PROGRAMMING

One shortcoming of GP, as noted by Zeleny and Cochrane [55] and by Cohon and Marks [12], is that the resulting solution is not necessarily the "best" one available to the decision maker because it may be dominated by another feasible solution. In a multicriteria problem with k objective functions, $\sum_{j=1}^{n} c_{ij}x_j = c^i(x)$, for $i = 1, \ldots, k$, the vector x^* is said to be dominated if and only if there exists another feasible x such that $c^i(x)$

$\geq c^i(x^*)$ for all $i = 1, \ldots, k$ and $c^i(x) > c^i(x^*)$ for some $i(i = 1, \ldots, k)$.

Figure 1 presents a graphic illustration of this shortcoming. The example is in objective function space (z_1, z_2). The region F where feasible solutions lie is ABCDEHIJA, and the set of efficient or nondominated points (points which are not dominated) lie on ABCDE. If the one-sided goals for the two objectives are to achieve at least g_1 and g_2 respectively, (g_1, g_2) is an optimal GP solution. However, this solution is inferior since it is dominated by all points in KLM. Also, point C is an extreme point which dominates (g_1, g_2) and is an alternative optimum of the GP problem.

Thus, alternative optima in a GP problem may be "better" solutions than the solution obtained. Hannan [26] extends the definition of a GP solution to that of a GP-nondominated solution and demonstrates how to determine when an inferior GP solution is obtained, and how to generate the set of GP-nondominated solutions. Suppose that $x^* = (x_1^*, \ldots, x_n^*)$, $w^* = (w_1^*, \ldots, w_k^*)$, $v^* = (v_1^*, \ldots, v_k^*)$ is an optimal solution to

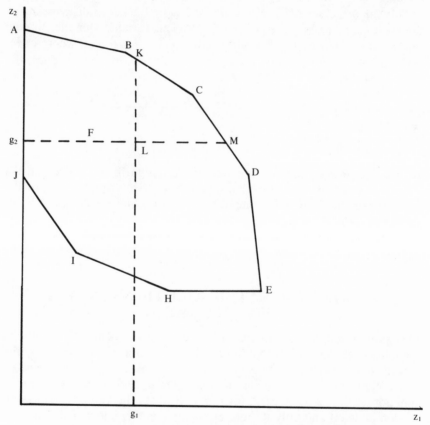

Figure 1. Inferiority of Some Goal Programming Solutions.

(1). Consider the problem:

$$\max \sum_{i=1}^{k} (s_i + t_i) = U \tag{2}$$

s.t. $\displaystyle\sum_{j=1}^{n} c_{ij}x_j - t_i \quad = g_i - w_i^* + v_i^* \quad$ if $P_i > 0$

$\displaystyle\sum_{j=1}^{n} c_{ij}x_j \quad + s_i = g_i - w_i^* + v_i^* \quad$ if $P_i' > 0$

$\displaystyle\sum_{j=1}^{n} c_{ij}x_j \quad = g_i - w_i^* + v_i^* \quad$ if $P_i'' > 0 \qquad i = 1, \ldots, k$

$Fx \le f$

$x \ge 0, \quad t \ge 0, \quad s \ge 0$

where $t = (t_1, \ldots, t_k)$ and $s = (s_1, \ldots, s_k)$.

If the optimal solution to (2) is zero, then $x = x^*$, $w = w^*$, $v = v^*$ is a GP-nondominated solution to (1). Otherwise $x = x^*$, $w = w^*$, $v = v^*$ is not a GP-nondominated solution, and it may be wise to generate one or more of them for consideration.

If

$$y_i = \sum_{j=1}^{n} c_{ij}x_j$$

is bounded for all i, the GP-nondominated solutions to (1) are the solutions to the following vector maximum problem:

$$\max \sum_{j=1}^{n} c_{ij}x_j \qquad \forall i:P_i > 0 \tag{3}$$

$$\max \sum_{j=1}^{n} (-c_{ij})x_j \qquad \forall i:P_i' > 0$$

s.t. $\displaystyle\sum_{j=1}^{n} c_{ij}x_j \ge g_i - w_i^* \qquad \forall i:P_i > 0$

$\displaystyle\sum_{j=1}^{n} c_{ij}x_j \le g_i \quad + v_i^* \qquad \forall i:P_i' > 0$

$\displaystyle\sum_{j=1}^{n} c_{ij}x_j = g_i - w_i^* + v_i^* \qquad \forall i:P_i'' > 0$

$Fx \le f$

$x \ge 0$

where $x = x^*$, $w = w^*$, $v = v^*$ is an optimal solution to (1).

Thus, problem (2) should be solved. If the optimal value is zero, the solution is GP-nondominated. If the optimal value is not zero, (3) should be solved. If a large number of solutions result from (3), this is an indication that some goals have been set too conservatively. One can obtain a more reasonable number of solutions from which to choose by setting more demanding goals or placing weights on the objectives in (3). These weights can either be preemptive priorities or Archimedean weights. However, the weights should reflect the relative values of extending the objectives once the goals have been satisfied to the fullest extent.

This method is important because it provides an avenue for dealing with nonefficient (dominated) GP solutions. If the original goals have been chosen too conservatively, it directs the DM to reformulate the goals in a more realistic manner, and it ensures that the resulting solutions will be efficient in a goal-oriented sense.

Another approach to obtaining efficient (nondominated) solutions via goal programming was presented by Ignizio [33] in 1981. This approach consists of finding an initial efficient solution to the vector maximum problem

$$\max \sum_{j=1}^{n} c_{1j}x_j$$

$$\max \sum_{j=1}^{n} c_{2j}x_j$$

$$\vdots$$

$$\max \sum_{j=1}^{n} c_{kj}x_j$$

$$\text{s.t.} \quad Fx \leq f$$

$$x \geq 0$$

by means of the preemptive GP problem

$$\min P_1w_1 + \cdots + P_kw_k$$

$$\text{s.t.} \quad \sum_{j=1}^{n} c_{1j}x_j + w_1 - v_1 + \cdots \qquad\qquad = g_1$$

$$\vdots$$

$$\sum_{j=1}^{n} c_{kj}x_j + \cdots \qquad\qquad + w_k - v_k \quad = g_k$$

$$Fx \leq f$$

$$x \geq 0$$

$$P_1 \ggg P_2 \ggg \cdots \ggg P_{k-1} \ggg P_k.$$

After the initial preemptive GP problem is solved, adjacent efficient extreme points are generated to see if they provide a more desirable solution than the initial one.

A drawback of this approach is that the initial GP solution is not necessarily efficient. The efficiency of this solution can be guaranteed only if $w_1, \ldots, w_k$ are all greater than zero. Consequently, the method is very dependent upon the a priori goals $g_1, \ldots, g_k$ stated by the DM. These goals must be extremely ambitious to ensure that all w_i values are positive. However, if this is done, the efficient points which are subsequently generated will not necessarily be in the region which is most preferred by the DM.

4. EXPLICIT SOLUTIONS IN GOAL PROGRAMMING

In 1975, Charnes et al. [11] demonstrated that a certain class of GP problems with separable goal functions could be solved explicitly without resorting to iterative techniques. In particular, problems of the form

$$\min \sum_{i=1}^{k} p_i(w_i + v_i) = z$$

$$\text{s.t.} \quad x_i + w_i - v_i = g_i \qquad i = 1, \ldots, k$$

$$\sum_{i=1}^{k} x_i \leq b_0$$

$$b_i \geq x_i \geq a_i \qquad i = 1, \ldots, k$$

$$x_i \geq 0 \qquad i = 1, \ldots, k$$

where $g_i(i = 1, \ldots, k)$ are goals and $b_0, a_i, b_i(i = 1, \ldots, k)$ are constants, can be solved explicitly.

The following theorem is instrumental in this process:

THEOREM 4.1. If x satisfies the constraints $\sum_{i=1}^{k} x_i \leq b_0, b_i \geq x_i \geq a_i$, for $i = 1, \ldots, k$, with some of its components $x_{i_0} > g_{i_0}$, then $\bar{x}$ with components

$$\bar{x}_i = \begin{cases} x_i, & i \neq i_0 \\ \text{Max}(a_{i_0}, g_{i_0}), & i = i_0 \end{cases}$$

also satisfies these constraints, and $z(\bar{x}) \leq z(x)$.

This theorem allows us to restate the above formulation after reducing the previous problem by setting $x_i = a_i$ when $g_i \leq a_i$ and omitting the variables x_i for which this occurs. The resulting formulation (assuming that the constraints are indexed so that $p_1 \geq p_2 \geq \cdots \geq p_k$) is

$$\max \sum_{i=1}^{k} p_i x_i$$

$$\text{s.t.} \quad \sum_{i=1}^{k} x_i \leq \hat{b}_0$$

$$\hat{b}_i \geq x_i \geq a_i$$

$$x_i \geq 0 \qquad\qquad i = 1, \ldots, k$$

where $\hat{b}_i \equiv \max(a_i, g_i)$ and $\hat{b}_0$ results from b_0 after the process of setting $x_i = a_i$ and omitting x_i when inequality $g_i \leq a_i$ holds.

The optimum (explicit) solution to this problem is

$$x_i^* = b_i \qquad\qquad i = 1, \ldots, j - 1$$

$$x_j^* = \hat{b}_0 - \sum_{i=1}^{j-1} \hat{b}_i - \sum_{i=j+1}^{k} a_i$$

where j is the smallest positive integer such that

$$\hat{b}_0 - \sum_{i=j+1}^{k} a_i \geq \sum_{i=1}^{j-1} \hat{b}_i$$

$$\hat{b}_0 - \sum_{i=j+1}^{k} a_i < \sum_{i=1}^{j} \hat{b}_i.$$

Although the format of this problem may not seem general enough, Charnes et al. indicate that Theorem 4.1 also applies when the constraints which involve more than one variable at a time have only nonnegative coefficients. Also, they demonstrate that the results hold not only for separable piecewise linear functions of the form $\sum_i p_i \mid x_i - g_i \mid$, as shown above, but also for general separable convex piecewise linear functionals.

5. GOAL PROGRAMMING WITH LINEAR FRACTIONAL CRITERIA

In practical optimization problems the objectives or goals are frequently of a ratio or fractional form. For example, return on investment, cost per patient, percent of students who are underclassmen, and market share are all fractional criteria. Awerbuch et al. [2] noted in 1976 that in fractional GP problems it does not suffice to merely multiply through by the denominator and solve the associated linear GP problem. That is, the problem

$$\min \left| \frac{u}{t} - g \right|, \qquad u, t \in K \qquad (4)$$

(where g is the goal and K is the nonempty convex set $\{(u,t) \in R^2 | u = a_1 \cdot x, t = a_2 \cdot y, Fx \le f\}$ with u, t, x, and f vectors, F a matrix, and $t \ne 0$) is not, in general, equivalent to the problem

$$\min | u - gt |, \qquad u, t \in K. \qquad (5)$$

A subsequent attempt by Hannan [25] to determine when problems (4) and (5) are equivalent was demonstrated to be incorrect by Soyster and Lev [50], who provided a counterexample and an auxiliary problem for determining when (5) could be substituted for (4). A minor error in this formulation was then corrected by Hannan [27]. The resulting formulation, due primarily to Soyster and Lev, is as follows:

(a) Solve the problem

$$\min_{u,t \in K} w + v$$

$$\text{s.t.} \quad u - gt - v + w = 0$$

$$v, w \ge 0.$$

(b) Suppose the optimal solution to (A) is $u = u^*, t = t^*$. If $u^* < gt^*$, delete v, let $g = u^*/t^*$, and change the right-hand side of the constraint to M where $u < M$ for all $u \in K$. If $u^* > gt^*$, delete w, let $g = u^*/t^*$, and change the right-hand side of the constraint to $-M$. Solve problem (a) with these changes.

(c) If the optimal objective value for the perturbed problem is M, the solution to (5) is optimal to (4). Otherwise, it is not and other methods must be employed.

The advantage of this method is that when the auxiliary problem proves that (4) and (5) are equivalent, nonlinear methods are not required. The disadvantage is that problems (4) and (5) are not always equivalent.

A more general method of dealing with this problem is to convert the fractional criterion problem into a linear problem which, although more complicated than formulation (5), will always provide a solution to the fractional criterion problem.

If some or all of the DM's criterion functions are of the form

$$\frac{c^i x + \alpha_i}{d^i x + \beta_i}$$

and there is only one fractional criterion function associated with each priority class, the linear fractional programming methods of Charnes and Cooper [6], Martos [45], or Bitran and Novaes [4] can be used in the following manner.

Suppose the first criterion function is fractional. Then the constraint

$$\frac{c^1 x + \alpha_1}{d^1 x + \beta_1} + w_1 - v_1 = g_1$$

can be added to the feasible region. Since $d^1 x + \beta_1 > 0$ by assumption, we obtain

$$(c^1 - g_1 d^1)x + w_1(d^1 x + \beta_1) - v_1(d^1 x + \beta_1) = g_1 \beta_1 - \alpha_1.$$

This equation is nonlinear, so we use the variable change

$$y_1^- = w_1(d^1 x + \beta_1) \text{ and } y_1^+ = v_1(d^1 x + \beta_1)$$

and formulate the GP problem as

$$\min \frac{p_1^- y_1^- + p_1^+ y_1^+}{d^1 x + \beta_1}$$

$$\text{s.t.} \quad (c^1 - g_1 d^1)x + y_1^- - y_1^+ = g_1 \beta_1 - \alpha_1$$

$$Fx \le f$$

$$x, y_1^-, y_1^+ \ge 0$$

where p_1^- and p_1^+ are *intragoal* weights.

This is a single objective linear fractional programming problem and the aforementioned references can be used to solve it. If g_1 is attainable, the constraint $(c^1 - g_1 d^1)x = g_1 \beta_1 - \alpha_1$ is added to the GP problem at the next priority level. If g_1 cannot be attained and $\hat{g}_1$ is the best possible value, the constraint $(c^1 - \hat{g}_1 d^1)x = \hat{g}_1 \beta_1 - \alpha_1$ is added at the next priority level.

This method is only possible when there is, at most, one fractional criterion for each priority level. Otherwise, the result is the sum of two or more linear fractionals, which is, in general, a quadratic function.

A more difficult problem arises when there are two or more fractional criteria for at least one priority class (or for a nonpreemptive GP problem). After using the variable change, we obtain

$$\min \sum_{i=1}^{k} \lambda_i \left(\frac{p_i^- y_i^- + p_i^+ y_i^+}{d^i x + \beta_i} \right) \tag{6}$$

$$\text{s.t.} \quad (c^i - g_i d^i)x + y_i^- - y_i^+ = g_i \beta_i - \alpha_i \qquad i = 1, 2, \ldots, k$$

$$Fx \le f$$

$$x, y^-, y^+ \ge 0$$

where λ_i is the weight associated with the ith fractional criterion.

This problem was addressed by Kornbluth and Steuer [39] in 1981. The method is derived from previous work done by the same two authors on the multiple objective linear fractional programming problem [40]:

$$\max \frac{c^1 x + \alpha_1}{d^1 x + \beta_1} = z_1$$

$$\vdots \qquad \vdots$$

$$\max \frac{c^k x + \alpha_k}{d^k x + \beta_k} = z_k$$

$$\text{s.t.} \quad Fx \leq f$$

$$x \in R^n$$

$$x \geq 0$$

where the α_i and β_i are constants and $d^i x + \beta_i > 0$ for all i and all feasible x.

Because of difficulties inherent in generating the set of efficient (non-dominated) points for the above problem, Kornbluth and Steuer [38] define a *weakly efficient* point $\bar{x} \in S = \{x \backslash Fx \leq f, \ x \in R^n, \ x \geq 0\}$ so that there does not exist another $x \in S$ such that $z_i(x) > z_i(\bar{x})$ for all i.

The authors solve problem (6) by finding all weakly efficient vertices, which is the set of all possible optimal solutions. The specific λ_i values can then be used to determine which of these solutions yield the minimum value.

In summary, this technique has the flexibility to handle more than one fractional criterion per priority level (or per problem, in the case of a GP problem without preemptive priorities). Also, this methodology allows problems with combinations of linear and fractional criteria to be solved.

6. GOAL INTERVAL PROGRAMMING

Charnes and Cooper [8] and Charnes et al. [10] have extended the typical goal programming formulation and also the simple goal interval of the form

$$\min p_1 w_1 + p_2 v_2$$

$$\text{s.t.} \quad f(x) + w_1 - v_1 \qquad \qquad = b_1$$

$$f(x) \qquad \qquad + w_2 - v_2 = b_2$$

$$x, w_1, w_2, v_1, v_2 \geq 0$$

which penalizes values of $f(x)$ outside the interval $[b_1, b_2]$ by using po-lygonal (piecewise linear and continuous) functions containing a variety of connected line segments, each with a different slope. An example of such a function is provided in Figure 2. The theory developed by Charnes et al. is dependent upon the following theorem:

THEOREM 6.1. Any polygonal function $f(x)$ may be represented as

$$f(x) = \sum_{j=1}^{N} \alpha_j \, | \, x - g_j \, | + \beta x + \gamma,$$

where $\alpha_j = \frac{1}{2}(k_{j+1} - k_j)$, $\beta = \frac{1}{2}(k_{N+1} + k_1)$, and $\gamma = \frac{1}{2}(a_{N+1} + a_1)$, in which

$$f(x) = k_r x + a_r \qquad (g_{r-1} \le x \le g_r).$$

Here k_r is the slope and a_r the intercept for the corresponding linear function in the section of the curve initiated at $x = g_{r-1}$, where $k_{r-1}x + a_{r-1}$ intersects $k_r x + a_r$, and terminated at $x = g_r$, where the latter intersects $k_{r+1}x + a_{r+1}$.

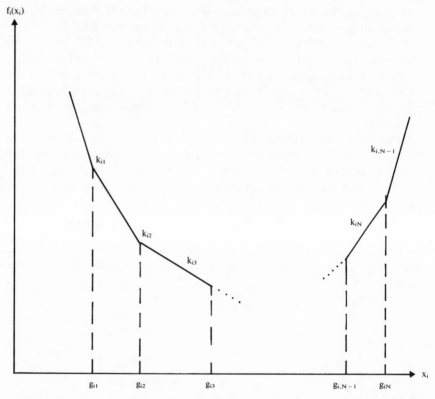

Figure 2. Graph for Goal Interval Functional with Varying Slopes.

The formulation which results is

$$\min \sum_{i=1}^{m} p_i \left[\sum_{j=1}^{n_i} \alpha_{ij}(w_{ij} + v_{ij}) + \beta_i x_i \right]$$

s.t. $\quad Fx \le f$

$$x_i + w_{ij} - v_{ij} = g_{ij} \qquad \text{for all i, j}$$

$$x_i, w_{ij}, v_{ij} \ge 0 \qquad \text{for all i, j.}$$

In this formulation, n_i is the number of goal segments corresponding to the ith goal.

Charnes and Cooper [8] note that both the p_i values, which are Archimedean and provide relative priorities between the goal functions $f_i(x_i)$, and the $\alpha_{ij} = \frac{1}{2}(k_{ij+1} - k_{ij})$ have an impact upon the relative weights of the functionals. This must be taken into consideration when choosing the p_i values.

It is also noted that the functions which are suitable for use as goal functionals are those for which

$$\sum_{j=1}^{N} \alpha_j > |\beta|$$

where N is the number of points at which the slope changes. Charnes and Cooper also cite other works which demonstrate how to convert piecewise linear and continuous functions which have local optima into GP formulations.

This study is important because it increases the flexibility of GP in providing a representation of the DM's actual preferences, while allowing the analyst to use the efficient LP-based solution procedures.

7. FUZZY GOAL PROGRAMMING

Two recent articles by Narasimhan [48] and Hannan [28] have explored the application of fuzzy set theory to goal programming. Fuzzy sets are used to describe imprecise goals of the DM by associating membership functions, with values ranging from 0 to 1, for various values pertaining to imprecise statements of the DM. For example, the fuzzy goal "a substantial profit" may be given the following membership function by the DM:

Profit x($)	5,000	6,000	7,000	8,000	10,000	12,000
Membership $\mu(x)$	0	.3	.5	.8	.9	1.0

For this function, $5,000 is in no sense a substantial profit and $12,000 is unquestionably a substantial profit; \$7,000 rates a .5 on a scale from 0 to 1.

Narasimhan used membership functions of the form

$$\mu_i\left(\sum_{j=1}^{n} c_{ij}x_j\right) = \begin{cases} 0 & \text{if } \sum_{j=1}^{n} c_{ij}x_j \le b_i - \Delta_i \\[2ex] \dfrac{\sum_{j=1}^{n} c_{ij}x_j - (b_i - \Delta_i)}{\Delta_i} & \text{if } b_i - \Delta_i \le \sum_{j=1}^{n} c_{ij}x_j \le b_i \\[2ex] \dfrac{b_i + \Delta_i - \sum_{j=1}^{n} c_{ij}x_j}{\Delta_i} & \text{if } b_i \le \sum_{j=1}^{n} c_{ij}x_j \le b_i + \Delta_i \\[2ex] 0 & \text{if } \sum_{j=1}^{n} c_{ij}x_j \ge b_i + \Delta_i \end{cases}$$

for the ith goal, $i = 1, \ldots, k$. This membership function is illustrated in Figure 3. The corresponding formulation can be reduced to

$$\max \lambda$$

$$\text{s.t.} \quad \frac{\sum_{j=1}^{n} c_{ij}x_j}{\Delta_i} + w_i - v_i = \frac{b_i}{\Delta_i} \qquad i = 1, \ldots, k$$

$$\lambda + w_i + v_i \le 1 \qquad i = 1, \ldots, k$$

$$x, \lambda, w_i, v_i \ge 0 \qquad i = 1, \ldots, k.$$

This formulation has the effect of maximizing the minimum membership function. The "maximin" concept is in keeping with the axioms of fuzzy set theory.

Narasimhan also extends the fuzzy GP problem to a problem involving fuzzy priorities. This is accomplished by defining a membership function which is a composite of the membership of the priority weights and of the goals.

Hannan demonstrates how any concave piecewise linear membership function representing the DM's imprecise goals can be incorporated in the fuzzy GP formulation. The goal interval programming methodology of Charnes et al. [8,10] (presented earlier) is the technique used to solve these more general problems. Hannan also illustrates how preemptive and nonpreemptive weights can be used in fuzzy GP problems in lieu of the somewhat arbitrary maximin approach.

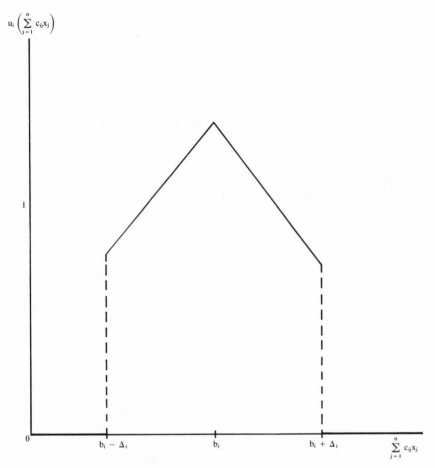

$u_i \left(\sum_{j=1}^{n} c_{ij}x_j \right)$

$b_i - \Delta_i$ b_i $b_i + \Delta_i$ $\sum_{j=1}^{n} c_{ij}x_j$

Figure 3. Graph of a Simple Membership Function.

The potential advantage of fuzzy goal programming techniques is their ability to allow the DM to be imprecise in his/her stipulation of goals. This would generally lead to the specification of a nonlinear function which represents this imprecision. It should be noted that fuzzy goal programming is closely akin to the a priori development of a utility function by the DM. The only difference is that the functions developed in fuzzy goal programming are based on statements of imprecision by the DM rather than statements of preference.

For example, in fuzzy GP, the DM might desire a "reasonable profit" and then specify what a reasonable profit is in terms of membership functions. In developing a utility function, the DM would immediately attribute different utilities to various profit values. To many, this may seem like a narrow distinction, and it is fair to say that the practical value of fuzzy GP is still open to question. Much of its future utility is dependent upon ongoing research pertaining to the means of combining goals and/or objectives.

8. RELATIONSHIP BETWEEN GOAL PROGRAMMING AND MULTIATTRIBUTE UTILITY THEORY

Some important insights about the relationship between goal programming and multiattribute utility theory (MAUT; see Keeney and Raiffa [36]) were provided in 1977 by Dyer [16]. This relationship is demonstrated in the following manner. Suppose there are two criterion functions, $h_1(x)$ and $h_2(x)$. Also, without loss of generality, assume that $0 \leq h_i(x) \leq 1$, for $i = 1, 2$. Suppose also that h_1 should be at least as large as g_1, but that values above g_1 have no marginal increase in value, and h_2 should be somewhere between g_{2L} and g_{2R}. Weights of relative importance (after norming) for the deviations of h_1 from g_1 and of h_2 from g_{2L} and g_{2R} are given to be the Archimedean weights p_1, p_2, and p_3, respectively. This problem can be formulated as follows:

$$\min p_1 w_1 + p_2 w_2 + p_3 v_3$$

$$\begin{aligned}
\text{s.t.} \quad h_1(x) - v_1 + w_1 & & &= g_1 \\
h_2(x) & - v_2 + w_2 & &= g_{2L} \\
h_2(x) & - v_3 + w_3 & &= g_{2R} \\
& & Fx &\leq f \\
& & v_i, w_i &\geq 0 \qquad i = 1, 2, 3 \\
& & x &\geq 0.
\end{aligned}$$

In this formulation,

$$w_1 = g_1 + v_1 - h_1(x).$$

Introducing the relationship $h_1(x) - v_{12} = 0$ as a new constraint and noting that g_1 is a constant, we conclude than minimizing $p_1 w_1$ is equivalent to minimizing $p_1(v_1 - v_{12})$.

Similarly, if we introduce the constraint $h_2(x) - v_{22} = 0$, minimizing $p_2 w_2$ is equivalent to minimizing $p_2(v_2 - v_{22})$, and minimizing $p_3 v_3$ is equivalent to minimizing $p_3(w_3 + v_{22} - g_{2R})$. The g_{2R} term is retained for purposes of graphic illustration.

After combining these results and rewriting the GP problem as a maximization problem, we obtain

$$\max p_1(v_{12} - v_1) + p_2(v_{22} - v_2) - p_3(v_{22} + w_3 - g_{2R})$$

s.t.
$$h_1(x) - v_1 + w_1 = g_1$$
$$h_2(x) - v_2 + w_2 = g_{2L}$$
$$h_2(x) - v_3 + w_3 = g_{2R}$$
$$h_1(x) - v_{12} = 0$$
$$h_2(x) - v_{22} = 0$$
$$v_i, w_i \geq 0 \quad i = 1, 2, 3$$
$$Fx \leq f \qquad v_{12}, v_{22} \geq 0.$$

These two piecewise linear functions are presented in Figures 4 and 5, taken from Dyer [16]. The dotted lines represent nonlinear functions u_1 and u_2, which could be represented by the piecewise linear functions. Obviously, there are other functions which could also be represented by these piecewise linear functions. Consequently, GP is an approximation to the problem

$$\max u_1(h_1(x_1, \ldots, x_n)) + u_2(h_2(x_1, \ldots, x_n)).$$

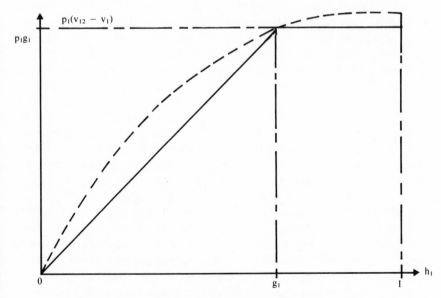

Figure 4. The Piecewise Linear Function $h_1(x)$.

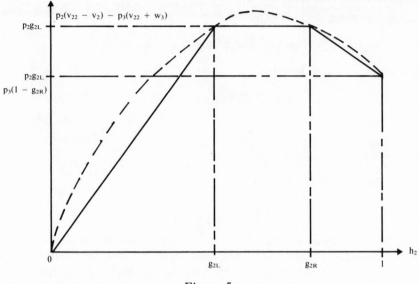

Figure 5.

Both u_1 and u_2 are conditional utility functions whose sum is an additive separable utility function. Thus, goal programming formulations implicitly assume the existence of an additive separable utility function.

As a result of this observation by Dyer, it follows that the existence of an additive separable utility function should be verified before using GP. Also, if the necessary conditions do not hold, an estimation of the error associated with using an additive separable function is desirable.

Because the GP problem is not related to risk, and because each goal is generally chosen independently of other goals, the special type of additive separable utility function that is required is a cardinal additive value function, which is a cardinal additive utility function under certainty. Two recent papers by Dyer and Sarin [17,18] indicate that this condition holds if the preference differences between two pairs of alternatives that differ in only one component do not depend upon the fixed values of the other components. This property is referred to as *difference independence.*

As an example of difference independence, suppose that the DM is confronted with goal vectors $A_1 = (10, 15, 30, 25)$; $A_2 = (5, 15, 30, 25)$; $B_1 = (10, 40, 10, 30)$; $B_2 = (5, 40, 10, 30)$. If "more is better" for the first goal, the DM should prefer A_1 to A_2 by the same amount as he/she prefers B_1 to B_2 if the difference independence property holds.

Dyer [16] then reports conflicting opinions regarding the significance of errors which result when the difference independence condition is not satisfied but the additive separable form is used as an approximation. He reconciles these views by stating that the additive separable form is a robust approximation but that serious errors can occur in "worst case" situations.

Dyer [16] continues by presenting the results of a study by Geoffrion [22] which demonstrates how goals, or goal intervals, can be chosen for each criterion so that the piecewise linear approximation to the implicit utility function provides the best fit. Dyer adds that in most cases the analyst would probably prefer to develop the best piecewise linear fit by asking a series of questions in order to provide a direct approximation of each utility function.

A study by Karwan and Wallace [35] compared the use of the goal interval programming approach by Charnes and Cooper (with the provision for revision of weighting factors) with the conjoint measurement approach to developing a utility function (see Luce and Tukey [44]). This was done for a U.S. Coast Guard resource allocation problem dealing with the protection of the marine environment from discharges of oil and other hazardous materials.

The conclusion of the Karwan–Wallace study was that although the conjoint measurement approach was relatively easy to use, when compared to the interactive GP approach, the quality of the resulting solution was unsatisfactory to the DM. The apparent reason for this dissatisfaction was the inability of the conjoint measurement approach to allow the DM to revise the weighting factors.

9. INTERACTIVE GOAL PROGRAMMING

Interactive techniques for solving multiple objective problems are based upon a search process which consists of periodic feedback from the DM, which serves to guide the direction of the search. Each cycle in the process contains an optimization phase and a DM evaluation phase. The true preference function of the DM remains unspecified, but the direction of the DM's preference is identified at each stage by presenting the DM with a trial solution.

Numerous interactive algorithms for obtaining preferred solutions to multiple objective linear programming problems have been proposed. These methods include attempts to have the DM sequentially specify weighting vectors or surrogate information from which to construct weighting vectors, construct payoff tables for reducing the feasible region, reduce weighting vector space on the basis of trade-off information, and reduce the convex cone generated by the gradients of the objectives.

This section will summarize only those papers devoted to goal programming interactive techniques. GP interactive techniques are defined as those interactive techniques in which each cycle contains the development of a set of new goals specified by the DM.

Several interactive GP approaches have been suggested in the last decade. In 1981, Masud and Hwang [46] presented an interactive approach

to attaining a "best compromise solution." This is referred to as interactive sequential goal programming (ISGP) by the authors.

Suppose that the multiple objective decision-making problem associated with (1) is the following:

$$\max h_1 = \sum_{j=1}^{n} c_{1j}x_j$$

$$\max h_2 = \sum_{j=1}^{n} c_{2j}x_j$$

$$\vdots \qquad\qquad \vdots$$

$$\max h_k = \sum_{j=1}^{n} c_{kj}x_j$$

$$\text{s.t.} \quad F_j(x_1, \ldots, x_n) - f_j \leq 0 \qquad j = 1, \ldots, m$$

$$x_1, \ldots, x_n \geq 0$$

where the functions and constants are as defined in (1). Also assume that
the larger the $\sum_{j=1}^{n} c_{ij}x_j$ values are, the better. Then the steps in the ISGP
approach are as follows:

1. Determine max $h_i = \sum_{j=1}^{n} c_{ij}x_j$ such that $F_j(x_1, \ldots, x_n) - f_j \leq$
    $0; j = 1, \ldots, m$ for each $i = 1, \ldots, k$. Let the solution to this
    problem be x_i^*, h_i^* for $i = 1, \ldots, k$. Also, let $h_{ji} = h_i(x_j^*)$ and h_{*i}
    $= \min_j h_{ji}$, for $j = 1, \ldots, k$.

This step generates a set of upper and lower bounds for the DM to use
in setting goals.

2. The DM sets the initial goals $g_1, \ldots, g_k$ ($h_{*i} < g_i \leq h_i^*$ for all i).
3. Solve the problem

$$\min P_1 \sum_i w_i + P_2 \sum_i (-v_i)$$

$$\text{s.t.} \quad F_j(x_1, \ldots, x_n) \qquad\qquad\qquad \leq f_j \qquad\qquad j = 1, \ldots, m$$

$$\sum_{j=1}^{n} c_{ij}x_j \qquad + q_iw_i - q_iv_i = g_i$$

$$w_i \qquad\qquad \leq 1 \qquad\qquad i = 1, \ldots, k$$

$$w_i, v_i \geq 0$$

$$P_1 \ggg P_2$$

where $q_i = g_i - h_{*i}$.

Suppose the solution is x^0, h^0. The first priority is to minimize the underachievement of the goals, and the second priority is to guarantee that the solution h^0 is undominated.

4. Solve, for $t = 1, \ldots, k$,

$$\min P_1 \sum_{\substack{i \\ i \neq t}} w_i + P_2 \sum_i (-v_i)$$

s.t. $F_j(x_1, \ldots, x_n)$ $\leq f_j \quad j = 1, \ldots, m$

$\quad h_t(x_1, \ldots, x_n) \qquad - q_t w_t \qquad\qquad = g_t$ ⎤

$\quad h_i(x_1, \ldots, x_n) \qquad\qquad + q_i w_i - q_i v_i = g_i$ ⎦ $\quad i \neq t$

$\qquad\qquad\qquad w_i \qquad\qquad\qquad \leq 1$

$\qquad\qquad\qquad w_i. \; v_i, \; v_t \geq 0$

$$P_1 \ggg P_2$$

where $q_i = g_i - h_{*i}$, for $i = 1, \ldots, k$. Suppose the solution to each of these problems is x^t, h^t, for $t = 1, \ldots, k$. This step generates solutions such that the intent of the t-th solution is to first satisfy the t-th goal.

5. Ask the DM if h^0 or any of the h^t values are satisfactory. If so, stop. Otherwise, the DM determines a modified g vector by comparing h^0 and the h^t values with the previous g vector.
6. Check to see if the modified g vector contains some goals which are less ambitious than the corresponding values in h^0 in order to compensate for the more ambitious goals. That is, there must be some i such that $g_i < h^0_i$.
7. Solve the problem

$$\min P_1 \sum_s w_s + P_2 \sum_i w_i + P_3 \sum_{i,s} (-v_i - v_s)$$

s.t. $F_j(x_1, \ldots, x_n)$ $\leq f_j \; j = 1, \ldots, m$

$\quad h_s(x_1, \ldots, x_n) + q_s w_s - q_s v_s \qquad = g_s$ for all s such that $g_s \leq h^0_s$

$\quad h_i(x_1, \ldots, x_n) \qquad\qquad + q_i w_i - q_i v_i = g_i$ for all i such that $g_i > h^0_i$

$\qquad\qquad\qquad w_s \leq 1$

$\qquad\qquad\qquad w_i \leq 1$

$$P_1 \ggg P_2 \ggg P_3$$

where $q_i = g_i - h_{*i}$, for $i = 1, \ldots, k$. Suppose the solution to this problem is x^0, h^0.

8. Solve, for $t = 1, \ldots, k$,

$$\min P_1 \sum_{\substack{s \\ s \neq t}} w_s + P_2 \sum_{\substack{i \\ i \neq t}} w_i + P_3 \sum_{i,s} (-v_i - v_s)$$

s.t. $F_j(x_1, \ldots, x_n)$ $\leq f_j$ $j = 1, \ldots, n$

$\quad f_t(x_1, \ldots, x_n) - q_t v_t$ $= g_t$

$\quad f_s(x_1, \ldots, x_n)$ $+ q_s w_s - q_s v_s$ $= g_s$ $\quad s \neq t$

$\quad f_i(x_1, \ldots, x_n)$ $+ q_i w_i - q_i v_i = g_i$ $\quad i \neq t$

$\quad\quad\quad\quad\quad\quad\quad\quad\quad w_s, w_i \leq 1$

$\quad\quad\quad\quad v_t, w_s, v_s, w_i, v_i \geq 0$ $\quad$ for all i, s

where $q_i = g_i - h_{*i}$, for $i = 1, \ldots, k$.

Suppose the solution to this problem is x^t, h^t. Go to step 5.

This method is advantageous because nondominated solutions are guaranteed, nonlinear problems can be solved, and a variety of solutions are presented to the DM at each iteration in order to guide him/her in future refinement of options. The disadvantages are the difficulty of finding an initial feasible solution and, more importantly, the difficulty of finding a feasible solution at step 8. This could necessitate a considerable amount of interaction with the DM. Also, the number of problems solved could be very high relative to other approaches, although this is probably not critical as a result of the efficiency of the solution techniques.

Another interactive goal programming algorithm, called interactive multiple goal programming (IMGP), is also a recent addition to the literature (see Spronk [51] and Nijkamp and Spronk [49]). The procedure consists of the following steps:

1. Assume that the DM's preferences can be described in terms of a (unknown) real-valued preference function u which is a concave function of $h_i(x_1, \ldots, x_n)$, for $i = 1, \ldots, k$ and $x_1, \ldots, x_n$. An optimal solution is defined by

$$\max u (h_1(x_1, \ldots, x_n), \ldots, h_k(x_1, \ldots, x_n))$$

$$\text{s.t.} \quad x \in S = \{x \backslash Fx \leq f, x \geq 0\}.$$

Also assume that $\partial u / \partial h_i > 0$ for $i = 1, \ldots, k$; that is, the higher the value of each goal variable, the better.

2. Identical to step 1 in the Masud and Hwang technique. Also, define

$$h_1^* \quad h_2^* \quad \ldots \quad h_k^*$$

as the potency matrix P_1.

$$h_{*1} \quad h_{*2} \quad \ldots \quad h_{*k}$$

3. For each goal g_i, the DM defines aspiration levels h_i^j, for $j = 2, \ldots, t - 1$ such that

$$h_{*i} = h_i^1 < h_i^2 < \cdots < h_i^{t-1} < h_i^t = h_i^*.$$

Define $\delta_i (i = 1, \ldots, k)$ as the difference between the lowest level of $h_i(x_1, \ldots, x_n)$ rejected by the DM so far and the highest level accepted so far. Initially, $\delta_i = 0$ for all i.

4. Define the initial solution as

$$R_1 = (h_1^1, h_2^1, \ldots, h_k^1).$$

Present this and the potency matrix to the DM.
5. If the proposed solution is satisfactory, the process is complete. Otherwise, continue after defining S_i as the subset of S defined by the goal levels in R_i.
6. Ask the DM which goal level should be improved first.
7. Suppose the DM wants to improve the jth goal level first. Construct a trial solution R_{i+1} which differs from R_i only with respect to the jth goal variable [these values are denoted by $(h_j)_{R_{i+1}}$ and $(h_j)_{R_i}$, respectively].
   If $\delta_j = 0$, propose the next higher aspiration level listed in step 3. If $\delta_j > 0$, define $(h_j)_{R_{i+1}} = (h_j)_{R_i} + \delta_j/2$.
   Also, introduce the constraint $h_j(x_1, \ldots, x_n) \geq (h_j)_{R_{i+1}}$.
8. Combine the constraints just formulated with those of the set S_i. Calculate a new potency matrix subject to the new feasible region. Label this potency matrix $\hat{P}_{i+1}$.
9. Present the DM with R_i and P_i and with $\hat{R}_{i+1}$ and $\hat{P}_{i+1}$.
   If the DM is dissatisfied with the new potency matrix, the proposed value of h_j is too high. Drop the constraint added in the previous step and continue to step 10.
   If the DM is satisfied with the new potency matrix, let $R_{i+1} = \hat{R}_{i+1}$ and $P_{i+1} = \hat{P}_{i+1}$. Also, let $\delta_j = \frac{1}{2}\delta_j$ in the algorithm and return to step 5.
10. Define $(h_j)_{R_{i+1}} = (h_j)_{R_i} + \delta_j/2$.
    Introduce the constraint $h_j(x_1, \ldots, x_n) \geq (h_j)_{R_{i+1}}$. Go to step 8.

This method is attractive because it allows the DM to improve goals in small increments without severely penalizing the achievement of other goals. Also, the DM does not have to specify the amount by which the unsatisfactory goal values would have to be raised. There is also a provision for changing more than one goal value simultaneously (not described here). The need to specify different gradations of aspiration levels for each goal (step 3) is a disadvantage of this method. Also, it may be difficult for the DM to decide whether he/she is satisfied with the potency matrices (see step 9).

Another interactive GP technique was developed by Benson [3] in 1975. Initially, the DM is asked to specify a set of minimally acceptable goal levels. Then the DM notes which of these levels is the least satisfactory. This goal level is then maximized, subject to the constraints on the other goal variables. If the resulting value is unsatisfactory to the DM, some of the other goal levels must then be relaxed. If the resulting goal level is satisfactory, the solution is either the desired solution or the resulting level is unnecessarily high. In the latter case, the DM specifies the maximal amount of relaxation which is acceptable for this variable and the process starts over by having the DM specify the least satisfactory goal level.

This method is advantageous because it can solve nonlinear problems. In addition, the idea of developing a set of minimal goal levels is good, but only if a feasible set can be easily developed. This may be difficult for the DM, and depends upon the DM's feel for the impact of the constraints. A disadvantage is that the process of maximizing the least desirable goal may tend to drive that value up too high at the expense of the other goals. This, in turn, could identify another (new) goal which is very close to the minimal level, maximizing it at the severe expense of at least one other goal, etc.

Van Delft and Nijkamp [52] presented a hierarchical interactive optimization technique in 1977. In this technique, they first assume that the objectives (not goals) can be prioritized. After maximizing the first objective (say g_1) and obtaining a value g_i^*, the constraint $g_1(x) \geq \beta_1 g_i^*$ (where $0 \leq \beta_1 \leq 1$) is added to the original constraint, which was set before maximizing the second objective. This process continues until all objectives are sequentially maximized. The procedure is an extension of the basic preemptive GP model in the sense that if $\beta_i = 1$ for all i, the problem is the preemptive GP model with unattainable goals.

An advantage of this method is its simplicity with regard to the solution technique as well as the DM interaction. A difficulty is that it would seem nearly impossible to assess in advance the combined impact of the prioritization and the tolerance parameters (β_i values). For example, if goal 1 is considered to have a higher preemptive priority than goal 2 but the tolerance parameters are .7 and .9, the true assessment of the relative degrees of importance of the goals is difficult to predict. This could be extremely confusing to the DM who is providing this information.

Monarchi et al. [47] developed a procedure whereby the DM inputs trial weights, aspiration levels (objective levels desired by the DM), and goals (minimum achievement levels desired by the DM). The aspiration levels may be desired upper bounds, lower bounds, or specific targets.

A dimensionless attainment indicator d_j, which generally is a nonlinear function of a goal variable, is defined. At each iteration, one main problem and m_i auxiliary problems are solved, where m_i is the number of goal variables not yet restricted ($m_1 = k$, $m_2 = k - 1$, $m_3 = k - 2$, etc.).

At the first iteration, the main problem is

$$\min \sum_{j=1}^{k} d_j$$

$$\text{s.t.} \quad Fx \leq f$$

$$x \geq 0$$

and the goal constraints and the auxiliary problems are:

$$\min \sum_{\substack{j=1 \\ j \neq j'}}^{k} d_j$$

$$\text{s.t.} \quad Fx \leq f$$

$$g_{j'}(x) \geq g_{j'} \qquad j' = 1, \ldots, k$$

$$x \geq 0$$

where $g_{j'}$ is the aspiration level for goal j'.

These problems are solved using a nonlinear GP algorithm. The results are presented to the DM, who then revises one of the aspiration levels. This revision is added to the above formulation as a constraint. The indicator corresponding to this goal variable is then dropped from the objective functions, and the process starts over. The process continues until a suitable solution is obtained.

An advantage of this method is its ability to solve nonlinear problems. One disadvantage is that it may be difficult to specify the upper and lower limits for aspiration levels. This, in turn, may have a bearing on the quality of the solutions generated. Another possible difficulty is that inconsistent constraint sets may result when more than one goal level is changed at one time. This leads to a random search to find a consistent set of goal levels.

10. ALGORITHMS AND COMPUTER CODES

The first computer code developed for preemptive priority GP problems was presented in 1972 by Lee [41]. A subsequent code was presented by Ignizio [30] in 1976. Both codes were written primarily to assist in formal course work in GP and were intended for relatively small problems. Both codes are based upon the Multiphase method, which is an extension of the Two-Phase method in linear programming.

Recently, alternatives have been proposed by Ignizio and Perlis [32] and by Arthur and Ravindran [1]. Ignizio and Perlis use the sequential linear goal programming (SLGP) method, which consists of first solving the problem for the first priority level only, setting the first goal equal to the level achieved, and adding this as a constraint. The problem is then solved for the second priority level only, and the resulting solution is added as a new constraint. The process is continued until there are no more priority levels. This is the essence of preemptive GP, and is explained by Kornbluth [37] and Dauer and Krueger [13].

Although a linear programming (LP) package can obviously be used to yield a solution, the drawback is the off-line manual effort which is needed to formulate the new LP problem at each stage. The purpose of the attempt by Ignizio and Perlis was to automate the SLGP algorithm so that the solution at one stage would be incorporated into the problem at the next stage without off-line effort. This was accomplished in conjunction with the IBM MPSX code. Problems with approximately 16,000 (goal and other) constraints, and as many variables as one can store, can be solved with the method. Ignizio and Perlis state that the SLGP code begins to dominate the Multiphase code in both speed and accuracy for problems with about 50 rows and 50 variables.

In order to achieve improved efficiency, Arthur and Ravindran use partitioning of constraints. The constraints are partitioned in order to form a nested series of GP problems, $S_1 \subset S_2 \subset \cdots \subset S_k$, where S_i designates the subproblem consisting of the goal constraints assigned to the first i priorities and the corresponding terms in the objective function.

Initially, the subproblem S_1, which consists of the goal constraints and corresponding objective function terms, is solved. The optimal tableau is then examined for alternative optimum solutions. If none exists, the solution is optimal with respect to all priorities. If there are alternative optimum solutions, the goal constraints and objective function terms corresponding to the second highest priority are added to the problem and the process resumes. The algorithm continues until, at some stage, there are no alternative optimum solutions.

The procedure also includes a variable elimination step, whereby all variables with positive relative costs in optimal tableau S_{i-1} are omitted from subproblem S_i, since they would never enter the basis to form an alternative optimum solution.

The procedure was coded in FORTRAN, and 31 test problems were compared with Lee's algorithm. The solution times ranged from 12 to 60 percent of those obtained with Lee's algorithm, with more efficiency occurring for larger problems.

Although the results of the Ignizio and Perlis and the Arthur and Ravindran studies are impressive in relation to the older Multiphase code results, it would be interesting to make these same comparisons with a Multiphase code which is written for large-scale problems.

11. DISCUSSION

This paper has discussed many of the methodological contributions to goal programming in the last decade. These contributions indicate that, in addition to GP's myriad applications, the computational power of GP has increased; a variety of nonlinear GP algorithms, which use the features of GP formulation for enhanced efficiency, have been developed; explicit solutions have been discovered for special cases of the GP problem; techniques have been developed for ensuring the efficiency of solutions; generalizations which include goal intervals and imprecise goals have been presented; a link between GP and utility functions has been established; and additional interactive methods have been suggested.

Despite this rosy picture, the literature is rife with researchers who dismiss GP as an inferior option when considering techniques for addressing multiple objective decision-making problems. The most recurrent criticisms relate to the use of preemptive priorities, the difficulty of choosing a priori weights (either in problems not involving preemptive priorities or intragoal weights for preemptive priority problems), and the difficulty in choosing goals. These are presented eloquently and succinctly by Zeleny [57] in a recent paper, and are certainly not insignificant criticisms.

With regard to preemptive priorities, it is contended that the use of preemptive priorities is inconsistent with having a utility function over the k objectives, which ultimately leads to decisions which are undesirable to the DM. Harrald et al. [29] present this argument and document that such problems were encountered in developing a multi-goal approach to resource allocation for a marine environmental protection program for the U.S. Coast Guard. This problem was subsequently circumvented, however, by using the goal interval programming approach developed (for this problem) by Charnes et al. [10].

The second major criticism has been directed toward the difficulty of specifying a priori weights for goals within preemptive priority classes or for goals in problems not involving preemptive priorities. This has been described in detail by Zeleny [56]. The problem stems from the fact that the polyhedron of optimal weighting vectors is more than a function of the DM's preferences. It is also very dependent upon the feasible region of the problem. It has been demonstrated that the same set of weighted preferences can lead to markedly different solutions by slightly altering the feasible region. The impact of the feasible region upon the solution is generally not known in advance, and even after obtaining a solution it is virtually impossible to accurately estimate the effects of changing the weights.

The third primary criticism concerns the difficulty of specifying a set of goals a priori without more knowledge of the feasible region. However, this criticism does not seem to be as vociferous or as well-founded as the other concerns. If the goals are too modest, nondominated solutions can be generated using the procedures mentioned by Hannan [26] or Masud and Hwang [46]. If some goals are too ambitious, they can be reduced after initiating further interaction with the DM.

Before any further attempt is made to address the future of goal programming, a very brief general discussion of the criteria for assessing multiple objective approaches is desirable. The variety of approaches which have been suggested differ with regard to several important considerations. Some of these are (1) the amount and type of prior information required from the DM; (2) the amount of interaction with the DM during the course of obtaining a "preferred" solution (using the term "optimal" seems preposterous since there are frequently thousands of nondominated solutions); (3) the number of solutions presented to the DM at various points of the solution process (including the end); (4) the quality of the resulting solution; (5) the amount of time required to obtain a "preferred" solution; and (6) the computer resources (CPU time, software, etc.) required to obtain a "preferred" solution.

Although there are undoubtedly other considerations which have been overlooked, each of the various techniques should be compared according to the aforementioned criteria. As Spronk [51] has noted, the evaluation of the appropriate multiple objective model to use is itself a multiple objective problem. Ignoring the obvious dilemma caused by this observation, let us proceed by comparing (to the extent which is possible) GP and other approaches to the multiple objective problem. This discussion refers to the standard GP method without incorporating formal interactive techniques.

The GP approach consists of eliciting more prior information than most other approaches. This can be an advantage if the DM is able to make reasonably accurate prior assessments for goals and weights. The quality of these estimates is dependent upon the familiarity of the DM with the problem and, in particular, with the feasible region. If the DM does not have a good feel for the problem, the a priori specification of goals and weights (especially preemptive weights) is not likely to be of much help. Instead, it may be preferable to have more of the interaction take place after some trial solutions have been generated.

With regard to computer resources consumed, GP is quite frugal. So-lutions can be generated quickly because the procedure is linear pro-gramming (LP) based, although to a certain extent, this criterion is de-pendent upon the number of iterations required before a satisfactory solution is obtained by the DM. However, the quality of the resulting solution when no formal interactive procedures are used is frequently suspect.

Theoretically, GP could be used to generate all efficient points of a problem by altering both the objective function and the right-hand-side vector of the problem, although it would be quite difficult to do this sys-tematically. In practice, GP without a systematized interactive protocol is most effective when the DM has a good idea of what goals can be achieved in view of the constraints of the problem. Unfortunately, this is probably too much to expect for most real-world problems.

Most formalized interactive methods do not suffer from the aforemen-tioned drawbacks of the standard GP approach. In particular, most sug-gested interactive GP approaches do not involve either the use of preemp-tive priorities or of a priori Archimedean weights. This relieves the DM of a substantial burden. The only a priori requirement of the DM for most of these approaches is the specification of a set of trial goals. Also, in these approaches the DM is generally apprised in advance of the best and worst possible attainments of the objectives as an aid in specifying these goals.

It should be reiterated that the primary characteristic being used here to distinguish between GP interactive methods and general multiple ob-jective programming interactive methods is the use of goals, or targets, at each iteration to guide the solution process in the GP methods. The use of these goals is intuitively appealing because the DM is more cog-nitively oriented toward achievement values for the objectives than to-ward indirect measures such as weights.

The merit of GP interactive methods vis-à-vis other interactive meth-ods, or vis-à-vis one another, has not been well-researched. Clearly the methods all have advantages and disadvantages relative to one another. Some characteristics which need to be considered for comparison have been presented above in the discussion of the criteria for assessing mul-tiple objective approaches in general. Also, the merit of each method is highly dependent upon the nature of the problem and the DM's familiarity with the problem.

Wallenius [53] and Dyer [15] have conducted studies which compare different approaches to multiple objective problems by developing solutions using each approach in conjunction with a set of DMs. The different approaches were compared with respect to the DM's confidence in the solution obtained, the ease of use of the method, the ease of understanding the logic of the method, the usefulness of the information provided to aid the DM, and the total time for solving the problem.

More studies of this nature are needed. In particular, it would be valuable to use different types of problems to compare competing methods. The DM's familiarity with the problem and its feasible region should be varied. Ideally, a scenario for choosing the best method to use for a given problem would consist of some initial questions to determine the extent of the DM's familiarity with the problem. After approximating the DM's degree of familiarity, the most effective method would be chosen on the basis of results from studies similar to those conducted by Wallenius and Dyer.

In summary, the last decade has seen GP become one of the most popular, if not the most popular, multiple objective technique employed in the operations research/management science (OR/MS) literature. Despite this fact, there has been much criticism of the assumptions required in GP methodology.

It is also becoming obvious that significant analyst–DM interaction is essential for complicated real-world problems, whether the analyst is using GP or other multiple objective methods. Furthermore, after the generation of a solution, a formalized interactive procedure seems to be preferable to ad hoc quizzing of the DM. Many formalized GP interactive methods exist, and surely more will be proposed. The notion of using a goal-based interactive procedure has an intuitively sound foundation, and most criticism of the standard GP methodology is not applicable to the interactive methods.

In my opinion, the future of GP, at least in the next decade, lies in the continued development of GP interactive techniques, in methods of comparing the effectiveness of these techniques with each other and with other multiple objective methods, and in the continued development of nonlinear methods to be incorporated into interactive techniques.

REFERENCES

1. Arthur, J. L. and A. Ravindran, "An Efficient Goal Programming Algorithm Using Constraint Partitioning and Variable Elimination." *Management Science* 24(8):867–868, 1978.
2. Awerbuch, S., J. G. Ecker and W. A. Wallace, "A Note: Hidden Nonlinearities in the Application of Goal Programming." *Management Science* 22(8):918–920, 1976.

3. Benson, R. G., "Interactive Multiple Criteria Optimization Using Satisfactory Goals." Ph.D. Thesis, University of Iowa, 1975.
4. Bitran, G. R. and A. G. Novaes, "Linear Programming with a Fractional Objective Function." *Operations Research* 21:22–29, 1973.
5. Charnes, A. and W. W. Cooper, *Management Models and the Industrial Applications of Linear Programming*, Vols. 1 and 2. New York: John Wiley, 1961.
6. Charnes, A. and W. W. Cooper, "Programming with Linear Fractional Functionals." *Naval Research Logistics Quarterly* 9:181–186, 1962.
7. Charnes, A. and W. W. Cooper, "Goal Programming and Constrained Regression— A Comment." *Omega* 3(4):403–409, 1975.
8. Charnes, A. and W. W. Cooper, "Goal Programming and Multiple Objective Optimizations, Part I." *European Journal of Operational Research* 1:39–54, 1977.
9. Charnes, A., W. W. Cooper and R. O. Ferguson, "Optimal Estimation of Executive Compensation by Linear Programming." *Management Science* 1(2):138–151, 1955.
10. Charnes, A., W. W. Cooper, J. Harrald, K. Karwan, and W. A. Wallace, "A Goal Interval Programming Model for Resource Allocation in a Marine Environmental Protection Program." *Journal of Environmental Economics and Management* 3:347–361, 1976.
11. Charnes, A., W. W. Cooper, D. Klingman, and R. J. Niehaus, "Explicit Solutions in Convex Goal Programming." *Management Science* 22(4):438–448, 1975.
12. Cohon, J. L. and D. H. Marks, "A Review and Evaluation of Multiobjective Programming Techniques." *Water Resources Research* 11(2):208–220, 1975.
13. Dauer, J. P. and R. J. Krueger, "An Iterative Approach to Goal Programming." *Operational Research Quarterly* 28(3):671–681, 1977.
14. de Kluyver, C. A., "On the Importance of Goal-Norming in Non-Preemptive Goal Programming." *Opsearch* 16(2 and 3):89–97, 1979.
15. Dyer, J. S., "An Empirical Investigation of a Man-Machine Interactive Approach to the Solution of the Multiple Criteria Problem." Pp. 202–216 in J. Cochrane and M. Zeleny (eds.), *Multiple Criteria Decision Making.* Columbia: University of South Carolina Press, 1973.
16. Dyer, J. S., "On the Relationship Between Goal Programming and Multiattribute Utility Theory." Discussion Paper No. 69, Graduate School of Management, University of California, Los Angeles, October 1977.
17. Dyer, J. S. and R. K. Sarin, "An Axiomatization of Cardinal Additive Conjoint Measurement Theory." Working Paper No. 265, Western Management Science Institute, University of California, Los Angeles, October 1977.
18. Dyer, J. S. and R. K. Sarin, "Measurable Multiattribute Value Functions." *Operations Research* 27:810–822, 1979.
19. Ferguson, R. O., L. F. Sargent, and N. V. Reinfeld, "Modified Regression Analysis As An Aid to Salary Classification." *Proceedings of a Conference in Modern Business Methods,* Sponsored by the American Statistical Association and the Graduate School of Industrial Administration, Carnegie Institute of Technology, 1952.
20. Freed, N. and F. Glover, "A Linear Programming Approach to the Discriminant Problem." *Decision Sciences* 12:68–74, 1981.
21. Freed, N. and F. Glover, "Simple But Powerful Goal Programming Models for Discriminant Problems." *European Journal of Operational Research* 7:44–60, 1981.
22. Geoffrion, A. M., "Objective Function Approximations in Mathematical Programming." *Mathematical Programming* 13:23–37, 1977.
23. Hannan, E. L., "A Graphical Interpretation of the Goal Programming Problem." *Omega* 4(6):733–735, 1976.

24. Hannan, E. L., "A Note on the Multidimensional Dual of the Linear Goal Programming Problem." *Proceedings of the Sixth Annual American Institute for Decision Sciences Conference of the Northeast Region.* Albany, New York, April 1977.

25. Hannan, E. L., "Effects of Substituting a Linear Goal for a Fractional Goal in the Goal Programming Problem." *Management Science* 24(1):105–107, 1977.

26. Hannan, E. L., "Nondominance in Goal Programming." *INFOR* 18(4):300–309, 1980.

27. Hannan, E. L., "On 'An Interpretation of Fractional Objectives in Goal Programming as Related to Papers by Awerbuch et al. and Hannan'." *Management Science* 27(7):847–848, 1981.

28. Hannan, E. L., "Linear Goal Programming with Multiple Fuzzy Goals." *Fuzzy Sets and Systems* 6:235–248, 1981.

29. Harrald, J., J. Leotta, W. A. Wallace, and R. E. Wendell, "A Note on the Limitations of Goal Programming as Observed in Resource Allocation for Marine Environmental Protection." *Naval Research Logistics Quarterly* 25:733–739, 1978.

30. Ignizio, J. P., *Goal Programming and Extensions.* Lexington, Mass.: D.C. Heath, 1976.

31. Ignizio, J. P., "A Review of Goal Programming: A Tool for Multiobjective Analysis." *Journal of the Operational Research Society* 29(11):1109–1119, 1978.

32. Ignizio, J. P. and J. H. Perlis, "Sequential Linear Goal Programming: Implementation Via MPSX." *Computers and Operations Research* 3(1):217–225, 1980.

33. Ignizio, J. P., "The Determination of a Subset of Efficient Solutions Via Goal Programming." *Computers and Operations Research* 8(1):9–16, 1981.

34. Ijiri, Y., *Management Goals and Accounting for Control.* Amsterdam: North Holland, 1965.

35. Karwan, K. R. and W. A. Wallace, "A Comparative Evaluation of Conjoint Measurement and Goal Programming as Aids in Decision Making for Marine Environmental Protection." In G. Fandel and T. Gal (eds.), *Multiple Objective Decision Making Theory and Application.* Berlin: Springer-Verlag, 1979.

36. Keeney, R. L. and H. Raiffa, *Decisions with Multiple Objectives: Preference and Value Tradeoffs.* New York: Wiley, 1976.

37. Kornbluth, J. S. H., "A Survey of Goal Programming." *Omega* 1(2):193–205, 1973.

38. Kornbluth, J. S. H. and R. E. Steuer, "On Computing the Set of All Weakly Efficient Vertices in Multiple Objective Linear Fractional Programming." In G. Fandell and T. Gal (eds.), *Multiple Objective Decision Making Theory and Application.* Berlin: Springer-Verlag, 1979.

39. Kornbluth, J. S. H. and R. E. Steuer, "Goal Programming with Linear Fractional Criteria." *European Journal of Operational Research* 8:58–65, 1981.

40. Kornbluth, J. S. H. and R. E. Steuer, "Multiple Objective Linear Fractional Programming." *Management Science* 27(9):1024–1039, 1981.

41. Lee, S. M., *Goal Programming for Decision Analysis.* Philadelphia: Auerbach, 1972.

42. Lee, S. M. and R. L. Morris, "Integer Goal Programming Methods." In M. K. Starr and M. Zeleny (eds.), *Multiple Criteria Decision Making.* New York: North Holland, 1977.

43. Lin, W. T., "A Survey of Goal Programming Applications." *Omega* 8(1):115–117, 1980.

44. Luce, R. and J. Tukey, "Simultaneous Conjoint Measurement: A New Type of Fundamental Measurement." *Journal of Mathematical Psychology* 1:1–27, 1964.

45. Martos, B., "Hyperbolic Programming." *Naval Research Logistics Quarterly* 11:135–155, 1964.

46. Masud, A. S. and C. L. Hwang, "Interactive Sequential Goal Programming." *Journal of the Operational Research Society* 32(5):391–400, 1981.

47. Monarchi, D. E., J. E. Weber, and L. Duckstein, "An Interactive Multiple Objective

Decision-Making Aid Using Non-Linear Goal Programming." In M. Zeleny (ed.), *Multiple Criteria Decision Making*. Kyoto: Springer-Verlag, 1975.

48. Narasimhan, R., "Goal Programming in a Fuzzy Environment." *Decision Sciences* 11:325–336, 1980.

49. Nijkamp, P. and J. Spronk, "Interactive Multiple Goal Programming: An Evaluation and Some Results." In G. Fandell and T. Gal (eds.), *Multiple Objective Decision Making Theory and Application*. Berlin: Springer-Verlag, 1979.

50. Soyster, A. L. and B. Lev, "An Interpretation of Fractional Objectives in Goal Programming as Related to Papers by Awerbuch et al. and Hannan." *Management Science* 24(14):1546–1549, 1978.

51. Spronk, J., *Interactive Multiple Goal Programming: Applications to Financial Planning*. Boston: Martinus Nijhoff, 1981.

52. Van Delft, A. and P. Nijkamp, *Multi-Criteria Analysis and Regional Decision Making*. Leiden/The Hague: Martinus Nijhoff, 1977.

53. Wallenius, J., "Comparative Evaluation of Some Interactive Approaches to Multicriteria Optimization." *Management Science* 21(12):1387–1396, 1975.

54. Widhelm, W. B., "Extensions of Goal Programming Models." *Omega* 9(2):212–214, 1981.

55. Zeleny, M. and J. L. Cochrane, "A Priori and Posteriori Goals in Macroeconomic Policy Making." Pp. 373–391 in J. L. Cochrane and M. Zeleny (eds.), *Multiple Criteria Decision Making*. Columbia: University of South Carolina Press, 1973.

56. Zeleny, M., "Compromise Programming." In J. L. Cochrane and M. Zeleny (eds.), *Multiple Criteria Decision Making*. Columbia: University of South Carolina Press, 1973.

57. Zeleny, M., "The Pros and Cons of Goal Programming." *Computers and Operations Research* 8(4):357–359, 1981.

FRACTIONAL PROGRAMMING IN MCDM

Jonathan S. H. Kornbluth

JONATHAN S. H. KORNBLUTH has reviewed the essentials of multiple objective linear fractional programming and its most promising application within goal programming types of models. This is a relatively new development, still rather technical and algorithmic, with a great potential for sound and relevant applications. It is with goals which are to be attained "precisely," both from below and from above, where goal programming has shown great promise and methodological distinction. And it is the fractional goals, or ratios, where such a "precise" attainment is usually desired in practice. Also, often we are interested in maximizing a rate of attainment rather than a particular attainment itself.

There is of course a well-developed methodology of linear fractional programming, characterized by a single fractional objective function, having several hundred papers to its credit, yet being very poorly represented in meaningful applications. In reality, fractional functions are always multiple and are often stated as goals or targets rather than simply objectives. It is therefore natural that it is the development of multicriterion fractional methodology which might lead to applicational breakthroughs.

One interesting and challenging property of fractional multiobjective programming is the nonconnectedness of nondominated extreme points of a convex polyhedron. The set of nondominated solutions, which is a fully connected set in multiobjective linear programming, is now disconnected—full of "gaps" and "holes." This poses some difficulties for a simple algorithmic tracing of nondominated solutions. At the least, the search procedure is likely to be more time consuming in the fractional case.

Kornbluth is one of the few authors who have engaged in exploring also the computational properties of multiobjective fractional programming, and some of his results are presented here.

Another topic of interest is goal programming and its suitability for treating fractionally defined goals. He dispels the simpleminded notion of some goal programming experts that fractions can be treated by simply cross multiplying the fractionals by the denominator function. This sort of applied "science" has lead to a serious degradation of some MCDM areas in recent years. Kornbluth outlines a correct approach to the fractional version of goal programming. Algorithmic connection to multiparametric programming is unmistakable and should be vigorously explored in the future.

Although the pervasive occurrence of ratio objectives and goals in financial and accounting decision problems is a sufficient guarantee for future applications, fractional programming still faces research issues of mostly algorithmic nature. For example, an interactive mode should be studied more creatively, nonlinear fractions should be dealt with, and a new, fast, and reliable test for fractional nondominance must be developed in order to improve computational attractiveness of this methodology.

1. INTRODUCTION

Over the past 10 years, many operations research (OR) tools that have dealt with single-objective function optimization have been extended to the MCDM environment. In mathematical programming this development has been evident in the interest in multiple objective linear programming (MOLP) models and the widespread use of goal programming (GP). The purpose of this paper is to review the parallel development in fractional programming (FP) and to document the advances in multiple objective linear fractional programming (MOLFP) and multiple objective linear fractional goal programming (MOLFGP). We will concentrate our attention on the similarities (and dissimilarities) between MOLFP and MOLP and relate them to the same comparison between LFP and LP.

In order to maintain a reasonable scope for this review, we will restrict our attention to the case where the fractional objectives are linear (i.e., ratios of linear functions) and the constraint set is linear. Some comments on the nonlinear case will be made at the end of the paper.

2. FRACTIONAL PROGRAMMING

Consider the problem

$$\max \left\{ Q(x) = \frac{N(x)}{D(x)} \middle| x \in S \right\} \tag{1}$$

$$S \in R^n, \quad N,D: \quad S \to R \text{ and } D \text{ positive}$$

and its linear form

$$\max \left\{ f(x) = \frac{c^T x + \alpha}{d^T x + \beta} \middle| Ax \le b, \ d^T x + \beta > 0 \right\} \tag{2}$$

Here, (2) is a linear fractional programming problem (LFP).

Fractional programming problems occur naturally in applications of management science where a rate (as opposed to an attainment) is to be optimized or where the degree of attainment is normalized by some variable scaling factor (e.g., return on assets, or output per employee). The earliest algorithms for solving LFP problems are those of Charnes and Cooper [5] and Dinkelbach [8]. Charnes and Cooper use a variable transformation and one of two auxilliary programs to find the optimal LFP solution. Instead of the LFP (2) they solve the following (LP) problem:

$$\max cy + \alpha t$$

$$\text{s.t.} \quad Ay - \alpha b \le 0$$

$$dy + \beta t = 0. \tag{3}$$

The variable transformation $y = tx$ maps from (3) to (2). If the original x variables are required to be positive, the constraints $y, t \geq 0$ are appended. Dinkelbach's algorithm uses the association between LFP and parametric programming by treating the denominator as a parameter (see also Ref. 18). Both demonstrate the close relationship between LP and LFP. This theme is developed by Martos [29], who delineates the natural extent to which simplex-type methods can be applied in mathematical programming. Martos's algorithm utilizes this direct analogy to LP [30]; Wagner and Yuan [44] show that the algorithm is equivalent to the original algorithm of Charnes and Cooper [5]. The simplex criterion used by Martos is based on the gradient function at the vertex; e.g., at x^0 we have

$$\frac{\partial f}{\partial x_i} = \frac{c_i(d^Tx^0 + \beta) - d_i(c^Tx^0 + \alpha)}{(d^Tx^0 + \beta^2)}. \tag{4}$$

(Note that at x^0 the denominator term is constant.) The algorithm relies on the fact that the fractional function is quasi-monotonic and that, if the reduced cost of a nonbasic variable x_j is positive, it will remain so along the entire edge of the simplex up to the next vertex solution. (For another approach to LFP see Bitran and Novaes [2].)

The close and natural association between LP and LFP has promoted many studies in the duality of LFP and the extent to which LP theorems can be held to apply in LFP. Major studies in LFP duality include those of Kydland [25], Schaible [33,35], Swarup [42], and Craven and Mond [7]. As is shown in Schaible [33], the most convenient definition of the LFP dual is to utilize (3)—the equivalent LP formulation. Thus the dual suggested by Schaible is

$$\min \lambda$$
$$\text{s.t.} \quad A^Tu + \lambda d = c \tag{5}$$
$$-b^Tu + \lambda\beta \geq \alpha$$
$$u \in R^m, \quad u \geq 0, \quad \lambda \in R.$$

The dual variables u and λ are clearly unique and can be related back to the original dual variables of (2). (See Ref. 21.) However, unlike the LP dual variables, those of LFP [in its original form, (2)] are not piecewise constant for changes in the right-hand side (rhs) but vary with the solution values themselves. A comparison between LP and LFP is given in Table 1.

By the very nature of the linear fractional function, LFP has many natural applications in finance and accounting, as well as general business applications. Schaible [33,35,37] has compiled a bibliography of several hundred theoretical and applied papers in fractional programming. A sim-

Table 1. Comparison of LP and LFP.

	LP	LFP
Definition	max c·x $x \in S = \{x \mid Ax \le b, \quad x \ge 0\}$	$\max(c^T x + \alpha)/(d^T x + \beta)$ $x \in S = \{x \mid Ax \le b, \quad x \ge 0\}$ $d^T x + \beta > 0$ for $x \in S$ (or $d^T x + \beta \ne 0$ for $x \in S$)
Solution algorithm	Simplex Method	Simplex type (Martos) and equivalent LP via variable transformation (Charnes and Cooper)
Solution	At vertex of S	At vertex of S
Duality	Direct LP duality	Duality most convenient via variable transformation and equivalent LP
	min π·b $\pi \cdot A \ge c$ $\pi \ge 0$	min λ $u \cdot A + \lambda d = c$ $-b^T u + \lambda \beta \ge \alpha$ $u \in R^m, \quad u \ge 0$ $\lambda \in R$
Dual variables (marginal values of resources)	Piecewise constant and unique (to the extent that degeneracy allows)	Variable (nonconstant) for rhs changes; same uniqueness as LP

ilar list is given in Ref. 41. Some problems arise in the application of LFP, and there are certainly fewer applications of the technique than might be expected. Typical of these is the application by Ziemba et al. [48], where FP is used in portfolio selection—with a denominator of the form $(\sum s_{ij} x_i x_j)^{1/2}$. This nonlinearity is overcome by Faaland and Jacob [12], who use a linear denominator. One reason for the relative dearth of LFP applications (as opposed to those of LP) may be due to the fact that where ratio functions do appear in optimization problems they appear both as objectives and as constraints; indeed, fractional functions appear to take a more natural role as part of an overall multicriterion optimization than as single-objective function criteria (see, e.g., Banker et al. [1]). Many applications (e.g., Refs. 32 and 37) have used fractional constraints in a goal programming environment. (The shortcomings of such applications will be discussed below.) Others (e.g., Chambers [3]) use ratio functions as hard constraints and have thus avoided the use of fractional functions as single (or multiple) objective functions or goals.

As with many areas of MCDM, the last 10 years have seen considerable development in the use of ratio functions in decision making, particularly in the areas of MOLFP and its extension to goal programming, MOLFGP, to which we will now turn our attention.

3. MULTIPLE OBJECTIVE LINEAR FRACTIONAL PROGRAMMING

The major efforts in extending the LP algorithm to include multiple objectives have been made by Charnes and Cooper [4], Evans and Steuer [11], and Zeleny [47], and more recently by Isermann [17]. Whereas in LP we attempt to find *the* optimal solution to a problem, in MOLP we attempt to find the *set* of efficient (nondominated, Pareto optimal) solutions, or at least the set of efficient vertex solutions. (See Ecker and Kouada [9] or Evans and Steuer [11].) For an MOLP with k objective functions $z_i(x)$, for $i = 1, \ldots , k$, an efficient solution is defined as follows:

DEFINITION 3.1. A point $\overline{x} \in S$ is efficient if and only if there does not exist another point $x \in S$ such that $z_i(x) \geq z_i(\overline{x})$ for all i and $z_i(x) > z_i(\overline{x})$ for at least one i.

The "MOLP problem" is defined as

$$\overline{\text{eff}}\ z(x) = \{z_i(x)\}$$

$$x \in S = \{x \in R^n \mid Ax = b, \quad x \geq 0, \quad b \in R^m\} \tag{6}$$

where $\overline{\text{eff}}$ denotes the search for the set of efficient (vertex) solutions in a maximizing sense and the functions $z_i(x)$ are linear (i.e., $z_i(x) = c^i x$).

The set of efficient extreme point solutions for (6) has been shown to be path connected by efficient edges [10] and to have close associations with parametric LP, with a single composite objective function of the form $\sum \lambda_i z_i(x)$, $\sum \lambda_i = 1$, $\lambda_i > 0$. (See Philip [31], Geoffrion [14], and Charnes and Cooper [4].) The property of path-connectedness in MOLP allows for the development of an algorithm based on the directional search from a given efficient vertex solution. Consider the situation at an efficient vertex solution x, for which

$$x_B = B^{-1}b - B^{-1}Nx_N$$

$$z = C_B B^{-1}b - (C_B B^{-1}N - C_N)x_B$$

$$R = C_B B^{-1}N - C_N$$

where B denotes basic; N denotes nonbasic; C is the k × n matrix of the coefficients of the objective functions; and A is the matrix of the technological coefficients partitioned into B and N. The following lemma is proposed by Evans and Steuer [11]:

LEMMA 3.1. Let x^0 be an efficient extreme point of S and let x_j be a nonbasic variable in the basic feasible solution associated with x^0. Then the adjacent extreme point with x_j a basic variable (with some currently basic variable converted to nonbasic status) is efficient if and only if the following version of problem (P) is consistent and bounded:

$$(P^j)\max\{e^T v: \quad Ru - r_j w + Iv = 0, \quad u \geqq 0, \quad v \geqq 0\}, \quad (7)$$

where $w \in R$ and r_j is the column of R associated with x_j.

The parametric approach of Charnes and Cooper relies on this lemma.

Note that the test (7) is carried out *at the actual vertex* x^0 and relies on local information similar to the reduced cost criterion of the standard LP simplex.

The domination structures associated with MOLP are considered by Yu and Zeleny [45], and other approaches to MOLP are given by Gal [13] and Isermann [17]. The basic MOLP algorithm has been extended to include interval criterion weights [38] and can be easily applied in situations where either total enumeration or interactive search is required. Several applications of MOLP are recorded in the literature (see, e.g., Refs. 39 and 40).

4. MULTIPLE OBJECTIVE LINEAR FRACTIONAL PROGRAMMING

The extension of MOLP to include linear fractional objectives is achieved by extending the definition of $z_i(x)$ in (6), such that

$$z_i(x) = \frac{c^i x + \alpha_i}{d^i x + \beta_i}$$

with $d^i x + \beta_i \neq 0$ for $x \in S$. (8)

(Note that MOLFP "includes" MOLP for $d^i = 0$, $\beta_i \neq 0$.)

Although such an extension is relatively simple in LP, the nonlinearities in the multiple objectives cause considerable algorithmic difficulties. Whereas in LP and LFP the set of alternative optimal vertex solutions is pathwise connected by optimal edges, and whereas in MOLP the set of efficient vertex solutions is pathwise connected by efficient edges, in MOLFP the set of efficient vertex solutions need not be pathwise connected. This "failure" automatically implies that a simple search procedure among the vertices will not necessarily identify the complete set of efficient vertex solutions. In Figure 1, x^1 and x^6 are efficient vertex solutions, yet the edge (x^1, x^6) is not efficient for its entire length.

In order to overcome this difficulty, the definition of efficiency is extended to weak efficiency and strong efficiency (w-efficiency and s-efficiency).

A point $\bar{x} \in S$ is defined to be w-efficient if and only if there does not exist another point $x \in S$ such that $z_i(x) > z_i(\bar{x})$ for all i. In other words there is no other point in S which *strongly dominates* $\bar{x}$.

A point $\bar{x} \in S$ is defined to be s-efficient if and only if there does not exist another point $x \in S$ such that $z_i(x) \geq z_i(\bar{x})$ for all i and $z_i(x) > z_i(\bar{x})$ for at least one i. In other words there is no other point in S which *weakly dominates* $\bar{x}$.

We must also differentiate between *extreme points* in the original feasible region S and those in the augmented feasible region created during the search (such as x^2). The latter are referred to as *vertices*. The set of all w-efficient solutions will be denoted by E^w. Here E^w_x and E^w_v are used to denote the set of all w-efficient extreme points and vertices, respectively, with similar definitions of E^S, E^S_x, and E^S_v. (See Ref. 22.)

As has been shown by Choo [6]:

(i) E^w is closed.

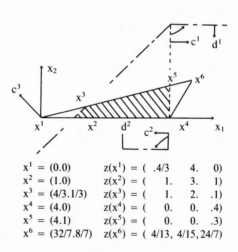

$$x^1 = (0.0) \qquad z(x^1) = (\ .4/3 \quad 4. \quad 0)$$
$$x^2 = (1.0) \qquad z(x^2) = (\ 1. \quad 3. \quad 1)$$
$$x^3 = (4/3.1/3) \quad z(x^3) = (\ 1. \quad 2. \quad .1)$$
$$x^4 = (4.0) \qquad z(x^4) = (\ 0. \quad 0. \quad .4)$$
$$x^5 = (4.1) \qquad z(x^5) = (\ 0. \quad 0. \quad .3)$$
$$x^6 = (32/7.8/7) \quad z(x^6) = (\ 4/13, 4/15, 24/7)$$

Figure 1.

(ii)   Assume S is bounded; then E_v^w is path-connected by a finite number of w-efficient line segments.

MOLFP is "solved" by enumerating E_v^w (from which E_x^S may be derived) [22]; some computational experience with an APL program is given in Ref. 24. The algorithm relies on an amended form of the efficient direction test of Evans and Steuer [11] and utilizes the classification of efficient MOLFP solutions derived by Tigan [43]. The latter paper also shows that $\bar{x}$ is s-efficient for (8) if $\bar{x}$ is s-efficient for the problem

$$\overline{\text{eff}} \{T(\bar{x})x \mid x \in S\} \tag{9}$$

where the ith row of $T(\bar{x})$ is the local gradient of the ith objective function of the MOLFP, evaluated at $\bar{x} \in S$. As is shown in Ref. 22, it is sufficient to define $T(\bar{x})$ using

$$T_i(\bar{x}) = (d^i\bar{x} + \beta_i)c^i - (c^i\bar{x} + \alpha_i)d^i.$$

The Tigan matrix used in (9) is a natural extension of the amended simplex criterion of Martos [30] in LFP, and can easily be amended to include w-efficiency at any vertex $x \in S$.

The search for w-efficient directions emanating from a w-efficient vertex is complicated by two factors:

(i)   an edge may appear to be w-efficient at a vertex and yet not actually be so at any distance δ away from the vertex, and
(ii)   an edge which is initially w-efficient may cease to be so *before* the adjacent vertex is reached.

Factor (i) implies that the w-efficiency edge test must be applied at a small distance δ away from the w-efficient vertex. (In MOLP the test is applied at the vertex.) Factor (ii) implies that even if a w-efficient direction has been identified, the *whole edge* must be tested, up to and including the adjacent vertex. This is done using the "weighted" sum of the reduced costs of the Tigan matrix. As is shown in [22], the edge is w-efficient for a distance θ_{max}, where θ_{max} is the maximum value of θ for which there is a solution for the system:

$$\lambda^T[\tilde{T}(x^0) + \theta H(x^0,j)] \geq 0$$

$$\lambda^T e = 1$$

$$0 \leq \lambda \in R^K \tag{10}$$

where j is the index of the incoming variable

$$\tilde{T}(x^0) = T_B(x^0)B^{-1}A_N - T_N(x^0)$$

and $H(x^0,j)$ is the matrix of changes in $\tilde{T}(x^0)$ as x_j is introduced into the basis. [Here $\tilde{T}(x^0)$ is similar to "$z_j - c_j$" in LP.].

If θ_{max} exceeds the simplex pivot criterion $\hat{\theta}(x_{B_i}/y_{ij})$, then the adjacent vertex is w-efficient and can be added to the list of discovered vertices in E_v^w. If θ_{max} is less than $\hat{\theta}$, then the edge is "broken," i.e., the edge is initially w-efficient but is not w-efficient along its entire length. In this case a cutting plane is added at the point corresponding to θ_{max}; this cutting plane augments the original feasible region S and allows the search to cut across S, and so ensures the path-connectedness of E_v^w required for the completion of the algorithm.

From these points it can be seen that the search procedure in MOLFP is considerably more time consuming than that of MOLP.

A comparison of MOLP and MOLFP is presented in Table 2. Computational experience with MOLFP is given in Ref. 24. The major advantage of the MOLFP algorithm is that it facilitates the inclusion of ratio criteria in a normative MCDM environment, and particularly in goal programming.

Table 2. Comparison of MOLP and MOLFP.

	MOLP	MOLFP
Definition	"max" $z(x) = (z_1(x), \ldots, z_K(x))$ $z_i(x) = c^ix$ $x \in S = \{x \mid Ax = b, \ x \geq 0\}$	"max" $z(x) = (z_1(x), \ldots, z_K(x))$ $z_i(x) = (c^ix + \alpha)/(d^ix + \beta)$ $x \in S = \{x \mid Ax = b, \ x \geq 0\}$ $d^ix + \beta \neq 0$ for any $x \in S$
Class of efficient solutions	Efficient (strongly efficient); properly efficient	Strongly and weakly efficient solutions
Closure of set of efficient solutions	E^S closed	E^w closed
Connectedness of set of efficient solutions	E_x^S connected	E_v^w path connected by a finite number of w-efficient line segments
Algorithm	Natural extension of LP; requires only local vertex information; size of constraint matrix is constant	Requires local vertex information plus a search along efficient edges; may require additional cutting planes to augment the constraint matrix

5. MULTIPLE OBJECTIVE LINEAR FRACTIONAL GOAL PROGRAMMING

The GP approach to MCDM uses the formulation:

$$\min \sum (w_i^- d_i^- + w_i^+ d_i^+)$$

s.t.   (i) $g_i(x) + d_i^- - d_i^+ = g_i^0$

        (ii) $x \in S = \{x \mid Ax = b, \quad x \geq 0\}$

       (iii) $d_i^-, d_i^+ \geq 0$ (11)

where the weights $\{w_i^+\}$ and $\{w_i^-\}$ can describe situations of preemptive goals or weighted goals. For linear $g_i(x)$, the method can be directly applied using only minor modifications of the LP algorithm (see, e.g., Ignizio [16] and Lee [27]; the literature abounds with literally hundreds of applications of linear GP, e.g., Lin [28]). For linear fractional $g_i(x)$, the method is not immediately applicable due to the presence of the denominator terms in (11(i)). (See Hannan [15].) Several authors (e.g., Sartoris and Spruill [32] and Zanakis and Maret [46]) have suggested that it is sufficient to cross multiply by the denominator function $d^i x + \beta_i$ and use new variables u_i^+ and u_i^- instead of $d_i^+(d^i x + \beta_i)$ and $d_i^-(d^i x + \beta_i)$.

The suggested formulation is

$$\min \sum (w_i^- u_i^- + w_i^+ u_i^+)$$

s.t.   (i) $(c^i x + \alpha_i) - g_i^0(d^i x + \beta_i) + u_i^- - u_i^+ = 0$

      (ii) $x \in S$

      (iii) $u_i^-, u_i^+ \geq 0$ (12)

This is not an accurate representation of the fractional GP since the variables u_i^-, u_i^+ are implicitly nonlinear. They do not measure the normal "distance" from goal attainment and will not reflect the true wishes of the decision maker as expressed via the weights $\{w_i^+\}$ and $\{w_i^-\}$.

As has been shown in [23], a more tractable version of the fractional GP problem is given by

$$\min \sum \lambda_i \left(\frac{w_i^- u_i^- + w_i^+ u_i^+}{d^i x + \beta_i} \right)$$

s.t.   (i) $(c^i x + \alpha_i) - g_i^0(d^i x + \beta_i) + u_i^- - u_i^+ = 0$

      (ii) $x \in S$

      (iii) $u_i^-, u_i^+ \geq 0$ (13)

and that (13) can be solved for the entire space of $\lambda_i \geq 0$, for $\sum \lambda_i = 1$, using the MOLFP algorithm. The advantage of such an approach is that it only requires the decision maker to weight overachievement versus underachievement for each goal (treated individually), i.e., w_i^+ versus w_i^-; the intergoal weights are provided by the λ_i, which can be analyzed *after* the solution set has been identified.

Multiple objective linear fractional goal programming can be used in many areas of decision making, e.g., manpower planning [19] (goals of required staffing ratios), analyses of equity and equal opportunity [20] (goals of desired proportions of the population or subgroups of the population), and many public and commercial decision-making situations where ratio functions are used as part of the normative evaluation process.

6. FUTURE DIRECTIONS

The major thrust in the use of fractional functions in MCDM has been that of developing algorithms. The developments of LP through MOLP and GP have been broadened to include linear fractional functions, both as objectives and goals, and the algorithms of MOLFP and MOLFGP are available in both total enumeration and interactive search modes. The widespread occurrence of ratio objectives and goals and the broad spectrum of applications of GP suggest that the technique of multiple objective linear fractional goal programming will find many applications in the future. In the short term, some aspects of MOLFGP present attractive areas for MCDM research: (i) algorithmic improvements in MOLFP; (ii) an analysis of total enumeration versus interactive search; and (iii) extensions of MOLFP to include nonlinear fractions. These are considered below:

i.   The major limitation in the MOLFP algorithm is the method of testing w-efficient edges (10). Improvements to this test would improve the speed of the algorithm and facilitate the solution of large-scale problems. An alternative approach might be to analyze MOLFP in the criterion space rather than in the decision space, (see Lazimy [26]).

ii.   The set E_v^w is generally much larger than E_x^S due to the inclusion of cutting planes. Research into the relationship between E^w and E^S and the required cutting planes are areas that will generally improve computation in MOLFP.

iii.   In many ratio applications of MCDM, the fractional function may be nonlinear (e.g., Ziemba [46]). In order to fully encompass the ratios used in financial planning (particularly for risk concepts) the MOLFP approach needs to be enhanced to include nonlinear fractional functions— particularly of the form $c(x)/d(x)^2$ and $c(x)/(d(x,x^2))^{1/2}$. This problem has already been covered for the single objective optimization (see, e.g.,

Schaible [35,36]). An enhancement of MOLFP to include nonlinear ratio objectives would represent a major breakthrough in MCDM model solution techniques.

REFERENCES

1. Banker, R. D., A. Charnes, W. W. Cooper and A. P. Schinner, "A Bi-Extremal Principle for Frontier Estimation and Efficiency Evaluations." *Management Science* 27(12):1370–1382, 1981.
2. Bitran, G. R. and A. G. Novaes, "Linear Programming with a Fractional Objective Function." *Operations Research* 1:22–29, 1973.
3. Chambers, D., "The Joint Problem of Investment and Financing." *Opl. Res. Q.* 22:267–295.
4. Charnes, A. and W. W. Cooper, *Management Models and Industrial Applications of Linear Programming.* New York: Wiley, 1961.
5. Charnes, A. and W. W. Cooper, "Programming with Linear Fractional Functionals." *NRLQ* 9:181–186, 1962.
6. Choo, E. U., "Multicriteria Linear Fractional Programming." Unpublished Ph.D. Dissertation, University of British Columbia, 1980.
7. Craven, B. D. and B. Mond, "The Dual of a Linear Fractional Program." *J. Math. Anal. Appl.* 42:507–512, 1973.
8. Dinkelbach, W., "Die Maximierung eines Quotienten zweier linearer Funktionen unter Linearen Nebendingungen." *Zeitschrift für Wahrscheinlichkeitstheorie und verwandte Gebiete* 1:141–145, 1962.
9. Ecker, J. G. and I. A. Kouada, "Finding An Efficient Extreme Point for Multiple Objective Linear Programs." *Math. Programming* 14:249–261, 1978.
10. Evans, J. P., "Connectedness of the Efficient Extreme Points in Linear Multiple Objective Problems." Graduate School of Business Administration and Operations Research and Systems Analysis Curriculum, University of North Carolina at Chapel Hill, 1972.
11. Evans, J. P. and R. E. Steuer, "A Revised Simplex Method for Linear Multiple Objective Programming." *Math. Programming* 5(1):54–73, 1973.
12. Faaland, B. H. and Nancy L. Jacob, "The Linear Fractional Portfolio Selection Problem." *Man. Science* 27(12):1383–1389, 1981.
13. Gal, T., "A General Method for Determining the Set of All Efficient Solutions to a Linear Vector Maximum Problem." *European Operational Research* 1:307–322, 1977.
14. Geoffrion, A. M., "Proper Efficiency and the Theory of Vector Maximization." *J. Math. Anal. Appl.* 22:618–630, 1968.
15. Hannan, E. L., "Effects of Substituting a Linear Goal for a Fractional Goal in the Goal Programming Problem." *Man. Science* 14(1):105–106, 1977.
16. Ignizio, J. P., *Goal Programming and Extensions.* Lexington, Mass.: Heath, 1976.
17. Isermann, H., "The Enumeration of the Set of all Efficient Solutions for a Linear Multiple Objective Program." *Operational Research Quarterly* 28(3):711–725, 1977.
18. Jagannathan, R., "On Some Properties of Programming Problems in Parametric Form Pertaining to Fractional Programming." *Man. Science* 12:609–615, 1966.
19. Kornbluth, J. S. H., "Manpower Planning with Structured Ratio Goals." Working Paper 81–07–03, Decision Sciences Dept. The Wharton School, University of Pennsylvania.

20. Kornbluth, J. S. H., "Planning for Equal Employment Opportunities, An Application of Ratio Goal Functions." Working Paper 81–07–02, Decision Sciences Dept., The Wharton School, University of Pennsylvania.

21. Kornbluth, J. S. H. and G. R. Salkin, "A Note on the Economic Interpretation of Dual Variables in Linear Fractional Programming." *ZAMM* 52:175–178, 1972.

22. Kornbluth, J. S. H. and R. E. Steuer, "Multiple Objective Linear Fractional Programming." *Man. Science* 27(9):1024–1039, 1981.

23. Kornbluth, J. S. H. and R. E. Steuer, "Goal Programming with Linear Fractional Criteria." *EJOR* 8:58–65, 1981.

24. Kornbluth, J. S. H. and R. E. Steuer, "On Computing the Set of All Weakly Efficient Vertices in Multiple Objective Linear Fractional Programming." Pp. 189–202 in G. Fandel and T. Gal (eds.), *Multiple Criteria Decision Making: Theory and Application,* Lecture Notes in Economics and Mathematical Systems, 177 (Springer, Berlin, 1979) 189–202.

25. Kydland, F., "Duality in Fractional Programming." *NRLQ* 19:691–697, 1972.

26. Lazimy, R., "An Enhanced Interactive Method for Solving the Multiple Criteria Problem." Working Paper, Jerusalem School of Business Administration, Hebrew University, Jerusalem, Israel.

27. Lee, S. M., *Goal Programming for Decision Analysis.* Philadelphia: Auerbach, 1972.

28. Lin, W. T., "A Survey of Goal Programming Applications." *Omega* 8(1):115–117, 1980.

29. Martos, B., "The Direct Power of Adjacent Vertex Programming Methods." *Man. Science* 12(3):241–252, 1965.

30. Martos, B., "Hyperbolic Programming." *NRLQ* 11:134–155, 1964.

31. Philip, J., "Algorithms for the Vector Maximum Problem." *Math. Programming* 2:207–229, 1972.

32. Sartoris, W. L. and Spruill M. L., "Goal Programming and Working Capital Management." *Financial Management* (Spring):67–74, 1974.

33. Schaible, S., "Fractional Programming. I: Duality." *Man. Science* 22(8):858–867, 1976.

34. Schaible, S., "Fractional Programming. II: On Dinkelbach's Algorithm." *Man. Science* 22(8):868–873, 1976.

35. Schaible, S., *Analysis and Applications of Fractional Programs* (Analyse und Anwendungen von Quotienten Programmen), Verlag Anton Hain (D-6554) Meisenheim am Glan, Mathematical Systems in Economics, Vol. 42 (1978).

36. Schaible, S., "A Survey of Fractional Programming, Generalized Concavity in Optimization and Economics." Pp. 417–440 in Schaible and Ziemba (eds.), *Proceedings of Nat. Advanced Study Institute.* Vancouver Conference, Aug. 1980.

37. Sealey, C. W. Jr., "Financial Planning with Multiple Objectives." *Financial Management* (Winter):17–23, 1978.

38. Steuer, R. E., "Linear Multiple Objective Programming with Interval Criterion Weights." *Man. Science* 23:305–316, 1978.

39. Steuer, R. E. and A. T. Schuler, "An Interactive Multiple Objective Linear Programming Approach to a Problem in Forest Management." *Operations Research* 26(2):254–269, 1978.

40. Steuer, R. E. and E. F. Wood, "A Weighted Tchebycheff Solution Procedure Applied to a Water Quality Multiple Criteria Optimization Problem." Working Paper 81–WR-3, Water Resources Program, Princeton University.

41. Stancu, Minasian, "Applications of Fractional Programming." *Economics, Computing and Economic Cybernetic Studies and Research* (Romania) 14(1):69–86, 1980.

42. Swarup, K., "Duality in Fractional Programming." *Unternehmensforschung* 12:106–112, 1968.

43. Tigan, S. T., "Sur le problème de la programmation vectorielle fractionnaire." *Mathematica—Revue d'Analyse Numérique et de Théorie de l'Approximation* 4(1):99–103, 1975.
44. Wagner, H. M. and J. Yuan, "Algorithmic Equivalence in Linear Fractional Programming." *Man. Science* 14:301–306, 1968.
45. Yu, P. L. and M. Zeleny, "The Set of All Nondominated Solutions in Linear Cases and a Multicriteria Simplex Method." *J. Math. Anal. Appl.* 49(2):430–468, 1975.
46. Zanakis, S. H. and M. W. Maret, "A Markovian Goal Programming Approach to Aggregate Manpower Planning." *JORSA* 32:56–63, 1981.
47. Zeleny, M., *Linear Multiobjective Programming*. Lecture Notes in Economics and Mathematical Systems, No. 95. New York: Springer Verlag, 1974.
48. Ziemba, W. T., C. Parkan and R. B. Hill, "Calculation of Investment Portfolios with Risk Free Borrowing and Lending." *Man. Science* 21:209–222, 1974.

MULTICRITERION DESIGN OF HIGH-PRODUCTIVITY SYSTEMS

Milan Zeleny

MILAN ZELENY presents further extensions and applications of the de novo programming approach, especially as it relates to MCDM. The basic idea is that in many production-mix problems of practical importance (those modeled by linear programming), there is a need for intelligent, optimal determination of resources levels (the right-hand sides) rather than for simply "optimizing" a "given" system.

So-called given systems are inherently suboptimal as they usually arise from the status quo, tradition, or arbitrary acquisition. Subsequent optimization then does not and cannot achieve the full potential available through restructuring or redesign of resources.

Any optimization theory appears to be incomplete if it concentrates on one part of the problem only: optimize the given system. Another, and perhaps more important, part is: design an optimal system.

Simultaneous determination of optimal decision variables and optimal right-hand sides turns out to be computationally trivial, collapsing into a simple continuous knapsack problem. This allows an optimal design of very large-scale linear programming systems. Such computational ease further allows for comprehensive and unlimited sensitivity analysis and postoptimality analysis. Demand changes and fluctuations, resource and product price changes and fluctuations, technological coefficients changes, and so on—all can be explored with convenient computational efficiency. It is obviously always better to design the system in the best possible way from the beginning rather than waste resources and time trying to improve something that has already been badly designed.

Such classical concepts as slack variables, shadow prices, and the entire duality theory lose their original meaning and acquire a new, more practical and more flexible power with full and meaningful economic interpretation.

Zeleny does not discount the role and usefulness of classical linear programming: it can still be successfully applied, this time to scientifically rather than to haphazardly or arbitrarily given systems. It is important to realize that any concept which leads inherently to wasted or underutilized resources cannot be effective under the conditions of limited and increasingly more expensive resources, sagging productivity, and uncertain demand fluctuations. The inescapable byproducts of linear programming—waste of resources, increased costs, and decreased profits—are no longer acceptable.

The multicriterion framework of the de novo approach appears to be extremely rich and fruitful in possible theoretical extensions and practical applications. It certainly deserves further research attention as it might lead to the rejuvenation of operations research in general and MCDM in particular, but most importantly to enhanced, economically grounded arguments in optimization theory.

ABSTRACT

High productivity, in any system, requires that resources be fully utilized or at least not wasted. In the linear programming framework this is not assured. Therefore, it is possible to design an optimal mix of resources (rather than simply optimize a given mix) which would assure a full utilization of all resources (leading to a fully degenerate LP formulation) and a real maximization of the objective function(s) under such circumstances. These considerations lead to a problem of optimal determination of the right-hand sides simultaneously with solving for decision variables. Through the de novo approach, it is now possible to determine both at the same time with minimum computational effort: computations can be carried out by hand within minutes for even the largest linear programming systems. A multicriterion version of the de novo approach reduces to designing a system which would make an ideal solution (or better) one of the feasible points. It is argued that the larger problem of optimization theory should be to design an optimal system, rather than to optimize a given system, and the larger problem of decision theory should be the choice among optimal systems, rather than among solutions to a given system.

1. INTRODUCTION

The philosophy of optimization as characterized by linear programming and dominating both strategic and tactical thinking of most managers can be simply expressed as follows: *Given* a set of available resources, what choice of production mix would be feasible under the resource constraints while optimizing a *given* figure of merit.

One can legitimately ask: Who has given the "givens" and how? Is the "given" system (or portfolio of resources) put together in the best possible, productivity-enhancing fashion, or was it construed in a suboptimal, arbitrarily conceived, and inherently wasteful way? If the latter is true, is it worthwhile to optimize such an inherently suboptimal system? Should not we pay as much attention to an optimal design of a portfolio of resources as we traditionally afford to its subsequent technical optimization?

Alternately, one may ask: In order to optimize a given figure of merit, how much and what kinds of resources should be acquired and put in place so that the resulting system would be the best possible under the circumstances? This is an entirely different proposition in that one tries to determine not only the optimal production mix but, at the same time, the necessary levels of resources that would ensure that such an optimal mix could be safely implemented.

It is proposed that the larger problem of *any* theory of optimization can be identified as follows: *design optimal systems; do not merely optimize given systems.*

This particular design-oriented methodology has been labeled as *de novo programming* in order to stress its emphasis on a new, optimally

171

constructed portfolio of resources rather than on accepting an existing mix of resources as given. Introductory details, examples, and potentials of the de novo approach have already been described in Refs. 4 through 6. The purpose of this chapter is to emphasize its further applications, multicriterion extensions, and computational attractiveness.

2. BASIC FORMULATION OF DE NOVO PROGRAMMING

Let us first consider the simpler, single-objective formulation as it arises naturally from traditional linear programming. Classical linear programming problem can be presented as follows:

$$\text{maximize} \quad f = \sum_j c_j x_j$$

subject to

$$\sum_j a_{ij} x_j \le b_i \qquad i = 1, \ldots, m \qquad (1)$$

$$x_j \ge 0 \qquad j = 1, \ldots, n.$$

The values of b_i represent the given, fixed levels of available resources. It is precisely these levels (as well as the a_{ij} in some cases) which one must be able to determine in an optimal manner in order to bring the notion of system optimality into the focus. Let us designate b_i as x_{n+i} (as they become additional variables rather than fixed constants). Then,

$$\text{maximize} \quad f = \sum_j c_j x_j$$

subject to

$$\sum_j a_{ij} x_j - x_{n+i} \le 0 \qquad i = 1, \ldots, m$$

$$\sum_i p_i x_{n+i} \qquad \le B \qquad (2)$$

$$x_j \ge 0 \qquad j = 1, \ldots, n + m$$

(where p_i are current unit prices of resources i, and B the total available budget) represents the de novo formulation. Observe that by solving problem (2) one determines not only the optimal levels of x_j but also the optimal levels of resources to be used [b_i in formulation (1)]. An optimal system is designed rather than a given system being optimized.

It appears that solving (2) is dramatically simpler than solving (1) even though much more information is obtained and more flexibility introduced into the system. Given the current market prices p_i, observe that $\sum_i p_i a_{ij}$

$= v_j$ represents the unit cost, in terms of stated resources, of producing product j. Using v_j we can reformulate (2) as follows:

$$\text{maximize} \quad f = \sum_j c_j x_j$$

subject to

$$\sum_j v_j x_j \leq B \tag{3}$$

$$x_j \geq 0 \qquad j = 1, \ldots, n.$$

Solving problem (3) is trivial because only one constraint is involved: Find $\max_j(c_j/v_j)$, say c_k/v_k; then $x_j^* = B/v_j$ for $j = k$, and 0 otherwise. This can of course be performed by hand or with the use of a pocket calculator for any number of variables, any number of resources, and any complexity of the matrix of technological coefficients.

3. NUMERICAL EXAMPLE

Consider the following linear programming problem:

$$\text{maximize} \quad 400x_1 + 300x_2$$

subject to

$$4x_1 \qquad\qquad \leq 20$$
$$2x_1 + \quad 6x_2 \leq 24$$
$$12x_1 + \quad 4x_2 \leq 60$$
$$3x_2 \leq 10.5$$
$$4x_1 + \quad 4x_2 \leq 26 \qquad x_1, x_2 \geq 0.$$

The above problem can be solved by regular linear programming method, giving $x_1 = 4.25$ and $x_2 = 2.25$ with the optimal value of the objective function $400(4.25) + 300(2.25) = 2375$. But what if the given right-hand sides are not "given" correctly? Would some other portfolio of resources, possibly of the same overall dollar value, lead to a better solution?

Let the current market prices of the listed resources be as follows: $p_1 = \$30$; $p_2 = \$40$; $p_3 = \$9.5$; $p_4 = \$20$; $p_5 = \$10$. Then the overall cost of the resource portfolio used above can be computed as follows:

$$\$30(20) + \$40(24) + \$9.5(60) + \$20(10.5) + \$10(26) = \$2600.$$

Can the same \$2600 be spent in a different, optimal way, so that a new system would be designed providing higher value of the objective function at the same cost?

Observe that the unit cost for products x_1 and x_2 are

$$v_1 = \$30(4) + \$40(2) + \$9.5(12) + \$20(0) + \$10(4) = \$354$$

$$v_2 = \$30(0) + \$40(6) + \$9.5(4) + \$20(3) + \$10(4) = \$378.$$

We can use v_1 and v_2 in the computational formulation (3):

maximize $400x_1 + 300x_2$

subject to

$$354x_1 + 378x_2 \leq 2600 \qquad x_1, x_2 \geq 0.$$

Since 400/354 is the largest ratio, the optimal solution will be $x_1^* = 2600/354 = 7.3446$ while $x_2^* = 0$. The value of the objective function has been increased to $400(7.3446) + 300(0) = 2937.84$. Thus, with the same amount of money spent (\$2600) we have been able to increase the objective function by 562.84.

The new, optimally designed linear programming system (with the *optimal portfolio of resources*) can be written as follows:

maximize $400x_1 + 300x_2$

subject to

$$4x_1 \qquad\qquad \leq 29.4$$

$$2x_1 + \quad 6x_2 \leq 14.7$$

$$12x_1 + \quad 4x_2 \leq 88$$

$$3x_2 \leq 0$$

$$4x_1 + \quad 4x_2 \leq 29.4 \qquad x_1, x_2 \geq 0.$$

Solving the above LP problem would lead to the same solution, $x_1 = 7.3446$ and $x_2 = 0$, as obtained earlier by inspection. The right-hand sides are obtained by simply substituting $x_1 = 7.3446$ in the set of constraint equations.

4. DISCUSSION OF DE NOVO RESULTS

The de novo approach is relevant to all practical product-mix problems. In most cases the resources are not fixed but must be acquired or purchased to form a desirable portfolio. Even if some resources are fixed in the short run, they should be changed and restructured (over the next planning periods or in the long run) in the direction of the optimal de novo design. Failing to do so leads to suboptimization and underutilization of scarce resources. Ultimately, all systems should be designed optimally; optimization of given systems should become rare because of its inherent wastefulness.

One important observation, stemming from the *unlimited demand assumption,* is that the optimal system design shall lead invariably to producing a single, most profitable product. This is theoretically and intuitively correct as there is no reason to produce anything else than as much as possible of the most profitable product. A system not designed to attain such solution is necessarily suboptimal.

The variety of production does evolve according to de novo recommendation: start with a single, most profitable product and produce as much of it as you can sell. After the demand for this product is satiated, move toward the production of the next most profitable product while continuing the necessary supply of the first product, and so on. In the course of time, depending on the structure and extent of demand, a variety of production is built up. The "variety" of production arising from the traditional linear programming (LP) solution simply reflects the suboptimality of a "given" portfolio of resources, has no economic interpretation, and results from a particular mathematical structure of the problem.

In traditional LP, the number of products recommended (the variety of production) is directly related to the number of stated mathematical constraints. Thus, one constraint would allow only one product to be recommended while a thousand such constraints should allow up to a thousand different products. Why this should be so is neither economically nor intuitively obvious; instead, it follows solely from the formal properties of the LP formulation.

It is a well-known fact that additional constraints can only limit, never enlarge, the set of feasible solutions. Why the largest possible variety of production should be associated with the most severely limited set of alternatives is not easily explainable. Decreasing or increasing the variety of production in practice has something to do with the limitations of demand and the number of criteria considered, nothing to do with the actual number of constraints stated in a mathematical LP formulation.

The de novo solution exhibits some other important properties. There are no underutilized resources; all slack variables must be equal to zero by the definition of optimality. No system can be considered optimal (at least not in the long run) if it leads to not fully utilized, idle resources. All resources must be fully utilized if we wish to speak of high-productivity systems. Idle resources are inadmissible according to most economic considerations.

Technically, then, since all slacks are zero, all shadow prices are positive; there are no "free goods." The solution to the optimal design problem is fully degenerate—the economically most desirable property of linear programming solutions. Why is degeneracy so desirable? No self-respecting manager would accept that some of his resources are (even temporarily) valueless; all resources should be used to full capacity, and none should be wasted; then all resources would and should have a nonzero value. Such desirable, ideal properties can only be obtained through totally degenerate systems, like those provided by the de novo approach. These and similar interpretations of LP degeneracy have also been explored in Refs. 2 and 3.

It is of course often desirable that not all resources be fully utilized; some types of resources should be available also in minimum safety or buffer amounts. This can only be handled by adding differentially determined safety percentages to individual, optimally designed levels of resources. It should never be a capricious outcome of a given mathematical structure, as Japanese zero-inventory ("just-in-time") systems demonstrate.

Because all resources are properly valued (nonzero shadow prices) in the economically most desirable system, the whole concept of duality and its use in so-called postoptimality analysis loses its original significance. There is less need to analyze the marginal impacts of marginal changes in individual resources (a one-by-one ceteris paribus approach) when one can change all resources at the same time toward the most desirable system. Also, the dual formulations for fully degenerate systems are not necessarily unique [5]: an infinite number of sets of dual variables exists that satisfy the duality theorem (the optimal value of the dual equals the optimal value of the primal). It appears that duality analysis is often economically unattractive, practically unjustifiable, and technically cumbersome.

The level of the budget B, as it appears as a single constraint in (3) is not really a constraint because the solution will remain the same for any level of B (only numerical values will change proportionally). Thus for B = 5200, the solution will still be x_1; this time $x_1 = 5200/354 = 14.69$, with individual resource levels being 58.8, 29.4, 176, 0, and 58.8, respectively. For *unlimited demand* there is only one optimal design structure with numerical properties proportional to the budget B.

It is only the external demand limitations and the number of criteria that can exert (and should exert) any influence on the variety of production and sensitivity to budget levels. For example, consider the following problem, already written in the continuous knapsack form (3):

$$\text{maximize} \quad 150x_1 + 50x_2 + 110x_3 + 65x_4$$

subject to

$$127.5x_1 + 47.5x_2 + 100x_3 + 62.5x_4 \leq B.$$

The ranking of products in the descending order of "profitability" is x_1, x_3, x_2, and x_4. Thus, if B = 5000, other things being equal, one would produce only x_1 = 5000/127.5 = 39.22 and none of the other products. Let us consider the following demand limits on the products: $x_1 \leq 25$; $x_2 \leq 10$; $x_3 \leq 10$; and $x_4 \leq 6$. This means that only 25 units of x_1 can be produced (instead of 39.22). Thus x_1 = 25 uses up 3187.5 of the 5000 budget, leaving B = 1812.5. This would allow producing the next most profitable product x_3 at x_3 = 18.125 (1812.5/100), but because of demand limit only x_3 = 10 can be produced. Similarly only x_2 = 10 can be produced; and because the demand on x_4 is nonbinding, only x_4 = 5.4 can be produced. Thus the optimal de novo solution under the given demand limitations is x_1 = 25; x_3 = 10; x_2 = 10; and x_4 = 5.4—to be undertaken in that order. (Details of this numerical example are given in the Appendix). As long as at least one product demand is unconstrained (or at least high enough to be nonbinding over the range of budget levels) the system will remain optimal for any budget size within that range. If all demand constraints become binding, there is a point beyond which further budget increases become meaningless.

Because of the trivial computational requirements of the de novo approach, the sensitivity analysis of the resulting system can assume entirely new dimensions: one can easily characterize the sensitivity of the optimal design not only with respect to changing budgets but also with respect to changes in any and all resource prices, any and all demand constraints, any and all objective function coefficients, any and all technological coefficients, and any and all combinations of these parameters—all at negligible computational expense.

As an optimal design is completed and optimal levels of desirable resources are established, it is time to establish proper levels of spare machine capacity, buffer stocks, safety cash, additional underemployed labor, and other safety additions and percentages. Determining these levels should not be entirely experiential or arbitrary, as they represent important tools for hedging against uncertainty—sort of uncertainty allowances. These uncertainty allowances could be either positive or negative with respect to the optimal (expected, most likely, or average) levels of resources. Such an approach was first proposed by R. B. Flavell in 1977 and appears to be highly adaptable to de novo design.

Dividing the level of each resource into two parts—the operational, most likely level, and the uncertainty allowance—represents a simple and useful way of handling uncertainty in linear programming. It does not compare with stochastic programming, which is mostly not practical, or with traditional postoptimality (sensitivity) analysis, which is usually limited to marginal changes in a single coefficient at a time.

As the underlying optimal solution is fully degenerate, the actual, uncertainty-adjusted system design will be necessarily nondegenerate, with some inefficiencies introduced as a hedge against future uncertainties. A numerical example of such uncertainty hedging is given in the Appendix.

In de novo programming, the single budgetary constraint is not the only way of conceiving the problem. Other constraint or set of constraints could serve the similar "budgetary" purposes. Some constraints simply must be fixed or are mandated to be fixed: such "hard" constraints cannot be "redesigned" de novo, and the optimal system must be built around them. This can be done by designing the "ideal" optimal design first, disregarding the hard constraint(s) temporarily, and then "regressing" from the ideal design by adjusting the levels of appropriate resources. This sequence approach is important as many "≤" or "≥" type constraints could turn out not to be violated by the de novo design and thus not be actually restrictive. It seems that only those constraints that are violated by the de novo optimal design *and/or* are otherwise unchangeable (cannot be purchased or installed on time) are the constraints of interest. These will usually be the strict " = " type of constraints. Essentially, a new definition of a constraint is needed: a constraint as a resource, the level of which is fixed or mandated in the sense that it cannot be (or should not be) purchased (or sold) at a price *and/or* which is not violated by the de novo optimal design. Such a definition reduces the number of constraints substantially and allows fast and efficient computation of large-scale, economically meaningful linear programming systems. It does preserve the attractiveness of LP's conceptual and computational package for a small, well-defined subset of theoretically interesting problems.

5. MULTIPLE OBJECTIVES: BASIC FORMULATIONS

De novo programming concepts can be easily extended to multicriterion situations:

$$\text{maximize} \quad f_1 = \sum_j c_j^1 x_j$$

$$\vdots \qquad \vdots$$

$$f_k = \sum_j c_j^k x_j \tag{4}$$

subject to

$$\sum_j a_{ij} x_j \leq b_i \qquad i = 1, \ldots, m$$

$$x_j \geq 0 \qquad j = 1, \ldots, n,$$

which is the linear multiobjective programming formulation with k linear objective functions. The conventional solution concept is the set of non-dominated solutions (see, for example, Ref. 4). Referring to formulation (3), we can reformulate (4) simply as:

$$\text{maximize } f_1 = \sum_j c_j^1 x_j$$

$$\vdots \qquad \vdots$$

$$f_k = \sum_j c_j^k x_j \tag{5}$$

subject to

$$\sum_j v_j x_j \le B$$

$$x_j \ge 0 \qquad j = 1, \ldots, n.$$

Observe that (5) is the multiobjective version of de novo programming with one budgetary constraint.

Another classical approach to solving (4) is the method of the displaced ideal or that of compromise programming (see Ref. 4). Should we maximize all objective functions with respect to a *given* constraint set, we would obtain k optimal values $f_1^*, \ldots, f_k^*$ and their corresponding solutions. This is the so-called *ideal point* (or ideal solution) in compromise programming. The multicriterion conflict exists only because such an ideal solution is generally infeasible: one cannot attain all $f_1^*, \ldots, f_k^*$ optimal values at the same time. It is self-evident that should such an ideal solution become feasible, no further decision making and compromising would be needed as *it* would become the most preferred solution for any decision maker.

Observe that setting some a priori desired goals for $f_1, \ldots, f_k$, say $f_1 = g_1, \ldots, f_k = g_k$, leads to a typical goal programming family of formulations. Compromise programming is concerned with identifying the solution(s) that is in some sense the closest to the otherwise infeasible ideal. See the chapter by Gearhart in this volume as well as Ref. 4

The de novo conceptual framework does not take the infeasibility of the ideal point as given but explores the conditions under which the ideal point itself could be made feasible, i.e., the multicriterion design. The infeasibility of the ideal comes from a suboptimal, arbitrary design of systems under consideration. If one is allowed to redesign the system, one can often make the original ideal feasible at lower total cost of resources, by means of trivial computational efforts, and with a potential for further increasing the values of all objective functions.

In Figure 1 we present a simple interpretation of the ideal point f* in linear multiobjective programming and its role in inducing the conflict

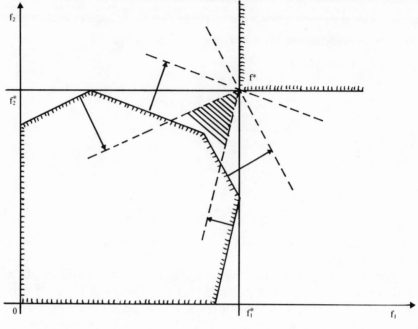

Figure 1.

calling for multicriterion resolution. One can see how redesigning the system could establish the feasibility of the ideal or even lead to an improvement in both objective functions above and beyond the "ideal" levels. The arrows leading from the original constraints to new (dashed lines), redesigned constraints indicate the necessary changes in all resource levels to ensure the feasibility of the ideal point. The lightly shaded area at the upper right denotes the high-productivity, new feasible set. The heavily outlined area dominating the ideal point $f^* = (f_1^*, f_2^*)$ represents the direction of further improvement, depending on the available budget levels.

The achievement of the ideal is demonstrated only for the purposes of systems comparison. Obviously, any change in the set of constraints may displace the location of the ideal. As soon as we allow to change the constraints (and thus displace the ideal) it no longer makes sense to design for an ideal corresponding to a *particular* constraint set. The only thing that is desirable is to define a *new* ideal corresponding to all possible extremes achievable on constraint sets described by the budget constraint. We shall return to these issues when discussing a *set of admissible systems*.

If one can design a system which includes the ideal (or better) as one of its feasible points, then not only will the multicriterion choice become highly simplified but in many cases it may be dispensed with as a minor problem. Under such conditions, MCDM ceases to exist as an outgrowth of classical operations research and moves to a new level of analysis, thus establishing the foundations for a new, design-oriented field of inquiry. Designing optimal systems under real or mandated (rather than arbitrary) constraints, creating new alternatives so that the old ideals can become feasible and surpassed in new systems, and dissolving the multicriterion conflict—these could become the activities of interest "beyond MCDM."

As an illustration, let us use the same numerical example discussed earlier (Section 3). Let the problem be:

$$\text{maximize} \quad f_1 = 300x_1 + 400x_2$$

and

$$\text{maximize} \quad f_2 = 400x_1 + 300x_1$$

subject to

$$
\begin{aligned}
4x_1 & & \leq 20 \\
2x_1 + & 6x_2 & \leq 24 \\
12x_1 + & 4x_2 & \leq 60 \\
& 3x_2 & \leq 10.5 \\
4x_1 + & 4x_2 & \leq 26 \qquad x_1, x_2 \geq 0.
\end{aligned}
$$

With respect to the first objective function, one obtains the optimal solution $x_1 = 3.75$, $x_2 = 2.75$ and the corresponding value $f_1^* = 2225$. With respect to the second objective, one obtains $x_1 = 4.25$, $x_2 = 2.25$ and $f_2^* = 2375$. Observe that the ideal point is ($f_1^* = 2225$, $f_2^* = 2375$)—an infeasible solution.

Recall that the total cost of all resources (all right-hand sides) in the above systems of constraints is \$2600. Can we redesign the system, not exceeding the \$2600 budget, so that the ideal point will become feasible? Consider:

$$\text{maximize} \quad f_1 = 400x_1 + 300x_2$$

and

$$\text{maximize} \quad f_2 = 300x_1 + 400x_2$$

subject to

$$4x_1 \quad\quad\quad \leq 16.12$$

$$2x_1 + \quad 6x_2 \leq 23.3$$

$$12x_1 + \quad 4x_2 \leq 58.52$$

$$3x_2 \leq \; 7.62$$

$$4x_1 + \quad 4x_2 \leq 26.28$$

Solving the above problem with respect to minimizing either f_1 or f_2 leads *in both cases* to $x_1 = 4.03$, $x_2 = 2.54$. (Unrounded figures are $x_1 = 4.0357145$, $x_2 = 2.5357142$.)

The values of objective functions are

$$f_1^* = 300(4.0357145) + 400(2.5357142) = 2224.9999$$

$$f_2^* = 400(4.0357145) + 300(2.5357142) = 2375.$$

One can see that the ideal solution $f^* = (2225, 2375)$ is now feasible: both of these originally separate maxima can now be achieved simultaneously.

Recalling the resource prices in the original example, the cost of the newly designed system can be computed as follows:

$$\$30(16.12) + \$40(23.3) + \$9.5(58.52) + \$20(7.62)$$

$$+ \$10(26.28) = \$2386.74$$

The total amount spent, $2386.74, is of course substantially lower than the cost of the original, crudely suboptimal system ($2600). Thus, given a system and the associated ideal solution, one can possibly design a cheaper system that will make such an ideal feasible. Obviously, if one were to spend the same $2600, i.e., $213.26 more than is necessary for securing the original ideal, one could correspondingly improve both objective functions beyond the original ideal levels.

Again, no linear programming is necessary for solving multicriterion design problem of any size; we can write:

$$\text{maximize} \quad 400x_1 + 300x_2$$

and

$$\text{maximize} \quad 300x_1 + 400x_2$$

subject to

$$354x_1 + 378x_2 \leq 2600.$$

If, instead of maximizing the above two objective functions, one would

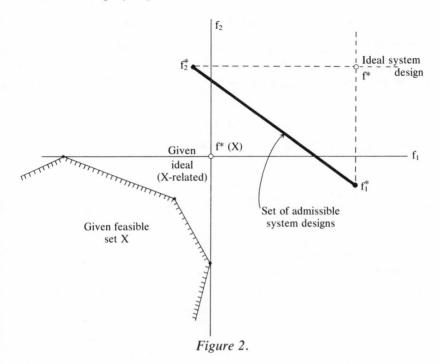

Figure 2.

determine their requisite a priori goal values (for example, the ideal 2225 and 2375), one simply solves a system of two equations. Obviously, any so-called goal programming problem can be similarly reduced to designing a system which would assure the feasibility of jointly desired goals.

We can see that the multicriterion problem has now shifted to a higher and more interesting level: that of *system* design. Obviously, we can improve the design substantially by utilizing the entire $2600 budget available.

Given the budgetary constraint of $2600, one can design the optimal system with respect to f_1, yielding $x_1 = 0$, $x_2 = 6.8783068$ and $f_1^* = 2751.3227$, $f_2 = 2063.492$. Similarly, the optimal design with respect to f_2 yields $x_1 = 7.344627$, $x_2 = 0$ and $f_2^* = 2937.853$, $f_1 = 2203.3898$. These solutions are the two extreme points of a *set of admissible systems*: a set of all systems (mathematical models) designed with respect to a given budgetary constraint and yielding only *nondominated values* with respect to f_1 *and* f_2. See Figure 2 for its graphical interpretation.

Observe that there is now infeasible *ideal system design* (not a solution to a given system) dominating the set of admissible systems: $f^* = (f_1^* = 2751.3227$, $f_2^* = 2937.853)$. This ideal can serve as a reference point for judging the multicriterion desirability of alternative (admissible) system designs. The ideal system design can no more be made feasible by restructuring the resource constraints, but only by increasing the budget itself. The optimal investment schedule can be computed to assure that additional budget leads always to optimal (admissible) design.

The problem of optimal design of systems is now extended to the problem of multicriterion choice among such optimally designed systems.

6. CONCLUSIONS

In optimization problems, as many constraints as possible should be redesigned and their levels so determined that the optimization of an objective function would be assured with respect to a given budget. In multicriterion situations this translates into designing a system which is admissible (in systems selection sense) and as close to the ideal *system* design as possible.

Such task is worthy of further research and study. For decades, operations research and related fields have been concerned with choosing the right solution to a given system when the problem has been, most of the time, that of choosing the optimal system to begin with. The problem of designing optimal systems and choosing among them, rather than optimizing a given system, stands now posed as one of the most important concerns for the MCDM research. Recognizing this could transform MCDM into a general field of inquiry of unquestionable practical importance. MCDM, being qualitatively different from and subsuming most operational sciences (OR/MS/DS) as a special case, deserves such practice-oriented restatement.

APPENDIX

Hedging for Uncertainty

The system below has been optimally designed:

$$\text{maximize} \quad 72x_1 + 60x_2 + 40x_3$$

subject to

$$2x_1 \quad\quad\quad + \quad x_3 \le 60$$
$$2x_1 + 3x_2 + \quad x_3 \le 60$$
$$x_1 + \quad x_2 + \quad x_3 \le 60,$$

giving the solution $x_3 = 60$ and the objective function value 2400. The managers argue that higher levels of resources are needed (higher right-hand sides) to hedge against absenteeism, rest times, and coffee breaks, unscheduled maintenance and machine breakdowns, and so on. They estimate that in order to maintain the designed levels de facto, a $\frac{1}{6}$ more of the first, $\frac{1}{5}$ more of the second, and $\frac{1}{12}$ more of the third constraint are needed. Thus, the actual, operating system would be:

$$\text{maximize} \quad 72x_1 + 60x_2 + 40x_3$$

subject to

$$2x_1 \quad\quad + \quad x_3 \le 60 + (10) = 70$$

$$2x_1 + 3x_2 + \quad x_3 \le 60 + (12) = 72$$

$$x_1 + \quad x_2 + \quad x_3 \le 60 + (\ 5) = 65.$$

Added safety levels are needed to ensure de facto functioning of the optimal system at the designed level of performance. Such underutilization of resources is quite different in spirit from that resulting from purely formal properties of LP.

The shadow prices associated with the optimal, fully degenerate system above satisfy the following:

$$w_1 + \quad w_2 \ge 32$$

$$-w_1 + 2w_2 \ge 20$$

$$w_1 + \quad w_2 \le 40 \quad\quad w_1, w_2 \ge 0, \quad w_3 = 40 - w_1 - w_2.$$

Obviously there are infinitely many different sets of shadow prices for the three resources, all corresponding to the same optimal solution of the primal; Eilon et al. concluded in their famous understatement [2]: "This leads us to question the economic significance of the dual LP."

Changing Coefficients; Quantity Discounts

The objective function coefficients do not have to be constant. They can depend functionally on a quantity produced (for example, with quantity discounting). Consider the following simplified example:

$$\text{maximize} \quad f_1(x_1)x_1 + f_2(x_2)x_2$$

subject to

$$4x_1 + \quad 2x_2 \le b_1$$

$$2x_1 + \quad 3x_2 \le b_2$$

$$10b_1 + \quad 8b_2 \le 1000$$

where $f_1(x_1) = 6$ for $0 \le x_1 \le 10$;
$\quad\quad f_1(x_1) = 4$ otherwise;
$\quad\quad f_2(x_2) = 4$.

The above problem transforms into a simple de novo design problem with multiple criteria:

$$\text{maximize} \quad 6x_1 + 4x_2 \quad \text{when } 0 \le x_1 \le 10$$

and

$$\text{maximize} \quad 4x_1 + 4x_2 \quad \text{otherwise}$$

subject to

$$56x_1 + 44x_2 \le 1000,$$

which can be solved by de novo inspection (no simplex method needed) to determine *both* the decision variables *and* the right-hand sides so that the piecewise linear objective function is maximized:

$$x_1 = 10, \quad x_2 = 10; \quad b_1 = 60, \quad b_2 = 50$$

This problem, restating b_1 and b_2 as variables and solving by the simplex method, could take up to seven iterations to solve. Observe that the size of the problem has no impact on the de novo inspection; it could however affect the simplex method efficiency quite unpleasantly.

De Novo Programming Under Demand Limitations

Consider the following problem:

$$\text{maximize } 150x_1 + 50x_2 + 110x_3 + 65x_4$$

subject to

$$x_2 + 2x_3 \le b_1$$
$$6x_1 + 2x_2 + 2x_3 \le b_2$$
$$3x_1 + x_2 + 2x_3 + 2x_4 \le b_3$$
$$2\tfrac{1}{2}x_1 + \tfrac{1}{2}x_2 + 2x_3 + 1\tfrac{1}{2}x_4 \le b_4$$
$$10b_1 + 5b_2 + 20b_3 + 15b_4 \le 5000.$$

The above assumes the prices of individual resources to be $10, $5, $20, and $15, respectively, and the total budget to be $5000. The problem is to determine $b_1, \ldots, b_4$ (not to cost more than $5000 at current market prices) and the corresponding $x_1, \ldots, x_4$ so that the stated objective function will reach its maximum. This is to be achieved under the limits on demand for $x_1, \ldots, x_4$ being 25, 10, 10, and 6, respectively.

Solving by de novo inspection, one obtains $x_1 = 25$, $x_2 = 10$, $x_3 = 10$, and $x_4 = 5.4$, suggesting the following optimal system of resources:

$$b_1 = 30, \quad b_2 = 190, \quad b_3 = 115.8, \quad b_4 = 95.6.$$

This portfolio of resources costs is

$$\$10(30) + \$5(190) + \$20(115.8) + \$15(95.6) = \$5000,$$

and the optimal value of the objective function is

$$150(25) + 50(10) + 110(10) + 65(5.4) = 5701.$$

REFERENCES

1. Eilon, A. and R. B. Flavell, "A Note on the Many-Sided Shadow Price." *Omega* 2(6):825–828, 1974.
2. Eilon, A., R. B. Flavell and G. R. Salkin, "Valuation of Resources." *Operational Research Quarterly* 28(4):807–816, 1974.
3. Gál, T. and J. Habr, "Linear System Programming 4. Economic-mathematic aspects of degeneracy." *Ekonomicko-matematický Obzor* 4:320–336, 1968.
4. Zeleny, M., "On the Squandering of Resources and Profits via Linear Programming." *Interfaces* 11(5):101–107, 1981.
5. Zeleny, M., *Multiple Criteria Decision Making*. New York: McGraw-Hill, 1982.
6. Zeleny, M., "De Novo Programming with Single and Multiple Objective Functions." Technical Report, TWISK 352, CSIR, Pretoria, August 1984, 20 p.

MULTICRITERIA DECISIONS IN POWER SYSTEMS PLANNING

Ibrahim Kavrakoğlu

IBRAHIM KAVRAKOĞLU has outlined a particular application of MCDM methodology, namely, multiobjective dynamic linear programming, to the types of decisions occurring in power systems planning. As a base he uses the case of Turkish electrical systems for the 1980–2000 period. Power systems planning has changed profoundly in the recent decade. The classical and simple criterion of economic efficiency is no longer sufficient and satisfactory. There are environmental concerns, problems of nuclear reactor safety, nuclear proliferation, radioactive waste disposal, oil price manipulations and oil supply cutbacks, and many other aspects or criteria for decisions.

Kavrakoğlu repeats the well-known fact that public sector decisions are inherently multidimensional, characterized by multiple criteria (this fact is not, however, yet reflected in the curricula of most programs of public administration, public decision making, or public planning). The public decision-making process is often devoid of proper knowledge or reference to multiple criteria in decision making. Inadequate and unscientific unidimensional cost/benefit ratios seem to dominate the lagging practical scene. Kavrakoğlu draws the reader's attention to this essential multidimensionality of public decision making in a convincing and engaging fashion.

In terms of methodological approach, Kavrakoğlu rejects the a priori articulation of preferences (utility theories) as inadequate. He also rejects the a posteriori approach characterized by generating all nondominated solutions and choosing from among them. His objections to the progressive articulation of decision maker's preferences, which arrives at a desirable solution in an interactive manner, are also understandable. So, he comes up with a simplified, small-scale approximation of the nondominated solutions generation technique which is intended to lead efficiently to identifying a handful of sufficiently distinct, meaningful alternatives.

Kavrakoğlu's dissatisfaction with the interactive approach is interesting and should perhaps be considered further. There is often a rather uncritical acceptance of interactive approaches, especially with the newly emerging decision support systems, and the related difficulties are often overlooked. For example, is it always possible to identify the decision maker unambiguously? If not, with whom is the model or the analyst supposed to interact? To what extent should the value system of an individual expert or "decision maker" be allowed to influence the outcome through such interaction? How can a desirable level of objectivity, representativeness, and responsibility be assured?

It seems that the so-called interactive approach should not only be related to the search for a solution but also to interactive evolvement of decision criteria and decision alternatives. Also, any interactive system of value must be confronted with more objective, less personal models and algorithms. It is through such confrontation of results and outcomes that a reliable, high-quality solution can be arrived at. Interactive systems devoid of such an "objective" computational matrix and algorithmic systems devoid of interactive features are equally deficient artifacts.

Kavrakoğlu skillfully uses the concept of "objective" or "implied" weights of attribute importance. The solutions are grouped in relation to the relative magnitudes of the values of objective functions.

ABSTRACT

Decision processes in planning electrical power systems are becoming more complex. New tools and techniques are needed in view of the multiplicity of criteria and the broad-based nature of the decision environment. In order that these techniques be successfully utilized, they must have certain qualities such as congruence, flexibility, transparency, efficiency, and accuracy.

The model proposed for analyzing decisions in power systems planning is one based on multiobjective dynamic linear programming. Model size has been kept as small as possible by representing only the most significant aspects of the system, and the influences of uncertain elements are analyzed by means of various future scenarios.

The model has been applied to the Turkish electrical system for the 1980–2000 period. Three criteria are used (cost, environmental impact, and risk) to evaluate the relative shares and timing of coal, hydro, and nuclear power plants. As a result of the analysis, four decision alternatives are identified: one of these alternatives complies with a least cost–least environmental damage–highest risk development program; another alternative is exactly the opposite; and the other two are compromise alternatives.

1. INTRODUCTION

Decisions in power system planning are becoming increasingly more complex. Until recently, the decision environment could be characterized by well-established guidelines (based primarily on economic efficiency) and clearly defined decision-making responsibilities. During the past decade or so, however, the decision procedures, the evaluation criteria, and the decision-making bodies have changed profoundly [2].

Typical of today's decision environment are the existence of a variety of regulatory authorities, the complexity of criteria, and the frequent public participation in crucial decisions. Certain key events and developments have lead to the present situation. The environmentalist movement; concern over reactor safety; nuclear proliferation and radioactive waste disposal; oil price increases and the threat of oil supply cutbacks—these are some of the major causes of the changes that we are witnessing.

Quite possibly, the present situation is a transitory one which will, in time, lead back to a stable decision environment, with established guidelines and decision-making procedures. Two aspects, however, are likely to remain permanent: (1) the multiplicity of evaluation criteria, and (2) the influences of different interest groups on the final decisions. Thus, a clear need for new planning procedures and tools is developing. It is understood that these procedures and methods will evolve gradually, going through phases of testing, application, evaluation, and acceptance.

This paper presents one possible approach that attempts to accommodate multiple criteria in power systems planning. The model is based on linear programming, and decision alternatives are generated by the clustering in the objective values.

Primary consideration has been given to transparency, flexibility in parametric analysis, and ease of communication. In order to illustrate the use of the model, it has been applied to the Turkish electrical power system.

2. DECISIONS IN THE PUBLIC SECTOR

Public sector decisions are inherently multidimensional. Economic costs are balanced against social benefits, which may involve increased service levels, redistribution of welfare, improvement in reliability, etc. Public projects induce economic gain, but usually over a rather long period, and in a diffuse, indirect way.

Long planning horizons imply the existence of considerable uncertainties and the need for sensitivity (or scenario) analyses on most public projects.

The existence of organized and unorganized interest groups, professional societies, and influential public figures—in addition to the officially designated bodies—complicate the public decision-making process.

In contrast to the complex, dynamic, uncertain, multidimensional, and multicentered decision environment, the (mathematical) tools available for aiding such decisions are quite simple and of limited capability. This is hardly surprising, however, since formal modeling of decision processes is a rather young discipline. Judging from the rapid advances made in the last three decades, there is reason to expect further, significant progress in the not-too-distant future.

3. MODELING POWER SYSTEM INVESTMENTS

Electrical power system projects can be characterized by large investments and long lead times. Coupled with the characteristics of the public decision environment, it is clear that the planning model has to satisfy certain requirements if it is to be at all useful in aiding the decisions. These requirements may be summarized as follows:

    a. *Congruence*—The characteristics of the power system, with regard to both the technical as well as the economic aspects, must be represented. In addition to this basic requirement, the model has to enable adequate representation of the decision makers' value system, especially incorporating multicriteria capability.

    b. *Flexibility*—Because of the long lead times, considerable uncertainties may exist in a number of system elements. Flexibility in model structure and solution method is highly desirable in evaluating the consequences of uncertain outcomes.

  c. *Transparency*—Since decision makers in the public sector are numerous and diffuse, the model that represents the system and its decision alternatives will stand a better chance of being used if it is sufficiently transparent.

  d. *Efficiency*—There is evidence that only efficient (nondominated) investment alternatives are considered in actual energy system expansions. The model, therefore, has to be able to eliminate dominated options from the set of viable decisions.

  e. *Accuracy*—Given the best available data, the model must be able to generate accurate results; i.e., the relative magnitude of errors in the solutions should be commensurate with that of the data and the way in which the solutions will be utilized.

The requirements just cited indicate a need for multicriteria decision making on the model structure itself, in view of the conflicting nature of the demands made of it! For example, congruence would call for a multicriteria, dynamic, nonlinear, stochastic model which contains all the necessary feedbacks that exist in the real system. Yet those characteristics would contradict the transparency requirement. Similarly, an attempt to reduce error margins via the inclusion of greater detail would diminish model flexibility.

Recognizing that the search for the "best" model is futile, we should try to construct what could be an "efficient" model—one that would have an appropriate balance among the desirable attributes that we are interested in.

The model proposed here for decisions in power system expansions is a multiobjective dynamic linear program of quite small dimensions. The optimization approach fits naturally with our aim for nondominated decision alternatives. The linearity assumption may be challenged on two grounds: (1) economies of scale considerations, and (2) resource depletion arguments. The first criticism is not valid since projects in the electrical system are usually very large, and certainly beyond the range where economies would be affected by size. Resource depletion characteristics, which would lead to nonlinear costs, on the other hand, can easily be modeled within the linear programming formulation, as these would result in convex cost functions.[1]

Stochastic aspects of the system are not explicitly modeled, but their influences are analyzed by means of "scenarios." In power systems planning, where the time horizon is of the order of decades, estimates of future values of parameters is, at best, a futile exercise. Besides, incorporating stochastic elements into a model not only causes computational difficulties but also makes the model more complex and the results more difficult to interpret.

The model, as presented here, does not include any interaction between the electrical system and the users of electricity.[2] Given a certain future demand for electricity, it tries to determine nondominated solutions for the timing of capacity additions and for the generation mix.

As for the method of obtaining nondominated solutions, the "generating technique" is utilized. A fast algorithm is used in determining the vertices of the solution space, from which all other nondominated solutions can be found. (See Appendix I for a description [3].)

A few words of explanation for choosing the generating approach would be in order. As is well known, there are three approaches in multicriteria decision processes:

a. *A priori* articulation of preferences, and generating a solution based on these preferences
b. *Progressive* articulation of preferences, and arriving at a desirable solution in an *interactive* manner
c. *A posteriori* articulation of preferences, i.e., generating all relevant solutions, then choosing from among them

Each of these processes has its strong as well as weak points. The first one places a considerable burden on the decision maker, who is forced to take a de facto decision in an information void. The last one overcomes that problem by deferring the decision until all relevant solutions have been obtained but creates the computational difficulty of actually finding the solutions. (For a linear program with N variables and M equations, the number of extreme points can be as large as $N!/[M!(N - M)!]$.) Assuming that the solutions have been found, there still remains the rather difficult task of analyzing such a large number of solutions and arriving at a desirable decision [1].

Theoretically, the interactive process overcomes the disadvantages of both methods, and it may even reduce the requirements on the formal modeling phase. Considering the nature of the decision environment in public sector investments, however, the interactive approach is probably the least feasible. To begin with, this process calls for continued cooperation between the analyst and the decision maker, who may be difficult to even identify, let alone cooperate with. Assuming that an expert may be called in to act as the decision maker, there still remains the objection that the value system of the expert will influence the outcome without being stated explicitly.

The diffuse nature of the decision maker renders the first method infeasible, also. The third method is not so easy to apply either, since a large number of decision alternatives may have to be considered. On the other hand, by keeping model size small, the number of solutions can be reduced significantly. Furthermore, as demonstrated below, the (non-dominated) solutions can be grouped systematically in order to arrive at only a handful of sufficiently distinct, meaningful alternatives.

4. THE MATHEMATICAL MODEL

Formally modeling the system expansion decisions poses considerable difficulties even when only a single criterion, say, cost, is specified. A variety of power plants exists with different fixed and variable costs, availability factors, capacities, etc.

On the demand side, the load is subject to seasonal, daily, and hourly variations. Furthermore, the expansion program has to be considered simultaneously with system operation in order to avoid suboptimal decisions.

In view of the dimensions and the complexity of the system, and given the uncertainties in various parameters, it is clear that a general-purpose model cannot be constructed. A natural approach is to first decide on the *overall strategy,* upon which detailed plans can be built. The aim of this paper is to present a model that allows multicriteria analyses of power system decisions from such a perspective. Especially in view of the changing nature of the decision environment, the model should prove to be useful in providing alternative courses of development which can be elaborated, discussed, and debated upon.

The general formulation, as well as a particular application of the model, is described next.

4.1. General Formulation

The model represents the capacity, generated electricity, and vintages of power plants in an aggregate manner and determines the nondominated solutions for the criteria specified. The time horizon is divided into T periods, each of n years duration, and the power plants (j) are grouped in terms of the primary source of energy, such as hydro, coal, nuclear, gas, or oil.

Three criteria are considered: (1) economic cost, (2) environmental impact, and (3) risk (or damage potential)

$$F_1 = \sum_{j \in J} \sum_{t=1}^{T} (1 + r)^{-t}(CP_{jt}P_{jt} + CE_{jt}E_{jt}) \tag{1}$$

$$F_2 = \sum_{j \in J} \sum_{t=1}^{T} I_{jt}E_{jt} \tag{2}$$

$$F_3 = \sum_{j \in J} \sum_{t=1}^{T} R_{jt} \sum_{k=0}^{t} P_{jk} \tag{3}$$

where   P is added power capacity [in GW (gigawatts)];
        E is energy generated [in TWH (terawatt-hours)];
        CP and CE are unit costs of power and generated energy;
        I is environmental impact associated with electricity generation;
        R is risk associated with installed power capacity;
        r is rate of interest (or opportunity cost);
        F_1, F_2, F_3 are objective functions associated with criteria specified;
        J is the set of relevant power plants;
        t is time period.

The constraints of the model are

$$\sum_{j \in J} E_{jt} \geq ED_t, \qquad \forall t \tag{4}$$

$$\sum_{j \in J} \sum_{k=0}^{t} P_{jk} \geq PD_t, \qquad \forall t \tag{5}$$

$$E_{jt} \leq f_j \sum_{k=0}^{t-1} P_{jk}, \qquad \forall jt \tag{6}$$

$$P_{jt} \leq a_j P_{jt-1}, \qquad \forall jt \tag{7}$$

$$E_{jt} \leq EP_j, \qquad \forall t \text{ for } j = \text{renewable resources} \tag{8}$$

$$\sum_{k=1}^{t} E_{jk} \leq ER_j, \qquad \forall t \text{ for } j = \text{depletable resources.} \tag{9}$$

In words, these constraints imply, respectively:

• Demand for energy (ED) and power (PD) has to be satisfied at all times.
• The energy that can be generated from any type of plant cannot exceed the existing production capacity, multiplied by the appropriate capacity factor, f (single period lag is assumed to exist between the construction and commissioning of a power plant).
• The additions of new capacity cannot exceed a certain rate of growth, a, for any type of power plant.
• Hydroelectric energy is restricted by existing hydropotential (EP).
• For depletable (and nonimportable) resources, more than the available reserve (ER) cannot be utilized.

In applying the model to a particular situation, special consideration has to be given to the characteristics of the system, such as a certain balance between hydro and thermal capacity, or nuclear power as a fraction of the total (from the point of system reliability, as a result of forced outage of a single, large unit, etc.).

As defined by the constraint set given above, the model may appear not as small as expressed to be desirable in Section 3. In applying the model to an existing system, however, the dimensions of the model will be reduced considerably. One reason for this is that it will not be possible to consider all combinations; another is the fact that trivial cases (such as obviously redundant constraints) will be left out.

Sensitivity of model solutions to uncertain elements in the system is a very important aspect of the decisions. The procedure in dealing with such elements will be illustrated best by means of a particular application of the model.

4.2. An Application of the Model

The model described above has been applied to the Turkish electrical power system, with the objective of determining system development options for the years 1980–2000, using the three criteria cited. In applying the model, the following observations have been made:

a. Only new coal, hydro, and nuclear power plants were considered, since there are practically no natural gas reserves and oil is expected to remain too expensive for electricity generation.

b. A 30-year time horizon was defined, with five 6-year time periods. It is sufficient to consider only the first 10- to 25-year planning period, since evaluations can be repeated; besides, uncertainties become too great beyond a planning horizon of 20 years.

c. The maximum hydro potential that was assumed to be realizable was taken as 130 TWh/year.

d. No limitation was placed on depletable resources.

The objective functions and the constraints of the model, as applied to the Turkish power system, took the following forms.

Objective functions for economic cost, environmental impact, and risk, respectively, were

$$F_1 = \sum_{j=1}^{3} \sum_{t=1}^{5} (1 + 0.1)^{-t} (CP_j P_{jt} + CE_j E_{jt}) \tag{10}$$

$$F_2 = \sum_{j=1}^{3} \sum_{t=1}^{5} I_j E_{jt} \tag{11}$$

$$F_3 = \sum_{j=1}^{3} \sum_{t=1}^{5} R_j \sum_{k=0}^{t} P_{jk} \tag{12}$$

where $j = 1$ for coal, $j = 2$ for hydro, and $j = 3$ for nuclear. (Only economic costs were discounted over time, since it is difficult to assign opportunity costs to nonfinancial quantities. Besides, it is not clear that we may wish to trade present environmental damage and risks with future ones.)

The constraints of the model were

$$\sum_{j=1}^{3} E_{jt} \geq ED_t, \qquad t = 1, 5 \tag{13}$$

$$\sum_{j=1}^{2} \sum_{k=0}^{t} P_{jk} \geq PD_t, \qquad t = 1, 2 \tag{14}$$

$$\sum_{j=1}^{3} \sum_{k=3}^{t} P_{jk} \geq PD_t, \qquad t = 3, 5 \tag{15}$$

$$E_{jt} \leq f_j \sum_{k=0}^{t-1} P_{jk}, \qquad j = 1, 2 \quad t = 1, 2 \tag{16}$$

$$E_{jt} \leq f_j \sum_{k=3}^{t} P_{jk}, \qquad j = 1, 3 \quad t = 3, 5 \tag{17}$$

$$P_{jt} \leq a_j P_{jt-1}, \qquad j = 1, 2 \quad t = 1, 5 \tag{18}$$

$$P_{3t} \leq a_3 P_{3t-1}, \qquad t = 3, 5 \tag{19}$$

$$E_{2t} \leq EP_2, \qquad t = 3, 5. \tag{20}$$

The factors that were considered to have the greatest significance were

a. The relative values of the coefficients CE, CP, I, and R
b. The extent to which the hydro potential can be developed within a given time period
c. The rate of growth of energy and power demand
d. The rate at which nuclear energy can penetrate, as a fraction of system total

Thus, sensitivity analyses were carried out on these factors.

In applying the model to the Turkish electricity system, the following strategy was observed (Figure 1):

• A BASE CASE scenario was defined.
• Power plant categories were ranked for each criterion, i.e., cost, environment, risk, and numerical values of CE, CP, I, and R for each type of plant (j) were assigned.

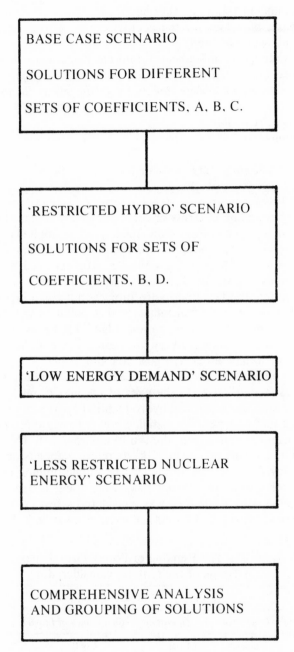

Figure 1. Steps Followed in Solution Strategy and Analysis of Results.

- Nondominated solutions were obtained.
- A new set of values for the coefficients were assigned, and new solutions were obtained.
- After studying the influence of different numerical values, the significance of certain policies such as *restricting rapid growth of hydro, slowing of energy demand growth,* and *reducing the constraint on nuclear energy* were analyzed by obtaining new solutions for these circumstances.
- Nondominated solutions that yielded similar objective values were grouped together, and systems expansion implications for each group of solutions were studied.

The ordinal ranking of power plants in terms of each criterion is shown in Table 1. The ranking in terms of economic cost was based on figures quoted for actual projects. Environmental impact, as implied here, relates to pollution and land use under *normal* operation conditions. Coal power plants are notorious for their air pollution property, and hydro plants cover large areas of land for their reservoirs. While the two involve different dimensions, the fact that hydro projects are given higher priority when all other things are equal indicates that pollution is usually more objectionable compared with occupation of land. Under normal operation conditions, nuclear plants have very low radioactive emissions, and they use less land area than either hydro or coal power plants.

Risk is also difficult to define. It could either be related to "perceived" risk or to "estimated" risk. In the eyes of the public, nuclear reactors pose greater risks compared with hydro plants. Experience to date, however, indicate that on a per GW installed power basis, hydro plants pose a greater danger to humans and the (built) environment. The choice between estimated versus perceived risk, therefore, depends on the extent to which policy decisions are influenced by public opinion or pressure. In this particular study, estimated risks were used; hence, hydro was considered most risky while coal was considered safest.

The numerical values for CE and CP were as given in Table 2.

Table 1. The Ranking of Power Plant Types
in Terms of the Criteria Considered

	Cost			
Ordinal Ranking	*Investment*	*Operating*	*Environmental Impact*	*Risk*
Highest	Nuclear	Coal	Coal	Hydro
	Hydro	Nuclear	Hydro	Nuclear
Lowest	Coal	Hydro	Nuclear	Coal

Table 2. Numerical Values of Economic Costs[a]

Type of Plant	CE (investment cost in $/W)	CP (operation cost in ¢/KWh)
Nuclear	1.62	1.25
Hydro	1.00	—
Coal	0.85	2.50

[a] Interconnection expenditures are included in investment costs, based on average distances from main load centers.

As for numerical values of environmental impact and risk, the following four sets of values were utilized (Tables 3 and 4).

In the BASE CASE (BC) runs, sets A, B, and C were utilized; in the RESTRICTED HYDRO runs, sets B and D were utilized; in the LOW ENERGY DEMAND and LESS RESTRICTED NUCLEAR ENERGY runs only set B was utilized.

RESTRICTED HYDRO (RH) implies that the rate of growth in hydro power was constrained, so that the realization of the full hydro potential of some 35 GW was not allowed within the 30-year time horizon.

LOW ENERGY DEMAND (LED) means that the growth rate in electricity demand was taken to be lower than the historical rate of around 11 percent per annum.

LESS RESTRICTED NUCLEAR ENERGY (LRNE) implies that the maximum factor by which nuclear power could grow in a 6-year period would be as high as 4.0, rather than the 1.5 used in other runs (Table 5).

Despite the considerable range of numerical values in different scenarios, runs 1, 2, and 3 yielded almost identical results. In each case, the number of nondominated solutions was around 30. Minor differences were observed in some of the other runs.

Analyzing the nondominated solutions in terms of objective values, one could group the solutions (the vertices in the solution space) as shown in Table 6, for runs 1 through 5. Evidently, solutions in Group I are associated with lowest financial cost and environmental impact and highest

Table 3. I Values for Environmental Impact

Type of Plant	Scenario			
	A	B	C	D
Coal	9	3	16	1.2
Hydro	3	2	4	1.1
Nuclear	1	1	1	1.0

Table 4.   R Values for Risk

Type of Plant	Scenario			
	A	B	C	D
Hydro	9	3	16	1.2
Nuclear	3	2	4	1.1
Coal	1	1	1	1.0

risk, while those in Group IV are associated with exactly the opposite; Groups II and III imply compromise solutions.

The resulting coal and hydro power capacities (for 1995) are shown in Figure 2. Coal and hydro power development to 1990 is shown in Figure 3. Group I solutions (least economic and environmental costs, high risk) involve greater hydro expansions. (Nuclear was restricted to later years in this example.)

Despite the rather large number of nondominated solutions, the ranges of outcomes for plausible expansion schemes are quite narrow. In addition, the outcomes are not so difficult to group, as demonstrated in this example. As a result, the decision maker is offered only a handful of choices, depending on his preferences. Furthermore, the trade-offs between different objectives can be easily evaluated. For example, by selecting a solution from Group II rather than Group I, risk is reduced by a factor of 2 while other costs increase only marginally.

Another way of evaluating model results is to analyze the "implied weights" of different objectives in the solutions. This additional information is valuable, especially for those more familiar with the classical approach of assigning weights (λ) to different criteria.

Table 7 gives the ranges of λ values for the four groups of solutions mentioned earlier. Here also it can be seen that Group I solutions correspond to greatest weight to economic cost and environmental impact, while Group IV solutions correspond to greatest weight to risk.

Table 5.   Identification of Model Runs

Run No.	Policy	Scenario
1	BC	A
2	BC	B
3	BC	C
4	RH	B
5	RH	D
6	LED	B
7	LRNE	B

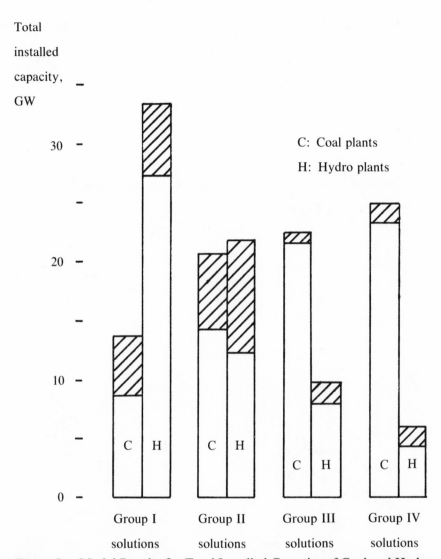

Figure 2.   Model Results for Total Installed Capacity of Coal and Hydro Plants for the Year 1995, in the LOW ENERGY DEMAND SCENARIO. Shaded Parts Indicate Range of Different Solutions. Number of Solutions in Each Group: 5, 5, 5 and 4, Respectively. (Nuclear Capacity was 1.0 - 2.5 GW in Each Group of Solutions and is not Shown Here.) Grouping is Based on the Clustering in Objective Function Values.

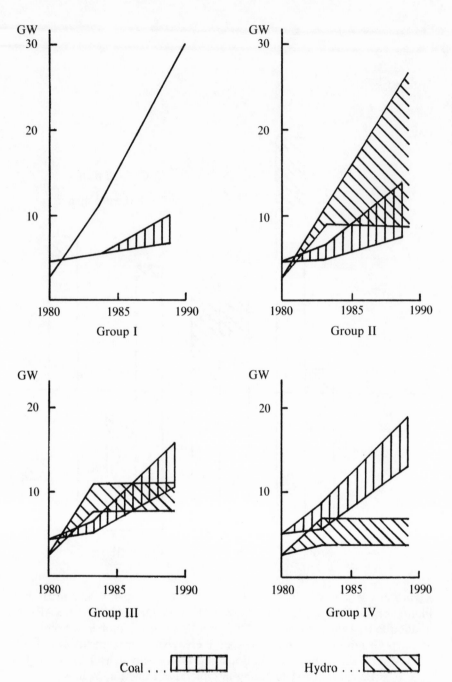

Figure 3. Growth of Installed Capacity for Coal and Hydro Plants up to the Year 1989 in the RESTRICTED HYDRO Scenario. The Ranges Indicate Different Values Corresponding to Grouping of Solutions.

Table 6. Clustering of Objective Values of Nondominated Solutions

| Group No. | No. of Solutions | Ranges of Objective Values | | |
		Economic Cost	Environmental Impact	Risk
I	14	1289–1333	1338–1500	91–137
II	6	1409–1427	1581–1642	57–65
III	3	1439–1463	1630–1657	54–55
IV	6	1505–1533	1672–1737	41–48

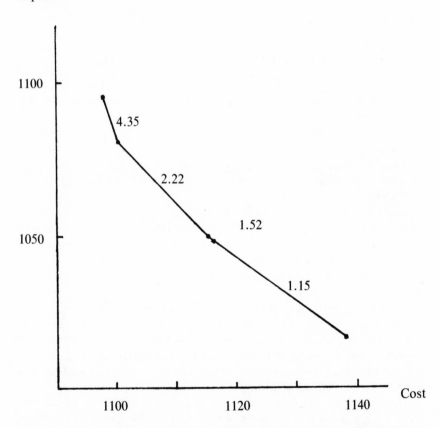

Figure 4. Tradeoff Function for Cost and Environmental Inpact. Numbers Refer to the Ratio ($\lambda c/\lambda e$) of Weights for Costs (λc) and Environmental Impact (λe) Implied for Different Nondominated Solutions.

205

Table 7. Ranges of Representative Objective Weights
(λ values) for Each Solution Group

Group No.	Economic Cost	Environmental Impact	Risk
I	0.18–0.33	0.04–0.33	0.33–0.64
II	0.11–0.18	0.02–0.14	0.73–0.79
III	0.04–0.18	0.02–0.12	0.79–0.85
IV	0.04–0.08	0.05–0.10	0.85–0.86

Trade-off functions between any two criteria can be generated directly by using the model. One such function is displayed in Figure 4 for the trade-off between economic cost and environmental impact.

The computation times required to obtain a set of solutions—for the size of model described here with 27 variables and 36 constraints—is of the order of 1 minute of computer time on a Univac 1106.

5. CONCLUDING OBSERVATIONS

Multicriteria analysis and decision making in public sector projects is, at best, a difficult undertaking. Thus, any method or technique developed with the objective of applicability has to satisfy rather tough requirements.

The modeling approach described, namely, that of generating efficient decision alternatives, is proposed not so much because it is the ideal technique but because the alternatives (interactive methods or prior articulation of preferences) are hardly feasible in the emerging decision environment.

The mathematical formulation does, however, combine certain desirable characteristics such as congruence, flexibility, transparency, and the ability to generate sufficiently accurate solutions. Improving upon only some of these attributes, while sustaining a loss in others, would not increase the chances of success in applying the model, since these attributes constitute a whole.

The modeling technique and the solution procedure employed in this study offers several advantages, especially when the characteristics of the decision environment are considered. A very significant aspect of the model is that it will yield reliable results even when only qualitative information exists. Hence, it is possible to accommodate dimensions which are otherwise difficult to model.

The modeling system and the solution algorithm allows the decisions to be analyzed from three points of view. One of these is to group efficient solutions based on the outcomes of the decision variables. The second approach is to group the solutions based on the relative magnitudes of objective weights. The third approach is to group the solutions based on the relative magnitudes of the objective values, as done in this study. This is also the most direct approach, since the desirability of the alternatives are measured by the values of the objective functions at the efficient solutions.

APPENDIX I:
THE SOLUTION ALGORITHM USED IN THE MULTIOBJECTIVE LINEAR PROGRAMMING MODEL

The solution algorithm is based on exploiting the equivalence of the multiobjective linear program to the multiparametric linear program. Either all efficient extreme points or any desired subset of such points are enumerated. The procedure is best described with the aid of the sketch in Figure 5.

Let us assume that points 1–5 denote the efficient vertices within the feasible region and that vertex 1 corresponds to the minimum of one of the objectives, k, with vertices 2–5 being numbered in nondecreasing values of the same objective. The algorithm starts by finding vertex 1. Then, referring to Figure 5, vertices 2 and 3 are found to be efficient and the next pivot is made to, say, vertex 2, and vertex 3 is stored to be visited later. At vertex 2, vertices 4 and 5 are identified as efficient and arbitrarily a pivot to 4 is made. At vertex 4 no further efficient vertex is identified, and next the last stored vertex, 5, is visited. Again at vertex 5 no further

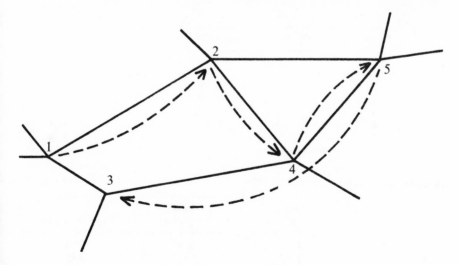

Figure 5. Sequence of Visits is Indicated by Broken Lines.

efficient vertex is identified, and the last vertex in storage, vertex 3, is visited. Here, the algorithm stops, as no new efficient vertex is identified and the storage is empty.

It should be noted that only adjacent vertices with nondecreasing values of the k objective are checked for efficiency. Those with increasing values of the k objective are either already identified or will anyway be identified later as being adjacent to one of the vertices in store. This procedure leads to computational advantages both in carrying out the efficiency checks and in eliminating those vertices which are already discovered from among the adjacent efficient vertices.

APPENDIX II:
DATA FOR MODEL APPLICATION TO TURKEY

Dates corresponding to the periods:

Period:	0	1	2	3	4	5
Midperiod year:	1977	1983	1989	1995	2001	2007

Beginning capacities:

$$P_{1,0} = 4 \text{ GW}$$

$$P_{2,0} = 4 \text{ GW}$$

$$P_{3,2} = 1 \text{ GW}$$

	Energy Demand (TWh)		Power Demand (GW)	
Period	High	Low	High	Low
1	30	30	6.21	6.21
2	60	50	12.44	10.37
3	108	90	22.37	18.63
4	170	150	35.25	31.13
5	240	220	49.77	45.66

Power plant data:

	Initial Cost (in $/W)	Operation Cost (in $/KWh)	Capacity Factor
Coal	0.85	2.50	0.70
Hydro	1.00	—	0.45
Nuclear	1.62	1.25	0.60

Capacity increase factors:

2.0   for coal and hydro

1.5   for nuclear (restricted)

4.0   for nuclear (less restricted)

ACKNOWLEDGMENT

The multiobjective dynamic linear programming model was developed with Dr. G. Kiziltan, who devised the multiobjective linear program (MOLP).

NOTES

1. A third source of nonlinearity would be the average load factors of different types of power plants, assumed to have constant values in the present model. Deviations of the optimum load factors from the a priori specified values, however, are usually small, and in any case lead to second-order errors in the objective value.

2. An "adaptive control, receding time horizon" version of the model has also been developed. In that modified form, the demand for a given time period is a function of the price of electricity, as determined from the solution of the model for the preceding time period.

REFERENCES

1. Cherniavsky, E. A., "Multiobjective Energy Analysis." In B. Bayraktar et al. (eds.), *Energy Policy Planning*. New York: Plenum, 1981.
2. Kavrakoğlu, I. (ed.), *Mathematical Modelling of Energy Systems*. Holland: Sijthoff and Noordhoff, 1981.
3. Kavrakoğlu, I. and G. Kiziltan, "Multiobjective Decisions in Power Systems Planning." Research Report, Bogazici University, Istanbul, 1980.

SUBOPTIMAL REGULATION WHEN ADDRESSING MULTIPLE ATTRIBUTES

Lester B. Lave

LESTER B. LAVE makes a convincing argument as to the multicriterion nature of governmental and public decision making, drawing especially from his experience in analyzing decision processes of regulatory agencies. Individually and independently mandated goals actually interact in practice, their attainment must be simultaneous, and they are contradictory in nature. Not recognizing these simple facts, a rule rather than an exception in governmental decision making, leads not only to suboptimization and a host of unanticipated, undesirable by-products but often to seemingly outright foolishness and an appearance of serious incompetence.

Lave uses sophomore calculus to show how simple such insights can be and how significant even the crudest recognition of these facts can be. If a decision-making body is incapable of recognizing inherent conflicts among the multiple legislative goals, if it cannot recognize even the multiplicity of goals itself, how can one even talk about any sort of decision making? As Lave points out, one hardly can. Actually, current congressional and regulatory agency decision behavior is two stages removed from decision making: it does not account for interactions among attributes, and it fails to optimize with respect to all criteria simultaneously.

For example, one can state as an objective the enhancement of automobile safety. This leads to higher costs, increased weight, and an increased consumption of gasoline. This all conflicts directly with the set standards for emissions and fuel economy, again increasing cost and degrading performance. Or take the disastrous idea of unleaded gasoline mandated for automobiles equipped with a catalytic converter. As a result, more petroleum raw material is needed, more energy is used up, and the cost is increased in order to produce the same amount of gasoline. As unleaded gasoline has lower performance, more is consumed. Because of the price differential, consumers are using leaded gasoline when even tiny amounts of lead render catalytic converters fully ineffective.

Lave also cites the case of the highly flammable fabrics for children's sleepwear. In order to increase mandated flame resistance, a carcinogenic chemical was added to children's sleepwear. This was subsequently banned and vast quantities of clothing had to be discarded. The problem is that children's sleepwear should not *just* be fire resistant; it should also be attractive, soft, durable, nontoxic, and inexpensive. Yet an agency like the Consumer Product Safety Commission would seem to be concerned with only one criterion, remaining totally oblivious to all other criteria.

Lave provides a number of other similar examples illustrating the pitfalls of ignoring the multicriterion nature of public decision making and regulation. He concludes on a pessimistic note, aware of his "counsel of despair," realizing that a full, multicriterion context of regulatory decision making may be forever beyond the grasp and comprehension of regulatory agencies. Yet, without such comprehension of the multiplicity of criteria, most regulatory outcomes will remain either ineffective or harmful.

ABSTRACT

Regulatory agencies generally consider only a single goal or attribute in regulating health, safety, and the environment. Congress initiates this behavior by dividing goals among different statutes, or even different agencies. When multiple goals are involved, univariate analysis is suboptimal, both from the standpoint of the multiple goals and even from the standpoint of the individual goal under consideration. Although consideration of multiple attributes imposes a substantially greater burden on Congress and the regulatory agencies, the costs of univariate consideration are sufficiently great that the burden is justified. Illustrations of the suboptimality of one attribute at a time consideration include regulation of safety, emissions, and fuel economy of the automobile, fire protection in children's sleepwear, lead content of gasoline, and population exposure to ionizing radiation from the nuclear fuel cycle. Reform requires Congress' specification of a multiple attribute goal (when individual goals conflict) and agency analysis of tradeoffs among attributes.

1. INTRODUCTION

More than a dozen times in the past decade and a half Congress has faced some untoward event, such as the Farmington coal mine disaster, the discovery that vinyl chloride monomer causes liver cancer in plastic workers, or the Love Canal catastrophe. Often, the response has been legislation which creates a new regulatory agency of increases the purview of an existing agency [2], Congress has instructed regulatory agencies to prevent such undesirable occurrences in the future, with feasibility generally being the only constraint on action.

This newly empowered agency's attempt to reach the congressionally defined goals often leads to unsatisfactory action and failure to attain the goals. Two difficulties block these goals. The first is that other goals mandated by Congress and consumer desires interact with, and often contradict, the attainment of the original goal [3]. The second difficulty is that goal attainment requires not only recognition of goal interaction but also simultaneous action in achievment of these goals.

The theory that models these phenomena, which relies on sophomore calculus, is almost absurdly simple. Even though elegant mathematical formulations rarely exist in practice, it is possible to apply these ideas, at least roughly, to improve current regulatory outcomes. The following section expounds the simple theory. Examples from various agencies are then cited to indicate the possibility of accounting for the interaction between mathematical formulation and regulatory outcome.

2. THEORY

Congress has instructed the Environmental Protection Agency (EPA) to regulate automobile emissions and fuel economy and the National High-

213

way and Traffic Safety Administration (NHTSA) to regulate safety. Congress does not appear to have recognized the inherent conflicts in defining the legislative goals.

Let x represent safety attributes, y represent fuel economy, e represent emissions control, z represent performance-comfort attributes, and p represent the price of a vehicle. The congressionally defined goals implicitly view these attributes as unrelated, except perhaps for some effect on price. Ignoring the differences between individual and societal goals, the utility or pleasure from an automobile is a function of these attributes:

$$f(x,y,z,e,p). \tag{1}$$

Each regulatory agency seeks to maximize the relevant attribute x, y, or e, without regard to other effects.

However, regulators enhance safety, fuel economy, or emissions control by requiring features that increase weight (w), decrease weight and horsepower (h) or increase emissions control equipment (c) and decreases horsepower, respectively. Thus $x(w)$, $y(w,h,c)$, $e(h,c)$, $z(w,h,c)$, and $p(w,h,c)$; each also depends on additional factors. The more informative way of writing Eq. (1) is

$$f\,[x(w),y(w,h,c),e(h,c),z(w,h,c),p(w,h,c)]. \tag{2}$$

The regulatory agency optimizing safety might calculate:

$$\frac{\partial f}{\partial x}\,\frac{\partial x}{\partial w} + \frac{\partial f}{\partial y}\,\frac{\partial y}{\partial w} + \frac{\partial f}{\partial z}\,\frac{\partial z}{\partial w} + \frac{\partial f}{\partial p}\,\frac{\partial p}{\partial w} = 0 \tag{3}$$

If the agency were seeking merely to optimize safety without attention to other effects, it would ignore the last three terms. If the agency were also willing to consider the increase in price resulting from safety regulations, it would ignore the middle two terms.

Note that the marginal utilities are positive, except for the negative effect of price on utility. Furthermore, additional weight increases safety and price while decreasing fuel economy and performance. Thus, if the agency seeks to maximize safety without qualifications, it will set regulations that increase weight until no greater safety can be achieved ($\partial x/\partial w = 0$). If price is taken into account, the fourth term will enter to give less safety at the optimal point. Finally, if the two interaction effects are also taken into account, these two terms will further decrease the amount of safety that is optimal.

But even this attempt to account for interactions is insufficient to optimize for all attributes. Instead of optimizing separately for each attribute, optimization should be done simultaneously for all attributes. Thus, the regulatory agencies and manufacturers should be looking at all three equations in (4); only by simultaneous maximization will the optimal solution arise:

$$\frac{\partial f}{\partial x}\frac{\partial x}{\partial w} + \frac{\partial f}{\partial y}\frac{\partial y}{\partial w} + \frac{\partial f}{\partial z}\frac{\partial z}{\partial w} + \frac{\partial f}{\partial p}\frac{\partial p}{\partial w} = 0$$

$$\frac{\partial f}{\partial y}\frac{\partial y}{\partial h} + \frac{\partial f}{\partial e}\frac{\partial e}{\partial h} + \frac{\partial f}{\partial z}\frac{\partial z}{\partial h} + \frac{\partial f}{\partial p}\frac{\partial p}{\partial h} = 0 \qquad (4)$$

$$\frac{\partial f}{\partial y}\frac{\partial y}{\partial c} + \frac{\partial f}{\partial e}\frac{\partial e}{\partial c} + \frac{\partial f}{\partial z}\frac{\partial z}{\partial c} + \frac{\partial f}{\partial p}\frac{\partial p}{\partial c} = 0.$$

The necessity for simultaneous optimiziation results from the fact that h and c must be at their optimal values in order for Eq. (3) to yield the correct value for w. If, for example, NHTSA attempted to solve Eq. (3) for w while assuming that horsepower and emissions control were at their 1968 levels, the wrong value of w would be chosen. Later, when EPA tried to solve the last equation in (4) for c, it would find that w and h had been set at nonoptimal levels, resulting in a need for more emissions control than would be necessary if they were at the optimal levels. The new h and c would mean that NHTSA should recalculate w.

Thus, current congressional and regulatory agency behavior is two stages removed from optimizing social welfare. The first is failing to account for interactions among attributes. The second is failing to optimize all attributes simultaneously. Each failure can be quantitatively important.

3. AUTOMOBILE REGULATION

Spokesmen for NHTSA have stated that the agency's objective is to require any change in design that will enhance safety [6]. While this is clearly an exaggeration, NHTSA does not accord additional cost or other effects much weight. Congress has set the standards for emissions and fuel economy; it does not give much, if any, weight to increased cost or degraded performance. Although manufacturers have attempted to estimate the increase in production cost and operating cost for each regulation, the costs are inherently difficult to characterize. As companies learn to meet the regulations more easily, costs will tend to fall over time.

It is possible to characterize each of the partial derivatives, although the estimates have many difficulties.[1] For example, analyses of cars during the early 1970s show that the chance of serious injury or fatality in an accident was 50 to 100 percent higher in a 3,000 pound car than in a 4,500 pound car. Although there is evidence that small cars have been redesigned to be safer, there still appears to be a large difference in safety.

Larry White estimates that the current emissions regulations decrease fuel economy by about 7 percent [10]. If so, the average car uses an additional 35 gallons of gasoline each year because of the emissions regulations.

Safety reduces fuel economy by adding weight. The package of required safety features increased weight by 200 pounds, leading to an increased consumption of gasoline of 22 gallons per car per year. These features provide a good illustration of the contradictory effects of regulation. This package of safety features is estimated to have increased automobile prices by $200 to $300 and saved about 7,900 lives and several times that many serious injuries, etc. I assume that the social value of saving injuries makes the total saved to be about equal to the value of lives saved; thus, the direct cost of preventing each "fatality equivalent" is $296,000 to $444,500. However, the additional weight, leading to additional fuel consumption, increases this cost per life by $247,000. Thus, the "secondary" effect is almost as large as the primary effect. Assuming society values the prevention of a fatality to be worth half a million dollars, this package of safety features would be worthwhile if the secondary effects were neglected, but not if they were taken into account. In the latter case, a more careful review of each feature would be required to excise the standards that contribute cost and weight but are not effective in reducing injury.

Less powerful engines are more fuel efficient. For example, for a 3,500 pound car, reducing engine size so that the time to accelerate from 0 to 60 miles per hour increases from 10 to 18 seconds will increase fuel economy from 18 to 21 miles per gallon.

Each of the partial derivatives can be estimated, at least roughly, including the increase in sticker price of the vehicle. There are no conceptual or data limitations on each agency examining the indirect effects of proposed regulations. If these interactions were taken into account, they would have a marked effect on regulations by tempering the current ones that have been formulated without consideration of the adverse effects on other attributes.

In practice, estimation of the partial derivatives is complicated by three factors. The first is that these derivatives are rarely constant. Thus, the magnitude of the interaction will depend on the point at which it is evaluated. This fact complicates estimation and calculation but poses no conceptual difficulty. The second is that technology is changing; thus, estimates are generally out of date as soon as they are made. There is little to be done about this complication, except to rely on a combination of out-of-date estimates and guesses about technological change. The third is that the regulations themselves are a major force shaping technological change. Emissions control standards awoke the moribund area of research on engine technology. Unfortunately, the cost of emissions regulation has been increased by congressional deadlines designed to force the development of new technology. While progress would surely have been slower without the pressure, the cost of such jerry-rigged solutions as the 1974 model emissions control suggests that cheaper ways must be found to provide the incentives for technological advances.

One way to do the maximization would be to approximate $\partial f/\partial x$ by dollar estimates of the value of saving lives, gallons of fuel, emissions of pollutants into the air, etc. With estimates of the other partial derivatives, this would provide at least a rough characterization of the sets of equations. For example, let us assume that the social value of saving a life ($\partial f/\partial x$) is \$500,000; the number of fatality equivalents saved by the current set of safety features is 15,800 ($\partial x/\partial w$); the social value of saving a gallon of gasoline is \$1.50 ($\partial f/\partial y$); the amount of gasoline "saved" by the additional 200 pounds of safety features is 22 pounds per car per year, or −2.42 billion gallons per year for the fleet ($\partial y/\partial w$); the social "value" of an additional dollar of price is −\$1 ($\partial f/\partial p$); and the additional annual cost of the safety features is \$50 per car or \$5.5 billion for the entire fleet ($\partial p/\partial w$). Neglecting the effect of the safety features on performance, Eq. (3) can be rewritten as (5a) by substituting the numerical values for each partial derivative:

$$.5 \times 10^6 \times 15,8000 - \$1.50 \times 2.42 \times 10^9 - \$1 \times 5.5 \times 10^9 \quad (5a)$$

Then we obtain

$$7.9 \times 10^9 - \$3.63 \times 10^9 - \$5.5 \times 10^9. \quad (5b)$$

Here, (5b) implies that neglecting secondary effects (the middle term), benefits exceed costs; indeed, the equation implies that additional safety features appear warranted. However, the middle term tips the balance the opposite way, indicating that the safety features are too expensive.

It would not be difficult to go on to flesh out the entire set of equations. However, rather than using numerical values for the partial derivatives, functional forms would have to be used since the optimal solution is likely to be somewhat removed from the current set of regulations and technology.

4. MAKING SLEEPWEAR FIRE RESISTANT

About a decade ago, Congress learned of a few incidents in which children had been severely burned because their sleepwear had caught fire and proved highly inflammable [1,9]. Upon investigation, it was found that fabrics that look and feel soft, precisely those characteristics desired for children's sleepwear, are highly flammable. Without establishing that this was a major hazard, that is, that more than a few children each year were affected, the Consumer Product Safety Commission (CPSC) acted to reduce the flammability of children's sleepwear.

Manufacturers were faced with a difficult choice. Sleepwear of about the same cost could be made flame resistant by changing the weave and fabric; unfortunately this made it feel and look less soft. Alternatively, more expensive fabrics and weaves could be used to produce sleepwear that looked and felt soft, but only at an increase in cost. If these were the only choices, CPSC would have had to look more deeply into the number of injuries that would be prevented each year and the additional cost of the less flammable sleepwear.

However, manufacturers discovered they could add a chemical, "tris" [i.e., tris(hydroxymethyl)aminomethane], to current fabrics to reduce flammability significantly. They did so, thereby satisfying the regulation at little cost. Unfortunately, not only was tris found to be carcinogenic in laboratory animals, it was also absorbed through the skin. Thus, a few children each year were being saved from bad burns at the cost of exposing all children to carcinogens.

Neither the manufacturers nor CPSC had done much testing of the toxic properties of tris. A chemical added to children's sleepwear could pose a health risk through contact with the child, through being sucked out of the fabric by the child, by contact with the mother, or by giving off fumes while being stored or cleaned.

There are many desirable properties for sleepwear. It should be attractive, soft, durable, nonflammable, nontoxic, and inexpensive. The regulatory process examined at most three of these attributes: softness, flammability, and price. Toxicity was considered only through the particular form of carcinogenicity. Few other toxic properties are ever investigated. Attractiveness and durability were not considered. The failure of the CPSC to consider all the relevant attributes simultaneously led to a situation where it seems likely that more harm was posed to children after regulation than before. Thus, suboptimization need not just be costly—it can also be dangerous. Before regulating one attribute, flammability, CPSC must examine the secondary effects of flammability on attractiveness, durability, softness, toxicity, and price.

5. UNLEADED GASOLINE

Airborne lead, primarily from tetraethyl lead used to raise octane in gasoline, is a major pollutant and has been subject to EPA regulation.[2] In addition to problems from the emission of lead, the primary technology for controlling automobile emissions is a catalyst that, in its current sophisticated version, both oxidizes carbon monoxide and hydrocarbons and reduces nitrogen dioxide. Unfortunately, even tiny amounts of lead in the gasoline poison the catalyst, making it totally ineffective. Thus, since the mid-1970s, EPA has ordered gasoline stations to offer unleaded gasoline and has designed a narrow gas tank opening for all cars requiring unleaded gasoline so that the standard size nozzle will not fit.

If tetraethyl lead cannot be added to gasoline to increase octane, additional refining is necessary, which both increases cost and uses energy. In particular, unleaded gasoline requires about 5 percent more petroleum input than leaded gasoline. Motorists are currently offered 87 octane unleaded gasoline at about 10 cents per gallon more than 89 octane leaded gasoline. Unleaded gasoline of the same octane would carry about a 15-cent premium.

Motorists are tempted to cheat by putting leaded gasoline into their cars, thus diabling their catalysts. Few states have inspection and maintenance programs that would catch the resulting high-emission cars, and it is doubtful that they would require owners to replace the catalysts even if they were discovered [4].

The suboptimization in this example is that EPA required that motorists be offered unleaded gasoline so that the catalysts would work. However, EPA had no control over the pricing of gasoline or even of the availability of unleaded gasoline. The U.S. Department of Energy (DOE) controls price and availability and is not concerned with curtailing emissions. The result is a strong set of incentives to use leaded gasoline, thereby disabling the catalyst. Alternatively, EPA has proposed to phase out the addition of lead to gasoline so that no leaded gasoline would be offered to the consumer. Short of that, the price of leaded gasoline could be raised so that it was actually more expensive for the same octane, thus inducing people to use unleaded gasoline.

This example is of suboptimization due not so much to the failure to see the secondary effects as to the separation of responsibility among agencies. EPA is responsible for emissions control, not ensuring the supply of gasoline, while DOE is responsible for the reverse. Wisdom calls for bringing both functions within the same agency.

6. IONIZING RADIATION FROM THE NUCLEAR FUEL CYCLE

Rather than deal with occupational and public health exposure to ionizing radiation from the entire fuel cycle, I will focus on general public exposure to radiation from reactors [5]. Here, radiation can come from two sources: the first is routine emissions of radionuclides and the second is emissions from accidents. A vast amount of attention has been given to the first source and to emissions from frequent small accidents; until recently, little attention has been given to releases from major accidents.

Ionizing radiation can cause cancer and genetic change. There is no known safe threshold for exposure, although "natural" (or background)

radiation provides one benchmark for comparison. It is possible to estimate the number of cancers and amount of genetic damage that would
occur from exposure to various levels of ionizing radiation [7].

Various ways can be found to reduce public exposure to radiation from
both the first and second category. Routine emissions can be reduced by
containing more of the long lived isotopes and by holding up the short
lived isotopes for a longer time. Obviously, both activities will increase
the cost of the electricity produced by a facility. Releases from accidents
are to be contained within one of three containment systems or, should
some radionuclides escape, exposure can be reduced by siting the reactor
in an area where few people reside. Additional layers of containment could
be added and siting could be more remote—although both activities would
increase the cost of the electricity.

During the early years, suboptimization led to considering only routine
emissions and small accidents, while ignoring the costs the regulations
imposed and the consequences of large accidents. More recently, large
accidents have been considered. However, the costs of the resulting regulations are not considered [8]. Thus, the Nuclear Regulatory Commission
has ordered changes which would reduce general population exposure to
ionizing radiation at a vast cost per cancer or genetic effect prevented.

7. CONCLUSION

The foregoing examples reveal myriad interactions and important suboptimization. Recommending that every regulatory issue be examined in its
full systems context is a counsel of despair. Regulatory decisions must
be timely; regulatory agencies have quite limited staff resources.

Instead, the issue is which problems have important interactions and
which interactions are first order? A major step forward would be to have
each agency identify the important interactions and to estimate their magnitude, at least roughly. For some major social issues, such as regulation
of the automobile, it may be possible to take the additional step of struc-
turing the systems problems—but even here, this will be difficult.

ACKNOWLEDGMENT

This research was supported by grants from the Sloan and Mellon and National
Science Foundations.

NOTES

1. See Lave [3].
2. See discussion in Lave [3].

REFERENCES

1. Blum, Arlene and Bruce N. Ames, "Flame-Retardant Additives as Possible Cancer Hazards." *Science* 195:17–23, 1977.
2. Lave, Lester B., *The Strategy of Social Regulation*. Washington, D.C.: Brookings Institution, 1981.
3. Lave, Lester B., "Conflicting Objectives in Regulating the Automobile." *Science* 212:893–899, 1981.
4. Lave, Lester B. and Gilbert S. Omenn, *Clearing the Air: Reforming the Clean Air Act*. Washington, D.C.: Brookings Institution, 1981.
5. Marnico, Ronald J., "An Examination of the Application of Quantitative Risk Analysis to Ionizing Radiation as Done by the EPA for 40 CFR 190." In Lester B. Lave (ed.), *Quantitative Risk Assessment for Regulation*. Washington, D.C.: Brookings Institution, in press.
6. Nash, Carl E., "A Regulator's View of Passive Restraints." In Robert W. Crandall and Lester B. Lave (eds.), *The Scientific Basis of Health and Safety Regulation*. Washington, D.C.: Brookings Institution, 1981.
7. National Academy of Sciences, Advisory Committee on the Biological Effects of Ionizing Radiations, *The Effects on Populations of Exposures to Low Levels of Ionizing Radiation*. Washington, D.C.: National Academy of Sciences, 1979.
8. Nuclear Regulatory Commission, *Safety Goals for Nuclear Power Plants: A Discussion Paper* (NUREG-0880). Washington, D.C.: Nuclear Regulatory Commission, 1982.
9. Prival, Michael J., Elena C. McCoy, Bezalel Gutter, and Herbert S. Rosenkranz, "Tris (2,3-Dibromopropyl) Phosphate: Mutagenicity of a Widely Used Flame Retardant." *Science* 195:76–78, 1977.
10. White, Lawrence J., "Air Pollution from Mobile Sources." Working Paper, New York University, 1981.

A COMPREHENSIVE BIBLIOGRAPHY ON MULTICRITERIA DECISION MAKING

Wolfram Stadler

ABSTRACT

This bibliography contains over 1700 references on MCDM, including more than 300 Russian citations with English title translations. In order to ensure ready accessibility no thesis, report, working paper, or preprint citations have been included in the Western literature; for the Russian literature completeness was the primary objective.

PART I. THE WESTERN LITERATURE

The bibliography has been compiled as an aid to those wishing to do research in MCDM. Every effort has been made to include all relevant citations, and the author regrets any inadvertent omissions which might have occured.

Multicriteria decision making and multicriteria optimization go hand in hand, since one obviously would like to obtain the best possible decision in any situation. These subjects have their origin in mathematical economics, in the work of Edgeworth and Pareto, whose approaches generally yielded an infinite number of optima. The usual scalarization to achieve a unique optimum has its roots in the early work of Marshall and Pigou on welfare theory. The subject branched out again with the inception of game theory by Borel. Today's form of these topics may be traced to Koopmans, who introduced the notion of the efficient point set, and to Kuhn and Tucker, who first gave a mathematically rigorous treatment of the vector maximum problem. The present treatment of these problems in abstract spaces would not be possible without the early work of Cantor and Hausdorff dealing with abstract ordered sets. Thus, although an attempt was made to include only material which pertains directly to MCDM, some digression into all of these areas could not be avoided; however, no effort was made to conduct specific literature searches in areas such as game theory or welfare theory.

In compiling the citations, accessibility of the citations to an international audience became an overriding concern. Abbreviations of journal titles were avoided; in many cases it was possible to establish the meaning of an abbreviation by consulting Alkire's *Periodical Title Abbreviations* [1] and *Ulrich's International Periodical Directory* [2]. Reports, working papers, and dissertations are not cited for the same reason. It is hoped that this approach will spare the reader the frustration of trying to determine, for example, that "Ann. Univ. Sci. Budapest., Sec. Math." means "Annales Universitatis Scientiarum Budapestiensis, Sectio Mathematica," or that the acronym IIASA stands for "International Institute for Applied System Analysis."

Clearly, this compilation strongly depended upon previous bibliographies as sources and checks. Stadler [3], Achilles et al. [4], and Zeleny [5] were particularly useful in this respect; Stadler [3] also includes reports, working papers, and dissertations, along with citations concerning related material—a total of more than 2,900 entries.

PART II. THE RUSSIAN LANGUAGE LITERATURE

There seems to be a special need to make Western readers aware of the Russian efforts in MCDM; the citations were therefore kept as complete as possible. Conversely, it is apparent from the primary sources of the Russian literature [4,6,7] that they seem almost unaware of the extensive Western literature. Most of these references are given in Cyrillic. In order to make this literature accessible to the Western reader, all of the titles have been translated and the transliteration scheme of the U.S. Library of Congress has been used. To allow an easy check of the citations in the Cyrillic bibliographies, the references in this section are given in Cyrillic alphabetical order. Unfortunately, it was not possible to ascertain the meaning of many of the abbreviations, and, with few exceptions, they were thus maintained as found in previous citations. As an additional aid to the reader, translations of some frequently used Russian phrases and words have also been included:

Avtomaticheskoe Upravlenie	Automatic Control
Avtomatika i Telemekhanika	Automation and Remote Control
Avtomatika i Vychislitelnaĩa Tekhnika	Automation and Computer Engineering
Avtoreferat Kandidatskoi Dissertatsii	Dissertation Abstracts
Chislennye Metody Neline ĭnogo Programmirovaniia	Numerical Methods in Nonlinear Programming
Differentsial'nye i Integralnye Uravnenĩia	Differential and Integral Equations
Differentsial'nye Igry s Nenulevoĭ Summoĭ	Differential Games with Non-Zero Sum
Doklady Akademiĭ Nauk SSSR	Proceedings of the Academy of Science USSR
Isvestiĩa Akademiĭ Nauk SSSR	Reports of the Academy of Science USSR
Kibernetika	Cybernetics
Mashinostroenie	Mechanical Engineering
Mathematicheskie Metody v Soĩsialnykh Naukakh	Mathematical Methods in the Social Sciences
Prilozhenĩia	Application

Referaty Dokladov [ ]	Abstracts of the [no.] All-Union
Vsesoi͡uznogo Soveshchanii͡a po	Conference on
Issledovanie Opera͡tsii	Operations Research
Matematike i Mekhanike	Mathematics and Mechanics
Problemam Upravlenii͡a	Control Problems
Teorii Igr	Game Theory
Slozhnyĭ	complex
Slozhnye Sistemy Upravlenii͡a	Complex Control Systems
Technicheska͡i͡a Kibernetika	Engineering Cybernetics
Upravlenie Dinamicheskimi	Control of Dynamic Systems
Sistemami	

The terms "Referaty Dokladov," "Tezisy," and "Tezisy Dokladov" all were translated as "Abstracts."

ACKNOWLEDGMENTS

The author wishes to thank Professor E. Axelrad for his valuable help in translating the Russian titles and to Mrs. Leila Stadler for her patience in typing the original manuscript from which these excerpts were taken.

REFERENCES

1. Alkire, L. G. Jr., *Periodical Title Abbreviations*, Second Edition, Gale Research Company, Book Tower, Detroit, Michigan, 1977.
2. *Ulrich's International Periodical Directory*, Nineteenth Edition (A Bowker Serials Bibliography), R. R. Bowker Company, A Xerox Publishing Company, New York and London, 1980.
3. Stadler, W., "A Comprehensive Bibliography on Multicriteria Decision Making and Related Areas," Progress Report under Contract No. NSF ECS–7813931, Department of Mechanical Engineering, University of California, Berkeley, California, 1981.
4. Achilles, A., K. H. Elster, and R. Nehse, *Bibliographie zur Vektoroptimierung* (*Theorie und Anwendung*), Optimization, Vol. 10, No. 2, pp. 277–321, 1979.
5. Zeleny, M., *Multiple Criteria Decision Making*, McGraw-Hill, New York, New York, 1982.
6. Salukvadze, M. E., *Vector Optimization Problems in Control Theory*, [in Russian], Metznierba, Tiflis, Republic of Georgia, USSR, 1975; English translation by J. L. Casti, Academic Press, New York, New York, 1979.
7. Tyni͡anskiĭ, N. T., and V. I. Zhukovskiĭ, *Non-Zero Sum Differential Games* (*Cooperative Version*), [in Russian], Itogi Nauki i Tekhniki, VINITI Seria Matematicheskiĭ Analiz, Moscow, No. 17, pp. 1–112, 1979.

PART I. THE WESTERN LITERATURE

Abad, P. and D. J. Sweeney, "An Interactive Algorithm for Optimal Control of a System with Multiple Criteria," *International Journal of Systems Science*, Vol. 8, No. 2, pp. 221–229, 1977.

Abelson, R. P. and J. W. Tukey, "Efficient Utilization of Non-Numerical Information in Quantitative Analysis: General Theory and the Case of Simple Order," *Annals of Mathematical Statistics*, Vol. 34, pp. 1347–1369, 1963.

Abrams, R., "Optimization Models for Regional Air Pollution Control," *Mathematical Analysis of Decision Problems in Ecology*, edited by A. W. Charnes and W. R. Lynn, Springer-Verlag, Berlin, New York, New York, pp. 116–137, 1975.

Achilles, A., K. H. Elster and R. Nehse, "Bibliographie zur Vektor-optimierung (Theorie und Anwendungen)," *Optimization*, Vol. 10, No. 2, pp. 277–321, 1979.

Adams, B. H. and C. E. Gearing, "Determining an Optimal Set of Research Experiments," *IEEE Transactions on Engineering Management*, Vol. EM-21, No. 1, pp. 29–39, February 1974.

Adams, E. W., "Elements of a Theory of Inexact Measurement," *Philosophy of Science*, Vol. 32, pp. 205–228, 1965.

Adams, E. W., "On the Nature and Purpose of Measurement," *Synthese*, Vol. 16, pp. 125–169, 1966.

Adams, E. W. and R. F. Fagot, "A Model of Riskless Choice," *Behavioral Science*, Vol. 4, pp. 1–10, 1959.

Adulbhan, P. and M. T. Tabucanon, "Bicriterion Linear Programming," *Computers and Operations Research*, Vol. 4, No. 2, pp. 147–153, 1977.

Agarwala, R., "Tests and Uses of Macro-Econometric Models: A Critical Survey," *Economics of Planning*, Vol. 9, pp. 235–257, 1969.

Agnew, N. H., R. A. Agnew, J. Rasmussen and K. R. Smith, "An Application of Chance Constrained Programming to Portfolio Selection in a Casualty Insurance Firm," *Management Science*, Vol. 15, pp. 512–520, 1969.

Akilov, G. P. and S. S. Kutateladze, *Ordered Vector Spaces* [in Russian], Novosibirsk, USSR, 1978.

Albers, S., "An Extended Algorithm for Optimal Product Positioning," *European Journal of Operational Research*, Vol. 3, pp. 222–231, 1979.

Alessio, F. J., "Multiple Criteria in Environmental Control: Use of Economic Maximization Rules to Determine Relative Standards," *Multiple Criteria Decision Making*, edited by J. C. Cochrane and M. Zeleny, University of South Carolina Press, Columbia, South Carolina, pp. 544–549, 1973.

Alexandre, A. and J. P. Barde, "L'Implantation des Aéroports—Peut On en Evaluer les Coûts et les Avantages?", *Analyse et Prévision*, Vol. 11, pp. 385–420, 1973.

Alexandrov, A. A., M. V. Petrova and K. T. Tsaturian, "Quantitative Comparisons of Alternative Variants or Strategies in Control Problems" [in Russian], *Proceedings of the 5th All-Union Conference on Control*, Part 1, Nauka, Moscow, USSR, 1971.

Allais, M., "La Psychologie de l'Homme Rationnel Devant la Risque, la Theorie et l'Experience," *J. Soc. Statist.*, Vol. 9c, pp. 47–73, 1953.

Allais, M., "Les Théories de l'Equilibre Economique Général et de l'Efficacité Maximale," *Revue d'Economie Politique*, Vol. 3, pp. 331–409, May–June 1971.

Allgaier, R., "Zur Lösung von Zielkonflikten," *Quantitative Methoden der Unternehmungsplanung*, Vol. 3, Anton Hain Verlag, Meisenheim am Glan, Germany, 1976.

Almogy, Y. and O. Levin, "A Class of Fractional Programming Problems," *Operations Research*, Vol. 19, pp. 57–67, 1971.

Anderson, N. H., "A Simple Model for Information Integration," *Theories of Cognitive Consistency: A Sourcebook*, edited by R. P. Abelson, E. Aronson, W. J. McGuire, T. M. Newcomb, M. J. Rosenberg and P. H. Tannenbaum, Rand McNally, Chicago, Illinois, 1968.

Andjelic, M., "On a Matrix Riccati Equation of Cooperative Control," *International Journal of Control*, Vol. 23, No. 3, pp. 427–432, 1976.

Andry, A. H., "Pareto Optimality and Systems Governed by Partial Differential Equations," *Proceedings of the IEEE Conference on Decisions and Control included in the 15th Symposium on Adaptive Processes*, Clearwater, Florida, pp. 107–110, 1976.

Aneja, Y. P., V. Aggarwal and K. P. K. Nair, "Maximization of the Vector-Flow in Multicommodity Networks," *INFOR*, Vol. 17, No. 3, pp. 276–286, 1979.

Aneja, Y. P. and K. P. K. Nair, "Bicriteria Transportation Problem," *Management Science*, Vol. 25, No. 1, pp. 73–78, 1979.

Angyris, C., *Integrating the Individual and the Organization*, John Wiley and Sons, New York, New York, 1964.

Aoki, M., J. S. Chipman and P. C. Fishburn, "A Selected Bibliography of Works Relating to the Theory of Preferences, Utility, and Demand," *Preferences, Utility, and Demand*, edited by J. S. Chipman, L. Hurwicz, M. K. Richter and H. F. Sonnenschein, Harcourt, Brace and Jovanovich, New York, New York, pp. 437–492, 1971.

Aoki, Y., K. Kobayashi, K. Kawamo, A. Tani and N. Sugimo, "Multi-objective Optimization Model for Transportation System Analysis," *Proceedings, 8th IEEE Conference on Cybernetics and Society*, Tokyo-Kyoto, Japan, November 3–7, 1978, pp. 772–775, 1978.

Aonuma, T., "An Algorithm for Vectoroptimization Problems; an Application to Generalized Linear Optimization Problems" [in Japanese], *Proceedings of the Kobe College of Commerce*, Vol. 18, No. 2, pp. 120–135, 1966.

Armstrong, R. D. and W. D. Cook, "Goal Programming Models for Assigning Search and Rescue Aircraft to Bases," *The Journal of the Operational Research Society*, Vol. 30, No. 6, pp. 555–562, 1979.

Armstrong, W. E., "A Note on the Theory of Consumer's Behavior," *Oxford Economic Papers*, Vol. 2, pp. 119–122, 1950.

Arrow, K. J., "A Difficulty in the Concept of Social Welfare," *Journal of Political Economy*, Vol. 58, No. 4, pp. 328–346, August 1950.

Arrow, K. J., "Alternative Proof of the Substitution Theorem for Leontief Models in the General Case," *Activity Analysis of Production and Allocation*, edited by T. C. Koopmans, John Wiley and Sons, New York, New York, pp. 155–164, 1951.

Arrow, K. J., "An Extension of the Basic Theorems of Classical Welfare Economics," *Proceedings of the Second Berkeley Symposium on Mathematical Statistics and Probability*, Berkeley, California, pp. 507–532, 1951.

Arrow, K. J., "Rational Choice Functions and Orderings," *Economica*, Vol. 26, (NS), 1959.

Arrow, K. J., "The Economic Implications of Learning by Doing," *Review of Economic Studies*, Vol. 29, pp. 155–173, 1962.

Arrow, K. J., *Social Choice and Individual Values*, First Edition 1951, Second Edition 1963, John Wiley and Sons, New York, New York.

Arrow, K. J., E. W. Barankin and D. Blackwell, "Admissible Points of Convex Sets," *Contributions to the Theory of Games II*, edited by H. W. Kuhn and A. W. Tucker, Princeton University Press, Princeton, New Jersey, 1953.

Arrow, K. J. and G. Debreu, "Existence of an Equilibrium for a Competitive Economy," *Econometrica*, Vol. 22, pp. 265–290, 1954.

Arrow, K. J. and F. H. Hahn, *General Competitive Analysis*, Holden Day, San Francisco, California, 1971.

Arrow, K. J., L. Hurwicz and H. Uzawa (eds.), *Studies in Linear and Nonlinear Programming*, Stanford University Press, Stanford, California, 1958; second printing, Oxford University Press, London, England, 1964.

Arrow, K. J., S. Karlin and P. Suppes (eds.), *Mathematical Methods in the Social Sciences*, Stanford University Press, Stanford, California, 1959.

Arrow, K. J. and T. Scitovsky (eds.), *Readings in Welfare Economics*, Irwin, Homewood, Illinois, 1969.

Arthur, J. L. and K. D. Lawrence, "A Multiple Goal Blending Problem," *Computers and Operations Research*, Vol. 7, No. 3, p. 125, 1980.

Arthur, J. L. and A. Ravindran, "An Efficient Goal Programming Algorithm Using Constraint Partitioning and Variable Elimination," *Management Science*, Vol. 24, No. 8, pp. 867–868, 1978.

Arthur, J. L. and A. Ravindran, "A Branch and Bound Algorithm with Constraint Partitioning for Integer Goal Programming Problems," *European Journal of Operational Research*, Vol. 4, No. 6, pp. 421–425, 1980.

Arthur, J. L. and A. Ravindran, "PAGP: A Partitioning Algorithm for (Linear) Goal Programming Problems," *ACM Transactions on Mathematical Software*, in press.

Ashton, D. J. and D. R. Atkins, "Multicriteria Programming for Financial Planning: Some Second Thoughts," *Multiple Criteria Analysis: Operational Methods*, edited by P. Nijkamp and J. Spronk, Gower Press, London, England, 1981.

Asimus, H. D., "De l'Optimisation à l'Analyse Multicritère: Le Modèle de Media Planning Automatisé: MOÏSE," *Metra*, Vol. 9, No. 4, pp. 531–558, 1970.

Athans, M. and H. Geering, "Necessary and Sufficient Conditions for Differentiable Nonscalar-Valued Functions to Attain Extrema," *IEEE Transactions on Automatic Control*, Vol. AC-18, No. 2, pp. 132–139, April 1973.

Attaway, L. D., "Criteria and the Measurement of Effectiveness," *System Analysis and Policy Planning*, edited by E. S. Quade and W. I. Boucher, Elsevier Publishing Company, New York, New York, pp. 54–80, 1968.

Aubin, J.-P., "A Pareto Minimum Principle," *Differential Games and Related Topics*, edited by H. K. Kuhn and G. P. Szegö, North-Holland Publishing Company, Amsterdam, Holland, pp. 147–175, 1971.

Aubin, J.-P., "Multi-Games and Decentralization in Management," *Multiple Criteria Decision Making*, edited by J. L. Cochrane and M. Zeleny, University of South Carolina Press, Columbia, South Carolina, pp. 544–549, 1973.

Aumann, R., "Measurable Utility and the Measurable Choice Theorem," *La Décision, Colloque Internationaux du Centre National Recherche Scientifique*, Paris, France, pp. 15–26, 1969.

Aumann, R. J., "Subjective Programming," *Human Judgments and Optimality*, edited by M. W. Shelly and G. L. Bryan, John Wiley and Sons, New York, New York, pp. 217–242, 1964.

Aumann, R. J., "A Survey of Cooperative Games Without Side Payments," *Essays in Mathematical Economics*, edited by M. Shubik, Princeton University Press, Princeton, New Jersey, pp. 3–27, 1967.

Aumann, R. J. and J. B. Kruskal, "The Coefficients in an Allocation Problem," *Naval Research Logistics Quarterly*, Vol. 5, pp. 111–123, 1958.

Aumann, R. J. and J. B. Kruskal, "Assigning Quantitative Values of Qualitative Factors in the Naval Electronics Problem, *Naval Research Logistics Quarterly*, Vol. 6, pp. 1–16, 1959.

Aumann, R. J. and M. Maschler, "The Bargaining Set for Cooperative Games," *Advances in Game Theory*, edited by M. Dresher, L. S. Shapley and A. W. Tucker, Annals of Mathematical Studies No. 52, Princeton University Press, Princeton, New Jersey, pp. 443–476, 1964.

Awerbuch, S., J. G. Ecker and W. A. Wallace, "A Note: Hidden Non-linearities in the Application of Goal Programming," *Management Science*, Vol. 22, No. 8, pp. 918–920, 1976.

Awerbuch, S. and W. Wallace, "A Goal-Setting and Evaluation Model for Community Development," *IEEE Transactions on Systems, Man, and Cybernetics*, Vol. SMC-7, No. 8, pp. 589–597, 1977.

Axelrod, R., "Schema Theory: An Information Processing Model of Perception and Cognition," *American Political Science Review*, Vol. 67, pp. 1248–1266, 1973.

Baas, J. M. and H. Kwakernaak, "Rating and Ranking of Multi-Aspect Alternative Using Fuzzy Sets," *Automatica*, Vol. 13, pp. 47–58, January 1977.

Bacopoulos, A., "Nonlinear Chebychev Approximation by Vectornorms," *Journal of Approximation Theory*, Vol. 2, pp. 79–84, 1969.

Bacopoulos, A. and I. Singer, "On Convex Vectorial Optimization in Linear Spaces," *Journal of Optimization Theory and Applications*, Vol. 21, No. 2, pp. 175–188, February 1977; Vol. 23, No. 3, pp. 473–476, November 1977.

Bacopoulos, A., G. Godini and I. Singer, "Infima of Sets in the Plane and Applications to Vectorial Optimization," *Revue Roumaine de Mathématiques Pures et Appliquées*, Vol. 23, pp. 343–360, 1978.

Baier, H., "Über Algorithmen zur Ermittlung und Charakterisierung Pareto-optimaler Lösungen bei Entwurfsaufgaben Elastischer Tragwerke," *Zeitschrift für Angewandte Mathematik und Mechanik*, Vol. 57, pp. 318–320, 1977.

Bailey, A. D. and W. J. Boe, "Goal and Resource Transfers in the Multigoal Organization," *Accounting Review*, pp. 559–573, July 1976.

Bajgier, S. M., et al., "Multiattribute Risk/Benefit Analysis of Citizen Attitudes Towards Societal Issues Involving Technology," *Multiple Criteria Problem Solving: Proceedings, Buffalo, N. Y. (U.S.A.), 1977*, Springer-Verlag, Berlin-New York, New York, pp. 424–448, 1978.

Bamba, E., "Constrained Optimization Under Vector-Valued Performance Index," *Systems and Controls*, Vol. 16, No. 5, pp. 405–418, 1972.

Bammi, D. and D. Bammi, "Land Use Planning: An Optimizing Model," *Omega*, Vol. 3, No. 5, pp. 583–594, 1975.

Bammi, De. and Da. Bammi, "Development of a Comprehensive Land Use Plan by Means of a Multiple Objective Mathematical Programming Model," *Interfaces*, Vol. 9, No. 2, pp. 50–63, 1979.

Banker, R. L. and S. K. Gupta, "A Process for Hierarchical Decision Making with Multiple Objectives," *Omega*, Vol. 8, No. 2, pp. 137–149, 1980.

Baptistella, L. F. B. and A. Ollero, "Fuzzy Methodologies for Interactive Multicriteria Optimization," *IEEE Transactions on Systems, Man, and Cybernetics*, Vol. SMC-10, No. 7, pp. 355–365, July 1980.

Barber, G., "Land-Use Plan Design via Interactive Multiple-Objective Programming," *Environment and Planning*, Vol. 8, pp. 625–636, 1976.

Barbut, M., "Note sur les Ordres Totaux à Distance Minimum d'une Relation Binaire Donnée," *Mathématiques et Sciences Humaines*, Vol. 17, 1966.

Baron, D. P., "Stochastic Programming and Risk Aversion," *Multiple Criteria Decision Making*, edited by J. L. Cochrane and M. Zeleny, University of South Carolina Press, Columbia, South Carolina, pp. 124–140, 1973.

Barone, E., "Il Ministero della Produzione nello Stato Colletivista," *Giornale degli Economisti e Revista di Statistica*, Vol. 37, pp. 267–293 and pp. 391–414, 1908; translation published under the title, "The Ministry of Production in the Collectivist State," edited by F. A. Hayek, *Collectivist Economic Planning*, London, England, 1935.

Barrett, J. H., *Individual Goals and Organizational Objectives: A Study of Integration Mechanism*, University of Michigan Press, Ann Arbor, Michigan, 1970.

Barrodale, J. and A. Young, "Algorithms for Best L_1 and L_∞ Linear Approximations on a Discrete Set," *Numerische Mathematik*, Vol. 8, pp. 295–306, 1966.

Barron, F. H. and H. B. Person, "Assessment of Multiplicative Utility Functions via Holistic Judgments," *Organizational Behavior and Human Performance*, Vol. 24, No. 2, pp. 147–166, 1979.

Bartel, D. L. and R. W. Marks, "The Optimum Design of Mechanical Systems with Competing Design Objectives," *ASME Transactions—Journal of Engineering for Industry*, Vol. 96, Ser. B, No. 1, pp. 171–179, 1974.

Barton, R. F., "Models with More Than One Criterion—or Why Not Build Implementation into the Model," *Interfaces*, Vol. 7, No. 4, pp. 71–75, August 1977.

Basar, T., "A New Dynamic Model for Duopoly Markets," *Proceedings, Eighth Princeton Conference on Information Sciences and Systems*, March 1974.

Basar, T., "Decentralized Multicriteria Optimization of Linear Stochastic Systems," *IEEE Transactions on Automatic Control*, Vol. 23, pp. 233–243, 1978.

Basile, G. and T. L. Vincent, "On the Many-Persons Cooperative Differential Game," *Proceedings, Third Hawaii International Conference on Systems Science*, Honolulu, Hawaii, 1970; Western Periodicals, North Hollywood, California, pp. 593–596, 1970.

Basile, G. and T. L. Vincent, "Absolutely Cooperative Solution for a Linear Multiplayer Differential Game," *Journal of Optimization Theory and Applications*, Vol. 6, No. 1, pp. 41–46, July 1970.

Bassler, J. F., et al., "Multiple Criteria Dominance Models: An Empirical Study of Investment Preferences," *Multiple Criteria Problem Solving: Proceedings, Buffalo, N. Y. (U.S.A.), 1977*, edited by S. Zionts, Springer-Verlag, Berlin-New York, New York, pp. 494–508, 1978.

Bauer, V. and M. Wegener, "Simulation, Evaluation, and Conflict Analysis in Urban Planning," *IEEE Proceedings*, Vol. 63, pp. 405–413, 1975.

Bauer, V. and M. Wegener, "A Community Information Feedback System with Multiattribute Utilities," *Conflicting Objectives in Decisions*, edited by D. E. Bell, R. L. Keeney and H. Raiffa, John Wiley and Sons, New York, New York, pp. 323–357, 1977.

Baum, S. and R. C. Carlson, "Multi-Goal Optimization in Managerial Science," *Omega*, Vol. 2, No. 5, pp. 607–623, 1974.

Baumgartner, T., T. R. Burns, P. DeVille and L. D. Meeker, "A System Model of Conflict and Change in Planning Systems with Multi-Level, Multiple Objective Evaluation and Decision Making," *General Systems Yearbook*, edited by A. Rapoport, Society for General Systems Research, Washington, D. C., pp. 167–184, 1975.

Baumol, W. J., "The Firm and Its Objectives," *Readings in Managerial Economics*, edited by K. S. Palda, Prentice-Hall, Englewood Cliffs, New Jersey, 1973.

Baumol, W. J. and D. F. Bradford, "Optimal Departures from Marginal Cost Pricing," *American Economic Review*, Vol. 55, pp. 265–283, 1970.

Becker, S. and S. Siegel, "Utility of Grades: Level of Aspiration in a Decision Theory Context," *Journal of Experimental Psychology*, Vol. 55, pp. 81–85, 1958.

Beckwith, N. E. and D. R. Lehmann, "The Importance of Differential Weights in Multiple Attribute Models of Consumer Attitude," *Journal of Marketing Research*, Vol. 10, pp. 141–145, May 1973.

Bedel'baev, A. A., J. A. Dubov and B. L. Smul'jan, "Adaptive Decision Procedures in Multicriterion Problems," *Automation and Remote Control*, Vol. 37, No. 1, pp. 76–85, 1976.

Beedles, W. L., "A Micro-Econometric Investigation of Multiobjective Firms," *Journal of Finance*, Vol. 32, pp. 1217–1234, 1977.

Beenhakker, H. L., "Optimization Versus Suboptimization," *The International Journal of Production Research*, Vol. 3, No. 4, pp. 317–325, 1964.

Beeson, R. M. and W. S. Meisel, "Optimization of Complex Systems with Respect to Multiple Criteria," *Proceedings, Joint National Conference on Major Systems*, Anaheim, California, pp. 144–149, October 25–29, 1971.

Behringer, F. A., "Eine Eindeutigkeitsaussage über ein vektorielles Tschebyscheffausgleichproblem," *Zeitschrift für Angewandte Mathematik und Mechanik*, Vol. 52, pp. T233–T236, 1972.

Behringer, F. A., "Tschebyscheff-Ausgleich überbestimmter Systeme linearer Gleichungen—Eindeutigkeit ohne Haarsche Bedingung durch lexikographischen Ausgleich," presented at GAMM Conference, Graz, Switzerland, 1976; to appear in *Zeitschrift für Angewandte Mathematik und Mechanik*.

Behringer, F. A., "Quasikonkav-quasikonvexe Spiele unter Ausnützung gegnerischer Schwächen und lexikographische Optimierung," *Mathematische Operationsforschung und Statistik*, Serie Optimization, Vol. 8, pp. 75–88, 1977.

Behringer, F. A., "Lexicographic Quasiconcave Multiobjective Programming," *Zeitschrift für Operations Research*, Vol. 21, No. 3, pp. 103–116, 1977.

Behringer, F. A., "Lexikographische Optimierung und Zweipersonennull summenspiele unter Ausnützung von Fehlern des Gegners," *Zeitschrift für Angewandte Mathematik und Mechanik*, Vol. 57, No. 6, pp. 345–346, 1977.

Belenson, S. M. and K. C. Kapur, "An Algorithm for Solving Multicriterion Linear Programming Problems with Examples," *Operational Research Quarterly*, Vol. 24, No. 1, pp. 65–77, March 1973.

Bell, D. E., "Interpolation Independence," *Multiple Criteria Problem Solving*, edited by S. Zionts, Lecture Notes in Economics and Mathematical Systems No. 155, Springer-Verlag, Berlin-New York, New York, 1978.

Bell, D. E., "Multiattribute Utility Functions: Decompositions Using Interpolation," *Management Science*, Vol. 25, No. 8, pp. 744–753, 1979.

Bell, D. E., R. L. Keeney and H. Raiffa (eds.), *Conflicting Objectives*, John Wiley and Sons, New York, New York, 1977.

Bellmore, M., H. J. Greenberg and J. J. Jarvis, "Generalized Penalty-Function Concepts in Mathematical Optimization," *Operations Research*, Vol. 18, No. 2, pp. 229–252, 1970.

Benayoun, R., J. de Montgolfier, J. Tergny and O. I. Larichev, "Linear Programming with Multiple Objective Functions; STEP Method (STEM)," *Mathematical Programming*, Vol. 1, No. 3, pp. 366–375, March 1971.

Benayoun, R., O. I. Larichev, J. de Montgolfier and J. Tergny, "Linear Programming with Multiple Objective Functions; the Method of Constraints," *Automation and Remote Control*, Vol. 32, No. 8, pp. 1257–1264, 1971.

Benayoun, R. and J. Tergny, "Critères Multiples en Programmation Mathématique: Une Solution dans le Cas Linéaire," *Revue Française d'Automatique, Informatique et de Recherche Opérationnelle*, Vol. 3, No. 5-2, pp. 31–56, 1969.

Benayoun, R., J. Tergny and D. Keuneman, "Mathematical Programming with Multiobjective Functions: A Solution by P.O.P. (Progressive Orientation Procedure)," *Revue Metra*, Vol. 9, No. 2, pp. 279–299, June 1970.

Bender, P. J., "Nonlinear Programming in Normed Linear Spaces," *Journal of Optimization Theory and Applications*, Vol. 24, No. 2, pp. 263–286, February 1978.

Ben-Israel, A., A. Ben-Tal and A. Charnes, "Necessary and Sufficient Conditions for a Pareto-optimum in Convex Programming," *Econometrica*, Vol. 45, No. 4, pp. 811–822, 1977.

Bennett, J. F. and W. L. Hays, "Multidimensional Unfolding: Determining the Dimensionality of Ranked Preference Data," *Psychometrika*, Vol. 25, pp. 27–43, 1960.

Benson, H. P., "Existence of Efficient Solutions for Vector Maximization Problems," *Journal of Optimization Theory and Applications*, Vol. 26, No. 4, pp. 569–580, December 1978.

Benson, H. P., "Vector Maximization with Two Objective Functions," *Journal of Optimization Theory and Applications*, Vol. 28, No. 2, pp. 253–257, June 1979.

Benson, H. P. and T. L. Morin, "The Vector Maximization Problem: Proper Efficiency and Stability," *SIAM Journal on Applied Mathematics*, Vol. 32, No. 1, pp. 64–72, 1977.

Benson, R. G., "Interactive Goal Programming Without Weights or Priorities," *Multiple*

Criteria Decision Making, edited by M. K. Starr and M. Zeleny, TIMS Studies in the Management Sciences, Vol. 6, North-Holland Publishing Company, Amsterdam, Holland, pp. 302–303, 1977.

Ben-Tal, A. and S. Zlobec, "Convex Programming and the Lexicographic Multicriteria Problem," *Mathematische Operationsforschung und Statistik*, Serie Optimization, Vol. 8, pp. 61–73, 1977.

Ben-Tal, A., "Characterization of Pareto and Lexicographic Optimal Solutions," *Multiple Criteria Decision Making Theory and Application*, edited by G. Fandel and T. Gal, Springer-Verlag, Berlin-New York, New York, pp. 1–11, 1980.

Benveniste, M., "Testing for Complete Efficiency in a Vector Maximization Problem," *Mathematical Programming*, Vol. 12, No. 2, pp. 285–288, 1977.

Bereanu, B., "Large Group Decision Making with Multiple Criteria," *Multiple Criteria Decision Making*, edited by H. Thiriez and S. Zionts, Lecture Notes in Economics and Mathematical Systems No. 130, Springer-Verlag, Berlin-New York, New York, pp. 87–102, 1976.

Bergson, A., "A Reformulation of Certain Aspects of Welfare Economics," *Quarterly Journal of Economics*, Vol. 52, pp. 310–334, 1938.

Bergson, A., *Socialist Economics, a Survey of Contemporary Economics*, Vol. 1, edited by H. S. Ellis, Irwin, Homewood, Illinois, pp. 412–447, 1948.

Bergstresser, K., A. Charnes and P. L. Yu, "Generalization of Domination Structures and Nondominated Solutions in Multicriteria Decision Making," *Journal of Optimization Theory and Applications*, Vol. 18, No. 1, pp. 3–13, January 1976.

Bergstresser, K. and P. L. Yu, "Domination Structures and Multicriteria Problems in N-Person Games," *Theory and Decision*, Vol. 8, No. 1, pp. 5–48, 1977.

Berhold, M., "Multiple Criteria Decision Making in Consumer Behavior," *Multiple Criteria Decision Making*, edited by J. L. Cochrane and M. Zeleny, University of South Carolina Press, Columbia, South Carolina, pp. 570–576, 1973.

Bernard, G. and M. L. Besson, "Douze Méthodes d'Analyse Multicritère," *Revue Française d'Automatique, Informatique et de Recherche Opérationelle*, Vol. 5, No. 5-3, pp. 19–64, 1971.

Bernardo, J. and J. M. Blin, "A Mathematical Model of Consumer Choice Among Multi-Attributed Brands," *Journal of Consumer Research*, Vol. 4, No. 2, pp. 111–118, September 1977.

Bernardo, J. and H. Lanser, "A Capital Budgeting Decision Model with Subjective Criteria," *Journal of Financial and Quantitative Analysis*, Vol. 12, No. 2, pp. 261–275, 1977.

Bernardo, J. J., "A Linear Assignment Formulation of the Multi-Attributed Purchase Decision," *Journal of Business Administration*, Vol. 7, No. 2, pp. 23–44, May 1976.

Bernstein, S. J. and G. W. Mellon, "Multi-Dimensional Considerations in the Evaluation of Urban Policy," *Multiple Criteria Decision Making*, edited by J. L. Cochrane and M. Zeleny, University of South Carolina Press, Columbia, South Carolina, pp. 530–543, 1973.

Bernstein, S. J., W. G. Mellon and L. E. Hoxie, "The Multi-Dimensional Allocation of Social Resources: The Assignment of Electromagnetic Spectrum," *The Journal of Socio-Economic Planning Science*, Vol. 5, pp. 449–466, 1971.

Bertier, P. and J. de Montgolfier, "Comment Choisir en Tenant Compte de Points de Vue Non Commensurable," *Analyse et Prévision*, Vol. 11, pp. 521–548, 1971.

Bertier, P. and J. de Montgolfier, "On Multicriteria Analysis: An Application to a Forest Management Problem," *Revue Metra*, Vol. 13, pp. 33–45, March 1974.

Bessler, S. A. and A. F. Veinott, "Optimal Policy for Dynamic Multiechelon Inventory Models," *Naval Research Logistics Quarterly*, Vol. 13, pp. 355–389, 1966.

Bettman, J., "A Graph Theory Approach to Comparing Consumer Information Processing Models," *Management Science*, Vol. 18, pp. P114–P129, Dec. 1971.

Bidlingmaier, J., *Zielkonflikte und Zielkompromisse im unternehmerischen Entscheidungsbereich*, Wiesbaden, Germany, 1968.

Bidlingmaier, J., "Unternehmerische Zielkonflikte und Ansätze zu ihrer Lösung," *Zeitschrift für Betriebswirtschaft*, Vol. 38, No. 3, pp. 149–176, 1968.

Bilkey, J. W., "Empirical Evidence Regarding Business Goals," *Multiple Criteria Decision Making*, edited by J. L. Cochrane and M. Zeleny, University of South Carolina Press, Columbia, South Carolina, pp. 613–634, 1973.

Billera, L. J., "Some Recent Results in n-Person Game Theory," *Mathematical Programming*, Vol. 1, No. 1, pp. 58–67, October 1971.

Billera, L. J. and R. E. Bixby, "A Characterization of Pareto Surfaces," *Proceedings of the American Mathematical Society*, Vol. 41, No. 1, pp. 261–267, November 1973.

Billera, L. J. and R. E. Bixby, "A Characterization of Polyhedral Market Games," *International Journal of Game Theory*, Vol. 2, No. 4, pp. 253–261, 1973.

Billera, L. J. and R. E. Bixby, "Pareto Surfaces of Complexity 1," *SIAM Journal on Applied Mathematics*, Vol. 30, No. 1, pp. 81–89, 1976.

Birkin, J. S. and J. S. Ford, "The Quantity/Quality Dilemma: The Impact of a Zero Defects Program," *Multiple Criteria Decision Making*, edited by J. L. Cochrane and M. Zeleny, University of South Carolina Press, Columbia, South Carolina, pp. 517–529, 1973.

Bischoff, M., "Multivariable Zielsysteme in der Unternehmensforschung," *Beiträge zur Datenverarbeitung und Unternehmensforschung*, Vol. 7, Anton Hain Verlag, Meisenheim am Glan, Germany, 1973.

Bitran, G. R., "Linear Multiple Objective Programs with Zero-One Variables," *Mathematical Programming*, Vol. 13, No. 2, pp. 121–139, 1977.

Bitran, G. R., "Theory and Algorithms for Linear Multiple Objective Programs with Zero-One Variables," *Mathematical Programming*, Vol. 17, No. 3, pp. 362–390, 1979.

Bitran, G. R., "Linear Multiple Objective Problems with Interval Coefficients," *Management Science*, Vol. 26, No. 7, pp. 694–706, 1980.

Bitran, G. R. and K. D. Lawrence, "Locating Service Facilities: A Multicriteria Approach," *Omega*, Vol. 8, No. 2, pp. 201–206, 1980.

Bitran, G. R. and T. L. Magnanti, "The Structure of Admissible Points with Respect to Cone Dominance," *Journal of Optimization Theory and Applications*, Vol. 29, No. 4, pp. 573–614, 1979.

Bitran, G. R. and T. L. Magnanti, "Duality Based Characterizations of Efficient Facets," *Multiple Criteria Decision Making Theory and Application*, edited by G. Fandel and T. Gal, Springer-Verlag, Berlin-New York, New York, pp. 13–23, 1980.

Blackwell, D., "An Analog of the Minimax Theorem for Vector Payoffs," *Pacific Journal of Mathematics*, Vol. 6, No. 1, pp. 1–8, March 1956.

Blair, D. H., G. Bordes, J. S. Kelly and K. Suzumura, "Impossibility Theorems without Collective Rationality," *Journal of Economic Theory*, Vol. 13, No. 3, pp. 361–379, 1976.

Blair, P. D., *Multiobjective Regional Energy Planning: Applications to the Energy Park Concept*, Martinus Nijhoff, Boston, Massachusetts, 1979.

Blaquière, A., "Sur la Géometrie des Surfaces de Pareto d'un Jeu Différentiel à N Joueurs," *Comptes Rendus Académie des Sciences de Paris*, Série A, Vol. 271, No. 15, pp. 744–747, 1970.

Blaquière, A. (ed.), *Topics in Differential Games*, American Elsevier Publishing Company, New York, New York, 1973.

Blaquière, A., "Further Topological Aspects of Vector-Valued Optimization in Multiplayer Quantitative Games," *Proceedings, IEEE Conference on Decisions and Control, 13th Symposium on Adaptive Processes*, Phoenix, Arizona, 1974, pp. 373–374, 1974.

Blaquière, A., "Vector Valued Optimization in Multiplayer Quantitative Games," *Multicriteria Decision Making*, edited by G. Leitmann and A. Marzollo, Courses and Lectures No. 211, International Center for Mechanical Sciences (CISM), Springer-Verlag, Wien-New York, New York, pp. 33–54, 1975.

Blaquière, A., "Une Généralisation du Concept d'Optimalité et de Certaines Notions Géometriques Qui s'y Rattachent," *Cahiers du Centre d'Études de Recherche Opérationelle*, Brussels, Belgium, Vol. 18, pp. 49–61, 1976.

Blaquière, A. and P. Caussin, "Jeux Différentiels Avec Retard, Propriétés Globales d'une Surface du Jeu," *Comptes Rendus Académie des Sciences de Paris*, Série A, Vol. 273, No. 5, pp. 326–328, 1971.

Blaquière, A., F. Gerard and G. Leitmann, *Quantitative and Qualitative Games*, Academic Press, New York, New York, 1969.

Blaquière, A. and L. Juricek, "Appendix—an Example of Duopoly," *Differential Games and Related Topics*, edited by H. W. Kuhn and G. P. Szegö, Elsevier Publishing Company, New York, New York, pp. 74–81, 1971.

Blaquière, A., L. Juricek and K. E. Wiese, "Sur la Géométrie des Surfaces de Pareto d'un Jeu Différentiel à N Joueurs; Théorème du Maximum," *Comptes Rendus Académie des Sciences de Paris*, Série A, Vol. 271, No. 20, pp. 1030–1032, 1970.

Blaquière, A., L. Juricek and K. E. Wiese, "Some Geometric Aspects of Pareto Surfaces of an n-Player Differential Game," *Proceedings, 4th Hawaii International Conference on Systems Science*, Honolulu, Hawaii, 1971; Western Periodicals, North Hollywood, California, pp. 27–29, 1971.

Blaquière, A., L. Juricek and K. E. Wiese, "Geometry of Pareto Equilibria and a Maximum Principle in N-Person Differential Games," *Journal of Mathematical Analysis and Applications*, Vol. 38, No. 1, pp. 223–243, 1972.

Blaquière, A., L. Juricek and K. E. Wiese, "Geometry of Pareto Equilibria in N-Person Differential Games," *Topics in Differential Games*, edited by A. Blaquière, Elsevier Publishing Company, New York, New York, pp. 271–310, 1973.

Blaquière, A. and K. E. Wiese, "Jeux Qualitatifs Multiétages à N-Personnes Coalitions," *Comptes Rendus Académie des Sciences de Paris*, Série A, Vol. 270, No. 19, 1970.

Bodily, S. E., "Evaluating Joint Life-Saving Activities Under Uncertainty," *Multiple Criteria Problem Solving*, edited by S. Zionts, Lecture Notes in Economics and Mathematical Systems No. 155, Springer-Verlag, Berlin-New York, New York, pp. 23–41, 1978.

Boebion, J. and L. Pun, "A Series-Parallel Multiple Criteria Model for a Scheduling Problem in the Dress-Making Industry," *Multiple Criteria Decision Making*, edited by H. Thiriez and S. Zionts, Lecture Notes in Economics and Mathematical Systems No. 130, Springer-Verlag, Berlin-New York, New York, pp. 305–318, 1976.

Bogardi, I., L. Duckstein and F. Szidarovszky, "Multiobjective Modelling for Regional Natural Resources Management," *Proceedings, Task Force Meeting*, NOTEC Regional Development Project, Jablonna, Poland, September 1978.

Bogardi, I., F. Szidarovszky and L. Duckstein, "Mining, Dewatering and Environmental Effects: A Multiobjective Approach," *Proceedings, International Congress for Energy and the Ecosystem*, Grand Forks, June 1978.

Bol, G., "Stetigkeit und Effizienz bei mengenwertigen Produktions funktionen," *Mathematical Systems in Economics*, Vol. 7, Anton Hain Verlag, Meisenheim am Glan, Germany, 1973.

Bol, G., "Effiziente Aktivitäten bei linearer Präferenz," *Proc. Oper. Res.*, Vol. 1, pp. 29–40, 1973.

Bol, G., "Continuity of Production Correspondences and a Relation Between Efficient Input and Output Vectors in Production Theory," *Lecture Notes in Economics and Mathematical Systems No. 99*, Springer-Verlag, Berlin-New York, New York, pp. 207–219, 1974.

Bol, G., "Ein funktionaler Zusammenhang zwischen Pareto-optimalen Input- und Output-vektoren," *Proc. Oper. Res.*, Vol. 3, pp. 356–359, 1974.

Boldur, G., "Metode Pentru Rezolvarea Problemelor Decizionale Complexe," *Studii și Cercetări de Calcul Economic și Cibernetică Economică*, No. 6, pp. 47–53, 1969.

Boldur, G., *Procese Informationale si de Decizie in Economie*, Editura Științifică, București, Romania, 1969.

Boldur, G., *Fundamentarea complexă a procesului decizional economic*, Editura Științifică, București, Romania, 1973.

Boldur, G. and J. M. Stancu-Minasian, "Méthodes de Resolution des Certains Problèmes de Programmation Linéaire Multidimensionelle," *Revue Roumaine de Mathématiques Pures et Appliquées*, Vol. 16, No. 3, pp. 313–326, 1971.

Boldur, G. and J. M. Stancu-Minasian, "Programmarea Liniară cu mai Multe Functii Objectiv," *Studii și Cercetări Matematice*, Vol. 24, No. 8, pp. 1169–1191, 1972.

Bona, B., D. Merighi and A. Ostanello-Borreani, "Financial Resource Allocation in a Decentralized Urban System," *Multiple Criteria Analysis: Operational Methods*, edited by P. Nijkamp and J. Spronk, Gower Press, London, England, 1981.

Bonnardeaux, J., J.-P. Dolait and J. S. Dyer, "The Use of the Nash Bargaining Model in Trajectory Selection," *Management Science*, Vol. 22, No. 7, pp. 766–777, 1976.

Borel, E., "La Théorie du Jeu et les Équations Integrals à Noyau Symétrique Gauche," *Comptes Rendus Académie des Sciences de Paris*, Vol. 173, pp. 1304–1308, 1921.

Borel, E., "Traité du Calcul des Probabilités et de ses Applications," *Applications des Jeux de Hasard*, Vol. 4, Part 2, Gauthier-Villars, Paris, France, 1938.

Borreani-Ostanello, A. and P. Capillaro, "Efficient Solutions of a Multiple-Objective Programming Method for a Problem of School Allocation and Dimensioning," *Advances in Operations Research*, edited by M. Roubens, North-Holland Publishing Company, Amsterdam, Holland, pp. 55–60, 1977.

Borwein, J., "Proper Efficient Points for Maximization with Respect to Cones," *SIAM Journal on Control and Optimization*, Vol. 15, No. 1, pp. 57–63, 1977.

Boulding, K. E., *Welfare Economics, a Survey of Contemporary Economics*, edited by B. F. Haley, Irwin, Homewood, Illinois, pp. 1–36, 1952.

Bowen, K. C., "Personal and Organizational Value Systems: How Should We Treat These in O.R. Studies?", *Omega*, in press.

Bowling, A. L. and J. F. Hair, Jr., "Optimal Decisions on Multiple Objectives Through Canonical Analysis," *Multiple Criteria Decision Making*, edited by J. L. Cochrane and M. Zeleny, University of South Carolina Press, Columbia, South Carolina, pp. 729–731, 1973.

Bowman, E. H., "Consistency and Optimality in Managerial Decision-Making," *Management Science*, Vol. 9, No. 2, pp. 310–321, 1963.

Bowman, V. J. Jr., "On the Relationship of the Tchebycheff Norm and the Efficient Frontier of Multiplecriteria Objectives," *Multiple Criteria Decision Making*, edited by H. Thiriez and S. Zionts, Lecture Notes in Economics and Mathematical Systems No. 130, Springer-Verlag, Berlin-New York, New York, pp. 76–86, 1976.

Boychuk, L. M. and V. O. Ovchinnikov, "Principal Methods for Solution of Multicriteria Optimization Problems (a Survey)," *Soviet Automatic Control*, Vol. 6, No. 3, pp. 1–4, 1973.

Bracken, J. and J. T. McGill, "Production and Marketing Decisions with Multiple Objectives in a Competitive Environment," *Journal of Optimization Theory and Applications*, Vol. 24, No. 3, pp. 449–458, March 1978.

Bradley, G. H. and M. Shubik, "A Note on the Shape of the Pareto Optimal Surface," *Journal of Economic Theory*, Vol. 8, pp. 530–538, 1974.

Bradley, J. and P. L. Yu, "A Concept of Optimality in Differential Games," *International Journal of Systems Science*, Vol. 7, No. 2, pp. 157–164, 1976.

Bragard, L., "Une Méthode Multicritère," *Proceedings of the First European Congress on*

Operations Research, North-Holland Publishing Company, Amsterdam, Holland, pp. 43–44, 1975.

Bragard, L., "Objectifs Discordants et Solutions Efficaces en Programmation Multicritère Linéaire," *Rev. Belge Statist. Inform. et Rech. Opér.*, Vol. 16, No. 3, pp. 43–49, 1976.

Bragard, L. and J. Vangeldère, "Points Efficaces en Programmation à Objectifs Multiples," *Bull. Soc. Roy. Sci. Liège*, Vol. 46, No. 1-2, pp. 27–41, 1977.

Brauers, W. K., "Multiple-Criteria Decision Making with a Special Application on Defense Problems," *Multiple Criteria Decision Making*, edited by H. Thiriez and S. Zionts, Lecture Notes in Economics and Mathematical Systems No. 130, Springer-Verlag, Berlin-New York, New York, pp. 199–200, 1976.

Brayton, R. K., G. D. Hachtel and A. L. Sangiovanni-Vincentelli, "A Survey of Optimization Techniques for Integrated-Circuit Design," *Proceedings of the IEEE*, Vol. 69, pp. 1334–1362, October 1981.

Breckner, W. W., "Dualität bei Optimierungsaufgaben in halbgeordneten topologischen Vektorräumen I," *Revue Analyse Numerique et Theorie Appr.*, Vol. 1, pp. 5–35, 1972.

Breckner, W. W., "Dualität bei Optimierungsaufgaben in halbgeordneten topologischen Vektorräumen II," *Revue Analyse Numérique et Théorie Appr.*, Vol. 2, pp. 27–35, 1973.

Breckner, W. W. and I. Kolumbán, "Dualität bei Optimierungsaufgaben in topologischen Vektorräumen," *Mathematika* (Cluj), Vol. 10, No. 2, pp. 229–244, 1968.

Breckner, W. W. and I. Kolumbán, "Konvexe Optimierungsaufgaben in topologischen Vektorräumen," *Mathematica Scandinavica*, Vol. 25, pp. 227–247, 1969.

Bredendiek, E., "Charakterisierung und Eindeutigkeit bei Simultanapproximationen," *Zeitschrift für Angewandte Mathematik und Mechanik*, Vol. 50, pp. 403–410, 1970.

Brill, E. D., "The Use of Optimization Models in Public-Sector Planning," *Management Science*, Vol. 25, No. 5, pp. 413–422, May 1979.

Brinck, F., L. Duckstein and J. Thames, "A Multiattribute Approach to the Reclamation of Stripmined Lands," *Proceedings, Hydrology and Water Resources in Arizona and the Southwest*, Vol. 9, Arizona Section, AWRA, Hydrology Section, AZ-NV Academy of Sciences, Tempe, Arizona, pp. 21–29, April 1979.

Briskin, L. E., "A Method of Unifying Multiple Objective Functions," *Management Science*, Vol. 12, No. 10, pp. 406–416, 1966.

Briskin, L. E., "Establishing a Generalized Multi-Attribute Utility Function," *Multiple Criteria Decision Making*, edited by J. L. Cochrane and M. Zeleny, University of South Carolina Press, Columbia, South Carolina, pp. 236–245, 1973.

Brucker, P., "Diskrete parametrische Optimierungsprobleme und wesentliche effiziente Punkte," *Zeitschrift für Operations Research*, Serie A-3, Vol. 16, No. 5, pp. 189–197, 1972.

Buffa, F. P., "A Goal Programming Approach for Simultaneous Determination of Safety Stock Levels," *Production and Inventory Management*, Vol. 17, No. 1, pp. 94–104, 1976.

Buffa, E. S. and J. S. Dyer, *Management Science/Operations Research* (Chapter 4, "Evaluative Models for Multiple Criteria"), John Wiley and Sons, New York, New York, 1977.

Buffet, P., J. P. Grémy, M. Marc and B. Sussmann, "Peut-on choisir en tenant compte de Critères Multiples? Une Méthode (ELECTRE) et trois Applications," *Revue Metra*, Vol. 6, No. 2, pp. 283–316, 1967.

Bühler, G., "Zur Theorie dynamischer, nichtkooperativer Zwei-Personen Spiele," *Zeitschrift für Operations Research*, Vol. A-17, No. 3, pp. 143–156, 1973.

Bühler, G., "Die Optimalitätsgleichung bei mehrstufigen Spielen und ihre Lösbarkeit," *Operations Research Verfahren*, Vol. 16, Anton Hain Verlag, Meisenheim am Glan, Germany, pp. 68–83, 1973.

Burmeister, E. and A. R. Dobell, "Guidance and Control of Free Market Economies: A New Interpretation," *IEEE Transactions on Systems, Man, and Cybernetics*, Vol. SMC-2, pp. 9–15, January 1972.

Burns, T. and L. D. Meeker, "A Mathematical Model of Multidimensional Evaluation, Decision-Making and Social Interaction," *Multiple Criteria Decision Making*, edited by J. L. Cochrane and M. Zeleny, University of South Carolina Press, Columbia, South Carolina, pp. 141–163, 1973.

Burros, R. H., "Axiomatic Analysis of Preference and Indifference," *Theory and Decision*, Vol. 5, pp. 187–204, 1974.

Burros, R. H., "Complementary Relations in the Theory of Preference," *Theory and Decision*, Vol. 7, No. 3, pp. 181–190, 1976.

Bussey, L. E., *The Economic Analysis of Industrial Projects* (Chapter 9, "Multiple Projects and Constraints II"), Prentice-Hall, Englewood Cliffs, New Jersey, 1978.

Buyanov, B. B. and V. M. Ozernoi, "Decision Method Using Vector Criterion," *Engineering Cybernetics*, Vol. 12, No. 3, pp. 49–54, 1974.

Callahan, J. R., "An Introduction to Financial Planning Through Goal Programming," *Cost and Management*, Vol. 47, No. 1, pp. 7–12, 1973.

Candler, W., "Linear Programming in Capital Budgeting with Multiple Goals," *Multiple Criteria Decision Making*, edited by J. L. Cochrane and M. Zeleny, University of South Carolina Press, Columbia, South Carolina, pp. 416–428, 1973.

Candler, W. and M. Boehlje, "Use of Linear Programming in Budgeting with Multiple Goals," *American Journal of Agricultural Economics*, Vol. 53, No. 2, pp. 325–330, 1971.

Candler, W. and W. Cartwright, "Estimation of Performance Functions for Budgeting and Simulation Studies," *American Journal of Agricultural Economics*, Vol. 51, No. 1, pp. 159–169, 1969.

Canon, M., C. Cullum and E. Polak, "Constrained Minimization Problems in Finite Dimensional Spaces," *SIAM Journal on Control*, Vol. 4, No. 3, pp. 528–547, 1966.

Cantley, M. F., "The Choice of Corporate Objectives," *Long Range Planning*, Vol. 3, No. 1, pp. 36–41, 1970.

Cantor, G., "Beiträge zur Begründung der Transfiniten Mengenlehre," *Mathematische Annalen*, Vol. 46, pp. 481–512, 1895, and Vol. 49, pp. 207–246, 1897; translated into English as *Contributions to the Founding of the Theory of Transfinite Numbers*, Dover Publications, New York, New York, undated. (See also *Gesammelte Abhandlungen [Collected Works]*, edited by E. Zermelo, Springer-Verlag, Berlin, Germany, 1932.)

Caplin, D. and J. S. H. Kornbluth, "Multiobjective Investments Planning Under Uncertainty," *Omega*, Vol. 3, No. 4, pp. 423–441, 1975.

Carlson, R. C. and H. H. Therp, "A Multicriteria Approach to Strategic Planning: An Application to Inventory Control," *Advances in Operations Research*, edited by M. Roubens, North-Holland Publishing Company, Amsterdam, Holland, pp. 75–83, 1977.

Carlsson, C., "An Approach to Adaptive Multigoal Control Using Fuzzy Automata," *Advances in Operations Research*, edited by M. Roubens, North-Holland Publishing Company, Amsterdam, Holland, pp. 85–93, 1977.

Carlsson, C., "Linking MP Models in a Systems Framework," *IEEE Transactions on Systems, Man, and Cybernetics*, Vol. SMC-9, No. 12, December 1979.

Carlsson, C., "Solving Complex and Ill-Structured Problems: An MCDM-Approach," *Multiple Criteria Analysis: Operational Methods*, edited by P. Nijkamp and J. Spronk, Gower Press, London, England, 1981.

Carmichael, D. G., "Computation of Pareto Optima in Structural Design," *International Journal for Numerical Methods in Engineering*, Vol. 15, No. 6, pp. 925–934, June 1980.

Carmichael, D. G., *Structural Modelling and Optimization: A General Methodology for*

Engineering and Control (Chapter 10, "Multicriteria Optimization"), Halsted Press, a Division of John Wiley and Sons, New York, New York, 1981.

Carrol, M. P., "Simultaneous L_1 Approximation of a Compact Set of Real Valued Functions," *Numerische Mathematik*, Vol. 19, pp. 110–115, 1972.

Carrol, M. P. and H. W. McLaughlin, "L_1 Approximation of Vector-Valued Functions," *Journal of Approximation Theory*, Vol. 7, pp. 122–131, 1973.

Case, J. H., "A Problem in International Trade," *Proceedings, 1st International Conference on the Theory and Applications of Differential Games*, Amherst, Massachusetts, s.l.s.a. pp. IV/8-IV/12, 1969.

Case, J. H., "Toward a Theory of Many Player Differential Games," *SIAM Journal on Control*, Vol. 7, No. 2, pp. 179–197, May 1969.

Case, J. H., "Applications of the Theory of Differential Games to Economic Problems," *Differential Games and Related Topics*, edited by H. W. Kuhn and G. P. Szegö, Elsevier Publishing Company, New York, New York, pp. 345–371, 1971.

Case, J. H., "Differential Trading Games," *Topics in Differential Games*, edited by A. Blaquière, Elsevier Publishing Company, New York, New York, pp. 377–400, 1973.

Case, J. H., "A Class of Games Having Pareto-Optimal Nash Equilibria," *Journal of Optimization Theory and Applications*, Vol. 13, No. 3, pp. 379–385, 1974.

Case, J. H., "A Game of Advertising Strategy," *Proceedings, 6th IFAC World Congress*, Cambridge, Massachusetts, 1975; Part 1, Pittsburgh, Pennsylvania, pp. 16.3/1–16.3/3, 1975.

Cassidy, R. G., C. Field and M. J. L. Kirby, "Solution of a Satisficing Model for Random Payoff Games," *Management Science*, Vol. 19, No. 3, pp. 266–271, November 1972.

Cassidy, R. G., M. J. L. Kirby and W. M. Raike, "Efficient Distribution of Resources Through Three Levels of Government," *Management Science*, Vol. 17, No. 8, pp. B462–B473, April 1971.

Castellani, G., "Explicit Solutions for a Class of Allocation Problems," *Multicriteria Decision Making*, edited by G. Leitmann and A. Marzollo, Courses and Lectures No. 211, International Center for Mechanical Sciences (CISM), Springer-Verlag, Wien-New York, New York, pp. 351–386, 1975.

Censor, Y., "Pareto Optimality in Multiobjective Problems," *Applied Mathematics and Optimization*, Vol. 4, pp. 41–59, 1978.

Censor, Y., "Necessary Conditions for Pareto Optimality in Simultaneous Chebyshev Best Approximation," *Journal of Approximation Theory*, Vol. 27, No. 2, pp. 127–134, October 1979.

Cesari, L. and M. B. Suryanarayana, "Existence Theorems for Pareto-Optimization in Banach Spaces," *Bulletin of the American Mathematical Society*, Vol. 82, No. 2, pp. 306–308, 1976.

Cesari, L. and M. B. Suryanarayana, "Existence Theorems for Pareto Problems of Optimization," *Calculus of Variations and Control Theory*, edited by D. L. Russell, Academic Press, New York, New York, pp. 139–154, 1976.

Cesari, L. and M. B. Suryanarayana, "An Existence Theorem for Pareto Problems," *Nonlinear Analysis, Theory, Methods and Applications*, Vol. 2, pp. 225–233, 1978.

Cesari, L. and M. B. Suryanarayana, "Existence Theorems for Pareto Optimization; Multivalued and Banach Space Valued Functionals," *Transactions of the American Mathematical Society*, Vol. 244, pp. 37–65, October 1978.

Chaiken, J. M. and P. Dormont, "A Patrol Car Allocation Model: Background, Capabilities and Algorithms," *Management Science*, Vol. 24, No. 12, pp. 1280–1300, 1978.

Champsaur, P., J. Drèze and C. Henry, "Stability Theorems with Economic Applications," *Econometrica*, Vol. 45, No. 2, pp. 273–294, 1977.

Chang, S. S. L., "General Theory of Optimal Processes with Applications," *Proceedings, IFAC Symposium*, Tokyo, Japan, 1965.

Chang, S. S. L., "General Theory of Optimal Processes," *SIAM Journal on Control*, Vol. 4, No. 1, pp. 46–55, 1966.

Chankong, V., "A Viewpoint Toward the Development of Multi-Objective Solution Techniques," *Multiple Criteria Decision Making*, edited by M. K. Starr and M. Zeleny, TIMS Studies in the Management Sciences, Vol. 6, North-Holland Publishing Company, Amsterdam, Holland, pp. 303–304, 1977.

Chankong, V. and Y. Y. Haimes, "The Interactive Surrogate Worth Trade-Off (ISWT) Method for Multiobjective Decision Making," *Multiple Criteria Problem Solving*, edited by S. Zionts, Lecture Notes in Economics and Mathematical Systems No. 155, Springer-Verlag, Berlin-New York, New York, pp. 42–67, 1978.

Chankong, V. and Y. Y. Haimes, *Multiobjective Decision Making: Theory and Methodology*, North-Holland Publishing Company, Amsterdam, Holland, 1983.

Chankong, V., Y. Y. Haimes and D. M. Gemperline, "A Multiobjective Dynamic Programming Method for Capacity Expansion," *IEEE Transactions on Automatic Control*, Vol. AC-26, No. 5, pp. 1195–1207, October 1981.

Chapman, D. W. and J. Volkman, "A Social Determinant of the Level of Aspiration," *Journal of Abnormal Psychology*, Vol. 34, pp. 225-238, 1939.

Charnes, A., et al., "A Goal Interval Programming Model for Resource Allocation in a Marine Environmental Protection Program," *Journal of Environmental Economics and Management*, Vol. 3, No. 4, pp. 347–362, December 1976.

Charnes, A., R. W. Clower and K. O. Kortanek, "Effective Control Through Coherent Decentralization with Preemptive Goals," *Econometrica*, Vol. 35, No. 2, pp. 294–320, 1967.

Charnes, A. and B. Collomb, "Optimal Economic Stabilization Policy: Linear Goal-Interval Programming Models," *Socio-Economic Planning Sciences*, Vol. 6, pp. 431–435, 1972.

Charnes, A. and W. W. Cooper, "Management Models and Industrial Applications of Linear Programming," *Management Science*, Vol. 4, No. 1, pp. 81–87, 1957.

Charnes, A. and W. W. Cooper, *Management Models and Industrial Applications of Linear Programming*, Vols. I and II, No. 5, John Wiley and Sons, New York, New York, 1961.

Charnes, A. and W. W. Cooper, "Systems Evaluation and Repricing Theorems," *Management Science*, Vol. 9, No. 1, pp. 33–49, 1962.

Charnes, A. and W. W. Cooper, "Deterministic Equivalents for Optimizing and Satisficing Under Chance Constraints," *Operations Research*, Vol. 11, No. 1, pp. 18–39, 1963.

Charnes, A. and W. W. Cooper, "Constrained Extremization Models and Their Use in Developing System Measures," *Views in General System Theory*, edited by M. D. Mesarović, John Wiley and Sons, New York, New York, pp. 61–88, 1964.

Charnes, A. and W. W. Cooper, "Elements of a Strategy for Making Models in LP," *System Engineering Handbook*, edited by R. E. Machol, W. P. Tanner and S. N. Alexander, McGraw-Hill, New York, New York, Chapter 26, 1965.

Charnes, A. and W. W. Cooper, "Some Network Characterizations for Mathematical Programming and Accounting Approaches for Planning and Control," *Accounting Review*, Vol. 42, No. 1, pp. 24–52, 1967.

Charnes, A. and W. W. Cooper, "Goal Programming and Constrained Regression—a Comment," *Omega*, Vol. 3, No. 4, pp. 403–409, 1975.

Charnes, A. and W. W. Cooper, "Goal Programming and Multiple Objective Optimization," *International Journal of Operations Research*, Vol. 1, No. 1, pp. 39–54, 1977.

Charnes, A., W. W. Cooper, J. K. de Voe, D. B. Learner and W. Reinecke, "A Goal Programming Model for Media Planning," *Management Science*, Vol. 14, No. 8, pp. 423–430, 1968.

Charnes, A., W. W. Cooper and J. P. Evans, "Connectedness of the Efficient Extreme Points in Linear Multiple Objective Programs," unpublished technical paper, 1972.

Charnes, A., W. W. Cooper and Y. Ijiri, "Breakeven Budgeting and Programming to Goals," *Journal of Accounting Research*, Vol. 1, No. 1, pp. 16–43, 1963.

Charnes, A., W. W. Cooper, D. Klingman and R. J. Niehaus, "Explicit Solutions in Convex Goal Programming," *Management Science*, Vol. 22, No. 4, pp. 438–448, 1975.

Charnes, A., W. W. Cooper, D. B. Learner and E. F. Snow, "Note on an Application of a Goal Programming Model for Media Planning," *Management Science*, Vol. 14, No. 8, pp. 431–436, 1968.

Charnes, A., W. W. Cooper, K. A. Lewis and R. J. Niehaus, "A Multi-Objective Model for Planning Equal Employment Opportunities," *Multiple Criteria Decision Making*, edited by M. Zeleny, Lecture Notes in Economics and Mathematical Systems No. 123, Springer-Verlag, Berlin-New York, New York, pp. 111–134, 1976.

Charnes, A., W. W. Cooper and R. J. Niehaus, "Dynamic Multi-Attribute Models for Mixed Manpower Systems," *Naval Research Logistics Quarterly*, Vol. 22, No. 2, pp. 205–220, 1975.

Charnes, A., W. W. Cooper, R. J. Niehaus and A. Stedry, "Static and Dynamic Assignment Models with Multiple Objectives and Some Remarks on Organization Design," *Management Science*, Vol. 15, No. 8, pp. 365–376, 1969.

Charnes, A., K. E. Haynes, J. Hazleton and M. J. Ryan, "An Hierarchical Goal Programming Approach to Environmental Land Use Management," *Mathematical Analysis of Decision Problems in Ecology*, edited by A. Charnes and W. R. Lynn, Springer-Verlag, Berlin, Germany, 1975.

Charnes, A., M. Kirby and W. Raike, "Chance-Constrained Games with Partially Controllable Strategies," *Operations Research*, Vol. 16, No. 1, pp. 142–149, January–February 1968.

Charnes, A., M. Kirby and W. Raike, "Zero–Zero Chance Constrained Games," *Theory of Probability and Its Applications*, Vol. 13, pp. 663–681, 1968.

Charnes, A. and K. O. Kortanek, "On Balanced Sets, Cores and Linear Programming," *Cahiers du Centre d'Études de Recherche Opérationelle*, Brussels, Belgium, Vol. 9, No. 1, pp. 32–43, 1967.

Charnes, A. and K. O. Kortanek, "On Classes of Convex and Preemptive Nuclei for n-Person Games," *Proceedings of the Princeton Symposium on Mathematical Programming*, edited by H. W. Kuhn, Princeton University Press, Princeton, New Jersey, pp. 377–390, 1975.

Charnes, A. and S. Littlechild, "On the Formation of Unions in n-Person Games," *Journal of Economic Theory*, Vol. 10, No. 3, pp. 386–402, June 1975.

Charnes, A., S. Littlechild and S. Sorensen, "Core-Stem Solutions of n-Person Essential Games," *Socio-Economic Planning Sciences*, Vol. 1, No. 6, pp. 649–660, December 1973.

Charnes, A. and W. R. Lynn (eds.), *Mathematical Analysis of Decision Problems in Ecology*, Springer-Verlag, Berlin-New York, New York, 1975.

Charnes, A. and S. Sorensen, "Constrained n-Person Games," *International Journal of Game Theory*, Vol. 3, No. 3, pp. 141–158, 1974.

Charnes, A. and A. Stedry, "Investigations in the Theory of Multiple Budgeted Goals," *Management Controls*, edited by C. P. Bonini, R. K. Jaedicke and H. M. Wagner, McGraw-Hill, New York, New York, 1964.

Charnes, A. and A. Stedry, "Search-Theoretic Models of Organization Control by Budgeted Multiple Goals," *Management Science*, Vol. 12, No. 5, pp. B457–B482, 1966.

Charnes, A. and J. Storbeck, "A Goal Programming Model for the Siting of Multilevel EMS Systems," *Socio-Economic Planning Sciences*, Vol. 14, No. 4, pp. 155–161, 1980.

Charnetski, J. R., "Multiple Criteria Decision Making with Partial Information: A Site Selection Problem," *Space Location and Regional Development*, edited by M. Chatterji, Pion, London, England, pp. 51–62, 1976.

Charnetski, J. R., "Linear Programming with Partial Information," *European Journal of Operational Research*, Vol. 5, No. 4, pp. 254–261, October 1980.

Charnetski, J. R. and R. M. Soland, "Multiple-Attribute Decision Making with Partial Information: The Comparative Hypervolume Criterion," *Naval Research Logistics Quarterly*, Vol. 25, No. 2, pp. 279–288, 1978.

Charnetski, J. R. and R. M. Soland, "Multiple-Attribute Decision Making with Partial Information: The Expected-Value Criterion," *Naval Research Logistics Quarterly*, Vol. 26, No. 2, pp. 249–256, 1979.

Charpentier, A. R. and E. Jacquet-Lagrèze, "La Promotion de Électricité dans l'Industrie et l'Utilisation de Méthodes Multicritères," *Multiple Criteria Decision Making*, edited by H. Thiriez and S. Zionts, Lecture Notes in Economics and Mathematical Systems No. 130, Springer-Verlag, Berlin-New York, New York, pp. 364–377, 1976.

Chateau, J. P. D., "The Capital Budgeting Problem under Conflicting Financial Policies," *Journal of Business Finance and Accounting*, Vol. 2, No. 1, pp. 83–103, 1975.

Chaudhary, B., "Multiobjective Spatial Planning in Developing Countries," *Multiple Criteria Decision Making*, edited by M. K. Starr and M. Zeleny, TIMS Studies in the Management Sciences, Vol. 6, North-Holland Publishing Company, Amsterdam, Holland, p. 305, 1977.

Chenery, H., "Economists' Production Functions from Engineering Data," *Studies in the Structure of the American Economy*, edited by W. Leontief, Oxford University Press, London, England, 1953.

Cherubino, S., "Ottimi Paretiani Dei Valori Nominale e Intrinseco della Produzione di un Sistema Economico e Analogihi," *Atti Accad. Naz. Lincei Rend. Cl. Sci. Fis. Mat.-Natur*, Vol. 38, No. 2, pp. 185–188, 1965.

Chichilinsky, G. and P. J. Kalman, "Application of Functional Analysis to Models of Efficient Allocation of Economic Resources," *Journal of Optimization Theory and Applications*, Vol. 30, No. 1, pp. 19–32, January 1980.

Chipman, J. S., "The Foundations of Utility," *Econometrica*, Vol. 28, pp. 193–224, 1960.

Chipman, J. S., "On the Lexicographic Representation of Preference Orderings," *Preferences, Utility, and Demand*, edited by J. S. Chipman, L. Hurwicz, M. K. Richter and H. F. Sonnenschein, Harcourt, Brace and Jovanovich, New York, New York, pp. 276–288, 1971.

Chipman, J. S., L. Hurwicz, M. K. Richter and H. F. Sonnenschein (eds.), *Preferences, Utility, and Demand*, Harcourt, Brace and Jovanovich, New York, New York, 1971.

Chisman, J. A. and D. Rippy, "Optimal Operation of a Multipurpose Reservoir Using Goal Programming," *Review of Industrial Management and Textile Science*, pp. 69–82, Fall 1977.

Choo, E. U. and D. R. Atkins, "An Interactive Algorithm for Multi-criteria Programming," *Computers and Operations Research: Special Issue on Mathematical Programming with Multiple Objectives*, edited by M. Zeleny, Vol. 7, No. 1–2, pp. 81–87, 1980.

Chu, K.-C., "On the Noninferior Set for Systems with Vector-Valued Objective Function," *IEEE Transactions on Automatic Control*, Vol. AC-15, No. 5, pp. 591–593, October 1970.

Churchman, C. W., "Morality as a Value Criterion," *Multiple Criteria Decision Making*, edited by J. L. Cochrane and M. Zeleny, University of South Carolina Press, Columbia, South Carolina, pp. 3–8, 1973.

Chyung, D. H., "Optimal Systems with Multiple Cost Functionals," *SIAM Journal on Control*, Vol. 5, No. 3, pp. 345–351, 1967.

Ciobanu, G., "Apliarea Simularii Digitale la Rezolvarea Problemelor de Programare Liniara cu mai Multe Functii Objectiv," *Studii şi Cercetări de Calcul Economic şi Cibernetică Economică*, Vol. 1, pp. 15–19, 1976.

Clarke, D. and B. H. P. Rivett, "A Structural Mapping Approach to Complex Decision

Making," *The Journal of the Operational Research Society*, Vol. 29, No. 2, pp. 113–128, 1978.

Claudy, J. G., "A Comparison of Five Variable Weighting Procedures," *Educational and Psychological Measurement*, Vol. 32, pp. 311–322, 1972.

Clayton, E. R. and L. J. Moore, "Goal vs. Linear Programming," *Journal of Systems Management*, pp. 26–31, November 1972.

Clemhout, S., H. Y. Wan and G. Leitmann, "A Differential Game Model of Duopoly," *Econometrica*, Vol. 39, No. 6, pp. 911–938, 1971.

Clemhout, S., H. Y. Wan and G. Leitmann, "A Differential Game of Oligopoly," *Kybernetika*, Vol. 3, No. 1, pp. 24–39, 1973.

Clemhout, S., H. Y. Wan and G. Leitmann, "Bargaining Under Strike: A Differential Game View," *Journal of Economic Theory*, Vol. 11, No. 1, pp. 55–67, 1975.

Clemhout, S., H. Y. Wan and G. Leitmann, "Equilibrium Patterns for Bargaining Under Strike: A Differential Game Model," *Proceedings, Conference on Directions in Decentralized Control, Many Person Games, Optimization and Large Scale Systems*, Plenum Press, New York, New York, 1976.

Clemhout, S., H. Y. Wan and G. Leitmann, "Equilibrium Patterns for Bargaining Under Strike: A Differential Game Model," *Proceedings, 6th IFAC World Congress*, Cambridge, Massachusetts, 1975; Part 1, Pittsburgh, Pennsylvania, pp. 16.5/1–16.5/12, 1978.

Cochrane, J. L. and M. Zeleny (eds.), *Multiple Criteria Decision Making*, University of South Carolina Press, Columbia, South Carolina, 1973.

Cohn, M. Z. and S. R. Parimi, "Multicriteria Probabilistic Structural Design," *Journal of Structural Mechanics*, Vol. 1, No. 4, pp. 479–496, 1973.

Cohon, J. L., "Applications of Multiple Objectives to Water Resources Problems," *Multiple Criteria Decision Making*, edited by M. Zeleny, Lecture Notes in Economics and Mathematical Systems No. 123, Springer-Verlag, Berlin-New York, New York, pp. 255–270, 1976.

Cohon, J. L., "Multiobjective Programming and Planning," *Mathematics and Science in Engineering*, Vol. 140, Academic Press, New York, New York, 1978.

Cohon, J. L., et al., "Application of a Multiobjective Facility Location Model to Power Plant Siting in a Six-State Region of the U.S.," *Computers and Operations Research: Special Issue on Mathematical Programming with Multiple Objectives*, edited by M. Zeleny, Vol. 7, No. 1-2, pp. 107–123, 1980.

Cohon, J. L. and D. H. Marks, "Multiobjective Screening Models and Water Resources Investment," *Water Resources Research*, Vol. 9, No. 4, pp. 826–836, August 1973.

Cohon, J. L. and D. H. Marks, "Multiobjective Analysis in Water Resources Planning," *Systems Planning and Design*, edited by R. de Neufville and D. Marks, Prentice-Hall, Englewood Cliffs, New Jersey, pp. 304–321, 1974.

Cohon, J. L. and D. H. Marks, "A Review and Evaluation of Multiobjective Programming Techniques," *Water Resources Research*, Vol. 11, No. 2, pp. 208–220, April 1975.

Cohon, J. L. and D. H. Marks, "Computational and Formulation Considerations in Multiobjective Analysis in Water Resource Planning," *Proceedings, 6th IFAC World Congress*, Cambridge, Massachusetts, 1975; Part 3, Pittsburg, Pennsylvania, pp. 48.5/1–48.5/7, 1975.

Cole, J. D. and A. P. Sage, "On Assessment of Utility and Worth of Multi-Attributed Consequences in Large Scale Systems," *Information Science*, Vol. 10, pp. 31–58, 1976.

Coleman, J. S., "Beyond Pareto Optimality," *Philosophy, Science and Method: Essays in Honor of Ernst Nagel*, edited by S. Morgenbesser, P. Suppes and M. White, St. Martin's Press, New York, New York, pp. 415–439, 1969.

Collins, D. C., "Applications of Multiple Criteria Evaluation to Decision Aiding," *Multiple Criteria Decision Making*, edited by J. L. Cochrane and M. Zeleny, University of South Carolina Press, Columbia, South Carolina, pp. 477–505, 1973.

Collins, D. C. and A. Jain, "Decision-Aiding Tools in Designing Health Care Delivery Systems," *Proceedings of the Hawaii International Conference on Systems Science*, University of Hawaii, Honolulu, Hawaii, January 1973.

Collins, D. C., W. S. Meisel, H. J. Payne and E. Polak, "An Algorithm for Bicriteria Optimization Based on the Sensitivity Function," *Proceedings, 1974 IEEE Conference on Decisions and Control, 13th Symposium on Adaptive Processes*, Phoenix, Arizona, November 20–22, 1974, pp. 30–34, 1974.

Colson, G. and M. Zeleny, *Uncertain Prospects Ranking and Portfolio Analysis under the Conditions of Partial Information*, Mathematical Systems in Economics, Anton Hain Verlag, Meisenheim am Glan, Germany, 1979/1980.

Colson, G. and M. Zeleny, "Multicriterion Concept of Risk under Incomplete Information," *Computers and Operations Research: Special Issue on Mathematical Programming with Multiple Objectives*, edited by M. Zeleny, Vol. 7, No. 1-2, pp. 125–141, 1980.

Contini, B. and S. Zionts, "Restricted Bargaining for Organizations with Multiple Objectives," *Econometrica*, Vol. 36, No. 2, pp. 397–414, 1968.

Contini, B. M., "A Decision Model Under Uncertainty with Multiple Payoffs," *Theory of Games, Techniques and Applications*, edited by A. Mensch, Elsevier Publishing Company, New York, New York, 1966.

Contini, B. M., "A Stochastic Approach to Goal Programming," *Operations Research*, Vol. 16, No. 3, pp. 576–586, May–June 1968.

Cook, R. L., "A Study of Interactive Judgment Analysis and the Representation of Weights in Judgment Policies," *Multiple Criteria Decision Making*, edited by M. K. Starr and M. Zeleny, TIMS Studies in the Management Sciences, Vol. 6, North-Holland Publishing Company, Amsterdam, Holland, p. 306, 1977.

Cook, W. D., "Zero-Sum Games with Multiple Goals," *Naval Research Logistics Quarterly*, Vol. 23, No. 4, pp. 615–621, 1976.

Cook, W. D. and L. M. Seiford, "Priority Ranking and Consensus Formation," *Management Science*, Vol. 24, No. 16, pp. 1721–1732, 1978.

Cook, W. D. and W. S. Shields, "Assignment of Military Officers to Groups: A New Multiattribute Team Balancing Problem," *INFOR*, Vol. 17, No. 2, pp. 114–123, 1979.

Corley, H. W., "New Scalar Equivalence for Pareto Optimization," *IEEE Transactions on Automatic Control*, Vol. AC-25, No. 4, pp. 829–830, August 1980.

Cornet, B., "Accessibilité des Optimums de Pareto par des Processus Monotones," *Comptes Rendus Académie des Sciences de Paris*, Série A, Vol. 285, No. 9, pp. 641–644, 1977.

Cottle, R. W. and A. F. Veinott, "Polyhedral Sets Having a Least Element," *Mathematical Programming*, Vol. 3, pp. 238–249, 1972.

Cournot, A., *Recherches sur les Principes Mathématiques de la Théorie des Richesses*, Hachette, Paris, France, 1838; translated into German by W. G. Waffenschmidt as *Untersuchungen über die mathematischen Grundlagen der Theorie des Reichtums*, Verlag von Gustav Fischer, Jena, Germany, 1924; translated into English by N. T. Bacon as *Researches into the Mathematical Principles of the Theory of Wealth*, The Macmillan Company, London, England, 1927.

Courtillot, M., "On Varying All the Parameters in a Linear Programming Problem," *Operations Research*, Vol. 10, No. 4, pp. 471–475, 1962.

Courtney, J. F., T. D. Klastorian and T. W. Ruefli, "A Goal Programming Approach to Urban-Suburban Location Preferences," *Management Science*, Vol. 18, No. 6, pp. 258–268, 1972.

Crawford, A. B., "Impact Analysis Using Differentially Weighted Evaluative Criteria," *Multiple Criteria Decision Making*, edited by J. L. Cochrane and M. Zeleny, University of South Carolina Press, Columbia, South Carolina, pp. 732–735, 1973.

Crawford, D. M., B. C. Huntzinger and C. W. Kirkwood, "Multiobjective Decision Analysis for Transmission Conductor Selection," *Management Science*, Vol. 24, No. 16, pp. 1700–1709, 1978.

Crowston, B. W. and P. R. Kleindorfer, "Coordinating Multi-Project Networks," *Multiple Criteria Decision Making*, edited by J. L. Cochrane and M. Zeleny, University of South Carolina Press, Columbia, South Carolina, pp. 668–685, 1973.

Czap, H., "The Dependency of Automatically Designed Multicriterion Decisions on Scale Transformations," *European Journal of Operational Research*, Vol. 5, No. 1, pp. 51–55, 1980.

Da Cunha, N. O. and E. Polak, "Constrained Minimization Under Vector Valued Criteria in Finite Dimensional Spaces," *Journal of Mathematical Analysis and Applications*, Vol. 19, No. 1, pp. 103–124, July 1967.

Da Cunha, N. O. and E. Polak, "Constrained Minimization Under Vector Valued Criteria in Linear Topological Spaces," *Mathematical Theory of Control*, edited by A. V. Balakrishnan and L. W. Neustadt, Academic Press, New York, New York, pp. 96–108, 1967.

Daellenbach, H. G. and C. A. De Kluyver, "Note on Multiple Objective Dynamic Programming," *The Journal of the Operational Research Society*, Vol. 31, No. 7, pp. 591–594, 1980.

Dalkey, N., "Toward a Theory of Group Estimation," *The Delphi Method: Techniques and Applications*, edited by H. Linstone and M. Turoff, Addison-Wesley, Reading, Massachusetts, 1975.

Dalkey, N. C., "Group Decision Analysis," *Multiple Criteria Decision Making*, edited by M. Zeleny, Lecture Notes in Economics and Mathematical Systems No. 123, Springer-Verlag, Berlin-New York, New York, pp. 45–74, 1976.

Dalkey, N. C. and O. Helmer, "An Experimental Application of the Delphi Method to the Use of Experts," *Management Science*, Vol. 9, No. 3, pp. 458–467, 1963.

Danilina, G. P. and V. S. Bovel, "A Certain Nonlinear Model with Several Specific Functions" [in Russian], *Vestnik Akademii Nauk Kazak.*, Vol. 25, No. 2, pp. 63–65, 1969.

Danskin, J. M., "The Theory of Max-Min with Applications," *SIAM Journal*, Vol. 14, No. 4, 1966.

Danskin, J. M., "On Suboptimization: An Example," *Operations Research*, Vol. 16, No. 3, pp. 680–681, 1968.

Dantzig, G. B., "The Programming of Interdependent Activities: Mathematical Model," *Activity Analysis of Production and Allocation*, Cowles Commission Monograph No. 13, edited by T. C. Koopmans, John Wiley and Sons, New York, New York, pp. 19–32, 1951.

Das, P. C. and R. R. Sharma, "On Optimal Controls with Vector-Valued Cost Functional," *Revue Roumaine de Mathématiques Pures et Appliquées*, Vol. 16, No. 3, pp. 341–354, 1971.

Das, P. and Y. Y. Haimes, "Multiobjective Optimization in Water Quality and Land Management," *Water Resources Research*, Vol. 15, No. 4, 1979.

Dauer, J. P., "An Equivalence Result for Solutions of Multiobjective Linear Programs," *Computers and Operations Research*, Vol. 7, Nos. 1-2, pp. 33–39, 1980.

Dauer, J. P. and R. J. Krueger, "An Iterative Approach to Goal Programming," *Operational Research Quarterly*, Vol. 28, No. 3, pp. 671–681, 1977.

Dauer, J. P. and R. J. Krueger, "Multiobjective Screening Model for Water Resources Planning," *Proceedings, First International Conference on Mathematical Modeling*, St. Louis, Missouri, Vol. 4, pp. 2203–2211, 1977.

Dauer, J. P. and R. J. Krueger, "A Multiobjective Optimization Model for Water Resources Planning," *Applied Mathematical Modeling*, Vol. 4, No. 3, pp. 171–175, June 1980.

David, L. and L. Duckstein, "Multicriteria Ranking of Alternative Long-Range Water Resources Systems," *Water Resources Bulletin*, Vol. 12, No. 4, pp. 731–754, 1976.

David, L., L. Duckstein and R. Krzysztofowicz, "Multiobjective Planning of Runoff Regulation under Uncertain Water Demands," *Applied Numerical Modelling: Proceedings of the 1st International Conference*, University of Southampton, pp. 13–22, July 1977.

Davis, M. D. and M. Maschler, "The Kernel of a Cooperative Game," *Naval Research Logistics Quarterly*, Vol. 12, No. 3-4, pp. 223–259, September–December 1965.

Davis, O. A., M. H. De Groot and M. J. Hinich, "Social Preference Orderings and Majority Rule," *Econometrica*, Vol. 40, pp. 147–158, 1972.

Dawes, R. M., "Social Selection Based on Multidimensional Criteria," *Journal of Abnormal and Social Psychology*, Vol. 68, pp. 104–109, 1964.

Dawes, R. M., "A Case Study of Graduate Admissions," *American Psychologist*, Vol. 26, No. 2, pp. 180–188, February 1971.

Dawes, R. M., "Objective Optimization Under Multiple Subjective Functions," *Multiple Criteria Decision Making*, edited by J. L. Cochrane and M. Zeleny, University of South Carolina Press, Columbia, South Carolina, pp. 9–17, 1973.

Dawes, R. M. and B. Corrigan, "Linear Models in Decision Making," *Psychological Bulletin*, Vol. 81, No. 2, pp. 95–106, 1974.

Dawes, R. M. and J. Eagle, "Multivariable Selection of Students in Racist Society: A Systematically Unfair Approach," *Multiple Criteria Decision Making*, edited by M. Zeleny, Lecture Notes in Economics and Mathematical Systems No. 123, Springer-Verlag, Berlin-New York, New York, pp. 97–110, 1976.

Day, R. H. and S. M. Robinson, "Economic Decisions with L** Utility," *Multiple Criteria Decision Making*, edited by J. L. Cochrane and M. Zeleny, University of South Carolina Press, Columbia, South Carolina, pp. 84–92, 1973.

Dean, J. H. and C. S. Shih, "Multiattribute Water Resources Decision Making," *AIIE Transactions*, Vol. 7, No. 4, pp. 408–413, 1975.

Debreu, G., "Representation of a Preference Ordering by a Numerical Function," *Decision Processes*, edited by R. M. Thrall, C. H. Coombs and R. L. Davis, John Wiley and Sons, New York, New York, pp. 159–165, 1954.

Debreu, G., "Valuation Equilibrium and Pareto Optimum," *Proceedings of the National Academy of Sciences, USA*, Vol. 40, pp. 588–592, 1954.

Debreu, G., *Theory of Value*, John Wiley and Sons, New York, New York, 1959; translated into German as *Werttheorie*, Springer-Verlag, Berlin-New York, New York, 1976.

Debreu, G., "Continuity Properties of Paretian Utility," *International Economic Review*, Vol. 5, pp. 285–293, 1964.

Debreu, G., "Smooth Preferences," *Econometrica*, Vol. 40, pp. 603–616, 1972.

Deckro, R. F., "Multiple Objective Districting: A General Heuristic Approach Using Multiple Criteria," *Operational Research Quarterly*, Vol. 28, No. 4, pp. 953–961, 1977.

De Kluyver, C. A., "An Exploration of Various Goal Programming Formulations—with Application to Advertising Media Scheduling," *The Journal of the Operational Research Society*, Vol. 30, No. 2, pp. 167–172, 1979.

de Montgolfier, J. and J. Tergny, "Les Décisions Partiellement Rationalisables (Avenir Incertain et Critères Multiples)," *Revue Metra*, Vol. 10, No. 2, pp. 267–279, 1971.

Dent, J. K., "Organizational Correlates of the Goals of Business Management," *Journal of Personnel Psychology*, Vol. 12, No. 3, pp. 1–22, 1959.

de Neufville, R. and R. L. Keeney, *Use of Decision Analysis in Airport Development for Mexico City, Analysis of Public Systems*, edited by A. W. Drake, R. L. Keeney and P. M. Morse, Massachusetts Institute of Technology Press, Cambridge, Massachusetts, 1972.

de Neufville, R. and R. L. Keeney, "Multiattribute Preference Analysis for Transportation Systems Evaluation," *Transportation Research*, Vol. 7, pp. 63–76, March 1973.

D'Errico, A., "Un Modello delle Preferenze nelle Operazioni Decisionali Multicriteriali," *Boll. Unione mat. ital.*, Vol. B13, No. 1, pp. 202–215, 1976.

Deshpande, D. V. and S. Zionts, "Sensitivity Analysis in Multiple Objective Linear Programming: Changes in the Objective Function Matrix," *Multiple Criteria Decision Making Theory and Application*, edited by G. Fandel and T. Gal, Springer-Verlag, Berlin-New York, New York, pp. 26–39, 1980.

Despontin, M. and P. Vincke, "Multiple Criteria Economic Policy," *Advances in Operations Research*, edited by M. Roubens, North-Holland Publishing Company, Amsterdam, Holland, pp. 119–128, 1977.

Devine, H., "Comment on Application Exampled in Management Science," *Multiple Criteria Decision Making*, edited by M. K. Starr and M. Zeleny, TIMS Studies in the Management Sciences, Vol. 6, North-Holland Publishing Company, Amsterdam, Holland, p. 307, 1977.

Diamond, P. A., "Cardinal Welfare, Individualistic Ethics and Interpersonal Comparisons of Utility: Comment," *Journal of Political Economy*, Vol. 75, pp. 765–766, October 1967.

Diaz, J. B. and H. W. McLaughlin, "Simultaneous Approximation of a Set of Bounded Real Functions," *Mathematics of Computation*, Vol. 23, pp. 583–594, 1969.

Diaz, J. A., "Solving Multiobjective Transportation Problems," *Ekonomicko-matematicky Obzor*, Vol. 14, No. 3, pp. 267–274, 1978.

Diaz, J. A., "Finding a Complete Description of All Efficient Solutions to a Multiobjective Transportation Problem," *Ekonomicko-matematicky Obzor*, Vol. 15, No. 1, pp. 62–73, 1979.

DiGuglielmo, F., "Nonconvex Duality in Multiobjective Optimization," *Mathematics of Operations Research*, Vol. 2, No. 3, pp. 285–291, 1977.

Diner, I. IĂ., "The Division of a Set of Vectors into Characteristic States and the Problem of Choosing a Solution," Problems of General and Social Prediction No. 2, *Operations Research Information Bulletin*, Vol. 29, No. 14, Moscow, USSR, 1969.

Diner, I. IĂ., "The Division of a Set of Vectors into Characteristic States and the Problems of Choosing a Solution," *Operations Research (Methodological Aspects)*, Nauka, Moscow, USSR, 1972.

Dinkel, J. J. and J. E. Erickson, "Multiple Objectives in Environmental Protection Programs," *Policy Sciences*, Vol. 9, pp. 87–96, 1978.

Dinkelbach, W., "Die Maximierung eines Quotienten zweier Linearer Funktionen unter linearen Nebenbedingungen," *Zeitschrift für Wahrscheinlichkeitstheorie und Verwandte Gebiete*, Vol. 1, No. 2, pp. 141–145, 1962.

Dinkelbach, W., "Unternehmerische Entscheidungen bei mehrfacher Zielsetzung," *Zeitschrift für Betriebswirtschaft*, Vol. 32, No. 12, pp. 739–747, 1962.

Dinkelbach, W., "Entscheidungen bei mehrfacher Zielsetzung und die Problematik der Zielgewichtung," *Unternehmerische Planung und Entscheidung*, edited by W. Busse, W. von Colbe and P. Meyer-Dohm, Bertelsmann, Bielefeld, Germany, 1968.

Dinkelbach, W., *Sensitivitätsanalysen und parametrische Programmierung*, Springer-Verlag, Berlin-New York, New York, 1969.

Dinkelbach, W., "Über einen Lösungsansatz zum Vektormaximumproblem," *Unternehmensforschung Heute*, edited by M. Beckmann, Lecture Notes in Operations Research and Mathematical Systems No. 50, Springer-Verlag, Berlin-New York, New York, pp. 1–13, 1971.

Dinkelbach, W. and W. Dürr, "Effizienzaussagen bei Ersatzprogrammen zum Vektormaximumproblem," *Operations Research Verfahren XII*, edited by R. Henn, H. P. Künzi and H. Schubert, Anton Hain Verlag, Meisenheim am Glan, Germany, pp. 117–123, 1972.

Dinkelbach, W. and H. Isermann, "On Decision Making Under Multiple Criteria and Under Incomplete Information," *Multiple Criteria Decision Making*, edited by J. L. Cochrane and M. Zeleny, University of South Carolina Press, Columbia, South Carolina, pp. 302–312, 1973.

Dinkelbach, W., "Multicriteria Decision Models with Specified Goal Levels," *Multiple Criteria Decision Making Theory and Application*, edited by G. Fandel and T. Gal, Springer-Verlag, Berlin-New York, New York, pp. 52–59, 1980.

Dinkelbach, W. and H. Isermann, "Resource Allocation of an Academic Department in the Presence of Multiple Criteria: Some Experience with a Modified STEM Method," *Computers and Operations Research: Special Issue on Mathematical Programming with Multiple Objectives*, edited by M. Zeleny, Vol. 7, No. 1-2, pp. 99–106, 1980.

di Roccaferrera, G. M. F., "Behavioral Aspect of Decision Making Under Multiple Goals," *Multiple Criteria Decision Making*, edited by J. L. Cochrane and M. Zeleny, University of South Carolina Press, Columbia, South Carolina, pp. 635–656, 1973.

Dixon, P. B., *The Theory of Joint Maximization*, North-Holland Publishing Company, Amsterdam, Holland; Elsevier Publishing Company, New York, New York, 1975.

Doležal, J., "Existence of Optima in General Discrete Systems," *Kybernetika*, Vol. 1, No. 4, pp. 301–312, 1975.

Doležal, J., "Some Properties of Nonzero-Sum Multistage Games," *Lecture Notes in Computer Science*, Vol. 27, pp. 451–459, 1975.

Doležal, J., "Necessary Optimality Conditions for N-Player Nonzero-Sum Multistage Games," *Kybernetika*, Vol. 12, No. 4, pp. 268–295, 1976.

Doležal, J., "Hierarchical Solution Concept for Static and Multistage Decision Problems with Two Objectives," *Kybernetika*, Vol. 12, No. 5, pp. 363–385, 1976.

Doležal, J., "Necessary Optimality Conditions for Discrete Systems with State-Dependent Control Region and Vector-Valued Objective Function," *Systems Science*, Vol. 3, No. 2, pp. 171–184, 1977.

Dorfman, R. and H. D. Jacoby, "A Model of Public Decisions Illustrated by a Water Pollution Policy Problem," *Public Expenditures and Policy Analysis*, edited by R. H. Haveman and J. Margolis, Markham Publishing Company, Chicago, Illinois, pp. 173–231, 1970.

Dorfman, R., P. A. Samuelson and R. Solow, *Linear Programming and Economic Analysis*, McGraw-Hill, New York, New York, pp. 408–416, 1958.

Dorfman, S., "Operations Research," *American Economic Review*, Vol. 50, No. 4, pp. 575–623, 1960.

Drăgusin, C., "Asupra Optimizarii Pareto," *Studii şi Cercetări Matematice*, Vol. 26, No. 10, pp. 1293–1326, 1974.

Drăgusin, C., "Functii de Penalizare in Criterii Optimale Vectoriale," *Bull. Univ. Brasov, Sec. C, Mat. Fiz. Chim. Sci. Natur.*, Vol. 16, pp. 25–34, 1974; *Mathematical Reviews*, Vol. 52, No. 5, p. 11712, 1976.

Drake, A. W., R. L. Keeney and P. M. Morse, *Analysis of Public Systems*, Massachusetts Institute of Technology, Cambridge, Massachusetts, 1972.

Dubois, T., "A Teaching System Using Fuzzy Subsets and Multicriteria Analysis," *International Journal of Mathematics, Education, Science and Technology*, Vol. 8, No. 2, pp. 203–217, 1977.

Dubov, Y. A. and B. L. Shmulyan, "Improvement of the Solution of Discrete Multicriterion Problem," *Automation and Remote Control*, Vol. 34, No. 12, pp. 1953–1959, 1973.

Dubov, Y. A., "Resource Allocation under Multiple Criteria," *Automation and Remote Control*, Vol. 38, pp. 1807–1814, 1977.

Duckstein, L., "Multiobjective Optimization in Structural Design: The Model Choice Problem," *Proceedings, International Symposium on Optimum Structural Design, 11th Naval Structural Mechanics Symposium*, University of Arizona, Tucson, Arizona, October 19–22, 1981.

Duckstein, L., D. Monarchi and C. Kisiel, "Interactive Multiobjective Decision Making under Uncertainty," *Theories of Decision in Practice,* Crane, Russak, New York, New York, Section 3, pp. 117–127, February 1976.

Duckstein, L. and S. Opricovic, "Multiobjective Optimization in River Basin Development," *Water Resources Research,* Vol. 16, No. 1, pp. 14–20, 1980.

Dudycha, L. W. and J. C. Naylor, "Characteristics of the Human Inference Process in Complex Choice Behavior Situations," *Organizational Behavior and Human Performance,* Vol. 1, pp. 110–128, 1966.

Dunham, C. B., "Simultaneous Chebyshev Approximation of Functions on an Interval," *Proceedings of the American Mathematical Society,* Vol. 18, pp. 472–477, 1967.

Dupre, R., K. Huckert and J. Jahn, "Lösung linearer Vektormaximum-probleme durch das STEM—Verfahren," *Ausgewählte Operations Research Software in Fortran,* edited by H. Späth, R. Oldenbourg Verlag, München-Wien, Germany, 1979.

Duris, C. S. and V. P. Sreedharan, "Chebyshev and L_1-Solutions of Linear Equations Using Least Squares Solutions," *SIAM Journal of Numerical Analysis,* Vol. 5, No. 3, 1968.

Dürr, W., "Stochastische Programmierungsmodelle als Vektormaximum-problem," *Proc. Oper. Res.,* Vol. 1, pp. 189–199, 1972.

Dwivendi, N. P., "Deterministic Optimal Maneuver Strategy for Multitarget Missions," *Journal of Optimization Theory and Applications,* Vol. 17, No. 1-2, pp. 133–153, 1975.

Dyer, J. S., "Interactive Goal Programming," *Management Science,* Vol. 19, No. 1, pp. 62–70, September 1972.

Dyer, J. S., "A Procedure for Selecting Educational Goal Areas for Emphasis," *Operations Research,* Vol. 21, No. 3, pp. 835–845, May–June 1973.

Dyer, J. S., "A Time-Sharing Computer Program for the Solution of the Multiple Criteria Problem," *Management Science,* Vol. 19, No. 12, pp. 1379–1383, 1973.

Dyer, J. S., "An Empirical Investigation of a Man-Machine Interactive Approach to the Solution of the Multiple Criteria Problem," *Multiple Criteria Decision Making,* edited by J. L. Cochrane and M. Zeleny, University of South Carolina Press, Columbia, South Carolina, pp. 202–216, 1973.

Dyer, J. S., "The Effects of Errors in the Estimation of the Gradient on the Frank-Wolfe-Algorithm with Implications for Interactive Programming," *Operations Research,* Vol. 22, No. 1, pp. 160–174, January 1974.

Dyer, J. S. and R. F. Miles, Jr., "Trajectory Selection for the Mariner Jupiter/Saturn 1977 Project," *Operations Research,* Vol. 24, pp. 220–244, 1975.

Dyer, J. S. and R. F. Miles, Jr., "Alternative Formulations for a Trajectory Selection Problem: The Mariner Jupiter/Saturn 1977 Project," *Conflicting Objectives,* edited by D. E. Bell, R. L. Keeney and H. Raiffa, John Wiley and Sons, New York, New York, pp. 367–388, 1977.

Dyer, J. S. and R. Sarin, "Cardinal Preference Aggregation—Rules for the Case of Certainty," *Multiple Criteria Problem Solving,* edited by S. Zionts, Lecture Notes in Economics and Mathematical Systems No. 155, Springer-Verlag, Berlin-New York, New York, pp. 68–86, 1978.

Dyer, J. S. and R. K. Sarin, "Multicriteria Decision Making," *Encyclopedia of Computer Science and Technology,* Vol. 11, Marcel Dekker, New York, New York, pp. 511–576, 1979.

Dyson, R. G., "Maximin Programming, Fuzzy Linear Programming, and Multi-Criteria Decision Making," *The Journal of the Operational Research Society,* Vol. 31, No. 3, pp. 263–267, 1980.

Eason, E. D. and J. M. Thomas, "Optimization of Multiple Safety Factors in Structural Design," *Proceedings, 11th Office of Naval Research (ONR) Naval Structural Mechanics Symposium,* Tucson, Arizona, October 19–22, 1981.

Easton, A., "A Forward Step in Performance Evaluation," *Journal of Marketing*, Vol. 30, pp. 26–32, 1966.

Easton, A., *Complex Managerial Decisions Involving Multiple Objectives*, John Wiley and Sons, New York, New York, 1973.

Easton, A., "One-of-a-Kind Decisions Involving Weighted Multiple Objectives and Disparate Alternatives," *Multiple Criteria Decision Making*, edited by J. L. Cochrane and M. Zeleny, University of South Carolina Press, Columbia, South Carolina, pp. 657–667, 1973.

Eatman, J. L. and C. W. Sealey, "A Multiobjective Linear Programming Model for Commercial Bank Balance Sheet Management," *Journal of Bank Research*, Vol. 9, pp. 227–236, Winter 1979.

Eaton, D. J., J. L. Cohon, C. S. ReVelle, W. S. Steele and K. Potter, "Grain Reserve Sizing: A Multiobjective and Probabilistic Analysis," *Proceedings, 7th IEEE Conference on Decisions and Control*, Clearwater, Florida, December 1–3, 1976; pp. 728–734, 1976.

Eckenrode, R. T., "Weighting Multiple Criteria," *Management Science*, Vol. 12, No. 3, pp. 180–192, 1965.

Ecker, J. G. and N. S. Hegner, "On Computing an Initial Efficient Extreme Point," *The Journal of the Operational Research Society*, Vol. 29, pp. 1005–1007, 1978.

Ecker, J. G., N. S. Hegner and I. A. Kouada, "Generating All Maximal Efficient Faces for Multiple Objective Linear Programs," *Journal of Optimization Theory and Applications*, Vol. 30, No. 3, pp. 353–382, March 1980.

Ecker, J. G. and I. A. Kouada, "Finding Efficient Points for Linear Multiple Objective Programs," *Mathematical Programming*, Vol. 8, No. 3, pp. 375–377, 1975.

Ecker, J. G. and I. A. Kouada, "Finding All Efficient Extreme Points for Multiple Objective Linear Programs," *Mathematical Programming*, Vol. 14, No. 2, pp. 249–261, 1978.

Ecker, J. G. and N. E. Shoemaker, "Multiple Objective Linear Programming and the Trade-off-Compromise Set," *Multiple Criteria Decision Making Theory and Application*, edited by G. Fandel and T. Gal, Springer-Verlag, Berlin-New York, New York, pp. 60–73, 1980.

Ecker, J. G. and N. E. Shoemaker, "Selecting Subsets from the Set of Efficient Vectors," *SIAM Journal on Control and Optimization*, in press.

Edgeworth, F. Y., *Mathematical Psychics*, P. Keagan, London, England, 1881.

Edwards, W., "The Theory of Decision Making," *Psychological Bulletin*, Vol. 51, pp. 380–417, 1954.

Edwards, W., "How to Use Multiattribute Utility Measurement for Social Decision Making," *IEEE Transactions on Systems, Man, and Cybernetics*, Vol. SMC-7, No. 5, pp. 326–340, 1977.

Edwards, W., "Use of Multiattribute Measurement for Social Decision Making," *Conflicting Objectives*, edited by D. E. Bell, R. L. Keeney and H. Raiffa, John Wiley and Sons, New York, New York, pp. 247–276, 1977.

Efstathiou, J. and V. Rajkovic, "Multi-Attribute Decision-Making Using a Fuzzy, Heuristic Approach," *IEEE Transactions on Systems, Man, and Cybernetics*, Vol. SMC-9, No. 6, pp. 326–333, 1979.

Eichhorn, W., "Effektivität von Produktionsverfahren," *Methods of Operations Research No. 12*, Anton Hain Verlag, Meisenheim am Glan, Germany, 1971.

Eichhorn, W., R. Henn, O. Opitz and R. W. Shepard, *Proceedings of an International Seminar*, University of Karlsruhe, 1973, Lecture Notes in Economics and Mathematical Systems No. 99, Springer-Verlag, Berlin-New York, New York, 1973.

Eilenberg, S., "Ordered Topological Spaces," *American Journal of Mathematics*, Vol. 63, No. 1, pp. 39–45, 1941.

Eilon, S., *Management Control*, The Macmillan Company, London, England, 1971.

Eilon, S., "Goals and Constraints in Decision Making," *Operational Research Quarterly*, Vol. 23, No. 1, pp. 3–15, 1972.

Einhorn, H. J., "The Use of Nonlinear, Noncompensating Models in Decision Making," *Psychological Bulletin*, Vol. 73, pp. 221–230, 1970.

Einhorn, H. J., "Equal Weighting in Multiattribute Models: A Rationale, an Example, and Some Extensions," *Proceedings of the Conference on Topical Research in Accounting*, edited by M. Schiff and G. Sorter, New York University Press, New York, New York, 1976.

Einhorn, H. J. and R. M. Hogarth, "Unit Weighting Schemes for Decision Making," *Organizational Behavior and Human Performance*, Vol. 13, pp. 171–192, 1975.

Einhorn, H. J. and W. McCoach, "A Simple Multi-Attribute Procedure for Evaluation," *Multiple Criteria Problem Solving*, edited by S. Zionts, Lecture Notes in Economics and Mathematical Systems No. 155, Springer-Verlag, Berlin-New York, New York, pp. 87–115, 1977.

Einhorn, H. J. and W. McCoach, "A Simple Multiattribute Utility Procedure for Evaluation," *Behavioral Science*, Vol. 22, No. 4, pp. 270–282, 1977.

El-Hodiri, M. A., "Constrained Extrema, Introduction to the Differentiable Case with Economic Applications," Lecture Notes in Operations Research and Mathematical Systems No. 56, Springer-Verlag, Berlin-New York, New York, 1971.

Ellis, H. M. and R. L. Keeney, "A Rational Approach for Government Decisions Concerning Air Pollution" (Chapter 18), *Analysis of Public Systems*, edited by A. W. Drake, R. L. Keeney and P. M. Morse, Massachusetts Institute of Technology Press, Cambridge, Massachusetts, 1972.

El-Sheshai, K. M., G. B. Harwood and R. H. Hermanson, "Cost-Volume-Profit Analysis with Integer Goal Programming," *Management Accounting*, pp. 43–47, October 1977.

Elster, K.-H. and R. Nehse, "Necessary and Sufficient Conditions for the Order-Completeness of Partially Ordered Vector Spaces," *Mathematische Nachrichten*, Vol. 81, pp. 301–311, 1978.

Emelyanov, S. V., V. I. Borisov, A. A. Malevic and A. M. Cercasin, "Models and Methods of Vector Optimization," *Engineering Cybernetics*, Vol. 11, No. 5, pp. 386–448, 1973.

Emelyanov, S. V., et al., "Problems of Solution Concepts in Organizational Systems," *Proceedings of the 5th All-Union Conference on Control*, Part 1, Nauka, Moscow, USSR, 1971.

Emelyanov, S. V., V. M. Ozernoi and M. G. Gaft, "Formulation of Decision Rules in Multicriterial Problems," *Soviet Physics-Doklady*, Vol. 21, pp. 249–250, 1976.

Encarnacion, J., "A Note on Lexicographical Preferences," *Econometrica*, Vol. 32, pp. 215–217, 1964.

Enzer, H., "On Two Nonprobabilistic Utility Measures for Weapon Systems," *Naval Research Logistics Quarterly*, Vol. 16, No. 1, 1969.

Ester, J., "Bestimmung der Kompromißmenge zweier Gütefunktionen mit Hilfe der Methode paralleler Gradienten," *Polyoptimierung*, pp. 46–53, 1975.

Ester, J., R. Müller and C. Riedel, "Dialogverfahren als Grundlage von Entscheidungen bei Kompromißsituationen," *Polyoptimierung*, pp. 65–74, 1975.

Ester, J., M. Peschel and C. Riedel, "Mathematische Grundlagen der Polyoptimierung," *Polyoptimierung*, pp. 15–27, 1975.

Ester, J. and C. Riedel, "Elementare Theorie der Zweierkompromisse," *Polyoptimierung*, pp. 28–38, 1975.

Ester, J., C. Riedel and M. Peschel, "Polioptimal Approach to the Control of Hierarchical Multilevel Systems," *Proceedings, 6th IFAC World Congress*, Cambridge, Massachusetts, 1975; Part 3, Pittsburgh, Pennsylvania, pp. 19.2/1–19.2/6, 1975.

Evans, J. P. and R. E. Steuer, "A Revised Simplex Method for Linear Multiple Objective Programs," *Mathematical Programming*, Vol. 5, No. 1, pp. 54–72, 1973.

Evans, J. P. and R. E. Steuer, "Generating Efficient Extreme Points in Linear Multiple Objective Programming, Two Algorithms and Computing Experience," *Multiple Criteria Decision Making*, edited by J. L. Cochrane and M. Zeleny, University of South Carolina Press, Columbia, South Carolina, pp. 349–365, 1973.

Fabozzi, F. J. and A. W. Bachner, "Mathematical Programming Models to Determine Civil Service Salaries," *European Journal of Operational Research*, Vol. 3, No. 3, pp. 190–198, 1979.

Fabre-Seneler, F. and R. Guesnerie, "Étude des Systèmes de Revenus Associés aux Optima Parétiens d'une Économie Convexe," *Bulletin de Mathématique Économique*, Vol. 6, 1973.

Falkson, L. M., "Discussion: 'Approaches to Multi-Objective Planning in Water Resources Projects,' by B. W. Taylor III, R. Davis, and R. M. North," *Water Resources Bulletin*, Vol. 12, No. 5, pp. 1071–1077, 1976.

Fama, E. F., "Efficient Capital Markets: A Review of Theory and Empirical Work," *Journal of Finance*, Vol. 25, pp. 383–417, May 1970.

Fandel, G., "Optimale Entscheidung bei mehrfacher Zielsetzung," Lecture Notes in Economics and Mathematical Systems No. 76, Springer-Verlag, Berlin-New York, New York, 1972.

Fandel, G., "Lösungsprinzipien und Lösungsalgorithmen zum Vektormaximumproblem bei Sicherheit und Unsicherheit," *Zeitschrift für Betriebswirtschaft*, Vol. 45, No. 6, pp. 371–392, 1975.

Fandel, G., "Öffentliche Investitionsentscheidung bei mehrfacher Zielsetzung: Dargestellt an einem Beispiel der Hochschulplanung," *Proc. Oper. Res.*, Vol. 6, pp. 110–122, 1976.

Fandel, G., "A Multiple-Objective Programming Algorithm for the Distribution of Resources Among Teaching and Research," *Production Theory and Its Application*, edited by H. Albach and G. Bergendahl, Lecture Notes in Economics and Mathematical Systems No. 139, Springer-Verlag, Berlin-New York, New York, pp. 146–175, 1977.

Fandel, G., "Public Investment Decision Making with Multiple Criteria: An Example of University Planning," *Multiple Criteria Problem Solving*, edited by S. Zionts, Lecture Notes in Economics and Mathematical Systems No. 155, Springer-Verlag, Berlin-New York, New York, pp. 116–130, 1978.

Fandel, G., "Perspectives of the Development in Multiple Criteria Decision Making," *Multiple Criteria Decision Making Theory and Application*, edited by G. Fandel and T. Gal, Springer-Verlag, Berlin-New York, New York, pp. ix-xvi, 1980.

Fandel, G. and J. Wilhelm, "Rational Solution Principles and Information Requirements as Elements of a Theory of Multiple Criteria Decision Making," *Multiple Criteria Decision Making*, edited by H. Thiriez and S. Zionts, Lecture Notes in Economics and Mathematical Systems No. 130, Springer-Verlag, Berlin-New York, New York, pp. 215–230, 1976.

Fandel, G. and J. Wilhelm, "Zur Entscheidungstheorie bei mehrfacher Zielsetzung," *Zeitschrift für Operations Research*, Vol. 20, Serie A-B, No. 1, pp. 1–21, 1976.

Farquhar, P. H., "A Fractional Hypercube Decomposition Theorem for Multiattribute Utility Functions," *Operations Research*, Vol. 23, No. 5, pp. 941–967, September-October 1975.

Farquhar, P. H., "Pyramid and Semicube Decompositions of Multiattribute Utility Functions," *Operations Research*, Vol. 24, pp. 256–271, 1976.

Farquhar, P. H., "A Survey of Multiattribute Utility Theory and Applications," *Multiple Criteria Decision Making*, TIMS Studies in the Management Sciences, Vol. 6, North-Holland Publishing Company, Amsterdam, Holland, pp. 59–89, 1977.

Farquhar, P. H., "Interdependent Criteria in Utility Analysis," *Multiple Criteria Problem Solving*, edited by S. Zionts, Lecture Notes in Economics and Mathematical Systems No. 155, Springer-Verlag, Berlin-New York, New York, pp. 131–180, 1977.

Farquhar, P. H. and V. R. Rao, "A Balance Model for Evaluating Subsets of Multiattribute Items," *Management Science*, Vol. 22, No. 5, pp. 528–539, January 1976.

Farquhavson, R., "Sur une Généralization de la Notion d'Équilibrium," *Comptes Rendus Académie des Sciences de Paris*, Vol. 240, No. 1, pp. 46–48, 1955.

Faulkner, F. D., "On Finding Solutions which Dominate Equilibrium Solutions to Some N-Person Differential Games," Lecture Notes on Economics and Mathematical Systems No. 106, Springer-Verlag, Berlin-New York, New York, pp. 155–167, 1974.

Fayette, J. R., "Appraisal of Non-Independent Projects," *Multiple Criteria Analysis: Operational Methods*, edited by P. Nijkamp and J. Spronk, Gower Press, London, England, 1981.

Feeney, G. J., "A Basis for Strategic Decisions on Inventory Control Operations," *Management Science*, Vol. 2, No. 1, pp. B69–B82, 1956.

Ferguson, C. E., "The Theory of Multidimensional Utility Analysis in Relation to Multiple Goal Business Behavior: A Synthesis," *Southern Economic Journal*, Vol. 32, No. 2, pp. 169–175, 1965.

Ferguson, C. E. and R. Blair, "Inferior Factors, Externalities and Pareto-Optimality," *Quarterly Review of Economics and Business*, Vol. 11, No. 3, pp. 17–27, 1971.

Fiala, J., "Optimierung der quantitativen röntgenographischen Phasenanalyse," *Kristall und Technik*, Vol. 12, No. 5, pp. 505–515, 1977.

Fichefet, J., "GPSTEM: An Interactive Multiobjective Optimization Method," presented at Colloq. Math. Soc. Janos Bolyai, Eger, Czechoslovakia, 1974; *Progress in Operations Research*, Vol. 1, edited by A. Prekopa, North-Holland Publishing Company, Amsterdam, Holland, pp. 317–332, 1976.

Field, D. B., "Goal Programming for Forest Management," *Forest Services*, Vol. 19, No. 2, pp. 125–135, 1973.

Firstman, S. I. and D. S. Stoller, "Establishing Objectives, Measures and Criteria for Multiphase Complementary Activities," *Operations Research*, Vol. 14, No. 1, pp. 84–99, 1966.

Fischer, G. W. "Experimental Applications of Multi-Attribute Utility Models," *Utility, Probability, and Human Decision Making*, edited by D. Wendt and C. Vlek, D. Reidel Publishing Company, Boston, Massachusetts, pp. 7–45, 1975.

Fischer, G. W., "Multidimensional Utility Models for Risky and Riskless Choice," *Organizational Behavior and Human Performance*, Vol. 17, pp. 127–146, 1976.

Fischer, G. W., "Convergent Validation of Decomposed Multiattribute Utility Assessment Procedures for Risky and Riskless Decisions," *Organizational Behavior and Human Performance*, Vol. 18, pp. 295–315, 1977.

Fischer, G. W., "Utility Models for Multiple Objective Decisions: Do They Accurately Represent Human Preferences?", *Decision Sciences*, Vol. 10, No. 3, pp. 451–479, 1979.

Fishburn, P. C., *Decision and Value Theory*, John Wiley and Sons, New York, New York, 1964.

Fishburn P. C., "Independence in Utility Theory with Whole Product Sets," *Operations Research*, Vol. 13, No. 1, pp. 28–45, 1965.

Fishburn, P. C., "A Note on Recent Developments in Additive Utility Theories for Multiple-Factor Situations," *Operations Research*, Vol. 14, pp. 1143–1148, November 1966.

Fishburn, P. C., "Additivity in Utility Theory with Denumerable Product Sets," *Econometrica*, Vol. 34, No. 2, pp. 500–503, 1966.

Fishburn, P. C., "Additive Utilities with Finite Sets: Applications in the Management Sciences," *Naval Research Logistics Quarterly*, Vol. 14, No. 1, pp. 1–10, 1967.

Fishburn, P. C., "Additive Utilities with Incomplete Product Sets: Applications to Priorities and Assignments," *Operations Research*, Vol. 15, No. 3, pp. 537–542, 1967.

Fishburn, P. C., "Methods of Estimating Additive Utilities," *Management Science*, Vol. 3, No. 7, pp. B435–B453, 1967.

Fishburn, P. C., "Utility Theory," *Management Science*, Vol. 14, No. 5, pp. B335–B378, 1968.

Fishburn, P. C., "A Study of Independence in Multivariate Utility Theory," *Econometrica*, Vol. 37, No. 1, pp. 107–121, January 1969.

Fishburn, P. C., "Preferences, Summation, and Social Welfare Functions," *Management Science*, Vol. 16, No. 3, pp. 179–186, November 1969.

Fishburn, P. C., "Intransitive Indifference in Preference Theory: A Survey," *Operations Research*, Vol. 18, No. 2, pp. 207–228, March–April 1970.

Fishburn, P. C., *Utility Theory for Decision Making*, John Wiley and Sons, New York, New York, 1970.

Fishburn, P. C., "Additive Representation of Real-Valued Functions on Subsets of Product Sets," *Journal of Mathematical Psychology*, Vol. 8, pp. 382–388, 1971.

Fishburn, P. C., "Lexicographic Orders, Utilities and Decision Rules: A Survey," Working Paper, Pennsylvania State University, University Park, Pennsylvania, 1972.

Fishburn, P. C., *Mathematics of Decision Theory*, Mouton, Paris, France, 1972.

Fishburn, P. C., "Bernoullian Utilities for Multiple Factor Situations," *Multiple Criteria Decision Making*, edited by J. L. Cochrane and M. Zeleny, University of South Carolina Press, Columbia, South Carolina, pp. 47–61, 1973.

Fishburn, P. C., "Lexicographic Orders, Utilities and Decision Rules: A Survey," *Management Science*, Vol. 20, No. 11, pp. B1442–B1471, 1974.

Fishburn, P. C., "Von Neumann-Morgenstern Utility Functions on Two Attributes," *Operations Research*, Vol. 22, No. 1, pp. 35–45, 1974.

Fishburn, P. C., "Axioms for Lexicographic Preferences," *Review of Economic Studies*, Vol. 42, pp. 415–419, 1975.

Fishburn, P. C., "Multiattribute Utilities in Expected Utility Theory," *Conflicting Objectives*, edited by D. E. Bell, R. L. Keeney and H. Raiffa, John Wiley and Sons, New York, New York, pp. 172–196, 1977.

Fishburn, P. C., "Approximations of Two-Attribute Utility Functions," *Mathematics of Operations Research*, Vol. 2, pp. 30–44, 1977.

Fishburn, P. C., "Multicriteria Choice Functions Based on Binary Relations," *Operations Research*, Vol. 25, pp. 989–1012, 1977.

Fishburn, P. C., "A Survey of Multiattribute/Multicriterion Evaluation Theories," *Multiple Criteria Problem Solving*, edited by S. Zionts, Lecture Notes in Economics and Mathematical Systems No. 155, Springer-Verlag, Berlin-New York, New York, pp. 181–224, 1978.

Fishburn, P. C. and R. L. Keeney, "Seven Independence Concepts and Continuous Multiattribute Utility Functions," *Journal of Mathematical Psychology*, Vol. 11, No. 3, pp. 294–327, 1974.

Fishburn, P. C. and R. L. Keeney, "Generalized Utility Independence and Some Implications," *Operations Research*, Vol. 23, No. 5, pp. 928–940, 1975.

Fisher, J., "Cournot and Mathematical Economics," *Quarterly Journal of Economics*, Vol. 12, pp. 119–138, 1898.

Fisk, J. C., "A Goal Programming Model for Output Planning," *Decision Sciences*, Vol. 10, No. 4, pp. 593–603, 1979.

Fiszel, H., "Uwzglednienie w rachunku optimalizacji wiecej niz jednej funkcjikryterium," *Przeglad Statystyczny*, Vol. 11, No. 4, pp. 401–403, 1964.

Flavell, R. F. and G. R. Salkin, "Resource Allocation in a Decentralized Organization,"

Advances in Operations Research, edited by M. Roubens, North-Holland Publishing Company, Amsterdam, Holland, pp. 169–175, 1977.

Fleming, M., "A Cardinal Concept of Welfare," *Quarterly Journal of Economics*, Vol. 66, pp. 366–384, 1952.

Focke, J., "Vektormaximumprobleme und Parametrische Optimierung," *Mathematische Operationsforschung und Statistik*, Vol. 4, pp. 365–369, 1973.

Foley, M. A., "On a Class of Nonzero-Sum Linear Quadratic Differential Games," *Journal of Optimization Theory and Applications*, Vol. 7, No. 5, pp. 357–377, 1971.

Ford, C. K., R. L. Keeney and C. W. Kirkwood, "Evaluating Methodologies: A Procedure and Application to Nuclear Power Plant Siting Methodologies," *Management Science*, Vol. 25, No. 1, pp. 1–10, January 1979.

Forsyth, J. D., "Utilization of Goal Programming in Production and Capital Expenditure Planning," *CORS Journal*, Vol. 7, No. 2, pp. 136–140, 1969.

Forsyth, J. D. and D. J. Laughhunn, "Capital Rationing in the Face of Multiple Organizational Objectives," *Multiple Criteria Decision Making*, edited by J. L. Cochrane and M. Zeleny, University of South Carolina Press, Columbia, South Carolina, pp. 439–446, 1973.

Franklin, B., "Letter to Joseph Priestley (1772)," *The Benjamin Franklin Sampler*, Fawcett, New York, New York, 1956.

Fraser, D. L. Jr. and S. W. Director, "Multiple Objective Functions Optimization of Digital MOSFET Circuits," *Proceedings, 11th IEEE International Symposium on Circuits and Systems*, New York, New York, May 17–19, 1978, pp. 1114–1115, 1978.

Frechet, M., "Emile Borel, Initiator of the Theory of Psychological Games and its Application," *Econometrica*, Vol. 21, pp. 95–127, 1953.

Frederick, D. G., "Multiple Objectives in Bayesian Analysis: An Applied Case," *Multiple Criteria Decision Making*, edited by J. L. Cochrane and M. Zeleny, University of South Carolina Press, Columbia, South Carolina, pp. 736–737, 1973.

Freeland, J. R., "A Note on Goal Decomposition in a Decentralized Organization," *Management Science*, Vol. 23, pp. 100–102, September 1976.

Freeland, J. R. and N. R. Baker, "Goal Partitioning in a Hierarchical Organization," *Omega*, Vol. 3, No. 6, pp. 673–688, 1975.

Freeman, A. M. III and R. H. Haveman, "Benefit-Cost Analysis and Multiple Objectives: Current Issues in Water Resources Planning," *Water Resources Research*, Vol. 6, No. 6, pp. 1533–1539, 1970.

Frehel, J., "Problèmes Multicritères: Théorie de la Domination de Yu et Efficacité de Pareto," *Cahiers du Centre d'Études de Recherche Opérationelle*, Vol. 16, No. 4, pp. 413–424, 1974.

Frehel, J., "Problèmes Multicritères: Théorie de la Domination de Yu et Efficacité de Pareto," *Revue Metra*, Vol. 13, No. 1, pp. 47–57, March 1974.

Freimer, M. and P. L. Yu, "The Application of Compromise Solutions to Reporting Games," *Game Theory as a Theory of Conflict Resolution*, edited by A. Rapoport, D. Reidel Publishing Company, Boston, Massachusetts, pp. 235–260, 1974.

Freimer, M. and P. L. Yu, "Some New Results on Compromise Solutions for Group Decision Problems," *Management Science*, Vol. 22, No. 6, pp. 688–693, 1976.

Friedmann, A., "Linear-Quadratic Differential Games with Nonzero-Sum and with N-Players," *Archives for Rational Mechanics and Analysis*, Vol. 34, No. 3, pp. 165–187, 1969.

Friedmann, B. M., "Optimal Economic Stabilization Policy: An Extended Framework," *Journal of Political Economy*, Vol. 80 pp. 1002–1022, 1972.

Gabbay, H., "A Note on Polyhedral Sets Having a Least Element," *Mathematical Programming*, Vol. 11, No. 1, pp. 94–96, 1976.

Gaft, M. G. and V. M. Ozernoi, "Isolation of a Set of Noninferior Solutions and Their

Estimates in Decision-Making Problems with Vector-Valued Criterion," *Automation and Remote Control*, Vol. 34, No. 11, pp. 1787–1795, 1973.

Gähler, S., "Eine Verallgemeinerung des Satzes von Dubovickij-Miljutin," *Mathematische Nachrichten*, Vol. 77, pp. 117–138, 1977.

Gähler, S., "Zur Polyoptimierung in verallgemeinerten topologischen Vektorräumen," *Abhandlungen der Akademie der Wissenschaften DDR*, Abteilung Mathematik, Naturwissenschaft, Technik, Vol. 1, pp. 319–326, 1977.

Gal, T., "Homogene mehrparametrische lineare Programmierung," *Zeitschrift für Operations Research*, Vol. 17, pp. 115–136, 1972.

Gal, T., "Eine Methode zur Bestimmung aller funktional effizienten Lösungen eines linearen Vektormaximumproblems," *Proc. Oper. Res.*, Vol. 6, pp. 89–98, 1976.

Gal, T., "A General Method for Determining the Set of All Efficient Solutions to Linear Vectormaximum Problems," *European Journal of Operational Research*, Vol. 1, No. 5, pp. 307–322, 1977.

Gal, T., "An Overview on Recent Results in Multiple Criteria Problem Solving as Developed in Aachen, Germany," *Multiple Criteria Problem Solving*, edited by S. Zionts, Lecture Notes in Economics and Mathematical Systems No. 155, Springer-Verlag, Berlin-New York, New York, pp. 225–248, 1978.

Gal, T., "A Note on Size Reduction of the Objective Functions Matrix in Vector Maximum Problems," *Multiple Criteria Decision Making Theory and Application*, edited by G. Fandel and T. Gal, Springer-Verlag, Berlin-New York, New York, pp. 74–84, 1980.

Gal, T., "Postefficient Sensitivity Analysis in Linear Vectormaximum Problems," *Multiple Criteria Analysis: Operational Methods*, edited by P. Nijkamp and J. Spronk, Gower Press, London, England, 1981.

Gal, T. and H. Leberling, "Über unwesentliche Zielfunktionen bei linearen Vektormaximumproblemen," *Proc. Oper. Res.*, Vol. 6, pp. 134–141, 1976.

Gal, T. and H. Leberling, "Redundant Objective Functions in Linear Vectorvalued Optimization and Their Determination," *European Journal of Operational Research*, Vol. 1, No. 3, pp. 176–184, 1977.

Gal, T. and H. Leberling, "Relaxation Analysis in Multi-Criteria Linear Programming: An Introduction," *Advances in Operations Research*, edited by M. Roubens, North-Holland Publishing Company, Amsterdam, Holland, pp. 177–180, 1977.

Gal, T. and J. Nedoma, "Multiparametric Linear Programming," *Management Science*, Vol. 18, No. 7, pp. B406–B421, 1972.

Gale, D., "Convex Polyhedral Cones and Linear Inqualities," *Activity Analysis of Production and Allocation*, edited by T. C. Koopmans, Cowles Commission Monograph No. 13, John Wiley and Sons, New York, New York, pp. 287–297, 1951.

Gale, D., H. W. Kuhn and A. W. Tucker, "Linear Programming and the Theory of Games," *Activity Analysis of Production and Allocation*, edited by T. C. Koopmans, Cowles Commission Monograph No. 13, John Wiley and Sons, New York, New York, pp. 317–329, 1951.

Gardiner, P. C. and W. Edwards, "Public Values: Multi-Attribute Utility Measurement for Social Decision Making," *Human Judgment and Decision Processes: Formal and Mathematical Approaches*, edited by S. Schwartz and M. Kaplan, Academic Press, New York, New York, pp. 1–37, 1975.

Garrod, N. W. and B. Moores, "An Implicit Enumeration Algorithm for Solving Zero-One Goal Programming Problems," *Omega*, Vol. 6, No. 4, pp. 374–377, 1978.

Gates, D. J. and J. A. Rickard, "Pareto Optimum by Independent Trials," *Bulletin of the Australian Mathematical Society*, Vol. 12, No. 2, pp. 259–265, 1975.

Gearhart, W. B., "On Vectorial Approximation," *Journal of Approximation Theory*, Vol. 10, pp. 49–63, 1974.

Gearhart, W. B., "On the Characterization of Pareto Optimal Solution in Bicriterion Optimization," *Journal of Optimization Theory and Applications*, Vol. 27, No. 2, pp. 301–308, February 1979.

Gearhart, W. B., "Compromise Solutions and Estimation of the Non-inferior Set," *Journal of Optimization Theory and Applications*, Vol. 28, pp. 29–47, May 1979.

Gearing, C. E. and B. H. Adams, "Determining an Optimal Set of Research Experiments," *IEEE Transactions on Engineering Management*, Vol. EM-21, No. 1, pp. 29–39, 1974.

Geering, H. P. and M. Athans, "Optimal Control Theory for Non-Scalar-Valued Performance Criteria," *Proceedings, 5th Annual Princeton Conference on Information Sciences and Systems*, Princeton, New Jersey, s.a., pp. 479–483, 1971.

Geering, H. P. and M. Athans, "The Infimum Principle," *Proceedings, IEEE Conference on Decisions and Control included in 12th Symposium on Adaptive Processes*, San Diego, California, 1973, pp. 577–593, 1973; *IEEE Transactions on Automatic Control*, Vol. AC-19, No. 5, pp. 485–494, October 1974.

Gehner, K. R., "Characterization Theorems for Constrained Approximation Problems Via Optimization Theory," *Journal of Approximation Theory*, Vol. 14, pp. 51–76, 1975.

Gembicki, F. W. and Y. Y. Haimes, "Approach to Performance and Sensitivity Multiobjective Optimization: The Goal Attainment Method," *IEEE Transactions on Automatic Control*, Vol. AC-20, No. 6, pp. 769–771, December 1975.

Geoffrion, A. M., "Solving Bicriterion Mathematical Programs," *Operations Research*, Vol. 15, No. 1, pp. 39–54, 1967.

Geoffrion, A. M., "Strictly Concave Parametric Programming, Part I: Basic Thoery," *Management Science*, Vol. 13, No. 3, pp. 244–253, 1967.

Geoffrion, A. M., "Strictly Concave Parametric Programming, Part II: Additional Theory and Computational Considerations," *Management Science*, Vol. 13, No. 5, pp. 359–370, 1967.

Geoffrion, A. M., "Stochastic Programming with Aspiration or Fractile Criteria," *Management Science*, Vol. 13, No. 9, pp. 672–679, 1967.

Geoffrion, A. M., "Proper Efficiency and the Theory of Vector Maximization," *Journal of Mathematical Analysis and Applications*, Vol. 22, No. 3, pp. 618–630, 1968.

Geoffrion, A. M., J. S. Dyer and A. Feinberg, "An Interactive Approach for Multicriterion Optimization with an Application to the Operation of an Academic Department," *Management Science*, Vol. 19, No. 4, pp. 357–368, December 1972.

Geoffrion, A. M. and W. W. Hogan, "Coordination of Two-Level Organizations with Multiple Objectives," *Techniques of Optimization*, edited by A. V. Balakrishnan, *Proceedings of the Fourth IFIP Colloquium on Optimization Techniques*, Academic Press, New York, New York, pp. 455–466, 1972.

Geogescu-Roegen, N., "Choice, Expectations and Measurability," *Quarterly Journal of Economics*, Vol. 68, No. 4, pp. 503–541, 1954.

Germeier, Y. B., "Multicriteria Optimization Problems and the Role of Information," *Proceedings of the 5th All-Union Conference on Control*, Part 1, Nauka, Moscow, USSR, 1971.

Germeier, Y. B., "Equilibrium Situations in Games with a Hierarchical Structure of the Vector of Criteria," *Lecture Notes in Computer Science*, Vol. 27, pp. 460–465, 1975.

Gershon, M., R. McAniff and L. Duckstein, "A Multi-objective Approach to River Basin Planning," *Proceedings, 1980 Meetings*, Arizona Section, AWRA and Hydrology Section, AZ-NV Academy of Sciences, Las Vegas, Nevada, pp. 41–50, April 1980.

Gerstenhaber, M., "Theory of Convex Polyhedral Cones," *Activity Analysis of Production and Allocation*, edited by T. C. Koopmans, John Wiley and Sons, New York, New York, 1951.

Giauque, W. C. and T. C. Peebles, "Application of Multidimensional Utility Theory in

Determining Optimal Test-Treatment Strategies for Streptococcal Sore Throat and Rheumatic Fever," *Operations Research*, Vol. 24, pp. 933–950, 1976.

Gibbs, T. E., "Goal Programming," *Journal of Systems Management*, Vol. 24, No. 5, pp. 38–41, 1973.

Giesy, D. P., "Calculation of Pareto-Optimal Solutions to Multiobjective Problems Using Threshhold-of-Acceptability Constraints," *IEEE Transactions on Automatic Control*, Vol. AC-23, No. 6, pp. 1114–1115, December 1978.

Gillies, D. B., "Solutions to General Nonzero-Sum Games," *Annals of Mathematical Studies*, Vol. 40, pp. 47–85, 1959.

Gindes, V. B., "A Problem of Optimal Joint Control," *SIAM Journal on Control*, Vol. 5, No. 2, pp. 222–227, 1967.

Giordano, J.-L. and J.-C. Suquet, "On Multicriteria Decision Making: An Application to a Work-Shop Organization Problem," *Advances in Operations Research*, edited by M. Roubens, North-Holland Publishing Company, Amsterdam, Holland, pp. 181–192, 1977.

Gittins, J. C., "A Generalization of a Result in Linear Programming," *Journal of the Institute of Mathematics and Its Applications*, pp. 193–201, 1967.

Gleason, J. M. and C. C. Lilly, "A Goal Programming Model for Insurance Agency Management," *Decision Sciences*, Vol. 8, pp. 180–190, January 1977.

Glover, F., "Surrogate Constraints," *Operations Research*, Vol. 16, No. 4, pp. 741–749, 1968.

Goffin, J.-L., "Conditions for Pareto Optimality in a Multicriterion System with Nondifferentiable Functions," *Proceedings of the 11th Annual Allerton Conference in Circuit and System Theory*, 1973.

Goffin, J.-L. and A. Haurie, "Necessary Conditions and Sufficient Conditions for Pareto-Optimality in a Multicriteria Perturbed System," *Proceedings of the 5th IFIP Conference*, Lecture Notes in Computer Science No. 3, Springer-Verlag, Berlin-New York, New York, pp. 184–193, 1973.

Goffin J.-L. and A. Haurie, "Pareto Optimality with Nondifferentiable Cost Functions," *Multiple Criteria Decision Making*, edited by H. Thiriez and S. Zionts, Lecture Notes in Economics and Mathematical Systems No. 130, Springer-Verlag, Berlin-New York, New York, pp. 232–246, 1976.

Goh, B., T. Vincent and G. Leitmann, "Optimal Control of the Prey-Predator System," 14th International Congress of Entomology, *Journal of Mathematical Biosciences*, Vol. 19, p. 263, 1974.

Goicoechea, A., "The Protrade-Method: A Multiobjective Approach to Decisionmaking," *Multiple Criteria Decision Making,* edited by M. K. Starr and M. Zeleny, TIMS Studies in the Management Sciences, Vol. 6, North-Holland Publishing Company, Amsterdam, Holland, p. 308, 1977.

Goicoechea, A., L. Duckstein and M. Fogel, "A Multiobjective Approach to Managing a Southern Arizona Watershed," *Proceedings, 6th Annual Joint Meeting*, AWRA and Arizona Academy of Sciences, Tucson, Arizona, pp. 233–242, April 1976.

Giocoechea, A., L. Duckstein and M. Fogel, "Multiobjective Programming in Watershed Management: A Study of the Charleston Watershed," *Water Resources Research*, Vol. 12, No. 6, pp. 1085–1092, December 1976.

Giocoechea, A., L. Duckstein and M. Fogel, "Multiple Objectives under Uncertainty: An Illustrative Application of PROTRADE," *Water Resources Research*, Vol. 15, No. 2, pp. 203–210, April 1979.

Goodman, D. A., "A Goal Programming Approach to Aggregate Planning of Production and Workforce," *Management Science,* Vol. 20, No. 12, pp. 1569–1575, August 1974.

Goodwin, G. C., P. V. Kabaila and T. S. Ng, "On the Optimization of Vector-Valued

Performance Criteria," *IEEE Transactions on Automatic Control*, Vol. AC-20, pp. 803–804, December 1975.

Goreux, L. M. and A. S. Manne, *Multilevel Planning: Case Studies on Mexico*, North-Holland Publishing Company, Amsterdam, Holland, 1973.

Gorman, W., "Separable Utility and Aggregation," *Econometrica*, Vol. 27, No. 3, pp. 469–481, July 1959.

Gorokhovik, V. V., "On the Problem of Vector Optimization," *Engineering Cybernetics*, Vol. 10, No. 6, pp. 995–1002, 1972.

Gorokhovik, V. V., "The Optimization of Systems with Vector-Valued Objective Function," *Multivariable Technology Systems,* proceedings of a symposium held at Manchester, England, 1974; London, England, pp. S32/1-S32/4, 1975.

Gourishankar, V. and A. Salama, "A Technique for Solving a Class of Differential Games," *International Journal of Control*, Vol. 15, No. 3, pp. 529–539, 1972.

Gray, D. F. and W. R. S. Sutherland, "Inverse Programming and the Linear Vector Maximization Problem," *Journal of Optimization Theory and Applications*, Vol. 30, No. 4, pp. 523–534, April 1980.

Green, P. E., "Multidimensional Scaling and Conjoint Measurement in the Study of Choice Among Muliattribute Alternatives," *Multiple Criteria Decision Making*, edited by J. L. Cochrane and M. Zeleny, University of South Caroline Press, Columbia, South Carolina, pp. 577–609, 1973.

Green, P. E. and F. J. Carmone, *Multidimensional Scaling and Related Techniques in Marketing Analysis*, Allyn and Bacon, Boston, Massachusetts, 1970.

Green, P. E. and F. J. Carmone, "Evaluation of Multiattribute Alternatives: Additive Versus Configural Utility Measurement," *Decision Sciences*, Vol. 5, pp. 164–181, April 1974.

Green, P. E. and V. R. Rao, *Applied Multidimensional Scaling: A Comparison of Approaches and Algorithms*, Holt, Rinehart and Winston, New York, New York, 1972.

Green, P. E. and Y. Wind, *Multiattribute Decisions in Marketing: A Measurement Approach*, Dryden Press, Hinsdale, Illinois, 1973.

Greenberg, H. J. and W. P. Pierskalla, "Surrogate Mathematical Programming," *Operations Research*, Vol. 18, No. 5, pp. 924–939, 1970.

Grote, J. D., "Dynamics of Cooperative Games," *International Journal of Game Theory*, Vol. 5, No. 1, pp. 27–64, 1976.

Guesnerie, R., "Optimum de Pareto et Ensembles de Production Non Convexes," *Bulletin of Mathematical Economics*, Vol. 2, pp. 32–59, 1969.

Guesnerie, R., "Pareto Optimality in Non-Convex Economics," *Econometrica*, Vol. 43, No. 1, pp. 1–29, 1975.

Guigou, J. L., "On French Location Models for Production Units," *Regional and Urban Economics*, Vol. 1, No. 2, pp. 107–138, 1971.

Guigou, J. L., *Analyse des Données et Choix à Critères Multiples*, Dunod, Paris, France, 1974.

Gum, R. L., T. G. Roefs and D. B. Kimball, "Quantifying Societal Goals: Development of a Weighting Methodology," *Water Resources Research*, Vol. 12, No. 4, pp. 612–622, 1976.

Gurin, L. S., "Some Aspects of Vectorial Optimization" [in Russian], *Avtomatika i Vychislitelnaya Tekhnika*, No. 4, pp. 40–44, 1974.

Gusev, M. J., "Vector Optimization of Linear Systems," *Soviet Mathematics-Doklady*, Vol. 13, pp. 1440–1444, 1972.

Gus'kov, Y. P., "Optimization of Discrete Stochastic Systems with Respect to Two Indicators of Quality" [in Russian], *Avtomatika i Telemekhanika*, No. 10, pp. 60–68, 1970.

Gus'kov, Y. P., "Automatic Landing as a Terminal Control Problem," *Proceedings, 5th IFAC World Congress*, Paris, France, 1972; Part II, Pittsburgh, Pennsylvania, Vol. 19, pp. 2/1-2/6, 1972.

Habenicht, W., "Efficiency in General Vector Maximum Problems," *Ricerca Operativa*, Vol. 8, No. 5, pp. 89–101, 1978.

Hacker, G., "Vektormaximierungsprobleme und Kennzahlen," *Proc. Oper. Res.*, Vol. 5, pp. 66–70, 1976.

Haimes, Y. Y., "Integrated System Identification and Optimization," *Advances in Control Systems Theory and Applications*, Vol. 10, edited by C. T. Leondes, Academic Press, New York, New York, pp. 435–518, 1973.

Haimes, Y. Y., "Coordination of Hierarchical Models via a Multiobjective Optimization Method," *Transactions of American Geophysical Union*, Vol. 55, p. 248, 1974.

Haimes, Y. Y., "Hierarchical Modeling of Regional Total Water Resources Systems," *Automatica*, Vol. 11, No. 1, pp. 25–36, January 1975.

Haimes, Y. Y., *Hierarchical Analyses of Water Resources Systems: Modeling and Optimization of Large-Scale Systems*, McGraw-Hill International Book Company, New York, New York, 1977.

Haimes, Y. Y., "The Surrogate Worth Trade-Off (SWT) Method and Its Extensions," *Multiple Criteria Decision Making Theory and Application*, edited by G. Fandel and T. Gal, Springer-Verlag, Berlin-New York, New York, pp. 85–108, 1980.

Haimes, Y. Y., "Hierarchical Holographic Modeling," *IEEE Transactions on Systems, Man, and Cybernetics*, Vol. SMC-11, No. 9, pp. 606–617, September 1981.

Haimes, Y. Y. and V. Chankong, "Kuhn-Tucker Multipliers as Trade-Offs in Multiobjective Decision Making Analysis," *Automatica*, Vol. 15, pp. 59–72, 1979.

Haimes, Y. Y., P. Das and K. Sung, "Level B Multiobjective Planning for Water and Land," *Journal of Water Resources Planning and Management Division*, Vol. 105, pp. 385–401, September 1979.

Haimes, Y. Y. and W. A. Hall, "Multiobjectives in Water Resources Systems Analysis: The Surrogate Worth Trade-Off Method," *Water Resources Research*, Vol. 10, No. 4, pp. 615–624, 1974.

Haimes, Y. Y. and W. A. Hall, "Analysis of Multiple Objectives in Water Quality," *ASCE Journal of the Hydraulics Division*, Vol. 101, No. 4, pp. 387–400, April 1975.

Haimes, Y. Y. and W. A. Hall, "Sensitivity, Responsivity, Stability and Irreversibility as Multiple Objectives in Civil Systems," *Advances in Water Resources*, Vol. 1, No. 2, 1977.

Haimes, Y. Y., W. A. Hall and H. T. Freedman, *Multiobjective Optimization in Water Resources Systems: the Surrogate Worth Trade-Off Method*, Elsevier Publishing Company, New York, New York, 1975.

Haimes, Y. Y., L. S. Lasdon and D. A. Wismer, "On a Bicriterion Formulation of the Problems of Integrated System Identification and System Optimization," *IEEE Transactions on Systems, Man, and Cybernetics*, Vol. SMC-1, No. 3, pp. 296–297, 1977.

Haimes, Y. Y., K. A. Loparo, S. C. Olenik and S. K. Nanda, "Multiobjective Statistical Method (MSM) for Interior Drainage Systems," *Water Resources Research*, Vol. 16, No. 3, pp. 465–475, June 1980.

Haimes, Y. Y. and D. Macko, "Hierarchical Structures in Water Resources Systems Management," *IEEE Transactions on Systems, Man, and Cybernetics*, Vol. SMC-3, No. 4, pp. 396–402, 1973.

Haimes, Y. Y. and K. Tarvainen, "Hierarchical Multiobjective Framework for Large Scale Systems," *Multiple Criteria Analysis: Operational Methods*, edited by P. Nijkamp and J. Spronk, Gower Press, London, England, 1981.

Haimes, Y. Y. and D. A. Wismer, "A Computational Approach to the Combined Problem of Optimization and Parameter Identification," *Automatica*, Vol. 8, No. 3, pp. 337–347, 1972.

Haith, D. A. and D. P. Loucks, "Multiobjective Water-Resources Planning," *Systems Ap-*

proach to Water Management, edited by A. K. Biswas, McGraw-Hill, New York, New York, 1976.

Halbritter, G., "Multiobjective Programming and Siting of Industrial Plants," *Optimization Techniques,* edited by A. V. Balakrishnan and M. Thoma, Springer-Verlag, Berlin-New York, New York, pp. 454–466, 1978.

Hall, W. A. and Y. Y. Haimes, "The Surrogate Worth Trade-Off Method with Multiple Decision-Makers," *Multiple Criteria Decision Making,* edited by M. Zeleny, Lecture Notes in Economics and Mathematical Systems No. 123, Springer-Verlag, Berlin-New York, New York, pp. 207–233, 1976.

Hammond, K. R., "Externalizing the Parameters of Quasirational Thought," *Multiple Criteria Decision Making,* edited by M. Zeleny, Lecture Notes in Economics and Mathematical Systems No. 123, Springer-Verlag, Berlin-New York, pp. 75–96, 1976.

Hammond, K. R., R. L. Cook and L. Adelman, "POLICY: An Aid for Decision Making and International Communication," *Columbia Journal of World Business,* Vol. 12, No. 3, pp. 79–93, Fall 1977.

Hammond, K. R., T. R. Stewart, B. Brehmer and D. Steinmann, "Social Judgment Theory," *Human Judgment and Decision Processes,* edited by M. F. Kaplan and S. Schwartz, Academic Press, New York, New York, 1975.

Hanieski, J. F., "Technological Change as the Optimization of a Multidimensional Product," *Multiple Criteria Decision Making,* edited by J. L. Cochrane and M. Zeleny, University of South Carolina Press, Columbia, South Carolina, pp. 550–569, 1973.

Hannan, E. L., "Using Duality Theory for Identification of Primal Efficient Points and for Sensitivity Analysis in Multiple Objective Linear Programming," *The Journal of the Operational Research Society,* Vol. 29, pp. 643–649, 1978.

Hannan, E. L., "Allocation of Library Funds for Books and Standing Orders—a Multiple Objective Formulation," *Computers and Operations Research,* Vol. 5, No. 2, pp. 109–114, 1978.

Hannan, E. L., "The Application of Goal Programming Techniques to the CPM Problem," *Socio-Economic Planning Sciences,* Vol. 12, No. 5, pp. 267–270, 1978.

Hannan, E. L., "Using Duality Theory for Identification of Primal Efficient Points and for Sensitivity Analysis of MOLP: Reply," *The Journal of the Operational Research Society,* Vol. 30, No. 3, pp. 287–288, 1979.

Hannan, E. L., "Nondominance in Goal Programming," *INFOR,* Vol. 18, No. 4, pp. 300–309, 1980.

Hansen, P., "Bicriterion Path Problems," *Multiple Criteria Decision Making Theory and Application,* edited by G. Fandel and T. Gal, Springer-Verlag, Berlin-New York, New York, pp. 109–127, 1980.

Hansen, P., M. Anciaux-Mundeleer and P. Vincke, "Quasi-Kernels of Outranking Relations," *Multiple Criteria Decision Making,* edited by H. Thiriez and S. Zionts, Lecture Notes in Economics and Mathematical Systems No. 130, Springer-Verlag, Berlin-New York, New York, pp. 53–63, 1976.

Hansen, P. and M. De Lattre, "Bicriterion Cluster Analysis as an Exploration Tool," *Multiple Criteria Problem Solving,* edited by S. Zionts, Lecture Notes in Economics and Mathematical Systems No. 155, Springer-Verlag, Berlin-New York, New York, pp. 249–273, 1978.

Harnett, R. M. and J. P. Ignizio, "A Heuristic Program for the Covering Problem with Multiple Objectives," *Multiple Criteria Decision Making,* edited by J. L. Cochrane and M. Zeleny, University of South Carolina Press, Columbia, South Carolina, pp. 738–740, 1973.

Harrald, J., et al., "A Note on the Limitations of Goal Programming as Observed in Resource Allocation for Marine Environmental Protection," *Naval Research Logistics Quarterly,* Vol. 25, No. 4, pp. 733–739, 1978.

Harrington, T. C. and W. A. Fischer, "Portfolio Modeling in Multiple-Criteria Situations under Uncertainty: Comment," *Decision Sciences*, Vol. 11, No. 1, pp. 171–177, 1980.

Harsanyi, J. C., "A Bargaining Model for the Cooperative n-Person Game," *Annals of Mathematical Studies*, Vol. 40, pp. 325–355, 1950.

Harsanyi, J. C., "Cardinal Welfare, Individualistic Ethics, and Interpersonal Comparison of Utility," *Journal of Political Economy*, Vol. 63, pp. 309–321, 1955.

Harsanyi, J. C., "A Bargaining Model for the Cooperative n-Person Game," *Contributions to the Theory of Games*, Vol. 4, edited by A. W. Tucker and R. D. Luce, Annals of Mathematical Studies, Princeton University Press, Princeton, New Jersey, pp. 325–356, 1959.

Harsanyi, J. C., "A General Theory of Rational Behavior in Game Situations," *Econometrica*, Vol. 34, pp. 613–634, 1966.

Harsanyi, J. C., "Games with Incomplete Information Played by 'Baysian' Players," Part 1, *Management Science*, Vol. 14, pp. 159–182, 1967.

Harsanyi, J. C., "Games with Incomplete Information Played by 'Baysian' Players," Parts 2 and 3, *Management Science*, Vol. 14, pp. 320–334 and pp. 486–502, 1968.

Harsanyi, J. C., "Nonlinear Social Welfare Functions," *Theory and Decision*, Vol. 7, pp. 61–82, 1974.

Harsanyi, J. C., *Rational Behavior and Bargaining Equilibrium in Games and Social Situations*, Cambridge University Press, Cambridge, England, 1977.

Hartley, R. V., *Operations Research: A Managerial Emphasis* (Chapters 8 and 14), Goodyear Publishing, Pacific Palisades, California, 1976.

Hartley, R., "Aspects of Partial Decisionmaking-Kernels of Quasiordered Sets," *Econometrica*, Vol. 44, pp. 605–608, 1976.

Hartung, J. G., "Über Ersatzprogramme bei der Vektoroptimierung," *Operations Research Verfahren No. 18*, edited by R. Henn, H. P. Künzi and H. Schubert, Anton Hain Verlag, Meisenheim am Glan, Germany, pp. 129–133, 1974.

Harwood, G. B. and R. W. Lawless, "Optimizing Organization Goals in Assigning Faculty Teaching Schedules," *Decision Sciences*, Vol. 6, No. 3, pp. 513–524, 1975.

Hasenauer, R., "Theoretical Analysis and Empirical Application of Goal Programming with Preemptive Priority Structures," *Multiple Criteria Decision Making*, edited by H. Thiriez and S. Zionts, Lecture Notes in Economics and Mathematical Systems No. 130, Springer-Verlag, Berlin-New York, New York, pp. 120–135, 1976.

Hatry, H. P., "Measuring the Effectiveness of Non-Defense Public Programs," *Operations Research*, Vol. 18, No. 5, pp. 772–784, 1970.

Haurie, A., "Jeux Quantitatifs Multi-Étages à M-Joueurs, Équilibres de Nash, Pareto-Optimalité, C-Optimalité," *Revue de Cethedec*, Vol. 30, No. 9, pp. 83–108, 1972.

Haurie, A., "On Pareto-Optimal Decisions for a Coalition of a Subset of Players," *IEEE Transactions on Automatic Control*, Vol. AC-18, No. 2, pp. 144–149, 1973.

Haurie, A., "Optimalité dans un Système Multicritère et Perturbe avec Application à Systèmes de Commande Linéaires à Coûts Quadratiques," *Revue Française d'Automatique, Informatique et de Recherche Opérationelle*, Vol. 7, No. 2, pp. 91–105, 1973.

Haurie, A., "A Note on Nonzero-Sum Differential Games with Bargaining Solution," *Journal of Optimization Theory and Applications*, Vol. 18, No. 1, pp. 31–39, January 1976.

Haurie, A. and M. C. Delfour, "Individual and Collective Rationality in a Dynamic Pareto Equilibrium," *Journal of Optimization Theory and Applications*, Vol. 13, No. 3, pp. 290–302, 1974.

Haurie, A. and M. C. Delfour, "Individual and Collective Rationality in a Dynamic Pareto Equilibrium," *Multicriteria Decision Making and Differential Games*, edited by G. Leitmann, Plenum Press, New York, New York, pp. 149–161, 1976.

Haurie, A. and J. L. Goffin, "Necessary Conditions and Sufficient Conditions for Pareto-

Optimality in a Multicriteria Perturbed System," *Proceedings, 5th IFIP Conference on Optimization Techniques*, Rome, Italy, 1973.

Hausdorff, F., "Untersuchungen über Ordnungstypen," *Berichte über die Verhandlungen der Königlich Sächsischen Gesellschaft der Wissenschaften zu Leipzig, Mathematisch-Physische Klasse*, Vol. 58, pp. 106–169, 1906.

Hausner, M., "Multidimensional Utilities," *Decision Processes*, edited by R. M. Thrall, C. H. Coombs and R. L. Davis, John Wiley and Sons, New York, New York, pp. 167–180, 1954.

Hawkins, C. A. and R. A. Adams, "A Goal Programming Model for Capital Budgeting," *Financial Management*, Vol. 3, No. 1, pp. 52–57, 1974.

Hax, H., "Bewertungsprobleme bei der Formulierung von Zielfunktionen für Entscheidungsmodelle," *Schmalenbachs Zeitschrift für betriebswirtschaftliche Forschung*, Vol. 19, pp. 749–771, 1967.

Hax, A. C. and K. M. Wiig, "The Use of Decision Analysis in Capital Investment Problems," *Conflicting Objectives*, edited by D. E. Bell, R. L. Keeney and H. Raiffa, John Wiley and Sons, pp. 277–297, 1977.

Heenan, D. A. and R. B. Addleman, "Quantitative Techniques for Today's Decision Makers," *Harvard Business Review*, Vol. 54, No. 3, pp. 32–62, 1976.

Hemming, T., "A New Method for Interactive Multiobjective Optimization: A Boundary Point Ranking Method," *Multiple Criteria Decision Making*, edited by H. Thiriez and S. Zionts, Lecture Notes in Economics and Mathematical Systems No. 130, Springer-Verlag, Berlin-New York, New York, pp. 333–340, 1976.

Hemming, T., *Multiobjective Decision Making under Certainty*, Economic Research Institute, Stockholm School of Economics, Stockholm, Sweden, 1978.

Hendrix, G. G. and A. C. Stedry, "The Elementary Redundancy-Optimization Problem: A Case Study in Probabilistic Multiple Goal Programming," *Operations Research*, Vol. 22, No. 3, pp. 610–621, 1974.

Herner, S. and K. J. Snapper, "Application of Multiple-Criteria Utility Model to Evaluation of Information Systems" *Journal of the American Society for Information Science*, Vol. 29, pp. 289–296, 1978.

Hettich, R., "Characterisierung Lokaler Pareto-Optima," *Proceedings of Oberwolfach Conference in Optimization and Operations Research*, edited by W. Oettli and K. Ritter, Lecture Notes in Economics and Operations Research No. 117, Springer-Verlag, Berlin-New York, New York, pp. 128–141, 1976.

Heuchenne, C., "Un Algorithme Général pour Trouver un Sousensemble d'un Certain Type a Distance Minimum d'une Partie Donnée," *Mathématiques et Sciences Humaines*, 1970.

Heyde, W. and O. Martens, "Methodische Probleme der Zielfunktionen bei der Ermittlung 'Optimales Produktionsprogramm' mit Hilfe der linearen Optimierung," *Wirtschaftswissenschaft*, Vol. 12, No. 6, pp. 898–908, 1964.

Hildenbrand, W., "Pareto-Optimality for a Measure Space of Economic Agents," *International Economic Review*, Vol. 10, pp. 363–372, 1969.

Hildenbrand, W., *Core and Equilibria of a Large Economy*, Princeton University Press, Princeton, New Jersey, 1975.

Hill, M., "Goals-Achievement Matrix for Evaluating Alternative Plans," *Journal of the American Institute of Planners*, Vol. 34, No. 1, pp. 19–28, 1968.

Hill, M., *Planning for Multiple Objectives*, Monograph 5, Regional Science Research Institute, Philadelphia, Pennsylvania, 1973.

Hill, M. and Y. Tzamir, "Multidimensional Evaluation of Regional Plans Serving Multiple Objectives," *Papers of the Regional Science Association*, Vol. 29, pp. 139–165, 1972.

Hindelang, T. J., "QC-Optimization through Goal Programming," *Quality Progress*, Vol. 6, No. 12, pp. 20–22, 1973.

Hirsch, G., "The Notion of Characteristic Set and Its Implication for the Analysis and Development of Multicriterion Methods," *Multiple Criteria Decision Making*, edited by H. Thiriez and S. Zionts, Lecture Notes in Economics and Mathematical Systems No. 130, Springer-Verlag, Berlin-New York, New York, pp. 247–262, 1976.

Hirshleifer, J., "Efficient Allocation of Capital in an Uncertain World," *American Economic Review*, Vol. 54, No. 3, pp. 77–85, May 1964.

Hisashi, M. and S. Harunori, "A Method of Determining Characteristic Functions for Co-operative Differential Games Without Side Payment," *Memoirs of the Faculty of Engineering, Kyoto University*, Vol. 38, No. 4, pp. 169–181, 1976.

Hitch, C. J., "Sub-Optimization in Operations Research," *Journal of Operations Research*, Vol. 1, No. 3, pp. 87–99, 1953.

Hitch, C. J., "On the Choice of Objectives in Systems Studies," *Systems, Research and Design*, edited by D. P. Eckmann, John Wiley and Sons, New York, New York, pp. 43–51, 1961.

Ho, Y. C., "Differential Games, Dynamic Optimization and Generalized Control Theory," *Journal of Optimization Theory and Applications*, Vol. 6, No. 3, pp. 179–209, 1970.

Ho, Y. C., "Comment on a Paper by J. Medanic and M. Andjelic," *Journal of Optimization Theory and Applications*, Vol. 10, No. 3, pp. 187–189, 1972.

Ho, Y. C. and K.-C. Chu, "Team Decision Theory and Information Structures in Optimal Control Problems," Part I, *IEEE Transactions on Automatic Control*, Vol. AC-17, pp. 15–22, February 1972.

Ho, Y. C. and K.-C. Chu, "Team Decision Theory and Information Structures in Optimal Control Problems," Part II, *IEEE Transactions on Automatic Control*, Vol. AC-17, pp. 22–28, February 1972.

Ho, Y. C. and S. K. Mitter (eds.), *Directions in Large-Scale Systems: Decentralized Control and Many-Person Optimization*, Plenum Press, New York, New York, 1976.

Hoag, M. W., "The Relevance of Costs in Operations Research," *Operations Research*, Vol. 4, No. 4, pp. 448–459, 1956.

Hobbs, B. F., "A Comparison of Weighting Methods in Power Plant Siting," *Decision Sciences*, Vol. 11, No. 4, pp. 725–737, 1980.

Hogan, W. W. and J. M. Warren, "Computation of the Efficient Boundary in the E-S Portfolio Selection Model," *Journal of Financial and Quantitative Analysis*, Vol. 7, pp. 1881–1896, 1972.

Holl, S. T. and J. P. Young, "Planning for Education in the Health Services: A Multicriterion Approach," *Socio-Economic Planning Sciences*, Vol. 14, No. 2, pp. 79–84, 1980.

Hopkins, D. S. P., J.-C. Larréché and W. F. Massy, "Multiattribute Preference Functions of University Administrators," *Multiple Criteria Decision Making*, edited by M. Zeleny, Lecture Notes in Economics and Mathematical Systems No. 123, Springer-Verlag, Berlin-New York, New York, pp. 284–286, 1976.

Horowitz, A. D., "The Competitive Bargaining Set for Cooperative n-Person Games," *Journal of Mathematical Psychology*, Vol. 10, No. 3, pp. 265–289, August 1973.

Houck, M. H. and J. L. Cohon, "Sequential Explicitly Stochastic Linear Programming Models: A Proposed Method for Design and Management of Multipurpose Reservoir Systems," *Water Resources Research*, Vol. 14, No. 2, pp. 161–169, April 1978.

House, P. W., "How do you know where you're going?", *Multiple Criteria Decision Making*, edited by J. L. Cochrane and M. Zeleny, University of South Carolina Press, Columbia, South Carolina, pp. 741–744, 1973.

Houthakker, H., "Revealed Preference and the Utility Function," *Economica*, Vol. 17, pp. 159–174, 1950.

Howard, R. A., "The Foundations of Decision Analysis," *IEEE Transactions on System Science and Cybernetics*, Vol. SSC-4, pp. 211–219, 1968.

Huang, S. C. "Optimal Control Problems with Vector-Valued Criterion Function," *Pro-*

ceedings of the IEEE Conference on Decisions and Control (International 10th Symposium on Adaptive Processes), Miami Beach, Florida, 1971; New York, New York, pp. 462–469, 1971.

Huang, S. C., "Note on the Mean-Square Strategy for Vector-Valued Objective Functions," *Journal of Optimization Theory and Applications*, Vol. 9, No. 5, pp. 364–366, 1972.

Huang, S. C. and A. Joshi, "Note on Non-Inferiority with Countably or Uncountably Many Performance Indices," *Proceedings, IEEE Joint Automatic Control Conference*, Austin, Texas, June 18–21, 1974, pp. 712–715, 1974.

Huber, G. P., "Multi-Attribute Utility Models: A Review of Field- and Field-like Studies," *Management Science*, Vol. 20, No. 10, pp. 1393–1402, June 1974.

Huber, G. P., "Methods for Quantifying Subjective Probabilities and Multiattribute Utilities," *Decision Sciences*, Vol. 5, pp. 430–458, July 1974.

Huckert, K., R. Rhode, O. Roglin and R. Weber, "On the Interaction Solution to a Multicriteria Scheduling Problem," *Zeitschrift für Operations Research*, Series A, Vol. 24, No. 1, pp. 47–60, February 1980.

Hughes, A. and D. Grawiog, *Linear Programming: An Emphasis on Decision Making*, Addison-Wesley, Reading, Massachusetts, 1973.

Humphreys, A. P. and P. C. Humphreys, "An Investigation of Subjective Preference Orderings for Multiattributed Alternations," *Utility, Subjective Probability and Human Decision Making*, edited by D. Wendt and C. Vlek, D. Reidel Publishing Company, Boston, Massachusetts, 1975.

Humphreys, P., "Applications of Multiattribute Utility Theory," *Decision Making and Change in Human Affairs*, edited by H. Jungermann and G. De Zeeuw, D. Reidel Publishing Company, Boston, Massachusetts, 1977.

Hurwicz, L., "Programming in Linear Spaces," *Studies in Linear and Nonlinear Programming*, edited by K. J. Arrow, L. Hurwicz and H. Uzawa, Stanford University Press, Standford, California, 1958; second printing, Oxford University Press, London, England, pp. 38–102, 1964.

Hurwicz, L. and H. Uzawa, "A Note on the Lagrangian Saddlepoints," *Studies in Linear and Nonlinear Programming*, edited by K. J. Arrow, L. Hurwicz and H. Uzawa, Stanford University Press, Stanford, California, 1958; second printing, Oxford University Press, London, England, pp. 103–113, 1964.

Hwang, C. L., K. C. Lai, F. A. Tillman and L. T. Fan, "Optimization of Systems Reliability by the Sequential Unconstrained Minimization Technique," *IEEE Transactions on Reliability*, Vol. R-24, pp. 133–135, 1975.

Hwang, C. L. and A. S. M. Masud, "Multiple Objective Decision Making--Methods and Applications," Lecture Notes in Economics and Mathematical Systems No. 164, Springer-Verlag, Berlin-New York, New York, 1979.

Hwang, C. L., A. S. M. Masud, S. R. Paidy and K. Yoon, "Mathematical Programming with Multiple Objectives: A Tutorial," *Computers and Operations Research: Special Issue on Mathematical Programming with Multiple Objectives*, edited by M. Zeleny, Vol. 7, No. 1–2, pp. 5–31, 1980.

Ignizio, J. P., "An Approach to the Capital Budgeting Problem with Multiple Objectives," *The Engineering Economist*, Vol. 21, No. 4, pp. 259–272, 1976.

Ignizio, J. P., *Goal Programming and Extensions*, Lexington Book, D. C. Heath and Co., Lexington, Massachusetts, 1976.

Ignizio, J. P., "A Review of Goal Programming: A Tool for Multiobjective Analysis," *The Journal of the Operational Research Society*, Vol. 29, No. 11, pp. 1109–1119, 1978.

Ignizio, J. P., "Antenna Array Beam Pattern Synthesis via Goal Programming," *European Journal of Operational Research*, Vol. 5, pp. 406–410, 1980.

Ignizio, J. P. and J. H. Perlis, "Sequential Linear Goal Programming: Implementation via MPSX," *Computers and Operations Research*, Vol. 6, No. 3, pp. 141–145, 1979.

Ijiri, Y., "A Historical Cost Approach to Aggregation of Multiple Goals," *Multiple Criteria Decision Making*, edited by J. L. Cochrane and M. Zeleny, University of South Carolina Press, Columbia, South Carolina, pp. 395–405, 1973.

Inagaki, T. K., K. Inoue and H. Akashi, "Interactive Optimization of System Reliability under Multiple Objectives," *IEEE Transactions on Reliability*, Vol. 27, No. 4, pp. 264–267, 1978.

International Institute for Applied Systems Analysis, *Proceedings of the Workshop on Decision Making with Multiple Conflicting Objectives*, Laxenburg, Austria, October 1975.

Isermann, H., "Lösungsansätze zum Entscheidungsproblem des Satisfizierers bei mehrfacher Zielsetzung," *Proceedings in Operations Research*, Vol. 3, edited by R. Gessner, R. Henn, V. Steinecke and H. Todt, Physica Verlag, Würzburg, Germany, 1974.

Isermann, H., "Proper Efficiency and the Linear Vector Maximum Problems," *Operations Research*, Vol. 22, No. 1, pp. 189–191, January-February 1974.

Isermann, H., "A Note on Proper Efficiency and the Linear Vector Maximum Problem," *Operations Research*, Vol. 22, No. 1, pp. 189–199, 1974.

Isermann, H., "Some Remarks on Optimising and Satisficing in Multiple Criteria Decision Problems," *The Role and Effectiveness of Theories of Decision in Practice*, edited by D. J. White and K. C. Bowen, Crane, Russak & Co., New York, New York, pp. 43–51, 1975.

Isermann, H., "Ein Algorithmus zur Lösung linearer Vektormaximumprobleme," *Proc. Oper. Res.*, Vol. 5, pp. 55–65, 1975.

Isermann, H., "Existence and duality in Multiple Objective Linear Programming," *Multiple Criteria Decision Making*, edited by H. Thiriez and S. Zionts, Lecture Notes in Economics and Mathematical Systems No. 130, Springer-Verlag, Berlin-New York, New York, pp. 64–75, 1976.

Isermann, H., "The Enumeration of the Set of all Efficient Solutions for Linear Multiple Objective Programs," *Operational Research Quarterly*, Vol. 28, No. 3, pp. 711–725, 1977.

Isermann, H., "The Relevance of Duality in Multiple Objective Linear Programming," *Multiple Criteria Decision Making*, edited by M. K. Starr and M. Zeleny, TIMS Studies in the Management Sciences, Vol. 6, North-Holland Publishing Company, Amsterdam, Holland, pp. 241–262, 1977.

Isermann, H., "Duality in Multiple Objective Linear Programming," *Multiple Criteria Problem Solving*, edited by S. Zionts, Lecture Notes in Economics and Mathematical Systems No. 155, Springer-Verlag, Berlin-New York, New York, pp. 274–285, 1978.

Isermann, H., "On Some Relations Between a Dual Pair of Multiple Objective Linear Programs," *Zeitschrift für Operations Research*, Vol. 22, pp. 33–41, 1978.

Isermann, H., "The Enumeration of All Efficient Solutions for a Linear Multiple-Objective Transportation Problem," *Naval Research Logistics Quarterly*, Vol. 26, No. 1, pp. 123–139, 1979.

Ishikawa, M., I. Matsuda and Y. Kaya, "Revised Multi-Objective Optimization in Industry Allocation Problem," *Proceedings, 8th IEEE Conference on Cybernetics and Society*, Tokyo-Kyoto, Japan, November 3–7, 1978, pp. 505–510, 1978.

Jääskeläinen, V., "A Goal Programming Model of Aggregate Production Planning," *Swedish Journal of Economics*, Vol. 71, No. 1, pp. 14–29, 1969.

Jääskeläinen, V., "Strategic Planning with Goal Programming," *Management Informatics*, Vol. 1, No. 1, pp. 23–31, 1972.

Jackman, H. W., "Financing Public Hospitals in Ontario: A Case Study in Rationing of Capital Budgets," *Management Science*, Vol. 20, No. 4 (Part 2), pp. 645–655, 1973.

Jacobson, D. H., "On Fuzzy Goals and Maximizing Decisions in Stochastic Optimal Control," *Journal of Mathematical Analysis and Applications*, Vol. 55, pp. 434–440, 1976.

Jacquet-Lagrèze, E., "L'Agrégation des Opinions Individuelles," *Informatique et Sciences Humaines*, Vol. 4, 1969.

Jacquet-Lagrèze, E., "Le Problème de l'Agrégation des Préférences; une Classe de Procédures à Seuil," *Mathématiques et Sciences Humaines*, Vol. 43, 1973.

Jacquet-Lagrèze, E., "How We Can Use the Notion of Semi-Orders to Build Outranking Relations in Multicriteria Decision Making," *Revue Metra*, Vol. 13, No. 1, pp. 56–86, 1974.

Jacquet-Lagrèze, E., "How We Can Use The Notion of Semi-Orders to Build Outranking Relations in Multicriteria Decision Making," *Utility, Probability, and Human Decision Making*, edited by D. Wendt and C. Vlek, D. Reidel Publishing Company, Boston, Massachusetts, pp. 87–111, 1975.

Jacquet-Lagrèze, E., "Explicative Models in Multicriteria Preference Analysis," *Advances in Operations research*, edited by M. Roubens, North-Holland Publishing Company, Amsterdam, Holland, pp. 213–218, 1977.

Jacquet-Lagrèze, E., "Modelling Preferences Among Distributions Using Fuzzy Relations," *Decision Making and Change in Human Affairs*, edited by H. Jungermann and G. De Zeeuw, D. Reidel Publishing Company, Boston, Massachusetts, 1977.

Jahn, J., "The Haar Condition in Vector Optimization," *Multiple Criteria Decision Making*, edited by G. Fandel and T. Gal, Lecture Notes in Economics and Mathematical Systems No. 177, Springer-Verlag, Berlin-New York, New York, 1980.

Jaikumar, R., "A Heuristic O-l-Algorithm with Multiple Objectives and Constraints," *Multiple Criteria Decision Making*, edited by J. L. Cochrane and M. Zeleny, University of South Carolina Press, Columbia, South Carolina, pp. 745–748, 1973.

Jain, R., "Decision Making in the Presence of Fuzzy Variables," *IEEE Transactions on Systems, Man, and Cybernetics*, Vol. SMC-6, pp. 698–703, 1976.

Jain, R., "A Procedure for Multiple-Aspect Decision Making Using Fuzzy Sets," *International Journal of Systems Science*, Vol. 8, No. 1, pp. 1–7, January 1977.

Jameson, G., "Ordered Linear Spaces," Lecture Notes in Mathematics No. 141, Springer-Verlag, Berlin-New York, New York, 1970.

Jasilionis, R. J. and P. E. Rybakovaite, "The Connection Between the Vector Minimizing Problem and Convex Programming Problem" [in Russian], *Litovskii Matematicheskii Sbornik*, Vol. 10, pp. 199–205, 1970.

Jemelyanov, S. V., O. J. Larichev, V. M. Ozernoy and A. J. Bogdanov, "Multi-Objective Decision Making Problems in R and D Planning," *Proceedings, 6th IFAC World Congress*, Cambridge, Massachusetts, 1975; Part 3, Pittsburgh, Pennsylvania, pp. 25.1/1–25.1/9, 1975.

Jemelyanov, S. V., V. M. Ozernoy and O. J. Larichev, "Problemy i metody podejmowania decyzji," *Przeglad "Pr. 10K,"* No. 32, 1976.

Jensen, M. C. and J. B. Long, "Corporate Investment Under Uncertainty and Pareto Optimality in the Capital Markets," *Bell Journal of Economics and Management Science*, Vol. 3, pp. 151–174, 1972.

Johnsen, E., *Studies in Multiobjective Decision Models*, Monograph No. 1, Economic Research Center, Berlingska Bohtryckeriet, Lund, Sweden, 1968.

Johnsen, E., "Experiences in Multiobjective Management Processes," *Multiple Criteria Decision Making*, edited by M. Zeleny, Lecture Notes in Economics and Mathematical Systems No. 123, Springer-Verlag, Berlin-New York, New York, pp. 135–151, 1976.

Johnsen, E., "Multiobjective Management of the Small Firm," *Multiple Criteria Problem Solving*, edited by S. Zionts, Lecture Notes in Economics and Mathematical Systems No. 155, Springer-Verlag, Berlin-New York, New York, pp. 286–298, 1978.

Johnson, E. M. and G. P. Huber, "The Technology of Utility Assessment," *IEEE Transactions on Systems, Man, and Cybernetics*, Vol. SMC-7, pp. 311–325, 1977.

Johnson, L. E. and D. P. Loucks, "Interactive Multiobjective Planning Using Computer

Graphics," *Computers and Operations Research: Special Issue on Mathematical Programming with Multiple Objectives*, edited by M. Zeleny, Vol. 7, No. 1–2, pp. 89–97, 1980.

Johnson, S. C., "Hierarchial Clustering Schemes," *Psychometrika*, Vol. 32, pp. 241–254, 1967.

Joksch, H. C., "Programming with Fractional Linear Objective Functions," *Naval Research Logistics Quarterly*, Vol. 11, pp. 197–204, 1964.

Joksch, H. C., "Constraints, Objectives, Efficient Solutions and Suboptimization in Mathematical Programming," *Zeitschrift für die Gesamte Staatswissenschaft*, Vol. 122, No. 1, pp. 5–13, 1966.

Joksch, H. C., "Mathematical Aspects of a Multi-Objective Optimizing Model Proposed by Leininger, et al.," *Accident Analysis and Prevention*, Vol. 3, No. 3, pp. 209–213, 1971.

Juralewicz, R. S., "Interpersonal Dimensions of Decision Making in a Cross-Cultural Setting," *Multiple Criteria Decision Making*, edited by J. L. Cochrane and M. Zeleny, University of South Carolina Press, Columbia, South Carolina, pp. 749–752, 1973.

Juricek, L., "Games with Coalition," *Topics in Differential Games*, edited by A. Blaquière, North-Holland Publishing Company, Amsterdam, Holland, pp. 311–344, 1973.

Jüttler, H., "Über spieltheoretische Entscheidungssituationen," *Konferenzprotokoll "Mathematik und Kybernetik in der Ökonomie,"* Teil 1, Akademie-Verlag, Berlin, Germany, pp. 103–110, 1965.

Jüttler, H., "A Linear Model with Several Objective Functions" [in Russian], *Ekonomika i Matematicheskie Metody*, Vol. 3, No. 3, pp. 397–406, 1967.

Jüttler, H., "Die lineare Quotientenoptimierung als Hilfsmittel für die Entscheidungsfindung," *Zeitschrift für Rechentechnik-Datenverarbeitung*, Vol. 4, No. 11, pp. 10–12, 1967.

Jüttler, H., "Zur Ermittlung von Kompromißlösungen für lineare Optimalprobleme mit unterschiedlichen Zielfunktionen," *Entwicklung der Mathematik in der DDR*, Verlag der Wissenschaften, East Berlin, German Democratic Republic, 1974.

Kafarov, V. V., G. B. Lazarev and V. I. Avdeev, "Multicriterial Problems in the Control of Complex-Engineering Systems," *Soviet Physics-Doklady*, Vol. 16, No. 5, pp. 344–345, 1971.

Kahne, S. J., "Optimal Cooperative State Rendez-Vous and Pontryagin's Maximum Principle," *International Journal of Control*, Vol. 2, No. 5, pp. 425–431, 1965.

Kalai, E., "Excess Functions for Cooperative Games without Side Payments," *SIAM Journal on Applied Mathematics*, Vol. 29, No. 1, pp. 60–71, 1975.

Kalai, E., E. A. Pazner and D. Schmeidler, "Collective Choice Correspondences as Admissible Outcomes of Social Bargaining Processes," *Econometrica*, Vol. 44, No. 2, pp. 233–240, 1976.

Kalinin, V. N., "Generalized Optimality Criteria, in Optimal Control Problems," *Automation and Remote Control*, Vol. 26, No. 2, pp. 359–364, February 1965.

Kannai, Y., "Existence of a Utility in Infinite Dimensional Partially Ordered Spaces," *Israel Journal of Mathematics*, Vol. 1, pp. 229–234, 1963.

Kantariya, G. V., "Optimal Choice of Strategy Based on Compromise Agreement Among Alternative Selection Criteria," *Engineering Cybernetics*, Vol. 12, No. 1, pp. 39–42, 1974.

Kantorovich, L. V., "Optimization Methods and Mathematical Models in Economics," *Uspekhi Math. Nauk*, Vol. 25, No. 5, 1970.

Kapur, K. C., "Mathematical Methods of Optimization for Multi-Objective Transportation Systems," *Socio-Economic Planning Sciences*, Vol. 4, No. 4, pp. 451–467, 1970.

Karpelevich, F. I. and V. A. Mukhina, "On One Method for Solving Multi-Objective Linear Programming Problems" [in Russian], *Avtomatika i Telemekhanika*, Vol. 7, pp. 153–155, 1975.

Karpelevich, F. I. and V. A. Mukhina, "On Some Solution Methods of Multi-Objective Problems" [in Russian], *Ekonomika i Matematicheskie Metody*, Vol. 11, No. 2, pp. 399–401, 1975.

Karwan, K. K., "MCDM and Public Program Management," *Multiple Criteria Decision Making*, edited by M. K. Starr and M. Zeleny, TIMS Studies in the Management Sciences, Vol. 6, North-Holland Publishing Company, Amsterdam, Holland, pp. 308–309, 1977.

Karwan, K. R. and W. A. Wallace, "A Comparative Evaluation of Conjoint Measurement and Goal Programming as Aids in Decision Making for Marine Environmental Protection," *Multiple Criteria Decision Making Theory and Application*, edited by G. Fandel and T. Gal, Springer-Verlag, Berlin-New York, New York, pp. 135–149, 1980.

Katopsis, G. A. and J. G. Lin, "Non-Inferiority of Controls Under Double Performance Objectives: Minimal Time and Minimal Energy," *Proceedings of the Seventh Hawaii International Conference on Systems Science*, Honolulu, Hawaii, pp. 129–131, 1974.

Katsutoshi, T., "Linear Optimal Problems with a Vector-Valued Performance Index," *Transactions of the Society of Instrument and Control Engineers*, Vol. 10, No. 6, pp. 749–755, 1974.

Keefer, D. L., "Allocation Planning for R&D with Uncertainty and Multiple Competing Objectives," *IEEE Transactions on Engineering Management*, Vol. EM-25, No. 1, pp. 8–14, 1978.

Keefer, D. L., "Applying Multiobjective Decision Analysis to Resource Allocation Planning Problems," *Multiple Criteria Problem Solving*, edited by S. Zionts, Lecture Notes in Economics and Mathematical Systems No. 155, Springer-Verlag, Berlin-New York, New York, pp. 299–320, 1978.

Keefer, D. L. and C. W. Kirkwood, "A Multiobjective Decision Analysis: Budget Planning for Product Engineering," *Operational Research Quarterly*, Vol. 29, p. 435, 1978.

Keefer, D. L. and S. M. Pollock, "Approximations and Sensitivity in Multiobjective Resource Allocation," *Operations Research*, Vol. 28, No. 1, pp. 114–128, 1980.

Keen, P. G. W., "The Evolving Concept of Optimality," *Multiple Criteria Decision Making*, edited by M. K. Starr and M. Zeleny, TIMS Studies in the Management Sciences, Vol. 6, North-Holland Publishing Company, Amsterdam, Holland, pp. 31–57, 1977.

Keeney, R. L., "Evaluating Multidimensional Situations Using a Quasi-Separable Utility Function," *IEEE Transactions on Man-Machine Systems*, Vol. MMS-9, No. 2, pp. 25–28, 1968.

Keeney, R. L., "Quasi-Separable Utility Functions," *Naval Research Logistics Quarterly*, Vol. 15, No. 4, pp. 551–566, 1968.

Keeney, R. L., "Utility Independence and Preferences for Multiattributed Consequences," *Operations Research*, Vol. 19, No. 4, pp. 875–893, 1971.

Keeney, R. L. "An Illustrated Procedure for Assessing Multiattributed Utility Functions," *Sloan Management Review*, Vol. 14, No. 1, pp. 37–50, 1972.

Keeney, R. L., "Utility Functions for Multiattributed Consequences," *Management Science*, Vol. 18, No. 5 (Part 1), pp. B276–B287, 1972.

Keeney, R. L., "A Decision Analysis with Multiple Objectives: The Mexico City Airport," *Bell Journal of Economics and Management Science*, Vol. 4, pp. 101–117, 1973.

Keeney, R. L., "A Utility Analysis for Response Time of Engines and Ladders to Fires," *Urban Analysis*, Vol. 1, pp. 209–222, 1973.

Keeney, R. L., "Concepts of Independence in Multiattribute Utility Theory," *Multiple Criteria Decision Making*, edited by J. L. Cochrane and M. Zeleny, University of South Carolina Press, Columbia, South Carolina, pp. 62–71, 1973.

Keeney, R. L., "Risk, Independence, and Multiattributed Utility Functions," *Econometrica*, Vol. 41, No. 1, pp. 27–39, 1973.

Keeney, R. L., "Multiplicative Utility Functions," *Operations Research*, Vol. 22, No. 1, pp. 22–34, 1974.

Keeney, R. L., "Examining Corporate Policy Using Multiattribute Utility Analysis," *Sloan Management Review*, Vol. 17, No. 1, pp. 63–76, 1975.

Keeney, R. L., "Quantifying Corporate Preferences for Policy Analysis," *Multiple Criteria Decision Making*, edited by H. Thiriez and S. Zionts, Lecture Notes in Economics and Mathematical Systems No. 130, Springer-Verlag, Berlin-New York, New York, pp. 293–304, 1976.

Keeney, R. L. and C. W. Kirkwood, "Group Decision Making Using Cardinal Social Welfare Functions," *Mangement Science*, Vol. 22, pp. 430–437, 1975.

Keeney, R. L., "A Utility Function for Examining Policy Affecting Salmon on the Skeena River,' *Journal of the Fisheries Research Board of Canada*, Vol. 34, pp. 49–63, 1977.

Keeney, R. L., "The Art of Assessing Multiattribute Utility Functions," *Organizational Behavior and Human Performance*, Vol. 19, pp. 267–310, 1977.

Keeney, R. L., "Evaluation of Proposed Pumped Storage Sites," *Operations Research*, Vol. 27, pp. 48–64, 1979.

Keeney, R. L. and G. L. Lilien, "A Utility Model for Product Positioning," *Multiple Criteria Problem Solving*, edited by S. Zionts, Lecture Notes in Economics and Mathematical Systems No. 155, Springer-Verlag, Berlin-New York, New York, pp. 321–334, 1978.

Keeney, R. L. and K. Nair, "Decision Analysis for the Siting of Nuclear Power Plants--the Relevance of Multiattribute Utility Theory," *Proceedings of the IEEE*, Vol. 63, pp. 494–501, 1975.

Keeney, R. L. and K. Nair, "Selecting Nuclear Power Plant Sites in the Pacific Northwest Using Decision Analysis," *Conflicting Objectives*, edited by D. E. Bell, R. L. Keeney and H. Raiffa, John Wiley and Sons, New York, New York, pp. 298–322, 1977.

Keeney, R. L. and H. Raiffa, *Decision Analysis with Multiple Conflicting Objectives*, John Wiley and Sons, New York, New York, 1976.

Keeney, R. L. and H. Raiffa, *Decisions with Multiple Objectives: Preferences and Value Tradeoffs*, John Wiley and Sons, New York, New York, 1976.

Keeney, R. L. and A. Sicherman, "Assessing and Analyzing Preferences Concerning Multiple Objectives: An Interactive Computer Program," *Behavioral Science*, Vol. 21, No. 3, pp. 173–182, 1976.

Keeney, R. L. and E. F. Wood, "An Illustrative Example of the Use of Multiattribute Utility Theory for Water Resource Planning," *Water Resources Research*, Vol. 13, No. 4, pp. 705–712, 1977.

Kendall, K. E., "Multiple Objective Planning for Regional Blood Centers," *Long Range Planning*, Vol. 13, No. 4, pp. 98–104, August 1980.

Keown, A. J., "A Chance-Constrained Goal Programming Model for Bank Liquidity Management," *Decision Sciences*, pp. 93–106, January 1978.

Keown, A. J. and C. P. Duncan, "Integer Goal Programming in Advertising Media Selection," *Decision Sciences*, Vol. 10, No. 4, pp. 577–592, 1979.

Keown, A. J. and J. D. Martin, "An Integer Goal Programming Model for Capital Budgeting in Hospitals," *Financial Management*, pp. 28–35, Autumn 1976.

Keown, A. J. and J. D. Martin, "A Chance Constrained Goal Programming Model for Working Capital Management," *The Engineering Economist*, Vol. 22, No. 3 pp. 153–174, 1977.

Keown, A. J. and B. W. Taylor, "A Chance-Constrained Integer Goal Programming Model for Capital Budgeting in the Production Area," *The Journal of the Operational Research Society*, Vol. 31, No. 7, pp. 579–589, 1980.

Keown, A. J., B. W. Taylor and C. P. Duncan, "Allocation of Research and Development Funds: A Zero-One Goal Programming Approach," *Omega*, Vol. 7, No. 4, pp. 345–354, 1979.

Khan, M. A. and S. Rashid, "Nonconvexity and Pareto Optimality in Large Markets," *International Economic Review*, Vol. 16, pp. 222–245, 1975.

Khairullah, Z. Y. and S. Zionts, "An Experiment with Some Algorithms for Multiple Criteria

Decision Making," *Multiple Criteria Decision Making Theory and Application,* edited by G. Fandel and T. Gal, Springer-Verlag, Berlin-New York, New York, pp. 178–188, 1980.

Killough, L. and T. Sanders, "A Goal Programming Model for Public Accounting Firms," *Accounting Review,* Vol. 48, No. 2, pp. 268–279, 1973.

Kirby, R. F., "A Preferencing Model for Trip Distribution," *Transportation Science,* Vol. 4, No. 1, 1970.

Kirkwood, C. W., "Parametrically Dependent Preferences for Multiattributed Consequences," *Operations Research,* Vol. 24, pp. 92–103, January 1976.

Kirkwood, C. W., "Superiority Conditions in Decision Problems with Multiple Objectives," *IEEE Transactions on Systems, Man, and Cybernetics,* Vol. SMC-7, No. 7, pp. 542–544, 1977.

Kirkwood, C. W., "Social Decision Analysis Using Multiattribute Utility Theory," *Multiple Criteria Problem Solving,* edited by S. Zionts, Lecture Notes in Economics and Mathematical Systems No. 155, Springer-Verlag, Berlin-New York, New York, pp. 335–344, 1978.

Klahr, D., "Multiple Objectives in Mathematical Programming," *Operations Research,* Vol. 6, No. 6, pp. 849–855, 1958.

Klahr, D., "Decision Making in a Complex Environment: The Use of Similarity Judgments to Predict Preferences," *Management Science,* Vol. 15, No. 11, pp. B595–B618, 1969.

Klinger, A., "Vector-Valued Performance Criteria," *IEEE Transactions on Automatic Control,* Vol. AC-9, No. 1, pp. 117–118, 1964.

Klinger, A., "Improper Solutions of the Vector Maximum Problem," *Operations Research,* Vol. 15, No. 3, pp. 570–572, 1967.

Klock, D. R. and S. M. Lee, "A Note on Decision Models for Insurers," *Journal of Risk and Insurance,* Vol. 16, No. 3, pp. 537–543, September 1974.

Knoll, A. L. and A. Engelberg, "Weighting Multiple Objectives--the Churchman-Ackoff Technique Revisited," *Computers and Operations Research,* Vol. 5, No. 3, pp. 165–177, 1978.

Knutson, D. L., et al., "A Goal Programming Model for Achieving Racial Balance in Public Schools," *Socio-Economic Planning Sciences,* Vol. 14, No. 3, pp. 109–116, 1980.

Kofler, E., "O Zagadnieniu Optymalizacji Weilocelowej," *Przeglad Statystyczny,* Vol. 14, No. 1, pp. 45–59, 1967.

Koivo, A. J., "On a Differential Game with Three Players," *Proceedings, International Conference on the Theory and Applications of Differential Games,* Amherst, Massachusetts, s.l.s.a. pp. VIII/18–VIII/19, 1969.

Koivo, A. J. and D. W. Repperger, "Optimization of Terminal Rendezvous as a Cooperative Game," 12th Joint Automatic Controls Conference, American Automatic Controls Council, St. Louis, Missouri, 1971; Technical Papers Preprints, New York, New York, pp. 508–516, 1971.

Koivo, A. J. and D. W. Repperger, "An Approach to Optimization of Terminal Rendezvous," *IEEE Transactions on Aerospace and Electronic Systems,* Vol. AES-8, pp. 218–228, March 1972.

Kojima, M., "Vector Maximum Problems," *Keio Engineering Report,* Vol. 24, No. 4, pp. 47–61, 1971.

Kojima, M., "Duality Between Objects and Constraints in Vector Optimum Problems," *Journal of the Operations Research Society of Japan,* Vol. 15, No. 1, pp. 53–62, 1972.

Konarzewska-Gubala, E. and S. Krawczyk, "Trzy modele optimalizacji wielokryteriowej," *Pr. nauk. AE Wroclawiu,* pp. 143–154, 1975.

Koopman, B. O., "The Optimum Distribution of Effort," *Operations Research,* Vol. 1, No. 2, pp. 52–63, 1953.

Koopman, B. O., "Fallacies in Operations Research," *Operations Research,* Vol. 4, No. 4, pp. 422–426, 1956.

Koopmans, T. C. (ed.), *Activity Analysis of Production and Allocation*, Cowles Commission Monograph No. 13, John Wiley and Sons, New York, New York, 1951.

Koopmans, T. C., "Analysis of Production as an Efficient Combination of Activities," *Activity Analysis of Production and Allocation*, edited by T. C. Koopmans, Cowles Commission Monograph No. 13, John Wiley and Sons, New York, New York, pp. 33–97, 1951.

Koopmans, T. C., "Objectives, Constraints and Outcomes in Optimal Growth Models," *Econometrica*, Vol. 35, pp. 1–15, 1967.

Koopmans, T. C. and S. Reiter, "A Model of Transportation," *Activity Analysis of Production and Allocation*, edited by T. C. Koopmans, Cowles Commission Monograph No. 13, John Wiley and Sons, New York, New York, pp. 222–259, 1951.

Korhonen, P., J. Wallenius and S. Zionts, "A Bargaining Model for Solving Multiple Criteria Problems," *Multiple Criteria Decision Making Theory and Application*, edited by G. Fandel and T. Gal, Springer-Verlag, Berlin-New York, New York, pp. 178–188, 1980.

Kornai, J. and T. Liptak, "Two-Level Planning," *Econometrica*, Vol. 33, pp. 141–169, 1965.

Kornbluth, J. S. H., "A Survey of Goal Programming," *Omega*, Vol. 1, No. 2, pp. 193–205, April 1973.

Kornbluth, J. S. H., "Accounting in Multiple Objective Linear Programming," *Accounting Review*, Vol. 49, No. 2, pp. 284–295, April 1974.

Kornbluth, J. S. H., "Duality, Indifference and Sensitivity Analysis in Multiple Objective Linear Programming," *Operational Research Quarterly*, Vol. 25, No. 4, pp. 599–614, December 1974.

Kornbluth, J. S. H., "The Fuzzy Dual: Information for the Multiple Objective Decision-maker," *Computers and Operations Research*, Vol. 4, No. 1, pp. 65–72, 1977.

Kornbluth, J. S. H., "Ranking with Multiple Objectives," *Multiple Criteria Problem Solving*, edited by S. Zionts, Lecture Notes in Economics and Mathematical Systems No. 155, Springer-Verlag, Berlin-New York, New York, pp. 345–361, 1978.

Kornbluth, J. S. H., "Using Duality Theory for Identification of Primal Efficient Points and for Sensitivity Analysis in MOLP: A Comment," *The Journal of the Operational Research Society*, Vol. 30, No. 3, pp. 285–287, 1979.

Kornbluth, J. S. H. and R. E. Steuer, "On Computing the Set of All Weakly Efficient Vertices in Multiple Objective Linear Fractional Programming," *Multiple Criteria Decision Making Theory and Application*, edited by G. Fandel and T. Gal, Springer-Verlag, Berlin-New York, New York, pp. 189–202, 1980.

Körth, H., "Zur Berücksichtigung mehrerer Zielfunktionen bei der Optimierung von Produktionsplänen," *Mathematik und Wirtschaft*, Vol. 6, Die Wirtschaft, Berlin, Germany, pp. 184–201, 1969.

Koski, J., "Multicriterion Optimization in Structural Design," *Proceedings, 11th Office of Naval Research (ONR) Naval Structural Mechanics Symposium*, Tucson, Arizona, October 19–22, 1981.

Koski, J. and R. Silvennoinen, "Pareto Optima of Isostatic Trusses," *Computer Methods in Applied Mechanics and Engineering*, Vol. 31, No. 3, pp. 265–279, 1982.

Kosmol, P., "Zur vektorwertigen Optimierung," *Operations Research Verfahren*, edited by R. Henn, Vol. 15, Anton Hain Verlag, Meisenheim am Glan, Germany, pp. 77–84, 1973.

Kosmol, P., "Grenzwerte des Polya-Algorithmus und Vektormaximumproblem," *Operations Research Verfahren*, Vol. 17, Anton Hain Verlag, Meisenheim am Glan, Germany, pp. 201–206, 1973.

Krajewski, L. J. and J. C. Henderson, "Decision Making in the Public Sector: An Application of Goal Interval Programming for Disaggregation in the Post Office," *Disaggregation, Problems in Manufacturing and Service Organizations*, edited by L. P. Ritzman, et al., Martinus Nijhoff, Boston, Massachusetts, 1979.

Krasnenker, A. S., "Method for Local Improvements in Vector-Optimization Problem," *Automation and Remote Control*, Vol. 36, pp. 419–422, 1975.

Krause, ___., "Analyse und Synthese von Präferenzen," *Operations Research Verfahren*, Vol. 15, Anton Hain Verlag, Meisenheim am Glan, Germany, pp. 108–116, 1973.

Kreisselmeier, G. and R. Steinhauser, "Systematic Controller Design by Optimization of a Vector Performance Index," *Regelungstechnik*, Vol. 27, No. 3, pp. 76–79, March 1979.

Krikelis, N. J., "A Linearization Method in N-Person Nonzero-Sum Differential Games," *Journal of Optimization Theory and Applications*, Vol. 9, No. 5, pp. 359–363, 1972.

Krikelis, N. J. and Z. V. Rekasius, "On the Solution of the Optimal Linear Control Problems Under Conflict of Interest," *IEEE Transactions on Automatic Control*, Vol. 16, No. 2, pp. 140–147, 1971.

Krueger, R. J. and J. P. Dauer, "Multiobjective Optimization Model," *SIAM Review*, Vol. 20, P. 629, 1978.

Kruskal, J. B., "Multidimensional Scaling by Optimizing Goodness of Fit to a Non-Metric Hypothesis," *Psychometrika*, Vol. 29, No. 1, pp. 1–27, 1964.

Krzysztofowicz, R., E. Castano and R. Fike, "Comment on 'A Review and Evaluation of Multi-Objective Programming Techniques' by J. L. Cohon and D. H. Marks," *Water Resources Research*, Vol. 13, No. 3, pp. 690–692, June 1977.

Krzysztofowicz, R. and L. Duckstein, "Assessment Errors in Multiattribute Utility Functions," *Organizational Behavior and Human Performance*, Vol. 26, pp. 326–348, 1980.

Kuhn, H. W. and A. W. Tucker, "Nonlinear Programming," *Proceedings of the Second Berkeley Symposium on Mathematical Statistics and Probability*, edited by J. Neyman, University of California Press, Berkeley, California, pp. 481–492, 1951.

Kuhn, H. W. and A. W. Tucker (eds.), *Contributions to the Theory of Games*, Annals of Mathematical Studies No. 28, Princeton University, Princeton, New Jersey, 1953.

Kulikov, V. A. and E. K. Gurjev, "Compromise Decision Making in the Two-Level Control System," *Proceedings, 8th IEEE Conference on Decisions and Control*, New Orleans, Louisiana, December 7–9, 1977, pp. 1373–1377, 1977.

Kulikowski, R., "A Dynamic Consumption Model and Optimization of Utility Functionals," *Conflicting Objectives*, edited by D. E. Bell, R. L. Keeney and H. Raiffa, John Wiley and Sons, New York, New York, pp. 222–231, 1977.

Kumar, P. C. and G. C. Philippatos, "Conflict Resolution in Investment Decisions: Implementation of Goal Programming Methodology for Dual-Purpose Funds," *Decision Sciences*, Vol. 10, No. 4, pp. 562–576, 1979.

Kumar, P. C., G. C. Philippatos and J. R. Ezzell, "Goal Programming and the Selection of Portfolios by Dual-Purpose Funds," *Journal of Finance*, Vol. 33, pp. 303–310, March 1978.

Kumbaraci, T. E., "The Judgment of Improvement--Choice for Decisions Relating to Medical Efficiency," *Multiple Criteria Decision Making*, edited by J. L. Cochrane and M. Zeleny, University of South Carolina Press, Columbia, South Carolina, pp. 753–754, 1973.

Kung, H. T., "On the Computational Complexity of Finding the Maxima of a Set of Vectors," *Proceedings of the 15th Annual IEEE Symposium on Switching and Automata Theory*, New Orleans, Louisiana, October 14–16, 1974, pp. 117–121, 1974.

Kung, H. T., F. Luccio and F. P. Preparata, "On Finding the Maxima of a Set of Vectors," *J. ACM*, Vol. 22, pp. 469–476, October 1975.

Kunreuther, H., "Extensions of Bowman's Theory on Managerial Decision Making," *Management Science*, Vol. 15, No. 8, pp. B415–B439, 1969.

Kusraev, A. G., "On Necessary Conditions for an Extremum of Nonsmooth Vector-Valued Mappings" [in Russian], *Dokladi Akademii Nauk, SSSR*, Vol. 242, No. 1, pp. 44–47, 1978; English translation in *Soviet Math. Dokl.*, Vol. 19, No. 5, pp. 1057–1060, 1978.

Kuzimin, I. V., E. O. Dedikov and B. Y. Kukharev, "Choice of Global Solution Criterion in Problems with Several Objective Functions," *Soviet Automatic Control*, Vol. 7, No. 4, pp 59–62, 1974.

Kvanli, A. H., "Financial Planning Using Goal Programming," *Omega*, Vol. 8, No. 2, pp. 207–218, 1980.

Kwak, N. K. and M. J. Schniederjans, "A Goal Programming Model for Improved Transportation Problem Solutions," *Omega*, Vol. 7, No. 4, pp. 367–370, 1979.

Kyrtavan, B., "Dynamic Two-Person, Two-Objective Control Problems with Delayed Sharing Information Pattern," *IEEE Transactions on Automatic Control*, Vol. 22, No. 4, pp. 659–661, 1977.

Ladany, S. P. and M. Aharoni, "Maintenance Policy of Aircraft According to Multiple Criteria," *International Journal of Systems Science*, Vol. 6, No. 11, pp. 1093–1101, 1975.

Lahdenpää, M., "On Phased Models and Managers' and Consumers' Decision Making, " *Multiple Criteria Decision Making*, edited by M. K. Starr and M. Zeleny, TIMS Studies in the Management Sciences, Vol. 6, North-Holland Publishing Company, Amsterdam, Holland, pp. 309–311, 1977.

Lahdenpää, M., *Multiple Criteria Decision Making: With Empirical Study on Choice of Marketing Strategies*, Acta Helsingiensis, ser. A:22, Helsinki School of Economics, Helsinki, Finland, 1977.

Landsberger, M. and A. Subotnik, "Optimal Behavior of a Monopolist Facing a Bicriteria Objective Function," *International Economic Review*, Vol. 17, No. 3, pp. 581–600, 1976.

Lange, O., "The Foundations of Welfare Economics," *Econometrica* Vol. 10, pp. 215–228, 1942.

Lantos, B., "Necessary Conditions for the Optimality in Abstract Optimum Control Problems with Nonscalar-Valued Performance Criterion," *Problems of Control and Information Theory*, Vol. 5, No. 3, pp. 271–284, 1976.

Lantos, B., "The Local Supremum Principle for Optimum Control Problems with Nonscalar-Valued Performance Criterion," *Period. Polytechn. Elec. Eng.*, Vol. 20, No. 3, pp. 313–323, 1976.

Larichev, O. I., "Man-Machine Procedures for Decision Making (Review)," *Automation and Remote Control*, Vol. 32, No. 12, pp. 1973–1983, 1971.

Larichev, O. I., "Method for Evaluating R&D Projects," *Automation and Remote Control*, Vol. 33, No. 8, pp. 1356–1360, 1972.

Larichev, O. I., "A Practical Methodology of Solving Multicriterion Problems with Subjective Criteria," *Conflictiing Objectives*, edited by D. E. Bell, R. L. Keeney and H. Raiffa, John Wiley and Sons, New York, New York, pp. 197–208, 1977.

Lata, M., "Strong Pseudo-Convex Programming in Banach Space," *Indian Journal of Pure and Applied Mathematics*, Vol. 6, No. 1, pp. 45–48, 1976.

LaValle, I. H., "On Admissibility and Bayesness When Risk Attitude but Not the Preference Ranking Is Permitted to Vary," *Multiple Criteria Decision Making*, edited by J. L. Cochrane and M. Zeleny, University of South Carolina Press, Columbia, South Carolina, pp. 72–83, 1973.

Lawrence, K. D. and J. J. Burbridge, "A Multiple Goal Linear Programming Model for Coordinated Production and Logistics Planning, " *The International Journal of Production Research*, Vol. 14, No. 2, March 1976.

Lawrence, K. D. and J. I. Weindling, "Multiple Goal Operations Management Planning and Decision Making in a Quality Control Department," *Multiple Criteria Decision Making Theory and Application*, edited by G. Fandel and T. Gal, Springer-Verlag, Berlin-New York, New York, pp. 203–217, 1980.

Lawser, J. J. and R. A. Volz, "some Aspects of Nonzero-Sum Differential Games," *Proceedings, 1st International Conference on the Theory and Applications of Differential Games, Amherst, Massachusetts, s.l.s.a. pp. IV/19–IV/22, 1969.

Lawser, J. J. and R. A. Volz, "Some Aspects of Nonzero-Sum Differential Games," IEEE Transactions on Automatic Control, Vol. 16, No. 1, pp. 66–69, 1971.

Lawser, J. J. and R. A. Volz, "A Nonzero-Sum Differential Game with Curious Solution Properties," IEEE Transactions on Automatic Control, Vol. 17, No. 5, pp. 717–718, 1972.

Leatham, A. L. and G. M. Anderson, "A Class of Nonzero-Sum Differential Games with Open Loop," Proceedings, 4th Hawaii International Conference on Systems Science, Honolulu, Hawaii, 1971; Western Periodicals, North Hollywood, California, pp. 199–241, 1971.

Lebedev, B. D., V. V. Podinovskii and R. S. Styrikovic, "An Optimization Problem with Respect to the Ordered Totality of Criteria" [in Russian], Ekonomika i Matematicheskie Metody, Vol. 7, pp. 612–616, 1971.

Le Boulanger, H. and B. Roy, "L'Enterprise Face à la Sélection et à l'Orientation des Projects de Recherche: La Méthodologie en Usage dans le Groupe," Sema, Metra International, Vol. 7, No. 4, 1968.

Lee, S. M., "Decision Analysis Through Goal Programming," Decision Sciences, Vol. 2, No. 2, pp. 172–180, 1971.

Lee, S. M., Goal Programming for Decision Analysis, Auerbach Publishers, Philadelphia, Pennsylvania, 1972.

Lee, S. M., "Goal Programming for Decision Analysis of Multiple-Objectives," Sloan Management Review, Vol. 14, No. 2, pp. 11–24, 1973.

Lee, S. M., "Interactive Integer Goal Programming: Methods and Applications," Multiple Criteria Problem Solving, edited by S. Zionts, Lecture Notes in Economics and Mathematical Systems No. 155, Springer-Verlag, Berlin-New York, New York, pp. 362–383, 1978.

Lee, S. M., "Goal Programming," Encyclopedia of Computer Science and Technology, Vol. 9, Marcel Dekker, New York, New York, pp. 83–104, 1978.

Lee, S. M., "Interactive Integer Programming Methods and Applications," Multiple Criteria Problem Solving: Proceedings, Buffalo, N.Y. (U.S.A.), 1977, edited by S. Zionts, Springer-Verlag, Berlin-New York, New York, pp. 362–383, 1978.

Lee, S. M. and M. M. Bird, Jr., "A Goal Programming Model for Sales Effort Allocation," Business Perspectives, Vol. 6, No. 4, pp. 17–21, 1970.

Lee, S. M. and D. L. Chesser, "Goal Programming for Portfolio Selection," Journal of Portfolio Management, Vol. 6, No. 3, pp. 22–26, 1980.

Lee, S. M. and E. R. Clayton, "A Goal Programming Model for Academic Resource Allocation," Management Science, Vol. 18, No. 8, pp. B395–B417, 1972.

Lee, S. M., E. R. Clayton and B. W. Taylor, "A Goal Programming Approach to Multi-Period Production Line Scheduling," Computers and Operations Research, Vol. 5, No. 3, pp. 205–211, 1978.

Lee, S. M. and L. S. Franz, "Optimising the Location-Allocation Problem with Multiple Objectives," International Journal of Physical Distribution and Materials Management, Vol. 9, No. 6, pp. 245–255, 1979.

Lee, S. M. and V. Jääskeläinen, "Goal Programming, Management's Mathematical Model," Industrial Engineering, Vol. 3, No. 2, pp. 30–35, February 1971.

Lee, S. M. and A. J. Lerro, "Optimizing the Portfolio Selection for Mutual Funds," Journal of Finance, Vol. 18, No. 5, pp. 1087–1101, 1973.

Lee, S. M. and A. J. Lerro, "Capital Budgeting for Multiple Objectives," Financial Management, Vol. 3, No. 1, pp. 58–66, 1974.

Lee, S. M. and L. Moore, "Optimizing Transportation Problems with Multiple Objectives," AIIE Transactions, Vol. 5, No. 4, pp. 333–338, 1973.

Lee, S. M. and L. J. Moore, "A Practical Approach to Production Scheduling," *Production and Inventory Management*, Vol. 15, No. 1, 1974.

Lee, S. M. and L. J. Moore, "Optimizing University Admissions Planning," *Decision Sciences*, Vol. 5, No. 3, pp. 405–414, July 1974.

Lee, S. M. and L. Moore, "Multicriteria School Bussing Models," *Management Science*, Vol. 23, No. 7, pp. B703–B715, 1977.

Lee, S. M. and R. L. Morris, "Integer Goal Programming Methods," *Multiple Criteria Decision Making*, edited by M. K. Starr and M. Zeleny, TIMS Studies in the Management Sciences, Vol. 6, North-Holland Publishing Company, Amsterdam, Holland, pp. 273–289, 1977.

Lee, S. M. and R. Nicely, "Goal Programming for Marketing Decisions: A Case Study," *Journal of Marketing*, Vol. 38, No. 1, pp. 24–32, 1974.

Lee, S. M., J. Van Horn and H. Brisch, "A Multiple Criteria Analysis Model for Academic Policies, Priorities, and Budgetary Constraints," *Multiple Criteria Decision Making Theory and Application*, edited by G. Fandel and T. Gal, Springer-Verlag, Berlin-New York, New York, pp. 218–237, 1980.

Lee, S. M. and A. J. Wynne, "Separable Goal Programming," *Multiple Criteria Analysis: Operational Methods*, edited by P. Nijkamp and J. Spronk, Gower Press, London, England, 1981.

Legasto, A. A., "A Multiple-Objective Policy Model: Results of an Application to a Developing Country," *Management Science*, Vol. 24, No. 5, pp. 498–509, 1978.

Lehmann, D. R., "Preference Among Similar Alternatives," *Decision Sciences*, Vol. 3, No. 4, pp. 64–82, 1972.

Lehmann, D. R. and W. Oettli, "The Theorem of the Alternative, the Key-Theorem, and the Vector-Maximum Problem," *Mathematical Programming*, Vol. 8, No. 3, pp. 332–344, 1975.

Leitmann, G., "Collective Bargaining: A Different Game," *Journal of Optimization Theory and Applications*, Vol. 11, No. 4, pp. 405–412, 1973.

Leitmann, G., *Cooperative and Non-Cooperative Many Player Differential Games*, Springer-Verlag, Vienna, Austria, 1974.

Leitmann, G., "Cooperative and Non-Cooperative Differential Games," *Theory and Application of Differential Games*, edited by J. D. Grote, D. Reidel Publishing Company, Boston, Massachusetts, pp. 85–96, 1975.

Leitmann, G., "Cooperative and Noncooperative Many Player Differential Games," *Multicriteria Decision Making*, edited by G. Leitmann and A. Marzollo, Courses and Lectures No. 211, International Center for Mechanical Sciences (CISM), Springer-Verlag, Wien-New York, New York, pp. 7–31, 1975.

Leitmann, G. (ed.), *Multicriteria Decision Making and Differential Games*, Plenum Press, New York, New York, 1976.

Leitmann, G., "Many Player Differential Games," *Proceedings, Workshop on Differential Games*, Twente University of Technology, Enschede Holland, 1977; Springer-Verlag, Berlin-New York, New York, 1977.

Leitmann, G., "Some Problems of Scalar and Vector-Valued Optimization in Linear Viscoelasticity," *Journal of Optimization Theory and Applications*, Vol. 23, No. 1, pp. 93–99, September 1977.

Leitmann, G., *The Calculus of Variations and Optimal Control* (Chapter 17, "Optimization with Vector-Valued Cost"), Plenum Press, New York, New York, 1981.

Leitmann, G. and P. T. Liu, "A Differential Game Model of Labor Management Negotiation During a Strike," *Journal of Optimization Theory and Applications*, Vol. 13, No. 4, pp. 427–435, 1974.

Leitmann, G. and P. T. Liu, "A Differential Game Model of Labor Management Negotiation

During a Strike," *Journal of Optimization Theory and Applications*, Vol. 14, No. 4, pp. 443–444, 1974.

Leitmann, G. and A. Marzollo (eds.), *Multicriteria Decision Making*, Courses and Lectures No. 211, International Center for Mechanical Sciences (CISM), Springer-Verlag, Wien-New York, New York, 1975.

Leitmann, G., S. Rocklin and T. L. Vincent, "A Note on Control Space Properties of Cooperative Games," *Journal of Optimization Theory and Applications*, Vol. 9, No. 6, pp. 379–390, 1972.

Leitmann, G. and W. Schmitendorf, "Some Sufficiency Conditions for Pareto-Optimal Control," 13th Joint Automatic Control Conference and American Automatic Control Council, Stanford, California, 1972; Technical Papers Preprints, New York, New York, pp. 1–7, 1972.

Leitmann, G. and W. Schmitendorf, "Some Sufficiency Conditions for Pareto-Optimal Control," *ASME Journal of Dynamical Systems, Measurement and Control*, Vol. 95, Series 6, No. 4, pp. 356–361, December 1973.

Leitmann, G. and W. Stadler, "Cooperative Games for the Experimentalist (Preliminary Results)," *Proceedings of the Fifth International Conference on Systems Science*, University of Hawaii, Honolulu, Hawaii, 1972.

Leitmann, G. and W. Stadler, "Cooperative Games for the Experimentalist," *Zagadnienia Drgan Nieliniowych [Journal of Nonlinear Vibration Problems]*, Warsaw, Poland, No. 18, pp. 273–286, 1974.

Levanon, Y. and U. Passy, "Condensing Multiple Criteria," *Multiple Criteria Problem Solving*, edited by S. Zionts, Lecture Notes in Economics and Mathematical Systems No. 155, Springer-Verlag, Berlin-New York, New York, pp. 449–461, 1978.

Levhari, D., J. Paroush and B. Peleg, "Efficiency Analysis for Multivariate Distributions," *Review of Economic Studies*, Vol. 42, pp. 87–91, 1975.

Levine, P., "Strategic 'Prejudgments' and Decision Criteria in N-Person Games," *Theory and Application of Differential Games*, Dordrecht, Boston, Massachusetts, pp. 121–132, 1975.

Levy, H. and J. Paroush, "Toward Multivariate Efficiency Criteria," *Journal of Economic Theory*, Vol. 7, pp. 129–142, 1974.

Lewis, K. A., "Planning Equal Employment Opportunities," *Multiple Criteria Decision Making*, edited by M. K. Starr and M. Zeleny, TIMS Studies in the Management Sciences, Vol. 6, North-Holland Publishing Company, Amsterdam, Holland, p. 312, 1977.

Lhoas, J., "Multi-Criteria Decision Aid Application to the Selection of the Route for a Pipe-Line," *Advances in Operations Research*, edited by M. Roubens, North-Holland Publishing Company, Amsterdam, Holland, pp. 265–273, 1977.

Lim, K. P., "Simultaneous Approximation of Compact Sets by Elements of Convex Sets in Normed Linear Spaces," *Journal of Approximation Theory*, Vol. 12, pp. 332–351, 1974.

Lin, J. G., "On N-Person Cooperative Differential Games," *Proceedings of the 6th Annual Princeton Conference on Information Sciences and Systems*, Princeton, New Jersey, 1972.

Lin, J. G., "Circuit Design Under Multiple Performance Objectives," *Proceedings of IEEE International Symposium on Circuits and Systems*, San Francisco, California, pp. 549–552, April 1974.

Lin, J. G., "Maximal Vectors and Multi-Objective Optimization," *Journal of Optimization Theory and Applications*, Vol. 18, No. 1, pp. 41–64, January 1976.

Lin, J. G., "Multiple-Objective Optimization: Proper Equality Constraints (PEC) and Maximization of Index Vectors," *Multicriteria Decision Making and Differential Games*, edited by G. Leitmann, Plenum Press, New York, New York, pp. 103–128, 1976.

Lin, J. G., "Multiple Objective Problems: Pareto-Optimal Solution by Method of Proper Equality Constraints," *IEEE Transactions on Automatic Control*, Vol. AC-21, No. 5, pp. 641–650, October 1976.

Lin, J. G., "Multiple-Objective Programming: Lagrange Multipliers and Method of Proper Equality Constraints," *Proceedings, Joint Automatic Control Conference*, West Lafayette, Indiana, 1976; New York, New York, pp. 517–523, 1976.

Lin, J. G., "Proper Equality Constraints and Maximization on Index Vectors," *Journal of Optimization Theory and Applications*, Vol. 20, No. 2, pp. 215–244, October 1976.

Lin, J. G., "Three Methods for Determining Pareto-Optimal Solutions of Multiple-Objective Optimization Problems," *Directions in Large-Scale Systems: Decentralized Control and Many-Person Optimization*, edited by Y. C. Ho and S. K. Mitter, Plenum Press, New York, New York, pp. 117–138, 1976.

Lin, J. G., "Proper Inequality Constraints and Maximization of Index Vectors," *Journal of Optimization Theory and Applications*, Vol. 21, No. 4, pp. 505–522, April 1977.

Lin, J. G., "Multiple-Objective Optimization by Method of Proper Equality Constraints Using Lagrange Multipliers," *Proceedings, IEEE Conference on Decisions and Control, including Symposium on Adaptive Processes*, San Diego, California, January 10–12, 1978, pp. 899–904, 1978.

Lin, J. G., "Multiple-Objective Optimization by a Multiplier Method of Proper Equality Constraints—Part I: Theory," *IEEE Transactions on Automatic Control*, Vol. 24, No. 4, pp. 567–573, August 1979.

Lin, J. G., G. Katopis, S. T. Patellis and H. N. Shen, "On Relatively Optimal Controls of Dynamic Systems with Vector Performance Indices," *Proceedings of the Seventh Annual Princeton Conference on Information Sciences and Systems*, Princeton, New Jersey, pp. 579–584, March 1973.

Lin, S. A. Y., "Dynamic Growth of the Firm Under Uncertainty with Multiple Goals," *Multiple Criteria Decision Making*, edited by J. L. Cochrane and M. Zeleny, University of South Carolina Press, Columbia, South Carolina, pp. 755–759, 1973.

Lin, W. T., "A Short Statement," *Multiple Criteria Decision Making*, edited by M. K. Starr and M. Zeleny, TIMS Studies in the Management Sciences, Vol. 6, North-Holland Publishing Company, Amsterdam, Holland, pp. 313–314, 1977.

Lin, T. W., "Application of Goal Programming in Accounting," *Journal of Business Finance and Accounting*, Vol. 6, No. 4, pp. 559–577, 1979.

Lin, T. W., "An Accounting Control System Structured on Multiple Objective Planning Models," *Omega*, Vol. 8, No. 3, pp. 375–382, 1980.

Lin, W. T., "Multiple Objective Budgeting Models: A Simulation," *Accounting Review*, Vol. 53, pp. 61–76, January 1978.

Lin, W. T., "A Survey of Goal Programming Applications," *Omega*, Vol. 8, No. 1, pp. 115–117, 1980.

Linstone, H. A. and M. Turoff (eds.), *The Delphi Method: Techniques and Applications*, Addison-Wesley, Reading, Massachusetts, 1975.

Little, I. M. D., *A Critique of Welfare Economics*, The Clarendon Press, Oxford, England, 1950.

Littlechild, S. C., "Peak-Load Pricing of Telephone Calls," *Bell Journal of Economics and Management Science*, Vol. 1, pp. 191–210, 1970.

Liu, P. T., "Nonzero-Sum Differential Games with Bargaining Solutions," *Journal of Optimization Theory and Applications*, Vol. 11, No. 3, pp. 284–292, 1973.

Lockett, A. G. and A. P. Muhlemann, "A Problem of Aggregate Scheduling: An Application of Goal Programming," *International Journal of Production Research*, Vol. 16, No. 2, pp. 127–136, 1978.

Logan, J., "Preferred Coalitions in Cooperative Differential Games," *Journal of Optimization Theory and Applications*, Vol. 13, No. 2, pp. 186–202, February 1974.

Lorentz, R. A., "Nonuniqueness of Simultaneous Approximation by Algebraic Polynomials," *Journal of Approximation Theory,* Vol. 13, pp. 17–23, 1975.

Lós, J., "Uwagi o lacznej optimalizacji kilku wielkósci," *Przeglad Statystyczny,* Vol. 12, No. 3, pp. 193–202, 1965.

Loucks, D. P., "Planning for Multiple Goals," *Economy Wide Models and Development Planning,* edited by C. R. Blitzer, P. Clerk and L. Taylor, Oxford University Press, London, England, pp. 213–233, 1975.

Loucks, D. P., "An Application of Interactive Multiobjective Water Resources Planning," *Interfaces,* Vol. 8, No. 1, pp. 70–75, November 1977.

Lucas, H. C. Jr. and J. R. Moore, Jr., "A Multiple Criterion Scoring Approach to Information System Project Selection," *Infor,* Vol. 14, No. 1, pp. 1–12, 1976.

Lucas, W. F., "A Game with No Solution," *Bulletin of the American Mathematical Society,* Vol. 74, No. 2, pp. 237–239, 1968.

Lucas, W. F., "Some Recent Developments in n-Person Game Theory," *SIAM Review,* Vol. 13, No. 4, pp. 491–523, 1971.

Lucas, W. F., "An Overview of the Mathematical Theory of Games," *Management Science,* Vol. 18, No. 5 (Part 2), pp. 3–19, 1972.

Luce, R. D., "Conjoint Measurement: A Brief Survey," *Conflicting Objectives,* edited by D. E. Bell, R. L. Keeney and H. Raiffa, John Wiley and Sons, New York, New York, pp. 148–171, 1977.

Luce, R. D. and H. Raiffa, *Games and Decisions: Introduction and Critical Survey,* John Wiley and Sons, New York, New York, 1957.

Luce, R. D. and J. W. Tukey, "Simultaneous Conjoint Measurement: A New Type of Fundamental Measurement," *Journal of Mathematical Psychology,* Vol. 1, pp. 1–27, 1964.

Lukka, M., "An Algorithm for Solving a Multiple Criteria Optimal Control Problem," *Journal of Optimization Theory and Applications,* Vol. 28, No. 3, pp. 435–438, July 1979.

MacCrimmon, K. R., "An Overview of Multiple Objective Decision Making," *Multiple Criteria Decision Making,* edited by J. L. Cochrane and M. Zeleny, University of South Carolina Press, Columbia, South Carolina, pp. 18–44, 1973.

MacCrimmon, K. R. and J. K. Siu, "Making Trade-Offs," *Decision Sciences,* Vol. 5, pp. 680–704, 1974.

MacCrimmon, K. R. and M. Toda, "The Experimental Determination of Indifference Curves," *Review of Economic Studies,* Vol. 36, pp. 433–450, 1969.

MacCrimmon, K. R. and D. A. Wehrung, "Trade-Off Analysis: The Indifference and the Preferred Proportions Approaches," *Conflicting Objectives,* edited by D. E. Bell, R. L. Keeney and H. Raiffa, John Wiley and Sons, New York, New York, pp. 123–147, 1977.

Macko, D. and Y. Y. Haimes, "Overlapping Coordination of Hierarchical Structures," *IEEE Transactions on Systems, Man, and Cybernetics,* Vol. SMC-8, No. 10, pp. 745–751, October 1978.

Mahmoud, M. S., "An Extension of Hierarchical Dynamic Control to Multiobjective Optimization," *Proceedings, 7th International Conference on Cybernetics and Society,* Washington, D.C., September 19–21, 1977, pp. 368–372, 1977.

Mahoney, F. J., "The Design of Regression Experiments with Multiple Objectives," *Multiple Criteria Decision Making,* edited by J. L. Cochrane and M. Zeleny, University of South Carolina Press, Columbia, South Carolina, pp. 760–763, 1973.

Major, D. C., "Benefit-Cost Ratios for Projects in Multiple Objective Investment Programs," *Water Resources Research,* Vol. 5, No. 6, pp. 1174–1178, December 1969.

Major, D. C., "Multiple Objective Redesign of the Big Walnut Project," *Systems Planning and Design,* edited by R. de Neufville and D. H. Marks, Prentice-Hall, Englewood Cliffs, New Jersey, pp. 322–337, 1974.

Major, D. C., *Multiobjective Water Resource Planning*, Water Resources Monograph, No. 4, American Geophysical Union, Washington, D.C., 1977.

Major, D. C. and R. Lenton, *Multiobjective, Multi-Model River Basin Planning: The MIT-Argentina Project*, Prentice-Hall, Englewood Cliffs, New Jersey, 1978.

Majumdar, M., "Some Approximation Theorems on Efficiency Prices for Infinite Programs," *Journal of Economic Theory*, Vol. 2, pp. 399–410, 1970.

Majumdar, M., "Efficient Programs in Infinite Dimensional Spaces: A Complete Characterization," *Journal of Economic Theory*, Vol. 7, No. 4, pp. 355–369, 1974.

Majumbar, M., T. Mitra and D. McFadden, "On Efficiency and Pareto Optimality of Competitive Programs in Closed Multisector Models," *Journal of Economic Theory*, Vol. 13, No. 1, pp. 26–46, 1976.

Malinvaud, E., "Capital Accumulation and Efficient Allocation of Resources," *Econometrica*, Vol. 21, pp. 233-268, 1953.

Manas, J. and J. Nedoma, "Finding All Vertices of a Convex Polyhedron," *Numerische Mathematik*, Vol. 12, pp. 226–229, 1968.

Mandelbrot, B., "Random Walks, Five Damage Amount and Other Paretian Risk Phenomena," *Operations Research*, Vol. 12, No. 4, pp. 582–585, 1964.

Manheim, M. L., *Hierarchical Structure: A Model of Design and Planning Processes*, Massachusetts Institute of Technology Press, Cambridge, Massachusetts, 1966.

Mao, J. C. T. and C. E. Särnal, "A Decision Theory Approach to Portfolio Selection," *Management Science*, Vol. 12, No. 8, pp. B323–B333, 1966.

Markowitz, H. M., *Portfolio Selection: Efficient Diversification of Investment*, John Wiley and Sons, New York, New York, 1959.

Marks, D. H., "Water Quality Management," *Analysis of Public Systems*, edited by A. Drake, R. Keeney and P. Morse, Massachusetts Institute of Technology Press, Cambridge, Massachusetts, pp. 356–375, 1972.

Marschak, J., "Elements for a Theory of Teams," *Management Science*, Vol. 1, No. 2, pp. 127–137, January 1955.

Marschak, J., "Decision Making: Economic Aspects," *International Encyclopedia of Social Sciences*, Vol. 4, edited by D. Sills, The Macmillan Company, London, England, pp. 42–55, 1968.

Marschak, J., "Guided Soul-Searching for Multi-Criterion Decisions," *Multiple Criteria Decision Making*, edited by M. Zeleny, Lecture Notes in Economics and Mathematical Systems No. 123, Springer-Verlag, Berlin-New York, New York, pp. 1–16, 1976.

Marshall, A., *Principles of Economics*, First Edition, London, England, 1890; Eighth Edition, London, England, 1920.

Marshall, A. W., "A Mathematical Note on Suboptimization," *Journal of Operations Research*, Vol. 1, pp. 100–102, 1953.

Marshall, H. E., "Cost Sharing and Multiobjectives in Water Resource Development," *Water Resources Research*, Vol. 9, No. 1, pp. 1–10, 1973.

Martin, W. S. and A. Barcus, "A Multiattribute Model for Evaluating Industrial Customer's Potential," *Interfaces*, Vol. 10, No. 3, pp. 40–44, June 1980.

Marusciac, I., "An Efficient Realization of an Algorithm to Compute the First Efficient Points of a Linear Multiobjective," *Studias Universitatis Babes-Bolyai Mat.*, Vol. 21, pp. 66–72, 1976.

Marusciac, I., "On the Hierarchy of the Efficient Extreme Points in Multiobjective Programming," *Studias Universitatis Babes-Bolyai Mat.*, Vol. 22, pp. 53–60, 1977.

Marusciac, I. and M. Radulescu, "Un Problème Général de la Programmation Linéaire à Plusieurs Fonctions Économiques," *Studias Universitatis Babes-Bolyai Mat.*, Vol. 1, pp. 55–65, 1970.

Marusciac, I. and M. Radulescu, "Un Problème de la Programmation Quadratique à Plusieurs Fonctions," *Studias Universitatis Babes-Bolyai Mat.*, Vol. 1, pp. 81–89, 1970.

Marusciac, I. and M. Radulescu, "Sur l'Ensemble des Points Efficients d'un Problème de la Programmation Mathématique," *Analele Stiintifice ale Universitatu 'Al. I. Cuza' din Iasi*, Vol. 18, No. 1, pp. 210–226, 1972.

Marzollo, A. and W. Ukovich, "A Support Function Approach to the Characterization of the Optimal Gain Vectors in Cooperative Games," *Proceedings of the 1974 IEEE Conference on Decisions and Control*, pp. 362–367, 1974.

Marzollo, A. and W. Ukovich, "Nondominated Solutions in Cooperative Games: A Dual Space Approach," *Proceedings, 6th IFAC Congress*, Boston, Massachusetts, 1975.

Marzollo, A. and W. Ukovich, "On Some Broad Classes of Vector Optimal Decisions and Their Characterization," *Multicriteria Decision Making*, edited by G. Leitmann and A. Marzollo, Courses and Lectures No. 211, International Center for Mechanical Sciences (CISM), Springer-Verlag, Wien-New York, New York, pp. 281–323, 1975.

Masakazu, K., "Vector Maximum Problems," *Keio Engineering Report*, Vol. 24, pp. 47–64, 1971.

Masser, I., P. W. J. Batey and P. J. B. Brown, "Sequential Treatment of the Multi-Criteria Aggregation Problem: A Case Study of Zoning System Design," *Spatial Representation and Spatial Interaction*, edited by I. Masser and P. Brown, Studies in Applied Regional Science, Vol. 10, Martinus Nijhoff, Boston, Massachusetts, 1978.

May, K. O., "Intransitivity, Utility, and Aggregation in Preference Patterns," *Econometrica*, Vol. 22, pp. 1–13, 1954.

McGinnis, L. F. and J. A. White, "A Single Facility Rectilinear Location Problem with Multiple Criteria," *Transportation Science*, Vol. 12, pp. 217–231, 1978.

McGrew, D. R. and Y. Y. Haimes, "Parametric Solution to the Joint System Identification and Optimization Problem," *Journal of Optimization Theory and Applications*, Vol. 13, No. 5, pp. 582–605, 1974.

McMillan, C. Jr., *Mathematical Programming* (Chapter 14, "Mathematical Programming with Multiple Objectives"), John Wiley and Sons, New York, New York, 1975.

Medanic, J., "Minimax Pareto Optimal Solutions with Application to Linear-Quadratic Problems," *Multicriteria Decision Making*, edited by G. Leitmann and A. Marzollo, Courses and Lectures No. 211, International Center for Mechanical Sciences (CISM), Springer-Verlag, Wien-New York, New York, pp. 55-124, 1975.

Medanic, J. and M. Andjelic, "Minimax Solution of the Multiple Target Problem," *IEEE Transactions on Automatic Control*, Vol. 17, No. 5, pp. 597–604, 1972.

Meisel, W. S., "Trade-Off Decisions in Multiple Criteria Decision Making," *Multiple Criteria Decision Making*, edited by J. L. Cochrane and M. Zeleny, University of South Carolina Press, Columbia, South Carolina, pp. 461–476, 1973.

Meisel, W. S. and R. M. Beeson, "Optimization of Complex Systems with Respect to Multiple Criteria," *Proceedings of the Systems, Man and Cybernetics Conference, Joint National Conference on Major Systems*, pp. 144–149, October 1971.

Mehta, A. J. and A. K. Rifai, "Application of Linear Programming vs. Goal Programming to Assignment Problem," *Akron Business and Economic Review*, pp. 52–55, Winter 1976.

Mellon, G. W., "Priority Ratings in More Than One Dimension," *Naval Research Logistics Quarterly*, Vol. 7, pp. 513–527, 1960.

Mendu, S. R., Y. Y. Haimes and D. Macko, "Computational Aspects of Overlapping Coordination Methodology for Linear Hierarchical Systems," *IEEE Transactions on Systems, Man, and Cybernetics*, Vol. SMC-10, No. 2, February 1980.

Menger, K., *Grundsätze der Volkswirtschaftslehre*, Braumüller, Wien, Austria, 1871.

Merkurev, V. V. and M. A. Moldavskii, "A Family of Convolutions of a Vector-Valued Criterion for Finding Points in a Pareto Set," *Automation and Remote Control*, Vol. 40, No. 1, Part 2, pp. 87–97, January 1979.

Mesarovic, M. D., D. Macko and Y. Takahara, *Theory of Hierarchical Multilevel Systems*,

Mathematics and Science in Engineering No. 68, Academic Press, New York, New York, 1970.

Meyer, R. F., "State Dependent Time Preference," *Proceedings of the Workshop on Decision Making with Multiple Conflicting Objectives*, International Institute for Applied Systems Analysis, Laxenburg, Austria, 1975.

Meyer, R. F., "State-Dependent Time Preference," *Conflicting Objectives*, edited by D. E. Bell, R. L. Keeney and H. Raiffa, John Wiley and Sons, New York, New York, pp. 232–246, 1977.

Michalson, E., E. Engelbert and W. Andrews (eds.), *Multiple Objectives Planning Water Resources*, Vol. 1, Idaho Research Foundation, Moscow, Idaho, 1974.

Michel, P., "Condition Nécessaire d'Optimalité de Pareto pour un System à Commande," *Comptes Rendus Académie des Sciences de Paris*, Série A, Vol. 280, pp. 1397–1399, 1975.

Micko, H. C. and W. Fischer, "The Metric of Multidimensional Psychological Spaces as a Function of the Differential Attention to Subjective Attribute," *Journal of Mathematical Psychology*, Vol. 7, pp. 118–143, 1970.

Miele, A., "On the Minimization of the Product of the Powers of Several Integrals," *Journal of Optimization Theory and Applications*, Vol. 1, No. 1, pp. 70–82, July 1967.

Miller, W. L. and D. M. Byers, "Development and Display of Multiple Objective Project Imports," *Water Resources Research*, Vol. 9, No. 1, pp. 11–20, 1973.

Miller, W. L. and S. P. Erickson, "The Impact of High Interest Rates on Optimum Multiple Objective Design of Surface Runoff Urban Drainage Systems," *Water Resources Bulletin*, Vol. 11, No. 1, pp. 49–59, 1975.

Minnehan, R. F., "Multiple Objectives and Multigroup Decision Making in Physical Design Situations," *Multiple Criteria Decision Making*, edited by J. L. Cochrane and M. Zeleny, University of South Carolina Press, Columbia, South Carolina, pp. 506–516, 1973.

Mishan, E. J., "A Survey of Welfare Economics, 1939–1959," *Economic Journal*, Vol. 70, pp. 197–265, 1960.

Mitroff, I. I., "On Being Consistent: The Management of Inquiry as a Multi-Criteria Decision Problem," *Multiple Criteria Decision Making*, edited by M. K. Starr and M. Zeleny, TIMS Studies in the Management Sciences, Vol. 6, North-Holland Publishing Company, Amsterdam, Holland, pp. 291–300, 1977.

Moinpur, R. and J. B. Wiley, "Application of Multi-Attribute Models of Attitude in Marketing," *Journal of Business Administration*, Vol. 5, No. 2, pp. 3–16, 1974.

Moiseev, N. N., "Computational Problems in the Theory of Hierarchical Control Systems," *Proceedings of the 5th All-Union Conference on Control*, Part 1, Nauka, USSR, 1971.

Molnar, Z., "Heuristicke konvergenti modely pro vicekriterialni optimalizaci," *Ekonomicko Matematický Obzor*, Vol. 12, No. 2, pp. 145–164, 1976.

Monarchi, D. E., C. E. Kisiel and L. Duckstein, "Interactive Multiobjective Programming in Water Resources: A Case Study," *Water Resources Research*, Vol. 9, No. 4, pp. 837–850, 1973.

Monarchi, D. E., J. E. Weber and L. Duckstein, "An Interactive Multiple Objective Decision-Making Aid Using Nonlinear Goal Programming," *Multiple Criteria Decision Making*, edited by M. Zeleny, Lecture Notes in Economics and Mathematical Systems No. 123, Springer-Verlag, Berlin-New York, New York, pp. 235–253, 1976.

Moore, J. C., "The Existence of 'Compensated Equilibrium' and the Structure of the Pareto Efficiency Frontier," *International Economic Review*, Vol. 16, No. 2, pp. 267–300, 1975.

Moore, J. M., "The Zone of Compromise for Evaluating Lay-Out Arrangements," *International Journal of Production Research*, Vol. 18, No. 1, pp. 1–10, 1980.

Moore, J. R. Jr. and N. R. Baker, "Computational Analysis of Scoring Models for R&D Project Selection," *Management Science*, Vol. 16, No. 4, pp. B212–B232, 1969.

Moore, L., "On Multiple Criteria Scoring Models," *Management Science*, Vol. 17, No. 4, 1970.

Moore, L. J., B. W. Taylor and S. M. Lee, "Analysis of a Transshipment Problem with Multiple Conflicting Objectives," *Computers and Operations Research*, Vol. 5, No. 1, pp. 39–46, 1978.

Morris, P. A. and S. S. Oren, "Multiattribute Decision Making by Sequential Resource Allocation," *Operations Research*, Vol. 28, No. 1, pp. 233–252, 1980.

Morris, W. T., *Engineering Economic Analysis* (Chapter 7, "Evaluating Outcomes—Multiple Criteria"), Reston Publishing Company, Reston, Virginia, 1976.

Morse, J. N., "Remarks on MCDM," *Multiple Criteria Decision Making*, edited by M. K. Starr and M. Zeleny, TIMS Studies in the Management Sciences, Vol. 6, North-Holland Publishing Company, Amsterdam, Holland, pp. 314–315, 1977.

Morse, J. N., "A Theory of Naive Weights," *Multiple Criteria Problem Solving*, edited by S. Zionts, Lecture Notes in Economics and Mathematical Systems No. 155, Springer-Verlag, Berlin-New York, New York, pp. 384–401, 1978.

Morse, J. N., "Reducing the Size of the Nondominated Set: Pruning by Clustering," *Computers and Operations Research: Special Issue on Mathematical Programming with Multiple Objectives*, edited by M. Zeleny, Vol. 7, No. 1–2, pp. 55–66, 1980.

Morse, J. N. and R. Clark, "Goal Programming in Transportation Planning: The Problem of Setting Weights," *Northeast Regional Science Review*, Vol. 5, pp. 140–147, 1975.

Morse, J. N. and E. B. Lieb, "Flexibility and Rigidity in Multicriterion Linear Programming," *Multiple Criteria Decision Making Theory and Application*, edited by G. Fandel and T. Gal, Springer-Verlag, Berlin-New York, New York, pp. 238–251, 1980.

Moscarola, J., "Multicriteria Decision Aid: Two Applications in Education Management," *Multiple Criteria Problem Solving*, edited by S. Zionts, Lecture Notes in Economics and Mathematical Systems No. 155, Springer-Verlag, Berlin-New York, New York, pp. 402–423, 1978.

Moscarola, J. and B. Roy, "Procédure Automatique d'Éxamen de Dossiers Fondée sur un Classement Trichotomique en Présence des Critères Multiples," *Revue Française d'Automatique, Informatique et de Recherche Opérationelle*, Vol. 11, No. 2, May 1977.

Moskowitz, H., S. M. Bajgier, A. Bartell and A. B. Whinston, "Multi-attribute Risk/Benefit Analysis of Citizen Attitudes Toward Societal Issues Involving Technology," *Multiple Criteria Problem Solving*, edited by S. Zionts, Lecture Notes in Economics and Mathematical Systems No. 155, Springer-Verlag, Berlin-New York, New York, pp. 424–448, 1977.

Moskowitz, H., G. Evans and I. Jimenez-Lerma, "Development of Multi-attribute Value Function for Long-Range Electrical Generation Expansion," *IEEE Transactions on Engineering Management*, Vol. EM-25, No. 4, pp. 78–87, 1978.

Mount, K. R. and S. Reiter, "Construction of a Continuous Utility Function for a Class of Preferences," *Journal of Mathematical Economics*, Vol. 3, No. 3, pp. 227–245, 1976.

Moursund, D. G., "Chebyshev Approximations of a Function and Its Derivatives," *Mathematics of Computation*, Vol. 18, pp. 382–389, 1964.

Muhlemann, A. P. and A. G. Lockett, "Portfolio Modeling in Multiple-Criteria Situations under Uncertainty: Rejoinder," *Decision Sciences*, Vol. 11, No. 1, pp. 178–180, 1980.

Muhlemann, A. P., A. G. Lockett and A. E. Gear, "Portfolio Modeling in Multiple-Criteria Situations under Uncertainty," *Decision Sciences*, Vol. 9, No. 4, pp. 612–626, 1978.

Mukai, H., "Algorithm for Multicriteria Optimization," *Proceedings, IEEE Conference on Decisions and Control, including Symposium on Adaptive Processes*, San Diego, California, January 10–12, 1978, pp. 892–896, 1978.

Mukundan, R. and W. B. Elsner, "Linear Feedback Strategies in Nonzero-Sum Differential Games," *International Journal of Systems Science*, Vol. 6, No. 6, pp. 513–532, 1975.

Müller, R., "Bestimmung der Kompromißmenge mit Hilfe der Teilzielmethode," *Polyoptimierung*, pp. 39–45, 1975.

Mundlak, Y. and Z. Volcani, "The Correspondence of Efficiency Frontier as a Generalization of the Cost Function," *International Economic Review*, Vol. 14, No. 1, pp. 223–233, 1973.

Muralidharan, R. and Y. C. Ho, "A Piecewise Closed Form Algorithm for a Family of Minimax and Vector Criteria Problems," *Proceedings, IEEE Conference on Decisions and Control, 13th Symposium on Adaptive Processes*, Phoenix, Arizona, 1974; New York, New York, pp. 350–361, 1974.

Muralidharan, R. and Y. C. Ho, "A Piecewise-Closed Form Algorithm for a Family of Minimax and Vector Criteria Problems," *IEEE Transactions on Automatic Control*, Vol. AC-20, pp. 381–385, 1975.

Musselman, K. and J. Talavage, "A Tradeoff Cut Approach to Multiple Objective Optimization," *Operations Research*, Vol. 28, No. 6, pp. 1424–1435, 1980.

Naccache, P., "Connectedness of the Set of Nondominated Outcomes in Multicriteria Optimization," *Journal of Optimization Theory and Applications*, Vol. 25, No. 3, pp. 459–468, July 1978.

Naccache, P., "Stability in Multicriteria Optimization," *Journal of Mathematical Analysis and Applications*, Vol. 68, No. 2, pp. 441–453, April 1979.

Nainis, W. S. and Y. Y. Haimes, "A Multilevel Approach to Planning for Capacity Expansion in Water Resource Systems" *IEEE Transactions on Systems, Man, and Cybernetics*, Vol. SMC-5, pp. 53–63, January 1975.

Nakayama, H., "Subjective Programming in Multi-Criterion Decision Making," *Multiple Criteria Decision Making Theory and Application*, edited by G. Fandel and T. Gal, Springer-Verlag, Berlin-New York, New York, pp. 252–265, 1980.

Nakayama, H., Y. Karasawa and S. Dohi, "Subjective Programming Applied to Optimal Operation in Automated Warehouses," *International Journal of Systems Science*, Vol. 11, No. 4, pp. 513–525, 1980.

Nakayama, H., V. Sawaragi and H. Sayama, "On an Optimization Problem with Min-Constraints," *International Journal of Systems Science*, Vol. 5, No. 10, pp. 995–1004, 1974.

Nakayama, H., T. Tanino and Y. Sawaragi, "An Interactive Optimization Method in Multicriteria Decisionmaking," *IEEE Transactions on Systems, Man, and Cybernetics*, Vol. SMC-10, No. 3, pp. 163–169, March 1980.

Narisimhan, R., "Goal Programming in a Fuzzy Environment," *Decision Sciences*, Vol. 11, No. 2, pp. 325–336, 1980.

Narula, S. C. and J. F. Wellington, "Linear Regression Using Multiple Criteria," *Multiple Criteria Decision Making Theory and Application*, edited by G. Fandel and T. Gal, Springer-Verlag, Berlin-New York, New York, pp. 266–277, 1980.

Neely, W. P., R. M. North and J. C. Fortson, "Planning and Selecting Multiobjective Projects by Goal Programming," *Water Resources Bulletin*, Vol. 12, No. 1, pp. 19–25, 1976.

Negoita, C. V., *Management Applications of System Theory*, Birkhäuser Verlag, Basel, Germany, pp. 136–143, 1979.

Negoita, C. V. and M. Sularia, "A Selection Method of Nondominated Points in Multicriteria Decision Problems," *Economic Computation and Economic Cybernetics: Studies and Research*, Vol. 12, No. 2, pp. 19–23, 1978.

Nehse, R., "Bemerkungen zu einem Ergebnis von J. Zowe," *Mathematische Operationsforschung und Statistik*, Vol. 6, pp. 929–931, 1975.

Nash, J., "Two-Person Cooperative Games," *Econometrica*, Vol. 21, pp. 128–140, 1953.

Nelson, W. L., "On the Use of Optimization Theory for Practical Control System Design,"

IEEE Transactions on Automatic Control, Vol. AC-9, No. 4, pp. 469–477, October 1964.

Neuman, S. P. and R. Krzysztofowicz, "An Iterative Algorithm for Interactive Multiobjective Programming," *Advances in Water Resources*, Vol. 1, No. 1, pp. 1–14, 1977.

Neumann, S., "Calibration of Distributed Parameter Groundwater Flow Models Viewed as a Multiple-Objective Decision Process under Uncertainty," *Water Resources Research*, Vol. 9, p. 1006, 1973.

Nievergelt, E., "Ein Beitrag zur Lösung von Entscheidungsproblemen mit mehrfacher Zielsetzung," *Die Unternehmung*, Vol. 25, No. 2, pp. 101–126, 1974.

Nijkamp, P., "Spatial Interdependencies and Environmental Effects," *Dynamic Allocation of Urban Space*, edited by A, Karlqvist, L. Lundqvist and F. Snickars, Saxon House, Farnborough, England, pp. 175–209, 1974.

Nijkamp, P., "A Multicriteria Analysis for Project Evaluation: Economic-Ecological Evaluation of a Land Reclamation Project," *Papers of the Regional Science Association*, Vol. 35, pp. 87–111, 1975.

Nijkamp, P. and P. Rietveld, "Multiobjective Programming Models (New Ways in Regional Decision Making)," *Regional and Urban Economics*, Vol. 6, No. 3, pp. 253–274, 1976.

Nijkamp, P. and P. Rietveld, "Conflicting Social Priorities and Compromise Social Decisions," *Analysis and Decision in Regional Policy*, edited by I. G. Cullen, Pion, London, England, pp. 153–177, 1979.

Nijkamp, P. and P. Rietveld, "Multilevel Multiobjective Models in a Multiregional System," *Multiple Criteria Analysis: Operational Methods*, edited by P. Nijkamp and J. Spronk, Gower Press, London, England, 1981.

Nijkamp, P. and W. H. Somermeyer, "Explicating Implicit Social Preference Functions," *Economics of Planning*, Vol. 11, No. 3, pp. 101–119, 1971.

Nijkamp, P. and J. Spronk, "Analysis of Production and Location Decisions by Means of Multicriteria Analysis," *Engineering and Process Economics*, Vol. 4, pp. 285–302, 1979.

Nijkamp, P. and J. Spronk, "Interactive Multiple Goal Programming: An Evaluation and Some Results," *Multiple Criteria Decision Making Theory and Application*, edited by G. Fandel and T. Gal, Springer-Verlag, Berlin-New York, New York, pp. 278–293, 1980.

Nijkamp, P. and J. Spronk, "Multicriteria Analysis: Theory and Reality," *Multiple Criteria Analysis: Operational Methods*, edited by P. Nijkamp and J. Spronk, Gower Press, London, England, 1981.

Nijkamp, P. and J. Spronk, (eds.), *Multiple Criteria Analysis: Operational Methods*, Gower Press, London, England, 1981.

Nijkamp, P. and A. van Delft, *Multi-Criteria Analysis and Regional Decision-Making*, Martinus Nijhoff, Leiden, Holland, 1977.

Nijkamp, P. and J. B. Vos, "A Multicriteria Analysis for Water Resource and Land Use Development," *Water Resources Research*, Vol. 13, No. 3, pp. 513–518, 1977.

Nurminen, M. I. and A. Paasio, "Some Remarks on the Fuzzy Approach to Multi-Goal Decision-Making," *Finnish Journal of Business Economics*, Special Edition 3, pp. 291–302, 1976.

Nutt, P. C., "Comparing Methods for Weighting Decision Criteria," *Omega*, Vol. 8, No. 2, pp. 163–172, 1980.

Nykowski, J., "Problem pogodzenia kilku kryteriow jednym programie liniowym," *Przeglad Statystyczny*, Vol. 13, No. 4, pp. 367–375, 1966.

Nykowski, J., "Multi-Criterion Linear Models," *Ekonomista*, Vol. 4, pp. 721–733, 1970.

Nykowski, J., "Rozwiazania kompromisowe w wielokriteriowym programowaniu liniowym," *Przeglad Statystyczny*, Vol. 24, No. 1, pp. 3–19, 1977.

Odom, P. R., "On Renewing the Innovative Thrust of Management Science Through MCDM

Research," *Multiple Criteria Decision Making*, edited by M. K. Starr and M. Zeleny, TIMS Studies in the Management Sciences, Vol. 6, North-Holland Publishing Company, Amsterdam, Holland, pp. 315–316, 1977.

Odom, P. R., R. E. Shannon and B. P. Buckles, "Multi-Goal Subset Selection Problems under Uncertainty," *AIIE Transactions*, Vol. 11, No. 1, pp. 61–69, 1979.

Oettli, W., "A Duality Theorem for the Nonlinear Vector-Maximum Problem," *Proc. Oper. Res.*, Eger 1974, Coloq. Math. Soc. János Bolyai, Vol. 12, pp. 697–703, 1976.

Oettli, W. and W. Prager, "Compatibility of Approximate Solution of Linear Equations with Given Error Bounds for Coefficients and Right Hand Sides," *Numerische Mathematik*, Vol. 6, pp. 405–409, 1964.

Oettli, W. and K. Ritter (eds.), *Optimization and Operations Research*, Lecture Notes in Economics and Mathematical Systems No. 117, Springer-Verlag, Berlin-New York, New York, 1976.

Ölander, F., "Search Behavior in Non-Simultaneous Choice Situations: Satisficing or Maximizing?", *Utility, Probability, and Human Decision Making*, edited by D. Wendt and C. Vlek, D. Reidel Publishing Company, Boston, Massachusetts, pp. 297–320, 1975.

Olech, G., "Existence Theorems for Optimal Problems with Vectorvalued Cost Function," *Transactions of the American Mathematical Society*, Vol. 136, pp. 159–180, 1969.

Olenik, S. C. and Y. Y. Haimes, "A Hierarchical-Multiobjective Method for Water Resources Planning," *IEEE Transactions on Systems, Man, and Cybernetics*, Vol. SMC-9, No. 9, 1979.

Olve, Nils-Göran, *Multiobjective Budgetary Planning*, Economic Research Institute, Stockholm School of Economics, Stockholm, Sweden, 1977.

Oppenheimer, K. R., "A Proxy Approach to Multi-Attribute Decision Making," *Management Science*, Vol. 24, No. 6, pp. 675–689, 1978.

Ören, T. I. and C. Y. Ören, "Solution Selection Techniques for Decision Making in Complex Systems," *Multiple Criteria Decision Making*, edited by J. L. Cochrane and M. Zeleny, University of South Carolina Press, Columbia, South Carolina, pp. 764–767, 1973.

Orne, D. L., A. Rao and W. A. Wallace, "Profit Maximization with the Aid of Goal Programming for Speculative Housing Estate Developers," *Operational Research Quarterly*, Vol. 26, No. 4, pp. 813–826, 1975.

Osborne, D. K., "Irrelevant Alternatives and Social Welfare," *Econometrica*, Vol. 44, pp. 1001–1015, 1976.

Osteryoung, J. S., "Multiple Goals in Capital-Budgeting Decision," *Multiple Criteria Decision Making*, edited by J. L. Cochrane and M. Zeleny, University of South Carolina Press, Columbia, South Carolina, pp. 447–457, 1973.

Osyczka, A., "An Approach to Multi-Criterion Optimization for Structural Design," *Proceedings, 11th Office of Naval Research (ONR) Naval Structural Mechanics Symposium*, Tucson, Arizona, October 19–22, 1981.

Ovchinnikov, V. O. and L. M. Boychuk, "Solving the Vector Optimization with a Supplementary Criterion" [in Russian], *Kibernetika i Vychislitelnaya Tekhnika*, No. 23, pp. 70–73, 1974.

Ozernoi, V. M. and M. G. Gaft, "Multicriterion Decision Problems," *Conflicting Objectives*, edited by D. E. Bell, R. L. Keeney and H. Raiffa, John Wiley and Sons, New York, New York, pp. 17–39, 1977.

Ozernoi, V. M., "Using Preference Information in Multistep Methods for Solving Multiple Criteria Decision Problems," *Multiple Criteria Decision Making Theory and Application*, edited by G. Fandel and T. Gal, Springer-Verlag, Berlin-New York, New York, pp. 314–328, 1980.

Paelink, J. H. P. and P. Nijkamp, *Operational Theory and Method in Regional Economics*, Saxon House, Farnborough, England, 1975.

Pareto, V., *Cours d'Économie Politique,* Volumes 1 and 2, F. Rouge, Lausanne, Switzerland, 1896.

Pareto, V., *Manuale di Economia Politica,* Società Editrice Librarià, Milano, Italy, 1906; Piccola Bibliteca Scientifica No. 13, Società Editrice Librarià, Milano, Italy, 1919; translated into French with Revised Mathematical Appendix, by Girard and Brière, as *Manuel d'Économie Politique,* Girard, Paris, France, First Edition 1909, Second Edition 1927; translated into English, by A. S. Schwier, as *Manual of Political Economy,* The Macmillan Company, London, England, 1971.

Pareto, V., *Sociological Writings,* selected and introduced by S. E. Finer, translated by D. Mirfin, Praeger, New York, New York, 1966.

Parks, R. P., "An Impossibility Theorem for Fixed Preferences: A Dictatorial Bergson-Samuelson Welfare Function," *Review of Economic Statistics,* Vol. 63, No. 3, pp. 447–450, 1976.

Pascoletti, A. and P. Serafini, "Comments on 'Cooperative Games and Vector-Valued Criteria Problems' by W. E. Schmitendorf," *IEEE Transactions on Automatic Control,* Vol. AC-21, No. 5, pp. 806–808, 1976.

Pascual, L. D. and A. Ben-Israel, "Vector-Valued Criteria in Geometric Programming," *Operations Research,* Vol. 19, No. 1, pp. 98–104, 1971.

Pask, G. S., "The Cybernetics of Behaviour and Cognition Extending the Meaning of 'Goal,'" *Cybernetica,* Vol. 13, Nos. 3–4, pp. 139–159, pp. 240–250, 1970.

Passy, U., "Cobb-Douglas Functions in Multiobjective Optimization," *Water Resources Research,* Vol. 14, pp. 688–690, 1978.

Passy, U. and Y. Levanon, "Multiobjective Considerations in the Planning and Management of Water and Related Land Resources," *Proceedings, 6th IFAC World Congress,* Cambridge, Massachusetts, 1975; Part 3, Pittsburgh, Pennsylvania, pp. 48.4/1-48.4/7, 1975.

Passy, U. and Y. Levanon, "Condensing Multiple Criteria," *Multiple Criteria Problem Solving,* edited by S. Zionts, Lecture Notes in Economics and Mathematical Systems No. 155, Springer-Verlag, Berlin-New York, New York, pp. 449–461, 1978.

Passy, U. and Y. Levanon, "Manpower Allocation with Multiple Objectives—the Min Max Approach," *Multiple Criteria Decision Making Theory and Application,* edited by G. Fandel and T. Gal, Springer-Verlag, Berlin-New York, New York, pp. 329–343, 1980.

Pasternak, H. and U. Passy, "Bicriterion Functions in Annual Activity Planning," *Operational Research '72,* edited by M. Ross, *Proceedings of the Sixth IFORS International Conference on Operations Research,* Dublin, Ireland, 1972; North-Holland Publishing Company, Amsterdam, Holland, pp. 325–341, 1973.

Pasternak, H. and U. Passy, "Bicriterion Mathematical Programs with Boolean Variables," *Multiple Criteria Decision Making,* edited by J. L. Cochrane and M. Zeleny, University of South Carolina Press, Columbia, South Carolina, pp. 327–348, 1973.

Pasternak, H. and U. Passy, "Finding Global Optimum of Bicriterion Mathematical Programs," *Operations Research Statistics and Economics,* Mimeograph Series No. 91, Faculty of Industrial Engineering, Technion, Haiffa, Israel, 1973.

Pasternak, H. and U. Passy, "Finding Global Optimum of Bicriterion Mathematical Programs," *Cahiers de Centre d'Études de Recherche Opérationelle,* Vol. 16, No. 1, pp. 67–80, 1974.

Pau, L. F., "Two-Level Planning with Conflicting Goals," *Multiple Criteria Decision Making,* edited by H. Thiriez and S. Zionts, Lecture Notes in Economics and Mathematical Systems No. 130, Springer-Verlag, Berlin-New York, New York, pp. 263–273, 1976.

Payne, J. H., E. Polak, D. C. Collins and W. S. Meisel, "An Algorithm for Bicriteria Optimization Based on the Sensitivity Function," *IEEE Transactions on Automatic Control,* Vol. AC-20, No. 4, pp. 546–548, August 1975.

Pearman, A., "A Weighted Maximum and Maximax Approach to Multiple Criteria Decision Making," *Operational Research Quarterly,* Vol. 28, pp. 584–587, 1977.

Pearman, A., "Approaches to Multiple Objective Decision Making with Ranked Criteria," *Analysis and Decision in Regional Policy*, edited by I. G. Cullen, Pion, London, England, pp. 136–152, 1979.

Pekelman, D. and S. K. Sen, "Mathematical Programming Models for the Determination of Attribute Weights," *Management Science*, Vol. 20, pp. 1217–1229, April 1974.

Peleg, B., "The Independence of Game Theory of Utility Theory," *Bulletin of the American Mathematical Society*, Vol. 72, pp. 995–999, 1966.

Peleg, B., "Efficiency Prices for Optimal Consumption Plans," *Journal of Mathematical Analysis and Applications*, Vol. 29, pp. 83–90, 1970.

Peleg, B., "Efficiency Prices for Optimal Consumption Plans II," *Israel Journal of Mathematics*, Vol. 9, pp. 222–234, 1971.

Peleg, B., "Topological Properties of the Efficient Point Set," *Proceedings of the American Mathematical Society*, Vol. 35, pp. 531–536, 1972.

Peleg, B., "Topological Properties of the Efficient Point Set," *Journal of Mathematical Analysis and Applications*, Vol. 63, No. 2, pp. 377–384, 1978.

Peressini, A. L., *Ordered Topological Vector Spaces*, Harper and Row, New York, New York, 1967.

Perlman, M. D., "Jensen's Inequality for a Convex Vector-Valued Function on an Infinite-Dimensional Space," *Journal of Multivariate Analysis*, Vol. 4, pp. 52–65, 1974.

Peschel, M., "Konvexität und Polyoptimierung," M. Peschel and C. Riedel, *Polyoptimierung*, Technik, Berlin, Germany, pp. 75–86, 1975.

Peschel, M., "Modellbildung und Polyoptimierung," M. Peschel and C. Riedel, *Polyoptimierung*, Technik, Berlin, Germany, pp. 123–131, 1975.

Peschel, M. and C. Riedel, "Mathematische Ungleichungen und Polyoptimierung," M. Peschel and C. Riedel, *Polyoptimierung*, Technik, Berlin, Germany, pp. 106–112, 1975.

Peschel, M. and C. Riedel, "Zur Parametrisierung widersprüchlicher Alternativsituationen," M. Peschel and C. Riedel, *Polyoptimierung*, Technik, Berlin, Germany, pp. 87–98, 1975.

Peschel, M. and C. Riedel, *Polyoptimierung—eine Entscheidungshilfe für ingenieurtechnische Kompromißlösungen*, Technik, Berlin, Germany, 1975.

Peschel, M. and C. Riedel, "Use of Vector Optimization in Multiobjective Decision Making," *Conflicting Objectives*, edited by D. E. Bell, R. L. Keeney and H. Raiffa, John Wiley and Sons, New York, New York, pp. 97–122, 1977.

Philip, J., "Algorithms for the Vector Maximization Problem," *Mathematical Programming*, Vol. 2, No. 2, pp. 207–229, 1972.

Philip, J., "An Algorithm for Combined Quadratic and Multiobjective Programming," *Multiple Criteria Decision Making*, edited by H. Thiriez and S. Zionts, Lecture Notes in Economics and Mathematical Studies No. 130, Springer-Verlag, Berlin-New York, New York, pp. 35–52, 1976.

Philip, J., "Vector Maximization at a Degenerate Vertex," *Mathematical Programming*, Vol. 13, No. 3, pp. 357–359, 1977.

Philippatos, G. C., "On the Specification of Viable Financial Goals," *Managerial Planning*, Vol. 20, No. 1, pp. 11–16, 1971.

Philippatos, G. C., "Behavioral Implications of Discrepancies in Expectations Between the Firm and Its Stockholders with an Application to Dividend Policies," *Multiple Criteria Decision Making*, edited by J. L. Cochrane and M. Zeleny, University of South Carolina Press, Columbia, South Carolina, pp. 768–770, 1973.

Philippe, M., "Condition Nécessaire d'Optimalité de Pareto Pour un Système à Commande," *Comptes Rendus Académie des Sciences de Paris*, Série A, Vol. 280, No. 20, pp. 1397–1399, 1975.

Philippe, V., "Problèmes Multicritères," *Cahiers du Centre d'Études de Recherche Opérationelle*, Vol. 16, No. 4, pp. 425–439, 1974.

Philipson, R. H. and A. Ravindran, "Application of Goal Programming to Machinability Data Optimization," *Journal of Mechanical Design*, Vol. 100, pp. 286–291, 1978.

Pigon, R., "O pewnym kryterium wyboru decyzji," *Pr. Nauk. AE Wroclawiu*, Vol. 70, pp. 101–121, 1976.

Pigou, A. C., *Economics of Welfare*, First Edition, London, England, 1920; Fourth Edition, London, England, 1934.

Pill, J., "The Delphi Method: Substance, Context, a Critique and an Annotated Bibliography," *Socio-Economic Planning Sciences*, Vol. 5, pp. 57–71, 1971.

Pindyck, R. S., "Optimal Economic Stabilization Policies Under Decentralized Control and Conflicting Objectives," *Proceedings, 7th IEEE Conference on Decisions and Control*, Clearwater, Florida, December 1–3, 1976, pp. 670–675, 1976.

Pitkanen, E., "Goal Programming and Operational Objectives in Public Administration," *Swedish Journal of Economics*, Vol. 72, No. 3, pp. 207–214, 1970.

Plisha, S. R., "Multiperson Controlled Diffusions," *SIAM Journal on Control*, Vol. 11, No. 4, pp. 563–586, 1973; *Mathematical Reviews*, Vol. 48, No. 7, p. 10523, 1974.

Pochtman, Y. M. and V. V. Skalozub, "On a Vector Model of the Problem of Optimal Design of Shells" [in Russian], *Stroitel'naya Mekhanika i Raschet Sooruzhenii*, No. 5, pp. 17–20, October 1979.

Podinovskii, V. V., "Lexicographical Problems of Linear Programming," *USSR Computational Mathematics and Mathematical Physics*, Vol. 12, pp. 249–253, 1972.

Podinovskii, V. V., "Lexicographic Games," *Advances in Game Theory, Proceedings, Second USSR Game Theory Conference*, Vilnius, USSR, 1973.

Podrebarac. M. L. and S. S. Sengupta, "Parametric Linear Programming: Some Extensions," *Infor*, Vol. 9, No. 3, pp. 305–319, 1971.

Polak, E., "On the Approximation of Solutions to Multiple Criteria Decision Making Problems," *Multiple Criteria Decison Making*, edited by M. Zeleny, Lecture Notes in Economics and Mathematical Systems No. 123, Springer-Verlag, Berlin-New York, New York, pp. 271–282, 1976.

Polak, E. and A. N. Payne, "On Multicriteria Optimization," *Directions in Large Scale Systems*, edited by Y. C. Ho and S. K. Mitter, Plenum Press, New York, New York, pp. 77–94, 1976.

Pollatscheck, A., "Personnel Assignment by Multiobjective Programming," *Zeitschrift für Operations Research*, Vol. 20, No. 5, pp. 161–170, 1976.

Powell, J. and R. Vergin, "A Heuristic Model for Planning Corporate Financing," *Financial Management*, Vol. 4, No. 2, pp. 13–20, 1975.

Prasad, V. R. and I. G. Sarma, "Stochastic Multicriterion Optimal Control Problems," *Proceedings, IEEE Conference on Decisions and Control (Symposium on Adaptive Processes)*, Austin, Texas, 1970; New York, New York, pp. XV/1-XV/5, 1970.

Prasad, V. R. and I. G. Sarma, "Theory of N-Person Differential Games," *Proceedings, 1st International Conference on the Theory and Applications of Differential Games*, Amherst, Massachusetts, s.l.s.a. pp. VIII/12-VIII/17, 1969.

Price, W. L., "Goal Programming and a Manpower Problem," *Mathematical Programming in Theory and Practice*, edited by P. L. Hammer and G. Zoutendijk, North-Holland Publishing Company, Amsterdam, Holland, pp. 395–416, 1974.

Price, W. L., "An Interactive Objective Function Generator for Goal Programmes," *Multiple Criteria Decision Making*, edited by H. Thiriez and S. Zionts, Lecture Notes in Economics and Mathematical Systems No. 130, Springer-Verlag, Berlin-New York, New York, pp. 147–158, 1976.

Price, W. L., "Solving Goal-Programming Manpower Models Using Advanced Network Codes," *The Journal of the Operational Research Society*, Vol. 29, No. 12, pp. 1231–1240, 1978.

Price, W. L. and W. G. Pisker, "The Application of Goal Programming to Manpower Planning," *Infor*, Vol. 10, No. 2, pp. 221–231, October 1972.

Pruzan, P. M., "Is Cost Benefit Analysis Consistent with the Maximization of Expected Utility?" *Operational Research of the Social Sciences*, edited by J. R. Lawrence, Tavistock Publications, Ltd., London, England, pp. 319–336, 1966.

Pruzan, P. M., "Measures of Performance for 'Significant' Planning Problems," *Erhversøkonomisk Tidsskrift*, Vol. 2, pp. 91–100, 1966.

Pruzan, P. M. and J. T. R. Jackson, "On the Development of Utility Spaces for Multi-Goal Systems," *Saertryk of Erhvervsokonomisk Tidsskrift*, Vol. 27, No. 4, pp. 257–274, 1963.

Pun, L., "Multicriteria Decision-Aid-Making in Production-Management Problems," *Multiple Criteria Decision Making Theory and Applications*, edited by G. Fandel and T. Gal, Springer-Verlag, Berlin-New York, New York, pp. 344-373, 1980.

Quirk, J. and R. Saposnik, *Introduction to General Equilibrium Theory and Welfare Economics*, McGraw-Hill, New York, New York, 1968.

Radner, R., "Mathematical Specifications of Goals for Decision Problems," *Human Judgments and Optimality*, edited by M. W. Shelly, II, and G. L. Bryan, John Wiley and Sons, New York, New York, pp. 178–216, 1964.

Radner, R., "A Note on Maximal Points of Convex Sets in l∞," *Proceedings, 5th Berkeley Symposium on Mathematical Statistics and Probability*, Berkeley, California, 1965–66; Vol. 1: *Statistics*, University of California Press, Berkeley, California, pp. 351–354, 1967.

Radner, R., "Satisficing," *Optimization Techniques (IFIP Technical Conference)*, edited by G. Marchuk, Springer-Verlag, Berlin-New York, New York, pp. 252–263, 1975.

Radner, R. and J. Marschak, "Note on Some Proposed Decision Criteria," *Decision Processes*, edited by R. M. Thrall, C. H. Coombs and R. L. Davis, John Wiley and Sons, New York, New York, pp. 61–86, 1954.

Radulescu, M., "La Programmation Vectorielle Convexe Avec des Restrictions Linéaires," *Abstracts of 3rd Conference on Mathematical Programming*, Matrafüred, pp. 53–57, 1975.

Radzikowski, W., "Methoden zur Einbeziehung mehr als einer Zielfunktion bei der Optimierungsrechnung," *Organizacja Samorzad Zarzadzanie*, Vol. 10, No. 10, pp. 43–52, 1965.

Radzikowski, W., "Die Berücksichtigung mehrer Zielfunktionen bei Aufgaben der linearen Optimierung," *Wirtschaftswissenschaften*, Vol. 15, No. 5, pp. 797–806, 1967.

Radzikowski, W., "Eine Methode der Berücksichtigung mehrer Zielfunktionen bei Aufgaben der linearen Optimierung," *Mathematische Methoden der Operationsforschung*, edited by B. Blumenthal, Die Wirtschaft, Berlin, Germany, pp. 116–130, 1970.

Rae, A. N., "A Note on the Solution of Goal Programming Problems with Preemptive Priority," *New Zealand Operational Research*, Vol. 2, No. 1, pp. 34–39, January 1974.

Raiffa, H., *Decision Analysis*, Addison-Wesley, Reading, Massachusetts, 1968.

Ramachandra, V. S., "Liberalism, Nonbinary Choice and Pareto Principle," *Theory and Decision*, Vol. 3, No. 1, pp. 49–54, 1972.

Rand, D., "Thresholds in Pareto Sets," *Journal of Mathematical Economics*, Vol. 3, No. 2, pp. 139–154, 1976.

Rao, S. S. and S. K. Hati, "Game Theory Approach in Multicriteria Optimization of Function Generating Mechanisms," *Journal of Mechanical Design, Transactions of the ASME*, Vol. 101, pp. 398–405, 1979.

Rapoport, A., "Interpersonal Comparison of Utilities," *Multiple Criteria Decision Making*, edited by M. Zeleny, Lecture Notes in Economics and Mathematical Systems No. 123, Springer-Verlag, Berlin-New York, New York, pp. 17–43, 1976.

Rasmusen, H. J., "Multi-Level Planning with Conflicting Objectives," *Swedish Journal of Economics*, Vol. 76, 1974.

Rauchhans, K., "Die Berücksichtigung mehrer Entscheidungskriterien bei ökonomischen Optimierungsrechnungen," *Wirtschaftswissenschaften*, Vol. 14, No. 4, pp. 580–601, 1966.

Reeves, G. R., "A Note on Quadratic Preferences and Goal Programming," *Decision Sciences*, Vol. 9, No. 3, pp. 532–534, 1978.

Reggiani, M. G. and F. E. Marchetti, "The Pseudometric View in Problems Involving Vector-Valued Performance Criteria," *Alta Frequenza*, Vol. 43, No. 7, pp. 462–467, July 1974.

Reid, R. W. and S. J. Citron, "On Noninferior Performance Index Vectors," *Journal of Optimization Theory and Applications*, Vol. 7, No. 1, pp. 11–28, 1971.

Reid, R. W. and V. Venkateswararao, "On the Noninferior Index Approach to Large-Scale Multicriteria Systems," *Journal of the Franklin Institute*, Vol. 291, No. 4, pp. 241–254, April 1971.

Rekasius, Z. V. and W. E. Schmitendorf, "On the Noninferiority of Nash-Equilibrium Solutions," *IEEE Transactions on Automatic Control*, Vol. AC-16, No. 2, pp. 170–173, April 1971.

Rekasius, Z. V. and W. E. Schmitendorf, "Comments on 'On the Noninferiority of Nash-Equilibrium Solutions,'" *IEEE Transactions on Automatic Control*, Vol. AC-17, p. 178, 1972.

Remak, R., "Kann die Volkswirtschaftslehre eine Exakte Wissenschaft Werden?", *Jahrbücher für Nationalökonomie und Statistik*, Vol. 76, pp. 703–735, 1929.

Resa, I. D. and L. Ladar, "Consideratii privind cumularea criteriilor de optimizat in programerera liniara," *Revista de Statistica*, Vol. 8, pp. 84–88, August 1973.

Rhodes, I. B., "On Nonzero-Sum Differential Games with Quadratic Cost Functionals," *Proceedings, 1st International Conference on the Theory and Applications of Differential Games*, Amherst, Massachusetts, s.l.s.a. pp. IV/1-IV/7, 1969.

Rice, J. R., "Approximation with Convex Constraints," *SIAM Journal*, Vol. 2, No. 1, pp. 15–32, 1963.

Richardson, M. W., "Multidimensional Psychophysics," *Psychological Bulletin of the American Psychological Association*, Vol. 35, pp. 659–660, 1938.

Richter, W., "Charakterisierung Pareto-effizienter Verteilungen in Ökonomien mit öffentlichen Gütern und einem Maßraum von Agenten," *Zeitschrift für Angewandte Mathematik und Mechanik*, Vol. 56, No. 3, pp. 357–359, 1976.

Rider, K. L., "A Parametric Model for the Allocation of Fire Companies in New York City," *Management Science*, Vol. 23, No. 2, pp. 146–158, 1976.

Riedel, C., "Technische Kompromißlösungen bei mehrfacher Zielstellung," M. Peschel and C. Riedel, *Polyoptimierung*, Technik, Berlin, Germany, pp. 3-14, 1975.

Riedel, C., "Verallgemeinerung des Optimalitätsprinzips der diskreten dynamischen Optimierung bei mehrfacher Zielsetzung," M. Peschel and C. Riedel, *Polyoptimierung*, Technik, Berlin, Germany, pp. 99–103, 1975.

Riedel, C., "Geometrische Optimierung und Polyoptimierung," M. Peschel and C. Riedel, *Polyoptimierung*, Technik, Berlin, Germany, pp. 113–122, 1975.

Riedel, C. and G. Timmel, "Statistische Suchverfahren zur Bestimmung der Kompromißmenge," M. Peschel and C. Riedel, *Polyoptimierung*, Technik, Berlin, Germany, pp. 54–64, 1975.

Rietveld, P., *Multiple Objective Decision Methods and Regional Planning*, Studies in Regional Science and Urban Economics, Vol. 7, North-Holland Publishing Company, Amsterdam, Holland, 1980.

Ritter, K., "Optimization Theory in Linear Spaces, Part I," *Mathematische Annalen*, Vol. 182, No. 3, pp. 189–206, 1969.

Ritter, K., "Optimization Theory in Linear Spaces, Part II: On Systems of Linear Operator Inequalities in Partially Ordered Normed Linear Spaces," *Mathematische Annalen*, Vol. 183, No. 3, pp. 169–180, 1969.

Ritter, K., "Optimization Theory in Linear Spaces, Part III: Mathematical Programming in Partially Ordered Banach Spaces," *Mathematische Annalen*, Vol. 184, No. 2, pp. 133–154, 1970.

Ritter, K., "Dual Nonlinear Programming Problems in Partially Ordered Banach Spaces," *Zeitschrift für Wahrscheinlichkeitstheorie und Verwandte Gebiete*, Vol. 14, pp. 257–263, 1970.

Ritzman, L., J. Bradford and R. Jacobs, "A Multiple Objective Approach to Space Planning for Academic Facilities," *Management Science*, Vol. 25, No. 9, pp. 895–906, 1979.

Ritzman, L. P. and L. J. Krajewski, "Multiple Objectives in Linear Programming—an Example in Scheduling Postal Resources," *Decision Sciences*, Vol. 4, No. 3, pp. 364–378, 1973.

Rivett, B. H. P. "Multidimensional Scaling for Multiobjective Policies," *Omega*, Vol. 5, No. 4, pp. 367–379, 1977.

Rivett, B. H. P., "Indifference Mapping for Multiple Criteria Decisions," *Omega*, Vol. 8, No. 1, pp. 81–94, 1980.

Rivett, B. H. P., "The Use of Local-Global Mapping Techniques in Analysing Multi-Criteria Decision Making," *Multiple Criteria Decision Making Theory and Application*, edited by G. Fandel and T. Gal, Springer-Verlag, Berlin-New York, New York, pp. 374–388, 1980.

Roba, E., B. Sussman and M. Theys, "Les Méthodes de Choix Multicritères Appliquées a la Sélection du Personnel," *Models of Manpower*, The English University Press, 1970.

Robers, P. D. and A. Ben-Israel, "An Interval Programming Algorithm for Discrete Linear L_1 Approximation Problems," *Journal of Approximation Theory*, Vol. 2, pp. 323–336, 1969.

Robinson, S. M., "An Inverse-Function Theorem for a Class of Multivalued Functions," *Proceedings of the American Mathematical Society*, Vol. 41, No. 1, pp. 211–218, 1973.

Rödder, W., "Der Sattelpunktbegriff für vektorwertige Funktionen und eine Anwendung auf lineare Vektoroptimumprobleme," *Proc. Oper. Res.*, Vol. 6, pp. 142–151, 1976.

Rödder, W., "A Duality Theory for Linear Vector Optimum Problems," *Advances in Operations Research*, edited by M. Roubens, North-Holland Publishing Company, Amsterdam, Holland, pp. 405–407, 1977.

Rödder, W., "A Generalized Saddle-Point Theory as Applied to Duality Theory for Linear Vector Optimization Problems," *European Journal of Operational Research*, Vol. 1, pp. 55–59, 1977.

Rödder, W., "A Satisfying Aggregation of Objectives by Duality," *Multiple Criteria Decision Making Theory and Application*, edited by G. Fandel and T. Gal, Springer-Verlag, Berlin-New York, New York, pp. 389–399, 1980.

Rom, W. O. and M. S. Hung, "Application of Primitive Sets to Multi-Criteria Optimization Problems," *Journal of Mathematical Economics*, Vol. 7, No. 1, pp. 77–90, 1980.

Rosenblatt, M. J., "The Facilities Layout Problem: A Multi-Goal Approach," *International Journal of Production Research*, Vol. 17, No. 4, pp. 323–332, 1979.

Rosenmüller, J., "Kooperative Spiele und Märkte," Lecture Notes in Operations Research and Mathematical Systems No. 53, Springer-Verlag, Berlin-New York, New York, 1971.

Rosinger, E. E., "Duality and Alternative in Multiobjective Optimization," *Proceedings of the American Mathematical Society*, Vol. 64, No. 2, pp. 307–313, 1977.

Rosinger, E. E., "Multiobjective Duality without Convexity," *Journal of Mathematical Analysis and Applications*, Vol. 66, pp. 442–450, 1978.

Rosinger, E. E., "Interactive Algorithm for Multiobjective Optimization," *Multiple Criteria Decision Making Theory and Application*, edited by G. Fandel and T. Gal, Springer-Verlag, Berlin-New York, New York, pp. 400–404, 1980.

Ross, G. T. and R. M. Soland, "A Multicriteria Approach to Location of Public Facilities," *European Journal of Operational Research*, Vol. 4, No. 5, pp. 307–321, 1980.

Rosser, J. B., "Problems and Methods with Multiple Objective Functions," *Mathematical Programming*, Vol. 1, No. 2, pp. 239–266, 1971.

Rothenberg, J. F., *The Measurement of Social Welfare*, Prentice-Hall, Englewood Cliffs, New Jersey, 1961.

Rothenberg, T., "Non-Convexity Aggregation and Pareto-optimality," *Journal of Political Economy*, Vol. 68, pp. 435–468, 1960.

Roy, B., "Classement et Choix en Présence des Critères Multiples (la méthode ELECTRE)," *Revue Française d'Automatique, Informatique et de Recherche Opérationelle*, Vol. 2, No. 8, pp. 57–75, 1968.

Roy, B., "Problems and Methods with Multiple Objective Functions," *Mathematical Programming*, Vol. 1, No. 3, pp. 239–266, 1971; French version in *Revue Metra*, Vol. 9, No. 1, 1972.

Roy, B., "Décisions avec Critères Multiples: Problèmes et Méthodes," *Revue Metra*, Vol. 11, No. 1, pp. 121–151, 1972.

Roy, B., "How Outranking Relations Helps Multiple Criteria Decision Making," *Multiple Criteria Decision Making*, edited by J. L. Cochrane and M. Zeleny, University of South Carolina Press, Columbia, South Carolina, pp. 179–201, 1973.

Roy, B., "Critères Multiples et Modèlisation des Préférences (l'Apport des Relations de Surclassement)," *Revue d'Economie Politique*, Vol. 84, No. 1, pp. 1–44, 1974.

Roy, B., "La Modelisation des Préférences: Un Aspect Crucial de l'Aide à la Décision," *Revue Metra*, Vol. 13, No. 2, pp. 135–153, 1974.

Roy, B., "Vers une Méthodologie Générale d'Aide à la Décision," *Revue Metra*, Vol. 14, No. 3, pp. 459–497, 1975.

Roy, B., "From Optimization to Multicriteria Decision Aid: Three Main Operational Attitudes," *Multiple Criteria Decision Making*, edited by H. Thiriez and S. Zionts, Lecture Notes in Economics and Mathematical Systems No. 130, Springer-Verlag, Berlin-New York, New York, pp. 1-34, 1976.

Roy, B., "Outranking and Fuzzy Outranking: A Concept Making Operational Partial Order Analysis," *Decision Making with Multiple Conflicting Objectives*, edited by H. Raiffa and R. L. Keeney, International Institute for Applied Systems Analysis, Laxenburg, Austria, 1976.

Roy, B., "Why Multicriteria Decision Aid May Not Fit In with the Assessment of a Unique Criterion," *Multiple Criteria Decision Making*, edited by M. Zeleny, Lecture Notes in Economics and Mathematical Systems No. 123, Springer-Verlag, Berlin-New York, New York, pp. 283–286, 1976.

Roy, B., "A Conceptual Framework for a Prescriptive Theory of 'Decision Aid,'" *Multiple Criteria Decision Making*, edited by M. K. Starr and M. Zeleny, TIMS Studies in the Management Sciences, Vol. 6, North-Holland Publishing Company, Amsterdam, Holland, pp. 179–210, 1977.

Roy, B., "Partial Preference Analysis and Decision-Aid: The Fuzzy Outranking Relation Concept," *Conflicting Objectives*, edited by D. E. Bell, R. L. Keeney and H. Raiffa, John Wiley and Sons, New York, New York, pp. 40–75, 1977.

Roy, B., "A Multicriteria Analysis for Trichotomic Segmentation Problems," *Multiple Criteria Analysis: Operational Methods*, edited by P. Nijkamp and J. Spronk, Gower Press, London, England, 1981.

Roy, B. and P. Bertier, "La Méthode ELECTRE II: Une Application au Media-Planning," *Operations Research '72*, edited by M. Ross, North-Holland Publishing Company, Amsterdam, Holland, pp. 291–302, 1973.

Roy, B. and E. Jacquet-Lagrèze, "Concepts and Methods Used in Multicriterion Decision Models: Their Applications to Transportation Problems," *Optimization Applied to Transportation Systems*, edited by H. Strobel, R. Genser and M. M. Etschmaier, International Institute for Applied Systems Analysis, Laxenburg, Austria, pp. 9–26, 1977.

Roy, B., P. Vincke and J.-P. Brans, "Aide à la Décision Multicritère," *Rev. Belge Statist. Inform. et Rech. Opèr.*, Vol. 15, No. 4, pp. 23–53, 1975.

Roy, G. G., "A Multicriteria Approach to Regional Planning Problems," *Environment and Planning*, Vol. 6, pp. 313–320, 1974.

Roy, G. G., "A Man-Machine Approach to Multicriteria Decision Making," *International Journal of Man-Machine Studies*, Vol. 12, No. 2, pp. 203–215, 1980.

Rudeanu, S., "Programmation Bivalente à Plusieurs Fonctions Èconomiques," *Revue Française d'Automatique, Informatique et de Recherche Opérationelle*, Vol. 3, No. 5–2, pp. 13–30, 1969.

Ruefli, T. W., "A Generalized Goal Decomposition Model," *Management Science*, Vol. 17, No. 8, pp. B505–B518, 1971.

Ruefli, T. W., "A Generalized Goal Decomposition Model," *Omega*, Vol. 17, No. 8, pp. 505–518, 1971.

Ruefli, T. W., "Linked Multi-Criteria Decision Models," *Multiple Criteria Decision Making*, edited by J. L. Cochrane and M. Zeleny, University of South Carolina Press, Columbia, South Carolina, pp. 406–415, 1973.

Rusu, I., "O metode de rezolvarea a problemelor de programarea liniara cu mai multe functii scop," *Studias Universitatis Babes-Bolyai Mat.*, Serie Oeconomica, Fasciculus 1, pp. 31–38, 1973.

Saaty, T. L., "Exploring the Interface Between Hierarchies, Multiple Objectives and Fuzzy Sets," *Fuzzy Sets and Systems*, Vol. 1, No. 1, pp. 57–68, 1978.

Sakawa, M., "An Approximate Solution on Linear Multicriteria Control Problems Through the Multicriteria Simplex Method," *Journal of Optimization Theory and Applications*, Vol. 22, No. 3, pp. 417–427, July 1977.

Sakawa, M., "Multiobjective Reliability and Redundancy Optimization of a Series-Parallel System by Surrogate Worth Trade-Off Method," *Microelectronics and Reliability*, Vol. 17, pp. 465–467, 1978.

Sakawa, M., "Solution of Multicriteria Control Problems in Certain Types of Linear Distributed-Parameter Systems by a Multicriteria Simplex Method," *Journal of Mathematical Analysis and Applications*, Vol. 64, pp. 181–188, 1978.

Sakawa, M., "Multiobjective Optimization by the Surrogate Worth Trade-Off Method," *The Journal of the Operational Research Society*, Vol. 31, No. 2, pp. 153–158, 1980.

Sakawa, M. and R. Narutaki, "Multi-Objective Optimization in Decentralized Management of Development in Large Production Organizations," *International Journal of Systems Science*, Vol. 8, pp. 9–16, 1977.

Sakawa, M., R. Narutaki and K. Sawada, "Vectoroptimization for a Nonlinear Dynamic Productionmodel" [in Japanese], *Systems and Controls*, Vol. 20, No. 7, pp. 388–390, 1976.

Sakawa, M., R. Narutaki and T. Suwa, "Application of Multicriteria Simplex Method to the Numerical Solution of Multicriteria Control Problems," *Memoirs of the Faculty of Engineering, Kobe University*, Kobe, Japan, Vol. 23, pp. 25–38, 1977.

Sakawa, M., R. Narutaki and T. Suwa, "Optimal Control of Linear Systems with Several Cost Functionals Through a Multicriteria Simplex Method," *International Journal of Control*, Vol. 25, No. 6, pp. 901–914, 1977.

Sakawa, M. and Y. Sawaragi, "Multiple-Objective Optimization for Environment Development Systems," *International Journal of Systems Science*, Vol. 6, No. 2, pp. 157–164, 1975.

Sakawa, M. and Y. Sawaragi, "Multiple-Criteria Optimization of Pollution Control Model," *International Journal of Systems Science*, Vol. 6, No. 8, pp. 741–748, 1975.

Sakawa, M. and Y. Sawaragi, "Multiple-Criteria Optimization for Environment Development System-Constrained Case," *Memoirs of the Faculty of Engineering, Kyoto University*, Kyoto, Japan, Vol. 37, No. 3, pp. 176–183, 1975.

Salama, A. I. A. and V. Gourishankar, "Optimization of a Deterministic System with Two Control Functions and Several Cost Functionals," *Proceedings, 4th Hawaii International Conference on Systems Science,* Honolulu, Hawaii, 1971; Western Periodicals, North Hollywood, California, pp. 371–373, 1971.

Salama, A. I. A. and Y. Gourishankar, "Optimal Control of Systems with a Single Control and Several Cost Functionals," *International Journal of Control,* Vol. 14, No. 4, pp. 705–725, 1971.

Salama, A. I. A. and M. H. Hamza, "On the Optimization of Static Systems with Several Cost Measures," *IEEE Transactions on Automatic Control,* Vol. AC-17, No. 1, pp. 170–172, 1972.

Salih, K., "Goal Conflicts in Pluralistic Multi-Level Planning for Development," *International Regional Science Review,* Vol. 1, pp. 49–72, 1975.

Salinetti, G., "Programmazione lineare cou piu' funzioni obiettivo," *Calcolo,* Vol. 9, pp. 293–322, 1972.

Salkin, G. R. and R. C. Jones, "A Goal Programming Formulation for Merger Strategy," *Applications of Management Science in Banking and Finance,* edited by S. Eilon and T. R. Fowkes, Gower Press, London, England, 1972.

Salles, M., "A General Possibility Theorem for Group Decision Rules with Pareto-Transitivity," *Journal of Economic Theory,* Vol. 11, No. 1, pp. 110–118, 1975.

Salukvadze, M. E., "On the Optimization of Vector Functionals, Part I: Programming Optimal Trajectories" [in Russian], *Avtomatika i Telemekhanika,* Vol. 32, No. 8, pp. 5–15, 1971; translation in *Automation and Remote Control,* Vol. 32, No. 8, pp. 1169–1178, 1972.

Salukvadze, M. E., "On the Optimization of Vector Functionals, Part II: Analytic Construction of Optimal Regulators" [in Russian], *Avtomatika i Telemekhanika,* Vol. 32, No. 9, pp. 5–15, 1971; translation in *Automation and Remote Control,* Vol. 32, No. 9, pp. 1347–1357, 1972.

Salukvadze, M. E., "On the Optimization of Control Systems with Vector Criteria," *Proceedings of the 5th All-Union Conference on Control,* Part 2, Nauka, Moscow, USSR, 1971.

Salukvadze, M. E., "On Optimization of Control Systems According to Vector-Valued Performance Criteria," *Proceedings, 5th IFAC World Congress,* Paris, France, Part IV, s.l.s.a., pp. 40-5/1-40-5/7, 1972.

Salukvadze, M. E., "On a Linear Programming Problem with a Vector-Valued Performance Criterion" [in Russian], *Avtomatika i Telemekhanika,* Vol. 31, No. 5, pp. 99–105, 1972; translation in *Automation and Remote Control,* Vol. 33, No. 6, pp. 794–799, 1972.

Salukvadze, M. E., "Vector Functionals in Linear Problems of Analytic Construction" [in Russian], *Avtomatika i Telemekhanika,* Vol. 34, No. 7, 1973.

Salukvadze, M. E., "On the Existence of Solutions in Problems of Optimization Under Vector-Valued Criteria," *Journal of Optimization Theory and Applications,* Vol. 13, No. 2, pp. 203–217, 1974.

Salukvadze, M. E., "Vector Optimization Problems in Control Theory" [in Russian], *Metzniereba,* Tiflis, Republic of Georgia, USSR, 1975; translated into English by J. L. Casti, Academic Press, New York, New York, 1979.

Salukvadze, M. E., "An Approach to the Solution of the Vector Optimization Problem of Dynamic Systems," to appear in *Journal of Optimization Theory and Applications,* 1982.

Salvia, A. A. and W. R. Ludwig, "An Application of Goal Programming at Lord Corporation," *Interfaces,* Vol. 9, No. 4, pp. 129–133, 1979.

Samuelson, P. A., "Efficient Portfolio Selection for Pareto-Levy Investments," *Journal of Finance and Quantitative Analysis,* pp. 107–122, June 1967.

Sandberg, I. W., "Public-Interest Type Results Concerning the Single Regulated Multiservice Firm and Multifirm Alternatives," *IEEE Transactions on Systems, Man, and Cybernetics*, Vol. SMC-6, pp. 740–746, 1976.

Sandor, P. E., "Some Problems of Ranging in Linear Programming," *CORS Journal*, Vol. 2, No. 1, pp. 26–31, 1964.

Sarin, R. K., "Interactive Evaluation and Bound Procedure for Selecting Multiattributed Alternatives," *Multiple Criteria Decision Making*, edited by M. K. Starr and M. Zeleny, TIMS Studies in the Management Sciences, Vol. 6, North-Holland Publishing Company, Amsterdam, Holland, pp. 211–224, 1977.

Sarin, R. K., "Ranking of Multiattribute Alternatives with an Application to Coal Power Plant Siting," *Multiple Criteria Decision Making Theory and Application*, Springer-Verlag, Berlin-New York, New York, pp. 405–429, 1980.

Sarles, M. D., "A Time-Fuel Optimum Controller," *IEEE Transactions on Automatic Control*, Vol. AC-11, pp. 306–307, April 1966.

Sarma, I. G. and R. K. Ragade, "Some Considerations in Formulating Optimal Control Problems as Differential Games," *International Journal of Control*, Vol. 4, No. 3, pp. 264–279, 1966.

Sartoris, W. L. and M. L. Spruill, "Goal Programming and Working Capital Management," *Financial Management*, Vol. 3, No. 1, pp. 67–74, 1974.

Saska, J., "Lineárni multiprogramováni," *Ekonomicko Mathematický Obzor*, Vol. 4, No. 3, pp. 359–373, 1968.

Sawaragi, Y., K. Inoue and H. Nakayama, "Multiobjective Decision Making with Applications to Environmental and Urban Design," *Conflicting Objectives*, edited by D. E. Bell, R. L. Keeney and H. Raiffa, John Wiley and Sons, New York, New York, pp. 358–366, 1977.

Sayeki, Y. and K. H. Vespers, "Allocation of Importance in a Hierarchical Goal Structure," *Management Science*, Vol. 19, No. 6, pp. B667–B675, 1973.

Scarf, H., "The Core of an n-Person Game," *Econometrica*, Vol. 35, pp. 50–69, 1967.

Scarf, H., "On the Existence of a Cooperative Solution for a General Class of n-Person Games," *Journal of Economic Theory*, Vol. 3, pp. 169–181, 1971.

Schiemenz, B., "Possibilities to Consider Multiple Criteria in Decision Situations," *Multiple Criteria Decision Making*, edited by H. Thiriez and S. Zionts, Lecture Notes in Economics and Mathematical Systems No. 130, Springer-Verlag, Berlin-New York, New York, pp. 274–292, 1976.

Schilling, D., "Dynamic Location Modelling for Public-Sector Facilities: A Multicriteria Approach," *Decision Sciences*, Vol. 11, No. 4, pp. 714–724, 1980.

Schmee, J., E. Hannan and M. P. Mirabile, "An Examination of Patient Referral Discharge Policies Using a Multiple Objective Semi-Markov Decision Process," *The Journal of the Operational Research Society*, Vol. 30, No. 2, pp. 121–129, 1979.

Schmidt, J. W. and G. K. Bennett, "Economic Multiattribute Acceptance Sampling," *AIIE Transactions*, Vol. 4, No. 3, pp. 194–199, 1972.

Schmitendorf, W. E., "Cooperative Games and Vector-Valued Criteria Problems," *Proceedings, IEEE Conference on Decisions and Control, 11th Symposium on Adaptive Processes*, New Orleans, Louisiana, 1972; New York, New York, pp. 340–344, 1972.

Schmitendorf, W. E., "Cooperative Games and Vector-Valued Criteria Problems," *IEEE Transactions on Automatic Control*, Vol. AC-18, No. 2, pp. 139–144, 1973.

Schmitendorf, W. E., "Optimal Control of Systems with Multiple Criteria When Disturbances Are Present," *Journal of Optimization Theory and Applications*, Vol. 27, No. 1, pp. 135–146, January 1979.

Schmitendorf, W. E. and G. Leitmann, "A Simple Derivation of Necessary Conditions for Pareto-Optimality," *IEEE Transactions on Automatic Control*, Vol. AC-19, No. 5, pp. 601–602, 1974.

Schmitendorf, W. F. and G. Moriarty, "A Sufficiency Condition for Coalitive Pareto-Optimal Solutions," *Journal of Optimization Theory and Applications*, Vol. 18, No. 1, pp. 93–102, 1976.

Schmitendorf, W. F. and G. Moriarty, "A Sufficiency Condition for Pareto-Optimal Solutions," *Multicriteria Decision Making and Differential Games*, edited by G. Leitmann, Plenum Press, New York, New York, pp. 163–172, 1976.

Schmitendorf, W. F. and J. A. Walker, "On the Equivalence of Some Necessary Conditions for Vector Valued Criteria Problems," *IEEE Transactions on Automatic Control*, Vol. AC-18, No. 6, pp. 664–665, 1973.

Schönfeld, P., "Some Duality of Theorems for the Non-Linear Vector Maximum Problem," *Unternehmensforschung*, Vol. 14, No. 1, pp. 51–63, 1970.

Schroeder, R. G., "Resource Planning in University Management by Goal Programming," *Operations Research*, Vol. 22, No. 4, pp. 700–710, 1974.

Schwartz, L. E., "Uncertainty Reduction Over Time in the Theory of Multiattributed Utility," *Multiple Criteria Decision Making*, edited by J. L. Cochrane and M. Zeleny, University of South Carolina Press, Columbia, South Carolina, pp. 108–123, 1973.

Schwartz, S. L. and I. Vertinsky, "Multiattribute Investment Decisions: A Study of R&D Project Selection," *Management Science*, Vol. 24, No. 3, pp. 285–301, 1977.

Schwartz, S. L., I. Vertinsky and W. T. Ziemba, "R&D Project Selection Behavior: Study Designs and Some Pilot Results," *Multiple Criteria Decision Making*, edited by H. Thiriez and S. Zionts, Lecture Notes in Economics and Mathematical Systems No. 130, Springer-Verlag, Berlin-New York, New York, pp. 136–146, 1976.

Schwartz, S. L., I. Vertinsky, W. T. Ziemba and M. Bernstein, "Some Behavioral Aspects of Information Use in Decision Making: A Study of Clinical Judgments," *Multiple Criteria Decision Making*, edited by H. Thiriez and S. Zionts, Lecture Notes in Economics and Mathematical Systems No. 130, Springer-Verlag, Berlin-New York, New York, pp. 378–391, 1976.

Sealey, C. W., "Financial Planning with Multiple Objectives," *Financial Management*, pp. 17–23, Winter 1978.

Seiford, L. and P. L. Yu, "Potential Solutions of Linear Systems: The Multi-Criteria Multiple Constraint Levels Program," *Journal of Mathematical Analysis and Applications*, Vol. 69, No. 2, pp. 283–303, June 1979.

Seinfeld, J. H. and W. Z. McBride, "Optimization with Multiple Performance Criteria," *I & EC Process Design and Development*, Vol. 9, No. 1, pp. 53–58, 1970.

Sen, A. K., *Collective Choice and Social Welfare*, Oliver and Boyd, Edinburgh, England, 1970.

Sengupta, S. S., M. L. Podrebarac and T. D. H. Fernando, "Probabilities of Optima in Multiobjective Linear Programmes," *Multiple Criteria Decision Making*, edited by J. L. Cochrane and M. Zeleny, University of South Carolina Press, Columbia, South Carolina, pp. 217–235, 1973.

Sfeir-Yonnis, A. and D. W. Bromley, *Decision Making in Developing Countries—Multiobjective Formulation and Evaluation Methods*, Praeger, New York, New York, 1977.

Shachtman, R., "Generation of the Admissible Boundary of a Convex Polytope," *Operations Research*, Vol. 22, No. 1, pp. 151–159, 1974.

Shapiro, J. F., "Multiple Criteria Public Investment Decision Making by Mixed Integer Programming," *Multiple Criteria Decision Making*, edited by H. Thiriez and S. Zionts, Lecture Notes in Economics and Mathematical Systems No. 130, Springer-Verlag, Berlin-New York, New York, pp. 170–182, 1976.

Shapley, L. S., "A Value for n-Person Games," *Contributions to the Theory of Games*, Vol. 2, edited by H. W. Kuhn and A. W. Tucker, Annals of Mathematical Studies No. 28, Princeton University Press, Princeton, New Jersey, 1953.

Shapley, L. S., "Equilibrium Points in Games with Vector Payoffs," *Naval Research Logistics Quarterly*, Vol. 6, No. 1, pp. 57–61, March 1959.

Shapley, L. S., "On Balanced Sets and Cores," *Naval Research Logistics Quarterly*, Vol. 14, No. 4, pp. 453–460, December 1967.

Shapley, L. S. and H. Scarf, "On Cores and Indivisibility," *Journal of Mathematical Economics*, Vol. 1, pp. 23–37, 1974.

Sharma, R. R., "On Optimal Controls with Vector-Valued Cost Functional," *Revue Roumaine de Mathématiques Pures et Appliquées*, Vol. 16, No. 3, pp. 341–354, 1971.

Shelly, M. W. and G. L. Bryan (eds.), *Human Judgments and Optimality*, John Wiley and Sons, New York, New York, 1964.

Shen, H. N. and J. G. Lin, "A Computational Method for Linear Multiple-Objective Optimization Problems," *Proceedings, IEEE Conference on Decisions and Control, including 14th Symposium on Adaptive Processes*, Houston, Texas, 1975; New York, New York, pp. 613–614, 1975.

Shen, H. N. and J. G. Lin, "Determining Sets of Pareto-Optimal Solutions for Linear Multiple-Objective Optimization Problems," *Proceedings, IEEE Conference on Decisions and Control, including Symposium on Adaptive Processes*, San Diego, California, January 10–12, 1978, pp. 897–898, 1978.

Shepard, R. N., "The Analysis of Proximities: Multidimensional Scaling with an Unknown Distance Function," Parts I and II, *Psychometrika*, Vol. 27, No. 2, pp. 125–140 and pp. 219–246, 1962.

Shepard, R. N., "On Subjectively Optimum Selection Among Multiattribute Alternatives," *Human Judgments and Optimality*, edited by M. W. Shelly and G. Bryan, John Wiley and Sons, New York, New York, pp. 257–281, 1964.

Shim, J. K. and J. Siegel, "Quadratic Preferences and Goal Programming," *Decision Sciences*, Vol. 6, No. 4, pp. 662–669, 1975.

Shim, J. K. and J. Siegel, "Sensitivity Analysis of Goal Programming with Pre-emption," *International Journal of Systems Science*, Vol. 11, No. 4, pp. 393–401, April 1980.

Shimizu, K. and E. Aiyoshi, "Theory for Multiobjective Decision Problems," *Proceedings, 8th IEEE Conference on Cybernetics and Society*, Tokyo-Kyoto, Japan, November 3–7, 1978, pp. 1135–1140, 1978.

Shimizu, K. and Y. Anzai, "Optimization of a Hierarchical System with Locally Independent Objective Functions" [in Japanese], *Transactions of the Society of Instrument and Control Engineers*, Vol. 10, No. 1, pp. 63–70, 1974.

Shimizu, K., S. Hiyoshi and T. Hirose, "Vectoroptimization Problems—Algorithms for Systems with Several Objective Functions" [in Japanese], *Transactions of the Society of Instrument and Control Engineers*, Vol. 11, No. 2, pp. 152–159, 1975.

Shubik, M., "Objective Functions and Models of Corporate Optimization," *Quarterly Journal of Economics*, Vol. 75, No. 3, p. 359, 1961.

Simon, C. P., "Conditions for Constrained Pareto-Optima on a Banach Space with a Finite Number of Criteria," *Dynamical Systems, Proceedings of a University of Florida International Symposium*, Academic Press, New York, New York, pp. 323–334, 1977.

Sinha, N. K., "Reduction of the Sensitivity of Optimal Control Systems by Using Two Degrees of Freedom," *Sensitivity, Adaptivity, and Optimality, Proceedings, 3rd IFAC Symposium*, Ischia, Italy, 1973; Pittsburgh, Pennsylvania, pp. 267–270, 1973.

Sinha, N. K., V. Temple and J. C. Rey, "A Vector Cost Function for Efficient Adaptation," *International Journal of Control*, Vol. 16, No. 6, pp. 1107–1120, 1973.

Sizer, P. W., "A Behavioral Model of Company Development," *Multiple Criteria Decision Making*, edited by H. Thiriez and S. Zionts, Lecture Notes in Economics and Mathematical Studies No. 130, Springer-Verlag, Berlin-New York, New York, pp. 392–401, 1976.

Slater, M., "Lagrange Multipliers Revisited," Cowless Commission Discussion Paper: Mathematics 403, November 7, 1950; reissued as Cowles Foundation Discussion Paper No. 80, 1959 and 1980.

Slovik, P., "Analyzing the Expert Judge: A Descriptive Study of Stockbrokers' Decision Processes," *Journal of Applied Psychology*, Vol. 53, No. 4, pp. 255–263, 1969.

Slovik, P., "Psychological Study of Human Judgment: Implications for Investment Decision Making," Research Monograph No. 11/1, Oregon Research Institute, Eugene, Oregon, September 1971.

Slovik, P., "Choice Between Equally Valued Alternatives," *Journal of Experimental Psychology: Human Perception and Performance*, Vol. 1, pp. 280–287, 1975.

Slovik, P. and S. Lichtenstein, "Comparison of Bayesian and Regression Approaches to the Study of Information Processing," *Judgment, Organizational Behavior and Human Performance*, Vol. 6, pp. 651–730, 1971.

Smale, S., "Global Analysis and Economics I: Pareto Optimum and Generalization of Morse Theory," *Dynamical Systems*, edited by M. Pexieto, Academic Press, New York, New York, pp. 531–544, 1973; *Mathematical Reviews*, Vol. 49, 6238, 1973.

Smale, S., "Global Analysis and Economics III: Pareto Optima and Price Equilibria," *Journal of Mathematical Economics*, Vol. 1, pp. 107–117, 1974.

Smale, S., "Global Analysis and Economics V: Pareto Theory with Constraints," *Journal of Mathematical Economics*, Vol. 1, pp. 213–221, 1974.

Smale, S., "Sufficient Conditions for an Optimum," *Proceedings of a Symposium on Dynamical Systems*, Warwick, England, 1974; Lecture Notes Math. No. 468, Springer-Verlag, Berlin-New York, New York, pp. 287–292, 1975.

Smale, S., "Global Analysis and Economics: Pareto Optimum and a Generalization of Morse Theory," *Synthese*, Vol. 31, No. 2, pp. 345–358, 1975.

Smale, S., "Global Analysis and Economics VI: Geometric Analysis of Pareto Optima and Price Equilibria Under Classicial Hypotheses," *Journal of Mathematical Economics*, Vol. 3, No. 1, pp. 1–14, 1976.

Smith, C. J., "Using Goal Programming to Determine Interest Group Disutility for Public Policy Choices," *Socio-Economic Planning Sciences*, Vol. 14, No. 3, pp. 117–120, 1980.

Smith, L. H., R. W. Lawless and B. Shenoy, "Evaluating Multiple Criteria—Models for Two Criteria Situations," *Decision Sciences*, Vol. 5, No. 4, pp. 587–596, 1974.

Smith, R. D. and P. S. Greenlaw, "Simulation of Psychological Decision Process in Personnel Section," *Management Science*, Vol. 13, No. 8, pp. B409–B419, 1967.

Snyder, W. W., "Economic Policy and Multiple Objective Decision Making, Lessons from the Postwar Period," *Multiple Criteria Decision Making*, edited by J. L. Cochrane and M. Zeleny, University of South Carolina Press, Columbia, South Carolina, pp. 771–773, 1973.

Sokolová, L., "Problem Viceparametrického Linearního Programováni" ["Linear Multi-Parametric Programming Problem"], Ekonomicko Matematický Obzor, Vol. 4, No. 1, pp. 44–68, 1968.

Soland, R. M., "Multicriteria Optimization: A General Characterization of Efficient Solutions," *Decision Sciences*, Vol. 10, No. 1, pp. 26–38, 1979.

Solich, R., "Zadanie programowania liniowego z wieloma funkcjami celu," *Przeglad Statystyczny*, Vol. 16, Nos. 3–4, pp. 351–359, 1969.

Sosinka, J., "Optimum Pareto dla programow liniowych i kryteriow rozlacznych," *Przeglad Statystyczny*, Vol. 18, Nos. 3–4, pp. 353–364, 1971.

Soyster, A. L. and B. Lev, "An Interpretation of Fractional Objectives in Goal Programming as Related to Papers by Awerbuch, et al., and Hannan," *Management Science*, Vol. 24, No. 14, pp. 1546–1549, 1978.

Soyster, A. L., B. Lev and D. I. Toof, "Conservative Linear Programming with Mixed Multiple Objectives," *Omega*, Vol. 5, No. 2, pp. 193–205, 1977.

Spagon, P. D., "Requirements for a Practical Public Sector Decision Making Process," *Multiple Criteria Decision Making*, edited by M. K. Starr and M. Zeleny, TIMS Studies in the Management Sciences, Vol. 6, North-Holland Publishing Company, Amsterdam, Holland, p. 317, 1977.

Spinetto, R., "The Geometry of Solution Concepts for N-Person Cooperative Games," *Management Science*, Vol. 20, No. 9, pp. 1291–1299, May 1974.

Spivey, W. A. and H. Tamura, "Goal Programming in Econometrics," *Naval Research Logistics Quarterly*, Vol. 17, No. 2, pp. 183–192, June 1970.

Spremann, K., "Über Vektormaximierung und Analyse der Gewichtung von Subzielen," *Optimization and Operations Research*, edited by W. Oettli and K. Ritter, Lecture Notes in Economics and Mathematical Systems No. 117, Springer-Verlag, Berlin-New York, New York, pp. 283–296, 1976.

Spronk, J., "Capital Budgeting and Financial Planning with Multiple Goals," *Multiple Criteria Analysis: Operational Methods*, edited by P. Nijkamp and J. Spronk, Gower Press, London, England, 1981.

Srinivasan, V. and A. D. Shocker, "Linear Programming Techniques for Multidimensional Analysis of Preferences," *Psychometrika*, Vol. 38, No. 3, pp. 337–369, September 1973.

Srinivasan, V. and A. D. Shocker, "Estimating the Weights for Multiple Attributes in a Composite Criterion Using Pairwise Judgments," *Psychometrika*, Vol. 38, No. 4, pp. 473–493, December 1973.

Srinivasan, V., A. D. Shocker and A. G. Weinstein, "Measurement of a Composite Criterion of Managerial Success," *Organizational Behavior and Human Performance*, Vol. 9, pp. 147–167, February 1973.

Srinivasan, V. and G. L. Thompson, "Alternative Formulations for Static Multi-Attribute Assignment Models," *Management Science*, Vol. 29, No. 2, pp. B154–B158, 1973.

Stadje, W., "On the Relationship of Goal Programming and Utility Functions," *Zeitschrift für Operations Research*, Vol. 23, No. 1, pp. 61–69, 1979.

Stadler, W., "Preference Optimality and Applications of Pareto-Optimality," *Multicriteria Decision Making*, edited by G. Leitmann and A. Marzollo, Courses and Lectures No. 211, International Center for Mechanical Sciences (CISM), Springer-Verlag, Wien-New York, New York, pp. 125–225, 1975.

Stadler, W., "Preference Optimality," *Optimization and Operations Research*, edited by W. Oettli and K. Ritter, Lecture Notes in Economics and Mathematical Systems No. 117, Springer-Verlag, Berlin-New York, New York, pp. 297–306, 1975.

Stadler, W., "Sufficient Conditions for Preference Optimality," *Journal of Optimization Theory and Applications*, Vol. 18, No. 1, pp. 119–140, January 1976.

Stadler, W., "Sufficient Conditions for Preference Optimality," *Multicriteria Decision Making and Differential Games*, edited by G. Leitmann, Plenum Press, New York, pp. 129–148, 1976.

Stadler, W., "Natural Shapes of Shallow Arches," *Journal of Applied Mechanics*, Vol. 44, No. 2, pp. 291–298, June 1977.

Stadler, W., "Natural Structural Shapes (The Static Case)," *Quarterly Journal of Mechanics and Applied Mathematics*, Vol. 31, No. 2, pp. 169–217, May 1978.

Stadler, W., "A Survey of Multicriteria Optimization or the Vector Maximum Problem, 1776–1960," *Journal of Optimization Theory and Applications*, Vol. 29, No. 1, pp. 1–52, September 1979.

Stadler, W., "Preference Optimality in Multicriteria Control and Programming Problems," *Journal of Nonlinear Analysis: Theory, Methods, and Applications*, Vol. 4, No. 1, pp. 51–65, 1979.

Stadler, W., "Stability Implications, and the Equivalence of Stability and Optimality Conditions in the Optimal Design of Uniform Shallow Arches," *Proceedings, Symposium on Structural Optimization, 11th Naval Structural Mechanics Symposium*, University of Arizona, Tucson, Arizona, October 19–22, 1981.

Stadler, W., "Engineering Applications of Multicriteria Optimization (a Survey)," *Proceedings of a Symposium on Multicriteria Decision Making*, American Association for the Advancement of Science, Washington, D. C., January 3–8, 1982.

Stainton, R. S., "Production Scheduling with Multiple Criteria Objectives," *Operational Research Quarterly*, Vol. 28, No. 21, pp. 285–292, 1977.

Stalbo, A. K., "Automatic Control System Optimization with Several Criteria" [in Russian], *Avtomatika i Sistemy Upravlenia*, No. 1, pp. 37–39, 1974.

Stalford, H., "Criteria for Pareto-Optimality in Cooperative Differential Games," *Journal of Optimization Theory and Applications*, Vol. 9, No. 6, pp. 391–398, June 1972.

Stancu-Minasian, I. M., "Stochastic Programming with Multiple Objective Functions," *Economic Computation and Economic Cybernetics, Studies and Research*, No. 1, pp. 49–67, 1974.

Stancu-Minasian, I. M., "Analiza unor puncte de vedere in programarea matematica eu mai multe funtii obiectiv," *Studii şi Cercetări de Calcul Economic şi Cibernetică Economică*, No. 3, 1975.

Stancu-Minasian, I. M., "Analyzing Several Points of View in Mathematical Programming with Several Objective Functions," *Economic Computation and Economic Cybernetics, Studies and Research*, No. 1, pp. 17–29, 1976.

Stancu-Minasian, I. M., "Asupra problemei en rise minim multiplu I: Cazul a două functii obiectiv," *Studii şi Cercetări Matematice*, Vol. 28, No. 5, pp. 617–623, 1976.

Stancu-Minasian, I. M., "Asupra problemei en rise minim multiplu II: Cazul a r (r > 2) functii obiectiv," *Studii şi Cercetări Matematice*, Vol. 28, No. 6, pp. 723–734, 1976.

Starr, A. W. and Y. C. Ho, "Nonzero-Sum Differential Games," *Journal of Optimization Theory and Applications*, Vol. 3, No. 3, pp. 184–206, March 1969.

Starr, A. W. and Y. C. Ho, "On Some Further Properties of Nonzero-Sum Differential Games," *Journal of Optimization Theory and Applications*, Vol. 3, No. 4, pp. 207–219, April 1969.

Starr, M. K. and L. H. Greenwood, "Normative Generation of Alternatives, with Multiple Criteria Evaluation," *Multiple Criteria Decision Making*, edited by M. K. Starr and M. Zeleny, TIMS Studies in the Management Sciences, Vol. 6, North-Holland Publishing Company, Amsterdam, Holland, pp. 111–127, 1977.

Starr, M. K. and I. Stein, *The Practice of Management Science* (Unit 5, "Decisions with Multiple Criteria"), Prentice-Hall, Englewood Cliffs, New Jersey, 1976.

Starr, M. K. and M. Zeleny, "MCDM—State and Future of the Arts," *Multiple Criteria Decision Making*, edited by M. K. Starr and M. Zeleny, TIMS Studies in the Management Sciences, Vol. 6, North-Holland Publishing Company, Amsterdam, Holland, pp. 5-29, 1977.

Starr, M. K. and M. Zeleny (eds.), *Multiple Criteria Decision Making*, TIMS Studies in the Management Sciences, Vol. 6, North-Holland Publishing Company, Amsterdam, Holland, 1977.

Stedry, A. C., "Aspiration Levels, Attitudes and Performance in Goal-Oriented Situation," *Industrial Management Review*, Vol. 3, No. 2, 1962.

Stedry, A. C. and A. Charnes, "Investigations in the Theory of Multiple Budgeted Goals," *Management Controls: New Directions in Basic Research*, edited by C. P. Bonini, R. K. Jaedicke and H. M. Wagner, McGraw-Hill, New York, New York, pp. 186–204, 1964.

Stern, R. J. and A. Ben-Israel, "On Linear Optimal Control Problems with Multiple Quadratic Criteria," *Multiple Criteria Decision Making*, edited by J. L. Cochrane and M. Zeleny, University of South Carolina Press, Columbia, South Carolina, pp. 366–372, 1973.

Stern, R. J. and A. Ben-Israel, "An Interior Penalty Function Method for the Construction of Efficient Points in a Multiple Criteria Problem," *Journal of Mathematical Analysis and Applications*, Vol. 46, No. 3, pp. 768–776, 1974.

Steuer, R. E., "Interval Criterion Weights Programming: A Portfolio Selection Example, Gradient Cone Modification and Computational Experience," *Proceedings of the 10th Southeastern TIMS Meeting*, pp. 246–255, October 1974.

Steuer, R. E., "ADBASE: An Adjacent Efficient Basis Algorithm for Solving Vector-Maximum and Interval Weighted-Sums Linear Programming Problems (in FORTRAN)," Abstract in *Journal of Marketing Research*, Vol. 12, pp. 454–455, November 1975.

Steuer, R. E., "A Five Phase Procedure for Implementing a Vector-Maximum Algorithm for Multiple Objective Linear Programming Problems," *Multiple Criteria Decision Making*, edited by H. Thiriez and S. Zionts, Lecture Notes in Economics and Mathematical Systems No. 130, Springer-Verlag, Berlin-New York, New York, pp. 159–169, 1976.

Steuer, R. E., "Multiple Objective Linear Programming with Interval Criterion Weights," *Management Science*, Vol. 23, No. 3, pp. B305–B316, 1976.

Steuer, R. E., "An Interactive Multiple Objective Linear Programming Procedure," *Multiple Criteria Decision Making*, edited by M. K. Starr and M. Zeleny, TIMS Studies in the Management Sciences, Vol. 6, North-Holland Publishing Company, Amsterdam, Holland, pp. 225-239, 1977.

Steuer, R. E., "Vector-Maximum Gradient Cone Contraction Techniques," *Multiple Criteria Problem Solving*, edited by S. Zionts, Lecture Notes in Economics and Mathematical Systems No. 155, Springer-Verlag, Berlin-New York, New York, pp. 462–481, 1978.

Steuer, R. E., "Goal Programming Sensitivity Analysis Using Interval Penalty Weights," *Mathematical Programming*, Vol. 17, No. 1, pp. 16-31, 1979.

Steuer, R. E. and F. W. Harris, "Intra-Set Point Generation and Filtering in Decision and Criterion Space," *Computers and Operations Research: Special Issue on Mathematical Programming with Multiple Objectives*, edited by M. Zeleny, Vol. 7, No. 1–2, pp. 41–53, 1980.

Steuer, R. E. and A. T. Schuler, "An Interactive Multiple Objective Linear Programming Approach to a Problem in Forest Management," *Operations Research*, Vol. 26, No. 2, pp. 254–269, 1978.

Steuer, R. E. and M. J. Wallace, "A Linear Multiple Objective Programming Model for Manpower Selection and Allocation Decisions," *Management Science Approaches to Manpower Planning and Organization Design*, edited by A. Charnes, W. W. Cooper and R. J. Niehaus, North-Holland Publishing Company, Amsterdam, Holland, pp. 193–208, 1978.

Stewart, T. J., "A Descriptive Approach to Multiple-Criteria Decision Making," *The Journal of the Operational Research Society*, Vol. 32, pp. 45–53, 1981.

Stigler, G. J., "The Development of Utility Theory," *Journal of Political Economy*, Vol. 58, pp. 307–327, 1950.

Sullivan, R. S. and J. A. Fitzimmons, "A Goal Programming Model for Readiness and the Optimal Replacement of Resources," *Socio-Economic Planning Sciences*, Vol. 12, No. 5, pp. 215–220, 1978.

Sundaram, R. M., "An Application of Goal Programming Technique in Metal Cutting," *International Journal of Production Research*, Vol. 16, No. 5, pp. 375–382, 1978.

Suryanarayana, M. B., "Remarks on Existence Theorems for Pareto Optimality," *Dynamical Systems (University of Florida International Symposium)*, edited by A. R. Bednarek and L. Cesari, Academic Press, New York, New York, pp. 335-347, 1977.

Sussman, B., P. Buffet, J. P. Gremy and M. Marc, "Point-On Choisir en Tenant Compte de Critères Multiples; Méthode (ELECTRE) et Trois Applications," *Revue Metra*, Vol. 4, No. 2, 1967.

Svensson, L. E. O., "Sequences of Temporary Equilibria, Stationary Point Expectations and Pareto Efficiency," *Journal of Economic Theory*, Vol. 13, No. 2, pp. 169-183, 1976.

Szaniawski, K., "Some Remarks Concerning the Criterion of Rational Decision Making," *Studia Logica*, Vol. 9, pp. 221-235, 1960.

Szidarovszky, F., I. Bogardi and L. Duckstein, "Use of Cooperative Games in a Multiobjective Analysis of Mining and Environment," *Proceedings, 2nd International Conference on Applied Numerical Modelling*, Madrid, Spain, September 11-15, 1978.

Tabak, D., "Numerical Aspects of Multicriteria Optimization in System Design," *Proceedings, 8th IEEE Conference on Cybernetics and Society*, Tokyo-Kyoto, Japan, November 3-7, 1978, pp. 1190-1193, 1978.

Tabak, D., "Computer Based Experimentation with Multicriteria Optimization Problems," *IEEE Transactions on Systems, Man, and Cybernetics*, Vol. SMC-9, No. 10, pp. 676-678, October 1979.

Tabak, D., A. A. Schy, D. P. Giesy and K. G. Johnson, "Application of Multiobjective Optimization in Aircraft Control System Design," *Automatica*, Vol. 15, pp. 595-600, 1979.

Taft, M. J. and A. Reisman, "A Proposed Generalized Heuristic Algorithm for Scheduling with Respect to N-Interrelated Criterion Functions," *The International Journal of Production Research*, Vol. 5, No. 2, pp. 155-162, 1966.

Takeda, E. and T. Nishida, "Multiple Criteria Decision Problems with Fuzzy Domination Structures," *Fuzzy Sets and Systems*, Vol. 3, No. 2, pp. 123-136.

Tamm, M. I., "Linear Programming Problem Solution with Several Objective Functions" [in Russian], *Ekonomika i Matematicheskie Metody*, Vol. 9, No. 2, pp. 328-329, 1973.

Tamura, H., "A Discrete Dynamic Model with Distributed Transport Delays and Its Hierarchical Optimization for Preserving Stream Quality," *IEEE Transactions on Systems, Man, and Cybernetics*, Vol. SMC-4, pp. 424-431, September 1974.

Tamura, K., "Linear Optimization Problems with Vectorvalued Objective Function" [in Japanese], *Transactions of the Society of Instrument and Control Engineers*, Vol. 10, No. 6, pp. 749-755, 1974.

Tamura, K., "A Method for Constructing the Polar Cone of a Polyhedral Cone, with Applications to Linear Multicriteria Decision Problems," *Journal of Optimization Theory and Applications*, Vol. 19, No. 4, pp. 547-564, 1976.

Tamura, K. and S. Miura, "On Linear Vector Maximization Problems," *Journal of the Operations Research Society of Japan*, Vol. 20, No. 3, pp. 139-149, 1977.

Tamura, K. and S. Miura, "Necessary and Sufficient Conditions for Local and Global Nondominated Solutions in Decision Problems with Multiobjectives," *Journal of Optimization Theory and Applications*, Vol. 28, No. 4, pp. 501-524, August 1979.

Tanino, T. and Y. Sawaragi, "Duality Theory in Multiobjective Programming," *Journal of Optimization Theory and Applications*, Vol. 27, pp. 509-529, April 1979.

Tanino, T. and Y. Sawaragi, "Stability and Nondominated Solutions in Multicriteria Decision Making," *Journal of Optimization Theory and Applications*, Vol. 30, No. 2, pp. 229-254, February 1980.

Tanino, T. and Y. Sawaragi, "Conjugate Maps and Duality in Multiobjective Optimization," *Journal of Optimization Theory and Applications*, Vol. 31, No. 4, pp. 473-499, 1980.

Tarvainen, K. and Y. Y. Haimes, "Hierarchical-Multiobjective Framework for Energy Storage Systems," *Multi-Criteria Problem Solving*, edited by J. Morris, Springer-Verlag, Berlin-New York, New York, 1981.

Tauxe, G. W., D. M. Mades and R. R. Inman, "Multiple Objectives Analysis by Dynamic Programming," *Transactions of American Geophysical Union*, Vol. 59, p. 1073, 1978.

Tauxe, G. W., R. R. Inman and D. M. Mades, "Multiobjective Dynamic Programming: A Classic Problem Redresses," *Water Resources Research*, Vol. 15, No. 6, pp. 1398-1402, December 1979.

Taylor, B. W. and A. J. Keown, "A Goal Programming Application of Capital Project Selection in the Production Area," *AIIE Transactions*, Vol. 10, pp. 52–57, 1978.

Taylor, B. W. and A. J. Keown, "Planning Urban Recreational Facilities with Integer Goal Programming," *The Journal of the Operational Research Society*, Vol. 29, 1978.

Taylor, R. L., "Consistent Multiattributed Decision Procedures," *Multiple Criteria Decision Making*, edited by J. L. Cochrane and M. Zeleny, University of South Carolina Press, Columbia, South Carolina, pp. 774–777, 1973.

Taylor, W. B. III, K. R. Davis and R. M. North, "Approaches to Multiobjective Planning in Water Resources Projects," *Water Resources Bulletin*, Vol. 11, No. 5, pp. 999–1008, 1975.

Tell, B., "A Comparative Study of Four Multiple-Criteria Methods," *Multiple Criteria Decision Making*, edited by H. Thiriez and S. Zionts, Lecture Notes in Economics and Mathematical Systems No. 130, Springer-Verlag, Berlin-New York, New York, pp. 183–198, 1976.

Tell, B., *A Comparative Study of Some Multiple-Criteria Methods*, Economics Research Institute, Stockholm School of Economics, Stockholm, Sweden, 1976.

Tell, B., "The Effect of Uncertainty on the Selection of a Multiple-Criteria Utility Model," *Advances in Operations Research*, edited by M. Roubens, North-Holland Publishing Company, Amsterdam, Holland, pp. 497–504, 1977.

Tell, B., "An Approach to Solving Multi-Person Multiple-Criteria Decision-Making Problems," *Multiple Criteria Problem Solving*, edited by S. Zionts, Lecture Notes in Economics and Mathematical Systems No. 155, Springer-Verlag, Berlin-New York, New York, pp. 482–493, 1978.

Tell, B., "Factor Analysis—a Method for Reducing the Number of Criteria in a Multiple-Criteria Model," *Omega*, Vol. 6, No. 5, pp. 451–454, 1978.

Terny, G., "D'une Rationalisation des Décisions Économiques de l'État à la Fonction de Préférence Étatique," *Analyse et Prévision*, No. 10, 1970.

Terry, H., "Comparative Evaluation of Performance Using Multiple Criteria," *Management Science*, Vol. 9, No. 3, pp. B431–B442, 1963.

Tersine, R. J., "Organizational Objectives and Goal Programming: A Convergence," *Managerial Planning*, Vol. 25, No. 2, pp. 27–40, 1976.

Thiriez, H. and D. Houri, "Multi-Person Multi-Criteria Decision Making: A Sample Approach," *Multiple Criteria Decision Making*, edited by H. Thiriez and S. Zionts, Lecture Notes in Economics and Mathematical Systems No. 130, Springer-Verlag, Berlin-New York, New York, pp. 103–119, 1976.

Thiriez, H. and S. Zionts (eds.), *Multiple Criteria Decision Making*, Lecture Notes in Economics and Mathematical Systems No. 130, Springer-Verlag, Berlin-New York, New York, 1976; *Proceedings of a Conference held at Jouy-en-Josas, France*, May 21–23, 1975.

Thomas, H. and A. R. Lock, "An Appraisal of Multi-Attribute Utility Models in Marketing," *European Journal of Marketing*, Vol. 13, No. 5, pp. 294–307, 1979.

Tintner, G., "A Note on Welfare Economics," *Econometrica*, Vol. 14, pp. 69–78, 1946.

Tischchenko, V. N., "Vector Optimization of an Ordered Set of Criteria" [in Russian], *Problemy Bioniki*, No. 13, pp. 66-70, 1974.

Tisdell, C., "Uncertainty and Pareto Optimality," *Econ. Rec.*, Vol. 39, No. 88, pp. 405–412, 1963.

Togsverd, T., "Multilevel Planning in the Public Sector," *Multiple Criteria Decision Making*, edited by H. Thiriez and S. Zionts, Lecture Notes in Economics and Mathematical Systems No. 130, Springer-Verlag, Berlin-New York, New York, pp. 201–214, 1976.

Tomlinson, J. W. C. and I. Vertinsky, "Selecting a Strategy for Joint Venture in Fisheries: A First Approximation," *Multiple Criteria Decision Making*, edited by H. Thiriez and

S. Zionts, Lecture Notes in Economics and Mathematical Systems No. 130, Springer-Verlag, Berlin-New York, New York, pp. 351–363, 1976.

Törn, A., "A Sampling-Search-Clustering Approach for Exploring and Feasible/Efficient Solutions of MCDM Problems," *Computers and Operations Research: Special Issue on Mathematical Programming with Multiple Objectives*, edited by M. Zeleny, Vol. 7, No. 1–2, pp. 67–79, 1980.

Trippy, R. R., "On the Evaluation of Investment Proposals Having Multiple Attributes," *Naval Research Logistics Quarterly*, Vol. 21, No. 2, pp. 327–332, 1974.

Trojanowski, S., "Wielokryteriowa optymalizacja w sensie Pareto niewspólmiernych funkcji celu," *Przeglad Statystyczny*, Vol. 22, No. 3, pp. 427–433, 1975.

Tversky, A., "Intransitivity of Preferences," *Psychological Review*, Vol. 76, pp. 31–48, 1969.

Tversky, A., "On the Elicitation of Preferences: Descriptive and Prescriptive Considerations," *Conflicting Objectives*, edited by D. E. Bell, R. L. Keeney and H. Raiffa, John Wiley and Sons, New York, New York, pp. 209–222, 1977.

Valadier, M., "Sous-Differentiabilité de Fonctions Convexes à Valeurs dans une Espace Vectoriel Ordonné," *Mathematica Scandinavica*, Vol. 30, pp. 65–74, 1972.

Van Wassenhove, L. N. and L. F. Gelders, "Solving a Bicriterion Scheduling Problem," *European Journal of Operational Research*, Vol. 4, No. 1, pp. 42–48, 1980.

Varga, Z., "Least Squares Solution for N-Person Multicriteria Differential Games," *Annales Universitatis Scientiarum Budapestiensio*, Sectio Mathematica, Vol. 21, pp. 139–148, 1978.

Vatcu, M. O., "O metodă de rezolvare a unei probleme de programarea liniara cu mai multe functii objectiv," *Studii şi Cercetări de Calcul Economic şi Cibernetică Economică*, No. 2, pp. 37–46, 1975.

Vatcu, M. O., "A Method of Solving a Linear Programming Problem with Several Objective Functions," *Economic Computation and Economic Cybernetics, Studies and Research*, No. 2, pp. 97–106, 1975.

Vedder, J. N., "Planning Problems with Multidimensional Consequences," *Journal of the American Institute of Planners*, Vol. 36, No. 2, pp. 112–119, March 1970.

Vedder, J. N., "Multiattribute Decision Making Under Uncertainty Using Bounded Intervals," *Multiple Criteria Decision Making*, edited by J. L. Cochrane and M. Zeleny, University of South Carolina Press, Columbia, South Carolina, pp. 93–107, 1973.

Vehovec, M., "Simple Criterion for the Global Regularity of Vector-Valued Functions," *Electronics Letters*, Vol. 5, pp. 680–681, 1969.

Velichenko, V. V., "Sufficient Conditions for Absolute Minimum of the Maximal Functional in the Multi-Criteria Problem of Optimal Control," *Optimization Techniques: IFIP Technical Conference*, edited by G. Marchuk, Lecture Notes in Computer Science No. 27, Springer-Verlag, Berlin-New York, New York, pp. 220–225, 1975.

Vemuri, V., "Multiple Objective Optimization in Water Resource Systems," *Water Resources Research*, Vol. 10, No. 1, pp. 44–48, 1974.

Villarreal, B., M. H. Karwan and S. Zionts, "An Interactive Branch and Bound Procedure for Multicriterion Integer Linear Programming," *Multiple Criteria Decision Making Theory and Application*, edited by G. Fandel and T. Gal, Springer-Verlag, Berlin-New York, New York, pp. 448–467, 1980.

Vincent, T. L. and J. E. Gayek, "A Game Theoretic Analysis for Renewable Resource Management," *Ecological Modelling (Special Issue on the Optimal Management of Renewable Resources)*, 1981.

Vincent, T. L. and W. J. Grantham, *Optimality in Parametric Systems*, Wiley Interscience, New York, New York, 1981.

Vincent, T. L. and G. Leitmann, "Control Space Properties of Cooperative Games," *Journal of Optimization Theory and Applications*, Vol. 6, No. 2, pp. 91–113, 1970.

Vincke, P., "Problèmes Multicritères," *Cahiers du Centre d'Études de Recherche Opérationelle*, Brussels, Belgium, Vol. 16, No. 4, pp. 425–439, 1974.

Vincke, P., "Une Méthode Interactive en Programmation Linéaire à Plusieurs Fonctions Économiques," *Revue Française d'Automatique, Informatique et de Recherche Opérationelle*, Vol. 10, No. 6, pp. 5–20, 1976.

Vincke, P., "A New Approach to Multiple Criteria Decision-Making," *Multiple Criteria Decision Making*, edited by H. Thiriez and S. Zionts, Lecture Notes in Economics and Mathematical Systems No. 130, Springer-Verlag, Berlin-New York, New York, pp. 341–349, 1976.

Vinogradskaya, T. M. and M. G. Gaft, "An Exact Upper Bound for the Number of Nonsubordinate Solutions in Multicriterion Problems," *Automation and Remote Control*, Vol. 35, No. 9, pp. 1474–1481, 1974.

Viswanathan, B., V. V. Aggarwal and K. P. K. Nair, "Multiple Criteria Markov Decision Processes," *Multiple Criteria Decision Making*, edited by M. K. Starr and M. Zeleny, TIMS Studies in the Management Sciences, Vol. 6, North-Holland Publishing Company, Amsterdam, Holland, pp. 263–272, 1977.

Vogel, W., "Ein Maximumprinzip fur Vektor-Optimierungsaufgaben," *Operations Research Verfahren*, Vol. 19, Anton Hain Verlag, Meisenheim am Glan, Germany, pp. 161–184, 1975.

Vogel, W., "Halbnormen und Vektoroptimierung," *Quantitative Wirtschaftsforschung-Festschrift für W. Krelle*, edited by H. Albach, E. Helmstädter and R. Henn, Tübingen, Germany, pp. 703–714, 1977.

Vogel, W., "Vektoroptimierung in Produkträumen," Mathematical Systems in Economics No. 35, Anton Hain Verlag, Meisenheim am Glan, Germany, 1977.

Vogel, W., "Vector Optimization Without the Use of Functions," *Methods of Operations Research*, Vol. 40, pp. 27–44, 1981.

Volkovich, V. L., "Multicriteria Problems and Their Methods of Solution" [in Russian], *Coll. Cybernetics and Computing Techniques*, No. 1, Naukova Dumka, Kiev, USSR, 1968.

Volkovich, V. L. and L. F. Darheyko, "On One Algorithm of Choosing a Compromise Solution for Linear Criteria" [in Russian], *Kybernetika*, No. 5, pp. 133–136, 1972.

Volkovich, V. L. and A. P. Gorchinskiy, "An Algorithm for Ordering the Versions of a Complex System on the Basis of Additive Criteria" [in Russian], *Coll. Cybernetics and Computing Techniques*, Naukova Dumka, Kiev, USSR, 1971.

Volkovich, V. L. and M. F. Radomskiy, "Preliminary Sifting of Nonpromising Versions of Complex Control Systems by Criteria in the Form of Concave Functions," *Soviet Automatic Control*, Vol. 8, No. 1, pp. 54–57, 1975.

von Neumann, J., "Zur Theorie der Gesellschaftsspiele," *Mathematische Annalen*, Vol. 100, pp. 295–320, 1928.

von Neumann, J. and O. Morgenstern, *Theory of Games and Economic Behavior*, Princeton University Press, Princeton, New Jersey, 1943.

von Winterfeldt, D., "Multi-Criteria Decision Making: Comments on Jacquet Lagrèze's Paper," *Utility, Probability, and Human Decision Making*, edited by D. Wendt and C. A. J. Vlek, D. Reidel Publishing Company, Boston, Massachusetts, pp. 47–85, 1975.

von Winterfeldt, D. and G. W. Fischer, "Multi-Attribute Utility Theory: Models and Assessment Procedures," *Utility, Probability, and Human Decision Making*, edited by D. Wendt and C. A. J. Vlek, D. Reidel Publishing Company, Boston, Massachusetts, pp. 47–85, 1975.

Voronin, A. N., "Vector Optimization of Multilink Dynamic Systems," *Soviet Automatic Control*, Vol. 12, No. 5, pp. 13–18, September-October 1979.

Wacht, R. F. and D. T. Whitford, "A Goal Programming Model for Capital Investment

Analysis in Nonprofit Hospitals," *Financial Management*, Vol. 5, No. 2, pp. 37–47, 1976.

Walker, J., "An Interactive Method as an Aid in Solving Bicriterion Mathematical Programming Problems," *The Journal of the Operational Research Society*, Vol. 29, No. 9, pp. 915–922, 1978.

Walker, J., "An Interactive Method as an Aid in Solving Multi-Objective Mathematical Programming Problems," *European Journal of Operational Reseach*, Vol. 2, pp. 341–349, 1978.

Wallenius, J., "Comparative Evaluation of Some Interactive Approaches to Multicriterion Optimization," *Management Science*, Vol. 21, No. 12, pp. B1387–B1396, August 1975.

Wallenius, J., "Interactive Multiple Criteria Decision Methods: An Investigation and an Approach," *Acta Academiae Oeconomicae Helsingiensis*, Series A, Vol. 14, Helsinki School of Economics, Helsinki, Finland, 1975.

Wallenius, H., J. Wallenius and P. Vartia, "An Approach to Solving Multiple Criteria Macroeconomic Policy Problems and an Application," *Management Science*, Vol. 24, No. 10, pp. 1021–1030, 1978.

Wallenius, J. and S. Zionts, "Some Tests of an Interactive Programming Method for Multicriterion Optimization and an Attempt at Implementation," *Multiple Criteria Decision Making*, edited by H. Thiriez and S. Zionts, Lecture Notes in Economics and Mathematical Systems No. 130, Springer-Verlag, Berlin-New York, New York, pp. 319–331, 1976.

Wallenius, J. and S. Zionts, "A Research Project on Multicriterion Decision Making," *Conflicting Objectives*, edited by D. E. Bell, R. L. Keeney and H. Raiffa, John Wiley and Sons, New York, New York, pp. 76–96, 1977.

Wallin, J., *Computer-Aided Multiattribute Profit Planning*, Skriftserie utgiven av Handelshögskolan vid Åbo akademi, Ser. A, No. 19, Åbo, Finland, 1978.

Walras, L., *Éléments d'Économie Politique Pure*, L. Corbaz and Companie, Lausanne, Switzerland, 1874–1877, Second Edition, 1889, Third Edition, 1896, Fourth Edition, 1900; Definitive Edition, F. Rouge, Lausanne, Switzerland, 1926; translation of the Definitive Edition into English by W. Jaffé as *Elements of Pure Economics*, George Allen and Unwin, London, England, 1954.

Walters, A., J. Mangold and E. Haran, "A Comprehensive Planning Model for Long-Range Academic Strategies," *Management Science*, Vol. 22, No. 7, pp. 727–738, 1976.

Waltz, F. M., "An Engineering Approach: Hierarchical Optimization Criteria," *IEEE Transactions on Automatic Control*, Vol. AC-12, No. 2, pp. 179–180, 1967.

Wan, Y. H.,"On Local Pareto-Optima," *Journal of Mathematical Economics*, Vol. 2, No. 1, pp. 35–42, 1975.

Warfield, J. N., "On Arranging Elements of a Hierarchy in Graphic Form," *IEEE Transactions on Systems, Man, and Cybernetics*, Vol. SMC-3, pp. 121–132, March 1973.

Warford, J. J. and D. S. Julius, "Multiple Objectives of Water Rate Policy in Less Developed Countries," *Water Supply Management*, Vol. 1, pp. 335–342, 1977.

Wedley, W. C. and A. E. J. Ferrie, "Duality and Vector Optima for Polyhedral Sets— Reply," *The Journal of the Operational Research Society*, Vol. 30, p. 84, 1979.

Wehrung, D. A., "Interactive Identifications and Optimization of Preferences in a Multiattributed Decision Problem," *Multiple Criteria Decision Making*, edited by M. K. Starr and M. Zeleny, TIMS Studies in the Management Sciences, Vol. 6, North-Holland Publishing Company, Amsterdam, Holland, pp. 318–320, 1977.

Wehrung, D. A., J. F. Bassler, K. R. MacCrimmon and W. T. Stanbury, "Multiple Criteria Dominance Models: An Empirical Study of Investment Preferences," *Multiple Criteria Problem Solving*, edited by S. Zionts, Lecture Notes in Economics and Mathematical Systems No. 155, Springer-Verlag, Berlin-New York, New York, pp. 494–508, 1978.

Wehrung, D. A., D. S. P. Hopkins and W. F. Massy, "Interactive Preference Optimization for University Administrators," *Management Science*, Vol. 24, No. 6, pp. 599–611, 1978.

Weiner, N. S., "Multiple Incentive Fee Maximization: An Economic Model," *Quarterly Journal of Economics*, Vol. 77, No. 4, pp. 603–616, 1963.

Weitzman, M., "Iterative Multilevel Planning with Production Targets," *Econometrica*, Vol. 38, No. 1, pp. 50–65, January 1970.

Welam, U. P., "Comments on Goal Programming for Aggregate Planning," *Management Science*, Vol. 22, No. 6, pp. 708–712, 1976.

Welling, P., "A Goal Programming Model for Human Resource Accounting in a CPA Firm," *Accounting Organization and Society*, Vol. 2, pp. 307–316, April 1977.

Wendell, R. E., "Multiple Objective Mathematical Programming with Respect to Multiple Decision-Makers," *Operations Research*, Vol. 28, No. 5, pp. 1100–1111, 1980.

Wendell, R. E., A. P. Hunter and T. J. Lowe, "Efficient Points in Location Problems," *Journal of Mathematical Analysis and Applications*, Vol. 49, No. 2, pp. 430–468, 1975.

Wendell, R. E., A. P. Hunter and T. J. Lowe, "Efficient Points in Location Problems," *AIIE Transactions*, Vol. 9, No. 3, pp. 238–246, 1977.

Wendell, R. E. and D. N. Lee, "Efficiency in Multiple Objective Optimization Problems," *Mathematical Programming*, Vol. 12, No. 3, pp. 406–414, 1977.

Wendt, D. and C. A. J. Vlek (eds.), *Utility, Probability, and Human Decision Making*, D. Reidel Publishing Company, Boston, Massachusetts, 1975.

Werczberger, E., "A Goal Programming Model for Industrial Location Involving Environmental Considerations," *Environment and Planning*, Vol. 8, p. 173, 1976.

Werczberger, E., "The Versatility Model in Decision Making under Uncertainty with Regard to Goals and Constraints," *Multiple Criteria Analysis: Operational Methods*, edited by P. Nijkamp and J. Spronk, Gower Press, London, England, 1981.

Wheeler, B. M. and J. R. M. Russell, "Goal Programming and Agricultural Planning," *Operational Research Quarterly*, Vol. 28, No. 1, pp. 21–32, 1977.

White, C. C. and K. W. Kim, "Solution Procedures for Vector Criterion Markov Decision Processes," *Journal of Large-Scale Systems*, Vol. 1, No. 2, p. 129, 1980.

White, C. C. and A. P. Sage, "A Multiple Objective Optimization-Based Approach to Choicemaking," *IEEE Transactions on Systems, Man, and Cybernetics*, Vol. SMC-10, No. 6, pp. 315–326, 1980.

White, C. M., "Multiple Goals in the Theory of the Firm," *Linear Programming and the Theory of the Firm*, edited by K. E. Boulding and M. A. Spivey, The Macmillan Company, London, England, pp. 181–201, 1960.

White, D. J., "Kernels of Preference Structures," *Econometrica*, Vol. 45, No. 1, pp. 91–100, 1977.

White, D. J., "Duality and Vector Optima for Polyhedral Sets," *The Journal of the Operational Research Society*, Vol. 30, pp. 81–83, 1979.

White, D. J., "Generalized Efficient Solutions for Sums of Sets," *Operations Research*, Vol. 28, No. 3, pp. 844–846, 1980.

White, D. J., "Multi-Objective Interactive Programming," *The Journal of the Operational Research Society*, Vol. 31, No. 6, pp. 517–523, 1980.

White, D. J., "Optimality and Efficiency I," *European Journal of Operational Research*, Vol. 4, No. 5, pp. 346–355, 1980.

Wicksell, K., "Vilfredo Pareto's Manuel d'Économie Politique," *Zeitschrift für Volkswirtschaft, Sozialpolitik, und Verwaltung*, Vol. 22, pp. 132–151, 1913; translated into English as "Vilfredo Pareto's Manuel d'Économie Politique," Kurt Wicksell, *Selected Papers on Economic Theory*, George Allen and Unwin, London, England, pp. 159–175, 1958.

Wiedemann, P., "Planning with Multiple Objectives," *Omega*, Vol. 6, No. 5, pp. 427–432, 1978.

Wierzbicki, A. P., "Penalty Methods in Solving Optimization Problems with Vector Performance Criteria," *Proceedings, 6th IFAC World Congress*, Cambridge, Massachusetts, 1975; Part 1, Pittsburgh, Pennsylvania, pp. 51.1/1-51.1/12 (A45-A46), 1975.

Wierzbicki, A. P., "Basic Properties of Scalarizing Functionals for Multiobjective Optimization," *Mathematische Operationsforschung und Statistik*, Serie Optimization, Vol. 8, pp. 55-60, 1977.

Wierzbicki, A. P. and S. Kurcyusz, "Projection on a Cone, Penalty Functionals and Duality Theory for Problems with Inequality Constraints in Hilbert Space," *SIAM Journal on Control and Optimization*, Vol. 15, No. 1, pp. 25-56, 1977.

Wierzbicki, A. P., "The Use of Reference Objectives in Multiobjective Optimization," *Multiple Criteria and Decision Making Theory and Application*, edited by G. Fandel and T. Gal, Springer-Verlag, Berlin-New York, New York, pp. 468-486, 1980.

Wilhelm, J., "Objectives and Multiobjective Decision Making Under Uncertainty," Lecture Notes in Economics and Mathematical Systems No. 112, Springer-Verlag, Berlin-New York, New York, 1975.

Wilhelm, J., "Ein verallgemeinertes Konzept von Lösungsprinzipien für Entscheidungsprobleme bei mehrfacher Zielsetzung," *Proc. Oper. Res.*, Vol. 6, pp. 123-133, 1976.

Wilhelm, J., "Generalized Solution Principles and Outranking Relations in Multi-Criteria Decision Making," *European Journal of Operational Research*, Vol. 1, No. 6, pp. 376-385, 1977.

Wilhelm, J. and G. Fandel, "Two Algorithms for Solving Vector-Optimization Problems," *Automation and Remote Control*, Vol. 37, pp. 1721-1727, 1976.

Wilkie, W. and E. A. Pessemier, "Issues in Marketing's Use of Multiattribute Attitude Models," *Journal of Marketing Research*, Vol. 10, pp. 428-441, 1973.

Williams, F. E., "On the Evaluation of Intertemporal Outcomes," *Multiple Criteria Decision Making*, edited by J. L. Cochrane and M. Zeleny, University of South Carolina Press, Columbia, South Carolina, pp. 429-438, 1973.

Wright, P. and F. Barbour, "Phased Decision Strategies: Sequels to an Initial Screening," *Multiple Criteria Decision Making*, edited by M. K. Starr and M. Zeleny, TIMS Studies in the Management Sciences, Vol. 6, North-Holland Publishing Company, Amsterdam, Holland, pp. 91-110, 1977.

Yager, R. R., "Multiple Objective Decision-Making Using Fuzzy Sets," *International Journal of Man-Machine Studies*, Vol. 9, No. 4, pp. 375-382, 1977.

Yager, R. R., "Fuzzy Decision Making Including Unequal Objectives," *Fuzzy Sets and Systems*, Vol. 1, No. 2, pp. 87-96, 1978.

Yager, R. R., "Extending Nash's Bargaining Model to Include Importances for Multiobjective Decisionmaking," *IEEE Transactions on Systems, Man, and Cybernetics*, Vol. SMC-10, No. 7, pp. 405-407, July 1980.

Yntema, D. and W. Torgerson, "Man-Computer Cooperation in Decisions Requiring Common Sense," *IRE Transactions on Human Factors in Electronics*, Vol. HFE-2, No. 1, pp. 20-26, 1961.

Young, H. P., "A Note on Preference Aggregation," *Econometrica*, Vol. 42, No. 6, pp. 1129-1131, 1974.

Yu, P. L., "A Class of Solutions for Group Decision Problems," *Management Science*, Vol. 19, No. 8, pp. B936-B946, 1973.

Yu, P. L., "Introduction to Domination Structures in Multicriteria Decision Problems," *Multiple Criteria Decision Making*, edited by J. L. Cochrane and M. Zeleny, University of South Carolina Press, Columbia, South Carolina, pp. 249-261, 1973.

Yu, P. L., "Cone Convexity, Cone Extreme Points and Nondominated Solutions in Decision Problems with Multiobjectives," *Journal of Optimization Theory and Applications*, Vol. 14, No. 3, pp. 319-377, 1974.

Yu, P. L., "Domination Structures and Nondominated Solutions," *Multicriteria Decision*

Making, edited by G. Leitmann and A. Marzollo, Courses and Lectures No. 211, International Center for Mechanical Sciences (CISM), Springer-Verlag, Wien-New York, New York, pp. 227–280, 1975.

Yu, P. L., "Cone Convexity, Cone Extreme Points, and Nondominated Solutions in Decision Problems with Multiobjectives," *Multicriteria Decision Making and Differential Games*, edited by G. Leitmann, Plenum Press, New York, New York, pp. 1–59, 1976.

Yu, P. L., "Decision Dynamics with an Application to Persuasion and Negotiation," *Multiple Criteria Decision Making*, edited by M. K. Starr and M. Zeleny, TIMS Studies in the Management Sciences, Vol. 6, North-Holland Publishing Company, Amsterdam, Holland, pp. 159–177, 1977.

Yu, P. L., "Toward Second Order Game Problems: Decision Dynamics in Gaming Phenomena," *Multiple Criteria Problem Solving*, edited by S. Zionts, Lecture Notes in Economics and Mathematical Systems No. 155, Springer-Verlag, Berlin-New York, New York, pp. 509–528, 1978.

Yu, P. L., "Second Order Game Problem: Decision Dynamics in Gaming Phenomena," *Journal of Optimization Theory and Applications*, Vol. 27, No. 1, pp. 147–166, January 1979.

Yu, P. L., "Behavior Bases and Habitual Domains of Human Decision/Behavior—Concepts and Applications," *Multiple Criteria Decision Making Theory and Application*, edited by G. Fandel and T. Gal, Springer-Verlag, Berlin-New York, New York, pp. 511–539, 1980.

Yu, P. L. and G. Leitmann, "Compromise Solutions, Domination Structures, and Salukvadze's Solution," *Journal of Optimization Theory and Applications*, Vol. 13, No. 3, pp. 362–378, 1974.

Yu, P. L. and G. Leitmann, "Nondominated Decisions and Cone Convexity in Dynamic Multicriteria Decision Problems," *Journal of Optimization Theory and Applications*, Vol. 14, No. 5, pp. 573–584, 1974.

Yu, P. L. and G. Leitmann, "Compromise Solutions, Domination Structures and Salukvadze's Solution," *Multicriteria Decision Making and Differential Games*, edited by G. Leitmann, Plenum Press, New York, New York, pp. 85–101, 1976.

Yu, P. L. and G. Leitmann, "Nondominated Decisions and Cone Convexity in Dynamic Multicriteria Decision Problems," *Multicriteria Decision Making and Differential Games*, edited by G. Leitmann, Plenum Press, New York, New York, pp. 61–72, 1976.

Yu, P. L. and G. Leitmann, "Confidence Structures in Decision Making," *Journal of Optimization Theory and Applications*, Vol. 22, No. 2, pp. 265–285, 1977.

Yu, P. L. and L. Seiford, "Multistage Decision Problems with Multicriteria," *Multiple Criteria Analysis: Operational Methods*, edited by P. Nijkamp and J. Spronk, Gower Press, London, England, 1981.

Yu, P. L. and M. Zeleny, "The Techniques of Linear Multiobjective Programming," *Revue Française d'Automatique, Informatique et de Recherche Opérationelle*, Vol. 8, No. 3, pp. 51–71, November 1974.

Yu, P. L. and M. Zeleny, "The Set of Nondominated Solutions in Linear Cases and a Multicriteria Simplex Method," *Journal of Mathematical Analysis and Applications*, Vol. 49, No. 2, pp. 430–468, February 1975.

Yu, P. L. and M. Zeleny, "Linear Multiparametric Programming by Multicriteria Simplex Method," *Management Science*, Vol. 23, No. 2, pp. B159–B170, 1976.

Yudin, D. B., "A New Approach to the Formalization of the Choice of a Solution in Complex Situations," *Proceedings of the 5th All-Union Conference on Control*, Part 1, Nauka, Moscow, USSR, 1971.

Yuttler, C., "Linear Models with Several Criterion Functions," *Economics and Mathematical Methods*, Vol. 3, No. 3, 1967.

Zadeh, L. A., "Optimality and Nonscalar-Valued Performance Criteria," *IEEE Transactions on Automatic Control*, Vol. AC-8, No. 1, pp. 59–60, 1963.

Zadeh, L. A., "Similarity Relations and Fuzzy Orderings," *Information Science*, Vol. 3, pp. 177–200, 1971.

Zadeh, L. A., "Outline of a New Approach to the Analysis of Complex Systems and Decision Processes," *Multiple Criteria Decision Making*, edited by J. L. Cochrane and M. Zeleny, University of South Carolina Press, Columbia, South Carolina, pp. 686–728, 1973.

Zak, Y. A., "Models and Methods of Constructing Compromise Plans in Problems of Mathematical Programming with Several Objective Functions" [in Russian], *Kybernetika*, No. 4, pp. 102–107, 1972.

Zangwill, W., "An Algorithm for the Chebyshev Problem with an Application to Concave Programming," *Management Science*, Vol. 14, No. 1, pp. 58–78, 1967.

Zeckhauser, R. J., "Voting Systems, Honest Preferences and Pareto Optimality," *American Political Science Review*, Vol. 3, pp. 934–946, 1973.

Zeckhauser, R. J. and M. C. Weinstein, "The Topology of Pareto-Optimal Regions with Public Goods," *Econometrica*, Vol. 42, No. 4, pp. 643–666, 1974.

Zeleny, M., "A Selected Bibliography of Works Related to Multiple Criteria Decision Making," *Multiple Criteria Decision Making*, edited by J. L. Cochrane and M. Zeleny, University of South Carolina Press, Columbia, South Carolina, pp. 779–796, 1973.

Zeleny, M., "Compromise Programming," *Multiple Criteria Decision Making*, edited by J. L. Cochrane and M. Zeleny, University of South Carolina Press, Columbia, South Carolina, pp. 262–301, 1973.

Zeleny, M., "A Concept of Compromise Solutions and the Method of the Displaced Ideal," *Computers and Operations Research*, Vol. 1, Nos. 3–4, pp. 479–496, 1974.

Zeleny, M., *Linear Multiobjective Programming*, Lecture Notes in Economics and Mathematical Systems No. 95, Springer-Verlag, Berlin-New York, New York, 1974.

Zeleny, M. (ed.), *Multiple Criteria Decision Making*, Lecture Notes in Economics and Mathematical Systems No. 123, Springer-Verlag, Berlin-New York, New York, 1976; *Proceedings of Multiple Criteria Decision Making Conference*, Kyoto, Japan, July 24–26, 1975.

Zeleny, M., "Games with Multiple Payoffs," *International Journal of Game Theory*, Vol. 4, No. 4, pp. 171–191, 1976.

Zeleny, M., "MCDM Bibliography 1975," *Multiple Criteria Decision Making*, edited by M. Zeleny, Lecture Notes in Economics and Mathematical Systems No. 123, Springer-Verlag, Berlin-New York, New York, pp. 291–321, 1976.

Zeleny, M., "Multicriteria Simplex Method: A Fortran Routine," *Multiple Criteria Decision Making*, edited by M. Zeleny, Lecture Notes in Economics and Mathematical Systems No. 123, Springer-Verlag, Berlin-New York, New York, pp. 323–345, 1976.

Zeleny, M., "On the Inadequacy of the Regression Paradigm Used in the Study of Human Judgment," *Theory and Decision*, Vol. 7, Nos. 1–2, pp. 57–65, 1976.

Zeleny, M., "The Attribute-Dynamic Attitude Model (ADAM)," *Management Science*, Vol. 23, No. 1, pp. B12–B26, 1976.

Zeleny, M., "The Theory of the Displaced Ideal," *Multiple Criteria Decision Making*, edited by M. Zeleny, Lecture Notes in Economics and Mathematical Systems No. 123, Springer-Verlag, Berlin-New York, New York, pp. 153–206, 1976.

Zeleny, M., "Conflict Dissolution," *General Systems Yearbook*, Vol. 21, pp. 131–136, 1976.

Zeleny, M., "Adaptive Displacement of Preferences in Decision Making," *Multiple Criteria Decision Making*, edited by M, K. Starr and M. Zeleny, TIMS Studies in the Management Sciences, Vol. 6, North-Holland Publishing Company, Amsterdam, Holland, pp. 146–158, 1977.

Zeleny, M., "Multidimensional Measure of Risk: Prospect Rating Vector (PRV)," *Multiple Criteria Problem Solving*, edited by S. Zionts, Lecture Notes in Economics and Mathematical Systems No. 155, Springer-Verlag, Berlin-New York, New York, pp. 529–548, 1978.

Zeleny, M. (ed.), *Computers and Operations Research: Special Issue on Mathematical Programming with Multiple Objectives*, Vol. 7, No. 1–2, 1980.

Zeleny, M., "Multiple Objectives in Mathematical Programming: Letting the Man In," *Computers and Operations Research: Special Issue on Mathematical Programming with Multiple Objectives*, edited by M. Zeleny, Vol. 7, No. 1–2, pp. 1–4, 1980.

Zeleny, M., "A Case Study in Multiobjective Design: De Novo Programming," *Multiple Criteria Analysis: Operational Methods*, edited by P. Nijkamp and J. Spronk, Gower Press, London, England, 1981.

Zeleny, M., "Descriptive Decision Making and Its Applications," *Applications of Management Science*, edited by R. L. Schultz, Vol. 1, JAI Press, Greenwich, Connecticut, pp. 327–388, 1981.

Zeleny, M., "Satisficing Optimization, and Risk in Portolio Selection," *Readings in Strategies for Corporate Investment*, edited by F. Derkinderen and R. Crum, Pitman Publishing, Boston, Massachusetts, 1981.

Zeleny, M., "The Pros and Cons of Goal Programming," *Computers and Operations Research* in press.

Zeleny, M., *Multiple Criteria Decision Making*, McGraw-Hill, New York, New York, 1982.

Zeleny, M. and J. L. Cochrane, "A Priori and Posteriori Goals in Macroeconomic Policy Making," *Multiple Criteria Decision Making*, edited by J. L. Cochrane and M. Zeleny, University of South Carolina Press, Columbia, South Carolina, pp. 373–394, 1973.

Zimmermann, H.-J., "Unscharfe Entscheidungen und Multi-Criteria-Analyse," *Proc. Oper. Res.*, Vol. 6, pp. 99–109, 1976.

Zimmermann, H.-J., "Fuzzy Programming and Linear Programming with Several Objective Functions," *Fuzzy Sets and Systems (An International Journal)*, Vol. 1, No. 1, pp. 45–56, January 1978.

Zionts, S. (ed.), *Multiple Criteria Problem Solving*, Lecture Notes in Economics and Mathematical Systems No. 155, Springer-Verlag, Berlin-New York, New York, 1978; *Proceedings of a Conference*, Buffalo, New York, August 22–26, 1977.

Zionts, S., "MCDM—If Not a Roman Numeral, Then What?", *Interfaces*, Vol. 9, No. 4, pp. 94–101, 1979.

Zionts, S., "Methods for Solving Management Problems Involving Multiple Objectives," *Multiple Criteria Decision Making Theory and Application*, edited by G. Fandel and T. Gal, Springer-Verlag, Berlin-New York, New York, pp. 540–558, 1980.

Zionts, S. and D. Deshpande, "A Time Sharing Computer Programming Application of a Multiple Criteria Decision Method to Energy Planning—a Progress Report," *Multiple Criteria Problem Solving*, edited by S. Zionts, Lecture Notes in Economics and Mathematical Systems No. 155, Springer-Verlag, Berlin-New York, New York, pp. 549–560, 1978.

Zionts, S. and D. Deshpande, "Energy Planning Using a Multiple Criteria Decision Method," *Multiple Criteria Analysis: Operational Methods*, edited by P. Nijkamp and J. Spronk, Gower Press, London, England, 1981.

Zionts, S. and J. Wallenius, "An Interactive Programming Method for Solving the Multiple Criteria Problem," *Management Science*, Vol. 22, No. 6, pp. B652–B663, 1976.

Zlobec, S., "Asymptotic Kuhn-Tucker Conditions for Mathematical Programming in a Banach Space," *SIAM Journal on Control and Optimization*, Vol. 9, pp. 505–512, 1970.

Zowe, J., "Fenchel Type Duality Theorems in Finite Dimensional Ordered Vector Spaces," *Mathematica Scandinavica*, Vol. 31, pp. 301–309, 1972.

Zowe, J., "Fenchelsche Dualitätsaussagen in endlichdimensionalen halbgeordneten Vektorräumen," *Zeitschrift für Angewandte Mathematik und Mechanik*, Vol. 53, No. 4, pp. 230–232, 1973.

Zowe, J., "Subdifferentiability of Convex Functions with Values in Ordered Vector Spaces," *Mathematica Scandinavica*, Vol. 34, pp. 69–83, 1974.

Zowe, J., "A Duality Theorem for a Convex Programming Problem in Order Complete Vector Lattices," *Journal of Mathematical Analyis and Applications*, Vol. 50, No. 2, pp. 273–287, 1975.

Zowe, J., "Der Sattelpunksatz von Kuhn und Tucker in geordneten Vektorräumen," *Lect. Notes Math.*, Vol. 477, pp. 285–294, 1975.

Zowe, J., "Der Sattelpunksatz von Kuhn und Tucker in geordneten Vektorräumen," *Zeitschrift für Angewandte Mathematik und Mechanik*, Vol. 55, No. 4, pp. 287–288, 1975.

Zowe, J., "The Saddle Point Theorem of Kuhn and Tucker in Ordered Vector Spaces," *Journal of Mathematical Analysis and Applications*, Vol. 57, No. 1, pp. 41–55, 1977.

Zrnovsky, P., "The Possibilities of Multigoal Optimization in Network Analysis," *Ekonomicko Matematický Obzor*, Vol. 2, pp. 174–190, 1972.

PART II. THE RUSSIAN LANGUAGE LITERATURE

Abramenko, V. I., V. E. Aleshin, P. G. Kas'ian and A. D. Puvnev, "Solution of the Multicriterion-Optimization Problem for Job Management by the Method of Random Search," *Identifik. i Optimiz. Komplekc.*, Institut Kibernet. AN USSR, Kiev, pp. 50–56, 1976.

Al'sevich, V. V., "Necessary Conditions for Optimality in Minimax Optimization," *Differents. Upravneniia*, Vol. 12, No. 8, pp. 1384–1391, 1976.

Azmetov, R. R., "An Algorithm for Vector Optimization by Graphical Methods," *Sb. Tr. Institut Probl. Upr.*, Vol. 10, pp. 31–35, 1976.

Aleksandrov, A. D., M. V. Petrova and K. T. Tsaturian, "Quantitative Comparisons of Alternative Variants or Strategies in Control Problems," *Abstracts of the 5th All-Union Conference on Control*, Part 1, Nauka, Moscow, 1971.

Amangel'diev, B. R. and M. N. Shigaev, "On the Automation of Decision Procedures Based on a Vector Criterion," *5th Kasakstan Intercollegiate Scientific Conference on Mathematics and Mechanics*, Part 2, Mathematics, Alma-Ata, 1974.

Amangel'diev, B. R., M. N. Shigaev and S. A. Shmulev, "On the Problem of Vector Optimization," *Optimiz. i Modelir. Slozhn. Sistem.*, Nauka, Alma-Ata, pp. 41–47, 1976.

Amangel'diev, B. R., M. N. Shigaev and S. A. Shmulev, "The Structure and Properties of Problems of Vector Optimization," *Optimiz. i Modelir. Slozhnykh Sistem.*, Nauka, Alma-Ata, pp. 48–62, 1976.

Balychavtsev, E. M. and E. K. Pavrovskiĭ, "On the Construction of the Pareto Set in Some Optimization Problems," *Isv. AN SSSR, Mekh. Tverdogo Tela*, No. 6, pp. 44–53, 1977.

Barantsev, A. V., "Factor Determination in the Problem of Vector Optimization," *Mat. Analiz. i ego Pril.*, Rostov Universitet, Rostov on the Don, pp. 184–190, 1975.

Bedel'baev, A. A., Iu. A. Dubov and B. L. Shmul'ian, "Adaptive Procedures of Decision Making in Multicriteria Problems," *Avtomatika i Telemekhanika*, No. 1, pp. 136–145, 1976.

Benaiiun, R., O. I. Larichev, Zh. Mongol'fe and Zh. Terni, "Linear Programming with Multiple Objective·Functions; the Method of Constraints," *Avtomatika i Telemekhanika*, No. 8, pp. 108–115, 1971.

Berezovskiĭ, B. A. and S. I. Travkin, "On the Distribution of the Elements of the Pareto Set," *Vopr. Kibernetiki*, Vyp. 83, Tashkent, pp. 7–18, 1975.

Bogdanovich, Z. P. and A. I. Iukhimenko, "Making Complex Multicriterion Decisions in Economic Systems," Preprint No. 71–31, Kiev, 1971.

Boĭchuk, L. M. and V. O. Ovchinnikov, "The Main Approaches to the Solution of Multicriteria Optimization Problems (a Review)," *Avtomatika* (Kiev), No. 3, pp. 3–7, 1973.

Boidareva, O. H., V. B. Vilkov, T. E. Kulakovskaia, H. M. Naumova and H. A. Sokolina, "A Review of Soviet Publications on the Theory of Cooperative Games," *Issled. Operatsii i Stat. Modelir*, Vyp. 4, Leningrad Universitet, pp. 81–126, 1977.

Borisov, V. I., "The Choice of a Solution in the Case of Several Criteria," *Problems of General and Social Forecasting*, Vyp. 2, *Issledovanie Operatsii, Informatsionnyi Biulleten*, Vol. 14, No. 29, Moscow, 1969.

Borisov, V. I., "Some Problems of Vector (Multicriteria) Optimization," *Proceedings of the 5th All-Union Conference on Control* Part 1, Nauka, Moscow, 1971.

Borisov, V. I., "Problems of Vector Optimization," *Issledovanie Operatsii, Metodologicheskie Aspekty*, Nauka, Moscow, pp. 72–91, 1972.

Borisov, V. I., "Discussion," *Issledovanie Operatsii*, Metodologicheskie Aspekty, Nauka, Moscow, 1972.

Borisov, V. I., "Some Problems of Vector Optimization," 1st All-Union Conference on Operations Research (Tez. Dokl.), Institut Matem. AN BSSR, 1972.

Borisov, V. I., "Vector Optimization Problems," *Issled. Operatsii*, Nauka, Moscow, pp. 72–91, 1972.

Byrliaeva, L. F., V. V. Kafarov, R. E. Kusin and A. V. Netushil, "Methods for the Calculation of Pareto-Optimal Decisions in Chemical Engineering Processes," *Isv. Akad. Nauk SSSR, Tekhn. Kibernet.*, Vol. 14, No. 4, pp. 196–199, 1976.

Buianov, B. B., "Multicriteria Decision Making Based on an Interval Utility Scale," *6th All-Union Conference on Control Problems 1974, Ref. Dokl.*, Part 2, Nauka, Moscow, pp. 57-60, 1974.

Buianov, B. B. and V. M. Ozernoi, "On One Method of Multicriteria Decision Making," *Isv. Akad. Nauk. SSSR. Tekhn. Kibernet.*, Vol. 12, No. 3, pp. 80–84, 1974.

Buianov, B. B. and V. M. Ozernoi, "Sufficient Conditions for Preferences in Multicriteria Decision Problems," *Vopr. Kibernetiki*, Vyp. 8, Moscow, pp. 60–70, 1975.

Vaisbord, E. M., V. I. Zhkovskii and V. S. Molostvov, "Some Results on Strategies in N-Person Differential Games," *Abstracts of the 3rd All-Union Conference on Game Theory*, Odessa, pp. 30–31, 1974.

Vankrinene, S., *Dynamic Nonantagonistic Two-Person Games*, Doctoral Dissertation, VGU, Vil'nius, 1972.

Vankrinene, S., "Cooperative Dynamic Nonantagonistic Two-Person Games," *Lit. Mat. Sb.*, Vol. 10, No. 3, pp. 453–461, 1970.

Varga, Z., *Antagonistic Differential Games with Vector Costs*, Mosk. Universitet, Moscow, 1977.

Varga, Z., "On a Cooperative Pursuit-Evasion Game," *Vest. Mosk., Universiteta*, Ser. Vych. Mat. i Kib., No. 1, 1979.

Velichenko, V. V., "On Sufficient Conditions for a Global Minimax," *Dokl. AN SSSR*, Vol. 219, No. 5, pp. 1045–1048, 1974.

Velichenko, V. V., "On the Extremal Field Method in Sufficient Conditions for Optimality," *Zh. Vychisl. Mat. i Mat. Fiz.*, Vol. 14, No. 1, pp. 45–67, 1974.

Velichenko, V. V., "On Minimax Conditions in Multicriteria Problems of Optimal Control," *Numerical Methods in Nonlinear Programming*, Materialy 1 Vses. Seminara, Kiev, pp. 19–26, 1976.

Ventsel, E. S., *Operations Research*, Sob. Radno., Moscow, 1972.

Vil'gel'm, I. and G. Fandel', "Two Algorithms for the Solution of Vector Optimization Problems," *Avtomatika i Telemekhanika*, No. 11, pp. 109–117, 1976.

Vilkas, E. I., "Existence of Effectively-Stationary Points in Problems of Vector Optimization," *Litovsk. Mat. Sb.*, Vol. 8, pp. 41–45, 1968.

Vilkas, E. I., "Utility Theory and Decision Making," *Mathematical Methods in Social Science*, Workshop, Vyp. 1, Vil'nius, 1972.

Vilkas, E. I., "Formalization of the Problem of Choosing a Gametheoretic Optimalitycriterion," *Mathematical Methods in the Social Sciences*, Vyp. 2, Vil'niūs, pp. 9–31, 1973.

Vilkas, É. Ĭ., "On the Cooperative Solution of a Game in Characteristic Function Form," *Mathematical Methods in the Social Sciences*, Vyp. 2, Vil'niūs, pp. 51–73, 1973.

Vilkas, É. Ĭ., "Multiobjective Optimization," *Mat. Metody v. Soĩs. Naukakh*, Vyp. 7, Vil'niūs, pp. 16–67, 1976.

Vilkas, É. Ĭ., "Utility Theory," *Probability Theory, Mathematical Statistics, Cybernetic Theory*, Itogi Nauki i Tekh. VINITI AN SSSR, Moscow, pp. 123–151, 1977.

Vilkas, É. Ĭ. and E. Z. Maĭmpinas, "On the Problem of the Complexity of a Solution (Statement and Approaches)," *Kibernetika*, No. 5, 1968.

Vinogradova, T. K. and V. F. Dem'iānov, "On Necessary Conditions in Minimax Control Problems," *Zh. Vychisl. Mat. i Mat. Fiz.*, Vol. 14, No. 1, pp. 233–236, 1974.

Vinogradskaiā, T. M., "The Use of Partially Ordered Sets in Problems of Multicriteria Decision Making," *Sb. Tr. Institut Probl. Upr.*, Vol. 5, pp. 56–60, 1974.

Vinogradskaiā, T. M., "The Mean of the Noninferior Solutions in Multicriteria Problems," *Isv. Akad. Nauk SSSR, Tekhn. Kibernet.*, Vol. 14, No. 2, pp. 36–38, 1976.

Vinogradskaiā, T. M., "Some Aspects of the Application of the Linear Model in Multicriteria Decision Making Problems," *Aktual'n. Vopr. Teorii i Prakt. Upr. Nauka*, Moscow, pp. 125–130, 1977.

Vinogradskaiā, T. M. and M. T. Gaft, "Exact Upper Bound on the Noninferior Solutions in Multicriteria Problems," *Avtomatika i Telemekhanika*, No. 9, pp. 111–118, 1974.

Volkovich, V. L., "Methods of Multicriteria Decision Making (a Review)," *Slozhnye Sistemy Upravleniiā*, Vyp. 1, IK AN USSR (Ukraine), Kiev, 1968.

Volkovich, V. L., "Multicriteria Problems and Methods for Their Solution," *Kibernetika i Vychislitel'naiā Tekhnika*, Naukova Dumka, Kiev, 1969.

Volkovich, V. L., "Multicriteria Problems and Solution Methods," *Slozhnye Sistemy Uprovleniiā*, Naukova Dumka, Kiev, 1969.

Volkovich, V. L., "Multicriteria Problems and Solution Methods," *Koll. Kibernetiki i Vychisl. Met.*, Naukova Dumka, Kiev, 1971.

Volkovich, V. L. and L. F. Dargeĭko, "An Algorithm for Choosing a Compromise Solution for Linear Criteria," *Kibernetika*, No. 5, pp. 133–136, 1972.

Volkovich, V. L. and L. F. Dargeĭko, "The Method of Constraints in Problems of Vector Optimization," *Avtomatika*, No. 3, pp. 13–17, 1976.

Vorob'ev, H. H., "The Contemporary State of Game Theory," *Uspekhi Mat. Nauk*, Vol. 25, No. 2, pp. 81–140, 1970.

Vorob'ev, H. H., "Game Theory," Lectures in Economics-Cybernetics, Leningrad Universitet, 1974.

Voronov, A. A. and A. I. Teĭman, "On Several Problems Arising in the Concept of a Solution in the Control of Large Systems Under Nonnegativity Conditions," *Trudy Ĭobileĭnoĭ Nauchnoĭ Seseii Obshchego Sobraniiā Mekhaniki i Proĭsessov Upravleniiā*, Akad. Nauk, SSSR, Moscow, 1971.

Gabasov, R. and F. M. Kirillova, *Qualitative Theory of Optimal Processes*, Nauka, Moscow, 1971.

Gabasov, R. and F. M. Kirillova, *Foundations of Dynamic Programming*, Belorus. Universitet, Minsk, 1975.

Gabasov, R. and F. M. Kirillova, "Methods of Optimal Control," *Sovrem. Probl. Mat.*, Vol. 6 (Itogi Nauki i Tekhn. VINITI AN SSSR), Moscow, pp. 133–261, 1976.

Gabrieliān, M. S., "The Problem of Approach for a Group of Guided Objects," *Isv. AN Arm. SSR, Mekhanika*, Vol. 29, No. 3, pp. 3–15, 1976.

Gabrieliān, M. S., "On the Problem of Conflicting Approach of a Group of Objects," *Uch. Zap. Erevan. Universiteta, Estestv. N.*, No. 3 (130), pp. 23–30, 1975.

Gabrielian, M. S., "On the Game Problem of Guidance on Convex Regions," *Uch. Zap. Erevan. Universiteta, Estestv. N.*, No. 1 (131), pp. 24-29, 1976.

Gabrielian, M. S., "A Stable Game of Pursuit for a Group of Objects," *Uch. Zap. Erevan. Universiteta, Estestv. N.*, No. 2 (135), pp. 27-35, 1977.

Gamidov, R. G., *On a Class of Problems of Vector Optimization*, Institut Kibernet. Az SSSR, Baku, 1976.

Gamidov, R. G. and M. Sh. Farber, "Parametrization of the Pareto Set," *Materialy Resp. Konf. Molodykh Uchenykh po Mat. i Mekh. Elm.*, Baku, pp. 175-179, 1976.

Gaft, M. G. and V. M. Ozernoĭ, "Discerning and Estimating the Set of Noninferior Decisions in Problems of Decision Making with a Vector Criterion," *Avtomatika i Telemekhanika*, No. 11, pp. 85-94, 1973.

Germeĭer, Iu. B., *Methodological and Mathematical Foundations of Operations Research and Game Theory*, MGU, Moscow, 1967.

Germeĭer, Iu. B., *Introduction to the Theory of Operations Research*, Nauka, Moscow, 1971.

Germeĭer, Iu. B., "On the Contraction of Vector Criteria to a Single Criterion in the Presence of Nonnegative Contraction Parameters," *Kibernetiku-na Sluzhbu Kommunizmu, Energiia*, Moscow, 1971.

Germeĭer, Iu. B., "Multicriteria Optimization Problems and the Role of Information," *Abstracts of the 5th All-Union Conference on Control*, Part 1, Nauka, Moscow, 1971.

Germeĭer, Iu. B., "Discussion," *Issledovanie Operatsii, Metodologicheskie Aspekty*, Nauka, Moscow, 1972.

Germeĭer, Iu. B., "Formulation of Objectives in Problems with Vector Criteria (Theses)," *Isv. Akad. Nauk SSSR, Tekhn. Kibernet.*, Vol. 12, No. 4, pp. 3-13, 1976.

Germeĭer, Iu. B. And I. A. Vatel', "Games with Hierarchical Objective Vectors," *Isv. Akad. Nauk SSSR, Tekhn. Kibernet.*, Vol. 12, No. 3, pp. 54-69, 1974.

Gorelik, V. A. and V. V. Fedorov, "On an Approach to the Solution of The Minimax Problems of Optimal Control," *Isv. AN SSSR, Tekhnich. Kibernetika*, No. 1, pp. 45-54, 1976.

Gorokhovik, V. V., "On the Problem of Vector Optimization," *Isv. Akad. Nauk SSSR, Tekhn. Kibernet.*, Vol. 10, No. 6, pp. 63-70, 1972.

Gorokhovik, V. V., *Some Problems of Vector Optimization and Differential Games*, Avtoreferat Kand. Dissertatsii, Minsk AN BSSR, 1973.

Gorokhovik, V. V., "Weak Efficiency Conditions in Finite Dimensional Problems of Vector Optimization," Preprint No. 12(12), Institut Mat. AN BSSR, Minsk, 1976.

Gorokhovik, V. V., "Necessary Conditions for Weak Efficiency in Control Problems with Vector Criteria," Preprint No. 13(13), Institut Mat. AN BSSR, Minsk, 1976.

Gorokhovik, V. V., "Optimization Problems with a Vector Criterion," *Probl. Upr. i Optimiz.*, Minsk, pp. 134-147, 1976.

Gorokhovik, V. V., "On Necessary Conditions for Weak Efficiency in Vector Criterion Control Problems," Preprint No. 4, Institut Mat. AN BSSR, Minsk, 1978.

Gorokhovik, V. V. and S. Ia. Gorokhovik, "Necessary Optimality Conditions for Singular Controls in Problems Having Trajectories with Movable Right-End Points," *Dokl. AN BSSR*, Vol. 20, No. 3, pp. 221-224, 1976.

Gorokhovik, V. V. and M. P. Dymkov, "The Optimization of Linear Systems with Vector Criteria," *Differents. i Integral'n. Uravneniia*, Vyp. 3, Irkutsk, pp. 245-256, 1975.

Gorokhovik, V. V. and F. M. Kirillova, "On the Scalarization of Vector Optimization Problems," *Dokl. Akad. Nauk, BSSR*, Vol. 19, pp. 588-591, 1975.

Gorokhovik, S. Ia., "Necessary Conditions for Multidimensional Singular Controls," *Differents. Uravneniia*, Vol. 9, No. 9, pp. 1721-1724, 1973.

Gorokhovik, S. Ia., "Necessary Optimality Conditions in Problems Having Trajectories with Movable Right-End Points," *Differents. Uravneniia*, Vol. 11, No. 10, pp. 1765–1773, 1975.

Gurin, L. G., "Some Problems of Vector Optimization," *Avtomat. i Vychisl. Tekhn.*, No. 4, pp. 40–44, 1974.

Gurin, L. G. and E. M. Stoliarova, "A Maximum Principle in a Minimax Problem," *Zh. Vychisl. Mat. i Mat. Fiz.*, Vol. 13, No. 5, pp. 1175–1185, 1973.

Gurman, V. N. and V. Dykhta, "Degenerate Problems of Optimal Control and the Method of Multiple Maxima," *Avtomatika i Telemekhanika*, No. 3, pp. 51–59, 1977.

Gusev, M. I., "Vector Optimization of Linear Systems," *Dokl. Akad. Nauk SSSR*, Vol. 207, No. 1, pp. 21–24, 1972.

Gusev, M. I., "Optimal Control for Linear Systems with Vector Criteria," *Ėkstremal'n. Strategii v Pozitsion. Differents. Igrakh*, Sverdlovsk, pp. 77–104, 1974.

Gusev, M. I. and A. B. Kurzhanskiĭ, "On the Location of Equilibria in Multicriteria Game Problems," *Dokl. Akad. Nauk SSSR*, Vol. 229, No. 6, pp. 1295–1298, 1976.

Gus'kov, Iu. I., "Optimization of Discrete Stochastic Systems with Two Criteria," *Avtomatika i Telemekhanika*, No. 10, pp. 60–68, 1970.

Gusiatnikov, P. B., "A Three-Dimensional Problem of Escape from Many Pursuers," *Isv. AN SSSR, Tekh. Kibernetika*, No. 5, pp. 30–36, 1976.

Gusiatnikov, P. B., "Escape and l-Escape in Many Person Differential Games," *Dokl. AN SSSR*, Vol. 232, No. 3, pp. 517–520, 1977.

Gusiatnikov, P. B. and L. P. Iugaĭ, "The Problem of Escape in Nonlinear Differential Games with a Complete Terminal Set," *Isv. AN SSSR, Tekhn. Kibernetika*, No. 2, pp. 8–13, 1977.

Gutkin, L. S., "On the Synthesis of Systems with Ill-conditioned Preference Criteria," *Isv. Akad. Nauk SSSR, Tekhn. Kibernet.*, Vol. 10, No. 3, 1972.

Gutkin, L. S., "On the Synthesis of Radio Systems with Several Criteria," *Radiotekh.*, No. 7, 1972.

Gutkin, L. S., "On the Application of the Method of Extreme Points for the Synthesis of Systems with Vector Criteria," *Isv. Akad. Nauk SSSR, Tekhn. Kibernet.*, Vol. 11, No. 4, 1973.

Danilov, N. N., "The Pareto-Set in Non-Strictly Competitive N-Person Differential Games," *Some Questions in Differential and Integral Equations and Their Application*, IaGU, Iakutsk, Vyp. 2, pp. 25–35, 1977.

Danilov, N. N., "The Structure of the Pareto-Set in Non-Antagonistic Differential Games," *Questions of Control of Mechanical Processes, Control of Dynamic Systems*, Isd. LGU, Leningrad, Vyp. 2, pp. 44–50, 1978.

Danilov, N. N., "Stability of the Solutions of N-Person Games with Terminal Cost," *Abstracts of the 4th All-Union Conference on Game Theory*, Gor'kiĭ, pp. 416–418, 1978.

Danilov, N. N., "Structure of the Pareto-Set in N-Person Differential Games," *Abstracts of the 4th All-Union Conference on Problems in Cybernetic Theory*, Novosibirsk, pp. 53–54, 1977.

Dargeĭko, L. F., "The Method of Constraints in Linear Problems of Vector Optimization," *Kibernet. i Vychisl. Tekhn., Resp. Mezhved.*, Sb. Vyp. 21, pp. 87–93, 1976.

Dzhibladze, N. I., et al., "The Optimization of Cooling Parameters for Water Cooling," *Isv. Akad. Nauk Belo. SSR*, No. 4, Minsk, 1970.

Diner, I. Ia., "The Division of a Set of Vectors into Characteristic States and the Problem of Choosing a Solution," *Problemy Obshcheĭ i Sotsial'noĭ Prognostiki*, Vyp. 2, *Issledovanie Operatsiĭ, Informatsionnyĭ Biulleten'*, Vol. 14 (29), Moscow, 1969.

Diner, I. Ia., "The Division of a Set of Vectors into Characteristic States and the Problem of Choosing a Solution," *Issledovanie Operatsiĭ, Metodologicheskie Aspekty*, Nauka, Moscow, 1972.

Dolodorenko, V. A. and É. I. Fedan, "On a Complex Optimal Control Problem of a Multiobjective System," *Slozhnye Sistemy Upravleniĭa*, pp. 96–110, 1976.

Dubov, Ĭu. A., "The Problem of One-Dimensional 'Rantse' with Vector Criterion," *Upr. Slozhn. Sistemami*. Nauka, Moscow, pp. 84–88, 1975.

Dubovitskii, A. Ĭa. and A. A. Miliutin, "Extremum Problems with Constraints," *Zh. Vychisl. Mat. Fiz.*, Vol. 5, No. 3, pp. 395–453, 1965.

Dudoladov, V. A., "The Principle of Minimum Complexity for Multicriteria Problems of Bivalent Programming," *Tr. Mosk. Tekhn. Uch-shcha Im.*, N. É. Baumana, Vol. 238, pp. 59–63, 1977.

Dymkov, M. R., "Solution Method for the General Multi-Criterion Linear Programming Problem," *Probl. Upr. i Optimiz.*, Minsk, pp. 147–157, 1976.

Dymkov, M. R., "One Method of Constructing a Set of Non-Inferior Values for a Functional in Problems of Vector Optimization," *Differential and Integral Equations*, Irkutsk, Vyp. 4, pp. 140–144, 1976.

Emel'ianov, S. V., V. I. Borisov, A. A. Malevich and A. M. Cherkashin, "Models and Methods of Vector Optimization," *Itogi Nauki Tekhn. Ser. Tekhn. Kibernetika*, Vol. 5, pp. 386–448, 1973.

Emel'ianov, S. V., E. B. Dudin, O. I. Larichev, A. A. Malevich, É. L. Napel'baim and V. M. Ozernoĭ, "Formulations and the Concept of a Solution for Organizational Control Systems," *Itogi Nauki Tekhn., Kibernetika*, Vol. 3, 1971.

Emel'ianov, S. V. and V. M. Ozernoĭ, "Problems and Methods in Decision Making in Vector Criteria Problems," *6th All-Union Conference on Control Problems, Ref. Dokladov*, Part 2, Nauka, Moscow, 1974.

Emel'ianov, S. V., V. M. Ozernoĭ and M. G. Gaft, "On the Construction of Contraction Rules in Multicriterion Problems," *Dokl. Akad. Nauk, SSSR*, Vol. 28, No. 1, pp. 56–58, 1976.

Emel'ianov, S. V., V. M. Ozernoĭ and O. I. Larichev, "Problems of Solution Concepts in Organizational Systems," *Abstracts of the 5th All-Union Conference on Control*, Part 1, Nauka, Moscow, 1971.

Emel'ianov, S. V., V. M. Ozernoĭ, O. I. Larichev, et al., "The Choice of Rational Variants for a Schematic Technological Mine Considering a Large Number of Criteria," *Gornyĭ Zhurnal*, No. 5, 1972.

Emel'ianov, S. V., V. M. Ozernoĭ and O. I. Larichev, "Problems and Methods of Decision Making (a Review)," *Mezhdunarodnyĭ Tsentr Nauchnoĭ i Tekhnicheskoĭ Informatsii*, Moscow, 1973.

Ermoleva, L. G., "On a Solution Method for Linear Vector Optimization Problems," *Matematicheskie Metody Issledovaniĭa i Optimizatsii Sistem*, Kiev, 1971.

Zhak, S. V., "Realization of the Trade-Off Method by Several Objective Functions," *Trudy Chetvertoĭ Zimneĭ Shkoly po Matematicheskomu Programmirovaniĭu i Smezhnym Voprosam 1971*, Vyp. 2, Moscow, 1971.

Zhukovskiĭ, V. I., "On Non-Zero Sum Several Person Differential Games," *Isv. AN SSSR, Tekhn. Kibernetika*, No. 3, pp. 3–13, 1971.

Zhukovskiĭ, V. I., "Optimality in a Several Person Differential Game," *Problems in Analytical Mechanics Theory of Stability and Control*, Nauka, Moscow, pp. 143–147, 1975.

Zhukovskiĭ, V. I., "On the Theory of Some Differential Games with Time Lag, Parts I, II and III," *Godishn. Bucsh. Tekhn. Uchebn. Zaved. Mat.*, Part I, Vol. 9, No. 1, pp. 7–21, 1973 (1974); Parts II and III, Vol. 9, No. 2, pp. 9–41, 1973 (1974).

Zhukovskiĭ, V. I. and N. B. Stoĭanov, "On the Pursuit Problem with Many Participants," *Prilozh. Mat.*, Vol. 10, No. 3, pp. 79–95, 1974 (1975).

Zabotin, V. I., "On the Optimization Problem with a Vector Criterion," *Tr. Kazan. Avnats. Instituta*, Vyp. 135, pp. 69–75, 1971.

Zabotin, V. I., "On Some Optimization Problems with a Set of Cost Functions," *Tr. Kazan. Avnats. Instituta*, Vyp. 147, pp. 14–17, 1972.

Zabotin, V. I., *Efficiency Conditions in Problems of Optimal Control and Nonlinear Programming*, Avtoreferat Kand. Dissertatsii, Kazan', KAI, 1973.

Zak, Iu. A., "Models and Methods for Compromising in Problems of Mathematical Programming with Several Objective Functionals," *Kibernetika*, No. 4, pp. 102–107, 1972.

Zak, Iu. A., "Setting Up Compromises for Complex Industrial Complexes with Several Objectives," *Upravliaiushehie Sistemy i Mashiny*, Vol. 5, pp. 8–14, 1974.

Zak, Iu. A., "A Modification of the Method of Successive Reduction in Vector Criterion Optimization Problems," *Avtomat. i Vychisl. Tekhn.*, No. 3, pp. 45–51, 1975.

Zak, Iu. A., "Multi-Stage Processes of Decision Making in the Problem of Vector Optimization," *Avtomat. i Vychisl. Tekhn.*, No. 6, pp. 41–45, 1976.

Zukhovskiĭ, S. I., R. A. Poliak and M. E. Prizhak, "On a Concave N-Person Game and a Production Model," *Dokl. AN SSSR*, Vol. 191, No. 6, pp. 1220–1223, 1970.

Ilyshev, V. M., "On the Theory of Optimal Systems," *Kibernetika*, No. 1, pp. 122–124, 1972.

Indzuki, I. and Iu. Nakamura, "A Study of Probabilistic Differential Games," *Bulletin of the Engineering Research Institute, Kyoto University*, Vol. 35, No. 34, 1969.

Intriligator, M., *Mathematical Methods of Optimization and Economic Theories*, Progress, Moscow, 1975.

Iskaraeva, R. T., I. I. Zapletin and V. I. Golovchenko, "Construction of an Optimality Criterion for Vector Parametric Programming Problems," *Trudy Dzhambul. Tekhnol. Institut Legk. i Pishch Promyshlennosti*, Vol. 4, pp. 131–149, 1973.

Kazakov, and A. A. Korbut, "Some Problems of Multicriteria Decision Making," VI Simpozium po Kibernetike (Tez. Dokl. Ch. III), Institut Kibernetiki AN Gruz. SSR, 1972.

Kantariia, G. V., "Optimal Choices of Strategy with Compromise Coordination Among Alternative Criteria," *Isv. Akad. Nauk SSSR, Tekhn. Kibernet.*, Vol. 12, No. 1, pp. 52–54, 1974.

Kantariia, G. V., "On the Application Procedure of Optimal Two-Level Coordinated Compromises," *Sakartveloe SSR Metsinerebasha Akademie Moambe, Soobshch. AN Gruz. SSR*, Vol. 85, No. 2, pp. 329–332, 1977.

Kantorovich, L. V., "Optimization Methods and Mathematical Models in Economics," *Uspekhi Mat. Nauk*, Vol. 25, No. 5, 1970.

Kantorovich, L. V. and V. L. Makarov, "Differential and Functional Equations Generated in Models of Dynamic Economics," *Sib. Mat. Zh.*, Vol. 11, No. 5, pp. 1046–1059, 1970.

Kaplinskiĭ, A. I. and A. S. Krasnenker, "On the Formulation of Dialogue Algorithms of Vector Optimization," *Avtomat. i Vychisl. Tekhn.*, No. 5, pp. 32–37, 1977.

Karlin, S., "Mathematical Methods in the Theory of Games," *Programming and Economics*, Mir, Moscow, 1964.

Karpelevich, F. I. and V. A. Mukhina, "On a Method of Solution of Multiobjective Problems," *Ékonom. i Mat. Metody*, Vol. 11, No. 2, pp. 399–401, 1975.

Karpelevich, F. I. and V. A. Mukhina, "On a Method of Solution of Multiobjective Problems," *Avtomatika i Telemekhanika*, No. 7, pp. 153–155, 1975.

Kafarov, G. M., G. B. Lazarev and V. I. Avdeev, "Solution Methods for Multicriteria Control Problems in Complex Chemical Engineering Systems," *Dokl. Akad. Nauk SSSR*, Vol. 198, No. 1, pp. 62–63, 1971.

Kigel', V. R. and V. Timann, "A General Method—Three Relative Reductions and an Algorithm for Solving Linear Bicriterion Problems," *Issled. Operatsii i ASU Mezhved. Nauchn.*, Sb. 9, pp. 42–50, 1977.

Kini, R., "Theory of Multicriteria Utility and Its Application," *Tr. Vses. Shkolyseminara po Upr. Bol'shimi Sistemami Tbilisi 1974*, Metsniereba, Tbilisi, pp. 143–157, 1976.

Kirillova, F. M., "On Problems of Analytic Construction of Regulators," *Prikl. Mat. i Mekh.*, Vol. 25, No. 3, 1961.

Kirillova, F. M., V. V. Gorokhovik and M. N. Dymkov, "On the Theory of Vector Optimization," *Materialy Vses. Simpoz. po Optimal'n. Upr. i Differents. Igram 1976*, Metsniereba, Tbilisi, pp. 139–145, 1977.

Kirillova, F. M. and N. A. Poletaeva, "On Some Problems of Pursuit," *Dokl, Mezhdunarodnogo Kongressa Matematikov*, Sektsiia 6, Nauka, Moscow, 1966.

Kleĭner, Ia. S. and A. D. Shapiro, "On the Solution of Linear Programming Problems with Several Objective Functions," *Avtomatizir. Sistemy Planir.*, Kiev, pp. 58–71, 1974.

Kozhinskaia, L. I. and L. I. Slutskiĭ, "The Role of the Method of Contraction in Vector Optimization," *Avtomatika i Telemekhanika*, No. 3, pp. 167–170, 1973.

Kozhukharov, A. N. and O. I. Larichev, "Multicriterion Problems with Uncertainty," *Avtomatika i Telemekhanika*, No. 7, pp. 71–88, 1977.

Kolmanovskii, V. B., "On Some Questions of Optimal Impulse Response in Stochastic Systems," *Probl. Upr. i Teorii Inform. (Vengr.)*, Vol. 4, No. 4, pp. 353–367, 1975.

Kolmanovskii, V. B., "On a Problem of Gyrostat Movement Control Under Random Perturbation," *Avtomatika i Telemekhanika*, No. 11, 1976.

Komlik, V. I. and V. I. Kurilenkov, "On the Structure of the Set of Non-Inferior Solutions," *Vests. Akad. Nauk BSSR, Ser. Fiz.- Mat. Nauk*, Vol. 4, pp. 132–133, 1976.

Kornienko, I. A., "Solution of Compromise Problems with the Aid of the Minimax Criterion," *Trudy Kazan. Aviatsion. Institut*, Vol. 135, pp. 50–56, 1971.

Kornienko, I. A., *Some Problems of Minimax Operator Theory with Application to the Problem of Interorbital Flight*, Avtoreferat Kand. Dissertatsii, Kazan', KAI, 1974.

Kornienko, I. A., "Sufficient Conditions for Optimal Control with a Vector Criterion and the Choice of the Efficient Solution," *Tr. Kazan. Avnats. Instituta*, Vyp. 161, pp. 55–60, 1974.

Kotov, N. V. and V. N. Zakharov, "Optimization of the Value Function by Decision Making," *Izv. Akad. Nauk SSSR, Tekhn. Kibernetika*, Vol. 15, No. 1, pp. 24–31, 1977.

Krasin, A. K., "Rapid Gas-Cooling of Reactors by Gaseous Dissociation," *Proceedings, Conference of MAGATE Experts*, Minsk, July 24–28, 1972.

Krasin, A. K., et al., "Physiko-Technical Foundations for the Construction of Nuclear Power Stations with Gas-Cooled Nuclear Reactors by Rapid Neutrons with Dissociated Heat Transfer by Tetranitrogen Oxide," *World Studies on Atomic Energy*, Vol. 5, 1972.

Krasnenker, A. S., "On the Behavior of Systems with Several Criteria," *Trudy Matematicheskogo Fakul'teta Voronezhskogo Gosudarstvennogo Universiteta*, Voronezh, 1971.

Krasnenker, A. S., "On the Adaptive Approach to the Problems of Decision Making with Several Criteria," *Voprosy Optimal'nogo Programmirovaniia v Proizvodstvennykh Zadachakh*, Voron. Gosudarstv. Universiteta, Voronezh, 1972.

Krasnenker, A. S., "On the Problem of Vector Optimization," *Trudy VI Zimp. Shkoly po Mat. Programmir. i Smezhn. Vopr.*, Drogobuch 1973, Moscow, pp. 90–99, 1975.

Krasnenker, A. S., "Problems and Methods of Vector Optimization," *Izmereniia, Kontrol'*, *Avtomatiz. Nauch.-Tekhn. Ref.*, Sb. 1, No. 3, pp. 51–56, 1975.

Krasnenker, A. S., "Method of Local Improvements in the Problem of Vectoroptimization," *Avtomatika i Telemekhanika*, No. 3, pp. 75–79, 1975.

Krasovskiĭ, N. N., *Game Problems on the Meeting of Motions*, Nauka, Moscow, 1970.

Krasovskiĭ, N. N. and A. I. Subbotin, *Positional Differential Games*, Nauka, Moscow, 1974.

Krivenkov, Iu. P., "Necessary Optimality Conditions for Linear Problems in the Mathematical Theory of Optimal Processes with Phase Restrictions," Novosibirsk, 1977.

Kryzhanovskiĭ, G. A., "Complex Criteria for Optimal Engineering Instruments," *Izmeritel'naia Tekhnika*, No. 3, 1971.

Kuz'min, I. V., É. A. Dedikov and B. E. Kukharev, "Methods for the Construction of Global Criteria in Mathematical Programming Problems," *Mekhanizaĭsiĭa i Avtomatizaĭsiĭa Upravleniĭa*, No. 6, pp. 11–12, 1971.

Kuz'min, I. V. and B. E. Kukharev, "Principles of Decision Making in Multi-Alternative Problems Subject to Vector Criteria," *Tezy Dokl. II-ĭ Vses. Nauchn.-Tekhn. Konf. Problemy Nauch. Organizaĭsii Upravleniĭa Sots. Promyshlennost'ĭu*, Moscow, pp. 168–179, 1972.

Kurzhanskiĭ, A. B., *Control and Observation Under Conditions of Uncertainty*, Nauka, Moscow, 1977.

Kutateladze, S. S. and M. M. Feldman, "Lagrange Multipliers in Vector Optimization Problems," *Dokl. Akad. Nauk SSSR*, Vol. 231, No. 1, pp. 28–31, 1976.

Kukharev, B. E., "Compromise Decision Choices Under Multicriterion Conditions," *Avtomatizir. Sistemy Upr. i Pribory Avtomatiki. Resp. Mezhved. Temat.Nauch.-Tekhn. Sb.*, Vyp. 35, pp. 6–12, 1975.

Labkovskiĭ, V. A., "On a Decision Making Model," *Adaptiv. Sistemy Upr.*, Kiev, pp. 13–18, 1977.

Larichev, O. I., "Man-Machine Procedures in Decision Making (a Review)," *Avtomatika i Telemekhanika*, No. 12, 1971.

Larichev, O. I., "A Method for the Evaluation of Plans of Realization of Applied Research and Development," *Avtomatika i Telemekhanika*, No. 8, pp. 121–127, 1972.

Lebedev, B. D., V. V. Podinovskiĭ and R. S. Styrikovich, "The Optimization Problem for an Ordered Set of Criteria," *Ėkonom. i Mat. Metody*, Vol. 7, No. 4, pp. 612–616, 1971.

Letov, A. M., "The Theory of Optimal Control (Review Lecture)," *Optimal'nye Sistemy, Statisticheskie Metody, Trudy II-go Kongressa IFAK*, Nauka, Moscow, 1965.

Lochmel', O. I., "On Multicriteria Problems in Operations Research," *Sb. Tr. Voen. Kafedry Estestv. Fak. Kibernetika*, Mosk. Universitet, Moscow, pp. 4–12, 1975.

Lur'e, Z. Ĭa. and B. S. Flanchik, "Multicriteria Optimization of Position Control Systems," *Avtomatizir. Sistemy Upr. i Pribory Avtomatiki, Resp. Mezhved. Nauch.-Tekhn. Sb.*, Vyp. 41, pp. 6–13, 1977.

Lutmanov, S. B., "On an Alternative in Several Person Differential Games," *Prikl. Mat. i Mekh.*, Vol. 41, Vyp. 5, pp. 813–818, 1977.

Lutmanov, S. B., "Theorem of the Alternative for k-Person Differential Games," *Tr. Instituta Mat. i Mekh. Ural'sk. Nauch. Ĭsentr. AN SSSR*, Vyp. 24, pp. 68–76, 1977.

L'ĭus, R. D. and Kh. Raĭfa, *Games and Decisions*, Izd-vo Inostr. Lit-ry, Moscow, 1961.

Liashko, I. I. and V. R. Kigel', "On Some Properties of Effective Schemes for Multicriteria Problems," *Nauch. Konf. Vychisl. Mat. v Sovrem. Nauch.-Tekhn. Progress*, 1974; Kiev, pp. 407–413, 1974.

Makarov, I. M. and T. M. Vinogradskaĭa, "On the Theory of Multicriterion Decision Making," *Dokl. Akad. Nauk SSSR*, Vol. 232, No. 1, pp. 47–49, 1977.

Makarov, I. M., V. M. Ozernoĭ and A. P. Ĭastrebov, "The Concept of a Solution in the Choice of a Variant of a Complex Control System," *Avtomatika i Telemekhanika*, No. 3, pp. 84–90, 1971.

Maksimov, A. N. and E. F. Filaretov, "The Application of a Quadratic Criterion for Complex Systems," *Isvestiĭa VUZOV, Mashinostroenie*, No. 9, pp. 61–65, 1976.

Maliukov, V. P., "Conflict-Type Interaction of Economies Within the Frame of the Leontiev Model with Incomplete Information," *Isv. AN SSSR, Tekhn. Kibernetika*, No. 5, pp. 3–10, 1974.

Marchenko, V. M., "Group Controllability of Dynamic Systems," *Vestn. Belorus. Universiteta*, Ser. 1, No. 3, pp. 72–73, 1974.

Maslov, E. P. and V. H. Kharchev, "A Comparison of Minmax Optimal and Optimal in Mean Square Strategy Pursuits," *Avtomatika i Telemekhanika*, No. 5, pp. 5–13, 1973.

Mashunin, Ĭu. K., "Solution Algorithms for Mathematical Programming Problems," Tikhookean Okeanol. Institut Dal'nevost. Nauch. T̃sentra Akad. Nauk SSSR, Vladivostok, 1977.

Metev, B. C. and I. I. Popchev, "A Solution Method for the Group Choice Problem Involving a Metric Space of Relations," *Avtomatika i Telemekhanika*, No. 2, pp. 81–87, 1977.

Metreveli, D. G., "Necessary and Sufficient Conditions for Efficiency in Vector Optimization Problems," *Sakartvelos SSR Met̃snierebata Akad. Moambe, Soobshch. AN Gruz. SSR*, Vol. 83, No. 3, pp. 585–588, 1976.

Metreveli, D. G., "On a Problem of Vector Optimization," *Sakartvelos SSR Met̃snierebata Akademis Marvis Sistemebis Institut i Shromebi, Tr. Institut Sistem Upr. AN Gruz. SSR*, Vol. 15, No. 1, pp. 94–104, 1976.

Metreveli, D. G., "On a Class of Vector Optimization Problems," *Sakartvelos SSR Metsnierebata Akad. Moambe. Soobshch. AN Gruz. SSR*, Vol. 84, No. 3, pp. 581–584, 1976.

Metreveli, D. G., "Necessary Conditions for Optimality in Vector Criterion Control Problems," *Tezesy Dokladov 1 Konf. Molodykh Uchenykh Zakavkaz'ĩa po Avtomat. Upravleniĩu*, Tbilisi, pp. 3–6, 1977.

Mirkin, B. G., *The Problem of Group Choice*, Nauka, Moscow, 1974.

Mishchenko, E. F., M. S. Nikol'skiĭ and N. Ĩu. Satimov, "The Encounter Evasion Problem in Many Person Differential Games," *Tr. MIAN*, pp. 105–128, 1977.

Mishchenko, E. F. and N. Ĩu. Satimov, "The Encounter Evasion Problem in Many Person Differential Games," *Materialy Vses. Simpoz. po Optim. Upr. i Differ. Igram*, Tbilisi, Metsniereba, pp. 214–215, 1977.

Moĭseev, N. N., "Computational Problems in the Theory of Hierarchical Control Systems," *Abstracts of the 5th All-Union Conference on Control*, Part 1, Nauka, Moscow, 1971.

Molostvov, V. S., *Some Game Problems in Systems Subjected to Random Excitations*, Avtoreferat Kand. Diss., MGU, Moscow, 1974.

Molostvov, V. S., "Pareto Optimality in Certain Differential Games," *Vestn. Mosk. Universiteta, Mat. Mekh.*, No. 2, pp. 91–96, 1974.

Molostvov, V. S., "On Pareto Strategies in Some Stochastic Several Person Differential Games," *Probl. Analit. Mekh. Teorii Ustoichivosti i Upr.*, Moscow, Nauka, pp. 217–221, 1975.

Molostvov, V. S. and Z. Varga, "Generalized Solution of a Differential Game with Vector Plateau," *Tezisy 4-go Vses. Soveshchaniĩa po Statist. Metodam Teorii Upravleniĩa*, Frunze, pp. 84–85, 1978.

Nikaido, Kh., *Convex Structures and Mathematical Economics*, Mir, Moscow, 1972.

Nikiforova, V. S., "Analysis of the Approaches to the Solution of Multi-Objective Planning and Control Problems," *Tr. Vses. n.-i. i Proekt.-Konstrukt. Institut Kompleks. Avtomatiz. Neft. i Gaz. Prom-sti*, Vol. 6, pp. 33–39, 1975.

Nogin, V. D., "On the Problem of Multiobjective Programming," Leningrad, 1975.

Nogin, V. D., "On the Existence of Efficient and Properly Efficient Points for Linear Vector Functions," *Vestnik Leningrad. Universiteta, Ser. Mat., Mekh., Astron.*, No. 1220-75, Leningrad, 1975.

Nogin, V. D., "A New Method for Narrowing the Bargaining Set," *Isv. Akad. Nauk SSSR, Tekhn. Kibernet.*, Vol. 14, No. 5, pp. 10–14, 1976.

Nogin, V. D., "On the Problem of Multiobjective Control," *Tezisy Dokladov Vses. Konf. po Kachestv. Teorii Different̃. Uravneniĭ*, Riãzan', pp. 218–219, 1976.

Nogin, V. D., "On the Problem of Vector Optimization in Multi-Level Decision Making Processes," *Dinamich. Modeli Prot̃sessov Priniãtiã Resheniĭ*, Vladivostok, pp. 111–116, 1976.

Nogin, V. D., "Duality in Multiobjective Programming," *Zh. Vychisl. Mat. i Mat. Fiz.*, Vol. 17, No. 1, pp. 254–258, 1977.

Ovchinnikov, V. A. and L. M. Boĭchuk, "On Solving Vector Optimization Problems Subject to an Additional Criterion," *Kibernet. i Vychisl. Tekhn. Resp. Mezhved. Sb.*, Vol. 23, pp. 70–73, 1974.

Ogorodneĭchuk, I. F., E. G. Kunik, A. Ĭa. Kuzemin, A. G. Osinevskiĭ and L. A. Golovko, "Methods of Multicriteria Optimization," *Pribory i Sistemy Avtomatiki, Resp. Mezhved. Temat. Nauchno-Tekhn Sb.*, Vol. 27, pp. 43–54, 1973.

Ozernoĭ, V. M., "Decision Making (a Review)," *Avtomatika i Telemekhanika*, No. 11, pp. 106–121, 1971.

Ozernoĭ, V. M., "Formulation and Application of Models of Multicriteria Decision Making Problems," *Sb. Tr. Institut Probl. Upr.*, Vol. 5, pp. 3–15, 1974.

Ozernoĭ, V. M., B. B. Buianov and L. M. Vas'kina, "An Algorithm for Finding the Set of Non-Inferior Solutions in Multicriterion Problems," *Sb. Tr. Institut Probl. Upr.*, Vol. 5, pp. 61–67, 1974.

Ozernoĭ, V. M. and M. G. Gaft, "A Set Theory Approach to Decision Making in Vector Criterion Problems," 6 Simpozium po Kibernetike, Part 2, Tbilisi, Nauka, Moscow, 1972.

Ozernoĭ, V. M. and M. G. Gaft, "Construction of Decision Making Rules in Multicriteria Decision Making Problems," *Sb. Tr. Institut Probl. Upr.*, Vol. 5, pp. 30–44, 1974.

Onishchenko, A. M., "An Optimality Criterion for Agricultural Production and Methods for Obtaining the Most Effective Plans Based on Several Criteria," Institut Ėkonomiki AN USSR, Kiev, 1976.

Ostapov, S. S., "On Multi-Criterion Linear Programming Problems," Matemat. Voprosy Formirovaniia Ėkonomicheskikh Modeleĭ, Institut Ėkonomiki i Organizatsii Promyshlennogo Proizvodstva SO AN SSSR, Novosibirsk, 1970.

Petrosian, L. A., "Differential Games of Survival with Many Participants," *Dokl. AN SSSR*, Vol. 161, No. 2, pp. 285–287, 1965.

Petrosian, L. A., "'Lifeline' Pursuit Games with Many Participants," *Izv. AN Arm SSR* (*Matem.*), Vol. 1, No. 5, pp. 331–340, 1966.

Petrosian, L. A., "Theoretical Game Problems of Mechanics," *Lit. Matem. Sb.*, Vol. 6, No. 3, pp. 423–433, 1966.

Petrosian, L. A., *Differential Games of Pursuit*, Avtoreferat Dokt. Dissertatsii, LGU, Leningrad, 1971.

Petrosian, L. A., "Stability Solutions in Differential Games with Many Participants," *Vestn. Leningr. Universiteta*, No. 19, pp. 46–52, 1977.

Petrosian, L. A., "Non-Antagonistic Differential Games," *Questions in Mechanical Control Processes, Control of Dynamical Systems*, Leningrad Universitet, Vyp. 2, pp. 173–181, 1978.

Petrosian, L. A. and N. B. Murzov, "Games of 'Winning Over' with Many Participants," *Vestn. Leningr. Universiteta*, Vyp. 3, No. 13, pp. 125–129, 1967.

Plotnikova, L. I., *Some Problems of Optimal Interaction of Several Controlled Objects*, Kandidatskaia Dissertatsiia, Novosibirsk, 1972.

Plotnikova, L. I., "On a Problem of Optimal Control," *Upravliaemye Sistemy*, Novosibirsk, Vyp. 6, pp. 36–43, 1970.

Plotnikova, L. I., "A Numerical Solution for the Problem of Search for the Point of Interception of Several Guided Objects," *Sb. Tr. Institut Mat. Sib. Otd. AN SSSR*, Vyp. 8, pp. 39–42, 1971.

Podinovskiĭ, V. V., "Application of the Procedure of Local Primary Criterion Maximization to the Solution of Vector Optimization Problems," *Upravliaemye Sistemy*, Vyp. 6, Novosibirsk, pp. 17–22, 1970.

Podinovskiĭ, V. V., "Methods of Multicriteria Optimization," *Trudy VIA Im. Dzerzhinskogo*, Moscow, 1971.

Podinovskiĭ, V. V., "Efficient Sequences and Their Properties," *Mat. Metody v Sots. Naukakh, Vil'nius*, Vyp. 2, pp. 75–88, 1972.

Podinovskiĭ, V. V., "Lexicographic Optimization Problems with Uncertainty," *Isv. Akad. Nauk SSSR, Tekhn. Kibernet.*, Vol. 11, No. 1, 1973.

Podinovskiĭ, V. V., "Decision Making Problems with Several Equal Homogeneous Criteria," *All-Union Conference on the Theory of Games*, Odesskiĭ Gosudarstv. Universitet, Odessa, pp. 131–132, 1974.

Podinovskiĭ, V. V., "Multi-Criterion Problems with Homogeneous Equally Important Criteria," *Zh. Vychisl. Mat. i Mat. Fiz.*, Vol. 15, No. 2, pp. 330–344, 1975.

Podinovskiĭ, V. V., "On the Solution of Multicriterion Problems as Single Criterion Problems Under Uncertainty," *Avtomat. i Vychisl. Tekhn.*, Vol. 2, pp. 45–49, 1976.

Podinovskiĭ, V. V., "Multicriterion Problems with Homogeneous Criteria Ordered in Accordance with Importance," *Avtomatika i Telemekhanika*, No. 11, pp. 118–127, 1976.

Podinovskiĭ, V. V. and V. M. Gavrilov, *Optimization in Accordance with Sequentially Applied Criteria*, Sovetskoe Radno, Moscow, 1975.

Poliak, R. A., "On an Approach to Multiobjective Programming Problems," *Tr. IV-i Zimn. Shkoly po Mat. Programmir. i Smezhnym Voprosam 1971*, Vyp. 2, Moscow, pp. 138–156, 1971.

Ponchev, I. and B. Metev, "Vector Optimization Methods Based on Partial Ordering Relations" [in Bulgarian], *Tekhn. Mysl'*, Vol. 12, No. 5, pp. 9–15, 1975.

Ponkov, Iu. S., B. L. Shmul'ian, N. V. Ikoeva and A. B. Kabakov, "A Multicriterion Approach to the Optimization of the Order of Construction in a City Addition," *Ispol'zovanie Prikladnogo Sistemnogo Analiza v Proektirovanii i Upravlenii Razvitiem Goroda*, Stroĭizdat, pp. 117–131, 1974.

Pontriagin, L. S., "On the Theory of Differential Games," *Uspekhi Mat. Nauk*, Vol. 21, No. 4, pp. 219–274, 1966.

Pontriagin, L. S., V. G. Boltianskii, R. V. Gamkrelidze and E. F. Mishchenko, *Mathematical Theory of Optimal Processes*, Nauka, Moscow, 1969.

Prasad, U. K. and N. D. Sarma, "Multicriterion Problems of Optimal Control: The Cooperative Game Solution of Nash-Harsanyi," *Avtomatika i Telemekhanika*, No. 6, pp. 95–105, 1975.

Prodan, N. V. and I. S. Chebotaru, "On Necessary Optimality Conditions in Games with Non-Conflicting and Conflicting Goals," *Issledovaniia po Algebre, Mat. Analizu i ikh Pril. Mat. Nauki*, Kishinev, pp. 104–109, 1977.

Pshenichnyĭ, B. N., "Simple Pursuit by Several Objects," *Kibernetika*, No. 3, pp. 145–146, 1976.

Radievskiĭ, A. E., "On the Existence of Solutions for the Multi-Criterion Synthesis of Linear Control Objectives," *Sistemy Prom. Kibern.*, Kiev, pp. 28–32, 1975.

Razumikhin, B. S., "Methods of Physical Modeling in Mathematical Programming and Economics, I–V," *Avtomatika i Telemekhanika*, Nos. 3, 4, 6 and 11, 1972; No. 2, 1973.

Rikhsiev, B. B., "Sufficient Conditions for Evasion for a Class of Many Person Differential Games," *Izv. AN Uz SSR, Ser. Fiz.-Mat. N.*, No. 3, pp. 69–70, 1977.

Ryzhova, V. E., *Some Guidance Problems with Parameterdependent Controls*, Kandidatskaia Dissertatsiia, MGU, Moscow, 1976.

Ryzhova, V. E., "On a Bicriterion Control Problem," *Nauch. Tr. Institut Mekh.*, Mosk. Universiteta, No. 40, pp. 30–47, 1975.

Ryzhova, V. E., "On the Problem of Vector Optimization," *Vest. Mosk. Universiteta, Mat. Mekh.*, No. 4, pp. 119–123, 1976.

Salukvadze, M. E., "On the Optimization of Vector Functionals: I. Programming Optimal Trajectories," *Avtomatika i Telemekhanika*, No. 8, pp. 5–15, 1971.

Salukvadze, M. E., "On the Optimization of Vector Functionals: II. The Analytical Design of Optimal Regulators," *Avtomatika i Telemekhanika*, No. 9, pp. 5–15, 1971.

Salukvadze, M. E., "On the Optimization of Control Systems with Vector Criterion," *Abstracts of the 5th All-Union Conference on Control*, Part 2, Nauka, Moscow, 1971.

Salukvadze, M. E., "On the Problem of Linear Programming with a Vector Criterion," *Avtomatika i Telemekhanika*, No. 5, pp. 99–105, 1972.

Salukvadze, M. E., "Vector Functionals in Linear Analytical Design Problems," *Avtomatika i Telemekhanika*, No. 7, pp. 5–12, 1973.

Salukvadze, M. E., *Vector Optimization Problems in Control Theory*, Metsniereba, Tbilisi, 1975.

Salukvadze, M. E. and D. G. Metreveli, "On the Problem of Optimal Flight to a Given Point in Space," *Avtomaticheskoe Upravlenie, Metsniereba*, Tbilisi, 1973.

Sarybekov, Zh. S., "A Multicriterion Approach to Strategy Choices Assuring Information Reliability in Complex Systems," *Tr. Vses. Shkoly-Seminara po Upr. Bol'shimi Sistemami 1974, Tbilisi*; Metsniereba, Tbilisi, pp. 185–188, 1976.

Saf'ian, A. C., "An Adaptive Procedure for the Evaluation of Lexicographic Preference Alternatives," *Isv. Akad. Nauk SSSR, Tekhn. Kibernet.*, Vol. 15, No. 2, pp. 196–206, 1977.

Sin, D. Kh., "Problems of Mathematical Programming with Several Criteria," *Optimizatsiia*, Vol. 35, No. 18, pp. 76–81, 1976.

Sivtsova, V. K., "Application of the Integral Minmax Principle to the Solution of Nonsmooth Optimal Control Problems," *Abstracts of the 3rd All-Union Conference on Operations Research*, Gor'kiĭ, pp. 342–343, 1978.

Skerus, S. L., *Some Coalitional Differential Games*, Avtoreferat Kandidatskoĭ Dissertatsii, VGU, Vil'niŭs, 1973.

Skerus, S. L. and I. P. Iachauskas, "A Three-Person Coalitional Differential Game," *Lit. Mat. Sb.*, Vol. 11, No. 4, pp. 887–898, 1971; *Abstracts of the 2nd All-Union Conference on Game Theory*, Vil'niŭs, pp. 103–105, 1971; *v Sb. Progress in Game Theory*, Vil'niŭs, p. 235, 1973.

Skerus, S. L. and I. P. Iachauskas, "A Coalitional N-Person Game," *Lit. Mat. Sb.*, Vol. 13, No. 2, pp. 163-175.

Skerus, S. L. and I. P. Iachauskas, "A Linear Coalitional Differential Game," *Sb. Mat. Metody v Sots. Naukakh, Vil'niŭs*, Vyp. 4, pp. 57-68, 1974.

Skerus, S. L. and I. P. Iachauskas, "On a Cooperative Differential Game," *Abstracts of the 3rd All-Union Conference on Game Theory*, Odessa, pp. 66–67, 1974.

Slobodinskaia, T. V. and L. A. Petrosian, "Simultaneous Games of Pursuit," *Mat. Metody v Sots. Naukakh, Vil'niŭs*, Vyp. 5, pp. 23–36, 1975.

Smol'iakov, E. R., "The Concept of a Solution for N-Person Coalitional Games with Transferability," *Dokl. AN SSSR*, Vol. 210, No. 6, pp. 1290–1292, 1973.

Stalbo, A. K., "Decision Making in Complex Situations and Multicriteria Problems," *Isv. Akad. Nauk SSSR, Tekhn. Kibernet.*, Vol. 13, No. 1, pp. 3–11, 1975.

Tadumadze, T. A., "Extremal Problems with Time Lags Characterized by Multidimensional Criteria," *Sakartvelos SSR Metsnierebata Akademia Martvis Sistemebis Instituti Shromebi, Tr. Instituta Sistem Upr. AN Gruz. SSR*, Vol. 13, No. 1, pp. 5–28, 1974.

Tadumadze, T. A., "A Maximum Principle for Some Guided Systems of Neutral Type," *Annotatsii Dokl. Seminar Instituta Prikl. Matem. Tbilisskogo Universiteta*, No. 9, pp. 9–13, 1974.

Tanabe, T., "On the Choice of Optimal Interception Type for Several Targets," *Upravlenie v Prostranstve*, Nauka, Moscow, No. 2, pp. 83–94, 1975.

Tamm, M. I., "A Compromise Solution in Complex Situations and Multicriteria Problems," *Ekonom. i Mat. Metody*, Vol. 9, No. 2, pp. 328–329, 1973.

Tarlinskiĭ, S. I., "On a Linear Differential Game of Approach for Several Guided Objects," *Dokl. AN SSSR*, Vol. 230, No. 3, pp. 534–537, 1976.

Teĭman, A. I., "On the Form of the Criterion in the Control of Large Systems," *Abstracts of the 5th All-Union Conference on Control*, Part 1, Nauka, Moscow, 1971.

Tkachenko, G. P., "Optimality Principles in Linear Multicriterion Games," *Teor.-Igrovye*

Voprosy Priniatiia Reshenii, Institut Sots.-Econ. Probl. AN SSSR, Leningrad, pp. 135–141, 1976.

Tynianskiĭ, N. T., *Investigations of Duality Theory for Nonlinear Programming and Differential Games*, Avtoreferat Dokt. Dissertatsii, Moscow, VTS AN SSSR, 1969.

Tynianskiĭ, N. T. and V. I. Zhukovskiĭ, "Non-Zero Sum Differential Games (Coalitionless Version)," *Itogi Nauki i Tekhn. VINITI Ser. Mat. Analiz.*, Moscow, No. 15, pp. 199–266, 1977.

Tynianskiĭ, N. T. and V. I. Zhukovskiĭ, "Non-Zero Sum Differential Games (Cooperative Version)," *Itogi Nauki i Tekhniki, VINITI Ser. Matematicheskiĭ Analiz.*, Moscow, No. 17, pp. 3–112, 1979.

Fedorov, V. V., "On a Two-Person Game with Vector Criteria," *Isv. Akad. Nauk SSSR, Tekhn. Kibernet.*, Vol. 13, No. 5, pp. 65–67, 1975.

Feĭgin, L. I., "Vector Optimization Problems with Incomplete Information in the Theory of Time Tables," *Isv. Akad. Nauk SSSR, Tekhn. Kibernet.*, Vol. 14, No. 5, pp. 3–9, 1976.

Formal'skiĭ, A. M., "Impulse Minimization and the Problem of Optimal Control with Two Functionals," *Nauch. Tr. Institut Mekh. Mosk. Universiteta*, No. 40, pp. 5–29, 1975.

Furasov, V. D., *Stability of Motion, Estimates and Stabilization*, Nauka, Moscow, 1977.

Khomeniŭk, V. V., *Optimal Control Systems*, Nauka, Moscow, 1977.

Khomeniŭk, V. V. and Iu. K. Mashunin, "An Application of Linear Multicriteria Programming to City Planning," *Ekon.-Mat. Metody Planir. i Upr. v Sisteme Gor. Khoziaĭstva*, Vladivostok, pp. 128–137, 1977.

Khomeniŭk, V. V. and M. B. Chemeris, "Application of the Entropy Criterion in Vector Optimization Problems," *Prikl. Metody Issled. Protsessov Priniatiia Reshenii*, Vladivostok, pp. 63–66, 1976.

Chebotaru, I. S., E. S. Naval and M. I. Sagaĭdak, "A Maximum Principle for an Optimization Problem," *Prikl. Mat. i Programmir.*, Kishinev, Vyp. 12, pp. 95–103, 1974.

Chemeris, M. B., "On the Problems of Vector Optimization," *Prikl. Metody Issled. Protsessov Priniatiia Reshenii*, Vladivostok, pp. 64–74, 1976.

Chemeris, M. B., "On an Approach to the Choice of Method of Normalization," *Prikl. Metody Issled. Protsessov Priniatiia Reshenii*, Vladivostok, pp. 75–82, 1976.

Chernous'ko, F. L. and V. B. Kolmanovskiĭ, *Optimal Control by Random Perturbations*, Nauka, Moscow, 1978.

Chernous'ko, F. L. and V. B. Kolmanovskiĭ, "Computational and Approximate Methods of Optimal Control," *Itogi Nauki i Tekhniki, Mat. Analiz. VINITI AN SSSR*, No. 14, pp. 101–166, 1977.

Chernous'ko, F. L. and A. A. Melikian, *Game Problems of Control and Search*, Nauka, Moscow, 1976.

Chikriĭ, A. A., "One Method of Evasion of Several Pursuers," *Avtomatika i Telemekhanika*, No. 8, pp. 33–37, 1978.

Chikriĭ, A. A., "Sufficient Conditions for Evasion in Nonlinear Several Person Differential Games," *Isv. AN SSSR, Tekhn. Kibernetika*, No. 6, pp. 22–29, 1978.

Chikriĭ, A. A., "Pursuit of an Evader by Several Guided Objects with Information Time Lag for the State of the Pursuer," Preprint, Institut IK AN USSR, No. 45, pp. 23–30, 1978.

Chikriĭ, A. A. and I. S. Rappoport, "The Problem of Approach in Linear Several Person Differential Games," *Predp. Institut Kibernet. AN USSR*, No. 88, 1977.

Chikriĭ, A. A. and I. S. Rappoport, "Linear Differential Games of Pursuit with Several Participants," *Dokl. AN USSR*, No. 6, pp. 553–556, 1978.

Chistiakov, S. V., "On N-Person Differential Games," *Mat. Metody v Sots. Naukakh*, Vil'nius, Vyp. 8, pp. 111–116, 1976.

Shvetsov, N. P., "Investigation of a Group Ergodic Differential Game Problem," *Ergatich.*

Dinamicheskie Sistemy Upr., Kiev, Naukova Dumka, pp. 122–132, 1975; *SI Tekhn. Kibern.*, Vol. 4, No. 21, p. 214, 1975.

Shevliakov, A. Iu., "On a Generalization of the Kalman-Bucy Equations," *Teoriia Sluchaĭnykh Protsessov*, Kiev, Naukova Dumka, Vyp. 3, pp. 142–149, 1975.

Shportiuk, Z. M., "On the Solution of a Problem of Evading a Coalition of Pursuers," *Nauchn. Konf. Vychisl. Mat. v Sovrem. Nauch.-Tekhn. Progresse 1974*, Vyp. 2, Kanev, pp. 286–289, 1974.

Errou, K. D., L. Gurvits and Kh. Udzava, "An Investigation of Linear and Non-Linear Programming," *Izd-vo Inostran. Lit-ry*, Moscow, 1962.

Iudin, D. B., "New Approaches to a Formalization of the Choice of a Solution in Complex Situations," *Abstracts of the 5th All-Union Conference on Control*, Part 1, Nauka, Moscow, 1971.

Iuttler, Kh., "Linear Model with Several Objective Functions," *Ekonomika i Matematicheskie Metody*, Vol. 3, No. 3, pp. 397–406, 1967.

Ianovskaia, E. B., "Optimality Criteria in Coalitionless Games," *Uspekhi Teorii Igr.*, Vil'nius, pp. 106–114, 1973.

MISCELLANEOUS (UNAUTHORED) REFERENCES

"Applied Research Methods for Decision Making Processes" (Prikladnye), Institut Avtomatiki i Protsessov Upr., Dal'nevost. Nauch. Tsentr AN SSSR, Vladivostok, 1976.

Differential Games, an Index of Russian and Foreign Literature for 1968–1976, AN SSSR, Ural'skiĭ Nauch. Tsentr. Sverdlovsk, 1978.

OWRT/WRSIC, "Multiobjective Water Resources Planning: A Bibliography," Water Resources Scientific Information Center, Washington, D. C., 1975.

"Polyoptimierung—Beiträge zur Optimierung bei mehrfacher Zielsetzung" (Material der Weiterbildungsveranstaltung Herbstkurs "Technische Kybernetik," 1975), Wissenschaftliche Schriftenreihe der Technischen Hochschule, Karl-Marx-Stadt, 1975.

BIOGRAPHICAL SKETCH OF
THE CONTRIBUTORS

Dr. William Gearhart obtained his Ph.D. in applied mathematics from Cornell University. During his graduate work, he was associated with the Department of Operations Research and Computer Science, and he worked in the Operations Research Department at the Cornell Aeronautical Laboratory. His work there concerned problems in the analysis and design of weapons and defense systems. Upon graduation, he joined the Mathematics Department at the University of Utah, where his teaching responsibilities were mainly in numerical analysis. His research there included Chebyshev approximation and methods for computing the parameters of systems described by differential equations. Later, Dr. Gearhart moved to the Division of Mathematics, Computer Science, and Systems Design at The University of Texas at San Antonio. In this position he has been involved in developing academic programs in the areas of statistics, operations research and actuarial science. His current research interests center around multi-criteria optimization.

Nicholas Georgescu-Roegen is distinguished professor emeritus of economics at Vanderbilt University. He is a Distinguished Fellow of the American Economic Association and a Fellow of the Econometric Society. His wide-ranging interests include economics, mathematics, statistics, and thermodynamics, fields in which he has written several books and numerous articles, including *Energy and Economic Myths* (Pergamon, 1976), *The Entropy Law and the Economic Process* (Harvard University Press, 1971). One area in which he made seminal contributions is the theory of choice. These are reprinted in his volume *Analytical Economics: Issues and Problems* (Harvard University Press, 1966).

Edward L. Hannan is Director, Bureau of Health Care Research and Information Services, Office of Health Systems Management, New York State Department of Health, Albany, New York and Adjunct Professor in the Institute of Administration and Management, Union College, Schenectady, New York.

Dr. Hannan received a B.S. in mathematics from Union College, an M.S. in mathematics from Syracuse University, an M.S. in operations research from Union College, and a Ph.D. in industrial engineering and operations research from the University of Massachusetts.

He has published articles in more than 20 refereed journals on a variety of topics, including: the analysis and evaluation of health care programs and facilities, goal programming, multiple objective linear programming, multiple objective integer programming, multiple payoff game theory, multiple objective semi-Markov processes, multiattribute utility theory, applications of the Analytical Hierarchy Process, inventory theory, applications of management science to sports (including tennis, swimming and jai-alai), and computer simulation models.

Dr. Hannan is a member of TIMS, AIDS, ORSA, JASA, APHA, Sigma Xi, Kappa Mu Epsilon, Alpha Pi Mu, and American Men and Women of Science.

Ibrahim Kavrakoğlu is jointly appointed as Visiting Professor in the Department of Industrial Engineering and Operations Research, and the Department of Mechanical Engineering, in University of California at Berkeley. His permanent tenure is at Bogazici University in Istanbul, where he is the Chairman of the Department of Industrial Engineering, and the former Dean of Engineering.

Professor Kavrakoğlu has wide research interests in engineering, operations research and economics. In addition to his work on mathematical programming, he has worked extensively on planning methodology in power and energy systems and developed models for macroeconomic analysis. His current research involves price-elastic dynamic optimization models, and simulation modelling of energy-economy interactions. The projects he has directed include the development of an energy model for Turkey, the analysis of nuclear alternatives for the Turkish Electricity Authority, and the rational pricing of electricity for the Greater Istanbul District. He has recently directed a NATO Advanced Study Institute on "Mathematical Modelling of Energy Systems". His contributions in the engineering sciences include: the analysis of turbulent flows; development of a theory for sound propagation from finite oscillating bodies; development of a transducer for measurements in dynamic pressure fields, and performance optimization in axial turbomachinery. His publications include six books and about seventy technical papers and reports.

Dr. Jonathan Kornbluth teaches Operations Research at the Jerusalem School of Business Administration of the Hebrew University, Jerusalem, Israel. He has a B.A. in Mathematics from Queens' College, Cambridge and a Ph.D. in OR from the Imperial College of Science and Technology of the University of London. His research interests include mathematical programming, financial planning and multicriteria decision making; he is the co-author of a book on Linear Programming and Financial Planning.

Lester B. Lave was born in Philadelphia, Pennsylvania, in 1939. He received his B.A. from Reed College (1960) and Ph.D. from Harvard University (1963). He has taught at Harvard University, Northwestern University, and the University of Pittsburgh, and was chair of the Department of Economics of Carnegie-Mellon University from 1971–1978. Dr. Lave is presently a Senior Fellow in the Economic Studies Program at the Brookings Institution and Professor of Economics at Carnegie-Mellon University.

Dr. Lave has received grants from both government agencies and foundations to support policy research on health care, the environment, automobile safety, bargaining behavior, the value of information dissemination, and energy, among other social issues. He has been a consultant to almost every Cabinet-level department as well as many private firms, and is a member of various professional associations. Dr. Lave has served on committees of the National Academy of Sciences and the American Association for the Advancement of Science. He is author of more than 150 publications, including two new books: *The Strategy of Social Regulation* and *The Scientific Basis of Health and Safety Regulation*. In addition, Dr. Lave is an associate editor of several journals.

Wolfram Stadler received his B.S. degree in Aerospace Engineering in 1963, an M.S. in Aerospace Engineering in 1964, an M.S. in Engineering Science and Mechanics in 1966, and a Ph.D. in Engineering Science and Mechanics in 1969, all from Georgia Tech. He was an Assistant Professor of Engineering Science and Mechanics and Applied Mathematics at Georgia Tech from 1967 to 1969. From 1970 to 1975 he was at the University of California, Berkeley, as a postdoctoral fellow and research associate in mechanical engineering. During that time, the emphasis of his studies was on control theory, programming, and mathematical economics. He was a visiting professor at the Institute for Applied Mathematics and Statistics at the Friedrich Wilhelm University, Bonn, Germany, in 1975, and at the Institute B for Mechanics at the Technical University, Munich, Germany, in 1976. He is now an Associate Professor in the Division of Engineering at San Francisco State University.

He has published papers in aeroelasticity, impact loading on shells, moving loads on beams and plates, convergence of Fourier transforms, and the axiomatics of dynamics. He introduced the concept of preference optimality in multicriteria optimization and the concept of natural structural shapes in optimal structural design. He has published two books, an expanded translation of *An Introduction to Optimal Control* by. G. Leitmann (from English into German), and a translation of *Nonlinear Oscillations* by P. Hagedorn (from German into English). He has been working in multicriteria decision making since 1971, and his current research interests center on the applications of multicriteria optimization in mechanics.

Mustafa R. Yilmaz is an Associate Professor of Business Administration at Northeastern University. He holds a B.S. degree in Mechanical Engineering from the Middle East Technical University (METU) in Ankara, Turkey, and a Ph.D in Mathematical Sciences from the Johns Hopkins University. Prior to joining Northeastern University, he served on the faculty of METU in the Department of Management and in the Department of Applied Statistics.

Dr. Yilmaz has published articles in the area of decision analysis. His research interests involve multiple criteria decision making and decisions under risk with particular interest in individual choice. He is a member of the Institute of Management Science and the Circle of Human Systems Management.

Po-Lung Yu is the Carl A. Scupin Distinguished Professor of the School of Business, The University of Kansas at Lawrence. Prior to joining the University of Kansas, he taught at the University of Texas at Austin, and before that he taught at the University of Rochester, New York. Professor Yu received a B.A. in Business Administration from the Taiwan University and a Ph.D. in Operations Research from the Johns Hopkins University. His active research and publication areas include Second Order Games, Behavior Bases for Decision Theory, Multi-criteria Decision Problems, Game Theory, Differential Games, Optimal Control Theory, Mathematical Programmings, Investment Models, Market Efficiency, Market Competition Models, Energy Conservation, and other related topics. He is an Associate Editor for the *Journal of Optimization Theory and Applications* and *Operations Research Letters*.

Milan Zeleny is Professor of Business Administration at Fordham University at Lincoln Center in New York City. His previous appointments include Columbia University, University of South Carolina, Copenhagen School of Economics and European Institute for Advanced Studies in Management in Brussels. Professor Zeleny serves on editorial boards of *Fuzzy Sets and Systems*, *Computers and Operations Research*, *Future Generations Computer Systems*, and *General Systems Yearbook*; he is the Policy Coordinator of *Human Systems Management*. Among his recent books are *Multiple Criteria Decision Making, Uncertain Prospects Ranking and Portfolio Analysis, Autopoiesis: A Theory of Living Organization, Linear Multiobjective Programming,* and many others. He has published more than 140 papers and articles in the areas of operations research, general systems theory, computer simulation, multiple criteria decision making, and socio-economic analysis. He was the recepient of von Humboldt award, Norbert Wiener award, and Scholar-in-residence at the Bellagio Study Center of the Rockefeller Foundation. His current interests involve high-technology management, socio-economic macrotrends and human systems management.

Index